Domino® System Administration

New Riders Professional Library

Planning for Windows 2000
Eric Cone, Jon Boggs, and Sergio Perez
ISBN: 0-7357-0048-6

Windows NT DNS
Michael Masterson, Herman Kneif, Scott Vinick, and Eric Roul
ISBN: 1-56205-943-2

Windows NT Network Management: Reducing Total Cost of Ownership
Anil Desai
ISBN: 1-56205-946-7

Windows NT Performance Monitoring, Benchmarking, and Tuning
Mark Edmead and Paul Hinsburg
ISBN: 1-56205-942-4

Windows NT Registry
Sandra Osborne
ISBN: 1-56205-941-6

Windows NT TCP/IP
Karanjit Siyan
ISBN 1-56205-887-8

Windows NT Terminal Server and Citrix MetaFrame
Ted Harwood
ISBN: 1-56205-931-9

Cisco Router Configuration and Troubleshooting
Mark Tripod
ISBN: 1-56205-944-0

Exchange System Administration
Janice Rice Howd
ISBN: 0-7357-0081-8

Implementing Exchange Server
Doug Hauger, Marywynne Leon, and William C. Wade III
ISBN: 0-7357-0024-9

Network Intrusion Detection: An Analyst's Handbook
Stephen Northcutt
ISBN: 0-7357-0868-1

Understanding Data Communications, Sixth Edition
Gilbert Held
ISBN: 0-7357-0036-2

Windows NT Power Toolkit
Stu Sjouwerman & Ed Tittel
ISBN: 0-7357-0922-x

Domino® System Administration

New Riders

201 West 103rd Street,
Indianapolis, IN 46290

Rob Kirkland

Domino System Administration

Rob Kirkland

International Standard Book Number: 1-56205-948-3

Library of Congress Catalog Card Number: 99-63588

Printed in the United States of America

First Printing: December, 1999

03 02 01 00   7 6 5 4

Interpretation of the printing code: The rightmost double-digit number is the year of the book's printing; the rightmost single-digit number is the number of the book's printing. For example, the printing code 99-1 shows that the first printing of the book occurred in 1999.

Trademarks

Warning and Disclaimer

Publisher
David Dwyer

Executive Editor
Al Valvano

Acquisitions Editor
Stacey Beheler

Managing Editor
Gina Brown

Development Editor
Christopher Morris

Project Editor
Linda Seifert

Technical Editors
Ronald Albuquerque
Dave Hatter
Adam Kornak
Karl Wabst

Indexer
Cheryl Landis

Proofreader
Debbie Williams

Compositor
Amy Parker

About the Authors

Rob Kirkland is an R3, R4, and R5 Certified Lotus Notes Instructor (CLI), principally certified in both system administration and application development. He is also a Certified NetWare Engineer (CNE) and a Microsoft Certified Product Specialist (MCPS) for Windows NT.

Rob is a preeminent author, speaker, consultant, and trainer on the topic of Lotus Notes, whose books and contributions include the *Professional Developer's Guide to Domino* (Que), *Special Edition Using Lotus Notes and Domino 4.5* (Que), *and Lotus Domino for AS/400* (AS/400 Press). Rob owns Stillwater Enterprises, Inc., a consulting firm located near Philadelphia, Pennsylvania.

Tim Bankes is a partner and Principal Information Systems Consultant with Definiti, Inc. (http://www.definiti.com), a Lotus Premium Business Partner and Microsoft Certified Solutions Provider located in Cincinnati, Ohio. Definiti improves corporate business results by implementing real business strategies for the Internet, Intranet, and Extranet. Tim helps provide consulting on Groupware, e-commerce, and e-business, which includes Web development and connectivity to the Internet. He has been working with Lotus Notes/Domino since version 3.0 and specializes in the design, development, and deployment of comprehensive Knowledge Management, Groupware/Workflow, and I-net solutions. Tim was has authored another title for New Riders Publishing, titled: *Lotus Notes and Domino Essential Reference Guide: a Java/LotusScript Guide to the Domino Object Model for Release 5*. He was also a coauthor for another Macmillian Publishing title: *Special Edition Using Lotus Notes and Domino 4.6*. Tim is a Certified Lotus Professional as a Principal Application Developer and System Administrator. He holds a B.B.A. in Information Systems, a B.B.A. in Management, and a certificate in International Business from the University of Cincinnati. Tim can be reached through email at tbankes@definiti.com or tim@bankes.net. In addition, you can visit his Web site at http://www.bankes.net.

Dorothy Burke is a Certified Lotus Instructor (CLI) and R5 Certified Lotus Professional (Principal). She teaches Domino system administration and application development, as well as Lotus Notes basics. She has been an independent consultant and trainer since 1988, following careers in sales, customer service, and writing. Dorothy was a contributor to *Special Edition Using PowerPoint 97*, and along with Jane Calabria, has coauthored books on the topics of Lotus Notes and Domino, Microsoft Windows, and Microsoft Word, Excel, and PowerPoint. Coauthoring efforts by Jane and Dorothy include: *Certified Microsoft Office User Exam Guide(s) for Microsoft Word 97, Microsoft Excel 97*, and *Microsoft PowerPoint 97*; *Microsoft Works 6-in-1, Microsoft Windows 95 6-in-1, Microsoft Windows 98 6-in-1, Using Microsoft Word 97 (Third Edition)*, and *Using Microsoft Word 2000*. Their Lotus Notes and Domino titles include: *The 10-Minute Guide to Lotus Notes Mail 4.5, Lotus Notes 4.5 and the Internet 6-in-1, The 10-Minute Guide to Lotus Notes 4.6*, and *The 10-Minute Guide to Lotus Notes Mail 4.6*. This year, they are collaborating on *Sams Teach Yourself Lotus Notes* and *Sams Domino 5*

Development in 21 Days, Sams Teach Yourself Lotus Notes 5 in 24 Hours, Sams Teach Yourself Lotus Notes 5 in 10 Minutes, and *How to Use Lotus Notes 5.*

Dave Hatter is a Principal Consultant with Definiti (`http://www.definiti.com`), a Lotus Premium Business Partner in Cincinnati specializing in Groupware and Intra/Extra/Internet software development. Dave has nearly nine years of programming experience using a variety of tools and has been working with Lotus Notes/Domino for nearly five years. He is a Principal Certified Lotus Professional Application Developer (R4, R5), Principal Certified Lotus Professional System Administrator (R4), Microsoft Certified Product Specialist, and holds a B.S. in Information Systems from Northern Kentucky University. Additionally, Dave served eight years as a Combat Engineer in United States Army Reserve.

He has coauthored seven books: *Lotus Notes and Domino Programmer's Essential Reference, Special Edition Using Lotus Notes 4.0, Special Edition Using Lotus Notes and Domino 4.5, Special Edition Using Lotus Notes and Domino 4.6, Using Lotus Notes 4.5, Windows NT Server Security Server Handbook*, and *Lotus Notes and Domino Server 4.6 Unleashed* all from Macmillan Computer Publishing (`http://www.mcp.com`). Additionally, he has served as technical editor for following titles: *Sams Teach Yourself Lotus Notes in 14 Days, Lotus Notes and Domino 4.5 Developer's Guide, Lotus Notes and Domino Server 4.6 Unleashed*, and *Sams Teach Yourself Lotus Notes in 24 Days* also from Macmillan Publishing. He has also contributed technology-related articles to several local newspapers including the *Recorder Newspapers, The Cincinnati Business Courier*, and NKU's alumni newspaper, the *NKUPDATE.*

Dave feels strongly about community service and stays active in his community in a number of ways: City Councilman and Webmaster for the City of Fort Wright, Kentucky (`http://www.fortwright.com`), Vice-Chair of the Telecommunications Board of Northern Kentucky, sound technician at Lakeside Presbyterian Church, founder of the NKU Information Systems Alumni Club, former Webmaster of the NKU Alumni Web site (`http://www.nku.edu/~alumni`), instructor for NKU's Community Education program and volunteer instructor for Senior Services of Northern Kentucky. He is a member of the following organizations: Redwood School Marketing Committee, American Legion, 4th District Republican Party Advisory Committee, Kenton County Republican Party Executive Committee, and is the Webmaster of the KCRP Web site (`http://www.kcrp.org`).

Dave was the proud recipient of NKU's 1997 Outstanding Young Alumnus award and the inaugural Senator Jim Bunning "Republican Man of the Year" award in 1998. Additionally, he is a regular guest on Intermedia Cable's Northern Kentucky Magazine show and occasionally appears on WKRC's 12 News Saturday program and WXIX's Morning News Program. Dave, his wife Leslee, and two sons, Samuel and Wyatt, are long-time residents of Fort Wright and can be reached via email at `dhatter@definiti.com` or `dhatter@one.net`, alternatively, you can visit his Web site at `http://w3.one.net/~dhatter`.

John C. Palmer is a Certified Lotus Professional, both as a Principal R5 Application Developer and a Principal R4 System Administrator. After 15 years in the computer field, as an analyst with a Fortune 100 company and with a Big Six consulting firm, he launched his career as an Independent Contractor in 1997. His company, John Palmer Associates, provides Lotus Notes/Domino consulting services to medium and large size companies and can be found on the Web at http://www.jpassoc.net. John lives in Chalfont, Pennsylvania with his wife and two sons. When not working or playing on the computer, John can be found working with the Boy Scouts or bicycling.

Karl Wabst is an independent consultant specializing in client/server computing. He has worked with Notes and Domino as a network architect, administrator, and applications developer over the last 10 years. During that time he has participated in large-scale commercial projects with IBM, Lotus Consulting, AT&T, and Bell Labs. Karl has also worked on the architecture and administration of several large corporate Notes/Domino projects, including one in South Korea for Hyundai Motor Corporation. In a previous life, Karl spent some 10 years working on Wall Street in corporate finance while becoming involved with network computing. This is Karl's second endeavor for Macmillan. He also contributed to Que's *Special Edition Using Notes 4*. Karl holds a B.A. in Psychology from SUNY at Stony Brook. In 1997, Karl founded Eagle Mountain Computing. Since then, he spends most of his time searching for new opportunities and adventures. Home is currently in Fort Worth, TX, although he does not remember actually spending much time there lately. Karl can be reached through email at karl.wabst@worldnet.att.net.

About the Technical Reviewers

Ronald Albuquerque is a software automation architect currently employed at Iris Associates, the developers of Lotus Notes/Domino. Ronald has over 10 years experience in the software industry. Starting out as a UNIX developer and administrator, he has focused his efforts in the last eight years on software test automation systems. He received his degree in Applied Mathematics from Dublin City University in Dublin, Ireland. During his university years and for a short while after, Ronald worked as a software consultant. In early 1993, he joined Segue Software and contributed significantly to the development and evolution of their premier test automation product, QA Partner (now called Silk). In early 1996, he joined New Era of Networks (NEON) in Denver, Colorado. At NEON, he developed a complete test automation system for NEONet, the company's cross-platform middleware product. He started his current post at Iris toward the end of 1997 and has developed several test automation tools for specific portions of the Notes/Domino system. His most recent contribution was the successful completion of test automation that certified the Java engine in Lotus Notes/Domino Release 5.

Ronald lives with his wife in Acton, Massachusetts, where he enjoys soccer, ocean kayaking, and hiking. His family and friends tolerate his passion for British soccer and love of puns.

He can be contacted through email at rja@netcom.com.

Adam Kornak is a Manager in the Systems Development & Technology Consulting Practice for Ernst & Young, LLP in Chicago, Illinois. His background includes over eight years of IT consulting experience focusing on the financial services industry and recently on e-commerce solutions. He has worked with Domino/network architecture and administration, Internet solutions, business/IT process reengineering, enterprise resource planning solutions, and e-commerce projects using Domino development.

Prior to joining Ernst & Young, Adam worked with IBM Global consulting services managing Domino implementations/migrations as well as Domino domain management. His work as an author began with *The Professional Developer's Guide to Domino* working with Jane Calabria and Rob Kirkland. He has also written several Domino/Lotus Learning Centers for Lotus/IBM including *Managing a Domino Deployment* and *Lotus 4.6 Development*. He is currently working on developing books in the e-commerce arena.

Adam and his wife Julie live in the Chicago area where they enjoy biking, golf, and travel. Adam can be reached through email at akornak@ibm.net.

In Memoriam

Weymouth S. Kirkland, 1919-1999

Dedication

I dedicate this book to my writing teachers:

To my father and mother, who taught me to speak "the King's English,"

To Miss Roberts, my second grade teacher, who, in an effort to help me stop missing writing deadlines, sat me down one afternoon and taught me the difference between long and short vowels;

To Miss McDougal, my seventh grade teacher, who was possibly the last English teacher in America to teach her students how to diagram a sentence;

To Miss Karl, my eleventh grade English teacher, a flint-edged old battle-ax whom I didn't much like, and who didn't care if I liked her or not, who espoused a five-step method for organizing an essay which I still use today, and who opened my eyes when she showed me how to rearrange a-few-words-here and a-couple-sentences-there to turn a god-awful first draft (my junior theme, for which she charitably gave me a D minus) into something passably good—the following year, I wrote a paper that I am still proud of today, and three years later, a college professor accused me of plagiarizing an essay that I submitted (no student as mediocre as I, she thought, could have written such a good essay on my own, but I showed her my research materials and proved my authorship)—thank you, Miss Karl;

To Jim McConnell, my first-year legal writing instructor, who taught me to write short, clear sentences that even a judge could understand, and never to use the word "subsequently" when "later" would do, and never, ever to use the word "said" as an adjective, as in "the said party did thus-and-such"—and, Jim, I haven't;

To Pam Woldow, my law partner and the best-ever legal writing partner, who taught me the value of writing a third draft—about the only reason I can think of why I would ever want to return to the practice of law would be to collaborate again with Pam in the creation of a pristine legal brief, knowing that the judge would be too busy to read it, but hoping to find the magical combination of words that would catch his eye, drag him in, and take his breath away;

And most of all, to Jane Calabria, my wife, who built the fire under me and kept it hot; without Jane's inspiration, vision, and encouragement, I could never have written this book at all, or the others. Now, if only I could learn from Jane how to meet a writing deadline....

Contents

Acknowledgements

When I began this book, I naively believed that I could write the whole thing myself. Such arrogance! Think of it—a whole book on the subject of administering Lotus Domino R5—the most comprehensive server software ever conjured—it can do anything! Software dedicated to group collaboration, no less! What's more, I thought I could do it in about six months, based on barely documented beta software that, like a chameleon, changed its appearance with every new build.

About nine months into the project (thank you, Lotus, for your lifesaving delays in releasing the product), with the end of the tunnel still a pinprick of light maybe two years distant (or was that the headlight of a train?), and my ever-more-surly editors snapping at my heels ("Sorry, Rob, but you just can't take three years to write a book that will have a shelf-life of maybe two years, if you're lucky."), and my income dwindling like the streams of Southeastern Pennsylvania during the drought of 1999, a cadre of Notes gurus came to my rescue. I thank them:

John Palmer, for writing Chapter 12, "User Maintenance and Troubleshooting";

Karl Wabst, for writing Chapter 13, "Client Maintenance and Troubleshooting"; Chapter 18, "Server Monitoring"; and Chapter 19, "Performance Tuning" (it killed me to give that one up).

Dorothy Burke, for taking time out from her own busy writing schedule to write Chapter 14, "Database Maintenance and Troubleshooting."

Dave Hatter, for writing Chapter 15, "Web Server Setup, Maintenance, Tuning and Troubleshooting"; and Tim Bankes, for writing Chapter 20, "Enhancing Data Availability."

You guys saved my life, and I owe you.

Thanks to Derek Bambauer of Lotus Development Corporation, who lent me much-needed help in unraveling the Lotus Notes R5 mail routing puzzle. I apologize, Derek, for any perceived incivility in my late-night emails.

Thanks to the people at Lotus Education: Nancy Leo and Chris Vasiliadis, for letting me participate in the development of Lotus's R5 system administration curriculum; and Lisa Tiernan, Judith Kaplan, Terri Karpel, Sharyn Richard, and Amy Hummel, with whom I worked there. At times, you all were darn near my only source of information about the product. Thanks to Elly Dombroski for riding herd over Lotus Accounts Payable. Thanks to Marjorie Kramer for referring me to Lotus Education in the first place, and to Debbie Lynd for your good words in my favor.

Thanks to Al Valvano, my executive editor, who went to bat for me again and again in those editorial reviews, explaining why the book was delayed yet again. The way I heard it, Al wore a Kevlar vest to those meetings.

Thanks to Stacey Beheler, my acquisitions editor. Stacey had the unenviable job of pestering me constantly about the state of my next chapter. She did her job all-too-well; I dreaded her phone calls.

Thanks to Chris Morris, my development editor, and Karl Wabst, Adam Kornak, Ronald Albuquerque, and Dave Hatter, my technical editors, and all the copy editors and whatever-other-kinds-of-editors-and-developers worked in the back rooms at New Riders Publishing, whose names I won't know until they appear on the mast-head of the printed version of this book. They all had to sit on their thumbs until the last minute, then give up their lives to meet their own deadlines because I could never meet any of mine.

Finally, thank you, Jane, for putting up with me for all these months, for bearing the load of life while I buried myself under the load of Lotus Notes, and for your love.

Tell Us What You Think!

As the reader of this book, you are our most important critic and commentator. We value your opinion and want to know what we're doing right, what we could do better, what areas you'd like to see us publish in, and any other words of wisdom you're willing to pass our way.

As the executive editor for the Networking team at New Riders Publishing, I welcome your comments. You can fax, email, or write me directly to let me know what you did or didn't like about this book—as well as what we can do to make our books stronger.

Please note that I cannot help you with technical problems related to the topic of this book, and that due to the high volume of mail I receive, I might not be able to reply to every message.

When you write, please be sure to include this book's title and author, as well as your name and phone or fax number. I will carefully review your comments and share them with the author and editors who worked on the book.

Fax:	317–581–4663
Email:	newriders@mcp.com
Mail:	Al Valvano
	Executive Editor
	New Riders Publishing
	201 West 103rd Street
	Indianapolis, IN 46290 USA

Introduction

At times, I have wondered why there are so many after-market books about software products that, at least occasionally, come with perfectly clear and well-written documentation. Take Lotus Notes and Domino, for example. The "yellow books" are very well-organized, well-written, and much more complete than any book I could write on administering Domino servers.

Well, okay, I admit that I really don't wonder for long. The reasons are obvious. For one, not everyone agrees with me about the quality of included documentation. For another, some of the concepts just need more than one explanation. For yet another, as well written as is documentation such as the yellow books, it is still incomplete, and inevitably so. Especially in a dot-zero release.

Think about it. The software is in beta, with next-to-no documentation. The eventual feature list of the final release is in constant doubt, as one feature after another hangs fire. The release date slips once, twice, three times. The trade press takes cynical pleasure in ridiculing the company for its inability to meet its ship dates. The developers are in lock-down for months on end, feverishly trying to whip the software into shape, debug it, find the right interface, polish it up, and get all the pieces to work together.

And, somehow, the documentation writers have to get the developers' attention long enough to find out what the new features are, how they relate to existing features, what value they contribute to the overall product, how to set them up, how to make them work, and how to tune and troubleshoot them. It's an impossible assignment. Nobody ever gets it right on the first try. Since I began writing this book I have developed great respect for those poor schmoes. The writers at Lotus did an excellent job, but they didn't—couldn't—meet all of your needs.

That's where this book comes in. My goal in writing it was to supplement the yellow books. To fill in the gaps in their coverage. To correct the errors in their coverage. To give you a second explanation of the difficult concepts. To help you understand the significance to *you* of this or that new feature. To explain *why* you should choose this option instead of that one, not merely what each option means.

Of course, like Lotus trying to write comprehensive, accurate documentation of behind-schedule beta software, we, too, did not and could not fully succeed in our quest. Sometimes we just couldn't get to the person who had the answers. And, we had to meet time or space limitations. Lotus covered Domino system administration in five books. We didn't have that luxury.

Two subjects that washed overboard along the way were the Server Web Navigator and the NNTP service. Something had to go and, as much as I like those aspects of Domino, there is a pretty small audience for those features. If you were in that audience, I apologize to you. Other aspects of Domino that got unavoidably short shrift were internationalization features and non-Windows platform support. There just wasn't time or space.

But, what is included in the final product is good, essential information. It is knowledge gained from painstaking research. It is street knowledge gained from years on the job.

How This Book Is Organized

This book is organized in three sections. Part I, "Getting Ready for R5 and Installation," is about setting up Domino and Notes. Part II, "Maintenance and Troubleshooting," is about maintaining a Notes domain. Part III, "Server Optimization," is about monitoring and tuning your domain.

Chapter 1 is an introduction to Domino and Notes R5. While an assumption of the book as a whole is that you are not new to Notes, the assumption in this chapter is that we are all new to R5. So, this chapter is an overview of Notes capabilities in general and new features of R5 in particular.

Chapters 2 through 6 are about as thorough coverage of planning and setting up a new Notes organization/domain as you are likely to read anywhere. About the only people in the world who get to set up a brand new Notes domain more than once or twice in their whole lives are the people who conduct classes in Domino system administration. We teachers get to set up new domains again and again and again. We system administration instructors, alone in all the world, know all the pitfalls, tricks, and tips involved in setting up a new Notes domain. So, if you are in the position of having to do that, this is the book for you. It is the fruit of years of experience.

Chapter 7 is for administrators who have to upgrade an R4 (or R3) domain to R5. Lotus did a really good job of documenting the process, so this chapter doesn't try to reinvent that wheel. Rather, it tries to clue you in on the problems you might encounter, the new features you should set up immediately, the ones you can hold off on, and other things that Lotus just didn't cover.

Chapters 8 through 14 cover the bread-and-butter features of Domino system administration—mail, replication, security, directories, user maintenance, Notes client maintenance, and database maintenance. These chapters tell you what you need to know and what you have to do.

Chapters 15 through 17 cover optional but important features of Domino, including the Domino Web service and the optional mail services. Like the previous set of chapters, these tell you what you need to know and what you have to do.

Chapters 18 through 20 cover more advanced but very important topics—how to keep your servers healthy, how to wring the best performance out of them, and how to connect them to other kinds of data sources. There's plenty of great stuff in them. Don't ignore them because they are at the end of the book.

Who Should Use This Book?

This book is for Domino system administrators, plain and simple. It assumes you know something about the subject already. But, it also assumes you may be new to Domino R5. It covers the basics quickly, then moves on to more advanced topics. It isn't intended to help you become certified (though I believe that's a valid goal for anyone). Rather, it's intended to help you get your job done. It's intended to give you the knowledge necessary to get your job done, to enable you to do your job intelligently, efficiently, even brilliantly.

Tips On Using This Book

In this book, the authors have tried to give you much more than the usual bare-bones instructions and descriptions. Wherever possible, we have tried to tell you the full consequences of your choices, whether they be policy decisions or fields in dialog boxes. For that reason, I encourage you to read the step-by-step instructions even for procedures that you already know. Especially read the steps that are long. Those are the ones with lots of hopefully interesting and useful information in them.

Lotus has a big naming problem. Some examples:

- First, there was Notes. Then there was Domino.
- First, there was the Public Name and Address Book. Then, there was the Public Address Book. Now, there is the Domino Directory.
- Here is Transaction Logging. Or is it Transactional Logging?
- Here is the Directory Catalog. It's on a Directory Server. There is the Catalog database. It's on a Catalog Server. Or is that a Search Server? And is it capitalized or lowercase?

Lotus knows they have this problem. They admit it. They lament it.

The problem arises mostly from the fact, I think, that they keep inventing new things. It's hard to find the right name for a unique new thing. When you find a name you think is good, it's hard to get everyone to agree on its particulars or, for that matter, that it really is the best name. When you do settle on a nice descriptive name, someone totally unrelated to the company comes along and popularizes some other name for the thing—like "directory" instead of "address book."

You may find this situation confusing. Sorry. Join the club. It's the absolute bane of the person who has to write about Domino-slash-Notes. But, there are some rules that have Lotus's official stamp of approval:

- The server is Domino. The client is Notes. The administration client is really Notes, but we call it Domino Administrator because we use it to administer Domino servers. The application development client is really Notes, but we call it Domino Designer, I guess because we use it to design applications that run on Domino servers.

- It's a Notes domain, not a Domino domain. This is official.
- It's a Notes organization, not a Domino organization.

If we say the wrong thing here or there or get the capitalization wrong, we apologize. Just hang in there. That's what we are all doing.

Enjoy this book. Believe it or not, it was enjoyable to write.

I

Getting Ready for R5 and Installation

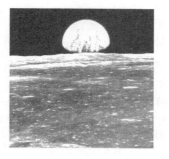

1

Features of Lotus Domino 5.0

To administer a Domino/Notes installation effectively, you obviously have to know how to perform administration chores, and that is what most of this book is about. More fundamentally, you have to understand the product's features and capabilities as well as Domino/Notes licensing options. This chapter provides important essentials you need to know about Domino R5 prior to administering the product.

Lotus Notes and Domino Features

Through its first three releases Notes was a mostly closed system. You had to use a Notes client to reach data on a Notes server. (Well, you could write your own client, using APIs that Lotus made available for C, C++, and Visual Basic, or using a precursor to LotusScript called Lotus Notes ViP. But you could not use standards-based clients like Web browsers.) You could think of the features of Notes as they existed in those releases as the "core" Notes functions, and the types of applications that Notes could accommodate as the "core" Notes applications.

Those features would include shared, document-oriented databases, and messaging; strong security features; distributed data kept in synch through replication; support for mobile, disconnected Notes users; and access to non-Notes data. The applications would include information repositories, discussion forums, project tracking applications, and business process or "workflow" applications.

Many organizations that use Notes and Domino today still use only the core features as described previously. However, as Release 3 matured it became more and more clear to Lotus (and everyone else) that the Internet was on its way to transforming how the world does business. Many people saw the emergence on the Internet of standards-based email (SMTP/MIME-based mail), discussion forums (Internet newsgroups), and information repositories (the World Wide Web) as spelling doom for the future of Notes.

Lotus saw the same trends as a great opportunity to expand the market for Notes by turning it into an extremely powerful platform for Internet applications. As a result, Lotus has added, with each 4.x and 5.x release of Notes, more and more Internet functionality to the server and client (and, in honor of the added functionality, renamed the server "Domino"). And to the "core" application types we can add one more: Web applications.

The essential features of Notes are the following:

- Client/Server architecture
- Nonrelational, object-oriented database architecture
- Messaging
- Distributed architecture and replication
- Security
- Support for mobile users
- Support for multiple computing platforms
- Comprehensive data access
- Integrated Development Environment
- Extensions and add-ins
- Web server
- Web browsers
- Directory services
- Manageability

Client/Server Architecture

From the beginning Notes databases have resided primarily on Notes or Domino servers and users have accessed the data via a client program running on their workstations. But Notes/Domino servers aren't file servers. Users don't retrieve whole databases; rather, they request specific data sets from the servers. The servers retrieve the requested data from the databases and deliver it to the users. Or users deliver new data to the servers, which then store it in the appropriate database. This is classic client/server architecture. Its goal is to maximize shared access to data while minimizing network traffic by separating the data storage and management functions from the data presentation function.

The client forwards user requests to the server, including requests to read and write data. The client also formats received data and displays it to the user.

Through Release 4.1, the sole off-the-shelf client was Lotus Notes (although it was possible for programmers to create their own client programs using APIs sold by Lotus). Beginning with Release 4.5 Lotus has enabled increasing data access via other standard client programs—first Web browsers, later Internet mail readers, news readers, and IMAP directory readers. Release 5 does not introduce any new clients over those introduced in Release 4.6. It does, however, add several important enhancements to the interaction between Domino and non-Notes clients. For example, Release 5 introduces CORBA/IIOP, which allows programmers to make Notes functionality available in Web browsers. It also enhances the interaction between Domino and other LDAP directory servers and clients.

Database Architecture

The heart of Notes is its unique object store, the NSF (Notes Storage Facility) file. Notes databases are called "object stores". They do not store data in the same way data is stored in most database architectures. Notes is designed to accommodate the kinds of information that knowledge workers generate, which is to say extremely diverse data.

Most database architectures store information in rigid structures—tables. Every record in a table must have the same array of fields, whether there is any information in the fields. The amount of storage space allotted to each field in a record is fixed in the field definitions before any records are actually created. If the actual data turns out to require more or less than the allotted space, that's too bad; it gets exactly the space allotted, no more, no less. This is a great design for large masses of uniform data, because it allows for fast retrieval of the information. But it is not the best design for the ad hoc kinds of data generated by knowledge workers.

Notes databases are much more flexible than tabular databases. Records are not stored in tables. Therefore, each record (called a "note" or a "document") can include only such fields that actually contain data. Each field can accommodate as much data as the user wants to enter, and occupies exactly that much storage space. Two records need not include the same array of fields. You can add new fields to a record at any time—creation time or some later time.

To make data stored in this way retrievable, Notes databases maintain indexed "views" of the data and, optionally, full-text indexes. A view is a tabular array of information from each record. Exactly what information appears in a view is up to the view's designer (who could be either the database designer or any user with at least Reader access to the database).

With each major release, Lotus has refined the database architecture, and Release 5 is no exception. In this release, Lotus has improved database integrity, reduced I/O costs, improved CPU and memory utilization, and made databases more scalable and more manageable.

Release 5 databases incorporate the following new features:

- Thirty-two gigabyte maximum database size
- Transaction logging. Changes to data are initially written to a transaction log, then to the database itself. If a malfunction occurs during a database write, so as to cause the corruption of data, the transaction logging process will detect and fix the problem automatically, assuring the ultimate integrity of the data.
- Online database backup and a backup API that backup software vendors can use to incorporate Domino backup capability into their backup software.
- Online, in-place compaction of databases.
- Optional recovery of deleted documents.

Messaging, Calendaring, and Scheduling

Notes has always included a ready-to-run email capability right out of the box, which Lotus has continually improved and refined over the years. What is most interesting about this feature is that all Notes databases can send and receive documents to each other—not just mail databases. So, in a sense, Notes Mail is just a by-product of a fundamental message-routing capability that is built-in to the Domino server and all Notes databases.

Of course, email is an essential application in today's networked world, and Lotus has never treated Notes Mail as a by-product of anything. Lotus knows that many Domino installations are strictly used for email, and that a company's email is part of its basic network infrastructure. Therefore, Lotus has made constant improvements in Notes Mail over the years, including group calendaring and scheduling in Release 4.5 and Internet mail access in Releases 4.5 and 4.6.

One of Lotus's main marketing themes with the release of Domino 5.0 has been to stress Domino's superiority to other products as a messaging infrastructure. In Release 5.0, Lotus added the following messaging enhancements:

- **Increased scalability and performance of servers.** Multiple mail box databases to increase mail router performance and scalability; Separate Directory servers to distribute the load of directory lookups so that mail servers can scale up to greater numbers of mail users.
- **Enhanced usability.** Faster name resolution to speed up addressing of messages; easier mail archiving; many interface improvements; mobile directory catalog; calendar lookups in nonadjacent Domino domains.

- **Manageability enhancements.** New, task-oriented administration interface; Pull router; Message tracking; Message routing controls, including antispam tools and control over message sizes; Improved reporting.
- **Improved integration with Internet standards.** Native MIME and SMTP; S/MIME support for sending encrypted messages to Internet mail recipients.

Directory Services

Notes has always provided a directory service which listed all Notes users, servers, groups, and server configuration information. Through Release 3.x the directory database was called the Public Name and Address Book. In Release 4.x, its name was shortened to Public Address Book. In Release 5, Lotus renamed it again, this time calling it the Domino Directory to bring its name in line with industry naming practice. Prior to Release 5, all Notes or Domino servers in a Notes or Domino domain maintained full local replica copies of the Public Address Book. Beginning with Release 5.1, a Domino server no longer needs to maintain a full local replica copy of the Domino Directory but can instead maintain a "userless" local directory that excludes Person, Mail-In Database, Resource, and Group documents.

When a server or user needs access to information stored in these documents, it can be looked up on a directory server instead. This reduces the footprint of the Domino Directory on most Domino servers, especially in large organizations with thousands of users. It also increases the efficiency, responsiveness, and scalability of mail and application servers, because they won't have to carry out name lookups anymore. Even directory lookups are faster because Lotus has made the name lookup process vastly more efficient.

As early as Release 2, administrators could set up multidomain directory services so that users could easily address mail to Notes users in Notes/Domino domains other than their own. Beginning with Release 4.6 and to a greater extent in Release 5, Lotus has extended this capacity to non-Domino domains by incorporating the Lightweight Directory Access Protocol (LDAP) into Domino directory services. This allows Domino servers to authenticate users listed in non-Domino directories. In addition, Lotus has added LDAP client services to Lotus Notes, so users can perform name lookups in LDAP directories.

Also in Release 5, Lotus has enhanced directory services in the following ways:

- Increased the maximum users per domain to one million (from 150,000 in Release 4.x).
- The Enterprise Directory Catalog stores just the essential information about users in a highly compact format—about 100 bytes per user and 255 users per document. This allows administrators to maintain a large directory on a small disk footprint, which in turn permits mobile users to keep a local replica copy of a whole enterprise directory without overwhelming their personal hard disk.

Distributed Architecture and Replication

Notes has always supported a distributed data architecture, in which replica copies of databases can reside on multiple servers. Users can access the server most convenient to them. The database replicas are by default peers of each other. That means that users can add data to any replica, and the servers will distribute the new data to the other replicas by a process called replication.

Over the years, Lotus has refined the replication process. Initially, if a change appeared in any field in a document, during replication the whole document would be transferred to the other servers. Beginning with Release 4.0, only the changed fields are transferred to the other servers.

While replication was developed specifically to allow distribution of Notes applications across multiple local servers, it has come in very handy as Lotus extends Domino functionality to the Internet. Take, for example, the problem of maintaining a Web site. Typically you develop and debug a Web site on a staging server, then transfer the files over to a production Web server exposed to the world. On most Web servers, this is a manual process, and it can be quite cumbersome to carry out when you consider that the staging server is behind the corporate firewall and the production server is in front of it.

For Domino servers, however, transferring the Web site from the staging server to the production server is an automatic and trivially easy procedure. You just establish replication between the two servers, and Domino takes care of the rest. You will need to open a port in the firewall, so the servers can communicate, but you would do that anyway.

For Release 5, Lotus has not changed the way replication works. But they have improved the tools for managing replication in two significant ways. First, they have added a replication topology map to the Administrator client. The map is a graphical representation of the replication relationships among your servers. Then there is a timeline showing recent past successful and unsuccessful replications and future scheduled replications of a server with all of its replication partners.

Security

Notes's developers knew from the beginning that people would be storing confidential information in Notes databases. So Notes has had tight security features built into it from its very first release. Notes security is comprehensive and granular. You can define who has access to servers, databases, forms, views, documents, and fields. Notes users and servers routinely and automatically establish each other's positive identity using certificate-based authentication licensed from RSA Data Security, Inc.

In Release 5, Lotus has enhanced Domino security in the following ways:

- **Password quality testing.** Administrators can require user passwords to meet any of five levels of quality, where the quality of passwords increases with more characters, nonalphabetic characters, and nonalphanumeric characters.

- **Recovery of lost passwords.** Administrators and users can now collaborate to unlock an ID file to recover a forgotten password.

- **Native support for X.509 certificates.** Notes IDs can store both native Notes certificates and X.509 certificates. This enables Notes users to carry out certificate-based authentication with both Domino servers and Internet servers that support SSL.

- **Support for S/MIME.** This enables Notes users to send and receive signed and encrypted mail when corresponding with anyone whose software also supports S/MIME.

- **Control over access to objects (HTML files, Java class files, GIF files, and so on) in the Domino server's file system.**

Support for Mobile Users

Notes provides comprehensive support for mobile users. First, they can connect to Domino servers either by network or by modem. By modem they can connect directly to dialup Domino servers or they can connect to a remote network, then access Domino servers across the network. Second, mobile users can pass through one or more Domino servers to reach others. This allows users to dial in to one server, then pass through it to reach multiple others. Finally, Notes clients can maintain local copies of databases and replicate the changes in them with servers. This enables remote users to work while disconnected from any server.

In Release 5, Lotus has added remote dynamic management of user desktops. In previous releases, Domino supported user profiles, which automated many aspects of user setup. The new aspect of this in Release 5 is that the user profile has ongoing influence over the user's client setup. If an administrator makes a change in the user profile, the user's client will be updated to reflect that change. This should make it easier for administrators to support mobile users.

Support for Multiple Computing Platforms

Both the Domino server and the Notes client operate on multiple hardware/OS platforms. This allows the user to deploy the product on the most convenient platform rather than deploy new, unfamiliar platforms. It also makes for great scalability of servers. Small organizations that use primarily PCs running Windows and Macintoshes can run their servers over Windows NT. Larger organizations can run larger, UNIX-based servers or even larger servers on AS/400 and S/390 platforms.

For Release 5, Lotus is refining this policy. It will stop supporting Novell NetWare as a Domino server platform and OS/2 and UNIX as Notes client platforms. Users on these platforms can continue to use Notes 4.x clients or can interact with Domino using Java-based client software that Lotus is developing.

Comprehensive Data Access

Lotus provides myriad tools for connecting to non-Notes data sources. The tools include @functions and LotusScript classes that Notes developers can use as well as add-in products that allow Domino servers to act as "middleware" servers between back-end data sources, such as relational databases and transaction systems, and front-end user access tools like Notes and Web browsers.

In Release 5, Lotus has enhanced these capabilities with the following enhancements:

- **Real-time, forms-based access to relational and transactional data with DECS (Domino Enterprise Connection Service).** This is a scaled-down version of Lotus NotesPump, incorporated in Domino.

- **Access to Notes/Domino services from a browser with CORBA/IIOP support.** This enables programmers to write Java applets that have access to Domino services and execute locally functions that it would otherwise have to ask a Domino server to execute. This offloads work from the server, empowers the browser, and reduces network traffic between them.

- **Real-time collaboration, including whiteboard and shared applications.** This is not actually included in Domino but rather in a separate Lotus client/server platform, Lotus SameTime, which you purchase separately and install on a separate server, but which works closely with Domino and Notes.

- **Domino Extended Search, an enhanced search engine that allows users to search simultaneously any indexes you want to make available to them.** This includes Domino domains, file systems, relational databases, Internet information repositories, and commercial information repositories. This is an add-on product, purchasable separately from Lotus.

- **Expanded Database Catalog (`catalog5.nsf`).** This permits domainwide searching of Notes databases and Domino server file systems.

Integrated Development Environment

Lotus recognized from the beginning that the sorts of problems that Notes could solve were so diverse that they themselves couldn't anticipate all of its potential applications. Therefore, Lotus added development tools so that users could develop applications tailored to their specific needs.

In Release 5, those tools include Domino Designer—development environment integrated designed specifically for development of Notes applications—as well as tools to allow developers to use other development environments. They also include openness to a whole array of languages, from the proprietary ones—formula language and LotusScript—to languages of general use. These would include C, C++, Java, Visual Basic, HTML, JavaScript, and CGI scripting languages.

Extensions and Add-Ins

Lotus continually extends Notes in an effort to meet the needs of Notes users and make the product as comprehensive as possible. To that end, Lotus markets a variety of products that add specialized capabilities to Notes. For example, you can add realtime collaboration tools, tools for wireless connection to Domino servers, and specific applications, such as Extended Search, an enhanced search engine, and Domino.Doc, a document management application.

Lotus also encourages third-party developers to develop products that add functionality to Notes. To that end, Lotus has developed a number of APIs that give third-party developers access to the Notes object classes. And of course there are products available from third-party developers.

Web Server

Domino's Web server first became available as an add-in as early as Release 4.1 and was fully incorporated into the server beginning with Release 4.5. It was the incorporation of the Web server (and the resultant opening of a whole new market for Notes servers) that prompted Lotus to adopt for its server the new name "Domino."

The Web server is a full-function Web server. Just like any other HTTP server it can serve up HTML files from its file system and interface with CGI programs. Unlike other HTTP servers, it can also serve up documents from Notes databases on the resident server.

In Release 5, Lotus added the following capabilities to the HTTP service:

- HTTP server clusters. Web users can (in the event of high user demand or a failed server) be transparently redirected to the least busy server in a cluster.
- Support for HTTP 1.1.
- Optional integration with Microsoft's Internet Information Server (IIS).
- File system ACLs.
- Byte range serving: permits restart of downloads, among other things.
- Reload HTTP configuration without restarting the server.
- Improved logging.

Because the inclusion of a Web server permits users to access Notes data with a Web browser, Lotus has also included the Domino HTTP stack in Notes Designer for Domino 4.6 and its successor, Domino Designer 5.0. This permits application developers to test their applications from the perspectives of both the Notes client and the browser client without ever leaving the design screens.

Web Browsers

Beginning with Release 4.0 Lotus incorporated a Web browser in the Notes/Domino server. Beginning with Release 4.5 they included a Web browser in the Notes client as well. These browsers supported most of the features of HTML 3.2. Beginning with Release 4.6 Lotus incorporated an embedded version of Microsoft Internet Explorer in the Notes client. This allowed Notes users to browse Web sites that supported HTML 4.0 without leaving Notes to open an external browser. Beginning with Release 5 Lotus has updated the internal Notes and Domino browsers to support HTML 4.0.

The server-based browser is a shared browser, usable by Notes clients, which send URLs to it for forwarding to Internet/intranet hosts. The server-based browser permits a company to offer Web browsing services to users who cannot browse directly, because their computers do not run TCP/IP or they do not have standalone browser software.

Management Tools

Lotus has always provided tools to facilitate management of a Notes/Domino installation. The tools haven't always been great, but in Release 5, Lotus made a big effort to provide really good management tools. The most obvious result of this effort is Domino Administrator, a task-oriented administrators' front-end that runs on Windows-based computers as an extension of the Notes client. This is a graphical management tool with a drag-and-drop interface, organized by tasks—database management, user and group management, server management, replication management, messaging management, and so on. The new administration interface is a huge improvement in the product. We will spend much of this book exploring it. Release 5 has introduced so many other management improvements that I won't try to catalog them all, but some especially significant ones include the following:

- A simpler installation program based on InstallShield. Also, improvements in automated installations.

- Improved HTTP-based management tools, including HTTP-based installation and setup, so that you can install, set up, and manage Domino servers from Web browsers.

- Improved user registration, including tools to register users in Windows NT domain directories and migrate users from cc:Mail, Microsoft Mail, and Microsoft Exchange Server mail systems.

- On-going, centralized control over user workstation configurations.

- Numerous improvements in statistics collection and presentation tools and in event notification.

- Added tools for monitoring Internet protocol servers and connections.

- Capability to start and stop network and dialup ports without shutting down the server. Administrators can reconfigure the HTTP service without bouncing the server.

- Enhanced Administration Process. For example, the administration process can work across domains and can produce server decommissioning analyses for organizations that need to consolidate servers.

Notes Applications

With its built-in messaging, shared, document-oriented databases, and application development tools, Notes was designed from the ground up with certain sorts of applications in mind. It of course lends itself to those types of applications. At the same time, it is totally unsuited to other kinds of applications. Applications that are good candidates for building in Notes include any involving document-oriented, loosely structured, highly diverse, or quickly evolving kinds of data. Applications that would more appropriately be built in a relational database include any that process transactions (such as accounting systems) or that involve highly structured, relatively static data, especially if there is a large mass of such data. Notes works well with relational databases and transaction systems, so applications that involve both kinds of data might be built using both kinds of systems—say, a Notes front end and a relational back end. I would classify Notes applications into the following categories:

- Messaging
- Personal information management
- Discussions
- Information repositories
- Project tracking and workflow

A comprehensive application of Notes/Domino to a specific business problem may well incorporate more than one of these types, but for purposes of understanding the basic functionality of Notes, I'll describe each of these application types separately.

Messaging

Messaging—the capability of Domino servers to deliver documents from any Notes database to any other Notes database or into or out of the Notes universe entirely—is a fundamental capability that permeates all of Notes and Domino. However, that is not the aspect of Domino messaging we want to talk about here. Rather, here we want to talk about simple email.

Email is the "killer app" of the Internet era. Lotus knows it and wants you to build your email-messaging infrastructure around Domino servers. To that end Lotus has continually improved and enhanced Domino's messaging and email capabilities. Lotus has optimized Domino servers to accommodate large numbers of mail users and to route mail efficiently and quickly. Lotus has developed powerful and usable tools so that administrators can easily set up, control, and troubleshoot the processes of routing, storing, and archiving mail. Lotus has refined the mail interface to make it inviting, intuitive, and useful. Lotus has incorporated industry mail standards into the product so as to enable seamless, full-fidelity transfer of mail between Notes users and users of other mail systems.

Most Notes/Domino applications are either you-build-it or you-customize-it in nature. This is because most of the business problems to which we apply Notes are unique and often they are in constant flux. So Lotus provides lots of templates and development tools and makes it easy to customize templates and change on-the-fly the way applications work.

But Notes Mail (while customizable) is one of the few applications that arrives ready-to-run, right out of the box, with little or no need for customization. You set up a Domino server, register or import users, then set up the users' mail software, which can be Lotus Notes or any SMTP or SMTP/MIME mail reader capable of accessing a POP3 or IMAPv4 server. And that's it. The users can send and receive mail. If their mail reader supports it, their messages can include formatting, attachments, and hypertext links to other objects on the net. If their mail reader supports it, they can encrypt their messages and affix either electronic or text signatures to them, they can request delivery confirmations or return receipts, and they can send out mail traces and probes.

Personal Information Management

Personal information management, as it functions in Notes, includes creation and maintenance of personal address books, calendars, to-do lists, and the like—things that are not "group" activities. In Notes it also includes group calendaring and scheduling. Calendaring as it now functions in Notes didn't appear until Release 4.5. Lotus refined it in Releases 4.6 and 5.0. They will undoubtedly refine it further in future releases. Like Notes Mail, it is functional right out of the box. The only thing special that it requires is creation and population of a resource reservations database, so people can reserve conference rooms and other resources when they schedule meetings.

Discussions

Notes database architecture has always allowed Notes documents to be classified into response hierarchies. Any Notes database can take advantage of this feature. The most fundamental application of it is the discussion database, in which groups of people can hold discussions in which the discussion threads are easy to follow because, in views, responses appear indented beneath the documents to which they respond.

Notes discussion databases are functionally identical to Internet newsgroups, Internet mailing lists, and CompuServe forums (to cite a few examples). This is why it was a relatively simple matter for Lotus to incorporate NNTP (Network News Transfer Protocol, the protocol that Internet News servers use) functionality into the Domino server. The functionality was already there; all Lotus had to do was add the transfer protocol to the list of transfer protocols Domino already supports.

Information Repositories

The simplest kind of Notes application is the database that holds announcements or reference information. Lotus would call a database that holds announcements a "broadcast" database and one that holds reference information a "reference" database. Both are knowledge bases and their hallmark is that they are maintained by a relatively small group of people for the read-only benefit of a much larger audience. In this way, they perform the same function as a typical Internet Web site.

The main difference between reference and broadcast databases is that the information in a reference database is of more enduring usefulness. The information in a broadcast database is more "timely" in nature—useful today, old news tomorrow, and would therefore change from day to day.

Any reference book is a good candidate to be stored online as a reference database. Examples of reference databases include the help databases that come with Notes and the knowledgebases about Notes, cc:Mail, and SmartSuite that Lotus maintains on the Internet and makes available to its business partners.

Candidates for broadcast applications include databases of product announcements, job openings, cafeteria menus, press releases, or anything that resembles a bulletin board.

Human Resources departments love both kinds of databases. A comprehensive HR application includes long-term reference information—company policy statements on everything from smoking to vacations to dress to illegal activities. It also includes current information—announcements of job openings, policy changes, promotions, holiday and vacation schedules, and the time and location of the annual picnic.

Tracking Applications

The tracking application is where Notes begins to rise above other "groupware" programs. Tracking applications typically consist of a database to which a relatively small "workgroup" or "team" has both read and write access. The purpose of the database is to enable the members of the team to keep track of each other's activities in furtherance of some team project, and the contents of the database include documents describing those activities as well as, perhaps, mission statements, timelines, milestones, and the like. The idea is that the team members can refer to the database at any time to discover the current status of the project. Whenever a team member moves the project forward in some tangible way, that member adds or updates a document to that effect, and the new status of the project is instantly available to the rest of the team.

Workflow Applications

Workflow applications, in general, are computerized versions of office workflows. They may be as simple as automated routing of forms to a series of people. Notes is fully capable of that sort of workflow. However, with its shared, mail-enabled database architecture, Notes is capable of a whole lot more.

A simple example of a workflow is a purchase requisition system. Say a team needs to acquire tools to get a job done. Typically someone will have to fill out a requisition form, one or more others will have to approve the requisition, then someone else will have to carry out the acquisition. The Notes version of this system might work something like this: The requisitioner could fill in the form in his own mail database, which would automatically mail it to a purchase requisition tracking database.

The arrival there of the new document would trigger an agent to run on the server. The agent would mail a notice form to the person responsible for approving the requisition. That person would click a link icon in the notice, which would automatically open the requisition form on the approver's computer. The approver could approve by simply clicking a box on the form. The approver could then save and close the form. This would in turn trigger another agent to run, which would mail a notice to the next designated actor, who might be another approver or the person designated to acquire the tools.

The benefits of a system designed like this are many. First, the form can never get lost because it is always in the tracking database. Second, the actors receive positive notice where they live—in their email—of the necessity to act. Third, if the requisitioner or anyone else involved in the transaction wants to find out or update the status of the requisition, he can simply look in the tracking database and open the form. In a paper- or email-based or forms-routing system he would have to track people down to find out if they had done their part yet.

Fourth, Notes security features can be applied to assure that only designated people can read the requisition documents or approve or update them. Lastly, Notes permits all sorts of refinements of this basic system so that, for example, reminders are sent out if an actor sits on a document for too long.

Web Applications

Domino Web applications are yet another refinement of the other kinds of applications. Web applications are simply the extension to the Internet, intranet, or extranet of the standard Notes applications. The power here is that they can be extended to anyone you want to extend them to. That may include not just people in your own company but suppliers, business partners, and customers. In the past, to extend Notes applications outside the company you had to convince outsiders to adopt Notes themselves. Now they can participate with off-the-shelf Web browsers. This makes possible a whole new world of applications—what IBM calls "market-facing" or "extended enterprise" applications—and a whole new way of doing business with people.

Release 5 Products

With Release 5.0, Lotus offers three versions of the Domino server, one version of the Notes client, and two Notes client add-ins—Domino Designer and Domino Administrator. The three Domino servers are as follows:

- **Domino Mail Server.** This low-end server offers basic email and collaboration services.

- **Domino Application Server.** This is the standard Domino server, similar to the Domino server of earlier releases. It includes the features of the Domino Mail Server and adds Web application services, CORBA/IIOP support, and connectivity to data sources external to Domino.

- **Domino Enterprise Server.** This includes all capabilities of the other servers and adds server clustering for increased data availability.

Domino Go

There is another Lotus product known as the Domino Go server. Domino Go is not a Domino server in the same sense as those listed above. It is actually a pure HTTP server without the Notes underpinnings. It is built on the same HTTP protocol stack that the Domino servers listed above use as their HTTP service, but other than that it is not related to them. We will not cover the Domino Go server in this book. To learn more about the Domino Go server, look for it at www.lotus.com.

The Domino Mail Server is intended to be an entry-level Domino server, aimed at organizations that want to get up and running quickly with basic Domino collaboration services—email, discussions, calendaring and scheduling, task management, and knowledge repositories.

The Domino Application Server is the standard Notes/Domino server of previous releases. It includes the services (HTTP, CORBA/IIOP) necessary to take full advantage of Domino's strengths as a Web application server, and is aimed at the organization that is ready to take Domino beyond simple email and collaboration services. The Domino Enterprise Server includes the services (server clustering, server partitioning, and billing) that were known in Release 4.x as the Domino Advanced Services. These are tools of particular use to large organizations and to Notes Public Networks—companies offering Domino server hosting to organizations that don't want to maintain their own servers. Server clustering (which in Release 5 also includes Web server clustering) is also useful to any organization that needs Domino-based data to be available on a 24x7 basis.

As in the past, Lotus supports the Domino server running on a variety of hardware/OS platforms. Release 5 server platforms include the following:

- Window 95 and Windows NT on Intel-based hardware
- Windows NT on Alpha-based hardware
- IBM OS/2
- IBM AIX
- Hewlett-Packard HP-UX
- Sun Solaris on SPARC-based hardware
- Sun Solaris on Intel-based hardware
- IBM OS/400
- IBM OS/390

Lotus has discontinued support for Novell NetWare, due to the relatively small demand for Domino on that platform.

All the Domino Release 5 servers actually include Domino server, Notes client, and Domino Administrator client software in the shrinkwrap. On the Windows-based Release 5 server platforms, the client runs on the server machine. On the other systems, the included client runs on a Windows-based machine.

The Domino client and its add-ins are

- **Notes Client.** This is *the* Lotus Notes client, intended for use by anyone looking for a good PIM and universal inbox. It is marketed, by the way, as *the best client* for a Domino server.

- **Domino Designer.** This is the Lotus Notes client with the new programmer's interface added. It is intended for Domino application developers.

- **Domino Administrator.** This is the Lotus Notes client with the administrator's interface added. It is intended for Domino system administrators.

Domino Designer and Domino Administrator are not really standalone clients at all. Rather, they are add-ins to the Notes client. When you buy a Domino Designer license you also get a Lotus Notes license, and you install them together. Domino Administrator is not a separately purchasable license. Rather, it comes with Domino, the server. You can install it over any installed copy of Notes.

The Notes Mail client, the Notes Desktop client, and the full Notes clients of Release 4 are gone. In Release 5, there is no equivalent of the Notes Mail client. The Release 5 Notes client is equivalent to the Notes Desktop license of Release 4 in that it includes all client services but does not include the design or administration interfaces. To set up the equivalent in Release 5 of the Release 4 full Notes client, you would choose during installation to install all three client interfaces.

The Notes client is available on the Window 95 and Windows NT and Apple Macintosh hardware/OS platforms.

Domino Designer and Domino Administrator are only available under Windows 95 and Windows NT.

In past versions, Lotus clients ran on OS/2 and the three server UNIX platforms. Beginning with Release 5, however, Lotus does not offer Notes clients for those platforms. Rather, Lotus offers Java applets that provide Notes functionality and run within the Lotus eSuite application package or a Web browser. System administrators either have to have a Windows machine so they can use Domino Administrator or they have to use the Web Administration tool, which is a Domino database, accessible only from a Web browser, that permits an administrator to perform most administrative tasks.

In this chapter, we have explored the capabilities of Notes and Domino. We have reviewed their components and the platforms on which they run. In the next four chapters, we'll focus on planning and executing the rollout of a Domino domain.

2

Planning an Installation

PLANNING AHEAD IS ESSENTIAL TO A SUCCESSFUL Domino/Notes deployment (no surprise there). Whether you are setting up a new Domino installation or extending an existing one, you need to determine beforehand what your needs are and how you will meet them. If you are setting up a new Domino installation—a new domain or organization—planning is especially important, because mistakes made in the initial setup tend to haunt you forever, and because a poorly planned and executed rollout may fail entirely. But even if you are just extending an existing installation, lack of adequate planning can lead to costly mistakes.

In this chapter we look briefly at the overall planning and rollout process. Then we look in detail at the technical issues that you have to iron out before installing the first Domino server. If you have already decided why you are installing Domino, who is going to do the work, and what your timelines are, and you are ready to install your first server, skip forward to the section "Establishing Domino's Internal Infrastructure," later in this chapter. But if Domino is new to you, remember that it is a fantastically versatile product. It can meet your company's needs in ways that you may not have considered. You may want to reassess your long-term plans for Domino even now. In that case, you should read Chapter 1, "Features of Lotus Domino 5.0" if you have not already done so, and read all of this chapter.

The Domino Rollout Process

There are many aspects to the planning process:

- You have to determine your needs, both functional and technical, and determine how Domino can meet them in both the short and long terms.

- You have to assemble a rollout team, which should include managers, user representatives and functional experts, and technical representatives.

- You have to identify current resources and determine what additional resources are needed.

- You have to develop a project plan and timeline. You have to establish accountability among team members for every task. You need to track the progress of the project and incorporate feedback about it into future planning.

- You may want to develop a pilot project—sort of a "beta rollout"—before doing a general, company-wide rollout.

Needs Assessment

This is a matter of asking yourself—and answering—many probing questions about the nature of your company's business as it relates to the kind of things that Domino can address. Recall the many ways Domino can serve you:

- Domino can be your company's messaging backbone.

- Domino can be a network of application servers and Web servers.

- As an information repository.

- Domino can automate workflows within the company and between the company and its suppliers, business partners, and customers.

Keeping these things in mind, consider the following business and technical issues:

- What information do you need to make available to people, and to whom? What information do you need to restrict access to?

- Does your company encourage the sharing of information now? Do departments have a vested interest in not sharing information? For example, Salespeople may not want their contacts or knowledge shared. This can affect the team that should be assembled and the way future applications are developed. Both of these may have an effect on hardware and training needs in the company.

- What corporate culture exists now? Will collaboration require a shift in the way a company does business? Who will drive the adoption of the project? Can you identify executives or influential persons in the company and how you can address their business needs/concerns with Notes?

- How do work and information flow through your company? How do they flow within and across workgroups and vertically? How do they flow between the company and its suppliers, partners, and customers?

- How is information stored, and where? How can you make that information more easily accessible? How can you capture the tacit expertise of individuals and make it available to others in the company?

- What are the processes that affect the success of your business? In what ways are these processes unsatisfactory? How can they be improved?

- What computing platforms does your company use? What software does your company use? Do you have company standards for selection of computing platforms?

- What computing platforms and software do your suppliers, business partners, and customers use? What are the interoperability and communication issues between your company and these other parties?

- How does communication take place within your company and between your company and third parties? Is it voice-based, paper-based, or computer-based? Are the methods reliable? How can communications be improved?

- What is the state of electronic communication within the company and between the company and third parties? What is the state of the hardware infrastructure? Is it easy to use? Is it reliable? Is it secure?

- How does your company use the Internet? World Wide Web? Messaging? If you have a Web site, how do you maintain it?

- How knowledgeable about and comfortable with computer technology are your employees, suppliers, business partners, and customers? As you move to Domino-based systems, how much resistance will you meet and how will you overcome it? How will you educate and train users in the new systems as you bring them online? How will you convince suppliers, partners, and customers to accept new systems?

Assembling a Team

The success of a Domino rollout depends on the team of people who will do the work. Who will compose the team depends on how large your company is and how far-reaching will be the planned rollout. The composition of the team may change as the Domino rollout progresses.

If your company is small or you are deploying Domino only in one department, your team may consist of just two or three people: the head of the department or company, an in-house computer technician, and perhaps an outside consultant with expertise in Domino/Notes. If the company is large and the rollout is company-wide, the team will consist of more people but in general should include the same types of people.

That is, there should be managers, end users, functional experts, and technicians on the team. You need managers on the team because a major Domino rollout will need the enthusiastic support of top management to succeed.

You need end users and functional experts because you want Domino to respond to their needs; you want them on the rollout team so that they can tell you how best to meet their needs. If the rollout includes Web or e-commerce functionality, then functional business representatives can test the application to determine if it meets business needs. Usually management can't do that, and users may not have the requisite expertise. For example, an e-commerce web site may require a marketing expert (who will not later be an end user) to test the site for functionality and end users to test for usability.

You need computer technicians because they are familiar with the company's current network infrastructure and they will implement the rollout. Your team should ideally include experts in network architecture, mail routing architecture, application development, Internet architecture, computer security, and Domino/Notes architecture. Development staff can also advise on the resources necessary to either update old Notes applications or create new ones. Application design frequently drives hardware and configuration needs.

Resource Identification

You need to determine what your current hardware, software, and network resources are, then determine what upgrades will be necessary to support your Domino rollout. You should develop a site map that identifies your hardware resources and the connections between them. You can use this map to determine what Domino servers you will need and where you should place them. You should continue to update the site map as the project progresses.

Consider the following items from the perspectives of their current state and your short-term and long-term future needs. Do not neglect future growth:

- **Servers.** What do you have now? What will Domino require? Can you install Domino on existing servers or will you need new ones? Consider operating systems, disk capacity, RAM, number and speed of processors, network connections, locations, access times, and workloads. Also consider new features of Notes/Domino Release 5. For example, if you want to take advantage of transaction logging in Release 5, you may well have to add or reconfigure disk drives on existing servers.

- **Workstations.** What do users have now? What will be required for Domino clients? Consider operating systems, disk capacity, RAM, number and speed of processors, and network connections. Will Notes client be used or browser? If Notes client, will it be loaded locally or reside on network drives? Are workstations backed up by the network or is it user responsibility?

- **Network resources.** What is in place? What will Domino require? Consider hardware such as cabling, NICs, bridges, routers, switches. Consider software, such as communication protocols, network operating systems, and backup programs. Examine network security: firewalls, access points, etc. Consider how users connect to the network. Consider bandwidth and throughput. Consider reliability, fault tolerance, and redundancies. Give some thought, also, to ways to improve service and reduce costs by incorporating technological advances introduced since your existing network was built. For example, while Notes and Domino *can* function on an IPX/SPX network, might this not be a good time to move to TCP/IP?

- **Remote and mobile users.** How do they connect to your network? How will they access Domino servers? How will you support them? Will the Notes client be used? How will users update installed code? What type of security/encryption is appropriate for laptop users?

- **Internet access.** What Internet access is currently in place? Will you need to upgrade? What security is in place? Will it continue to be adequate?

Project Plan

A Domino rollout is a complex project that requires the timely cooperation of many people. To insure success, you should develop a plan of action, assign individual responsibility for each action item, and track your progress in some reliable way. This will help you to meet milestones in a timely, relatively painless way. It will also help you to incorporate feedback so that you learn from mistakes and don't repeat them.

You should determine what resources will be necessary—human, financial, and computer—to carry out the plan, and allocate sufficient resources to get the job done.

You should assign responsibility for specific parts of the plan to specific people, then hold them accountable to their responsibilities. I'll emphasize that last point. If nobody is responsible for getting a job done, it won't get done. If two people are responsible for getting a job done, it might get done or it might not, and if it doesn't, each respondent will point a finger at the other and say, "I thought she was going to do it." But if one person is responsible, then it will get done (or, if it doesn't, you'll know exactly whom you can't rely on).

You also need to track the progress of the rollout. For this purpose, you may want to use standard project management software. In addition (or instead), I would recommend that you also consider using Domino and the TeamRoom application template, which is included with the Domino R5 Application and Enterprise servers. You might think of setting this up as sort of a "pre-pilot" project.

TeamRoom provides a shared resource, an electronic forum where a project team can work together on the project. Team members can raise and discuss issues, set up meeting agendas, and track the resolution of action items.

When you set up a TeamRoom application, you define the team's name and purpose, the team leader, facilitator, and members, general categories that people can assign to documents they create, and types of documents that people can add to the database. You can define subteams and their membership. You can define events and milestones.

TeamRoom includes agents that can 1) automatically remove old documents from lists of active documents, 2) notify team members by email when new documents of interest to them appear in the database, and 3) send email reminders to people when action is due on any item.

TeamRoom is especially useful if your rollout team is geographically dispersed and not all members have Lotus Notes, which is very likely at the earliest stages of the process. You can set it up on an Internet- or intranet-accessible Domino server. Team members can access it either with a Notes client or a Web browser.

Pilot Project

A large, companywide rollout is a major undertaking, fraught with opportunities for failure. You may want to do a "beta rollout" in the form of a pilot project—a localized rollout of a single application. If you decide to do this, consider carefully the application that you will roll out. Ideally, you want to choose an application that will roll out easily and be a wild success. Enthusiasm for a product by current users can overcome a lot of resistance in prospective users.

Fitting Domino into Your Existing Infrastructure

To determine how Domino will fit into your existing infrastructure, you have to consider the following issues:

- How will you use Domino, both short-term and long-term? Will you use Domino companywide or just departmentally? Will people outside the company (suppliers, business partners, customers) have access to your servers?
- How will Domino integrate into your existing network infrastructure?
- What hardware and software upgrades to existing systems will be required to accommodate Domino?
- What corporate culture exists now? Will collaboration require a shift in the way a company does business?
- Who will drive the adoption of the project? Can you identify executives or influential persons in the company and how can you address their business needs/concerns with Notes?

Usage Considerations—How Will You Use Notes?

How and where you set up your Domino servers, what clients you use, and how you connect everything together depends on what you plan to do with Domino/Notes. It also depends on who will be using it. Will you roll out Domino companywide or just within certain departments? For example, if Domino is destined to become the company's messaging backbone, you may need to install Domino Mail servers, whereas if you are setting up Domino to support specific applications, you will need to install Domino application servers. For Domino to support mission-critical applications requiring 24x7 availability, you will need to install Domino Enterprise servers.

If the rollout is localized or the company is located primarily in one location, you may install a small number of high-capacity servers all in one location. If the rollout is company-wide and the company has widely scattered offices, you may install more servers, they may be lower-capacity servers, and they may be located in multiple locations. Consider also the administrative implications to your design. For example, if servers are distributed among local offices, will you administer them centrally or locally? How much control do you want local administrators to have?

If users are exclusively employees of the company you may decide to install Notes clients on every desktop. But if customers or business partners will be using certain applications, you may need to set up those applications on Web-accessible servers and the users may use Web browsers to access the servers.

Network Considerations—How Will Domino Integrate into Your Network?

Exactly what servers you set up and where depends also on the current and future makeup of your local and wide-area networks. Your goals in deciding what servers to set up and where include the following:

- Minimize network traffic
- Maximize user convenience
- Minimize administration overhead
- Maximize hardware uptime

Some of these goals may conflict with each other. For example, you can serve user convenience by placing Domino servers close to users, so that they don't have to endure slow WAN connections when connecting to servers. But to minimize administration overhead, you may prefer to locate servers in a central location. Your goal is to find the best compromise for your organization.

Minimize Network Traffic

As a general principle, you want to minimize network traffic because the network tends to be a bottleneck. Also, the more network traffic you have, the more network bandwidth you have to install and maintain—faster media and more bridges, routers, and switches. This in turn means you need more and better-trained people to manage the network.

Domino servers tend to generate a lot of network traffic. Their client/server architecture minimizes network traffic as much as possible. But Notes applications by their nature generate network traffic, as users and servers transfer messages back and forth and changes replicate to databases located on multiple servers.

In general, you can minimize Domino-generated network traffic by minimizing the number of Domino servers. Fewer Domino servers mean less replication of databases and less message traffic between servers.

In other words, you want to install Domino on large, powerful computers that can accommodate the demands of large numbers of users. To this end Lotus has designed Domino to scale up easily. You can scale up an individual server by increasing the amount of RAM and the number of processors on the computer hosting it. The more RAM a Domino server has, the more simultaneous user sessions it can handle. The more processors a Domino server has, the faster it can respond to user demands. You can scale up even more by hosting Domino on computers running UNIX, OS/400, or OS/390 rather than Windows or OS/2.

Maximize User Convenience

You want your users to like using Notes. It can make them much more productive if they use it effectively. But if they have to reach the nearest Domino server via a slow or unreliable WAN link or dial-up connection, or if the server is unresponsive, they may well decide they don't like Notes and, as a result, they may use it ineffectively or not at all.

This may not be an issue if all of your users work in the same building. But if your company has widely dispersed offices, then either you have to invest in a fast enough, reliable enough WAN to accommodate the demands of users hitting your servers from tens, hundreds, or thousands of miles away, or you have to disperse your servers. This may mean that, instead of a few very powerful servers located in one raised-floor room at headquarters, you may have many not-so-powerful servers located locally to your users, that is, at their offices.

Which is the better strategy? The answer (as usual) is: It depends.

- It depends on what applications you are using. Some applications require constant, fast access to a server. Other applications don't.

- It depends on what in your users' opinions constitutes adequate server response time. If it's a hassle or takes a long time to connect to the server, the users won't. If they have to wait what seems like forever between mouse clicks, the users won't. If the users won't use an application, then you wasted good time and money rolling it out. Consider also that some users may require faster access than others.

- It depends on the current status of your WAN and how much money you can spend on upgrading it. If you can't feasibly establish a fast enough (say, according to a Compaq rule of thumb, 75kbps per active user), reliable enough WAN link between a set of users and their server, then you need to set up a server locally. The server, being a patient computer, will tolerate a slow, unreliable WAN link. Users won't.

- It depends on the availability and quality of network support personnel in the satellite offices. If you don't have good, reliable support in a remote office, perhaps you don't want to set up high-maintenance hardware/software there. You can set up Domino servers so they are all but 100 percent remotely maintainable. But for some administrators this may not be good enough; they need the servers to be where they can easily touch them.

- It depends on the security of the server at the remote office. Domino security depends, in part, on the servers being physically secure. If you don't feel you could make a server physically secure enough at a given location, maybe you shouldn't place it there.

The possibilities for connecting remote offices together vary depending on the number of offices, the actual distance between them, the locations of the offices, and your budget. If your offices are close enough together (and your budget big enough and your in-house expertise adequate to the job), you might be able to lay your own cable or set up a line-of-sight microwave link between them. If your offices are so remote from civilization that standard telephone services are not available, you may have to rely on satellite links or some equally exotic technology. If you have access to cable television service and your cable provider is way ahead of the rest of them, you may be able to use television cables to connect your offices (but probably not).

For the rest of us, the likely choices all mean connecting through the public telephone networks and all involve contracting with a service provider, either your local phone companies or a network service provider. The choices, generally from fastest and most expensive to slowest and cheapest, are as follows:

- Set up a private WAN using dedicated, leased telephone lines.

- Connect via leased lines to a semiprivate WAN such as the phone companies' frame relay networks.

- Connect via leased lines, Digital Subscriber Line (DSL), or modem or ISDN dialup to the public WAN, (that is, to the Internet).

- Connect as needed via dialup either computer-to-computer or LAN-to-LAN.

Of these choices, setting up your own, private WAN using dedicated, leased telephone lines between your offices is the most reliable, potentially the fastest, and certainly the most expensive way to establish communication among them. The great thing about leased phone lines is that you don't have to share them with anyone else—the only traffic on them is that which you yourself generate.

The downside of leased lines is that, because the local phone companies still have a monopoly on the telephone connection to your office, leased lines are expensive. Until the monopoly breaks (and the phone companies are holding on to it for dear life), private, leased lines will always be the rich man's solution to interoffice connectivity. If you don't have a fat budget, leased lines are feasible, in general, only if you have just a few offices to connect and if the offices aren't too far apart (because you pay for leased lines by the mile).

With leased telephone lines you also pay for transmission capacity (that is, bandwidth). The lowest available transmission speed with leased lines is 9600bps or, more realistically for our purposes, 56kbps. The upper end is limited, really, only by your budget. Beyond 56kbps you can install T-1, which has throughput of 1.544mbps, or T-3, which has throughput of 45mbps. If you don't need full T-1 or T-3 throughput, many vendors will sell you "fractional" T-1 or T-3, in which you install hardware with the full transmission capacity but then only use and pay for an agreed upon fraction of the full capacity. If you need more than T-1 or T-3 capacity, you can aggregate T-1 or T-3 lines. (T-1 and T-3 are North American standards. Outside North America you can arrange similar types of phone service that are different from T-1 and T-3 only in name and other minor details.)

Semiprivate WANs such as frame relay networks are the next most reliable and expensive solution. Speeds are generally the same as with leased lines—they begin at 56kbps and go up in 128kbps increments to full T-1 (or higher) capacity. However, on frame relay networks you share the network with other users. While the phone companies (and other entities that offer these services) guarantee that you'll always have access to at least the amount of bandwidth that you pay for, that doesn't mean that you actually will receive that much capacity. The guarantee is merely that, if they don't meet the contracted bandwidth guarantee, you don't have to pay for it.

You still have to set up a dedicated, leased telephone line to connect each of your offices to the provider's frame relay network. But you will pay a minimal amount for the leased lines because you only have to pay for it between your office and the provider's local POP—presumably only a few miles distant.

The next possibility is to use the Internet as your WAN. You can set up connections to the Internet in a variety of ways. First, you can set up leased lines from each of your offices to the nearest POP of an Internet service provider.

Second, you may be able (depending on the ISP) to set up Digital Subscriber Line (DSL) service for each office to an ISP. Like leased lines, this provides an office with a constant connection to the Internet, at a cost and at speeds that are generally lower than for leased lines.

Third, you can establish dialup connectivity to an ISP. In general, any computer that will be accessed by other computers over the Internet needs to be constantly connected via leased line or DSL. Any computer that will not be accessed but will only initiate access to other computers on the Internet may only need dialup connectivity.

The benefit of using the Internet as your WAN is the low cost—you don't have to pay for long-distance leased lines or for use of a service provider's privately maintained wide area network. The offsetting penalties are less reliability and lower security.

Because nobody owns the Internet, nobody really controls the traffic. Therefore, nobody can guarantee the availability of a specific minimum bandwidth. At any given moment, without any notice, the rate of transfer between two computers might slow to a crawl or, worse, shut down entirely for an unpredictable length of time. You can minimize the incidence of this by contracting with a large national or international ISP, one that maintains its own WAN, to provide connectivity for all of your offices. Chances are all or most of the data traffic between your offices will travel over the ISP's own backbone instead of other, generic Internet backbones. When traffic bogs down on other parts of the Internet, you may be unaffected. Of course, such an ISP will charge higher prices than other ISPs.

The other Internet issue is security. Because you share the Internet with everyone else on and off the planet, people can intercept your transmissions and read them or tamper with them. Also, total strangers, competitors, and corporate spies can try to access your Internet-connected servers either to gain unauthorized access to data or to disrupt your servers' proper functioning.

Domino is designed to minimize these dangers. It includes certificate-based authentication so only authorized entities can access servers and so third parties cannot impersonate servers. It includes optional encryption of all transmissions over a given port, so interlopers cannot read or tamper with intercepted transmissions. It includes support for Internet-standard and de facto standard security protocols, including SSL 2.0, SSL 3.0, X.509, and SMIME. It includes a built-in application-level proxy server in the form of pass-through server capabilities, as well as support for HTTP and SOCKS proxy servers and packet-filtering firewalls.

The last option in the preceding bullet list is direct dialup access either to your servers or to a LAN (then across the LAN/WAN to your servers). Domino supports both. Dialup access is the slowest form of access, but also the cheapest and the most secure. You can dial into a server or LAN using either standard modems or ISDN terminal adapters or routers. Modems support transmission speeds ranging realistically from 14.4kbps up to 56kbps or 112kbps if using dual modems. ISDN supports speeds of either 64kbps or 128kbps.

Of these connectivity schemes, which is best for you? Only you can decide that. But bear in mind that users cannot tolerate slow connections, long server response times, and constantly breaking connections. Servers can. Your trade-off, then, is between these two options:

- Set up your servers in one central location (or maybe a few central locations) and establish a connectivity scheme that can accommodate a lot of user traffic without slowing down. This would be one of the wide area network schemes— a private WAN based on leased lines, a semi-private WAN such as a frame relay network, or high-speed connections to the Internet.

- Distribute your servers so users have LAN access or local, high-speed WAN access to them and establish a connectivity scheme that the servers can tolerate. Servers are more tolerant of slow and unreliable connections than are people, so you can get by with a much slower, less expensive WAN than if people are using it. For that matter, you can function with no WAN at all if you feel that dialup access among the servers is adequate to meet your needs.

Minimize Administration Overhead

You want to minimize the administrative burden because, well, you're overworked and, well, your boss doesn't want to hire more high-priced people like you to help out. The more servers you set up, the more administration you will have to do. So minimize administration by setting up fewer, more powerful servers.

Of course, if you have concluded that for your users' convenience (which does after all come first) you need to set up a lot of servers, not to worry. Domino Release 5 is an administrator's dream come true. The administrator's interface puts 99 percent of your tasks right in front of you, all in one place, organized by task. Furthermore, the only administrative task you cannot perform remotely is to reboot the server, and even that you can manage with the right software. And even the most illiterate computer klutz can be walked by phone through the process of restarting a computer (well, okay, maybe that's going too far).

Maximize Hardware Uptime

Hard drives crash. Electronic circuits fail. Software has bugs. People unplug wires. You need to decide whether and to what degree your organization can tolerate such faults, then build in enough redundancy and backup to insure that the organization never has to tolerate more fault than it comfortably can. How much fault is tolerable will be different for every organization. It will depend on what Notes applications you are using, how costly downtime would be, and how costly it would be to insure that downtime does not occur.

The kinds of failure that can occur are as follows:

- Electric power failures
- Disk drive failures
- Whole server failures
- LAN/WAN failures
- Building failures

Electric Power Failures

Poor quality electrical power (brownouts, surges, spikes, and noise) can cause all sorts of obscure and mysterious problems. Power outages (blackouts) are just plain crippling. At a minimum, you should provide your servers with high quality UPSes and configure the software that comes with the UPSes to shut your servers down in an orderly manner. Whether you want to take further measures (all the way to setting up emergency power generation) depends on your own needs.

Disk Drive Failures

Although disk drives are far more reliable than they used to be, they are still prone to failure, and the consequences of a disk drive failure can be devastating. To protect against disk drive failure you should certainly implement some form of backup procedures, such as backup to magnetic tape.

From time to time you should review your backup procedures to assure that you are in fact backing up what you think you are. You should also review your media retention policy to make sure you are retaining backed up data for a sufficiently long period to protect against data loss but not so long that the organization is needlessly exposed to legal risk. Finally, when you install Domino Release 5, you should probably update your current backup procedures to accommodate transaction logging, a new feature in Domino Release 5.

You should also consider whether to incorporate RAID functionality into your servers. RAID stands for "Redundant Array of Inexpensive/Independent Drives" and refers to a series of ways to write data redundantly onto disk drives, so that if one drive fails, you don't lose the data written onto it. Of course, you won't lose the data if it was backed up to tape. But with tape backup, you do lose access to the data until the failed drive is replaced and the backed up data is restored to the replacement drive. This can be a very time consuming process. With RAID, even though you lose access to a disk drive, you don't lose disk access to the data because it was written redundantly to more than one drive.

The types of RAID that are commonly used in servers include the following:

- RAID 1. Two disk drives mirrored: All data is written to both drives simultaneously. If one dies, all data is still available on the other one. The advantage over other RAID architectures is read/write speed. The drawback of RAID 1 is that it is expensive, requiring two full disk drives for every one drive's worth of data.

- RAID 5 (stripe sets with parity). Data is "striped" (or "stripped" as some say) across three or more disk drives. Each data "stripe" (or "strip") includes parity information. If any one disk drive dies, the data written to it can be reconstructed because of the parity information. It can be reconstructed in real time until the dead drive can be replaced. Later, it can be reconstructed onto the replacement drive. RAID 5 is less wasteful of disk space than RAID 1 because it does not require that every bit be written to two different drives. The more drives in an array, the more economical is RAID 5. The downside is that calculation of parity slows down disk access.

- RAID "10" (RAID 0 plus RAID 1, that is, two nonparity stripe arrays (RAID 0) mirrored). Striping data onto three or more disks is a really fast way to write and read data (because multiple read-write heads work simultaneously). This setup combines that speed with the protection of mirroring. In effect, you have two mirrored stripe sets of disks. The gain here over RAID 1 and RAID 5 is speed, not data integrity.

Whole Server Failures

Whole server failures include motherboard and power supply failures as well as software failures. To guard against both, you can buy computers with redundant motherboards and power supplies. To guard against hardware failures (and, in some cases, software failures,) you can set up server clusters. You can implement server clusters at the OS level, in Domino, or in both. OS-level server clusters come generally in two types: passive and active.

In a passive server cluster, two computers share one or more disk drives. One server "owns" them and runs the software located on them. The other server passively waits for the first server to fail, at which time it claims ownership of the shared disk drives and takes over running the software on them. The drawback of this scheme is that you have to run two computers but only one actually does any work.

In an active server cluster, each server owns one or more of the shared disk drives and runs the software on them. If either server fails, the other claims ownership of the failed server's drives and runs the software on them. The benefit here is that you don't spend all that money on a computer just to have it idle forever, as it would in the passive clustering scheme.

The drawback of this scheme is that you may not want or be able to run Domino on these servers. For example, under Windows NT you shouldn't, as a general rule, run any other programs on a computer running Domino. If one of the two servers in an active cluster runs, say, an Oracle server, and the other runs a Domino server, then, upon failure of one the other will run both, with unpredictable consequences. Alternately, if you try to run Domino on each server, then upon failure the remaining server will try to run two Domino servers. To make this work properly, you have to run Domino Enterprise Server on both computers and install the Domino servers as partitioned servers. One partitioned server runs on each computer. When one computer fails, the second partitioned Domino server on the second computer starts, with the end result being that both Domino servers are now running on the second box.

Under Domino server clustering (which comes with the Domino Enterprise Server), between two and six Domino servers can work together to balance the workload among themselves. If any server in the cluster becomes overworked or fails, new users will automatically fail over to other servers in the cluster. Read about this in more detail in Chapter 20, "Enhancing Data Availability."

To guard against software-caused server failures you can take a number of steps. Some operating systems (for example, OS/400) can detect if Domino malfunctions and force it to restart. For other Domino platforms you can buy monitoring software that can force Domino to restart in the event of a malfunction. An example of this is Intelliwatch by Candle, and there are others. You can also buy products that will reboot a computer if the OS or other software running on it fails. To guard against the risk that third-party software running on the Domino server locks up Domino, you should obey Lotus's directive never to run other types of servers on the machine running your Domino server. (This is primarily a problem for Windows NT.)

Organizations that require high availability of their servers and applications may very well use all of these tools to ensure that availability. Not only will the computers on which the servers run employ redundant hardware components, but the Domino servers running on them will be partitioned across OS clusters *and* combined into Domino clusters. They will also run monitoring software that watches the health of the running servers and takes various actions in response to developing problems.

LAN/WAN Failures

LAN and WAN failures are rare but potentially devastating when they occur. If you feel the need to protect against LAN failures, you can do so by installing redundant equipment: hot spare file servers, dual LAN adapters, and backup LANs. Your Domino installation can actually benefit from dual LANs in that your servers can communicate with each other over one LAN while users communicate with Domino servers over another LAN.

If you have a private WAN you could use Internet connections as a backup. If you use a frame relay network or the Internet as your WAN you could have redundant connections to one or more POPs. You could also implement backup dialup connections between your Domino servers and for mobile users.

Building Failures

To protect against such calamities as fires and natural disasters, you would normally set up a whole secondary set of servers, located distant—hundreds of miles—from your primary facilities. As a less costly alternative, consider contracting with a Domino hosting service to host servers for you. CompuServe, Interliant, NetCom, and US West are some but not all of the companies that host Domino servers.

Network Protocols

Domino servers and Notes clients are very flexible when it comes to network protocols. They can use the protocols listed in Table 2.1 to communicate with each other.

Table 2.1 **Network Protocols Supported by Domino and Notes**

Protocol	Description
TCP/IP	The protocol suite of the Internet and UNIX networks. The best protocols for large networks. As of Windows NT 4.0 Microsoft adopted it as its default protocol. As of Novell NetWare 5.0 Novell adopted it as its default protocol.
NetBIOS over IP	A Domino or Notes computer running TCP/IP can alternatively communicate using NetBIOS over IP instead of TCP over IP.
IPX/SPX	The native protocol suite of Novell NetWare networks. Also available on Microsoft Windows NT 3.5 networks and later. A fast protocol on small networks. Works on bridged or routed networks.

Protocol	Description
NetBIOS over IPX	A Domino or Notes computer running IPX/SPX can alternatively communicate using NetBIOS over IPX instead of SPX over IPX.
NetBEUI/NetBIOS	The native protocol suite of Microsoft's and IBM's early networking products including Microsoft Network, the family of network server operating systems co-developed by 3Com and Microsoft and marketed under various names by different OEMS (e.g., Microsoft LAN Manager, IBM LAN Server, DEC PathWorks), and Windows NT 3.1 and later. A fast protocol on small networks. Works on bridged but not routed networks.
Vines	The native protocol suite of Banyan Vines networks. Vines networks also support TCP/IP.
AppleTalk	The native protocol suite of Apple Macintosh networks. Apple networks also support TCP/IP.

Domino and Notes use NetBIOS when running on a NetBEUI network and can use NetBIOS when running on computers running TCP/IP or IPX/SPX. The benefit of running Domino or Notes with NetBIOS over IP or IPX is that two computers not running the same underlying protocol (TCP/IP, IPX/SPX, or NetBEUI) could still communicate with each other because all three of these protocol suites support NetBIOS. NetBIOS is native to NetBEUI. The IP and IPX suites support NetBIOS as alternatives to TCP and SPX, respectively.

In the past couple of years, as the Internet and the Internet protocol suite have become ascendant, everyone in the world has been more and more favoring TCP/IP over the other protocols. Lotus is no exception. While Domino and Notes continue to support the other protocols, certain features of Domino work best if communication takes place over TCP/IP, and other features only work over TCP/IP.

For example, the automatic failover and load balancing features of Domino server clusters work best if the clients are communicating with the server via TCP/IP. Also, Internet clients can only use TCP/IP. A Web browser or POP3 or IMAP mail reader cannot communicate with a server not running TCP/IP.

There are good reasons (other than the ascendancy of the Internet) why TCP/IP is being favored over the other network protocols. In many ways it is superior to the others. In particular, with its built-in support of DNS, ARP, RARP, and NIS, it is the most efficient protocol to use on a large network. And all of our networks are growing, getting more internally complex, and interconnecting with one another.

The bottom line here is that you can use any of the supported protocols when you set up Domino and Notes in your organization, but if TCP/IP is one of the options, you should probably treat it as the preferred option. And you can use any combination of the supported protocols. For example, a given server or Notes client can run both TCP/IP and IPX/SPX if need be.

Just remember that, to communicate with each other at all, two computers must use the same protocol, whatever you choose. That is, if a server uses TCP/IP and a Notes client uses AppleTalk, the two will not be able to communicate directly. If one server uses TCP/IP and a second server uses IPX/SPX, they will not be able to replicate or route mail directly. (In both these examples the two computers may be able to communicate indirectly, via a pass-through server running both protocols, if pass-through is otherwise properly set up to allow them to communicate.) Also, if you have to choose between implementing multiple protocols on servers and implementing them on user workstation, you will be much better off implementing them on servers.

Hardware Considerations: What Hardware and Software Upgrades Will Be Required?

At the end of Chapter 1, I listed the hardware/OS platforms on which Domino and Notes run. Most companies decide which platforms to use based on what they already know how to administer. Historically, for most companies, that has been Windows NT. But if you are looking at really large numbers of users per server or you will need rock-solid reliability, take a close look at the UNIX, AS/400, and S390 platforms. In general, they are more scalable and reliable than Windows NT has been historically.

A much more difficult issue facing anyone planning a Domino rollout is how much raw server power you should install—whatever the platform. How many servers do you need and, in each server, how many processors, how much RAM, and how much disk capacity are necessary to support a given number of users. The question, "How many servers do you need?" we have dealt with elsewhere in this chapter. But its answer also depends on how many users each server can accommodate, and that depends on disk, RAM, and processors, considered later. So read on. The answer to "How much disk capacity?" is relatively easy and I'll deal with it next. The answers to "How many processors, how much RAM?" are difficult and I'll deal with them last.

How Much Disk Capacity (and What Disk Configuration)?

Beyond the axiom that you can never have too much disk capacity, it is perhaps not so easy to predict how much disk capacity you will need. Lotus says you need 270MB just to install Domino and recommends 1GB total free disk space for program and data. But that's really just for starters. For anything more than a test platform, you will sooner or later need more disk space than that. Also, you will want more than one physical disk drive.

A rule of thumb that I have heard for mail servers (which are by far the biggest disk hogs among Domino servers) is to provide 50MB per mail user. It seems as though, no matter how hard you try (and Domino gives you the tools), you'll never be able to control some users' penchants for saving everything forever.

For other types of servers, you can consult with the designers of the applications that the servers will be hosting to determine what those applications' disk needs will be. If the designers are not available or are otherwise not helpful, you can run tests on the applications themselves to determine how much disk space various kinds of documents will occupy, then estimate the numbers of documents that are likely to accumulate. Rather than try to predict your ultimate disk capacity needs, you may prefer to configure your servers with disk hardware that is easily expandable.

However, much disk capacity you decide to install, you should configure your servers' disk capacity as follows:

- You want your servers to have at least two separate disk drives and preferably three. Your operating system and Domino program directories will reside on the first drive. Your Domino data directories will reside on the second drive. Your transaction logs will reside on the third drive if you have one, on the first drive if you only have two drives.

   The important point here is that the transaction logs should reside on a different drive than the data files that they back up. Domino writes to Notes databases randomly but to the transaction logs serially. If they reside together on the same physical disk, the constant switching between modes will cause delays in writes to the transaction logs and excessive disk head thrashing. The first is not good for your data. The second is not good for your hardware.

- You want to use RAIDs rather than single disk drives (see the section "Disk Drive Failures" earlier in this chapter). At minimum, the drive on which your transaction logs reside should be a RAID, preferably RAID 1 or RAID 10, because they provide the fastest data access. For full protection, your program and data files should reside on RAIDs as well. RAID 5 may be acceptable here, because access speed is not as important for these files as it is for the transaction logs. Of course, you may consider proprietary RAID schemes, such as RAID 7, if you feel they offer better speed or safety than RAIDs 1, 5, and 10.

How Many Processors, How Much RAM?

The bare minimum and recommended minimum RAM for a Domino server are 48MB and 96MB for the Windows and OS/2 platforms and 64MB and 128MB for the UNIX platforms—and one processor. But those are hardly more than marketing numbers. You will need more than the minimums if the server will be accommodating more than a small group of users. (50? 100? 200? Read on)

Exactly how many processors and how much RAM a server needs depend mostly on how many users the server will accommodate at any one time and what those users will be doing. Some user activities work the server harder than others. For example, users who generate large documents, run agents, do full-text searches, and replicate with servers work the server much harder than users who only read and write mail memos.

Some user activities are more subject than others to certain kinds of bottlenecks. For example, heavily used discussion or tracking databases are subject to contention problems as multiple users try to access them simultaneously. Because of this, a given server might support several times more mail users than users of discussion, tracking, and workflow applications.

This variability makes it very difficult to predict necessary server capacity. To start with, you may be unable to predict what the mix of workloads will be on your servers. Maybe you can predict the total number of users in your organization. But can you predict how many will use given Domino services at any one time? Can you predict what combination of activities your users will perform? Even if you *can* predict your workload mix, how do you translate those loads into recommended hardware configurations? This is not an easy problem. The difficulty is compounded by the fact that Lotus has optimized the server in a number of ways going from R4 to R5, such that a computer running R5 can support as many as five times more users than the same computer could support under R4.6. This makes whatever performance metrics that may have developed over the life of R4 all that much harder to apply.

Lotus does supply some tools to help you determine what hardware capacity you will need, including Lotus NotesBench, Domino Server.Planner, and Domino Server.Load. There are also tools and services available from third parties to assist in this task.

- Lotus NotesBench is a benchmarking program that hardware manufacturers can use to generate Notes capacity and performance data for given hardware configurations. Under NotesBench, testers run scripts that simulate user workloads on the tested platform. Testers gradually increase the number of simulated users logged in and performing various kinds of tasks. NotesBench collects ongoing statistics on such useful parameters as server response times, numbers of transactions performed per minute, CPU utilization, memory utilization, and I/O utilization. The scripts and test conditions are standardized and test results are audited. This ensures that all manufacturers play by the same rules and that different manufacturers' test results are comparable and uniform. Audited NotesBench test results take two forms—a summary test report and a dataset. The test report is a narrative summary intended for human consumption. The dataset (aka a Vendor Database) is a read-only Notes database intended to be used as a data input by Domino Server.Planner.

- Domino Server.Planner is a set of Notes database templates that are included with Domino and which you can use to compare NotesBench test results with your intended server workloads to determine what tested hardware configurations would meet your projected needs. You enter your own requirements—numbers of users for various types of workloads—and Server.Planner tells you which hardware configurations from among those on datasets chosen by you can support those workloads.

- Domino Server.Load is a scripting tool from Lotus that simulates various workloads on an existing, Windows/Intel-based Domino server. It includes ready made scripts, a scripting language, and an interface for controlling script variables in real time. Download it at `www.lotus.com/performance`. This tool is of value to current Domino users who need to evaluate the capacity of existing hardware, not to prospective Domino users.

- The following performance and capacity planning tools are available from Lotus Business Partners: ProActive Assistant from G2 Associates (`www.g2sys.com`); GroupSizr Pro, MailSizr, and WebSizr from Technovations, Inc. (`www.technovations.com`); Intelliwatch Pinnacle from Candle (`www.candle.com`); and inter.action (`www.interdotaction.com`). Like Domino Server.Load, these tools are mostly of value to existing Domino users, not prospective ones.

Unfortunately using these tools to generate data that will help you decide what your server configurations should be is not a simple or straightforward matter. One problem is that the hardware manufacturers don't publish the datasets that Server.Planner needs (so you can ignore the instruction in Server.Planner to retrieve the datasets from the notesbench.org Web site—they aren't there). In fact, the only thing most of the manufacturers do publish is summary test results that show their servers in the best possible light. They use the Mail Only test script, which assumes light demand on the server by users and therefore shows the highest numbers of supported users for any given hardware configuration. Your users will probably make heavier use of server resources. Therefore you will never be able to support the numbers claimed in these published test summaries.

So what should you do? You have four options, which I list below in order of increasing accuracy and expense:

- You can make a rough guess based on published data.

- You can discuss your needs with server hardware vendors.

- You can contract with someone to generate NotesBench data in a lab, using your predicted mix of workloads.

- You can run real-world, on-site pilot tests in your own environment.

Regarding the first option ("rough guess"), here are some things you should keep in mind:

- You can find published summary reports of NotesBench test results at www.notesbench.org and at the Web sites of various computer manufacturers including IBM, Sun, Hewlett-Packard, Compaq (www.compaq.com, www.digital.com), and Dell. As I write this, all published test results are for Domino 4.x. I hope there will be some test results for Domino 5.x by the time you read this.

- Almost all the published test results will be for the Mail workload, the lightest of them all. (The manufacturers are no fools; they know that people look at the maximum number of users first, and ask questions later, if at all.)

- As a rule of thumb for Domino 4.6 Mail workload test results, divide the highest number of users achieved in the test by 3, then (to give your server some headroom) deduct another 25 percent from the resulting number. This should give you a rough real-world user count for the hardware configuration tested. But then multiply the result by about 1.8 to adjust for Domino 5.0's greater capacity.

- There is no comparable rule of thumb for translating Domino 5.0 NotesBench user counts into real world user counts, because there isn't any real world data yet. But the NotesBench workloads are being redesigned to achieve a closer correspondence between NotesBench numbers and real world numbers, so hopefully you won't have to reduce the Domino 5.0 NotesBench results by nearly as much as the Domino 4.6 results. Get the latest information on this fast evolving situation at www.notesbench.org/guestdsc.nsf.

- Find out what loads other Domino users have achieved. Look in two places: The NotesBench Consortium at www.notesbench.org/guestdsc.nsf and success stories at www.lotus.com/performance.

- Another method that I have seen recommended for obtaining a rough estimate of your server's minimum RAM requirement is to multiply the projected number of users by 300KB. I don't know where this number came from or how reliable it is.

- The number of user sessions that your server can accommodate is limited by RAM. The amount of time it takes the server to respond to user requests is affected by the number of processors.

- As I write this, Lotus is not sure how many processors Domino R5 will be able to use effectively. They think, conservatively, 6–8 RISC processors, 3–4 Intel processors. To get the latest information, visit `www.notesbench.org/guestdsc.nsf`.

Regarding the second option for estimating your hardware configuration needs—discussing it with your hardware vendor—I can't tell you how useful it will be. But Lotus highly recommends it. If you buy hardware from a Lotus Alliance Hardware Vendor (Compaq/Digital, Hewlett-Packard, IBM, or Sun Microsystems), they undoubtedly will work with you on this. These vendors all conduct NotesBench tests on their products, so they should have the datasets Server.Planner needs. In fact, I would recommend you ask your hardware vendor to run NotesBench workloads to your specifications. Then, see if they will do the analyses in Server.Planner for you as well.

If you can't talk your hardware vendor into producing the NotesBench datasets that you need, you could hire a third party to produce them for you. Lotus Consulting will do it and so will some Lotus Business Partners. You can get names of Lotus Business Partners who are qualified to consult with you on your capacity planning and/or run NotesBench tests for you from Lotus's Web site (`www.lotus.com/performance`).

Finally, as Lotus will tell you again and again, the best way to determine your hardware needs is to run, in your own environment, a pilot rollout of the applications you intend to implement, then analyze the results. The same business partners that can produce NotesBench datasets for you can help you stage an in-house pilot program and analyze the results.

Establishing Domino's Internal Infrastructure

When you set up your first Domino server you have to supply a domain name, an organization name, a server name, and the name of one user. You also have to put Domino's security into place. Before you ever get to this point, however, you should have established a security policy for Domino and decided on an overall naming policy. To do this properly you have to understand how Domino organizes itself and you have to decide how Domino's organization will fit into your company's organization.

In this chapter, we consider the following issues:

- **Domino domain considerations.** How many domains? What domain name or names?

- **Organization considerations.** How many Domino organizations? How many Domino organization levels? How should the Domino organization scheme reflect the company's organization? What names?

- **Domino Named Network considerations.** How many named networks? How will the named networks map to the underlying network architecture? What names?

- **Domino security considerations.** How much do you care about security and what measures should you take to assure security adequate to your needs?

You also need to establish topologies, schedules, and policies for database replication and mail routing. However, it isn't as important that you decide these issues at this stage, so we'll defer our discussion of them until later chapters.

How Domino Organizes Itself: Domains, Organizations, Named Networks

Domino servers organize themselves in three ways, by domain, organization, and named network. Each server exists in a Domino domain. Each server belongs to an organization that forms the basis for the server's name. Each server is in one or more Domino named networks, which reflect the server's relationship to the network on which it exists.

If you are rolling out Domino for the first time in your company, you have to determine how many Domino domains, organizations, and named networks there will (or may eventually) be and how they will be named. If you are rolling out Domino servers into a company in which Domino already has a presence, you have to decide how the new servers will fit into the existing infrastructure. In both cases you have to place your new servers and users in the correct places in the organization hierarchy and name them in accordance with the established naming conventions.

Domains

Domino domains define boundaries for mail delivery and server management and consist of a group of Domino servers that share a common Domain Directory database. That is, a given Domino Directory defines the membership of a single Domino domain. Every Domino server is a member of the Domino Domain represented by the Domino Directory located on that server. (If multiple Domino Directories reside on a server, the one that defines the server's domain is the one with filename *names.nsf*.) See Figure 2.1.

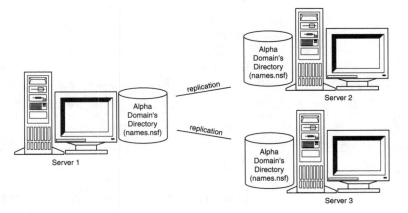

Figure 2.1   All servers in a domain maintain
replica copies of the domain directory (names.nsf).

Each server in a domain is represented in the Domain Directory by a Server document that defines the server and acts as a configuration document for it. A server's domain name appears in the Domain field of its Server document, and appears again in the "Domain" variable in the server's notes.ini file (a text file stored on the server computer and containing more configuration information for the server).

The server's domain name must appear in both of these places and the domain name entered in both of these places must be the same as for all the other servers in the domain. Any server whose domain name is incorrectly listed in either of these places will not function properly.

Users belong to a Domino domain as well. Each user is a member of the same domain as his/her home server and has a Person document in the Domain Directory describing him or her. Each user's domain name appears in the Domain field of his/her Person document and in the Domain field of all of the Location documents in his or her Personal Address Book.

Domino domains define the boundaries of numerous functions. Chief among these is mail delivery. Mail addressed to Notes mail users must be addressed to "Username @ Domainname," See Figure 2.2. (If you address mail just to "Username," Notes assumes that the user is in the same domain as you and supplies that information for you, automatically expanding the name to "Username @ Domainname.")

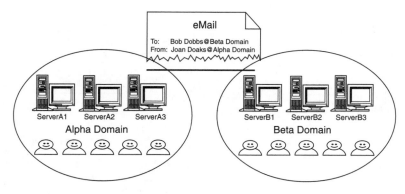

Figure 2.2 Mail addressed to a user in another Domino domain must be addressed "username @ domainname."

Other functions that are bounded by the domain include the Database Catalog, Domain Search, Statistics Reporting and Event Dispatching, and the Administration Process. Each of these functions creates and maintains one or more databases on the servers on which it runs. If these services run on more than one server in the domain, their respective databases are automatically replicas of each other, because their replica IDs are generated from the Domain Directory's replica ID.

Domino domains are independent of Internet domains, Windows NT domains, LAN Manager, LAN Server, and PathWorks domains, and Novell NetWare directory trees. They are strictly a creature of Domino, intended to streamline the management of Domino servers.

How Many Domino Domains Should You Set Up?

You can set up as many Domino domains as you like within a company. However, more domains generally mean more administration, so you want to minimize the number of domains. There are all sorts of reasons why a company might have more than one domain:

- Very large companies may have established multiple domains in earlier releases of Domino/Notes in order to keep the Public Address Book (now the Domain Directory) manageably small. Earlier versions of Domino/Notes could not accommodate databases nearly as large as Release 5 Domino can. If a company intended to set up tens or hundreds of thousands of Notes seats, they might have planned up front for multiple domains. Even now a company with many self-managed, quasi-independent business units might prefer, in the name of distributed management, that each business unit maintain its own Domino domain.

- Two companies that both use Notes independently might merge.

- Notes might grow from the ground up in a company, with different divisions within the company setting it up unbeknownst to each other.

- Many companies allow subsidiaries a high degree of independence. In the spirit of that independence, some subsidiaries will prefer to set up and maintain their own Domino domains rather than give up that control to the parent company.

- A company might set up a "firewall" domain separate from its principle domain, so that it can selectively share data with outsiders. The internal domain directory, accessible only by company insiders, contains lots of information about company employees. But the firewall domain directory, accessible by outsiders, contains no such information. Databases containing sensitive internal information reside only on internal domain servers. Databases containing public information reside on the firewall domain servers.

- A company might set up a separate domain for its public Web servers so that the names of Web visitors don't get commingled with those of company insiders in a single domain directory.

I have seen or heard of instances of each of the scenarios described above. However, you should understand that most companies only have one domain or, at most, an internal domain and maybe a firewall or Web domain. Because more domains mean more administration, I highly recommend that you set up just one internal domain if you don't have an overriding reason to set up more than one.

Domino Domain Naming Recommendations

Domino domain names should somehow reflect the name of the entity they represent. If you have a registered Internet domain name, you might also use that as your Domino domain name. (In fact, beginning with R5, the server setup program for the first server in an organization uses your Internet domain name by default if it can find it in the server's IP stack. For example, if your Internet domain name is "planetnotes.com," Notes uses "planetnotes" as the default Domino domain name.) Some people suggest that the domain name of a company should be the company name as outsiders refer to it (since outsiders are the most likely to need to know the domain name—for mail addressing reasons). The popup help for the Domain Name field in the Domino Setup database (where you actually enter the domain name for the first time) recommends that, for ease of administration, your domain name not use spaces. I personally can think of no reason why you shouldn't use spaces if you want to. But I would recommend you keep the name short and sweet so that people who have to type it out in the future will not curse you under their breath as they do so.

Domino domain names A–Z, a–z, 0–9, & (ampersand), – (dash), . (period), _ (underscore), ' (apostrophe), and spaces. They should begin with a letter of the alphabet. Finally, use proper case. It will make your domain name much more pleasant to read than all uppercase or all lowercase. (Users will be able to use upper case, lower case, or mixed case, because Domino domain names are not case-sensitive.)

Organizations

The Domino Organization is not a monolithic thing like the domain. Rather, it is a hierarchical naming scheme that defines the name of every Domino server and Notes user. It is very important in that it is the bedrock on which all Domino security is built. (Domino servers have to know who you are if they are to grant you the correct level of data access.)

The Domino naming scheme was originally modeled on the International directory standard known as X.500, the Directory Access Protocol (DAP) but now also complies with the Lightweight Directory Access Protocol (LDAP), which is itself a simplified subset of X.500 and an emerging Internet standard. X.500 also forms the basis of the Novell Directory Service and (at least loosely) the Internet Domain Name System (DNS). LDAP forms the basis of the Microsoft Active Directory, due for release with Windows 2000, the Netscape Directory Server, and numerous public Internet directory services. If you understand how any of these name/directory services work, you are already familiar with the general characteristics of the Domino organization.

In a DAP or LDAP naming scheme all server and user names are hierarchical. They consist of two or more parts that identify the server or user and tell others where the server or user fits in the organization hierarchy. Names in this format are called "fully-distinguished" names because they serve to distinguish people even if they have the same name. Domino names look something like this:

These examples use just the CN and O components:

Server1/Acme or

CN=Server1/O=Acme

Rob Kirkland/Stillwater or

CN=Rob Kirkland/O=Stillwater

These examples use varying numbers of OU components:

Server2/Servers/Stillwater or

CN=Server2/OU=Servers/O=Stillwater

Bob Dobbs/Acctg/MarshCreek/Stillwater or

CN=Bob Dobbs/OU2=Acctg/OU1=MarshCreek/O=Stillwater

This example uses the C component:

Joe Doaks/AR/Acctg/London/Acme/UK or

CN=Joe Doaks/OU3=AR/OU2=Acctg/OU1=London/O=Acme/C=UK

Notice that each name in the preceding list appears twice. The first instance of each name just shows the components of the name separated by slashes. The second instance of each name includes labels that identify the type of each component of the name. The first form is called "abbreviated" format. The second form is called *canonicalized* format.

Notice also that, in the names that include OU components, the OU numbers descend from left to right.

The possible parts of a Domino server name or Notes user name include the following:

- **Common Name ("CN").** This part of the name corresponds to your or my actual name: "Rob Kirkland", or to a server's "host" name. Every name must include a common name component. In a nonhierarchical naming system, the common name would be the full name.

- **Organizational Units ("OU" or "OUn", where n is a number from 1 to 4).** This part of the name identifies where in the organizational hierarchy a server or user fits. Domino allows up to four levels of organizational units but they are entirely optional. You need not define any OUs if you don't want to.

- **Organization ("O").** This part of the name identifies the organization to which you belong. Every name must include an organization component.

- **Country ("C").** This part of the name identifies in which country an entity exists. It is optional. You need not use the C component if you don't want to.

To understand how a hierarchical name reflects a user's place in the hierarchy, you can draw a hierarchical diagram, such as the one in Figure 2.3.

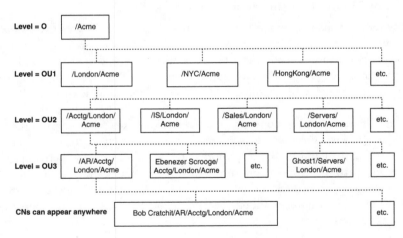

Figure 2.3   Domino names show where an entity fits in the hierarchy of an organization.

The Domino organization is embodied in a series of small binary files called ID files. There is one organization certifier ID that has a name in the form /O=Acme (or simply /Acme). By default its filename is cert.id. You can change the file name to anything you want (say, in our example, acmecert.id). Whatever you name the file, you should retain the ".id" extension so that it appears in lists of ID files.

There is an organization unit certifier ID for each organizational unit that you define. The name of each organizational unit is its own name plus the name of its parent (the O or a higher level OU). Thus, in Figure 2.3, the London OU is a child of /O=Acme, so its name is /OU=Servers/O=Acme. The filename in this case would default to london.id, but you could change it. The O and OU ID files should be stored where only authorized users have access to them.

Each server and user also has an ID file. These are not called "certifier" IDs but rather "server" IDs or "user" IDs. The name of each user or server is his/her/its common name plus the full name of his/her/its parent certifier ID. User file names default to user.id. Server file names default to server.id. In both cases you may want to rename them to make it clear which user or server they belong to.

There is no "country" ID file to represent the C component (if your company uses it). The C component appears as the last part of the entity's name in certifier, server, and user IDs. Most organizations don't use the C component.

How Many Domino Organizations Should You Set Up?

You may set up as many Domino organizations as you want. However, even more than with Domino domains, you probably want to have just one organization. Servers and users in an organization can automatically authenticate each other. Servers and users not in the same organization can only authenticate each other if they (or their parent OUs or Os) have been cross-certified, which is something administrators have to do manually.

You might want part of a company to be in a separate organization from the rest of the company if it is a very independent entity or if you anticipate its being spun off from the rest of the company. Other than that, the usual reason why there might be multiple organizations within a company is that one company was acquired by another company. For example, Lotus was acquired by IBM. Employees of Lotus are members of the /Lotus organization, whereas employees of IBM are members of the /IBM organization.

How Should OUs Be Organized?

The guidelines regarding formation of OUs are as follows:

- Keep your organization shallow. Very small organizations—consulting firms, for example—might not use OUs at all. Larger companies should use as few OUs as practicable. Even the largest companies should not use all four levels of OUs, because you want to reserve OU4 to resolve name conflicts within an OU.

- Assign OUs (if at all) to entities within the company that have some permanence. This minimizes the necessity to rename users when an entity identified by one of their OUs is dissolved.

- Servers should reside in their own OU or OUs, separate from people. This gives you better control over their creation, administration, and cross-certification. Even companies that don't plan to use OUs at all for people should consider putting their server or servers in an OU.

- If internal politics is going to make it difficult to reach agreement on what OUs to set up, consider forgetting about user OUs entirely. You can always move users into OUs later. But once a server is set up, it is very difficult to move it to a new OU, so at least try to arrive at agreement regarding server OUs.

- Geographically dispersed companies typically use OU1 to identify the cities where offices are located. Companies with only one office (colleges, for example) typically use OU1 to identify divisions or departments. But don't feel compelled to adhere rigidly to such classifications. For example, your company might primarily use city names at OU1; but you might decide that it makes sense for Manufacturing to be an OU1 classification as well.

Domino Organization Naming Recommendations

The guidelines regarding naming of the organization, OUs, servers, and people are as follows:

- The organization name, OU names, and server names should not contain spaces. This makes for easier administration of servers. User common names may contain whatever spaces they do in real life.

- Country names, if you use them, must consist of the two-letter abbreviations assigned to each country by the ISO.

- The organization name must be at least three characters and not more than 64 characters in length. Keep it short but identifiable.

- By default, Notes will assign the same name to your domain and organization. Consider making them different. This will make it easier in the future for people to recognize which one they are looking at. Some companies name their domain as outsiders know the company ("Winkin, Blinkin, and Nod") and their organization as insiders refer to it ("WBN").

- OU names can be as short as a single character and as long as 32 characters. For the sake of those who have to type them out, make them as short as possible but long enough to be meaningfully descriptive.

- Server common names should be unique across the organization. In fact, server common names should be unique across all organizations and domains within your control. This minimizes the possibility of a user reaching ServerX/Acme when really intending to reach ServerX/Bard.

- Consider using server common names that will be easy for users to remember, whimsical even, instead of the deadly meaningless combinations of code letters and numbers typically assigned to computers by IS departments. The computer's host name or NetBIOS name can adhere to the IS department's standard naming scheme, if you want. But there's no need to inflict that on your Notes users.

- Users' common names are usually each person's real name. Decide whether or not to use full names with middle initials ("Guy R. Kirkland") or just nicknames and last names ("Rob Kirkland"), then follow that rule when registering users. (But if a given user doesn't like his full name and wants you to use a nickname, go along with the user's wishes if you want. Remember, also, that you can add aliases to a user's Person document, so that he can be known by more than one name.)

- If you decide to use users' middle initials in their common names, decide whether to use trailing periods. Consistency makes the environment less frustrating for users.

- If you want to use something other than users' real names to identify them (for example, login IDs), you may. The only name field that requires an entry is the Last Name field.

- The maximum size of any user's or server's fully distinguished name is 128 characters. For the sake of those who have to type out the names, I hope you never approach that limit.

How Domino Domains and Organizations Relate to Each Other

Technically, there is no relationship between Domino domains and organizations. They serve two different purposes and exist independently of each other. But it may help you to understand them if you think about the fact that a company might have one of each, more than one of either, or more than one of both. The simplest scenario, easiest to manage, and the most common, is one of each. A company has one domain and one organization, and the two may or may not have the same name. Mail addressed to a user in such a company might look like this: *Joe Doaks/Acme @ Acme.* This situation is illustrated in Figure 2.4 as Company 1. If you are setting up Domino for the first time in a small or medium-size company, this is the recommended setup.

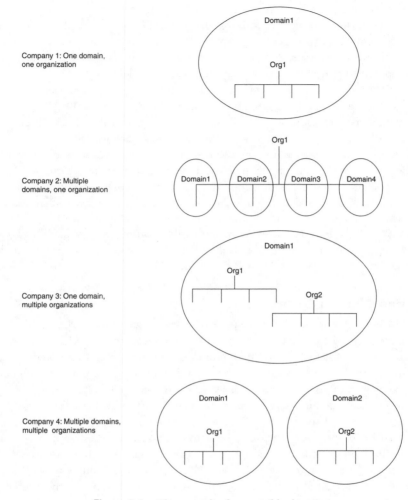

Figure 2.4   These are the four possible domain/
organization configurations in a company.

Large companies with many independent business units that roll out Domino company-wide might find that a single organization spread across multiple domains makes the most sense. All servers and users are members of the same corporate organization but the business units each administer their own domain directories. This is illustrated in Figure 2.4 as Company 2. Mail addressed to two users in this situation might look like this: *Joe Doaks/AcmeConsulting/Acme @ Acme Consulting* and *Bob Dobbs/ AcmeWidgets/Acme @ Acme Widgets.*

The third scenario—one domain and more than one organization—might arise where more than one company work together closely. They want to set themselves up in a single domain for management purposes. But they want user names to accurately reflect each user's corporate identity. This is illustrated in Figure 2.4 as Company 3. Mail addressed to two users in this situation might look like this: *Joe Doaks/ AcmeConsulting @ Acme Holdings* and *Bob Dobbs/AcmeWidgets @ Acme Holdings*.

The last scenario—multiple domains and organizations—is most likely to arise inadvertently, either because separate divisions of a company rolled out Domino independently of and unbeknownst to each other, or from an acquisition of one company by another. But you can imagine a situation—a composite of the second and third scenarios above—in which a holding company would want each of its subsidiaries to manage their own domains and retain their subsidiary corporate identities in their naming schemes, or in which the subsidiaries are independent of each other and free to do what they want regarding Domino. This scenario is illustrated in Figure 2.4 as Company 4. Mail addressed to two users in this situation might look like this: *Joe Doaks/Acme @ Acme* and *Bob Dobbs/Bard @ Bard*. There is no indication here at all that these two people work for related companies.

Domino Named Networks

The third organizing principle of Domino is Domino named networks, which allow administrators to relate Domino servers to the topology of the underlying network. Every Domino server belongs to one Domino named network for each network communication port that it recognizes. You can define a network port for each network protocol running on a server. If a server has multiple network interface cards, you can optionally define a separate port for each NIC/protocol combination.

Not that you want to do these things. Every protocol running on a computer consumes RAM and processor time. I recommend that you minimize the number of protocols running on any computer as much as possible. Some operating systems (well, okay, Windows) may automatically set themselves up running multiple network protocols. Notes/Domino, in turn, will by default enable ports for every protocol installed on the computer at setup time. I recommend that you remove any superfluous protocols from the underlying operating system of any computer running Notes or Domino and that in every copy of Notes or Domino you disable any superfluous network communication ports.

Domino named networks are important in two ways:

- Domino servers in the same Domino named network route mail to each other automatically and immediately, without intervention by administrators. All other Domino servers have to route mail as scheduled by Connection documents in the Domain Directory. For this reason, you may want to consolidate the servers in as few named networks as possible.

- In the Open Database dialog box (as well as other dialogs), when a user chooses Other to see a list of servers, the list includes only servers in the user's home server's Domino named network for the port on which the user communicates with his/her home server. It is well known that the average user becomes paralyzed when confronted with too long a list of server names; to avoid this, you will want to limit the number of servers in each named network.

You *may* place two servers in the same Domino named network if they meet two conditions:

1. They must use the same network communication protocol.

2. They must be constantly connected to each other by LAN or bridged or routed WAN.

The operative word here is "*may.*" Just because you *may* put two servers in the same named network does not mean that you *have* to or that you *should.* And you *can* put two servers in the same named network even if they don't meet the two conditions, but you do so at your peril.

It is important that you set up Domino named networks correctly in your domain for two reasons:

1. By judiciously choosing which servers go in which named networks you can avoid injury to users' brains caused by exposure to too long a list of servers and you can discourage users from opening databases on servers to which they are connected only by slow or high-traffic links.

2. If you put two servers in the same named network even though they do not meet the two conditions for doing so, you will cripple mail transfers between them and possibly between other servers as well.

The last point is really important. Two servers in the same Domino named network will assume they are connected by LAN/WAN. If they are really only connected by telephone, they will try many times to connect and route mail by LAN/WAN. Only after numerous failed attempts to connect by LAN will they try the phone connection. This will cause mail routing between these two servers to slow to a crawl.

If other servers think the fastest mail route to each other is via the nonexistent LAN connection between the first two computers, mail routing between them will suffer, too. Because mail will eventually route over the telephone link, you may only realize there is a problem when the volume of user complaints about slow mail deliveries reaches a deafening level.

It is really easy to make this mistake because, in Releases 4.6 and later, the Domino server setup process enters a default named network name for each enabled port. If you set up servers on LANs connected to each other only by telephone, and you accept the default network names without thinking, you are dead meat.

You can name Domino named networks any way you want. But Lotus and I both recommend you name them such that their names identify the two conditions that they meet. That is, if a group of servers will communicate on the TCPIP port and they are located on the same LAN in the company headquarters, you might put them all in a named network called "TCPIP_HQ."

By default, the server setup process will call the named networks for each enabled port "*Portname* Network," where *portname* is the name of the network communication port to which the named network is assigned. I highly recommend you change those names, following the naming convention described in the previous paragraph, so as to avoid the problem of inadvertently assigning two remote servers to the same named network.

Here, then, are the rules of thumb for setting up Domino named networks:

- Consolidate servers in as few named networks as possible, subject to the following limitations.

- Limit the number of servers in each named network to, say, seven or less.

- Do not put servers connected by slow WAN links in the same named network.

- Do not put two servers connected only by phone or remote LAN link in the same named network.

- Do not accept the default network names. Change them so that they describe the port and location of each named network

Security Considerations

Domino is a very secure system by default, and its security is very granular. If you need a secure system for storing data, Domino is unsurpassed. If, on the other hand, you really don't care much about security issues, Domino lets you turn off many of its security features.

The first thing you have to decide when planning a Domino installation is how much you care about security. If you don't intend to store sensitive data on Domino servers, then maybe you shouldn't get too worked up about security. But if you intend to use Domino servers to store sensitive or secret information either in the short-term or down the road, you must take control over Domino's security features from the moment of creation of the first server in your organization. If you are lax about security at this time (or at any time thereafter), it may be very hard to be sure your organization is still secure when you finally do conclude that you care about security.

What I'm referring to here is the fact that Domino uses certificate-based authentication. Domino servers are charged with the responsibility of doling out information only to and accepting it only from authorized users. A server can only determine if a user is authorized if it can positively identify the user.

Domino recognizes three kinds of users: those identified through certificate-based authentication, those identified though challenge-response authentication, and anonymous users. Users authenticated on the basis of a certificate are the most securely identified, because they possess and present to the server a certificate signed by a trusted third party positively tying a public key to their name. If you don't have that properly signed certificate, you will be unable to convince the server of your identity and it won't do business with you.

The trusted third party who signs your certificate is known in Notes as a "certifier" and in SSL as a "certificate authority" or "CA." The certifier or CA can sign your certificate because he/she/it possesses a public/private key pair. In the Notes security scheme, these keys are stored in a password-encrypted file called a certifier ID file. This file is the ultimate key to all Domino security. The possessor of the file (and the password that decrypts it) has the power to break every Domino security feature except one—field encryption. Therefore it is very important that this file not get into the wrong hands.

The Organization certifier ID (the highest level of certifier in Notes) is created automatically during the process of setting up the first server in an organization. (Or you can set it up manually ahead of time.) It is a binary file named cert.id, about 2200 bytes in size, more or less. It's an insignificant looking thing sitting there in the server's data directory. It is easy to overlook it. It is also easy for anyone with access to the server to copy it to a floppy disk or to one's home directory, and to rename it. (It may be a little harder for someone to guess the password if he doesn't already know it.)

If you care (or think you will someday care) about the security of the data on your Domino servers, it is imperative that you take positive steps from the moment the cert.id file comes into existence to protect if from falling into unauthorized hands and being used in an unauthorized manner. As you use it later on to create lower level (Organizational Unit) certifier IDs, you must take similar measures to protect them as well.

3

First Server Installation and Setup

SETTING UP THE FIRST DOMINO SERVER IN an organization is a process fraught with pitfalls. Thankfully, most administrators never have to do it. They inherit a fully configured system. Most of the rest of us may have to do it once. A few of us—consultants and instructors mostly—have to do it again and again. Those who do it a lot know where the pitfalls are and how to avoid them. Those who have to do it once are the ones who get caught in the pitfalls. If you are one of those people, this chapter is for you.

Setting up the first server in an organization is a three-step process. First, you make a bunch of decisions. Second, you install the server software on the computer. Third, you configure it.

The preliminary decisions consist primarily of coming up with a naming scheme and a security policy. During the configuration process you will have to feed names to Notes and make initial decisions regarding the long-term security of the data in your Notes database. You might be inclined to wing the first step, to just come up with the names and security decisions off-the-cuff at configuration time. But that would be a mistake. You will have to live with those names and decisions for a long time. So, you need to give them some thought. We discussed these issues in the Chapter 2, "Planning an Installation." You might want to read it now if you skipped over it.

Installing the Server Software

The second step—installing Domino on the computer—is easy. Shut down any running programs, including screen savers and antivirus programs, then run the installation program and follow the steps.

If you are installing Domino on a Windows system, the installation program is InstallShield Wizard, the standard installation program for Windows software. You can run InstallShield Wizard from the Domino CD-ROM or you can copy the contents of the CD-ROM to a network file server and run InstallShield Wizard from there. You can run it manually by double-clicking `setup.exe` in Windows Explorer or you can run it automatically from the CD-ROM's AutoPlay front-end (which you can also run from the CD-ROM or a file server).

- **Running AutoPlay from the CD-ROM.** If the CD-ROM doesn't AutoPlay automatically, you can AutoPlay it manually by right-clicking the CD-ROM icon in Windows Explorer and choosing AutoPlay from the context menu. If your monitor is set up for only 16 colors, an error message will appear. Override the error message and AutoPlay anyway.

- **Running AutoPlay from a file server.** If you installed the entire contents of the Domino CD-ROM into a set of directories on a file server identical in structure to the directories on the CD-ROM, you can run the AutoPlay front-end from the file server by running `setup.bat`. It should be located in the topmost directory into which you copied the contents of the CD-ROM.

- **Running InstallShield Wizard from the AutoPlay front-end.** Choose Install, then Servers, then the server you want to install. Then, choose Custom Install or Standard Install. If you choose Custom Install, then when InstallShield Wizard runs, it will display a screen in which you will be able to choose which individual sets of files to install. If you choose Standard Install, InstallShield Wizard will skip that screen.

- **Running InstallShield Wizard manually.** Its filename is `setup.exe`. If you run it from the Domino CD-ROM, it will be located in the \Servers\W32Intel or \Servers\W32Alpha folder. If you run it from a file server, it will be in a similarly named folder.

InstallShield Wizard prompts you step by step for all the information it needs to install Domino. Precisely what information it will prompt you for depends on whether you started it manually or from the CD-ROM's AutoPlay front-end. If you start it from the front-end, you will make some choices there, and InstallShield Wizard won't prompt you a second time for the choices you made in the front-end.

The decisions you have to make during the installation process (whether in the AutoPlay front-end, InstallShield Wizard, or the installation program on one of the other Domino platforms) are in the list that follows. The details described here are for Windows, but the principles are the same for the other operating systems.

- **Which server to install.** Your choices are Domino Mail Server, Domino Application Server, and Domino Enterprise Server. Choose the one for which you bought a license.

- **Standard or Customized Installation.** If you choose Customized, an additional screen will appear in which you will be able to select/deselect individual classes of files to install. If you are installing over Windows NT, one reason to choose Customized is so that you can install Domino as an NT Service. If you choose a Standard install, Domino as an NT Service will not install, and you will have to rerun InstallShield Wizard later to install it. (The reason to install Domino as an NT Service is so that Domino will start automatically when the computer starts, then continue to run independently of any user session. On other platforms you will write batch files or scripts to accomplish the same result. See details at the end of this chapter.)

- **Partitioned Server Installation.** If you intend to put multiple partitioned Domino servers on this computer, select "Partitioned Server Installation." (If you're not sure whether to do this, don't.)

- **File locations (nonpartitioned servers).** You will have to choose the locations of Domino program files and data files. If you have never installed Domino on this computer before, and it is a Windows or OS/2 computer, the default file locations are `c:\lotus\domino` for the program files and `c:\lotus\domino\data` for data files. (If you have installed Domino on this computer before, the install program might detect that fact and offer the previous file locations as the default choices.) If your server has more than one physical disk drive, place the program files on one drive and the data files on the other. For example, if you have two drives, put the program files in `c:\lotus\domino` and the data files in `d:\data`. See Chapter 2 for a discussion of the reasons for this.

- **File locations (partitioned servers).** If you chose Partitioned Server Installation, you will have to choose the location of the program files in one step and the locations of the data files for each partitioned server in later steps. Otherwise the procedure is the same as for nonpartitioned servers. As with nonpartitioned servers, if you have two or more disk drives, put the program files on one and the data files on the other(s). Finally, name each server's data folder in such a way as to make it obvious later on which folder belongs to which server. For example, name the data folders with each server's intended common name (for example, `d:\osprey`).

- **Shortcut or icon locations.** For Windows installation, InstallShield Wizard creates a shortcut for starting each server. For OS/2, the install program creates icon(s) in a program group. By default, the Windows shortcut(s) appears in the menu under Programs\Lotus Applications. The OS/2 icons appear in a group called "Lotus Applications." You can choose a location other than "Lotus Applications" if you want.

InstallShield Wizard installs most of the program files in the program folder you specify, with some Web server executables in a subfolder called configuration files in a subfolder called data files in the data folder you specify, with special files in a series of subfolders. These include help databases in a subfolder called help, sample Web site databases in a subfolder called sample, modem command files in a subfolder called modems, and files associated with Lotus SmartIcons in a subfolder called W32. It installs data files specific to Domino's HTTP service in a set of folders under a folder called domino. Finally, if you installed partitioned servers, each partition has a complete set of data folders and files.

The other server platforms have a similar folder hierarchy but in some cases the folders have different names. For example, under OS/2 the SmartIcon files are stored in a folder called OS2 (instead of W32 as in Windows).

If you installed an unpartitioned server, the program folder includes a text file called `notes.ini`. If you installed one or more partitioned servers, an instance of this file (with settings appropriate to each server) is located in each partitioned server's data folder. `Notes.ini` is a configuration file. It consists of a list of variables and their values. When you start Domino (or Notes), it looks for this file, then sets itself up in memory according to the dictates of the variables it finds. If it cannot find `notes.ini`, Domino (or Notes) will be unable to start.

InstallShield Wizard also creates a shortcut with which to start Domino. The shortcut appears in the Windows menu under the name you specified during installation (by default, under "Lotus Applications"). For an unpartitioned Windows/Intel-based server, the command line for the shortcut is as follows:

```
[path]\nserver.exe
```

For each partitioned Windows/Intel-based server, the command line for the shortcut is as follows:

```
[path]\nserver.exe =[path]\notes.ini
```

In each example, `[path]` is the location on disk of each file. In our example, if we placed the program files in `c:\lotus\domino` and the data files in `d:\osprey`, the command line would be one of the following.

For an unpartitioned server:

```
c:\lotus\domino\nserver.exe
```

For a partitioned server:

```
c:\lotus\domino\nserver.exe =d:\osprey\notes.ini
```

The second argument of the partitioned server command line begins with an equal sign. There is no space between the equal sign and the pathname that follows it. The second argument enables Domino to find the `notes.ini` file, and therefore to run. If you try to start Domino some other way (by clicking `notes.exe` or `server.exe` in Windows Explorer, for example), it may not be able to find `notes.ini`, or therefore to start.

Notice also in the previous Domino command lines that the name of the executable that starts the Domino server is `nserver.exe`. This file on the Windows/Alpha platform is named `aserver.exe`, on the OS/2 platform is named `iserver.exe`, and on the UNIX platforms is called `server`.

On all these platforms, the Domino server actually consists of an entire series of executable programs that run simultaneously. You start the database server (`nserver.exe`) with the command line. The database server then reads the *servertasks* variable in `notes.ini`, and starts each program named there. Each one is responsible for one of the Domino services.

Under Windows/Intel, each executable is named `n*.exe`, where `*` is the name of the service listed in servertasks. For example, if *servertasks* includes `router`, `replica`, `update`, `amgr`, `adminp`, and `stats`, `nserver.exe` loads the executables called `nrouter.exe`, `nreplica.exe`, `nupdate.exe`, `namgr.exe`, `nadminp.exe`, and `nstats.exe`. Under Windows/Alpha, the corresponding filenames all begin with the letter "a", under OS/2 they begin with the letter "i", and under UNIX they have no prefix.

Configuring the First Domino Server

The third step in setting up the first server is to configure it. This is a two-part process. In the first part, you run Domino (not Notes) on the server machine, fill in a form, then wait while Notes (if running under Windows) or Domino (if running under any other OS) creates a new Domino Directory, some IDs, and a few other things. In the second part, you run through a whole checklist of steps to clean up miscellaneous loose ends that Notes didn't take care of automatically.

But wait! There may be one more preconfiguration step to perform first. Whether you want to start configuring now depends on the naming scheme you settled on in the planning step, covered in the previous chapter. If you decided not to use Organizational Units in your naming scheme, you can proceed with the configuration process, and you can skip over the next section. If you intend to use Organizational Units in your naming scheme, you need to read the following section, about moving the first server to its OU.

Moving the First Server to Its OU

When you fill in the form during the first part of the server configuration process, you enter, among other things, the names of the new domain and organization, the server you are setting up, and one user. Notes then creates these objects and names them as you instructed. By default, the server and user are named *servername/orgname* and *username/orgname*, where *servername*, *username*, and *orgname* are the names you supplied for the server, user, and organization, respectively.

If you intend to set up an organization without any Organizational Units (see the previous chapter), this is good, because that's just what first server setup does. But if you intend your servers and users to be members of Organizational Units, you have a problem. Your initial server and user are not members of Organizational Units, and you have to do something about it.

Let's say, for example, that you have decided to call your organization Stillwater. You have decided that your servers will be in an Organizational Unit called Servers. Your users will be in Organizational Units too, the names of which should indicate the location of the office out of which the user works. The servers are to be called *servername*/Servers/Stillwater. Your first server, Osprey, should therefore be Osprey/Servers/Stillwater. The users are to be called *username*/*OUname*/Stillwater. If your first user is Rob Kirkland and he works out of the Marsh Creek office, his fully distinguished name should be Rob Kirkland/MarshCreek/Stillwater. (I'll remind you again to consider carefully whether to use OUs and, if you decide to use them, to choose their names carefully; it's a hassle to change your mind later. See the previous chapter for details.)

But the first server setup process does not automatically set up the first server and user in their intended OUs. By default it sets them up in the O instead. In our example, it sets them up as Osprey/Stillwater and Rob Kirkland/Stillwater.

You have to manually override this. There are three ways to do so:

- Before running first server setup, you can create ID files for the organization, one or more Organizational Units, the first server, and (optionally) the first user. Later, at first server setup, you can feed those IDs to the first server configuration form when you fill it out. The result is that the first server and (optionally) the first user are properly named.

- After first server setup, you can generate the proper Organizational Unit IDs, then use them to rename the first server and user.

- You can create a "throwaway" first server and user at first server setup, then register and set up your Organizational Units and your *real* servers and users in their proper OUs, then "throw away" the first, wrongly named server and user.

Unfortunately, none of these methods is clean and neat. They all require you to tie off a bunch of loose ends. But if you are going to use Organizational Units in your naming scheme, you have to pick one of these methods and fight your way through it. In Release 5, I prefer the third method, but I'll describe them all. Pick the one that looks the least painful to you.

Method One: Create the IDs Beforehand

By this method you preregister your organization, Organizational Unit(s), and first server before you ever get around to setting up your first server. In doing so, you create a set of ID files. Then, during first server setup, you tell Notes that you are supplying the ID files for the organization and first server. When Notes prompts you for them, you feed these IDs to it. After the first server is set up, you will have to perform two cleanup operations. First, you will have to manually re-create the Certificate document(s) for the OU certifier ID(s) that you preregistered. Second, you will have to manually repaste the server's public key into the Server document.

You could also preregister the first user. But you don't really want to. Our goal here is to avoid the monumental hassle of renaming the server. Renaming the user isn't a hassle, so there's no need to avoid it by preregistering the first user. Besides, the more OUs you preregister, the more cleanup work you have to do after setting up the first server. So we minimize hassles by preregistering just the server OU(s) and the first server, but not the user OU(s) or the first user.

To use this method, you need access to a Notes workstation and Domino server before you get to first server setup. (In earlier versions of Notes you could use this method without access to a server, but not in Release 5.) If you are a consultant and your client has hired you to help with his first server setup, do this in your office, then take the new IDs with you to the client's office on the day you plan to set up the client's first server. Better yet, do it on your laptop PC at your client's office the day you set up the first server (assuming, of course, that your laptop has a Domino server on-board or access to one via LAN or modem). Create the IDs directly on a floppy disk. That way your client knows for sure that no other, unauthorized copies of the IDs can be floating around.

(If you are new to Notes, couldn't hire a Notes consultant to midwife your first server setup, and you have to do it on your own, I suggest you abandon this method. To use this method, you have to set up a Domino server, Notes client, and Domino Administrator client ahead of time, just for the purpose of generating the IDs. If you want to do all that as a dry run, just for the practice or fun of it, then you can stay with this method. But don't do it just for the sake of being able to preregister IDs; it's not worth the effort.)

You do not at this time want to generate all of the OUs that your naming scheme calls for. Rather, you only want to generate the ones that will allow you to generate the first server's ID. In our example, in which our server will be named `Osprey/Servers/Stillwater`, we have to create only three IDs, the /Stillwater organization certifier ID, the /Servers/Stillwater OU1 certifier ID, and the Osprey/Servers/Stillwater server ID. If you have decided to put your first server in a level 2 or 3 OU, then you would have to create additional OU certifier IDs.

To generate the IDs, follow this procedure:

1. Decide what minimum quality password your IDs will have. Domino Administrator defaults to a minimum password quality of 10 (on a scale from 0 to 16) for certifier IDs, 8 for user IDs, and 0 for server IDs (but in certain publications Lotus recommends a minimum password quality of 14). What, for example, a minimum password quality of 10 means is that the ID will be required to have a password at least 10 same-case alphabetic characters in length or 9 mixed-case or mixed alphabetic and nonalphabetic characters in length.

If you are a consultant, make sure your client understands the significance of password quality and preapproves the password quality you intend to set for IDs before you create them. To learn more about ID passwords, see Chapter 20, "Enhancing Data Availability."

2. Register the Organization (O) certifier ID.

3. Use the O certifier ID to register the first level Organizational Unit (OU1) certifier ID for the first server.

4. Use the OU1 certifier ID to register the second level Organizational Unit (OU2) certifier ID beneath it (if any) or (if no OU2) to register the first server.

5. If you registered an OU2, use it to register the OU3 beneath it (if any) or the first server.

6. And so on.

Register an organization certifier in Notes R5 as follows:

1. Run Domino Administrator.

2. Choose the Configuration tab (see Figure 3.1).

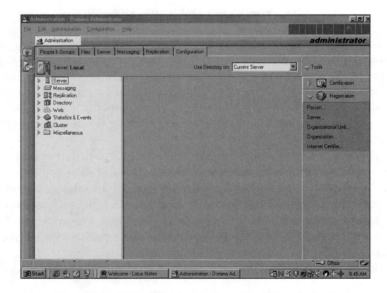

Figure 3.1 The registration tools are located in the Tools pane of the Configuration page in Domino Administrator.

3. Expand Registration, then click Organization to open the Register Organization Certifier dialog box (see Figure 3.2).

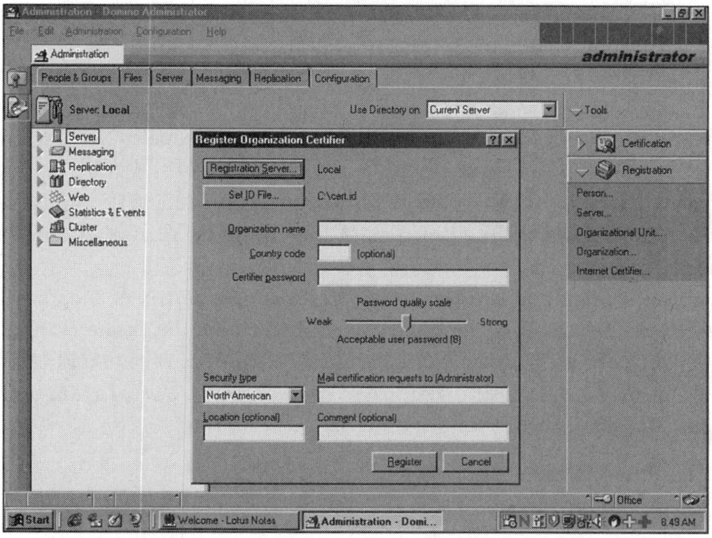

Figure 3.2 Enter the name of certifier and its password. The other fields are optional.

4. Set the Registration Server field to the name of a server to which you have access.

5. Click the Set ID file button and enter the pathname of the ID file you are about to create. You should save it to a floppy disk, so its pathname should be a:*filename*.id, where *filename* is the name of the organization or maybe a name like "o-xyz", where "o" tells you this is the organization certifier for XYZ and "xyz" is the name of the organization.

6. Enter the organization name in the Organization field. In our example, this would be Stillwater. If you decided to use country codes, enter the two-letter ISO code for the country in the Country code field.

7. Set the Password quality scale and enter a password in the Password field.

8. If you are using a North American version of Domino Administrator to generate IDs for a non-North American organization (non-U.S., non-Canadian), choose International in the Security type field. The resulting ID file will use security that complies with U.S. export laws. See Chapter 20.

9. The other fields supply information to the Certificate document that Domino Administrator is about to create. You can either fill them in, then paste the Certificate document into the new Domain Directory after you create the first server. Or you can leave these fields blank and re-create the Certificate document by hand after you create the first server.

10. Click Register. Domino Administrator creates the new certifier ID.

Domino Administrator generates a public/private key pair, creates the ID with the keys in it, and creates a Certificate document with a copy of the public key in it. It saves the certifier ID file in the location you specified in the Set ID file field. It creates the Certificate document in the Directory of the computer named in the Registration Server field.

Next, you will create one or more organizational unit certifiers. Don't create all of them at this time. Create only the ones necessary to create the first server's ID. In our example, in which the first server will be named `Osprey/Servers/Stillwater`, you only have to create a single Organizational Unit certifier—`/Servers/Stillwater`. To create an OU1 certifier ID, follow these steps:

1. Run Domino Administrator.

2. Choose the Configuration tab.

3. Expand Registration, then click Organizational Unit. Domino Administrator displays one of two dialog boxes. If the floppy disk with the last used certifier ID is in the disk drive, the Enter Password dialog box for that certifier ID appears. If that disk is not in the disk drive, the Choose Certifier ID dialog box appears.

   If the Enter Password dialog box appears, look closely to verify that Domino Administrator picked the correct ID, the certifier ID that you just created. If it did, enter the password and click OK. If it did not, press Cancel, which will display the Choose Certifier ID dialog box.

   If the Choose Certifier ID dialog box appears, choose the certifier ID that you created in the previous step, then click Open. The Enter Password dialog box appears. Enter the password and click OK.

4. A warning appears to the effect that the certifier ID has no ID/password recovery information. For the time being, you can ignore this warning. Choose Yes.

5. The Register Organizational Unit dialog box appears. With two exceptions it is identical to the Register Organization dialog box. The exceptions are that it has a Certifier ID button and it lacks a field for a country code. If you chose the wrong certifier ID in the previous step, you can click the Certifier ID button and choose again. You don't need a field for the country code because the ID you are creating will inherit the organization certifier's country code.

6. Fill in the fields the same way you did for the organization certifier. In our example, the OU name is `Servers`. Choose Register when you are finished.

Domino Administrator again generates public and private keys, creates the ID file, and creates a Certificate document.

If you need to create an OU2 certifier or an OU3 certifier, follow the preceding procedure, with one exception. Don't choose the certifier ID in step 3. Rather, choose the OU1 certifier when you create the OU2 certifier, and choose the OU2 certifier when you create the OU3 certifier. The same goes when you create the first server ID —choose the OU (1, 2, or 3) certifier that will be the server's parent OU. The steps for creating the server ID file are as follows:

1. Run Domino Administrator.

2. Choose the Configuration tab.

3. Expand Registration, then click Server. As in the previous procedure, Domino Administrator displays either the Enter Password dialog box or the Choose Certifier ID dialog box.

   If the Enter Password dialog box appears, look closely to verify that Domino Administrator picked the correct ID—the OU certifier ID that you intend to be the server's parent OU. In our example, that would be the OU named /Servers/Stillwater. If that is the certifier for which you are being prompted for a password, enter the password and click OK. If it is not, click Cancel, and the Choose Certifier ID dialog box will appear.

   If the Choose Certifier ID dialog box appears, choose the correct OU certifier ID, then click Open. The Enter Password dialog box appears. Enter the password and click OK.

4. A warning appears to the effect that the certifier ID has no ID/password recovery information. For the time being, you can ignore this warning. Choose Yes.

5. The Register Servers dialog box appears. It has four fields. You only need to focus on three, Registration Server, Certifier ID, and Security type.

   Registration Server. Click Registration Server to change the value from "Local" to the name of a Domino server to which you have access.

   Certifier ID. If you chose the wrong certifier ID in step 3, click Certifier ID to choose again.

   Security Type. If you are using a North American version of Domino Administrator to register a server that will be located elsewhere than the United States or Canada, choose International in the Security type field.

6. Click Continue to display the second Register Servers dialog box. Here, again, you only need to focus on some of the fields, specifically, Server Name, Password, Password quality scale, Domain, Administrator, and the Store Server ID fields.

   Server Name. Enter the name of the first server. In our example, that would be Osprey.

   Password. For most servers, you want to leave this blank, because if the server has a password, it will not restart automatically after a crash. You only want a server to have a password if the computer it will eventually run on will not be physically secure.

   Password quality scale. If you want to leave the password blank, you must leave this field set to 0 – Password optional.

   Domain. Put anything here. We don't care about this field, but you are required to put something in it.

   Administrator. Same as Domain.

7. Click Other to see the other fields.

   Store Server ID. Select In file. Deselect In Domain Directory. Because of our special circumstances (creating a server ID for a domain not yet in existence) we don't want to store the new server ID in the domain directory.

   Set ID file. Click the button, then choose the file's pathname. If you are storing the IDs on a floppy disk, the pathname would be (in our example) `a:\osprey.id`. (We name the ID file with the server's common name.)

8. Click Register. Domino Administrator creates the ID file. Then it creates a Server document for this new server in the Domain Directory on the server you chose in the Registration Server field. You should delete the Server document.

Now you have a set of IDs you can use when setting up your first server. When you finish that process, your first server will be correctly named, and you won't have to go through the hassle of renaming it or decommissioning it. You will have some manual cleanup to do after setting up the first server. You will also have to rename the first user, who we did not bother to generate a correct ID for (because renaming users is easy). However, we'll wait until after the server is set up to go into the sordid details.

Method Two: Rename the First Server and User Afterward

Instead of generating a correctly named server ID file ahead of time (see the previous section), you can just go ahead and set up an incorrectly named first server and user in the default way, then rename them. This is easy to do for the user, because the Domino Administration Process does most of the work. It is not hard, exactly, for the first server. You just have to do all the work yourself, and there are a lot of details. If you miss a step or make a mistake, it can be a real headache to track down and correct the error. For that reason I prefer either of the other methods to this one. Because you do all the work after setting up the first server, we will hold off on describing the details until after we describe first server setup, later in this chapter.

Method Three: Create a "Throwaway" First Server, Delete It Later

The third method is to go ahead and create an incorrectly named first server and user, as in method two. But instead of using the names of a real server and user, use throwaway names like Temp1 for the server and any cute name for the user. (Go ahead, be creative.) But then, instead of renaming the first server and user, you register the appropriate OU certifiers, then use them to register your real servers and users, correctly named. Then you set up a second server and decommission the first server. You should not yet have set up a user workstation, so you don't have to worry about breaking it down. You can just delete the first user. You could rename the first user, but it's a lot less work to just throw him away, because you can't *just* rename this user. You also have to transfer him to another mail server.

As in method two, you do all of this after setting up the first server, so we'll cover the details then.

First Server Configuration

When you are ready to finish setting up the first server in your organization, run Domino on the server. In Windows 9x/NT/Intel you choose Domino in the menu. On the other platforms you run Domino with a special command line that starts up a browser-based setup application. Under Windows NT/Alpha the command is [path]\ahttp httpsetup. Under OS/2 the command is [path]\ihttp httpsetup. Under UNIX the command is /opt/lotus/bin/http httpsetup.

Under Windows/Intel, Domino will try to run but will fail because it hasn't been configured yet. If you watch closely, you will see an error message to that effect on the screen. But then, somewhat miraculously, Notes will start up. A variable in notes.ini (SetupDB=Setup.nsf) causes Notes to open the Domino Configuration database (setup.nsf), which was installed by the install process in the data directory. In the database, a multiscreen Configuration form automatically opens. You fill in the fields on four screens of the form, specifying the details about how the server should be set up, then click the Finish button on the form.

If you are running OS/2, UNIX, or Windows NT/Alpha, an abbreviated form of Domino will start and you will then be able to access the Domino Web Setup database with a browser. There you complete the setup form and submit it. To access the server from a browser, use the server's IP address in your URL (for example, http://192.168.0.9).

Notes (on Windows/Intel) or Domino (on the other platforms) then performs the lion's share of the first server setup process:

- It populates `notes.ini` with the necessary variables for Domino to run properly, including those that enable network and serial ports and one that identifies the server's domain.

- It creates the Domain Directory (`names.nsf`) from the Domain Directory design template (`pubnames.ntf`). It adds the first user and first server to the Domain Directory's ACL as managers and makes the first server the Administration Server of the Domain Directory.

- It creates the organization certifier ID (or you supply one) and creates a corresponding Certificate document in the Domain Directory.

- It creates a user ID (or you supply one) for the first user, and creates a Person document for him in the Domain Directory. If it creates the user ID, it stores it in the Person document. It also creates a subfolder called mail under the data folder and creates there a mail database for the first user.

- It creates a server ID (or you supply one) for the first server, creates a corresponding Server document in the Domain Directory, and adds the server to the already existing LocalDomainServers group in the Domain Directory.

When Domino finishes these steps, it presents a final screen to you, in which it informs you of the results of its initial pass at configuring the server, and presents you with the option of configuring some groups.

To fill in the Domino Configuration form in Windows NT/Intel, follow these steps (the procedure on the other platforms is similar):

1. The first screen of the form appears. Choose First Domino Server, then click the right-arrow button to move to screen two. Notice that this and all the screens that follow display lots of information onscreen. I encourage you to read these screens carefully, and to move freely forward and backward through them, comparing the alternatives. If you planned your system carefully and completely, as recommended in Chapter 2, you should pretty much know ahead of time which options you will choose. But, I still recommend that you read each screen carefully.

2. Choose either Quick and Easy Configuration or Advanced Configuration, then click the right-arrow button to move to screen three. Unless you know you won't set up any optional services on this computer, I recommend using Advanced Configuration. With Quick and Easy Configuration you will have to make fewer choices on screens three and four. But you may find that, with Quick and Easy Configuration, you install more of each optional service than you wanted. For example, you might want to install the POP3 and SMTP mail

services but not the IMAP mail service. With Quick and Easy Configuration, it's all or none. Feel free, however, to explore both the Quick and Easy and Advanced screens and decide for yourself which is best for you. Until you click the Finish button on screen four, you are free to change your mind as often as you want.

3. If you chose Quick and Easy Configuration in screen two, screen three offers you options to set up Domino for access by 1) Web browsers, 2) Internet mail programs, and 3) Internet news readers, and for access to back-end data sources via Domino Enterprise Connection Services (DECS). Advanced Configuration offers more detailed options in each of these areas, plus options not to set up certain basic Domino services. We will look at each option in detail a little further on. But first, let's see what happens when you move to screen four.

4. In both Quick and Easy Configuration and Advanced Configuration, screen four is where you enter the domain name, the organization name, the first server name, the name of the first user, and network and serial port options. The available options are more detailed in Advanced Configuration. We will look at each option in detail a little further on. In either case, when you finish setting up all the options, you can click the Finish button in the upper-right corner of the form. Doing this closes the form and triggers the automatic setup process described previously.

5. When the automatic setup process is complete, the last screen of the setup form appears. It presents you with the following information and options:

   - It displays the names of the first server and user, and the certifier and user passwords. Before you close the form, commit the passwords to memory. This is the last time Notes will display them to you. If you forget them you will be locked out of the IDs with no back door. Are they memorized? Good!

   - It informs you of any errors that may have occurred and offers solutions to them.

   - It presents you with one last option, described in detail in its own section later, to add a Manager entry to the ACLs of all existing databases. I recommend you choose this option.

   - It informs you that, before you can do any further configuration, you need to install a copy of Domino Administrator. I'll describe how to do this later in this chapter.

6. After performing the ACL option, close the form by clicking the Exit Configuration button. This shuts down Notes entirely.

Domino Configuration Options, Screen Three

After you click Finish in the preceding step 4, Notes will install a standard set of basic Domino services plus the services you selected in screen three of the setup form (see Figure 3.3).

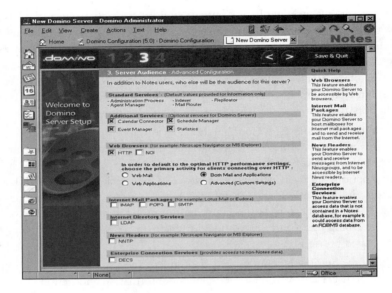

Figure 3.3   Notes automatically sets up the Domino services you select in screen three of the Server Configuration form.

The nonoptional standard Domino services include the following (with their Windows NT/Intel filenames listed in parentheses):

- The Administration Process (`nadminp.exe`), a program which automates a wide variety of administrative tasks.

- The Agent Manager (`namgr.exe`), a program which controls the running of Notes agent programs on the server.

- The Indexer (`nupdate.exe`), which maintains view and full-text indexes in Notes databases.

- The Mail Router (`nrouter.exe`), which transfers mail to other servers and delivers mail to recipients on this server.

- The Replicator, (`nreplica.exe`), which controls database replication between servers.

Quick and Easy Configuration also sets up the following basic Domino services, which are optional under Advanced Configuration:

- Schedule Manager (nsched.exe), which maintains the Free Time database (busytime.nsf), which contains information about all local mail users' calendar entries so that users can see when others are busy and can plan meetings accordingly.

- Calendar Connector (ncalconn.exe), which retrieves users' free time information from other Domino servers.

- Event Manager (nevent.exe), which watches for occurrences of defined events and notifies administrators in designated ways when such events take place.

- Statistics (nstats.exe), which enables collection of server operating statistics either by mail or on command.

Both Quick and Easy Configuration and Advanced Configuration allow you to set up the following optional services: Domino Web server, Internet mail and directory services, Network News server, and Enterprise Connection Services. The Advanced Configuration further breaks these services down as follows:

- Domino Web services
  - HTTP service (nhttp.exe), which is the Domino HTTP stack. If you select this option, another field appears in which you have to select the primary activity that Web visitors will perform: browsing, working with their mail databases, both, or something else.
  - Domino Internet Inter-ORB Protocol (DIIOP) service (ndiiop.exe), which enables Domino CORBA/IIOP functionality, which in turn allows non-Notes clients to perform Notes-like functions.
- Internet mail services
  - IMAP server (nimap.exe), which provides mail services to users with Internet Mail Access Protocol version 4 (IMAP4) mail readers, such as Netscape Communicator.
  - POP3 server (npop3.exe), which provides mail services to users with Post Office Protocol version 3 (POP3) mail readers, such as Eudora and Microsoft Exchange Client.
  - SMTP server (nsmtp.exe), which provides mail transfer services under the Simple Mail Transfer Protocol (SMTP) for all Internet mail composers, including Lotus Notes.
- Internet (LDAP) directory services (nldap.exe), which provides directory services under the Lightweight Directory Access Protocol (LDAP). Quick and Easy Configuration includes this under Internet mail services.

- Internet Newsgroup (NNTP) Server (`nnntp.exe`), which provides discussion forums under the Network News Transfer Protocol (NNTP).

- Domino Enterprise Connection Service (`ndecs.exe`), which provides forms-based, real-time connectivity between Notes databases and other data sources, such as ODBC and SQL-based relational database management systems and transaction systems.

You should exercise restraint when deciding which of these services to set up. Only set up the ones you know you will use on this server. If there is any doubt, don't set up a service. You can always set up any of these services later.

Domino Configuration Options, Screen Four

If you are using Advanced Configuration, screen four opens in Edit Mode (see Figure 3.4). If you are using Quick and Easy Configuration, it opens in Read Mode and you have to click the Edit button to open an Edit Mode version of it in a dialog box. The screen four options differ somewhat, depending on whether you chose Quick and Easy Configuration or Advanced Configuration. All of them appear here, and I note the differences between Quick and Easy Configuration and Advanced Configuration.

- **Domain Name**. Enter the domain name you decided on as part of your naming scheme. Notes provides your Internet domain name (as it appears in the computer's TCP/IP setup and minus the superdomain (org, net, and so on) component) as a default.

- **Certifier Name**. This is where you put your organization name, that is, the name you chose as the O component of your user and server names. Notes provides the computer's host name as a default.

- **Certifier Country Code**. If you decided, in your naming scheme, to use Country (C) codes (for example, `CN=Osprey/OU=Servers/O=Stillwater/C=US`), enter the ISO two-letter country code for the organization certifier ID here. Otherwise leave it blank.

- **Certifier ID**. If you created a certifier ID ahead of time, as described previously, choose "Use existing certifier ID" here. Otherwise, leave it set to "Allow Setup to create new certifier ID" (Advanced Configuration) or "Create new certifier ID" (Quick and Easy Configuration).

- **Certifier Password**. This field appears if you set the Certifier ID field to "Allow Setup to create new certifier ID." Enter a password here. Notes automatically sets the minimum password quality to 8. This means your password must be no shorter than 8 characters in length—more or less. If it consists of dictionary words in all lowercase, the program may require as many as 12 characters. If it consists of mixed case letters, numbers, punctuation characters, and/or meaningless words, the password could be as few as 6 characters. It is the difficulty of decrypting that determines the quality of a password.

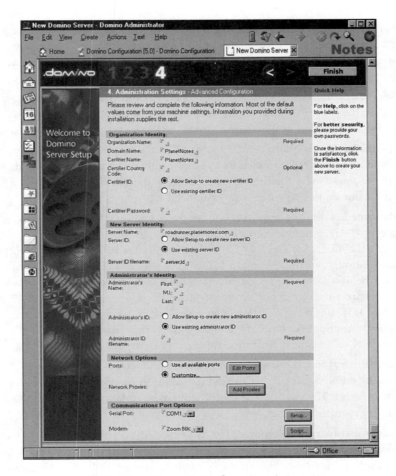

Figure 3.4   Advanced Configuration gives you a
detailed list of services to set up on your new server.

- **Certifier ID filename.** This field appears if you set the Certifier ID field to
  "Use existing certifier ID". Enter the pathname of the certifier ID file you
  created as described earlier in this chapter. In our example, this would be
  `a:\stillwater.id`.

- **Server Name.** Enter here the CN component of your first server's name.
  Notes supplies as a default the computer's host name as it appears in the computer's TCP/IP setup.

- **Server's Hostname.** Notes populates this field itself, getting its value from the
  IP stack.

- **Server ID.** If you created a server ID ahead of time, as described earlier in this chapter, choose "Use existing server ID." Otherwise, choose "Allow Setup to create new server ID" (or, if using Quick and Easy Configuration, "Create new server ID").

- **Server ID filename.** This field appears only if you chose "Use existing server ID" in the Server ID field. Enter the pathname of the server ID file you created as described earlier in this chapter. In our example, this would be `a:\osprey.id`.

- **Administrator's Name.** Enter the name of the first user. Use your own name if you haven't already decided on another name. Use a fictitious name if you plan to throw away the first server and user as described earlier in this chapter. First name and middle initial are optional. Last name is required.

- **Password.** This field appears if you set the Administrator's ID field (described later) to "Allow Setup to create new administrator ID" (or "Create new administrator ID" in Quick and Easy Configuration). Enter a password here. Notes automatically sets the minimum password quality to 8. This means your password must be no shorter than 8 characters in length—more or less. If it consists of dictionary words in all lowercase, the program may require as many as 12 characters. If it consists of mixed case letters, numbers, punctuation characters, and/or meaningless words, the password could be as few as 6 characters. It is the difficulty of decrypting that determines the quality of a password.

- **Administrator's ID.** If you created a server ID ahead of time, choose "Use existing administrator ID". Otherwise, choose "Allow Setup to create new administrator ID" (or, if using Quick and Easy Configuration, "Create new administrator ID").

- **Administrator ID filename.** This field appears only if you chose "Use existing administrator ID" in the Administrator's ID field. Enter the pathname of the user ID file you previously created. As an example, this might be `a:\kirkland.id`.

- **Ports.** This option is available only if you are using Advanced Configuration. Under Quick and Easy Configuration, Notes automatically sets up all available ports. If you choose "Use all available ports," Notes will enable every network port that is currently enabled in the operating system. If you choose "Customize," the Edit Ports button appears. When you click it, the Port Setup dialog box appears. It is a table in which each row represents one of the available network ports. All you really need to do here is disable the ports you don't want the server to use.

- **Network Proxies.** This option is available only if you are using Advanced Configuration. If the server will need to access other servers outside a proxy server firewall, you will need to define the host name(s) or IP address(es) of the proxy server(s). To do this, click the Add Proxies button. This opens the Proxy Server Configuration dialog box. Domino supports HTTP, Socks, and Notes RPC proxy servers, and the dialog box provides a field for each type. For each type of proxy server that the new Domino server will have to interact with, enter its host name or IP address in the appropriate field. If you don't want the new server going through the proxy server to reach other servers on the inside of the firewall, enter the domain names, host names, or IP addresses of those servers in the field labeled "No proxy for these hosts or domains." Of course, if you don't know any of this information, you can always enter it later, after the server is running.

- **Serial Port.** If the server will have use of one or more modems, you can choose the COM port for one of the modems here. (The others you will have to set up after the server is running.)

- **Modem.** If the server will use a modem, you can optionally choose a modem driver from the list in this field. The modem drivers that appear in this list are the `*.mdm` files that appear in the modems subfolder of the server's data folder.

- **Setup.** After you have selected a COM port and modem in the previous two fields, you can click this button to display the Additional Setup dialog box. There you can set various modem parameters. We discuss this dialog box in detail in Chapter 4, "Additional Server Setup."

- **Script.** If your modem will be dialing into an X.25 or Frame Relay network, you can set up a script to negotiate the connection. Click the Script button to display the Connect Script dialog box, where you can select a script from a list of available scripts and enter arguments for the script. The scripts that appear in the list are the `*.scr` files that appear in the modems subfolder of the server's data folder.

Domino Configuration Options, Last Screen

The last server configuration screen (labeled Congratulations!), presents you with (among other things) one last configuration option—a button labeled Set Access Control List Entry. I recommend you exercise the option. Click the button to display the Set Default Database Access dialog box. In it you have two options:

- To add a group or a person as Manager to the ACLs of all existing databases. I recommend that you accept the default, which is to add a group called Administrators. If you do accept this default, Domino will create the group document, then add the group name as Manager to the ACLs of all existing databases.

- To add "Anonymous" to the ACLs of all existing databases with a status of "No Access." I recommend you check this check box as well.

When you make these choices and click OK, Domino immediately updates all databases, then returns you to the Congratulations! screen, with the ACL update option now replaced by a message that you either succeeded in adding the ACL entries to x databases or that you failed and the reasons why. Record any errors that appear, commit passwords to memory, then click the Exit Configuration button. This shuts down Domino entirely. The next time you start it, the server will run in its normal way.

Start the First Server

For now, you can start up the first server by choosing its shortcut in the menu. Later, you will set up the server to start automatically. (At the end of this chapter, if you're still awake, I'll also show you how to create shortcuts that start and stop the Domino NT service.) As the server starts up, watch the console screen that appears. You will see one service after another start up for the first time. As they start, many of the services look for special databases. If they don't find them, they create them. You might also see error messages. Keep track of those so that you can eliminate their causes later.

The services that typically start up on a new server, in the order that they typically start up, include the following:

- Mail Router. Creates and maintains one or more Incoming Mail databases, called `mail.box` if only one or `mailn.box` (where *n* is an integer from 1 to 9) if more than one. (See Chapter 8, "Mail Routing Setup and Maintenance," for information about setting up multiple mailbox databases.)

- Replicator

- Indexer

- Agent Manager

- Administration Process. Creates and maintains the Administration Requests database (`admin4.nsf`)

- Java Class Loader and the ISpy class

Other services that might start, depending on your choices you made in screen three of the Server Configuration document, include:

- Schedule Manager. Creates and maintains the Free Time database (`busytime.nsf`)

- Calendar Connector

- Stats. Creates the `[servername] Stats/[organizationname]` database (`statmail.nsf`) and a Mail-In Database document for it, then monitors that database for the arrival of mailed-in requests for statistics reports.

- Events. Creates and monitors the Statistics & Events database (`events4.nsf`). Creates and maintains the Statistics Reports database (`statrep.nsf`).

Setting Up the First User

Now that the first Domino server is capable of running, you need to finish configuring it. To do so, you have to be able to run Domino Administrator, which, if you've been following my instructions, we haven't installed yet. You have three options for installing Domino Administrator:

- You can install it on the same machine as Domino, and in the same program and data folders as Domino.
- You can install it on the same machine as Domino, but in a different data folder than Domino. (The executables can reside in the same or a different program folder, whichever you want.)
- You can install it on a different machine altogether.

Lotus recommends that you choose the third alternative or, if you must install client software on the server, the second alternative. I agree with Lotus's recommendations. There are several good reasons not to install any client on the server machine.

First, running any foreground program on the server puts a big burden on the processor. This in turn significantly impairs the server's ability to meet the demands of remote clients.

Second, permitting local access to a server compromises Domino's security. The local user may be able to manipulate data in otherwise unauthorized ways. Also, making changes while logged in using the server's ID obliterate Domino's audit trail.

Finally, it's simply unnecessary to install Domino Administrator directly on the server. Veteran R4 Notes/Domino administrators are accustomed to running Notes locally at the server to administer it. Many administrators do it all the time and are sort of addicted to it, and are probably very uncomfortable at the thought of not having that ability in R5. But in R5 it is no longer harder to do most things remotely.

In fact, about the only reason I can think of to administer an R5 server locally (other than to start it up) is if you get locked out of a database ACL. Local access would give you Manager access to the ACL (if Domino/Notes aren't enforcing a consistent ACL—see Chapter 20). But to access an ACL you need Notes, not Domino Administrator; and Notes is installed (on Windows/Intel servers) along with Domino, in the form of `nlnotes.exe`.

To run Notes at the server, you have to execute `nlnotes.exe`. If `notes.ini` is in the Domino program folder or in any other folder in the Windows search path, the command to start Notes is as follows:

```
[path]\nlnotes.exe
```

If `notes.ini` is in the Domino data folder (which it would be if the server is partitioned) or otherwise not in the Windows search path, the command to start Notes is as follows:

```
[path]\nlnotes.exe =[path]\notes.ini
```

In both of these examples, [path] stands in for the actual location of each file.

So, we conclude that you should almost always install Domino Administrator on any computer other than the server computer itself. The only exceptions I can think of are situations in which there is only one computer at hand. For example, you might set up a lone Domino server at your ISP. Or you might set up a test or demo server on your laptop computer.

In such a situation, I recommend you install Domino Administrator in a separate set of folders from Domino. If you are short of disk space, you could install them both in the same program folder but at least install their data files in separate folders.

If you decide to install both Domino and Notes in one program folder, be sure to move the notes.ini file created during your first install to the data folder. Otherwise, your second install will overwrite the first notes.ini file. Also, be sure to edit the shortcuts of the first install to reflect the fact that you moved the notes.ini file out of the program folder.

When you install Domino Administrator, both that and Notes will be installed. Because Domino Administrator and Domino Designer are really just alternate front-ends to Notes, InstallShield always installs the standard Notes client along with them. InstallShield will also, among other things, add shortcuts to the menu for each of the client front-ends that you install.

Start the client for the first time by choosing any of the shortcuts but preferably Domino Administrator, because that is the one you will use to finish up the server configuration process. The first time Notes starts up, the Lotus Notes Client Configuration Wizard will appear. As its opening screen points out, it will present you with several options, including connecting to a Domino server and connecting to one or more Internet servers. Our goal in setting up this client is to finish configuring our first server, so in the description that follows, we will focus only on those options. We will look at the other options in Chapter 5, "User Registration and Client Setup."

Here are the instructions for answering the wizard's prompts:

1. Read the opening screen, then click Next.

2. Accept the default, "I want to connect to a Domino server," then click Next.

3. Choose the default connection method: Set up a connection to a local area network (LAN). Click Next.

4. Enter the name of the first server. In our example, it is Osprey/Stillwater or Osprey/Servers/Stillwater or Temp1/Stillwater (depending on which, if any, method you chose in the beginning of this chapter for setting up the first server and user in OUs). Click Next.

5. Next, tell Domino the identity of the first user. You have two options here:

    - If you preregistered a user (which we did not cover in this chapter), choose the first option, My Notes User ID has been supplied to me in a file, and complete the File name field. Click Next. If the file you specify is not already located in your Notes data folder, you will be asked if you want it copied there. Choose Yes. Then, you will be prompted for your password. Enter it and press OK.

    - If you did not preregister the first user , the first user's ID file is attached to his/her Person document. In that case, choose the second option, Use my name as identification, and enter the Common Name portion of your user name (that is, in my case, just Rob Kirkland). Click Next.

6. Notes will try to establish a LAN connection to the server. If it succeeds, a screen will appear telling you so. Click Next. If it fails, a screen will appear in which you can correct the server's name or enter its network address and specify what network protocol Notes should use. When you enter that information and click Next, Notes will try again to connect to the server. If it succeeds, a screen will appear telling you so. Click Next. If it fails, one of the following error messages will appear:

    - **Server not responding.** This is caused by one of the following conditions:

        - You entered an erroneous network address or protocol. Correct it, then try again.

        - The Domino server is not running. Start it, then try again.

        - The network protocol software is not properly set up on your computer or the server. Shut down Notes, correct the problem, and then try again.

        - The network itself is blocking a connection between the workstation and server, due to a network hardware or software problem. Shut down Notes, correct the problem, and then try again.

    - **Connection denied. The server you connected to has a different name from the one requested.** You may have entered the server's name incorrectly. Verify the server's fully distinguished name and reenter it. Alternatively, there may be more than one server on your network using the same common name. If so, you need to shut down one of the servers and either decommission it or disconnect it from the network.

7. The wizard asks you next if you want to set up an Internet mail account. If you choose to do so, it will conduct you through a series of screens in which it prompts you for that information.

8. Finally, Notes announces that you are finished. Click Finish.

9. Notes then connects to the server. It verifies your identity in the Domain Directory, then finishes setting up Notes. If you supplied a name in step 5, Notes prompts you for the password of the attached ID file, then copies it to your local data directory with the file name user.id. Notes then proceeds to set up your workstation. When it is finished, it tells you so. Click OK. After some more configuration, the Domino Administrator (or Notes) interface will appear.

The Domino Administrator Interface

If you have never seen the Domino Administrator interface, you should look it over at this time. You can start Domino Administrator from Windows by clicking on its shortcut in the menu. You can also start it from within Notes by clicking its bookmark on the left side of the screen. See Figure 3.5. Lastly, you can start it by choosing Tools, Server Administration in Notes's File menu.

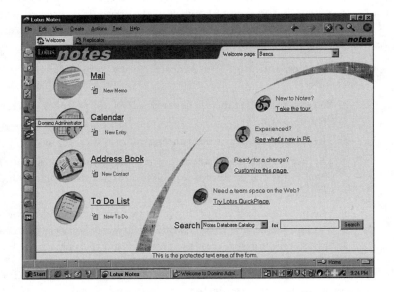

Figure 3.5 Click the Domino Administrator bookmark (highlighted) to run Domino Administrator from within Notes.

I could lull you to sleep with in in-depth description of the interface and features of Domino Administrator, but I think you'll prefer to discover it for yourself. Start out by exploring the Welcome page, which appears when you first run Domino Administrator. Click the labels—Server Bookmarks, Task Buttons, and so on—on the left side of the screen to see illustrated descriptions of the program's main features on the right side of the screen.

For further orientation, open the Help menu and run the Guided Tour, an animated, interactive slide show about the program. Finally, explore the program on your own. Here are some things to take note of as you explore:

- **Context-sensitive help.** As you work with Domino Administrator, if you run across something about which you'd like more information, press F1 to display the pertinent pages from the Domino 5 Administration Help database.

- **Menus, tools, and pop-up menus.** You can accomplish most tasks three different ways—look in the Actions menu at the top of the screen, look in the Tool pane on the right side of the screen, or right-click on an object to pop up a menu of available actions.

- **Panes are resizeable, closable, and pinnable.** You can drag the borders between panes to resize them. You can close the Tools and Servers panes or you can pin them so they stay open.

- **Drag-and-drop interface.** You can drag a user's name to a server to change the user's mail server. You can drag a database's name to a server to copy a database to that server.

- **Administration preferences** (in the File menu under Preferences). Here's where you can specify what Domino domains you will administer, what columns will appear in file listings in the Files tab, and default settings for the registration screens. You can also fine-tune server monitoring settings here.

- **Refresh Server List** (in the Administration menu). Choose this to update the list of servers whenever you add a new server to or remove one from an administered domain.

Finishing First Server Configuration

Now that both your first server and a Domino Administration client are initially configured and running, you can complete the first server configuration. You will have to do the following:

- (Optional) Add or remove ports.
- Set up Domino Named Networks.
- Create administrative groups.
- Set up the Administration Process
- Edit access lists in the Server document.
- (Optional) Edit certain other fields in the Server document.
- (Optional) Create Certificate documents and recopy the server's public key from the server ID file to the Server document. You only have to do these things if, in your first server configuration, you used certifier and server IDs created beforehand.

- (Optional) Rename the user and either rename the server or create a new server and decommission this server. You only have to do these things if you want the server and user to be in OUs and you allowed the Server Configuration program to create the certifier and server IDs. But if you have to do this, I highly recommend you do it before creating any other servers or users.

Set Up Ports

If you did not specify which network ports the server should use in the Server Configuration form (and you only could have if you used Advanced Configuration), Notes configured all possible network ports. You should review those port settings now, with a view to possibly disabling any that you know the server won't use. This conserves RAM and saves on processor cycles.

Furthermore, if you plan to use multiple LAN adapters on this server (say, one for user-to-server communication, another for server-to-server communication) you might need to create one or more new ports at this time. For example, you may need to create a second TCP/IP port.

Likewise, if you plan to enable a COM port on this server (for modem access) and you did not enable it in the Server Configuration form, you can enable it now. Or if you plan to set up this server to use multiple modems (the Server Configuration form only allows you to enable one), you can enable the others now.

Finally, if you plan to use any Internet ports or proxy servers to reach the Internet, you may want to configure them now.

You can enable and disable, create, rename, and remove ports in three different places: in Notes, Domino Administrator, or the Domino console. Doing it in Notes only works locally and the server can't be running when you do it, so you will really only use Notes to enable/disable ports on workstations. For servers, you will either use Domino Administrator or the Domino console. Both allow you to enable/disable ports without bringing down the server. Domino Administrator has the additional advantage of working remotely.

To enable or disable a port in Domino Administrator, follow these steps:

1. Make sure the server whose ports you want to enable/disable is selected. (When you first start Domino Administrator, Local is selected. Click the [domainname] bookmark on the left side of the screen, then choose a server.)

2. Go to the Server page. Choose Server, Port Information in the Tools pane or the Server menu. If you can watch the server console as you do this, you'll see that Domino Administrator sends a series of Show Configuration commands to the server to collect information about the current status of its ports. It then displays that information in the Ports Setup for [servername] dialog box.

3. In the Communication Ports list, select the port you want to enable/disable, then select/deselect Port Enabled.

4. Choose OK. Again, if you can watch the server console as you do this, you'll see
    that Domino Administrator sends a series of console commands to the server,
    this time Set Configuration commands, which actually change the server's
    configuration.

To enable or disable a port from within the Domino console you can simply enter
one of the following commands:

```
start port [portname]
```

or

```
stop port [portname]
```

where [portname] is the name of a defined port.

To find out what ports are currently enabled on a server, enter the following
command:

```
show config ports
```

To find out what other ports are defined on a server, enter the following command:

```
show config disabledports
```

These commands work for both network ports and serial ports.

Enabling or disabling a network port is actually a two-part process, of which the
preceding description is only the first part. To complete the process you have to
change the Enabled field for the port in the Server document. To do this, open the
Server document in Edit Mode, go to the Ports/Notes Network Ports page, and
change the field to Enabled or Disabled.

To fully configure a serial port you have to choose a modem driver and configure
it. See Chapter 4, "Additional Server Setup," for details on that topic.

To create, remove, or rename ports in Domino Administrator, use the same procedure as described previously for enabling/disabling ports. The only difference is, in the
Port Setup dialog box (step 3), choose the New, Rename, or Delete buttons.

When creating a second port for a given protocol (say, a second TCP/IP port),
consider naming it descriptively, that is, so that its purpose is obvious. At the same
time, consider renaming the first port so that it, too, is descriptively named. For example, if you have two TCP/IP ports, one for communication with users, the other for
communication with other servers in a cluster, name them *TCPIP-Users* and *TCPIP-
Cluster*.

Set Up Named Networks

Notes automatically assigned Domino Named Network names to every enabled port
during first server configuration. I highly recommend you rename them. As I pointed
out in Chapter 2, leaving the default network names in place can get you in trouble as
you add more servers to your domain.

For example, if two servers both have TCP/IP ports but only connect to each other via modem, leaving the default network names in place will drastically slow down mail transfers, not only between these two servers but potentially among all the servers in your domain as well. If Server A and Server B share a network name, they will assume they have a constant connection to each other over the network port represented by that network name. They will try repeatedly to transfer mail to each other over that port, and will only try the modem connection after multiple failures.

Other servers will also assume that Server A and B have a constant network connection. If the other servers conclude that the fictional route via Server A and Server B is lower cost than other, actual routes, they will try to route mail via them as well, with similar dismal results.

If you never set up any servers in your domain that connect only to some other servers by modem, this problem will not affect you. But if there is even the slightest possibility that a future server may only be able to connect via modem to another server in the domain, forestall this problem by renaming all of the Domino named networks now. It's easy to do:

1. Open the Server document for this server in Edit Mode (and every future server).

2. Choose the Ports tab.

3. Choose the Notes Network Ports tab.

4. For each port, rename the Domino Named Network in the Notes Network column. If you followed my advice in Chapter 2 and created a comprehensive naming plan before installing the first server, you already know what names you want to assign to each network. If you did not follow my advice (shame on you!), call each network *location protocol*, where *location* is the name of the city/office/LAN where the server will be located and *protocol* is the protocol name. For example, server Osprey is located in Marsh Creek and uses TCP/IP. That port is on a network that I might name Marsh Creek TCP. (Notice that spaces *are* permitted in the network name.)

Set Up Administrative Groups

In a later step you will edit several access lists in the Server document for your new server. Those access lists will include mostly names of groups. The job of editing those lists will be easier (and less error prone) if you create ahead of time the groups that you will add to them.

As with all the other named entities in Notes, you should have developed a policy for the creation and naming of groups before ever setting up the first server in your domain. Among the groups you should have decided to establish are at least two that you will want to create now:

- A group to hold the names of all of your Domino administrators. It might be named Administrators, Admins, DominoAdmins, or GlobalAdmins). If you chose the Set Access Control List Entry option at the end of the initial server configuration process (described earlier in this chapter), Domino already created this group for you. It also populated it with the name of your first user and added it as Manager to the ACLs of all existing databases.

- A "deny access" group to hold the names of all entities (people, groups, and servers) that are *persona non grata* in your domain. No such entities will exist at this time, but this group will grow over time, as (for example) employees leave the company. This group might be called Terminated, Inactive Users, Outlaws, or any other name that conveys its purpose.

You will want to create at least these two groups ahead of time, and maybe others. To create a group, follow these steps:

1. Open the Groups view of the Domain Directory. In Domino Administrator, this is on the People and Groups page. (You'll notice that two groups already exist—LocalDomainServers and OtherDomainServers.)

2. Create a new Group document. (In Domino Administrator, you can click Add Group in the toolbar above the Groups view, or in the menu you can choose People, Groups, Create, or in the Tools pane you can choose Groups, Create.)

3. Fill in the fields:

   - **Group name.** This is the name by which the group will be identified in all lists. The group name may include spaces. For readability, it should be proper case. It should also be descriptive without being verbose.

   - **Group type.** For your Administrators group choose either "Multi-purpose" or "Access Control List only." For your Inactive Users group, choose "Deny List only." As a general rule, you should not leave any group as a "multi-purpose" group unless you know the group name will be used both in access lists and as a mailing list. Domino creates an index for every possible function of the group. Therefore, it has to work harder to maintain multipurpose groups than single-purpose groups. You can improve the overall performance of your servers by using single-purpose groups whenever possible.

- **Description.** Always enter a description of the group you are creating that will convey to you a year from now (and to your successors) this group's purpose. Eventually, you will have a lot of groups and inevitably you will forget (or a successor will have to figure out) each group's original purpose. Having an informative description will make it much easier.

- **Members.** Add members to the group either by typing their names (but watch out for typos—they can kill you) or, better yet, clicking the helper button next to the field and adding members' names in the Names dialog box. Members can be people, servers, and other groups. You can nest groups up to five levels deep for mail routing, six levels deep for other purposes. However, those are theoretical limits. I don't recommend you ever nest groups that deep in real life.

- **Owners.** Notes will enter your name in this field by default. That means you can edit this document in the future. You might want to add or substitute a group name.

- **Administrators.** Notes will enter your name in this field by default. That means you will be able to edit this document in the future. You might want to add or substitute a group name.

- **Foreign directory sync allowed**. The default, Yes, allows Domino to send information about this group to foreign directories.

4. Save and close the document.

The Administrators group appears in the Groups view. The Inactive Users group does not, because it is a Deny Access group. Such groups only appear in the Deny Access view, which you can see if you open the Deny Access Groups view (which only administrators can see) of the Domain Directory. To open this view in Domino Administrator, go to either the People and Groups tab or the Configuration tab and, in the View menu, choose Server, Deny Access Groups.

Set Up the Administration Process

The Administration Process is a service that runs on the server and automates numerous tasks that would be difficult or tedious to perform manually. Using the Administration Process is optional, but it is so beneficial that there is no reason at this time why you would not want it running. It sets itself up automatically in Domino R5, except for a couple items, which you have to set up manually.

The requirements for the Administration Process to function properly are as follows:

- The adminp server task runs on all servers in the domain.
- A proper replica copy of the Administration Requests database (admin4.nsf) exists on all servers in the domain.

- An Administration Server is designated for the Domain Directory.

- Administration Servers are designated for other databases.

- A Certification Log database (`certlog.nsf`) exists on every server that will be used as a registration server when registering certifiers, users, and servers.

The first three items in the preceding list are requirements for the Administration Process to function, and Domino takes care of them automatically. The last two items are optional and you have to take care of them manually.

Designate Administration Servers

Among the things the Administration Process will do is update databases. If you rename a person or remove a person from the system, the Administration process can update database ACLs and Authors and Readers fields. But it can do these things only if you designate an Administration Server to update each database. So it is in your best interest to make sure every database in your system has an Administration Server designated.

The Administration Process works more or less as follows:

1. A user or a process creates a request in the Administration Requests database on one server. (Users never make requests by actually composing a document in Administration Requests. Rather, they choose an item in the Actions menu, usually in the Domain Directory, and, in response, the system generates the request.

2. By replication, the request appears in the replica of Administration Requests on all servers in the domain. (Depending on configuration documents, the request might also replicate to other domains as well.)

3. The servers continuously monitor Administration Requests for changes. If a request appears for which a given server is responsible (because it is the Administration Server of a given database or group of databases), that server carries out the request (for example, renames a person in the ACL of a database).

4. Upon carrying out the request, successfully or not, the server updates the Administration Requests database. It creates a document responding to the original request document, either declaring its success or detailing the problem that caused it to fail. If successful, the server may also generate other requests in furtherance of the overall process of, say, renaming a person.

5. Replication causes each server's contributions to the furtherance of each process to appear in each other server's copy of the Administration Requests database. Over time, all the steps necessary to carry out each request will take place throughout the domain. At some point after the last step of a given process has been carried out successfully, the system will purge that set of documents from the database.

You can designate the Administration Server of a database either in the ACL of that database or on the Files page in Domino Administrator. Use the ACL if you only need to designate the Administration Server of one database, say, a new one that you just added to the system. Use Domino Administrator if you need to designate Administration Servers for multiple databases, such as when you are setting up a new domain—in other words, right now.

To designate an Administration Server for a single database, using its ACL, follow these steps:

1. Open the ACL of the database in question.

2. Choose Advanced.

3. Under Administration Server, choose Server, then either enter the fully distinguished name of a server (`Osprey/Servers/Stillwater`, *not* just `Osprey`) or pick it from the list of servers. Click OK.

To designate an Administration Server for one or more databases in Domino Administrator, follow these steps:

1. Select a server on which the database(s) in question is/are located.

2. Go to the Files page. There, in the list of databases, select the database or databases you want to affect. Select only those databases that you want to set alike.

3. Choose Database, Manage ACL either in the Tools pane or in the Files menu.

4. In the ACL Management dialog box, choose Advanced.

5. In the Advanced pane, select Modify Administration Server setting, then choose Server and either type in the fully distinguished name of a server or pick a server from the list.

6. Select Modify fields of type Reader or Author if you want the Administration Process to update such fields. Usually you do, but in some cases you do not. Selecting this option requires the Administration Server of a database to search every document in the database. For a large database that could take a lot of time. So (especially if you know a database does not have Readers or Authors fields or that their contents won't ever change) you might not want to select this option for such databases.

7. Click OK.

Which server should you choose to be Administration Server of a given database? In general, it does not matter. All R4 and R5 servers can fill that role. But some administrators like to consolidate the Administration Process as much as possible on a single server, perhaps a hub server. So, they designate one server to be the Administration Server of all databases as far as possible. Of course, some databases may not reside on that server. For example, people's mail databases usually reside only on their mail server. For such databases, you will have to designate the server on which the database resides.

What about databases that reside only on people's workstations? These include one's Personal Address Book and Headlines databases, among others. Users can enter their own names in the Server field on the Advanced pane of the ACL of those databases. (For example, I would enter `Rob Kirkland/MarshCreek/Stillwater`.) When a user accepts a name change, his copy of Notes will update those databases at that time.

Create the Certification Log Database

The Certification Log is a database in which Domino servers store information about (you guessed it) certifications. All new registrations of certifier IDs, servers, and users are recorded here. All recertifications and renamings are recorded here.

This database has to reside on any server that serves as a registration server or where you request new names. You can maintain nonreplica copies on each server by creating one separately on each server. But the database is more useful if you maintain replica copies on each server, because then each copy retains a record of all certifications throughout the domain. If you ever need to search for information about a certification, you'll appreciate not having to look through multiple, nonreplica Certification Logs. To replicate a single Certification Log to a group of servers, create the database on one server then make replicas on the other servers.

To create the Certification Log, follow these steps:

1. In the File menu, choose Database, New.

2. In the New Database dialog box, edit the following fields:

   - **Server.** Enter (or pick from the list) the fully distinguished name of the server on which the database will be created. In our example we would enter Osprey/Stillwater or Osprey/Servers/Stillwater.

   - **Title.** Enter Certification Log.

   - **File Name.** Enter `certlog.nsf`. You must use this filename.

   - **Template Server.** The Certification Log template (`certlog.ntf`) resides only on servers, so if you are not running a copy of Notes or Domino Administrator that shares a data directory with a server, you must change this field from Local to a server's name. Do so by clicking the Template Server button, entering or choosing a server, then clicking OK. The list of database templates will change to show the templates on that server. Scroll through the new list and select Certification Log.

3. Leave the other fields unchanged. Choose OK when finished. If you have the right to create new databases on the named server (which you should this early in the configuration process), Domino will create the new Certification Log. (Otherwise, it would display an error message.)

Because you haven't created any other server yet, we won't discuss making replicas of this database on them at this time. You can learn how to make new replicas in Chapter 9 "Replication."

Set Up Server Access Fields

Several fields in the Server document define server access lists. They define who can access the server for various purposes, and server configuration is not complete until you have populated those fields. As a general rule, you should populate them with group names and wildcards. The server won't automatically recognize when you change the contents of many of the fields. You have to bounce the server—bring it down, then restart it (you can do both with the Restart Server console command)—to force it to recognize those changes. But if you populate the fields with group names, you can add entries to or remove them from the groups. The server will recognize the changes without the need to bounce it.

You can also add wildcard names to the fields. For example, you could add `*/MarshCreek/Stillwater`. This would permit anyone in the MarshCreek OU to perform the activity that membership in the field permits. Using just an asterisk stands in for all users named in the Domain Directory.

You can also populate the fields with names of Domain Directory views. Enter an asterisk followed by the view name. All entities listed in the view will be affected by the field's restrictions.

The fields you need to populate are as follows:

Basics page, Basics heading:

- **Administrators.** People named in this field can

  - Send commands to the server via Domino Administrator and the Remote Console

  - Designate Administration Servers for databases on the server

  - Compact databases on the server

  - Create, update, and delete full text indexes on the server

  - Create, update, and delete folders and directory and database links on the server.

Security page, Server Access heading:

- **Allow server access only to users listed in this Directory.** This field defaults to No and you normally want to leave it that way. Setting it to Yes allows only people represented by Person documents in this directory to access this server. It also denies access to *all* other servers. If you set this field to No, you have to add to the Access server field the names of any servers, server groups, or server OUs (for example, `*/Servers/Stillwater`) that you want to be able to access this server.

- **Access server.** Default (blank) allows anyone to access the server. Adding anything to this field limits access to only the entities named in this field. It also may lengthen the amount of time it takes to log in to the server, so leave this field blank unless you have a specific reason for limiting access to this server. If you enter anything in this field, be sure to also add entries (such as "LocalDomainServers") to allow other servers to access this server for replication and mail routing purposes.

- **Not access server.** Anyone listed in this field will be barred from the server even if they are also listed in the "Access server" field. This field overrides. If you leave the field empty, you deny access to nobody. You should at this time add the name of your Inactive Users group to this field.

- **Create new databases.** Unless this field is blank, only those listed in it will be permitted to create new databases (File, Database, New) on this server. If left blank, everyone will be able to create new databases. As a general rule, you should allow only administrators and application developers (who might be collected in a group named Designers) should be able to create new databases.

- **Create replica databases.** Only those listed in this field can create replicas of databases (choose File, Replication, New Replica) on this server. If the field is left blank, nobody will be able to create new replicas. At this time add the LocalDomainServers and Administrators groups.

- **Allowed to use monitors.** Only those listed can set perform headline monitoring on this server. Users set up headline monitoring by creating subscriptions to databases. Their headlines databases will then search subscribed databases for designated changes. The more such monitoring takes place, the more performance suffers. In this field, you can define who is allowed to set up headline monitors on this server. If blank, everyone (except entities listed in the following field) can set headline monitors.

- **Not allowed to use monitors.** Those listed cannot subscribe to databases on this server.

- **Administer the server from a browser.** Only those listed can use the Domino Web Administrator application to administer this server from a Web browser. If this field is blank, nobody can use the Domino Web Administrator to administer this server. (Of course, if the server won't be accessible by HTTP at all, then this field is not used.)

Security page, Passthru Use heading:

- **Access this server.** Only entities listed here can access this server via passthru. If this field is blank, this server is not reachable via passthru.

- **Route through.** Only entities listed here can pass through this server to reach another Domino server. If this field is blank, this server cannot be passed through.

- **Cause calling.** Only entities listed here can cause this server, acting in the capacity of a passthru server, to dial up another server via modem or remote LAN. If this field is blank, nobody can do so.

- **Destinations allowed.** Lists the servers that can be reached from this server acting as a passthru server. If this field is blank, all servers can be reached.

Security page, Agent Restrictions heading:

- **Run Personal Agents.** Entities listed here can run personal agents on this server. If this field is blank, all can run personal agents. If you populate this field, entities named in this and the two following fields will be able to run personal agents on this server.

- **Run restricted LotusScript/Java agents.** Entities listed here can run some LotusScript and Java agents, depending on what the agents do. If this field is blank, nobody can run LotusScript/Java agents except those listed in the next field. You should add LocalDomainServers and Administrators here. You may want to add groups (such as OtherDomainServers) that encompass servers from other domains.

- **Run unrestricted LotusScript/Java agents.** Entities listed here can run any LotusScript or Java agent, including those that manipulate system time, file I/O, and the OS. If you leave this field blank, nobody can run such agents. One could use these agents to steal or destroy data and otherwise bypass security barriers, so you want to authorize only the most trusted users to run such agents.

Security page, IIOP Restrictions heading: Entities listed in these two fields can, via IIOP from a browser, direct the server to run CORBA-enabled LotusScript and Java agents.

- **Run restricted Java/Javascript.** The same rules apply here as for regular restricted LotusScript/Java agents. See the bullet points in the immediately preceding section. If you leave this field blank, nobody can run such agents.

- **Run unrestricted Java/Javascript.** The same rules apply here as for regular unrestricted LotusScript/Java agents. See the bullet points in the immediately preceding section. If you leave this field blank, nobody can run such agents. One could use these agents to steal or destroy data and otherwise bypass security barriers, so you want to authorize only the most trusted users to run such agents.

Most other fields on the Server document were correctly populated when Notes created the document. But, there are some other fields that you may need to edit at this time.

Set Up Other Server Fields

Other (nonaccess) fields in the Server document, which you may want to edit at this time, include the following:

Basics page, Basics heading:

- **Server's phone number(s).** If the server will receive incoming phone calls on a modem and you know its phone number(s), enter it/them here.

Basics page, Server Location Information heading: Update these fields if this server will be dialing out or receiving calls by modem.

- **Prefix for outside line.** If the server will be dialing out on a modem and has to dial a prefix to reach an outside line, enter the prefix here.

- **International prefix.** Enter here the prefix for making an international call from the server's location. For servers located in the United States, this is 011.

- **Country code at this location.** Enter the code for the country in which this server will be located. If in the United States, this is 1.

- **Long distance prefix.** Enter the prefix for dialing a long-distance call from the server's location. The default is 1, the prefix used in the United States.

- **Area code at this location.** Enter the area code where this server will be located. For example, in Marsh Creek this is 610. In other countries this would be a city code. For example, the city code for Melbourne, Australia is 3.

- **Calling card access number.** If this server will bill outgoing calls to a credit card, enter here the phone number the server must dial to place such calls. for example, for AT&T in the United States, the phone number is 800–225–5288.

- **Calling card number.** If this server will bill outgoing calls to a credit card, enter the credit card number here.

- **Network Dialup idle timeout.** Enter here the number of minutes after which, if no activity has taken place over the phone line, the server should terminate a Microsoft RAS connection. If left blank, the server will terminate RAS connections as soon as it completes all scheduled transactions. Normally you should leave this field blank.

Basics page, Servers heading: These fields are relevant only if a Notes client shares this server's data folders.

- **Mail Server.** This is the mail server of the Notes client (if any) sharing this server's data folders.

- **Passthru server.** This is the default passthru server of the Notes client (if any) sharing this server's data folders. If Notes needs to reach another server for which no connection is defined, the server will ask the default passthru server to connect it.

- **InterNotes server.** This is the proxy Web browsing server of the Notes client (if any) sharing this server's data folders. Such a Notes client only needs an InterNotes server if no TCP/IP port is enabled for this server.

Security page, Security Settings heading:

- **Compare Notes public keys against those stored in Directory.** Default is No. Changing it to Yes will cause the server to match the public key presented by a user to the public key stored in the user's Person document in the Domain Directory. If the keys don't match, the user cannot authenticate with the server and is locked out. You can use this feature to lock out unauthorized holders of ID files or people for whom no Person document exists. Setting this to Yes slows the authentication process.

- **Allow anonymous Notes connections.** Allows Notes users to access the server without authenticating. Because they don't have to authenticate, the server does not know their identity—they are anonymous. If you intend to allow anonymous Notes users into the server, you should update server and database access lists to include the entry "Anonymous." You would normally enable this option only on servers intended for public access. There are corresponding fields on the Internet Ports page which can allow or deny anonymous access for Web, LDAP directory, news, and IIOP users, as well as inbound mail exchangers.

- **Check passwords on Notes Ids.** Default is disabled. Enabling it causes the server to check during authentication that the password protecting a user's ID file is the same as on file in the Person document. If they are not the same, the user is required to update the password on the ID to match the one on file. This makes it possible to lock out unauthorized holders of IDs and to force users to update their passwords periodically. If you enable this feature, you also have to enable it on Person documents. Warning: Enabling this feature prevents access to this server by Notes clients earlier than Release 4.5. It also alters the IDs of users and servers that access this server, which in turn prevents them from accessing servers earlier than Release 4.5. Any user who needs to access servers of both kinds will have to maintain multiple, separate copies of his/her ID file.

Ports page, Proxies page, Proxy Configuration heading. If the server will be passing through a firewall to connect with other servers and you didn't identify proxy servers at first server setup, you can do so in this section of the Server document. In the appropriate fields, enter the name of each kind of proxy server in the form *hostname:portnumber*, where *hostname* is the proxy server's fully qualified domain name (FQDN) and *portnumber* is the IP port that the proxy server will be monitoring. If you do enable one or more proxy servers but you want to server to bypass the proxy to reach other local servers, enter the domain names, host names or IP addresses of the other local servers in the "No proxy for these hosts and domains" field.

Miscellaneous page, Contact Information heading: Use the fields under this heading to further identify each server. As a general rule, you can never have too much identifying information, but you can easily have too little. These fields will be especially useful to new hires or if you plan to set up numerous, widely dispersed servers.

Miscellaneous page, Administration heading:

- **Owner.** Enter here the names of individuals or groups that you want to authorize to edit this Server document.

- **Administrators.** Enter here the names of individuals or groups that you want to authorize to edit this Server document.

Transactional Logging page: Transactional logging is a new feature of R5 Domino servers. It greatly enhances the integrity, security, and manageability of the data residing on the server. It promotes faster restarts after server crashes. It promotes faster responses to user requests because the server can defer database updates until periods of low demand. It simplifies backup procedures because you can perform daily incremental backups of the transaction logs rather than full database backups.

On the other hand, enabling transaction logging raises administrative issues that you should understand and be prepared to deal with. For example, certain operations which you can perform without major consequence on an unlogged database may require an unscheduled full backup of a logged database. In addition, you *shouldn't* set up transaction logging on a computer with only one hard disk drive or with only one disk controller. There are other examples, as well.

Because of these issues, I recommend that you hold off on enabling transaction logging at this time unless you are familiar with its implications and you had already set up this server with the intention of enabling transaction logging. For a more detailed discussion of transaction logging, see Chapter 14, "Database Maintenance and Troubleshooting," and Chapter 19, "Performance Tuning."

- **Transactional logging.** Transactional logging is disabled on a new server by default. Enable it by setting this field to Enabled.

- **Log path.** Enter here the pathname of the folder in which the transactional log files will be maintained. If you just enter a folder name (for example, logdir), the folder will be created under the Domino data folder. For optimal performance, however, you should set up the transactional logs on a mirrored, separate physical disk drive, dedicated to that purpose. For example, you might dedicate drive G: to the transactional logs, in which case you might enter in this field `g:\logdir`. Alternatively and next best is to set up transaction logs on any physical drive other than that on which databases will be stored. For example, you might keep the OS, Domino program files, and transaction logs on c: and databases on d:.

- **Use all available space on log device.** Select Yes if dedicating a disk drive to transactional logs. Otherwise select No.

- **Maximum log space.** This field appears only if you select No in the preceding field. Enter the maximum amount of disk space, in megabytes, to be allocated to the transactional logs on a nondedicated disk drive. The default (and minimum) is 192MB. The recommended minimum is 1GB. The maximum possible for circular logging is 4GB, with no maximum for archive logging (see last bullet).

- **Automatic fixup of corrupt databases.** Enabled by default. If this option is enabled and Domino cannot restore a database from transaction logs, Domino will automatically run Fixup to restore the database. If this option is not enabled, Domino will notify the administrator of the need to run Fixup.

- **Runtime/Restart performance.** Default is Standard, which is a compromise between the other two choices, faster runtime performance or faster restart performance. If you choose to favor faster runtime performance, Domino will force database updates less often. That is, it will allow the transaction logs to accumulate more transactions before forcing them to be written to the database. This corresponds to a longer recovery time in the event of a server crash. If you choose to favor faster restart performance, Domino will force database updates more often. This means shorter recover time in the event of a server crash but could slow performance of other services on a busy server.

- **Logging style.** Choose circular or archive logging. Circular is the default; archive is recommended. Circular logs are reused continuously, with the oldest log records being overwritten as needed. You can't back up circular logs, so you may not be able to recover from a media failure. Under archive logging you use an R5-compliant backup utility to backup logs. The system never overwrites an existing log until it is backed up. Because the logs are backed up, you can always recover from a media failure. Use archive logging if you have an R5-compliant backup program in place. Otherwise use circular logging.

Optional Cleanup Chores

Earlier in the chapter we learned that, if servers in this organization are to be part of an OU, we have to jump through extra hoops during first server configuration, because, by default, it creates the first server and user using at the O level within the organization. We learned that there were three ways to approach this problem:

- Create O, OU, and the first server's ID ahead of time, then feed them to the Server Configuration form during first server configuration.

- Rename the first server and user.

- Create a temporary first server then throw it away after creating, configuring one or more additional servers.

Whichever solution we implement, we have to follow a checklist of cleanup items. Those checklists appear in the following sections.

IDs Created Ahead of Time

If you created the O, OU, and Server IDs before running first server setup, you have to perform two items of cleanup. You have to create one or more Certificate documents and you have to copy the server's public key from its ID file to the Server document. Normally, when you create OU certifier IDs, Notes creates (along with the ID) a Certificate document in the Domain Directory (or Personal Address Book). Because you created the IDs for the Organization, server OU, and server (and possibly other entities) before first server configuration, the corresponding certificate documents were created in another directory—not the new one created at first server configuration.

At first server configuration a new certificate document was created in the new Domain Directory for the O certifier ID (if that was the one you fed to the Server Configuration form). But no certificate document exists for the server OU (or any other OUs that you pre-created). You either have to create those documents manually or, if the directory in which they were originally created is still accessible, copy them over from it to the new directory.

Creating a Certificate document is easy. You only have to fill in three fields. But it is tricky in a couple ways. First, you have to do it indirectly. Second, you have to paste the public key in from the ID file. From Domino Administrator, follow these steps:

1. Switch to the server.
2. Switch to the Configuration tab.
3. In the Tools pane, choose Certification, ID Properties.
4. In the Choose ID File to Examine dialog box, find the certifier ID file for which you are creating a Certificate document. Select it and choose Open.
5. Enter the password for the certifier ID file. The User ID dialog box opens.
6. Choose More Options, Copy Public Key, then OK. A copy of the ID's public key is now in the Clipboard.
7. In the Task pane (left side of screen) choose Miscellaneous, Certificates. The Certificates view appears, showing all existing certificates, which, at this early stage, should include only the O certifier. (But it might show only an OU certifier.)
8. Click Add Certifier. Fill in the fields as follows:

   - **Certifier name.** Enter the name of the OU for which you are creating this document. In our example, the server OU is named /Servers/Stillwater. Enter the name in that format (that is, with the leading slash character).

   - **Issued by.** Enter the name of the OU's issuer. In the case of /Servers/Stillwater, the issuer is /Stillwater. In the case of /Servers/MarshCreek/Stillwater, the issuer is /MarshCreek/Stillwater. Enter the name in that format (that is, with the leading slash character).

- **Certified public key.** Paste the public key that you copied in step 6.

    Optionally, fill in the fields on the other tabs, especially the contact fields on the Contact Information tab.

9. Save and close the document. Repeat this process for each OU that you preregistered.

For a reason that I have never uncovered, the public key in the Server document does not match that in the server ID when you generate the server ID ahead of time. This produces the following error message when you start the server: `Error updating local ID file: The information in the supplied certificates from the Address Book entry is out of date.` To fix this problem, paste a new copy of the server's public key from its ID file to the Server document. Follow these steps:

1. In Domino Administrator, choose the Configuration tab.

2. In the Tools pane, choose Certification, ID Properties.

3. In the Choose ID File to Examine dialog box, find the Server's ID file. Select it and choose Open.

4. If prompted for a password (you probably won't be), enter the server's password.

5. In the User ID dialog box, choose More Options, Copy public key, and then OK. A copy of the public key is now in the Clipboard

6. Back on the Configuration page, choose the server if necessary, then choose Server, Current Server Document in the Task pane. The Server document opens.

7. When the Server document appears, choose Edit Server.

8. Open the Administration page.

9. Select the contents of the Certified public key field, then choose Edit, Paste. The copy of the public key that was in the Clipboard replaces the copy that was in this field.

10. Save and close the Server document.

11. If the server is running, bounce the server (Console command: restart server) for it to discover the new copy of its public key in the Server document.

Rename the Server and User

If you opted to let the first server configuration process generate your organization, server, and user IDs for you, you now need to rename the user and either rename the server or create another server, properly named, and decommission the first server. Renaming the person and server means moving them to OUs that you haven't yet created. So first you have to create the OUs into which you intend to move them. Then you can tell Domino to rename the user for you and it will take care of all the messy details. But for the server you have to take care of the messy details yourself.

We covered registering OU certifier IDs earlier in this chapter. But just as a reminder, you can register OUs from the Configuration tab in Domino Administrator. Choose Registration, Organizational Unit in the Tools pane. To register an OU certifier ID you have to have possession of and know the password of the certifier ID representing the parent O or OU of the OU you want to create. You need this because Domino Administrator will use the private key in the parent ID to certify the public key of the child OU that you are creating.

After you have created the OU certifier IDs representing the OUs in which your first server and user will reside, you can use them to rename the server and user.

Rename the User

If you sort of ignore the endless number of steps that follow, renaming the user is comparatively easy:

1. Go to the People & Groups page in Domino Administrator.

2. Select the People view in the Navigator pane on the left.

3. Select the person in the Person view in the View pane.

4. Choose People, Rename in the Tools pane.

5. In the Certify Selected Entries dialog box (yes, you could rename multiple people at once), choose Request Move to New Certifier.

6. In the Choose Original Certifier ID dialog box, find the O certifier. In our example, it is `stillwater.id`. Select it and choose Open. Enter the password when prompted.

7. In the Request Move For Selected Entries dialog box, enter the name of the OU that you will move the user into. In our example, this is `/MarshCreek/Stillwater`. Then click Submit Request. Domino Administrator processes your request, then displays the results (success or failure). Click OK when prompted.

8. Go to the Files page of Domino Administrator. Find the Administration Requests (`R5.0`) (`admin4.nsf`) database and double-click it to open it.

9. If the About Administration Requests screen appears, read it then close it to reveal the All Requests by Server view. Change to the Name Move Requests view.

10. In the Name Move Requests view, your user's name should appear. Select it, then choose Complete Move for selected entries in the Actions menu.

11. Find the new OU certifier ID in the Choose Certifier ID dialog box. This is the ID for the OU to which you are moving the user. Select it and click Open. Enter its password.

12. In the Complete Move For Selected Entries dialog box, edit the field entries if you want (but you probably won't want), then click Certify. Domino Administrator will process your request, then inform you of the results (success or failure). Click OK when prompted.

Now, you just sort of sit back and wait. In the fullness of time (maybe 24 to 48 hours), Domino will perform all the steps necessary to rename this user. At some point along the way, when someone logs in as that user, a dialog box will appear prompting you to accept the name change. You should accept the name change. The name change can't proceed until you take this manual step.

You can hurry the renaming process along as follows:

1. Go to the Server tab in Domino Administrator. Switch to your server, if necessary. Select Admin Process in the list of server tasks.

2. Choose Tasks, Tell, and choose All requests (everything). Alternatively, choose Console, then enter the following command on the Command line at the bottom of the screen: `tell adminp process all`.

3. Log in as the renamed user. (If you are currently logged in as that user, you can press F5 to clear your login, then open any database on the server to relog.) The Name update request found on the server dialog box will appear, asking you to accept the user's new name. Click Yes.

4. The rest of the renaming process will take place without any intervention by you. But if you want, you can reenter the `tell adminp process all` command several more times to hurry along the various steps of the process.

To learn more about the process of renaming a user, see Chapter 5.

Rename the Server

Renaming the server is a lot more work than renaming a user, because you have to do it all manually. Here is what you have to do:

1. Rename the server in the server ID file by recertifying it with the appropriate OU certifier.

2. Manually (or by agent) change the server's name everywhere it appears.

3. Restart the server.

The places where the server name may appear include:

- Documents in the Domain Directory and each user's Personal Address Book. See later in this section for a list of documents that could include the server's name.

- Database ACLs. Look in the ACL of every database and design template on the server.

- The server's `notes.ini` file. Open it in a text editor and run a text search for the server's common name.

- The `notes.ini` file of each user for whom the server is the mail server (hopefully, that's only the first user at this time). Open it in a text editor and run a text search for the server's common name.

- Documents in various other databases. The only database that should exist at this early stage that might have the server's old name in it is Statistics & Events—the Server Statistic Collection Profile in the Server Statistic Collection view.

- Database titles. At least two databases include the server's fully distinguished name in their titles—the Notes Log and the Stats database. Change their titles in their respective Database Properties boxes (choose File, Database, and then Properties).

The documents in the Domain Directory and user Personal Address Books that might contain references to the server include:

- Server documents (Domain Directory). The "Server name" field. The "Mail server," "Passthru server," and "InterNotes server" fields. Server access fields.

- Group documents (Domain Directory and existing Personal Address Books). The Members field. Especially the LocalDomainServers group for this domain and the OtherDomainServers groups of other domains.

- Person documents (Domain Directory). The "Mail server" field.

- Mail-in Database documents (Domain Directory). The "Server" field.

- Resource documents (Domain Directory). The "Server" field.

- Connection documents (Domain Directory and existing Personal Address Books). "Source server" and "Destination server" fields. Might appear in other domains also.

- Location documents (Domain Directory and existing Personal Address Books). Several server fields.

- Certificate documents (Domain Directory and existing Personal Address Books). "Notes mail server" field.

- Configuration documents (Domain Directory). Group or Server name field. "Allowed to track messages" field. "Allowed to track subjects" field.

- Domain documents (Domain Directory of other domains, both Domino and foreign). "Calendar server" field.

- External Domain Network Information documents (Domain Directory) "Requesting server" and "Information server" fields. Might appear in other domains also.

- Program documents (Domain Directory). "Server to run on" field.

- User Setup Profile documents (Domain Directory). Numerous fields.
- Web Configuration documents (Domain Directory). "Applies to" field of "Web Realm" documents.

It is because the server's name appears in potentially so many places that you want to change its name (if at all) as soon as possible. The number of places you have to look for and potentially change the name grows with each new OU, server, user, database, and document that you create. Of course, you can use various tricks to automate the process. For example, if you temporarily full-text index the Domain Directory, a search for the server's name should turn up a list of all documents that include it. As another example, a Decommission Server analysis should turn up a list of places where the server's name appears. But the bottom line is that renaming a server is not an automatic process and not a chore to be taken on lightly.

To recertify the server so that its name includes its OU, follow these steps:

1. Make sure you have possession of both the server ID file and the OU certifier ID file for the OU in which you want to server to reside.

2. Make a backup copy of the server ID file.

3. In Domino Administrator, choose Certification, Certify from the Tools pane on the Configuration page.

4. In the Choose Certifier ID dialog box, locate the server's intended OU certifier ID file. In our example, that would be the file for /Servers/Stillwater. Select it and choose Open. Enter the OU certifier's password when prompted and press Enter or click OK.

5. In the Choose ID to Certify dialog box, locate the server ID file. In our example, that would be the file for Osprey/Stillwater, and the filename is probably server.id. Select it and choose Open.

6. In the Certify dialog box, choose Re-certify.

7. In the Certify ID dialog box, edit the following fields:

   - **Server.** If the word "Local" appears to the right of the Server button, click the Server button, then enter or choose the original name of the server from the list. In our example, that would be Osprey/Stillwater. This will be the Registration Server, where the certification process will look for the Certification Log database and the Domain Directory database, both of which it will update.

   - **Expiration date.** By default, server certifications expire after 100 years and user certifications expire after only two years. But it is a little unusual to recertify a server, and Notes has mistakenly assumed a two-year expiration for this server recertification. Change the expiration date to 100 years from today's date.

8. Leave all other fields unchanged. Click Certify.

Notes recertifies the server ID, updates the Certification Log, updates the Server name field in the Server document, and adds the new server name to the LocalDomainServers group. It does *not* remove the old server name from the LocalDomainServers group or update the server's name in any other field of any other document, not even other fields (such as the "Mail server" field) in the Server document.

Throwaway Server

With the throwaway server, you avoid the necessity of manually finding and editing the name of the renamed server. Instead you have to find and delete the name of the server. Also, you have to designate a new Administrative Server for the Domain Directory. I'm not sure there is substantially less work involved.

One tool that should be very useful in this scenario is the Decommission Server Analysis, which will provide you with a checklist of things you have to do to successfully decommission a server. Run the Decommission Server Analysis as follows:

1. Make sure the server to be decommissioned and the server that will take over its duties are both running and available from your workstation.

2. On the Server/Analysis page of Domino Administrator, choose Analyze, Decommission Server in the Tools pane or Decommission Server Analysis in the Analysis menu. The Decommission Server Analysis dialog box appears.

3. In the Source Server field, enter the fully distinguished name (or choose it from the list) of the server to be decommissioned. In the Target server field, enter or choose the server that will replace the first server.

4. Click OK. Domino Administrator runs a comparison of the two servers and enters the results into the Decommission Server Analysis database on your workstation.

When the analysis is complete, the database opens on your screen. It consists of a set of documents covering all of the areas in which the second server may have to take over the responsibilities of the first. The areas in which the second server cannot currently do so are marked on the view with a red X and the exact nature of each problem is described in the marked document (see Figure 3.6). Your goal is to eliminate the causes of all the red Xs. Then you can shut down the first server for good.

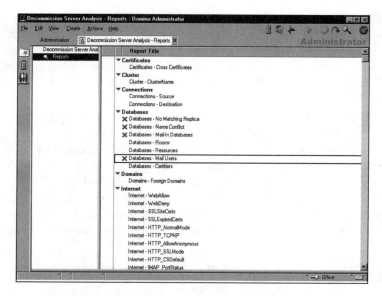

Figure 3.6   Discrepancies between the
two servers are marked with a red X.

Other Good Things to Do

There are lots of other things that you might have to do to complete the configuration of the first server. Most of them depend on what services the server will provide and we cover them in later chapters. But the following are a few things you should do on this and every server:

- Automate server startup
- Set up more shortcuts
- Secure the data folders at the OS level

Automating Server Startup

Normally, you want a Domino server to start up automatically, as soon as the computer starts up. So far we have not taken care of that. For most of the server platforms, you would do this by adding a command line to a startup batch file or script. In Windows NT, you have to install Domino as an NT service, then configure the service to start automatically. There are two benefits to doing this. First, Domino *will* start when the computer starts. Second, it will run independently of any user session.

For example, under Windows NT you can log on as an NT user, then log off, and all the time Domino will run. You will see and be able to interact with Domino when you are logged on, and you will be able to stop it if necessary and restart it. But, you don't have to remain logged on to keep the server running, as you would have to if you did not start it as an NT service.

If you installed a server under Windows NT, InstallShield Wizard installed Domino as an NT service *only if you chose to do a Customized install*. If you just picked a server type, InstallShield Wizard did not set up the server as an NT service. In that case you would have to re-run InstallShield Wizard and choose Customize or Custom Install at the appropriate point. You could then deselect every option except Domino as an NT Service. Installing only that option, InstallShield Wizard would take only a few seconds to run.

You can tell if Domino is installed as an NT service by opening the Windows NT Control Panel, then opening Services. In the Services dialog box, look for "Lotus Domino Server." It will be listed alphabetically. If you don't see it, then re-run InstallShield as described in the preceding paragraph.

If Domino is listed in the Services dialog box, you can see whether it is started and how it starts: Automatic, Manual, or Disabled. It must be set at Automatic to start when the computer starts. If it is not, set it by clicking the Startup button. That displays the Service dialog box, where you can choose Automatic, then OK (see Figure 3.7).

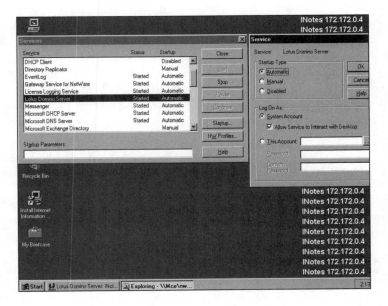

Figure 3.7　To set a service's startup options, click Startup in the Services dialog box (on the left) to open the Service dialog box (on the right).

You can also manually start and stop the Domino server from the Services dialog box. Choose Start to start it and Stop to shut it down. Stop only works, of course, if Domino is running as a service. You can also stop Domino in the usual way (by entering "quit," "q," "exit," or "e" at the server console) whether or not it is running as an NT service.

Adding Windows Shortcuts

Whether you run Domino as an NT service or from the menu, you might find yourself wishing, sooner or later, for more convenient manual ways to start and stop the server. For example, it might be nice to have a shortcut on the Windows desktop, so you don't have to open the menu to start the server. That's easy to do—just copy it from the menu. Better yet, it would be really nice to have shortcuts in the menu or on the Windows desktop for starting and stopping the Domino NT service, rather than having to open first the Windows Control Panel, then the Services dialog box every time.

Copying a Shortcut to the Windows Desktop

To copy the Domino startup shortcut from the menu to the Windows Desktop, you need to find the shortcut that InstallShield created when it installed Domino, then just copy it to the Clipboard and paste it to the Windows Desktop.

The tricky part of all this is finding the shortcut. It is located in the Folder you told InstallShield to put it in. That folder, in turn, is located in a folder named Programs, which is itself in a folder named Start Menu, which (under Windows NT) is in a folder named for the account under which you were logged on when you ran InstallShield. For example, if you were logged on under the Administrator account, the Start Menu folder will be in a folder named Administrator. That folder, in turn, is in a folder named Profiles, which is, finally, in your Windows NT folder. Got that?

Try it this way. In Windows Explorer, go to the Windows NT folder and find the Profiles folder. There you will see a folder for every local user account. Every one of those folders has a Start Menu folder in it, and a Programs folder. Your Domino folder and shortcut are in one of the Programs folders. Find the shortcut, copy it, and then paste in onto the Windows Desktop.

Moving a Shortcut to the All Users Profile

A problem with the Domino shortcut as InstallShield creates it is that it appears in the menu only when you are logged in using the same account as when you installed Domino on this computer. That means all administrators, when they want to interact locally with Domino, have to log on using that account. You might prefer that each administrator log on with his/her own account. That way, you have an audit trail. If something goes wrong, you can find out who was logged on at the time.

If you like this idea, you need to copy the Domino folder and shortcut from the Programs folder of the user account where InstallShield put it to the Programs folder in the All Users profile. This will cause the Domino folder and shortcut to appear in the bottom half of every user's menu when they log on (see Figure 3.8).

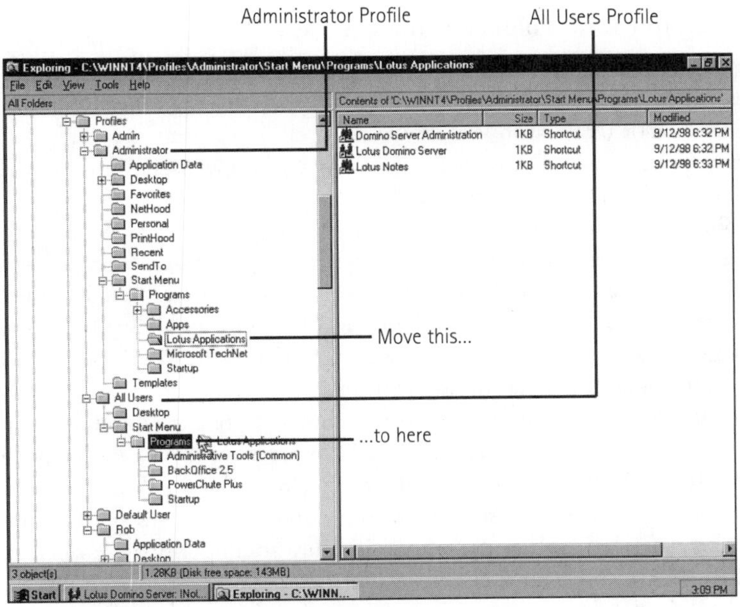

Figure 3.8   Move this folder to here so that the Domino shortcut will appear in the menus of all users.

Creating NT Service Start/Stop Shortcuts

If you create shortcuts for manually starting and stopping Domino as an NT service, you can avoid the hassle of opening the Services dialog box. Create them on the Windows Desktop, in the menu, or both. To create a shortcut on the Windows Desktop, right-click the Windows Desktop, then choose New, Shortcut. To create a shortcut in a menu folder, select the folder, then choose New, Shortcut in the File menu. In both cases, the Create Shortcut wizard appears. There, you have to enter a command line and a shortcut title.

The command line for starting Domino as an NT service is as follows:

```
%windir%\system32\net.exe start "Lotus Domino Server"
```

The command line for stopping Domino as an NT service is as follows:

```
%windir%\system32\net.exe stop "Lotus Domino Server"
```

%windir% is a standard Windows NT environment variable that holds the path name of your Windows NT folder.

Secure Domino Data Folders at the OS Level

The job of a Domino server is to allow only authorized users to access the data in its databases. It can only do that job effectively if users have to go through the server to get at the data. For that reason you should close all other avenues to the databases on your server. (That is why Lotus recommends that you not install Notes in the same program and data folders as Domino uses.)

The obvious avenue to the databases, other than through Domino and Notes, is to access them directly through the operating system. To close this door, you should make sure that the Domino data folder and its descendants are not accessible either across the network or, if possible, locally. All Domino OS platforms allow you to block network access to individual folders. You just have to make sure you know how to do it on your platform and that you do in fact do it.

Under Windows NT, that means that you should share the Domino data folder but then set Permissions so that "Everyone" has "No access." It is not sufficient that the data folder is not shared at all, because the root folder of every disk drive under Windows NT is automatically shared for administrative purposes as [driveletter]$, that is, C$, D$, E$, whatever the drive letter is. Only administrative users can make use of this share. But you should really block out the administrators too. A positive share will accomplish that for all users except the owner of the shared resource, in this case the user account named Administrator.

In addition, don't allow such services as FTP or NFS to run (or even to be installed, if possible) on the computer that hosts Domino. If such a service *must* run, then configure it to disallow access to Domino's folders.

You can also (and should) block local OS access to the Domino data folders, at least if your OS file system allows it. Under Windows NT, you can block local access to folders on NTFS partitions, but not on FAT partitions. Under OS/2 you can block local access to folders on HPFS partitions. Under UNIX, you can block access to folders on all kinds of partitions. If you are running under Windows NT, make sure your data is on an NTFS partition. If you are running under OS/2, make sure your data is on an HPFS partition. If you have to run on a FAT partition, consider securing the server in some other way, such as removal or locking of the keyboard.

Remember, finally, that you can use the Set Secure command at the Domino console as a partial barrier to local data access. A server secured in this way won't accept certain commands, such as tell and load, and requires that you append the password to others (for example, quit [password]).

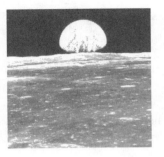

4

Additional Server Setup

I N THE PRECEDING CHAPTER WE SET UP THE FIRST server in a domain. In this chapter, we set up the rest of the servers. We also learn ways to automate server setup.

Setting Up Additional Servers

Setting up additional servers in a domain is similar to setting up the first server. The primary difference is that the additional servers have to obtain a replica of the Domain Directory from a preexisting domain server. The first server, being the first server in the domain, has to create the Domain Directory from scratch. Another difference is that, because the domain now has more than one server, you have to set up interserver communications.

The overall process of setting up a new server in an existing domain is as follows:

1. Register the new server. By this process you create a server document and a server ID file containing public and private keys and a certificate signed by a certifier ID file. Registration also adds the new server to the LocalDomainServers group.

2. Install the server software on its computer and configure it. Among other things, this means the new server must connect to an existing server in the domain and retrieve a replica copy of the Domain Directory from it.

3. Set up ports, replication, and mail routing between the new server and existing servers.

4. Optionally set up and configure other server tasks, depending on the intended use of the server.

Registering Server IDs

Before you can set up a new server in a domain, you have to register the server. The procedure for registering a server ID is similar to that described in the previous chapter, but not necessarily identical. So I'll describe it again here, briefly:

1. You have to possess the certifier ID (and know the password) of the organization or organizational unit in which you intend the new server to reside. If you've followed my earlier recommendations, this is an OU just for servers. You also should have Editor or higher access to the Certification Log database on the registration server (which you will designate in step 5).

2. You can register servers in Domino Administrator, from either the People & Groups screen or the Configuration screen, by choosing Registration, Server from the Tools list (or, in the People & Groups screen by choosing Registration, Server from the People menu).

3. If Domino Administrator can locate the last Certifier ID it used, it will display the Enter Password (or Enter Passwords) dialog box for that ID. If this happens and Domino Administrator chose the ID you want to use, go ahead and enter the password (or passwords). Otherwise choose Cancel.

4. If Domino Administrator could not locate the last Certifier ID it used or if you chose cancel in step 3, the Choose Certifier ID dialog box appears. Locate and select the ID you intend to use. Choose Open, then enter the ID's password or passwords.

5. The Register Servers dialog box appears. It has four fields, which you should set as follows:

   Registration Server. This is the server in whose copy of the Domain Directory the newly registered server's Server document will be created. Unless you are working in a copy of Domino Administrator that shares a data directory with a server, you should set this field to a server's name, not "Local." Also, the server you enter in this field should be one to which that Domino Administrator has current access. If you can't meet both of these conditions, Domino Administrator will not be able to create the new Server document.

   Certifier ID. If you chose the wrong Certifier ID in the previous steps, you can switch to the correct one now by clicking this button.

Security type. If the Certifier ID you have chosen uses North American security but the server will be using International security, choose International in this field. You should choose International if this server will reside anywhere but in the United States or Canada or a territory or possession of either. Choosing International as the security type causes the server to use weaker keys for encryption. For simplicity's sake, administrators of international organizations sometimes prefer to use International security for all of their servers, both International and North American. But this isn't strictly necessary because servers created with North American security have both North American and International-strength public keys and will automatically use the International ones when communicating with International-only servers and users.

Certificate expiration date. For servers, this defaults to 100 years. Most people accept the default.

6. When these fields are correctly set, choose Continue to open the Register Servers dialog box. It has two screens: Basics and Other. In Basics, complete the fields as follows:

Server Name. Enter the common name of the server. (The rest of the server's name it inherits from its certifier.)

Password. For most servers you want to leave this blank. You only want a server to have a password if the computer it will eventually run on will not be physically secure. The reason for this is that a server with a password-protected ID file will not start until some human enters a password. This can be a problem if a server goes down in the middle of the night or over the weekend.

Password quality scale. If you want to leave the password blank, you must set this field to 0 - Password optional.

Domain. Enter the name of the domain here. If you are not sure what you should enter here, you can find the domain name in several places: the title of the Domain directory (*Domainname*'s Directory), the Domain field of numerous documents, including Server and Person documents, and the Domain variable in each existing server's `notes.ini` file.

Administrator. The contents of this field are entered into the two Administrators fields on the server document (one at the beginning, the other at the end). It also becomes the value of the Admin variable in the server's `notes.ini` file. Enter either a group name or a fully distinguished user name. I always enter the name of the server administrators' group.

7. Click Other to see the other fields.

   Server Title. Optional. Enter descriptive information about the server.

   Network. This is the Domino Named Network that is set up when you set up this server. This field defaults to Network1. *Important: Do not leave it at the default setting.* Change it to the actual Domino Named Network that this server will reside in for the port you will use at initial server setup to connect to an existing server. If you leave this at the default setting, you risk crippling the mail routing performance of this server and others in your domain.

   Local Administrator. The contents of this field are entered in the Owner field in this server's Server document. Enter either a group name or a fully distinguished user name. I usually enter the name of the server administrators' group. But if an individual administrator will be responsible for administering just this server, you could enter that person's name.

   Store Server ID. You can store the ID file (which will be created when you choose Register) in the Server document as an attachment (In Address Book), in a file (In file), or in both places. If you select In Address Book, you will be required to enter a password in the Password field in the Basics screen, even if you set Password Quality Scale to 0. Later, after you have set up the server, you will have to manually clear the password. Domino requires this to protect you from the folly of making a password-free server ID available to anyone with Reader access to the Domino Directory (that is, to everyone in the domain). Someone might detach a copy of the ID and use it later to gain unauthorized access to sensitive data. Many administrators prefer to select In file and deselect In Address Book. This avoids both the hassle of having to clear the password after the server is set up and the security risk of making even a password-protected server ID available to everyone in the domain.

   Set ID file. If you chose In file in the previous field, Domino will create the new ID file by default on a floppy disk in drive A:. The filename will be *servername*.id (where *servername* is the first eight characters of the server's common name). To change either the location or the name of the new ID file, click the button, then choose the file's location and enter its filename.

8. When all fields are filled in to your satisfaction, choose one of the following:

   Next to add another server (or review other added servers if you have already chosen Previous)

   Previous to review and edit any previously entered servers

   Delete to clear all fields in this server entry

   Register to register this server (and all others that you set up during this session)

After you choose Register, Domino Administrator completes the server registration process by doing the following things (and informing you of its progress):

- It connects to the Registration Server.

- It creates an ID file in memory. In the process it generates a public/private key pair, which it stores in the ID file.

- It creates a certificate for the new server and stores it (along with copies of the certifier's own certificate and those of any of the certifier's ancestors) in the ID file.

- It updates the Certification Log database on the Registration Server.

- It creates a Server document for the newly registered server in the Registration Server's copy of the Domain Directory.

- It adds the newly registered server to the membership list of the LocalDomainServers document in the Registration Server's copy of the Domain Directory.

- Depending on your choices in the Register Servers dialog box, it saves the ID file as an attachment to the Server document, as a file in the file system, or in both places.

Setup Procedures

After you have registered a new server you have to set it up on its computer and configure it. For the first server in the domain you had to set up the computer first, then configure it. For the later servers, you can reverse the order if you want. You can do much of the configuration first, then set up the servers on their computers. Or you can set them up, then configure them. I prefer to do as much configuration up front as I can, and I will present the setup process to you in the order I would approach it: pre-setup configuration, then setup, then post-setup configuration.

Pre-Setup Configuration

The configuration steps that you can complete before actually setting up the new servers on their computers include the following:

- Add Servers to Group documents
- Edit access lists in the Server documents

The Group documents you have to edit depend on what Group documents you have created. Domino Administrator automatically adds new servers to the LocalDomainServers group during registration. But you are responsible for updating any other server groups you might be using.

The fields you need to edit in each server's Server document are listed in Chapter 3 "First Server Installation and Setup," and I won't repeat them here. If you only have one or two new servers to configure, you can edit each Server document individually. But if you have a lot of servers to set up, you might want to create an agent to automate the process.

The details of the agent vary depending on your situation, but the method of creating the agent is straightforward. The hardest part of setting up the agent is figuring out what the names are of the fields we want the agent to update. Let's say, for example, that you want to add a group called "InactiveUsers" to the "Not access server" field of every server document. "Not access server" is not the real field name but just the label that identifies the field's purpose to the user. To update the field with an agent, we need to find out its actual field name.

The easiest way to do that is to open the Server form in Design mode. That is easy to do if you have Manager or Designer access to the Domain Directory (and a copy of Domino Designer installed). But if you have a lower level of access, it is a little harder to do, because the server won't let you open the Server form in Design mode.

If you don't have Designer access to the Domain Directory, try to convince the database manager to give it to you. If that fails, create a local replica or copy of the Domain Directory, then open that copy in Design mode (in Domino Designer).

To make a local copy of the Domain Directory, follow these steps:

1. Right-click the Domain Directory in the Bookmarks list in Notes. Then, from the context menu, choose Database, New Copy.

2. In the Copy Database dialog box, change the filename in the File Name field. This is very important because you don't want to overwrite your Personal Address Book, which, like the Domain Directory, is named `names.nsf`.

3. Optionally deselect Access Control List. Choose OK.

To make a local replica of the Domain Directory, follow these steps:

1. Right-click the Domain Directory in the Bookmarks list in Notes, then, from the context menu, choose Replication, New Replica.

2. In the New Replica dialog box, change the filename in the File Name field. This is very important because you don't want to overwrite your Personal Address Book, which, like the Domain Directory, is named `names.nsf`.

3. Optionally deselect Copy Access Control List. Choose OK.

After you have Designer or higher access to a database based on the `pubnames.ntf` template, you can open the Server form in Design mode (in Domino Designer) and see the actual field names of every field on the form. In our example, we discover that the field labeled "Not access server" is really named "DenyAccess." See Figure 4.1. In your case, I would recommend you write down the field name of every field to which you want to add values.

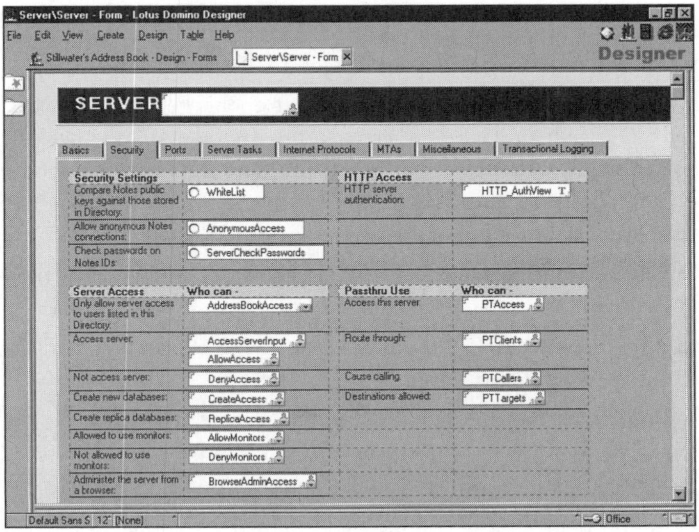

Figure 4.1   The easiest way to discover the field names in a
large form such as the Server form is to open it in Design mode.

To create an agent to insert values into fields, follow these steps:

1. Open the database in which you will change the field values. In our case, this is
    the Domain Directory.

2. In the Create menu, choose Agent. An Untitled Agent window opens. See Figure 4.2.

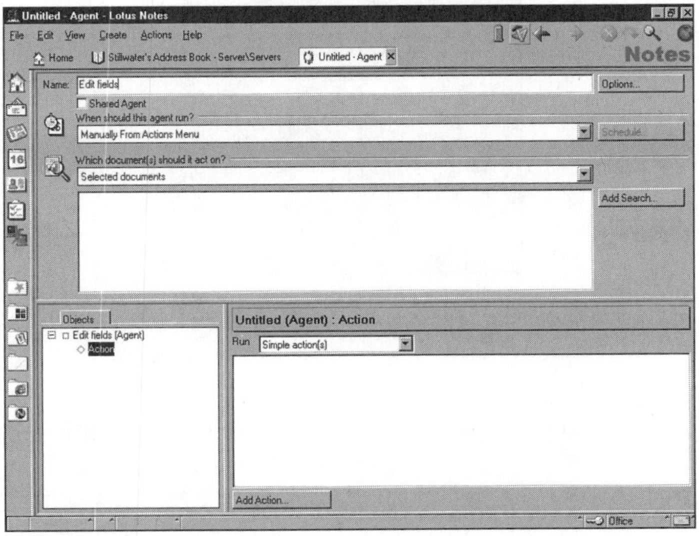

Figure 4.2   For our agent, we can accept the default
values of most of the fields in the Agent window.

3. In the Name field, enter a name, such as Edit fields. When you want to run the agent, you will open the Actions menu and select this name.

4. If the Shared Agent field is available, leave it unchecked. It is only available if you have Designer or Manager access to the database. If you check it, anyone can run this agent (though it won't actually write to any document unless the person running it has author access to the document). But this agent is only for your use, so you don't want to share it with others anyway.

5. In the When should this agent run? field, choose Manually from the Actions Menu (which is the default selection).

6. In the Which document(s) should it act on? field, choose Selected documents (which is the default selection).

7. In the Run field, you could choose Simple action(s) (which is the default choice) or Formula. For our purposes, Simple action(s) is sufficient.

8. Click the Add Action button. The Add Action dialog box appears.

9. In the Action field, choose Modify Field (which is the default choice).

10. In the Field field (no, that's not a typo), choose the field name of the field you want to modify. In our case we choose DenyAccess. If you start scrolling, you will discover that the Server document has a phenomenal number of fields. To speed things up, press the letter D on the keyboard. This jumps you to the first field that begins with the letter D. Scroll from there.

11. In the Value field, enter the value you want inserted into the DenyAccess field. In our example, enter InactiveUsers. See Figure 4.3.

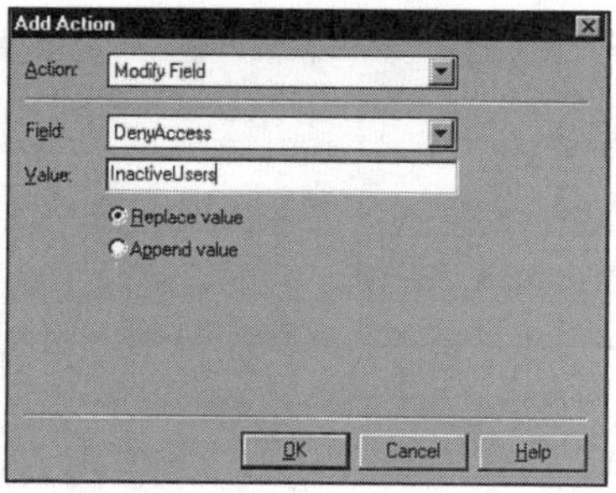

Figure 4.3 The Add Action dialog box allows you
to create agents without resorting to programming.

12. Choose either Replace value or Append value. In our example it doesn't matter which we choose because nothing will have been entered in the DenyAccess field when we run this agent.

13. Choose OK. A label describing your choices appears in the Action window. If you made a mistake you can either double-click the label to reopen the Add Action dialog box or delete the label and start over.

14. If you want to add more actions, repeat steps 9 through 13. Say, for example, you want to add the names of the Administrators, Designers, and LocalDomainServers groups to the field labeled Create new databases and named CreateAccess. You would enter all three values in the Value field in step 11. (Use commas or semicolons to separate multiple values.) When you close the Add Action dialog box, a second (or third or fourth) label would appear in the Action window. See Figure 4.4.

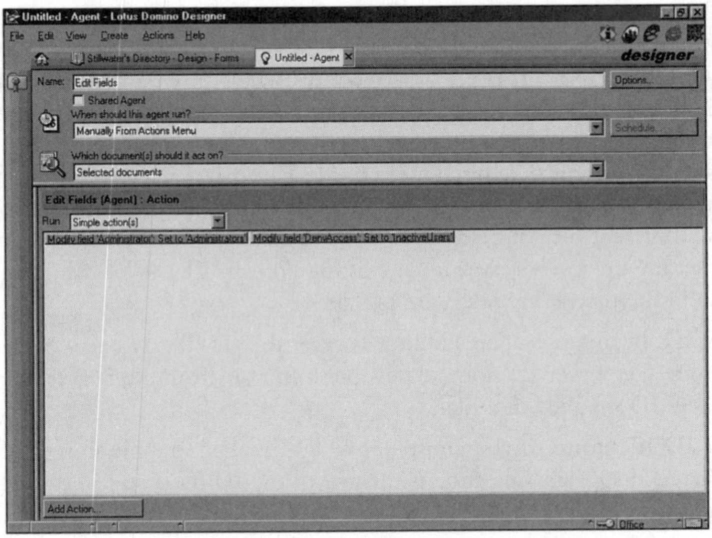

Figure 4.4   The Action window shows the two actions that this agent will perform.

15. Close the Agent Window when you are finished. Choose Yes if prompted to save the agent.

The agent you created now appears in the Actions menu and in the Agents list.

- To see the Agents list, choose Agents from the View menu or, if you are in Domino Designer, from the Bookmarks list (the list of databases that appears when you click a bookmark on the left side of the screen).

- To edit your agent, double-click it in the Agents list.

- To run your agent, open the Servers view, select the Server document or documents you want to edit, then choose your agent from the Actions menu.

Be careful to select the proper documents before running this agent. If it runs against the wrong server document, it may (depending on your choice in step 12) overwrite values that you wanted to retain. If it does, you will have to manually restore those values; there is no "undo" for the changes your agent makes.

Setup

Installation and initial setup of additional servers in a domain is largely identical to first server installation and setup. The differences between them are minor and stem from the fact that, during first server setup, you are also setting up a new domain and organization. Additional server setup sets up a new server, preregistered server in an existing domain and organization.

In both cases you install the server software on the computer, then perform some initial configuration by running Domino and filling in a Configuration form in the Domino Configuration database. I described this whole process in great detail in Chapter 3, so I won't repeat it here, except to describe the differences between first server setup and additional server setup.

The first difference is that, instead of choosing First Domino Server in Screen 1 of the Configuration form, you choose Additional Domino Server. This causes Screen 4 to present a different mix of fields from the first server setup. It presents fields appropriate for setting up a new server in an existing domain. The fields, which are different from those in the first server setup, are as follows:

Server ID. In the case of an additional server the ID already exists. So your choices are Get server ID from address book (that is, from the Server document) and Server ID supplied in a file.

Server ID filename. If you chose Server ID supplied in a file in the previous field, this field appears. Enter the pathname of the ID file. Later in the setup process this file will be copied to the server's data folder.

Get address Book from which Server?. Enter the name of an existing server to which the new server will be able to connect to retrieve a replica of the Domain Directory.

After you complete the Configuration form and choose Finish, Notes performs the following tasks:

- It populates `notes.ini` with the necessary variables for the server to run properly.

- It copies the server's ID file to the server's data folder. If it copies the ID file from the Server document, it also deletes it from the Server documents.

- It connects to the existing Domino server you specified and retrieves a replica of the Domain Directory from it.

- If you chose any specialized server tasks in Screen 3 of the Configuration form, it may modify its own Server document, create other documents in the Domain Directory, or create other databases. To learn the details of server setup for each specialized server task, see the appropriate chapters later in this book.

The other difference from first server setup is that you may have a large number of additional servers to set up, in which case you might want to automate the process. To this end you can create server configuration documents ahead of time, then just click the Finish button at setup time. You can do this because the Configuration form is a form in the Domino Configuration database (`setup.nsf`) which is copied to every server as part of the installation routine. When you run a Windows-based Domino server for the first time, it opens the Configuration form in this database because it encounters the variable *SetupDB=setup.nsf* in its `notes.ini` file.

You don't have to wait until the first time you start a server to fill in a server configuration form for it. You can create a server configuration document ahead of time in any copy of the Domino Configuration database. Then you can copy that database onto the new server (overwriting the copy placed there by the installation routine) before running Domino for the first time. When you run Domino it will open the Configuration form as usual. But, instead of filling it in, you can close it and open the configuration document that you created earlier for this server, then just click the Finish button.

Post-Setup Configuration

Post-setup configuration includes setting up or disabling network and/or modem ports, setting up connections between the new server and existing servers, and setting up or fine-tuning the operation of various server tasks. We discussed setup and breakdown of network ports in Chapter 3, so I won't discuss it again except to remind you to disable any ports you know your server won't use and to assign network names to every network port. I've said this in every chapter so far but it bears repeating: Don't accept the default network names assigned during the automated server setup process. Assign unique network names. See Chapter 3 for details.

Regarding modem ports, see "Setting up Modem Communications," later in this chapter. Regarding server connections, see "Setting Up Mail Routing" and "Setting Up Replication," both in this chapter. All other aspects of server setup are covered either in separate sections of this chapter or, in the case of certain specialized server tasks, in separate chapters.

Setting Up Modem Communications

If two servers are not on the same LAN or WAN, they must connect to each other by modem. Even if they are on the same WAN (the Internet, for example), you might want to provide them with a modem connection for backup purposes. This can be a "direct dialup" connection, a "pass-thru" connection, or a "network dialup" connection.

Direct dialup connections can occur when two servers both have modems connected to telephone lines. (The calling server could actually have access to a modem pool instead of having its own modem.) Either server can dial up the other directly. Figure 4.5 illustrates a direct dialup connection.

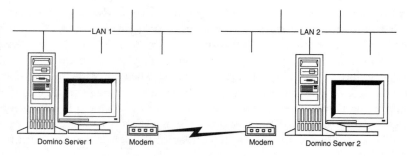

Figure 4.5 Using Notes Direct Dial-up, Domino Server 1 and Domino Server 2 communicate directly, using their own modems.

Pass-thru connections aren't strictly related to modem communications but can be used in a variety of circumstances. With a pass-thru connection, a server uses another Domino server's resources to connect to a third Domino server. The first server "passes through" the second server to reach the third server and does not necessarily have to have a modem of its own.

Network dialup connections can occur if one or both servers are on a network that includes a communications server. In a network dialup connection you establish a modem connection between a server and a remote network, then the servers communicate across the modem connection as if they were connected by LAN. Figure 4.6 illustrates two variations of a network dialup connection.

In the first variation in Figure 4.6, Domino Server 1 uses its own modem to call Comm Server 2 on LAN2. It establishes a connection to the LAN to which Domino Server 2 is connected. Through the LAN it then connects to Domino Server 2. In the second variation in Figure 4.6 neither Domino server has a modem. Domino Server 3 acquires a modem from Comm Server 3, then uses it to dial up Comm Server 2. To set up direct dialup modem communications on Domino servers you have to do the following:

- Install modems on the calling and answering servers. Alternatively, install software on the calling server that gives it access to a modem pool maintained by a communication server on its LAN.

- Set up ports in Domino (on both servers) for each modem it will use. This includes configuring the modem drivers.
- Create a direct dialup connection document on the calling server.

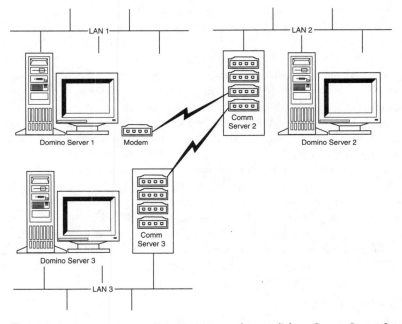

Figure 4.6 Domino Server 1 uses its own modem to dial up Comm Server 2, then connects to Domino Server 2 across LAN 2. Domino Server 3 acquires a modem on Comm Server 3, uses the modem to dial up Comm Server 2, and then connects to Domino Server 2 across LAN 2.

To set up network dialup modem communications on Domino servers you have to do the following:

- Install a modem on the calling server. Alternatively, install software on the calling server that gives it access to a modem pool maintained by a communication server on its LAN.
- Set up ports in Domino on the calling server for each modem it will use. This includes configuring the modem drivers.
- Set up Microsoft Dial-up Networking software (also known as Microsoft Remote Access Service or "RAS") on the calling server and on a computer running the Windows NT Server OS on the responding server's LAN. On the calling server RAS must be configured to dial out and should not be configured to answer calls. On the answering computer, RAS must be configured to answer calls and can be configured to dial out.
- Create a network dialup connection document on the calling server.

How you install a modem on a computer depends on the computer's operating system, among other things. Beyond suggesting that you make sure before you buy a modem that it will work with Domino, we won't discuss modem installation here. Refer to the documentation that came with the computer and its operating system.

To give a computer access to a modem pool, you must install special software on the calling server. The server comes with the communication server that controls the modem pool. Refer to the communication server's documentation for directions.

To have your Domino server acquire a modem automatically from the modem pool, without manual intervention from a human being, you will have to set up an "acquire script." This is a text file containing commands, keywords, and arguments that tell Domino what commands to issue to the communication server, and when. Ideally the communication server software includes a script that you can use or you can download one from the communication server maker's Web site. Failing those happy alternatives, you can write your own script or modify one of the sample scripts that come with Domino. Domino scripts are named *filename*.scr (where *filename* is any filename) and are located in the modems subfolder under the Domino data folder. The sample acquire scripts include comserv.scr and sprntpad.scr.

Microsoft Dial-up Networking software comes with Windows NT OS software. You set it up as a networking service (Control Panel, Networking, Services). You configure it in the Control Panel under Networking and Dial-Up Monitor. For details, refer to Windows NT documentation and online help.

Setting Up a Port

You set up a modem port (or a LAN port) by setting a series of variables in the server's notes.ini file. These include the <portname>, Ports, and DisabledPorts variables. If you look in notes.ini, you will see something such as the following:

```
TCPIP=TCP, 0, 15, 0
LAN0=NETBIOS, 0, 15, 0
LAN1ipx=NETBIOS, 1, 15, 0
LAN2ip=NETBIOS, 2, 15, 0
SPX=NWSPX, 0, 15, 0
VINES=VINES, 0, 15, 0
AppleTalk=ATALK, 0, 15, 0
LAN3=NETBIOS, 3, 15, 0
LAN4=NETBIOS, 4, 15, 0
LAN5=NETBIOS, 5, 15, 0
LAN6=NETBIOS, 6, 15, 0
LAN7=NETBIOS, 7, 15, 0
LAN8=NETBIOS, 8, 15, 0
COM1=XPC,1,15,0,
COM2=XPC,2,15,0,,12292,115200,,usrspx2.mdm,60,15
COM3=XPC,3,15,0,
COM4=XPC,4,15,0,
COM5=XPC,5,15,0,
Ports=TCPIP,SPX,LAN0,LAN1ip,LAN2ipx
DisabledPorts=VINES,AppleTalk,LAN3,LAN4,LAN5,LAN6,LAN7,LAN8,COM1,COM3,COM4,COM5
```

In this listing, the `Ports` variable lists the ports currently in use. Notes or Domino will try those ports in the order they appear here. The `DisabledPorts` variable lists all the other ports. Together, the `Ports` and `DisabledPorts` variables include all defined ports, which is all ports represented by a `<portname>` variable. The `<portname>` variables actually define the ports. This listing includes ports named TCPIP, SPX, Vines, AppleTalk, all of which run the LAN protocol represented by their names. Also included are LAN0, LAN1ipx, LAN2ip, and LAN3-LAN8, all of which run NetBIOS. LAN1ipx runs NetBIOS over IPX. LAN2ip runs NetBIOS over IP. All the other LAN* ports run NetBIOS over NetBEUI. Finally, ports COM1 through COM5 are the serial ports, and they all run the X.PC protocol, which is a modem communication protocol.

All the ports in this listing were set up automatically by Notes when it set up this server. It automatically enabled TCPIP, SPX, LAN0, LAN1ipx, and LAN2ip because TCPIP and SPX were enabled in the underlying OS.

The LAN `<portname>` variables and the unconfigured COM `<portname>` variables include the following parameters:

`driver`: The filename of the DLL file that drives the port.

`unit_ID`: The logical number assigned to the port. Corresponds to the n in LANn and COMn.

`max_sessions`: The maximum number of concurrent sessions allowable on the port.

`buffer_size`: The size in kilobytes of the memory buffer assigned to the port.

The configured COM `<portname>` variables include the previous parameters, plus the following:

`null`: Contains no value.

`flags`: Contains a sum of numbers representing which of a group of flags is turned on. The flags include most of the settings in the Additional Setup dialog box.

`modem_speed`: The speed at which the modem will operate (in kbps).

`modem_volume`: The modem sound volume and its dialing mode.

`modem_filename`: The filename of the modem command file used. The modem command files are in the modems subfolder of the data folder.

`dial_timer`: The connection timeout (in seconds).

`hangup_timeout`: The idle time (in minutes) after which Domino will terminate the modem connection.

Of course, the `notes.ini` settings are too arcane to set manually, and nobody does it if they can avoid it. It's much easier to let Notes or Domino Administrator set them for you by making choices in dialog boxes. When you click OK in the dialog box, the settings there are translated into variable settings in `notes.ini`.

There are two different dialog boxes where you can set up modem ports. In Notes, you can use the User Preferences dialog box. See Figure 4.7. You open the dialog box by choosing Preferences in the File menu, then choosing User Preferences. When the dialog box appears, choose Ports.

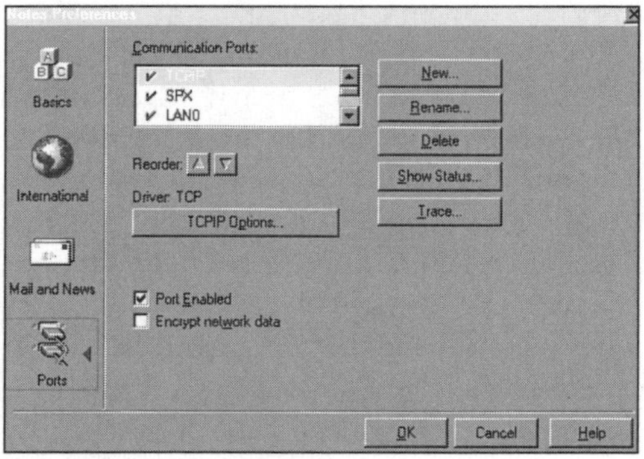

Figure 4.7   Set up ports for the current copy of Notes or Domino in User Preferences.

In Domino Administrator, you can use either the User Preferences dialog box (the same as in Notes) or the Port Setup for <*servername*> dialog box. See Figure 4.8. You open the Port Setup dialog box from the Server screen of Domino Administrator. First, you choose the server you want to work on in the Bookmarks pane on the left side of the screen. Then, you open the dialog box from either the Server menu or the Tools pane, in both cases by choosing Server, then Setup Ports.

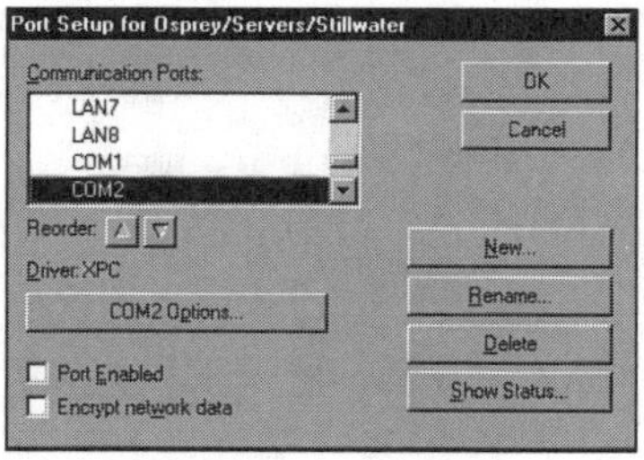

Figure 4.8   Set up ports for any accessible Domino server in Setup Ports.

Both dialog boxes let you do the same things, so use whichever one is most convenient. If you have to configure server ports, the Port Setup for <*servername*> dialog box is usually more convenient because it lets you set up ports remotely on any accessible server. Also, it lets you enable and disable server ports without first shutting down the remote server. Notes Preferences only lets you set up ports for the copy of Notes in which you are currently working. If that copy of Notes shares its `notes.ini` file with a Domino server, you must bring the server down before you can enable or disable ports in Notes Preferences.

To set up a modem port in either dialog box, follow these steps:

1. Choose the port you want to set up in the "Communication Ports" field. The available choices include LAN ports and serial ports. Modems attach to serial ports, so you should choose the serial ports that your modems are connected to. On Windows and OS/2 computers the serial ports are named COM1, COM2, and so on. On UNIX computers the outbound serial ports are called /dev/cua0, /dev/cua1, and so on, and the inbound serial ports are called /dev/tty0, /dev/tty1, and so on.

2. Reorder the ports, if desired, by clicking the up and down Reorder buttons. If a connection document doesn't tell it which port to use, Notes/Domino will try the ports in the order they appear here.

3. Place a checkmark in the "Port Enabled" field. (If you are in the Notes Preferences dialog box on the server, and the server is running, you won't be allowed to check this box.)

4. Optionally put a checkmark in the "Encrypt network data" field. Checking this box increases overhead and slows down transmissions, so do this only if you are concerned that eavesdroppers may intercept sensitive data in transit.

5. Click the "*<portname>* Options" button. This opens the Additional Setup dialog box.

6. Fill in the fields in the Additional Setup dialog box. When setting up a modem, the Additional Setup dialog box has the following fields:

   Modem type. This is a list of modem command files. It is actually a list of files in the data\modems directory that have the extension `mdm`. Choose one that your modem can work with. With luck, one will be listed that was designed to work with your make and model of modem. If you're not so lucky, you will have to try out different ones until you find one that works with your modem. If you are really unlucky, you won't be able to find one that works with your modem.

   Maximum port speed. This is a list of standard modem port speeds. Choose the fastest one your modem and serial port will support.

   Speaker volume. Use this to control the volume of the modem's speaker when it is dialing out. The general rule here is you want the speaker loud enough so you can hear what it is doing while you are testing it, but turned off entirely otherwise.

   Dial mode. Your choices are Tone and Pulse. Choose Tone if your phone system supports tone dialing.

Log modem I/O. Turn this on only when you are testing your modem's ability to connect with another modem. When you check this box, every command Notes/Domino sends to your modem and every response from the modem will be recorded in the Notes Log database. This is useful for debugging but generates a lot of information in your log. So, the general rule here is leave this turned off except when testing the modem.

Log script I/O. You only need to turn this on if you are testing a script, which you will only ever do if you have to acquire a modem from a modem pool, dial into an X.25 network to reach a server, or dial into a security device. As with logging modem I/O, turning this on causes every script command and response to be recorded in the Notes Log, so you can see where errors occur. Leave it turned off when you aren't actually debugging a script.

Hardware flow control. This is on by default. Leave it on unless you know that your modem only supports software flow control. These days that's a rare modem.

Wait for dialtone before dialing. This is on by default. Turn it off only if you cannot otherwise get the modem to work properly.

Dial timeout. This is set to 60 seconds by default. It defines the amount of time within which your modem must establish a connection with another modem. If the modem has not connected within that time, Notes will abort the effort and retry later from the beginning. In general, leave this alone unless you have a specific reason to change it.

Hang up if idle for. This is set to 15 minutes by default. It is the amount of time after which, if no modem activity has occurred, Notes/Domino will automatically disconnect. In general, leave this alone unless you have a specific reason to change it.

Port number. This is the operating system's number for this port. In Windows and OS/2, it is the same number as n in COMn, and you shouldn't change it. If you ever create a new serial port or rename one using a name other than COMn, you can use this field to identify the OS port which your port uses.

Modem File. Click this button to edit the modem command file listed in the Modem type field. A modem command file is a text file consisting of variables and their values. The variables are keywords describing things the modem can do. The values are the actual key sequences that tell the modem to do the things. You can click this button just to look, if you want, but in general you should only edit a file if it isn't working properly and you can't find any other file that *does* work properly with your modem.

Acquire Script. If the modem that this port will access is part of a modem pool maintained by a communication server, click here to choose an acquire script. The Acquire Script dialog box will appear, displaying a list of scripts. It is actually a list of files in the data\modems directory that have the extension .scr. Choose one, then choose Edit to edit it or OK to return to the Additional Setup dialog box.

7. When finished in the Additional Setup dialog box, click OK to close it and return to the Port Setup or Notes Preferences dialog box. Click OK to close that dialog box.

Creating a Connection Document

To complete the process of establishing modem communications between servers, you have to create one or more Connection documents in the Domain Directory. A Connection document tells Domino (or Notes) how to connect to another computer, when to do so, and what to do when it connects. Here we are concerned with enabling modem communications between Domino servers, so we need to know about three kinds of Connection documents: Direct Dial-up, Network Dial-up, and Pass-thru.

Create a Connection document as follows:

1. Run Domino Administrator. Go to the Configuration screen. If the currently selected server is Local, change the selection to a currently accessible server. Alternatively, choose a server in the Use Directory on field. If you don't do one of these, you will create the new Connection document in the Personal Address Book of the local workstation, using a form intended not for Server-to-Server connections but for Person-to-Server connections. Preferably, change to the server for which you are creating the new Connection document. But if it isn't running or is not otherwise accessible to you, then choose any other server in the same domain as the intended server.

2. Choose Server, then Connections in the Navigator (left) pane. The Server, Connections view of the Domain Directory will appear in the View (right) pane. This consists of a list of existing Connection documents.

3. Click Add Connection at the top of the view. A new, blank Server Connection document will appear.

4. Fill in the fields as described next, then save and close the document. Your new Connection document will appear in the Connections view.

The Connection form that appears in step 3 has five tabs. See Figure 4.9. We will focus only on the Basics tab. First select a connection type in the Connection type field. Your choice there will affect what other fields are available to be filled in.

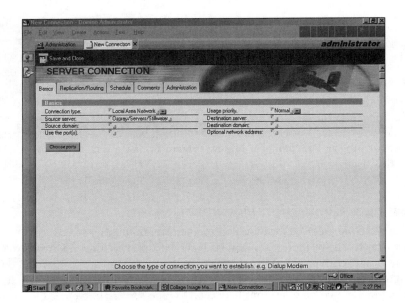

Figure 4.9 The fields that make up this section of a Connection document vary depending on your choice in the Connection type field.

Fields to fill in for all Connection types include the following:

Connection type. It defaults to Local Area Network. Choose Notes Direct Dialup if this server will use its own modem (or will access a modem pool) to dial another Domino server's modem (as in Figure 4.5). Choose Network Dialup if this server will use its own modem (or will access a modem pool) to connect to a Microsoft Dial-Up Networking server (first scenario in Figure 4.6), also known as a Microsoft Remote Access Server (RAS) or to an AppleTalk Remote Access server.

Usage priority. Determines whether Domino will look for this Connection document first or will wait until after it has exhausted all other connection options before relying on this Connection document. Select Normal for modem connections. The other choice is Low, which is really only relevant when two servers can communicate by a choice of LAN protocols. If Domino has a choice between two or more Connection documents it will choose among them in the following order of precedence: local area network, network dial-up, direct dial-up, pass-thru server, hunt group of pass-thru servers.

Source server. Enter the fully distinguished name of the server that will initiate the connection between servers. Defaults to the name of the server whose copy of the Domain Directory you are using to create this Connection document.

Destination server. Enter the fully distinguished name of the server to which the source server will connect.

Source domain and Destination Domain. Enter each server's domain name. If both the source and destination servers are in the same domain, you may leave these fields blank.

Use the port(s). Enter the name of one or more ports. If you enter more than one port, Domino will try the ports in the order you enter them. If you chose Local Area Network as the Connection type, you can click the Choose Ports button and choose one or more ports from a list. Also, if you chose Local Area Network as the Connection type, you can leave this field blank, in which case Domino will try all available LAN ports, starting with the last port successfully used.

An additional field to fill in for local area network and network dial-up connection types includes the following:

Optional network address. If you chose TCP/IP in the "Use the port(s)" field, you may optionally enter the destination server's fully distinguished hostname or IP address here. Entering the IP address saves Domino the trouble of querying the IP protocol stack for the destination server's IP address. But if the destination server's IP address ever changes, you would have to change it here as well. If you enter the destination server's hostname, Domino will use that hostname when querying the IP protocol stack for its IP address. If you leave this field blank, Domino will use the destination server's Notes common name to query the IP protocol stack for its IP address.

An additional tab called Network Dialup appears on network dial-up connection documents. It includes a field called Choose a service type, in which the choices are AppleTalk Remote Access, Microsoft Dial-Up Networking, and Macintosh PPP. What other fields appear on this page depend on your choice in the first field. Because I consider it unlikely that a server will ever dial up another server via AppleTalk Remote Access or Macintosh PPP, I later describe only the fields that appear if you choose Microsoft Dial-Up Networking. You enter the values in a dialog box that appears when you click the Edit Configuration button. Two of the fields are labeled one way in the dialog box, but another way on the form. In the listing that follows, the form label appears in parentheses after the dialog box label. The fields are as follows:

Dial-Up Networking name (Remote connection name). Enter the name of a connection defined in Microsoft Dial-up Networking.

Login name (Remote network login name). Optionally enter the name under which the server will log in to the remote network.

Password. Optionally enter the password the server must use to log in to the remote network.

Country code, Area code, and Phone number. Optionally enter the country code, area code, and phone number the server must dial to log in to the remote network.

Dial-back phone number. Optionally enter the source server's phone number (including, if necessary, the area code or city code and country code).

The optional fields listed previously are necessary only if, first, the component is necessary to complete the connection and, second, if the corresponding fields in the Microsoft Dial-up Networking connection were left blank. For example, you only need to use a country code if, one, the source and destination servers are not located in the same country and, two, the country code is *not* entered in the Microsoft Dial-up Networking connection. If you enter a value in an optional field and there is also a value in the corresponding field in the Microsoft Dial-up Networking connection, the Notes value will override the Microsoft Dial-up Networking value. Finally, when you save the document, Domino automatically encrypts the password field with the private keys of the source server and the people individually named in the Owners and Administrators fields (on the Administration page).

Additional fields to fill in for the Notes direct dialup connection type include the following:

Destination country code, Destination area code, and Destination phone number. The phone number is mandatory. The country and area codes are optional.

Always use area code. Default is No. Change to Yes if the area code is required to dial local calls.

Login script file name. Enter the filename of a connect script if you must use one to access the destination server. An example of this would be to dial up a public server on CompuServe's network. After dialing, but before reaching the server, you must provide a CompuServe user ID and password.

Login script arguments. Enter up to four values that the connect script will send to the destination login program. In the CompuServe example you would use only two arguments, the CompuServe user ID and the password.

Unfortunately, Notes doesn't encrypt the password information in a Direct Dial-up connection document as it does with a Network Dialup connection document. If you want to hide, say, the CompuServe password from prying eyes, you have to find a different way to do it. Probably the easiest way is to restrict who can read the document. Do this as follows:

1. Save and close the connection document.
2. Right-click the document in the Connections view. This pops up a context menu. Choose Document Properties. This displays the Document properties box.
3. Choose the Security ("key") tab in Document Properties.
4. Under Who can read this document deselect All readers and above. Then select authorized readers in the list appearing below the All readers and above checkbox. If a person, server, or group that you want to select doesn't appear in the list, click the icon to the right of the list. A Names dialog box appears, where you can choose names of people, servers, and groups from any Address Book or

Directory listed in the field in the upper left corner of the dialog box. Authorized readers should include the source server of the connection document. In addition to those you add here, anyone listed in the Owners or Administrators fields or assigned the [NetModifier] role will be able to read the document (as well as edit it).

Alternatively, you could enable encryption of the fields you want to hide. This would require you to make design changes in a subform in the design template for the Domain Directory. This involves a whole set of Notes application development skills that I can't assume you have, so I won't go into the details here. However, I will say that, although lots of people would go ahead and make such design changes, I prefer to avoid doing so because customization of core databases like the Domain Directory complicates the upgrade process.

Setting Up Server Pass-thru

Server pass-thru, by which a computer passes through one or more Domino servers to reach a destination Domino server, is most useful in setting up modem-based users to reach networked, modemless servers, and we discuss that aspect of server pass-thru in the next chapter. But servers can benefit from it in circumstances such as the following:

- Server 1 does not have a modem but instead passes-through one or more servers, which do have modems, to reach Server 4 on a remote LAN. See Figure 4.10.
- Server 1 (configured with TCP/IP) passes through Server 2 (configured with TCP/IP and IPX/SPX) to communicate with Server 3 (configured with IPX/SPX) on the same LAN. Server 2 translates for Servers 1 and 3, which could not otherwise communicate with each other.

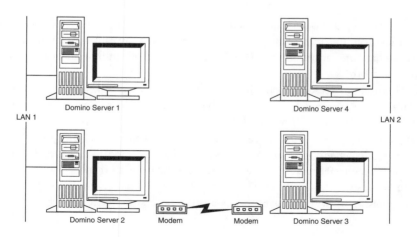

Figure 4.10 Server 1 can pass through Servers 2 and 3 to reach Server 4. A server can pass through up to 9 other servers to reach a 10th server.

To establish pass-thru communications between servers, you have to create one or more Server Pass-thru connection documents. A Server Pass-thru connection document is just like any other connection document except that, instead of specifying a port through which to access the destination server, you specify a pass-thru server. Just select Passthru Server in the Connection type field and enter the name of the pass-thru server in the Use passthru server or hunt group field.

The pass-thru server must know how to reach the destination server. It may have its own connection documents telling it how or a name service may inform it. So, for example, in Figure 4.10:

1. Server 1 knows from a pass-thru connection document that, to reach Server 4, it must pass through Server 2. It knows how to reach Server 2 because they are on the same LAN and share a common protocol. For example, if they both use TCP/IP, then Server 1 can query either a local hosts file or a DNS name server for the address of Server 2.

2. Server 2 knows from a pass-thru connection document that, to reach Server 4, it must pass through Server 3. Server 2 also knows from a Notes Direct Dialup connection document how to reach Server 3.

3. Server 3 can find the route to Server 4 via a name service (just as Server 1 was able to find Server 2 in step 1).

Setting Up Replication

In order for the new server and existing servers in a Domino domain to work with each other, they must be able to share information with each other. Each server must know the names of the other servers. Each server must be able to determine how to contact the other servers. Each server needs to know what services the other servers provide.

The servers keep track of each other by jointly maintaining a series of databases in which they store this information. That is, all servers in a domain maintain local copies of a set of databases, including the Domain Directory, the Administration Requests database, and others.

In addition, one reason you might be setting up an additional server is so that it can maintain duplicate copies of end-user databases, either for user convenience or to ensure high availability of those databases.

Whatever the reason, Domino servers typically maintain duplicate copies of certain databases. If a change occurs in one server's copy of a database, that change has to propagate to the other servers' copies of the same database, so that the servers can continue to work smoothly together. The process by which changes in databases propagate is called replication. We will cover the replication process in detail in Chapter 9,

"Replication." For now, we merely need to realize that, except within Domino clusters, which are a special case (see Chapter 20, "Enhancing Data Availability"), replication does not take place automatically between Domino servers. You have to force it. Although you can and occasionally will force a one-time replication by issuing a command, what you really want to do is set up replication to occur on a schedule, without human intervention. To do this, you must create one or more connection documents in which you enable the replication task and scheduled connections.

If you have planned thoroughly before setting up your servers, you should already know at this time what connection documents you need to create to assure that replication will take place smoothly between your new server and existing servers in its domain. If you have been following this book, then you may not have planned this part yet, because we don't discuss replication in detail until Chapter 9.

For now (that is, for the purpose of describing how to ensure that your additional server replicates properly with existing servers), let's assume that the first server in your domain will initiate replication with your new server(s). To extend the example we have been using, Osprey/Servers/Stillwater will initiate replication with Kestrel/Servers/Stillwater. To accomplish this we have to set up a connection document with at least the following fields completed:

On the Basics tab:

Source server: Osprey/Servers/Stillwater

Destination server: Kestrel/Servers/Stillwater

On the Replication/Routing tab:

Replication task: Enabled.

(Optionally) Routing task: -None-. If the source and destination servers are both in the same Domino Named Network, set this field to -None-. If they are in different named networks, you may optionally use this connection document to accomplish both replication and mail routing between the two servers. For details on setting up and maintaining mail routing, see Chapter 7.

On the Schedule tab:

Schedule: Enabled.

All other fields: Accept the defaults for now.

Depending on how the two servers connect to each other, you may have to change the default entries in the other fields on the Basics tab of the connection document. But other than that, you can accept the default settings of all other fields.

Notice that this one connection document will establish replication in both directions between the two involved servers. That is because the Replication Type field (on the Replication/Routing tab) defaults to "Pull Push." In this type of replication, the source server first pulls changes from the destination server's copy of each database to its own copy, then pushes changes in its own copy of each database to the destination server's copy. You should take as a rule of thumb that, under ordinary circumstances, only one connection document is necessary to ensure that all necessary replication takes place between two servers.

Notice also that if, as in the preceding example, you set up replication between your first server (Osprey in our example) and each new server that you bring on line, you need not set up replication between each new server and any other server. Because Osprey replicates with every other server, changes that occur on any server will eventually replicate to every other server that Osprey replicates with.

This is an example of hub-and-spoke replication topology, which is the most efficient replication topology. In our example, Osprey is the hub and Kestrel and all other servers set up similarly are the spokes. See Chapter 8, "Mail Routing Setup and Maintenance," for a more detailed explanation.

Setting Up Mail Routing

You might not have to set up mail routing between your new server and existing servers. If two servers are in the same Domino Named Network, they will automatically route mail to each other, and you don't have to set up anything. If two servers are not in the same Domino Named Network, you might have to set up one or more connection documents to enable mail routing between them. Or they might route mail to each other via other servers that already have connection documents in place.

If you want to enable mail routing between your new server and servers in another Domino domain, or between your new server and a non-Notes mail system, such as cc:Mail, SMTP, or X.400, you generally don't have to do anything special. You will, of course, have to configure mail routing connections between at least one "gateway" server in your domain and one or more mail servers outside your domain. But, having done that, you don't have to do anything special to enable other servers in your domain to benefit from that connection. As long as the other servers in the domain can route mail to the "gateway" server, either directly or indirectly, they will automatically benefit from the interdomain mail connection.

In other words, whether you have to configure mail routing for a given new server depends on its relationship to other servers in the domain and what mail routing connections have already been put in place. To learn the details of all this, see Chapter 8 . For now, you need to keep three things in mind.

First, all Domino servers need to be able to send mail to and receive it from other servers in the domain, even if they are not "mail" servers per se. All Notes databases can be mail-enabled. That is, they can send documents to each other via Domino mail routing. So any server might find that it must transfer mail to another server.

Second, if you do have to create a connection document to enable mail routing between a new server and other servers in the domain, you have to be sure to enable mail routing in both directions. In releases of Domino and Notes before 5.0, this meant you had to create two connection documents, because mail routing was a push-only proposition. Each server had to initiate its own connection with, then push outgoing mail to the receiving server. Release 5 servers can initiate "Pull Push" mail routing with a single connection document. Therefore, only a single connection document is necessary, in which the following field values are set:

On the Replication/Routing tab:

Routing task: Enabled.

Router type: Pull Push. If you choose any other routing type, you must create a second connection document to enable mail routing in the opposite direction of that chosen.

On the Schedule tab:

Schedule: Enabled.

All other fields: Accept the defaults for now.

Third, the default time range for mail routing in a connection document is from 8 a.m. to 10 p.m. However, the default time range for the routing of low priority mail is from 12 midnight to 6 a.m. If you don't change one or the other default time range so that they overlap, low priority mail will be undeliverable. Therefore, in any circumstance which requires that you create connection documents to enable mail routing, you need to change one or the other. To change the low priority mail delivery time, set the following variable in the server's `notes.ini` file:

```
MailLowPriorityTime=time-range
```

where `time-range` is in 24-hour format. For example,

```
MailLowPriorityTime=21:00-23:00
```

sets the low priority mail delivery time to between 9 p.m. and 11 p.m.

Setting Up the Administration Process

The administration process is a server task that performs a wide variety of tedious and complex chores that an administrator would otherwise have to perform manually. Among the tasks performed are the following:

- **Name management.** For example, rename users and groups, delete users and groups, delete servers, recertify users, and store internet certificates.
- **Mail file management.** For example, move and delete mail files.
- **Server document management.** Automatic update of various fields in Server documents.

The administration process runs automatically on every server, because `adminp` is included in the Servertasks variable in each server's `notes.ini` file. You can stop the administration process by issuing the command `tell adminp quit` at the server console. You can restart the administration process with the command `load adminp`. The administration process also uses a database, Administration Requests (`admin4.nsf`), to track the progress of tasks as it performs them. You can read and edit documents in this database, but you never create documents manually. Rather, the administration process itself creates all documents in the database, in response either to requests made by administrators or to events that take place on the server.

Many tasks performed by the administration process have to be performed on multiple servers either simultaneously or in series. Therefore, Administration Requests is replicated to all servers (R4.0 or higher) in the domain. As each server performs its part of a task, it updates its copy of the database, either by modifying a request or by adding a response document. By replication, the update makes its way to the other servers. In this way, all the servers can track the progress of all tasks and do their parts at the appropriate stages.

The servers that actually carry out the requests that appear in Administration Requests are called administrative servers. You designate administrative servers for individual databases. Each database can have a single designated administrative server (or it can have no administrative server). Also, for databases that reside only on users' workstations, you can designate the user as the administrative server. When the user logs in to his/her home server, Notes polls the Administration Requests database on that server for requests affecting databases for which the user is the administrative server, and carries them out at that time if it finds any.

The administrative server of the Domain Directory has a relatively heavy burden. It changes the contents of documents in the Domain Directory. It also changes the contents of the ACL of the Domain Directory. Administrative servers of other databases generally have a lighter burden. They make changes to the database ACL and, optionally, to Reader and Author fields.

Reader and Author are data types of two kinds of fields that hold user names. Not all databases have fields of these types. When you designate an administrative server for a database, you have to decide whether the server will make changes in Reader and Author fields or just in the ACL. If a database does not have any Reader or Author fields, it is pointless to make the administrative server check for changes in them, and you should not check off that option.

If you are not sure whether a database has any Reader or Author fields, the most painless way to find out is to ask the developer. Alternatively, you can use Domino Designer to generate a design synopsis of the database. If you generate a design synopsis, include all forms, subforms, and shared fields in the synopsis. Then use Find/Replace to locate the words "author" and "reader." What you are looking for is fields of data type author or reader. So if Find/Replace locates either word, make sure the word appears to the right of the word "datatype."

One organizational issue that you have to resolve in the on-going setup of your Domino domain is which servers will administer which databases. You can distribute or consolidate administrative tasks. The most important determining factor is probably user convenience. You want servers to be as responsive as possible to your users. So you should avoid designating servers with a heavy user load to perform database administration tasks. Designate nonuser servers, such as replication hubs, instead.

You probably won't be able to relieve any server entirely of the burden of administering databases, because every server has some databases that reside only on it. For example, user mail databases typically reside only on mail servers. So, even though your mail servers may groan under the weight of heavy user demand, you still must designate them as administrative server of their mail databases. But avoid designating a heavily used mail or application server to administer databases that do not reside exclusively on it.

Several conditions must be in place for the administration process to work properly. We listed them in Chapter 3 but will repeat them briefly here:

- Adminp must run continuously on every server that participates in the administration process. This occurs by default.

- A replica copy of Administration Requests must exist on every server that participates in the administration process. Adminp creates this database automatically the first time it runs.

- One server must be designated the administration server of the Domain Directory. This is the server that makes all changes called for by the administration process to the Domain Directory. By default, the first server in the domain assumes this role. You can set another server to perform this role.

- Any server that may be the Registration Server during a recertification or renaming of users must have a Certification Log database (certlog.nsf). This may or may not be a replica of the Certification Log database on other servers in the domain. You must create this database. We reviewed the steps for creating it in Chapter 3.

- An administrative server should be designated for every server-resident database in the domain. Any database that does not designate an administrative server will not get updated by the administration process.

To create a new replica of an existing Certification Log database, follow these steps:

1. Start Domino Administrator on any workstation. Log in using the ID of a user authorized to create new replicas on the server in question.

2. Click the Files tab. A screen should appear similar to that in Figure 4.11.

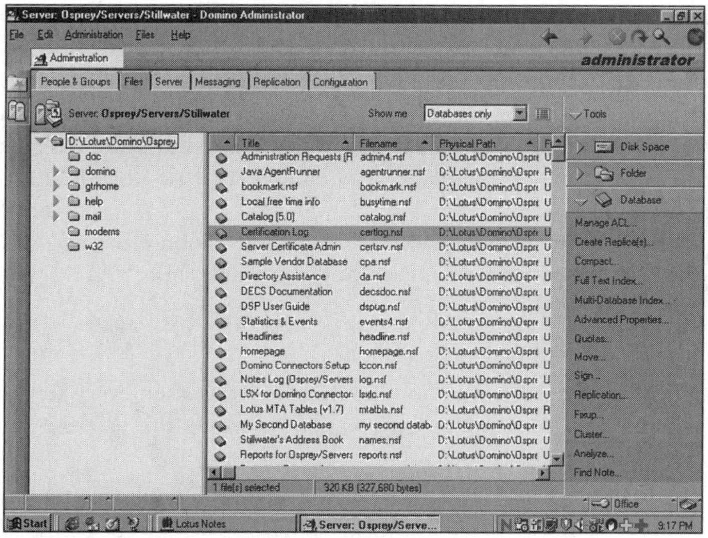

Figure 4.11　The Files screen displays folders and files in the Data folder of the selected server, and provides tools for manipulating those files.

3. In the Bookmarks pane (left side of screen), select any currently running (and accessible) server on which a copy of the Certification Requests database exists. (You can click the icon for your domain, then click the desired server.) The name of the server you chose should appear below the tabs at the top of the screen. The files in its data directory appear onscreen.

4. Select the Certification Log database in the list of files. Then, open the Create Replica dialog box. You can do this three different ways. First, you can choose Create Replica(s) in the Tools pane. Second and third, you can choose New, then Replica(s) in either the File menu or the context menu that appears when you right-click the Certification Log database listing.

5. In the Create Replica dialog box, select the name(s) of the server(s) on which you want to create the new replica(s). If a server does not appear in the list, choose Other and either enter the name of your server or choose the server from the drop-down list, then choose OK. Do *not* change the path or filename of the new replica database. On each server it should be located in the main data

directory and be named `certlog.nsf`. Click OK when all desired servers are selected. Within the next couple of replication cycles, the administration process will create new replica stubs on each server, and the replication process will populate them with existing documents.

There are two ways to designate an administrative server for a database—by directly editing the database's ACL or by directing the administration process to update the database's ACL. Use either method if you need to designate the administrative server for only one database. Use the second method if you have to designate administrative servers for multiple databases.

To designate an administrative server by updating a database ACL directly, follow these steps:

1. Log in to Notes as a user with Manager access to the database in question. Alternatively, run Notes locally on a server on which the database is stored.

2. Select or open the database in question. Then, in the File menu, choose Database, then Access Control. Alternatively, choose Database, then Access Control in the context menu that appears when you right-click the database icon.

3. The Access Control List dialog box opens. Choose Advanced. Then, under Administration Server, choose Server. Enter the fully distinguished name of the server in the Server field (or choose the server from the drop-down list).

4. Choose whether the administration process should modify Reader and Author fields in this database. For the Domain Directory and any databases that do not have Reader or Author fields, select Do not modify Reader or Author fields. For all other databases, select Modify all Reader and Author fields. Choose OK when finished.

To designate an administrative server by directing the administration process to update the ACLs of one or more databases, follow these steps:

1. Log in to Domino Administrator using the ID of a person with Manager access to the databases you want to change. In the Bookmarks pane, select the server on which the databases reside.

2. In the Files screen, choose one or more databases. In later steps you will designate an administrative server and whether that server should modify Reader and Author fields. Therefore, in this step you should choose only the databases that will have the same settings in both of those fields.

3. In the Tools pane, expand Database, then choose Manage ACL. Alternately, in the Files menu, choose Access Control, then Manage.

4. The Multi ACL Management dialog box opens. Choose Advanced, then select Modify Administration Server setting. Choose Server, then enter the fully distinguished name of the server you want to designate as administration server or choose the server from the drop-down list.

5. For the Domain Directory and any databases that do not have Reader or Author fields, deselect Modify fields of type Reader or Author. For all other databases, select this box.

6. Choose OK to close the ACL Management dialog box. If you want to apply different settings to other databases, select them now, then repeat steps 3 through 5.

You can verify that the administration process is functioning properly on a server by checking the Administration Requests database. Soon after starting up the first time, a new server generates requests to put its build number, number of CPUs, and OS platform information into its server document. If those requests appear, the administration process is working properly on that server.

If replication is also properly set up for that server and the Domain Directory's administration server, then within about an hour of receiving those requests into its own replica of the Administration Requests database, the Domino Directory's administrative server should carry out the requests. It will add responses to the Administration Requests database indicating that it did so (or tried and failed to do so).

Setting Up the Agent Manager

The agent manager is a server task that manages the running of agents on the server. Agents can consume lots of server resources, so we have to ration the resources to them. Agents can also run out of control, so we need a way to kill them if necessary. The agent manager keeps agents from taking over the computer.

The agent manager runs automatically on all servers because `amgr` is included in the `servertasks` variable of each server's `notes.ini` file. You can stop the agent manager by issuing the command `tell amgr quit` at the server console. You can restart the agent manager with the command `load amgr`.

You configure the agent manager in two places, both in the server document. One is the Agent Restrictions section under the Security tab. Here you designate who will be allowed to run agents of various kinds on the server. We discussed these fields in Chapter 3.

The other place is the fields under the Agent Manager Tab, which is under the Server Tasks tab. These fields let you configure the parameters of the agent manager. As is plain from a study of Figure 4.12, the agent manager runs differently during daytime hours than during nighttime hours. It permits less agent activity during the day, when users are presumably making greater demands on the server, than at night. You can redefine the time ranges when the agent manager runs in daytime versus nighttime mode. You can change the number of agents the agent manager will allow to run concurrently and the maximum runtime of an agent. The rule of thumb here is that you really don't need to change any of these parameters unless specific agents running on a server make unusual demands or you have unusual patterns of user demand on a server.

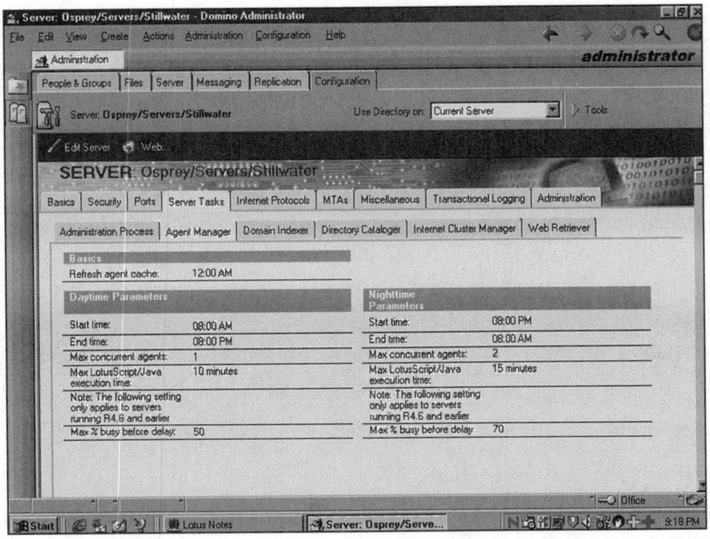

Figure 4.12   The Agent Manager manages agents differently during daytime hours than at night. You can define daytime and nighttime hours and how agents are allowed to run during each period.

Setting Up Transaction Logging

As with the first server, you need to consider whether each additional server will use transaction logging and then tailor it to each server's hardware configuration. Lotus, of course, highly recommends that you enable transaction logging, because it provides tremendous benefits, including greater database integrity, more responsiveness to user demands on busy servers, and faster, more reliable recovery from system failures. However, enabling transaction logging affects your backup procedures as well as when, how, and if you run certain utilities, such as fixup and compact. Be sure you understand all the issues and their implications before you enable transaction logging. For details of how to set up transaction logging, as well as a discussion of the implications of doing so, see Chapter 14, "Database Maintenance and Troubleshooting."

Special-Purpose Servers

If a server will be put to a specialized use, you may need to configure it differently. The principal server specialties and their special setup needs appear in the next sections.

Mail Servers

Mail servers are the custodians of the users' mail databases. Notes mail databases include standard email functions as well as calendaring and task management functions. Many users live inside these applications. They create mail messages, tasks, and calendar entries. They receive messages here from others. They usually save a copy of everything they send. Their mail databases can get quite large.

Many organizations will dedicate one or more servers just to this purpose. This practice is so common, in fact, that one version of Domino, the Domino Mail Server, is intended just for this purpose. And the most common NotesBench figure that server manufacturers cite is the Mail benchmark.

The special setups that you might perform on a mail server include the following items, each of which is covered in detail elsewhere in this book, as noted in the list:

- Create multiple Outgoing Mail databases. See Chapter 8.
- Set up shared mail. See Chapter 8.
- Set up Internet mail functions, including SMTP, POP3, IMAP, and LDAP. See Chapters 8, 16, 17, and 11.
- Run HTTP so that mail users can access their mail databases via browser. See Chapter 15.
- Set up Message Tracking. See Chapter 8.
- Set up a Resources database so calendar users can reserve resources such as conference rooms when scheduling meetings and other events. See Chapter 8.
- Offload certain tasks, such as directory lookups, to other servers. See Chapter 11.

Application Servers

Application servers are the custodians of Domino applications other than mail, calendaring, and task management. These may include everything from simple discussions and document repositories to complex workflow applications. Application servers are likely to run the HTTP, DIIOP, and NNTP server tasks, because Domino apps these days are accessed from browsers and news readers as often as from Notes clients. We cover configuration of the HTTP and DIIOP tasks in Chapter 15.

If no applications running on this server use the sched and calconn server tasks, you may want to disable them. These tasks manage the group calendaring function, which is ordinarily a function of mail servers. To stop running these functions, enter tell sched quit and tell calconn quit at the server console. To keep them from starting the next time the server starts, remove them from the servertasks variable in the server's notes.ini file.

Dialup/Pass-Thru Servers

Organizations that have a lot of mobile users connecting to their servers from outside the firewall may designate one or more servers to manage this traffic. The trend toward universal connectivity to the Internet is gradually obviating the need for dialup/pass-thru servers. But the idea behind them is that you can designate one or more servers to accept all incoming modem traffic. Users who dial in can call a dialup server, then pass through it to reach their mail and application servers, which are accessible only via LAN. You needn't provide direct modem access to your mail and application servers. Users only need to make one phone call to reach all of their servers.

Dialup/pass-thru servers typically are stripped down servers attached to a phalanx of modems. You can disable all tasks on them except `router`, `update`, `adminp`, and `amgr`.

If mobile users typically maintain local replicas of certain databases, you might consider putting copies of those databases on the dialup server, then setting up the users to replicate directly with the dialup server to update those databases. This would minimize LAN traffic. A likely candidate for this treatment would be the Directory Catalog database, which is specifically intended for local replication by mobile users.

Mail and Replication Hubs

As the number of servers that you manage increases beyond three or four, you have to concern yourself with replication and mail routing topologies. Specifically, you quickly reach a point at which it becomes unwieldy to allow every server to replicate with (and perhaps route mail to) every other server and you have to set up hub-and-spoke replication (and perhaps mail routing). (For the reasons behind this problem, see Chapters 7 and 8.) So you may designate one or more servers as hub servers—replication hubs and possibly mail routing hubs.

A hub server is generally a powerful server that does not serve users directly—often only administrators and other servers may access it directly. Lowly users only have access to their mail and application servers.

An especially busy replication hub will typically run multiple replicators. You can set a server to run *n* replicators by setting the variable *replicators=n* in the server's `notes.ini`. How many replicators should a replication hub run? The general rule is no more than two replicators per processor. A single processor server should run no more than two replicators. A dual processor server should run no more than four. Chances are you won't need to run that many anyway. Domino replication is a phenomenally efficient process. You really have to generate a lot of replicable data on a lot of spoke servers to overwork a hub replicator process. But see Chapter 8 for details.

If you need to set up a mail hub, you will no doubt want to set up multiple Outgoing Mail (mail.box) databases on it.

If a hub server will be the focus of a lot of network traffic, you might want to isolate it on its own high-speed LAN, connected to the rest of the world via switch. Finally, because a hub server is a single point of failure, you might want to set it up on OS-partitioned computers. It runs on one computer in the partition. But if that computer fails, a backup computer takes ownership of the disk array on which Domino resides, as well as the failed computer's IP address and host name. Domino restarts with only a few minutes' downtime.

Shared Browser Servers

Back in January 1996, when the World Wide Web was young and most of us didn't yet know what a browser was, let alone have one, Lotus introduced (with Notes Release 4.0) a shared browser service. It allowed Notes users to browse the World Wide Web via a Notes server (they weren't yet called Domino servers). The Notes users didn't need to run IP locally and they didn't need to have any other browser. The server running the shared browser service (called Web Retriever) was designated the "InterNotes" server.

Notes users could click a URL or enter one into a dialog box. Notes would submit the URL to the InterNotes server, which would in turn submit it to the appropriate Web server. The Web server would send an HTML document back to the InterNotes server, which would convert it to a Notes document and store it in the InterNotes Web Navigator database. Then it would deliver the now Notes document to the requesting user.

The Web Retriever was a really slow browser, and people who had surfed the Web with a real browser generally disdained it. But it had some nice features, not the least of which was the fact that all retrieved pages were stored in a shared Notes database. This meant that whole groups of Notes users could benefit from each other's Web discoveries. The Web Navigator database included several agents that leveraged this feature.

Nowadays, most Notes users are on IP LANs connected to the Internet and they have their own browsers. In fact, since Release 4.1 the Notes client has had browser capabilities built into it. So, even though the server-based Web Retriever is still available, hardly anybody cares because hardly anybody needs it.

However, the Web Retriever still exists in Domino and it has some features that certain companies might find attractive. For example, an administrator can prohibit users from retrieving pages from unauthorized Web sites. Also, the Web Navigator database is very customizable. And the Domino server running the Web Retriever is a very cheap, effective firewall that requires no expertise to set up. So for a company that has grave reservations about permitting users to surf the Web or is nervous about opening up its internal networks to the Internet, the Web Retriever may offer value yet.

If you want to learn how to set up and configure Web Retriever on a Domino server, and how to set up Notes clients to use it, see Chapter 25 "Administering the Domino System" of the Lotus "yellow book," which came with your server software.

Internet Servers

Although you can set up the HTTP or NNTP services on any Domino application server, most likely you will do so only to make applications available to internal users who don't have a Notes client. If you want to make applications available to outside users, you won't just open up the firewall and let them hit any old Domino server. Rather, you will designate one or more servers to sit outside the firewall, connected directly to the Internet. These are your company Web servers and your company News servers. You won't put just any databases on them. Rather, you will put only those databases on them that you are willing to expose to the world.

When you set up such servers, you must lock them down carefully so that outsiders can't gain access to nonpublic data. They will replicate with inside servers. You should use selective replication to insure that only documents approved for public exposure replicate to them.

In addition, if you open the firewall to let outsiders connect to internal servers, either directly or by proxy, you need to secure those servers carefully as well. The servers that you are most likely to set up this way are your mail servers.

Firewall Servers

Most companies are very wary of letting traffic pass from the Internet onto their private networks (or "intranets"), and they are well-justified in their caution. They have erected firewalls, consisting of packet-filtering routers and hosts as well as various kinds of proxy servers, to lock unauthorized network traffic out of their private networks.

Among the kinds of proxy servers used on the firewall are "application-level" proxy servers, which are designed to work with network packets generated by a particular application. Domino servers are all capable of acting as application-level proxy servers for each other. When you set up a pass-thru Domino server, you are setting it up as an application-level proxy server.

In the context of a firewall between the Internet and a company's intranet, a pass-thru Domino server is accessible from the Internet and has the right to send and receive information through any filtering routers to Domino servers on the other side of the router. You can use a firewall server to allow your Notes users to access internal Domino servers from the Internet. To do this, you have to perform the following steps:

- In Internet-based users' "Internet" Location documents, designate the firewall server as the default pass-thru server.
- In the firewall server's Server document, give Internet-based users the right to pass through it to reach other Domino servers.
- In the Server documents of the internal servers, give Internet-based users the right to reach them via pass-thru.
- In any packet-filtering router that sits between the firewall server and the internal servers, open port number 1352, which is the well-known port for Domino and Notes traffic.

A lightly used Domino public Web or NNTP server could serve double-duty as a fire-wall server. So could a Domino mail server that offers mail services to external, Internet-based users.

Directory Servers

Domino server setup automatically sets up basic Domino directory services. First server setup (described in Chapter 3) creates the domain directory database (names.nsf). Additional server setup (the subject of this chapter) replicates the domain directory to each additional server at setup time. Ongoing replication among the servers keeps each one's copy of the domain directory in synch with the others.

The Domino directory provides essential services to users and servers. It provides users an easy way to address mail to each other and to look up information about each other. It allows servers to find each other, to determine what services each server provides, and to determine how to route mail to users and databases.

A closed, single-domain system with no mobile users needs no more directory services than this. However, your system is probably not that simple, and you may need to consider setting up additional directory services. Other Domino directory services that you should consider setting up include the following:

- **Server and mobile directory catalogs.** A directory catalog is a specialized Notes database (based on dircat5.ntf) that collects the most frequently looked-up information from one or more Domino directories into a single, light-weight directory, optimized to provide very fast lookups. A server directory catalog resides on a Domino server. A mobile directory catalog resides on a Notes user's workstation.

- **Directory assistance.** Enables Notes users to do lookups in multiple Domino and LDAP directories. Enables Domino servers to use credentials located in LDAP directories to authenticate Web users. Allows a Domino LDAP server to refer LDAP clients to other LDAP directories.

- **Dedicated directory servers.** By default Domino mail servers also provide directory lookup services for Notes mail users. You can off-load directory services to another server, so the mail server can provide faster mail services to more mail clients while the directory server provides faster directory lookups.

- **LDAP directory services.** LDAP is a standardized protocol for providing and accessing directory services. It is widely used by Internet programs. A Domino server running LDAP directory services becomes an LDAP directory server. It can permit LDAP clients to read from and write to the Domino directory. It can do lookups in other LDAP directories. It can refer LDAP clients to other LDAP directories.

Examples of situations in which you may want or need to set up additional directory services include the following:

- You want to provide the fastest possible name lookup services to your Notes users. Set up a server directory catalog.

- You have mobile users who are not always connected to a Domino server. Set up a mobile directory catalog that mobile users can easily carry with them.

- You have lots of mail users. They make heavy demands on the mail servers. Consider setting up one or more directory servers.

- You have more than one Domino domain. Set up Domino directory assistance and directory assistance to make each domain's directory available to the users in the other domains.

- You authenticate various Internet clients (Web/IIOP, POP3, IMAP, NNTP, and LDAP) as well as Notes clients. You can more easily keep track of the different kinds of clients you serve by setting them up in separate directory databases (for example, Notes users in the Domino Directory (`names.nsf`), non-Notes users in one or more other directories, for example `inetnames.nsf`). To make all of these directories available to Notes users for name lookups, you can set up directory assistance and a directory catalog.

- You serve POP3 or IMAP mail clients. To make the Domino Directory available to them, you need to set up LDAP directory services.

Consider the following rules of thumb:

- Set up a directory catalog even if you administer just one, small Domino domain.

- Set up both a directory catalog and directory assistance if you have to administer multiple related Domino domains or if you provide LDAP services.

- Consider setting up one or more dedicated directory servers if you have large numbers of mail users.

- Set up LDAP services if you serve non-Notes clients or if you want to use an LDAP directory to authenticate Web users.

We cover the details of setting up each of these directory services in Chapter 11, "Domino Directory Services."

Domain Catalog/Search Servers

Domino R5 includes a search capability called Domain Search, which permits users to search an entire Domino domain for the contents of Notes databases and file systems. To set up Domain Search you have to designate one or more servers as Domain Catalog servers. Servers so designated maintain a catalog of databases in the domain and a full-text index (called the Domain Index). The Domain Index includes databases and file systems earmarked for such inclusion. Thereafter, users can search the index for text strings included in documents in the indexed databases, in files attached to those documents, and in files in the indexed file systems. The search engine will return only such documents, attachments, and files as the searching user has Reader or higher access to.

Domain Catalog/Search servers should have considerable processor power, RAM, and disk space. The catalog task (which runs nightly at 1:00 a.m.) and the indexer task (which by default runs hourly) are both processor- and RAM-intensive. The full-text index occupies a lot of disk space. Lotus recommends that a domain catalog server running under Windows NT be configured, at minimum, with a 266mhz Pentium processor, 256MB RAM, and free disk space (for the full-text index) equal to 75 percent of the size of the databases and files being indexed. (The preceding recommendation is a low-ball figure; elsewhere Lotus recommends that the Domain Catalog server have multiple processors.) Lotus further recommends that, if your domain has more than, say, eight servers, the Domain Catalog server be relieved of all other tasks. Finally, Lotus recommends that you consider clustering Domain Catalog servers for reliability, fault-tolerance, and load balancing. To learn how to set up a Domain Catalog/Search server, see Chapter 7, "Upgrading from Domino 4.x to 5.0."

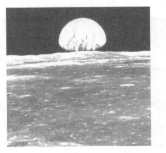

5

User Registration and Client Setup

IN THIS CHAPTER WE'LL COVER THE PROCESS OF SETTING UP generic Notes users, that is, users who come into the office everyday and use Notes at their desks, and who use Notes mail and databases, but don't necessarily use Notes as an Internet client. (We'll cover mobile Notes users and those who will use Notes to connect to Internet mail, directory, and news servers in Chapter 6, "Advanced Client Setup.")

The steps involved in setting up new users include the following:

- Create user OU certifiers (if you plan to use them and they don't exist yet).
- Add alternate languages to O and OU certifiers (if you plan to use alternate names).
- Create User Setup Profiles
- Set up a default Execution Control List and sign any unsigned databases.
- Set up ID/password recovery
- Register users
- Install and configure Notes on user computers

Most of the items in the preceding list are optional. But many of the options will save you lots of busy work and grief over time, and I highly recommend most of them to you. For example:

- **User Setup Profiles** will provide a single place for you to define lots of user settings that you would otherwise have to set individually for each new Notes user during the configuration process.

- Setting up **ID/password recovery** will make your life much easier when users forget their passwords or lose or corrupt their ID files.

- The **Execution Control List** limits the actions that programs can take on users' workstations. This is a protection against mail viruses and other nasty surprises.

There's one little problem here. You want to set up ID/password recovery before registering users. If you do, the recovery information gets written into users' IDs automatically at registration time. If you register users first, then set up ID/password recovery, you have to mail ID recovery information to the users, and they in turn have to accept the information, then mail a copy of their ID file to a special database.

This is a semiautomated process, of course. But users are generally too busy or preoccupied with their own business to cooperate with administrators in any active way. Or they're afraid to push a button without first consulting you. So, you want to set up ID/password recovery first.

But you have to set up at least some administrative users before you set up ID/password recovery, because the public keys of the administrators who will recover IDs and passwords have to be available at the time you set up ID/password recovery. Because of that, in this chapter we'll approach the user setup tasks in the following order:

- **User setup profiles.** We'll set up a profile for administrative users first.
- **Default execution control list**
- **OU certifiers**
- **Alternate name languages**
- **Basic user registration**. So you can register your administrative users.
- **ID/password recovery.** Once this is set up (and nonadministrative user profiles defined), you can register the rest of your users.
- **Basic Notes installation and configuration**

Creating User Setup Profiles

You definitely want to employ user setup profiles. They cut down on the amount of work you have to do to set up each new user. They ensure uniformity of user setups. And they allow you to update existing users' workstations over time. To set one up, follow these steps:

1. Open Domino Administrator to the People & Groups tab.

2. In the Servers pane, choose the server in whose copy of the Domain Directory you will set up the profile.

3. In the Tasks pane, choose the Setup Profiles view in your domain's directory. Any user setup profiles that already exist will appear in the Results pane.

4. Click Add Setup Profile in the action bar above the Results pane. A User Setup Profile form appears.

5. Fill in the fields, then save and close the form.

The fields in the User Setup Profile form are as follows:

Basics tab

- **Profile name.** Enter any descriptive name here. When registering new users, the name you enter here will appear in a list of available profiles.

- **Internet browser.** Choose the browser Notes will run when a user clicks on or enters a URL. This fills in the Internet browser field in the user's location documents. The choices are:

  - **Notes.** Notes is a browser compliant with HTML 4.0.

  - **Notes with Internet Explorer.** This is IE running embedded in the Notes window.

  - **Netscape Navigator.** Runs in a separate window from Notes.

  - **Microsoft Internet Explorer.** This is IE running in a separate window from Notes.

  - **Other.** If you choose this, the user can choose any third-party browser (but you can't choose it for them in this profile).

- **Directory server.** Enter the fully distinguished name of the server on which users will do name lookups.

- **Catalog/Domain Search server.** Enter the fully distinguished name of the server on which users will do domain searches.

- **Retrieve/open pages.** Choose how the user will retrieve Web pages. These choices are only relevant if you chose "Notes" in the Internet browser field:

- **from InterNotes server.** Choose this for users who won't have their own browsers but will use a Domino-based "InterNotes" server.

- **from Notes Workstation.** Choose this for users who will have and use their own browsers.

- **no retrievals.** Choose this for users who will not have any access to the World Wide Web.

Databases tab. You can insert database links in each of the fields on this tab. To insert a database link, follow these steps:

1. Open the database.
2. Choose Edit, Copy as Link, Database Link
3. With the text cursor in the field, choose Edit, Paste.

- **Default databases added to bookmarks.** Insert a database link for each database you want to add to the users' workspaces.

- **Create As new replicas on user's machine.** Insert a database link for each database that you want to replicate to the users' workstations.

- **Mobile directory catalogs.** Insert a database link for each mobile directory catalog you want to replicate to the users' workstations.

Dial-up Connections tab, Default Passthru Server fields. Use these fields to set up a default passthru server. The server name you enter will appear in the Passthru Server field on the users' location documents. This also results in the creation of a direct dial-up connection document to the passthru server in the users' personal address books.

- **Server name.** Enter the fully distinguished name of the default passthru server.

- **Country code.** Enter the country code (if any) of the default passthru server.

- **Area code.** Enter the area code or city code (if any) of the default passthru server.

- **Phone number.** Enter the local phone number (if any) of the default passthru server.

Dial-up Connections tab, Default Connections to Other Remote Servers fields. Use these fields to set up a connection information for remote servers. When you set up a user based on this profile, Notes will create a direct dial-up connection document for each listed server.

Each field can have multiple entries. Use commas, semicolons, or carriage returns to separate multiple entries in each field.

There should be an entry in each field for each server, and the entries for each server should fall in the same place in each field. That is, entries for the first listed server should appear first in each field, entries for the second listed server should appear second in each field, and so on.

- **Server names.** Enter the fully distinguished names of remote servers.
- **Country Codes.** Enter the country codes of remote servers.
- **Area Codes.** Enter the area codes or city codes of remote servers.
- **Phone Number.** Enter the local phone numbers of remote servers.

Accounts tab. Use these fields to set up information Notes needs to connect with Internet servers. For each account listed, the workstation setup program will create an account document in the users' personal address books.

Each field can have multiple entries. Use commas, semicolons, or carriage returns to separate multiple entries in each field.

There should be an entry in each field for each server, and the entries for each server should fall in the same place in each field. That is, entries for the first listed server should appear first in each field, entries for the second listed server should appear second in each field, and so on.

- **Account Names.** Enter descriptive names that will become the names of the account documents that will appear in users' personal address books.
- **Server Addresses.** Enter the fully distinguished host name or IP address of each account server.
- **Protocols.** Enter the Internet protocol of each account server (for example, LDAP, POP, IMAP, or SMTP).
- **Use SSL Connection.** For each listed account, enter 0 (if not using SSL to connect) or 1 (if using SSL to connect to the server).

Name Servers tab. In these fields you can designate a fallback Domino server that Notes will seek if it can't find the designated home server. Complete these fields only if they apply.

- **Secondary TCP/IP Notes name server.** Enter the fully distinguished Notes name of the secondary server if it is reachable by TCP/IP.
- **Secondary TCP/IP host name or address.** Enter the secondary server's fully distinguished host name or its IP address.
- **Secondary NDS Notes name server.** Enter the fully distinguished Notes name of the secondary server if it is a registered object on a Novell Name Server.
- **Secondary NDS name server address.** Enter the secondary server's fully distinguished Novell name.

Applet Security tab. Java applets can cause network connections with other computers and set up communications with them. This is a potential security problem. On this tab, you can limit the network access Notes will permit of Java applets.

- **Trusted hosts.** These are hosts or domains from which any received applets are assumed to be benign. Enter host names, domain names, and partial or complete IP addresses (for example, 205.159.212.*). If you leave the field blank, all hosts are assumed to be trusted.

  - **Network access for trusted hosts.** Choose one of the degrees of network access. The choices include:
  - **Disable Java.** Java applets won't be allowed to run.
  - **No access allowed.** Java applets won't be allowed to communicate with other computers.
  - **Allow access only to originating host.** Java applets will be allowed to communicate only with the host from which the applet was received.
  - **Allow access to any trusted host.** Java applets will be allowed to communicate only with hosts listed in the Trusted hosts field.
  - **Allow access to any host.** Java applets will be allowed to communicate with any reachable host.

- **Network access for untrusted hosts.** Choose one of the degrees of network access. The choices are: Disable Java; No access allowed; Allow access only to originating host. These are the three most restrictive choices listed previously.

Proxies tab. If users will have to pass through any proxy server(s) to reach other servers, enter the IP address(es) and port(s) of the proxy server(s) here.

- **HTTP proxy.** Enter the host name or IP address and port number (for example., 192.168.0.12:8080).
- **Use HTTP proxy for all Internet protocols.** Set this to Yes if the proxy server listed in the HTTP proxy field also serves as an FTP, Gopher, and SSL Security proxy. Then you can leave the next three fields blank.
- **FTP proxy.** If the second field is set to No, enter this proxy's host name or IP address and port number.
- **Gopher proxy.** If the second field is set to No, enter this proxy's host name or IP address and port number.
- **Security proxy.** If the second field is set to No, enter this proxy's host name or IP address and port number.
- **HTTP Tunnel proxy.** Enter this proxy's host name or IP address and port number.
- **SOCKS proxy.** Enter this proxy's host name or IP address and port number.

- **No proxy for these hosts and domains.** These are servers or hosts that users should access directly—without passing through a proxy server. Usually these are servers or hosts on the user's own LAN. Enter domain names, host names, and IP addresses. Use "★" as a wildcard for any part of a name or address (for example, 192.168.0.★).

MIME tab. This tab has one field, Format for messages addressed to internet addresses which cannot be found when sending. The choices are "Notes Rich Text Format" (the default) and "MIME format." Your choice here will become the setting for the "Format for messages addressed to internet addresses" field in the users' Location documents. When a Notes user sends a message, Notes looks in various directories for a Person document for the addressee and if it finds one, checks a field called "Format preference for incoming mail" to determine how it should format the message for that addressee—in Notes Rich Text format or MIME format. If Notes can't find a Person document for the addressee or the choice in the field is "No Preference," Notes will use the setting that you enter here.

Administration tab. The two fields under this tab, Owners and Administrators, serve the same purpose as they serve on all other documents in the Domain Directory—to designate editors for this document. They both default to the name of the author of the document, but you can add names of other users, servers, or groups.

Setting Up the Default Execution Control List

The Execution Control List (ECL) is a feature of the Notes client intended to protect the user from maliciously written programs running inside Notes, that is, from email viruses and the like. In the Notes client, you can access the ECL on the Basics page of the User Preferences dialog box by clicking the Security Options button. This opens the Workstation Security: Execution Control List dialog box, as depicted in Figure 5.1.

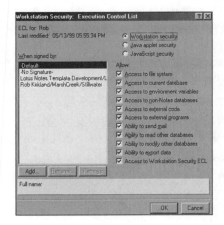

Figure 5.1   By default, LotusScript programs can perform all actions.

The ECL looks and works much like a database access control list. You can add user names, group names, server names, or wild cards representing organizations or organizational units to the "When signed by" list on the left. Then you can select one of the entities and, to the right, check off as many of the "Allow" boxes as you want. The "Allow" boxes represent potentially dangerous actions that programs running in Notes can carry out. Notes maintains three separate lists of entities and allowed actions, represented by the three radio buttons in the top-right corner of the dialog box:

- **Workstation security.** Protects against potentially dangerous LotusScript actions and formulas.

- **Java applet security.** Protects against potentially dangerous actions that Java applets can perform.

- **JavaScript security.** Protects against potentially dangerous JavaScript actions.

When a program tries to carry out one of the actions in the lists, Notes determines whether the signer of the program is authorized to carry out the action. If the signer is not listed or the program is not signed, Notes permits the program to carry out the actions allowed by the entries "–Default–" or "–No Signature–."

If a program tries to perform an action not permitted in the ECL, Notes will display an Execution Security Alert to the user, similar to the one that appears in Figure 5.2.

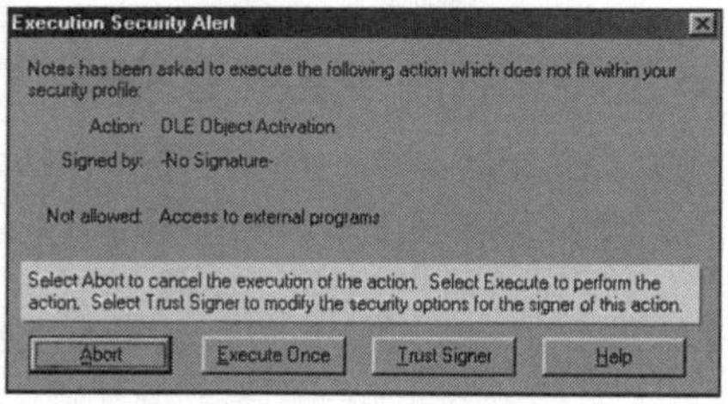

Figure 5.2   This dialog box appears if a program attempts to perform an action not authorized to its signer in the workstation's ECL.

The user will have to decide whether to allow the program to proceed, by choosing one of the buttons in the Execution Security Alert dialog box. The choices are

- **Abort.** Notes will not execute the requested action

- **Execute Once.** Notes will execute the requested action. If the same signer needs to execute the same action again later, the dialog box will reappear.

- **Trust Signer.** Notes will execute the requested action and update the ECL to authorize the signer to execute the same kind of action later without having to ask permission again.

- **Help.** Opens the Administrative Help database to the appropriate page for this dialog box.

By default the ECL is disabled. That is, all listed signers, including –Default– and –No Signature–, can perform all actions. Administrators can change the default, so that when they set up new users, the users' ECLs do restrict program execution in any ways the administrators desire. To change the default ECL, follow these steps:

1. In Domino Administrator, choose the Files tab.

2. In the Server pane, choose any accessible server in your domain.

3. Open the Domain Directory.

4. In the Actions menu, choose Edit Administration ECL. The Administration ECL appears, looking just like a workstation ECL. Change it as desired, then close it.

When you set up new users in the domain, Notes will inherit the defaults you set here. You can also push the changes to existing workstations. We'll cover that in Chapter 10, "Security."

One thing you may want to do at this time is designate a standard signer for your company, add it to the Administration ECL, and give it full execution rights. As your company develops new applications, you can have the designated signer sign them so that all users can run the applications without invoking Execution Security Alerts like the one in Figure 5.2.

The designated signer can be any registered user in your company, including one created just for the purpose of signing design templates. You can see an example of just such a signer in Figure 5.2—"Lotus Notes Template Development/Lotus Notes." This is an ID file that Lotus uses (or is supposed to, anyway) to sign Notes database templates that it includes with the Notes and Domino distribution disks.

Our example company, Stillwater Enterprises, might register a user called "Stillwater Template Development/Stillwater," then use that ID to sign databases that it develops or distributes to its users. You could also use it to sign templates and databases distributed with Notes and Domino that Lotus forgot to sign. There are quite a few of them in Release 5.0.

If you don't sign them, your users will be harassed by Execution Security Alerts. Then, they will discover that they can make the Execution Security Alerts disappear forever by choosing "Trust Signer." But, by doing that, they will effectively be telling Notes to trust unsigned programs to carry out the actions designated in the Execution Security Alerts. Later, when a malicious, unsigned program arrives in an email, the ECL won't be able to protect against it.

Whether you go to all this trouble depends on your company's security policies. Lotus distributes Notes with the ECL disabled by default, because it recognizes that most of its customers don't care enough about this threat to tangle with the ECL. If your company does care, you need to set up the ECL now, before you have set up lots of workstations, because it's harder to push your ECL onto established users than on new ones.

OU Certifiers

If you haven't created user organizational units yet (and you intend to assign users to them), now is the time to create them. Whether you will use OUs depends on policies that you should have established before now. If you haven't made that decision yet, read Chapter 2, "Planning an Installation," now to learn the pros and cons.

The detailed instructions for registering organizational units are in Chapter 3, "First Server Installation and Setup." We'll review the procedure briefly here. When you register an OU1 certifier, you use the O certifier to certify it. When you register an OU2 certifier, you use an OU1 certifier to certify it, and so on. To register any certifier, do the following:

1. Open the Configuration tab in Domino Administrator.

2. In the Tools pane, choose Registration, Organizational Unit.

3. Choose the new OU's parent certifier and enter its password.

4. Complete the fields in the Register Organizational Unit Certifier dialog box, then choose Register.

Alternate Names and Languages

If your organization has an International presence, you should enable the alternate names and languages feature. This allows you to assign two names to each user—a primary, internationally recognized name and a secondary name in the user's native language and character set. Notes can then display Notes documents and name lists to that user in either language.

This solves all sorts of problems. For example, in China, people's surnames come first and their given names last—just the opposite of European names. The alternate name feature would allow Chinese speakers to see their names in the correct order for them, and using Chinese characters. But Europeans would see the Chinese names in European order and using the Latin alphabet.

Another example is Latin American names, in which a person's written surname is composed of his father's and mother's last names, separated by a hyphen. When speaking, one usually refers to the person only by the name preceding the hyphen (his father's surname). But English speaking Americans typically blow it and use the name following the hyphen, because it's the "last" name. The alternate name feature would allow the Spanish speaker's surname to appear internationally as just his father's name, but to Spanish speakers as the hyphenated name.

To use this feature, you have to add alternate languages to the certifier IDs, starting with the O certifier. You can add as many languages to the certifier IDs as there are language specifiers recognized by Notes (38 languages as of R5.0). The O certifier must include every alternate language that you intend to use. The OU certifiers can include subsets of the languages included in the O certifier. User IDs can only include two languages, a subset of the languages its parent certifier includes.

For example, say /Stillwater includes four languages. /MarshCreek/Stillwater could include all four of those languages or any subset of them, but it couldn't include any languages other than those four, because you can only add languages to an OU that are already included in its parent. User ID Rob Kirkland/MarshCreek/Stillwater could include any two of the languages that /MarshCreek/Stillwater includes, but no languages other than those, and no more than two.

To add an alternate language and name to a certifier, you have to recertify it. You can add an alternate language and name to a user ID either during registration or by recertifying it.

Adding an Alternate Language to a Certifier ID

The procedure for adding an alternate language to a certifier ID is as follows:

1. Open the Configurations tab in Domino Administrator.

2. In the Tools pane, choose Certification, then choose Certify.

3. In the Choose Certifier Id dialog box, locate and select a certifier. If you are certifying the O certifier, choose the O certifier. If you are certifying an OU certifier, choose its parent certifier. Enter the password of the chosen certifier.

4. In the Choose ID to Certify dialog box, select the certifier to be recertified. If you are recertifying the O certifier, choose it again. Enter the certifier's password.

5. The Certify ID dialog box appears. The field Subject name list appears in it. Choose Add.

6. The Specify Alternate Organization Name (or Specify Alternate Organizational Unit Name) dialog box appears. Fill in the fields:

   - **Language.** Choose an alternate language. If you are certifying the O certifier, all language specifiers recognized by Notes are available. If you are certifying an OU certifier, only the languages included in its parent are available.

   - **Country code.** This field is optional and only available when adding a name to the O certifier. OU certifiers inherit the O certifier's country code. Enter a 2-character ISO country code here only if your organization has decided as a policy to use the country code as part of the organization's name.

   - **Organization.** This field appears when recertifying an O certifier. You have to choose a new, unique name, not used by any other language specifier. For example, say in our example organization that we chose Spanish as an alternate language. Its English name is /Stillwater. Notes won't let its Spanish name be /Stillwater. We have to come up with something different and unique. It could be a Spanish equivalent—say, for example, /AguaSerena. Or it might simply be something like /Stillwater.sp.

- **Org Unit.** This field appears when recertifying an OU certifier. Here (unlike in the alternate O name) you *do not* have to supply a unique name. For example, if a certifier's name in English is /MarshCreek/Stillwater, its Spanish name could be /MarshCreek/AguaSerena. Because the O component of the name provides uniqueness, the OU component need not be unique.

7. Choose OK. The alternate name and language appear in the Subject name list.

8. Repeat steps 5 through 9 to add other alternate languages. You can also choose Rename or Remove if you change your mind about the alternate name or the inclusion of an alternate language.

9. If you are recertifying an OU certifier, check the Expiration date field. The expiration date of this ID file was originally set 100 years from the date the O certifier was created. But when you recertify an OU, Domino Administrator (R5.0) wants to reset the expiration date to two years from today's date. You may prefer not to accept the default, but rather to set the expiration date about 100 years into the future, as it was originally set.

10. When finished, choose Certify.

What Happens When You Add a Language to a Certifier?

What happens during the recertification process is that the parent certifier issues new certificates to the child certifier (except that the O certifier issues new certificates to itself). In this case, the parent certifier issues certificates that identify all of the child's alternate names with the child's public key. You can see what I mean by examining the contents of an ID that includes an alternate name. To do so, follow these steps:

1. Open the Configuration tab in Domino Administrator.

2. In the Tools pane, choose Certification, ID Properties.

3. Locate and choose the ID you want to examine. Enter its password.

4. The "User ID – *IDname*" dialog box appears. Choose Certificates. There you'll see all certificates issued to the ID and to each of its ancestor certifiers, and the identities of the issuers. See Figure 5.3.

In the ID displayed in Figure 5.3, the Certificate issued by list shows /Stillwater three times (implying that the ID includes at least three certificates issued by /Stillwater). The first certificate is selected and the Certificate issued to list displays the entities to whom the certificate was issued. In this case, the certificate was issued to /Marshcreek/Stillwater and /MarshCreek/AguaSerena. That is, the certificate identifies the MarshCreek certifier's public key (in this case the International version of the public key) with both of its names.

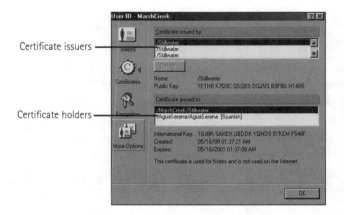

Certificate issuers

Certificate holders

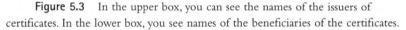

Figure 5.3   In the upper box, you can see the names of the issuers of certificates. In the lower box, you see names of the beneficiaries of the certificates.

We can't see it in Figure 5.3, but the second certificate was also issued to both /MarshCreek/Stillwater and /MarshCreek/AguaSerena, but in that case it identifies the North American version of the public key with the two names. The third certificate is a copy of the one /Stillwater issued to itself, and it binds Stillwater's public key to all of Stillwater's alternate names. (If this discussion makes your eyes glaze over, see Chapter 10, "Security," for an even more eye-glazing discussion of this topic.)

Basic User Registration

A full-fledged Notes user has a Person document in the domain Directory, is a member of various groups, has a mail database on a mail server, and has an ID file. The ID file includes at least one certificate signed by a certifier (that is, by you, the possessor of the certifier ID) and identifying the user with a unique public key. That public key and its corresponding private key are also stored in the ID file.

Luckily, you don't have to set all this stuff up by hand. Domino Administrator automatically generates the keys, the certificate(s), the ID file, the Person document, and the mail database, and adds the person to designated groups, all as part of the registration process. All you have to do is fill in a registration form, thereby providing Domino Administrator with the information it needs about the new user.

Prerequisites for the Registrar

However, before you can fill in the form, you have to meet certain conditions:

- You need access to or possession of the certifier ID that will certify the users you intend to register, and knowledge of its password.

- Your workstation needs access to the Domino server that will act as registration server.

- You need to be assigned the UserCreator role and at least Author Access to the Domain Directory on the registration server.

- You need at least Editor access to the certification log (certlog.nsf) on the registration server.

- You need "Create new databases" access to each new user's mail server if you plan to create his/her mail files during registration. (Alternatively, you can choose to create new users' mail databases when you set up their workstations, but in that case each new user must have "Create new databases" access to his/her mail server, and by default they do.)

If you are setting up a new domain and you followed the instructions in Chapters 3 and 4, all of these conditions will automatically be in place.

Setting Registration Defaults

In addition, you may want to set some registration defaults before you begin registering users. You can do this in Administration Preferences. In the File menu, choose Preferences, Administration Preferences. In the Administration Preferences dialog box, choose Registration. The options you can set include the following:

- **Registration domain.** Enter the name of the domain for which you are most likely to register users.

- **Registration server.** Enter the fully distinguished name of the server whose copy of the Domain Directory will receive the new Person document and changes to Group documents.

- **Certifier ID.** Locate and choose the certifier ID you are most likely to use when registering new users. You will be prompted for the password of the ID that you choose.

- **Mail system.** Choose the mail system most registered users will use. The choices are Lotus Notes, Other Internet, POP, IMAP, Other, and None. The next two fields only appear if you choose Lotus Notes, POP, or IMAP.

- **Mail server.** Choose or enter the fully distinguished name of the server on which newly registered users will access their mail databases.

- **Mail template.** Select the mail template on which the mail databases of most newly registered users will be based.
- **ID file folders.** Enter the path names of the folders in which new ID files (person, server, and certifier) should be saved.
- **Password quality settings.** Use the slider to set the default minimum password quality for each type of ID file (person, server, certifier). Lotus defaults them to 8 for people, 0 for servers, and 10 for certifiers. The scale is from 0 (password optional) through 16 (very strong passwords). Lotus chooses 0 for servers because they are usually located in secure areas and servers without passwords can restart unattended after a power failure. For people and certifiers, Lotus defaults to password qualities that should be hard to crack. How and if you reset these depend on your own organization's security policies.
- **Internet domain.** Enter the name of the Internet domain in which most newly registered users will dwell.
- **User setup profile.** Select from the list of available profiles the one which most newly registered users will fit.

You may want to make a habit of reviewing the registration defaults in Administration Preferences each time you are about to register a new group of users. If you have a lot of new users to register, setting correct defaults here can save you a lot of work later. Also, be sure to proofread your entries here before accepting them. An error here can cause lots of extra work for you later.

Filling in the Registration Form

Having met the preceding list of prerequisites and set the registration defaults, you are ready to register new users. Do so as follows:

1. Make sure you have the preceding described items in place before you start.
2. In Domino Administrator, choose either the People & Groups tab or the Configuration tab. You can register users from either place.
3. In People & Groups, choose Tools, People, Register. In Configuration, choose Tools, Registration, Person.
4. Domino Administrator tries to locate the certifier ID file named in the registration defaults. If none is named, it tries to locate the last used certifier. During this process you will see one or more of the following dialog boxes:
   - **Enter Password.** You have to enter the correct password to gain access to the contents of the certifier ID. When you see the Enter Password dialog box, make sure it is prompting you for the password of the certifier ID that you really want to use. If it is, enter the password and choose OK,

then proceed to step 5. If it is not, choose Cancel to choose another certifier ID. If users remain in the registration queue from a previous registration session, and they were defined to be registered with different certifiers than the current default, you will be prompted for the passwords of all certifiers involved.

- **Choose Certifier ID.** If Domino Administrator couldn't find an ID file or found one other that the one you want to use and you chose Cancel, it displays the Choose Certifier ID dialog, where you can locate and choose the correct certifier ID.

- **Domino Administrator.** If you have not yet installed ID recovery information in the certifier ID (and you would not have if you are following the procedures as outlined in this book—that's in the next section of this chapter), this dialog box may appear to warn you that the certifier ID contains no recovery information. Choose Yes or No to close it.

5. Finally a dialog box titled Register Person — New Entry appears. This dialog box is a relatively complex affair. See Figure 5.4 and the bullet list that follows for details.

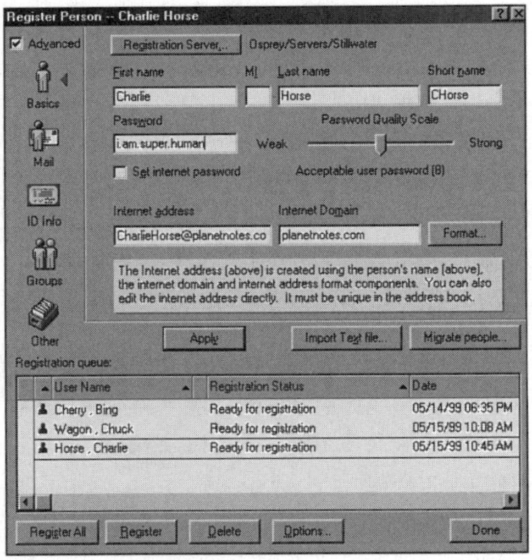

Figure 5.4   This is the "Advanced" user entry screen. Deselect Advanced to hide the Mail, ID Info, and Other screens. Users ready to be registered appear in the Registration Queue.

- **Registration form.** The top half of the dialog box consists of either two or five screens (depending on whether you select Advanced in the top-left corner of the dialog box) of fields (described later) for you to complete.

- **Registration queue.** The bottom half of the dialog box is the registration queue, a list of users ready to be registered.

- **Add Person.** You will fill in the two or five screens of information for each user, then choose Add Person. The person will appear in the registration queue list.

- **Import Text file.** Instead of entering people manually in the Register Person dialog, you can import them via a delimited text file. For the details of this technique, see Chapter 6, "Advanced Client Setup."

- **Migrate people.** Domino Administrator can migrate users from other systems, including Lotus cc.Mail, Windows NT, Microsoft Exchange, Microsoft Mail, LDAP directories (via LDIF file), Novell GroupWise 4.1 and 5.0, and Netscape Messaging Server. For details of this technique, see Chapter 6, "Advanced Client Setup."

- **Register** and **Register All.** When you are finished adding new people (or before you are finished—it doesn't really matter when), you can choose either Register or Register All to cause Domino Administrator to finish the registration process on either selected users in the queue or all users in the queue. Unless you changed the way the registration process works (see "Options" later in this list), successfully registered users will disappear from the registration queue, and unsuccessfully registered users will show a changed status in the queue.

- **Apply.** You can select one or more users in the registration queue, then edit choices you made earlier for them in the top half of the screen. The Add User button becomes the Apply button when you make edits to users already in the Registration Queue. Choose Apply to accept the changes and change the label back to Add User.

- **Delete.** You can choose Delete to remove selected users from the registration queue.

- **Options.** You can also choose Options to change several aspects of the way the Register Person dialog works.

  - **Do not continue on registration errors.** If the registration process encounters an error, it normally stops trying to register the person for whom it encountered the error and continues registering the rest of the people in the list. Checking this box causes the registration process to halt entirely upon occurrence of an error.

  - **Keep successfully registered people in the queue.** People normally disappear from the queue when registered successfully. Checking this box causes them to remain, showing a status of Registered.

- **Try to register queued people with error status.** If you check this box, the registration process will try to register a person despite the occurrence of an error that would normally cause failure.

- **Allow registration of previously registered people.** I'm not sure why you would want to do this, but it is an option.

- **Don't prompt for a duplicate person.** Normally, if a registrant has the same full name or short name as an existing user, Domino Administrator will ask you if you want to update the existing user with the new information. If you check this box and choose "Skip the person registration," attempts to register a person with a duplicate name will automatically fail. If you choose "Update the existing address book entry," Domino Administrator will update the existing user without asking your permission.

- **Don't prompt for a duplicate mail file.** Normally, if a mail file already exists with the same filename as that chosen for the registrant, Domino Administrator will prompt you to change the filename. If you check this box, you have three options. Choose "Skip the person registration" to have such a condition result in automatic failure. Choose "Generate a unique mail file name to have Domino Administrator change the filename for you. Choose "Replace the existing mail file" to have Domino Administrator overwrite the existing mail file without asking your permission. The last choice will work only if you have Manager access to the existing mail file. Also, it will fail if the Administration Process will be required to create the mail file. This would be the case if you choose "Create file in background" on the Mail screen of the registration form.

- **Done.** When you are finished registering users (or if you get interrupted before you finish), choose Done to close the dialog box. If there are unregistered users in the queue (or there is an un-added person in the top half), you will be prompted to save the unregistered users. If you save, the data will be stored in a local database called User Registration Queue (userreg.nsf) and will reappear in the queue next time you register users at the same workstation.

Fields in the Register Person Dialog Box

The fields you have to fill out to register a person depend on whether you choose Advanced in the Register Person dialog box. If you don't choose Advanced, you only have to enter the user's name and password and choose to what groups the person will be added. All other fields get default settings. If you have a lot of users to register, you definitely want the system to set as many fields as possible. To that end, if the default settings won't accommodate all users to be registered, here are a couple strategies that can automate data entry for you:

Strategy one: Set defaults in Administration Preferences as described earlier. Then, with Advanced deselected, enter all users by entering just their names and passwords. Then go through the list in the registration queue, selecting users who will have similar settings. (To select multiple users, click in the leftmost column to add a checkmark next to each user you want to select.) Select Advanced and enter data that is incorrect but unique to this group. Fields that must be unique for each user are grayed out. Choose Apply to apply the changed settings to all selected users. Repeat this process until settings for all users in the registration queue are correct.

Strategy two: Select Advanced, then enter data for one user, and add the user to the registration queue. Deselect Advanced and add other users, entering only their names and passwords (and groups, if you want). Their nonunique settings will be the same as the first user you entered. Repeat this process for each group of users whose settings are unique.

The idea here, of course, is to minimize tedium and time spent. In the process, you also minimize the opportunity to commit error. Which brings me to one last point: Be careful entering data. Proofread everything you enter. Errors create future hassles. Errors applied to multiple users create multiple future hassles.

The fields in the Register Person form are in Table 5.1.

Table 5.1   **Fields in Register Person Form**

Field Name (An entry is optional in all fields unless otherwise indicated.)	Description
	BASICS
First name	The user's given name.
MI	The user's middle initial. You can enter up to two characters in this field, enough for a letter and a period, if desired. Decide as a policy whether to use a period with middle initials. That is, use a period either always or never.
Last name	Required field. The user's surname.
Short name	Domino Administrator automatically creates this, using the user's first initial and last name. This name should be unique in the domain. If you know that it is not, change it. If you're not sure, leave it. At registration time, if it is not unique, Domino Administrator will by default notify you and give you an opportunity to change it.

continues

Table 5.1 **Continued**

Field Name (An entry is optional in all fields unless otherwise indicated.)	Description
	BASICS
Password	Required field (unless the Password Quality Scale is set to 0). This is the password that unlocks a user's ID file. You should encourage users to change their password immediately after their workstation is set up. You can encourage users to do this by making the password either hard to remember (using random characters) or very long. If you don't use a standard password for all users, be sure to write down the password somewhere. After the user name disappears from the registration queue, Notes will no longer display the password anywhere.
Password Quality Scale	Sets the minimum password quality, ranging from 0 (password optional) to 16 (very strong). Use the slider to change it. Notes judges a password's quality according to an algorithm that takes into account whether the password includes words in the Notes spell check dictionary, and whether it includes mixed case characters, numbers, spaces, and non-alphanumeric characters. Depending on the mix of characters used, a password consisting of anywhere from 6 to 12 characters would be necessary to equal a quality of 8 on the scale.
Set internet	This is not the same password as the password described previously. It corresponds to a field in the Person document and is the password a Web user would have to enter to authenticate with a Domino Web server. If the field is blank in the Person document, the user will not be able to authenticate from a Web browser. Consider leaving this field blank and letting users enter an Internet password themselves in their Person document when and if they are ready to use a Web browser to access Domino Web servers.
Internet address	Domino Administrator creates an Internet mail address for the user automatically, using the user's name and the data in the Internet Domain field, and formatting it as directed in the Format button. Alternatively, you can edit the field directly to create any legal Internet mail name you want. If you don't provide Internet mail connectivity or you don't have a registered Internet domain name, you can leave this field blank.

Field Name (An entry is optional in all fields unless otherwise indicated.)	Description
	BASICS
Internet Domain	Enter the Internet domain (if any) in which the user resides.
Format	Clicking this button opens the Set Internet Address Format dialog box. There you can choose the Internet address name format and the separator to be used between the components of the user's Internet mail name. The defaults are FirstName Lastname with no separator. This would set my Internet mail name to RobKirkland@domainname. Other choices include variations of the user's first name, last name, and initials. You can choose an underscore, a dot, or an equal sign to separate the components.
	MAIL
Mail Server	This is the server on which the user's mail database will reside.
Mail file template	This is the design template on which the user's mail database will be based. Use Mail (R5.0) for users of Notes 5 or for users of POP or IMAP mail clients. Use one of the earlier mail templates for users of Notes 4.x.
About	Click this button to see the About This Database document of the selected design template.
Set database quota	Check the box and enter a number of megabytes to set the maximum size the user's mail database will be permitted to reach. After it reaches the quota size, the user won't be able to save mail messages.
Set warning threshold	Check the box and enter a number of megabytes to set a warning threshold for the user's mail database. When the databases reaches the threshold size, a warning message will appear in the Notes Log on the user's mail server. You can also set up the server to notify you when such a warning message appears. See Chapter 18, "Server Monitoring."
Mail system	The choices include Lotus Notes, Other Internet, POP, IMAP, Other, and None. Domino servers support Lotus Notes, POP, and IMAP mail. If you choose anything other than one of those, the next two fields will gray out.

continues

Table 5.1 **Continued**

Field Name (An entry is optional in all fields unless otherwise indicated.)	Description
	MAIL
Mail file name	Domino Administrator uses the user's short name as the mail database's filename. If you know of an existing mail file with the same name, you can edit the name directly to change it. If you are not sure if there is a conflict, you can leave the name as is. When you register the person, if a conflict exists, Domino Administrator will by default notify you and give you an opportunity to edit the file name.
Mail file owner	By default users have the highest possible access— Manager—to their own mail files. Some administrators prefer to give users lesser access, to keep inquisitive users out of trouble.
Create file now Create file in background	Choose one. "Create file now" is the default. If you choose "Create file in background," the Administration Process on the mail server will create the file later. This causes the registration process to proceed more quickly (because it won't have to wait while the mail file is created) but it may cause the registration to fail if a mail file of the same name already exists.
Create full text index	If you check this box, Domino Administrator will create a full text index for the mail database when it creates it. Full text indexes enable fast searches of databases but take up a lot of space on disk.
	ID INFO
Certifier ID	Click here to change the certifier ID for this user.
Security type	Choose International if setting up users who will be located outside of the United States and Canada.
Certificate expiration date	Defaults to two years from the current date, at which time the user will have to be recertified. Change it to any date you wish, but keep in mind that it is a good thing that IDs expire periodically. Otherwise, as time passes, employees come and go, and unused IDs accumulate, your exposure to the possibility of unauthorized server access increases.

Field Name (An entry is optional in all fields unless otherwise indicated.)	Description
	ID INFO
Location for storing user ID: In Domino directory In file	You can choose to store the newly created ID in the new user's Person document, as an ID file on disk, in both places, or no place. If you choose "In file," you can click the Set ID File button to choose the disk location and filename. Store new ID files in the Person document if you use hard-to-guess passwords. Store new ID files on disk if you use easy-to-guess passwords. Deselect both boxes when creating non-Notes users (for example, POP and IMAP mail users).
	GROUPS
Assign person to group(s)	A list of groups in the Domain Directory. Click a group to select it or select multiple groups by clicking in the left column to add checkmarks next to the groups you want to select.
Selected groups	Groups appearing in this column are the ones that the user will be added to.
Add, Remove, Remove All	Click the Add button to add groups selected in the left column to the right column. Click Remove to remove selected groups from the right column. Click Remove All to remove all groups from the right column.
	OTHER
Setup profile	Choose the user setup profile for this user.
Unique org unit	The purpose of fully distinguished names is to ensure than no two users have the same name. But the remote possibility exists that two people with the exact same first name, middle initial, and last name belong in the same OU. If you encounter that situation, enter a unique OU name in this field to differentiate this user from the other. No actual OU certifier exists for this OU. It is simply a standard method of differentiating same-name users.

continues

Table 5.1 **Continued**

Field Name (An entry is optional in all fields unless otherwise indicated.)	Description
	OTHER
Location	This field is purely for informational purposes. The information here will transfer to the Location field on the user's Person document.
Local administrator	You can enter the names of users or groups here. The users whose names appear here (if they have Author access to the Domain Directory) will be transferred to the Administrators field of this user's Person document and will have authority to edit this user's Person document. Use this field to assign highly limited administrative authority.
Comment	This field is purely for informational purposes. The information here will transfer to the Comment field on the user's Person document.
Alternate name language	If you use alternate name languages, choose a language from this list. See "Alternate Names and Languages" earlier in this chapter for more information.
Alternate name	Enter the user's name as it is written in the chosen alternate language.
Alternate org unit	If the user has been assigned a unique OU, enter here the OU name as it should appear in the chosen alternate language.
Add this person to Windows NT	Check this box if you want Domino Administrator to create an NT user account for this user. Clear this with your Windows NT administrators first.
Windows NT user name	If you checked the box in the previous field, enter the user's NT account name here.
Add person to Windows NT group	If you checked the box in the earlier field, choose an NT group here to add him to (for example, Domain Users).

Adding Recovery Information to Certifier IDs

Now that you have registered some administrative users (at least), you can set up ID and password recovery. New in Release 5, this feature automates the recovery of lost IDs and rehabilitation of IDs whose owners have forgotten their passwords. Under earlier versions of Domino/Notes you can replace an ID with an archive copy of it. But that isn't an ideal solution to the problem because the archive copy would most likely not reflect changes that had taken place in the ID over time—recertifications, addition of encryption keys, name changes, and the like. Also, under the archiving schemes used by most Notes organizations, the administrators keep unencrypted backup copies of all IDs and know their passwords, which makes the IDs vulnerable to misuse.

Under Release 5's new ID and password recovery scheme, the information necessary to open an ID in the event of a lost password is written right into the ID. The archive copy of each ID (needed to replace lost IDs) is stored in a Notes database in an encrypted form. And a new backup copy of each ID is automatically forwarded to the backup database whenever a change occurs in the user's working copy.

To take advantage of R5's ID recovery functions, you have to add recovery information to the IDs. The best time to do that is when the IDs are first created, because then it is added automatically. If you don't get around to initializing the recovery system until after you have created lots of servers and users, it's harder to initialize those IDs because the owners of those IDs have to cooperate in the process. And users are often too busy or preoccupied with their own business to cooperate with administrators in any active way. It's especially difficult to initialize IDs for people who have multiple copies of their ID. They (or you) have to perform each ID for recovery separately or they have to copy the ID that has recovery information added to it over the other copies of the ID.

In other words, you want to initialize the ID/password recovery process now, before you register any more servers or users. There's one catch, though. You have to register the administrators who will participate in ID recovery before you set it up, because their public keys are needed at setup time.

Under R5 ID and password recovery, an encrypted copy of each user's ID file is stored in a database created for that purpose. The ID file is encrypted with one or more randomly generated passwords, each of which is itself encrypted with an administrator's public key. Thus, to decrypt the archived ID file, the administrator associated with each encrypted password must decrypt it.

When you set up ID/password recovery, you have to decide how many administrators must cooperate to decrypt an ID file. It can be as few as one, but Lotus recommends at least three, so as to make it difficult for administrators to decrypt users' IDs for unauthorized purposes. You can set it up so that, for example, IDs are encrypted with five different administrators' public keys, but that only three (any three) of those five are necessary to decrypt. That way, if administrators A and B are not available to decrypt, administrators C, D, and E can still get the job done.

Just how many "decrypters" you should designate depends on your organization's security policies. I consider 3–5 to be very secure. You may feel comfortable requiring only two people to decrypt and ID, or even one if the danger of impostors using stolen IDs doesn't exactly keep you awake nights.

If you don't have enough administrators to fill every signer role that you want to create, you can designate nonadministrators as signers as well. Just be sure to designate people you judge to be relatively stable, long-term members of your organization. Over time, as designated decryptors leave your organization for greener pastures, you'll have to update the password recovery information in your certifier IDs. As you do, Notes will automatically refresh the information in the IDs of existing users.

Some organizations may decide to create fictional IDs for this purpose, to be switched to just for the purpose of decrypting IDs. This is similar to a not uncommon practice in the Notes community of designating a fictional ID to be used when carrying out any administrative chores. One consultant I know always uses the name "Primary Administrator" during first server setup, then has his client administrators switch to the "Primary Administrator" ID when performing administrative chores. This is similar to the practice whereby network administrators login as "Admin," "Administrator," "Supervisor," "SuperUser," or "root," when carrying out network administration chores.

I personally don't recommend the use of "designated" administrator IDs. They defeat the whole Notes scheme of positively identifying users. If you have several administrators walking around, all of them switching to "Primary Administrator/Stillwater" whenever they do any administrative work, you lose your audit trail. You have no way of knowing who did what.

To set up ID/password recovery you have to do the following things:

1. Create a mail-in database for storage of backup copies of users' ID files.

2. Add recovery information to certifier ID files. That information includes:

   - The names of administrators who will participate in the recovery process
   - The Mail-In name of the mail-in ID storage database
   - The number of administrators required to recover an ID file

3. Update any preexisting user IDs with the recovery information. (IDs registered with certifier IDs that already contain recovery information automatically have that information added to them.)

Creating the Mail-In Database

When you create the mail-in database in step 1, you can use any database template. Lotus suggests the mail template. If you have disk space to burn, that will be okay. However, I suggest you create your own database instead. Maybe I'm just getting old, but the notion of using the mail template with its 5.3MB of bells and whistles to store backup ID files, when a simple 400MB database with a single view and a single form would do the job just as well, sort of sticks in my craw. So, I suggest you create a database based on no design template and then create the view and form yourself. I'll explain what the form and view need to contain a little further on.

But first you need to create a mail-in database. Follow these steps:

1. In Domino Administrator, choose File, Database, New. The New Database dialog box opens. Fill in the fields as follows (see Figure 5.5):

    - **Server.** Choose the server on which the database will reside. Do not leave the field set to Local unless you are using a copy of Domino Administrator that shares data folders with a server.

    - **Title.** Enter any title, up to 32 characters in length. For example: **ID Recovery Database**.

    - **File name.** Enter any filename. For example: **idrecovery.nsf**.

    - **Encryption.** Don't enable local encryption of this database. Each entry is automatically encrypted by the Administration Process.

    - **Template Server.** Either leave as is and leave the item "-Blank-" selected or change it to the name of the server on which the database will reside, then choose the mail template, "Mail (R5.0)." (An R4 mail template would be acceptable too.)

2. Choose Advanced. In the Advanced Database Options dialog box, check the following items:

    - Don't maintain unread marks

    - Don't Support specialized response hierarchy

    - Don't allow headline Monitoring

3. Choose OK to return to the New Database dialog box. Choose OK again. The database will be created on the server with your name and the server's name set as Manager in the ACL. And it will be open on your screen.

4. With the new database open on the screen, choose File, Database, Access Control. The Access Control List Dialog box opens. Set -Default- to No Access. Add your Administrators group and set its user type to Person Group and its access to Reader. Choose OK to close the dialog box. You can also close the database at this time.

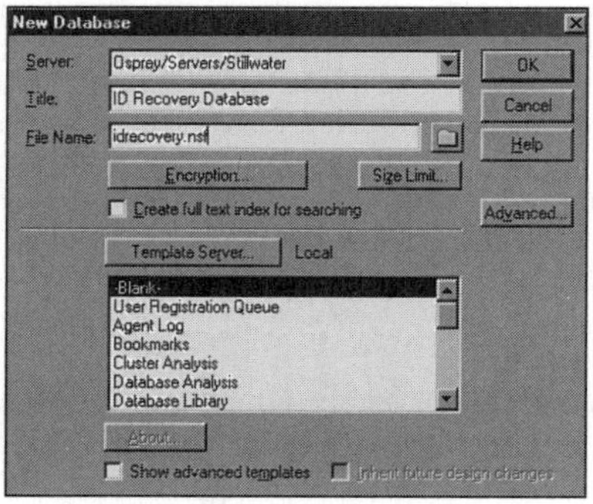

Figure 5.5   You only have to choose a server,
a title, and a filename to create an ID recovery database.

Creating a Mail-In Database Document

Your database isn't a mail-in database yet. To complete the process, follow these steps:

1. In Domino Administrator, make sure a server in your domain is selected, then go to People & Groups.

2. Choose Mail-In Databases & Resources in the Tasks pane (left side of screen). That view will appear in the Results pane (center of screen).

3. Click the Add Mail-In Database action (center of screen above the view). This opens a Mail-In Database form. Fill in the fields as follows:

   Basics Tab:

   - **Mail-In Name.** Enter any descriptive name. For example: ID Recovery Archive. It does not have to be the same as the filename or title of the database you just created, but it may be if you wish. What you enter here will be used as the database's mailing address, and you will reenter it later, when you add recovery information to the certifier ID.

   - **Description.** Enter any descriptive text that will remind you or your successor in the future of the purpose of this document. For example: "The ID and Password Recovery database."

   Database Information tab:

   - **Domain.** Enter your domain name. In our example: Stillwater.

   - **Server.** Enter the fully distinguished name of the server on which the database is stored. (If stored on more than one server, enter only one server name.) In our example: Osprey/Servers/Stillwater.

- **Filename.** Enter the filename of the database on the server named in the preceding field. In our example: **idrecovery.nsf**.

4. Save and close the new mail-in database document.

Creating a Form and a View

If you didn't use a design template when you created the ID recovery database, you need to create a form and a view, so Administrators can find people's backup ID files. To do this, you'll need to work in a copy of Domino Designer.

Creating the Form

The form will have three fields: a text field named "From," a Date/Time field called "ComposedDate," and a rich text field called "Body." See Figure 5.6.

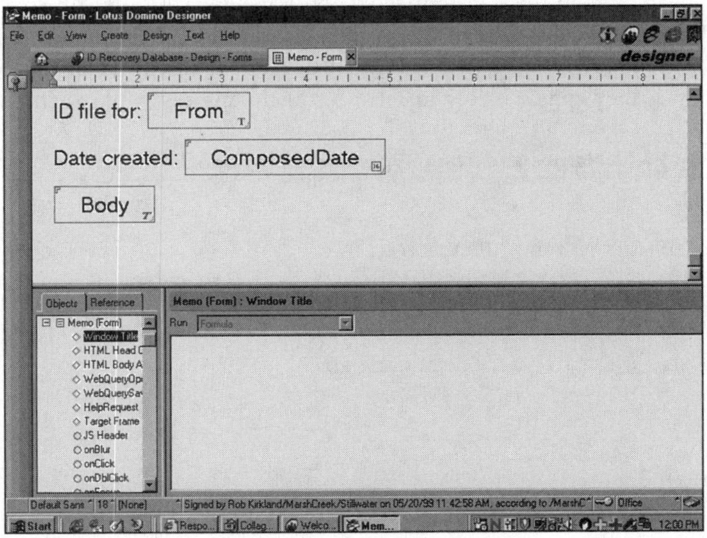

Figure 5.6   In a small form like this one, make the text as large as you want. The text here is 18-point.

To add this form to the database, follow these steps:

1. Open your database in Domino Designer. You can do this in several ways. One easy way, if it is open on your screen, is to choose Design in the View menu.

2. The database will open to the Forms view. If it doesn't, click the Recent Databases bookmark (on the right edge of screen) to open the Design pane. An icon for your database will appear there. Expand the icon to show the views. Choose Forms. An empty list of forms will appear in the Work pane.

3. Click the New Form button at the top of the Work pane. A new form will appear.

4. In the menu, choose Design, Form Properties.

5. In Form Properties, Form Info tab, complete the following fields, then close the Properties box:

   - **Name.** Call this form "Memo."

   - **Display.** Deselect the "Include in menu" checkbox.

   - **Options.** Select "Default database form."

6. Type two field labels into the form on separate lines: "ID file for:" and "Date created:." Include the spaces following the colons. Refer to Figure 5.6.

7. Add two fields to the right of the field labels and a third field on the next line below them. To add a field, place the text insertion bar where you want the field to appear, then, in the Create menu, choose Field. Each time you create a new field, the field will appear in the form and the Field Properties box will open. Enter the following data in Field Properties for each field. Enter the field names exactly as they appear below in Table 5.2, including case and spacing.

Table 5.2 **Field Names and Data Types for the Memo Form**

For Field...	...Enter
FIRST FIELD (NEXT TO LABEL "ID FILE FOR: ")	
Name	From
Type	Text, Editable
SECOND FIELD (NEXT TO LABEL "DATE CREATED: ")	
Name	ComposedDate
Type	Date/Time, Editable
THIRD FIELD	
Name	Body
Type	Rich Text, Editable

8. Save and close the form.

Creating the View

Next we'll turn the existing untitled view into something usable. We'll name it "By Name" and set up two columns, the first column to hold the Author's name, the second to show the Creation Date. Both columns will be sorted ascending. See Figure 5.7.

Figure 5.7   If you point to a tab in a Properties box for a second or two, the tab's name will appear in a pop-up box.

To create this view, follow these steps:

1. In Domino Designer, click the Recent Databases icon (right edge of screen) to open the Design pane. Under the icon for your database, choose Views. A list of forms will appear in the Work pane.

2. Open the view called (Untitled) by double-clicking it.

3. In the menu choose Design, View Properties to open the View Properties box.

4. In View Properties, View Info tab, in the Name field, enter "By Name."

5. There is currently one column in the view. In its column header a pound sign (#) appears. Double-click the column header at that point. The View Properties box becomes the Column Properties box. Make the changes as shown in Table 5.3.

Table 5.3   **Column Properties for Column One**

Label	Action
	COLUMN INFO TAB
Title	Delete the pound sign (#)
	SORTING TAB
Sort	Ascending

6. Making sure the header over the first column is still selected, choose "Simple Function" and "Author(s) (Simple Name)" in the Programmer's Pane (bottom right pane).

7. In the menu, choose Create, Append New Column.

8. In the Column Properties box for the new column, make the changes as in Table 5.4.

Table 5.4 **Column Properties for Column Two**

Label	Action
	SORTING TAB
Sort	Ascending
	DATE AND TIME FORMAT TAB
Show	Date only

9. Close the Column Properties box.
10. Making sure the header over the second column is still selected, choose Simple Function and Creation Date in the Programmer's pane (bottom right pane).
11. Save and close the view.

Adding Recovery Information to the Certifier ID

To add recovery information to a certifier ID, follow these steps:

1. In Domino Administrator, be sure a server is selected, and choose the Configuration tab.
2. In the Tools pane, choose Certification, Edit Recovery Information.
3. In the Choose Certifier ID dialog box, choose a certifier ID that will be used to register people. Choose Open. Enter the ID's password. The Edit Master Recovery Authority List dialog box opens (see Figure 5.8).

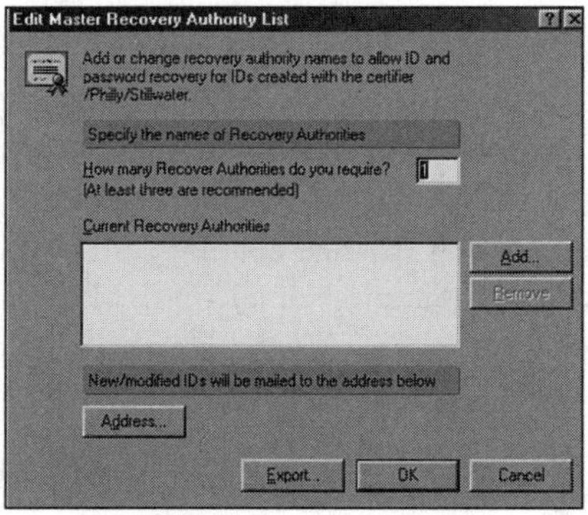

Figure 5.8 Add administrator names to the Current Recovery Authorities list. Insert the mail-in database name with the Address button. Decide how many administrators must act together to recover an ID.

4. Enter a number in the How many Recovery Authorities do you require? field. The more you are concerned about ID security, the more recovery authorities you should require to act. The number should be less than the number of people's names in the Current Recovery Authorities field and probably not more than 3.

5. Choose the Add button to add the names of administrators to the Current Recovery Authorities field. To be added, one must have a Person document in an available directory and a valid public key in the Person document (see the Notes certified public key field of the Person document).

6. Either choose OK to close the dialog box or choose Export to export the new recovery information to existing users certified with this certifier. See the details of the export procedure in the next section.

Exporting Recovery Information to Existing Users

At this time, you should export the new recovery information to existing users certified with the updated certifier ID. Follow these steps:

1. Reopen the Edit Master Recovery Authority List dialog box, if you closed it in the preceding step 6.

2. Choose Export. Enter the certifier ID's password.

3. The Mail ID File Recovery Information dialog box appears. Add the names of existing users to the To field. Remember to add only users who were certified by this certifier ID. To tell more easily who those users are, press the Address button, change "List by name" (lower left corner of the Select Addresses dialog box) to "Notes name hierarchy", then expand the O or OU represented by the certifier ID you are currently working with. The names of people you want to add will be listed beneath that O or OU.

4. You may optionally add information to the other fields. For example, you might want to add some explanation to the body field, something such as, "This will allow us to recover your password should you forget it or to recover your ID file should it become lost or corrupted in the future."

5. Click Send to send this message to the addressees and close the dialog box. Click OK to close the Edit Master Recovery Authority List dialog box.

When an addressee of the mail message receives it, he should choose Accept Recovery Information in his Action menu. When he does, he'll be prompted for his password, then the Backup ID File dialog box will appear. The addressee should choose Send.

   This causes the recovery information to be merged into the user's ID file, and a copy of the ID file to be mailed to the ID recovery database, where it will be stored until needed. The mailed copy of the user's ID will be encrypted with a random encryption key which will in turn be encrypted by the public keys of the current recovery authorities, therefore only decryptable by them.

A few final points:

- All users registered with this certifier ID in the future will automatically have a copy of their ID placed in the ID recovery database at registration time.

- If, at a future time, you change the recovery information in a certifier ID (perhaps by adding a new recovery authority or removing one), you should export the new recovery information to all then-current users, and they should accept it, just as described previously.

- In the "unlikely event" that a user actually loses or corrupts an ID file or forgets a password, see Chapter 12, "User Maintenance and Troubleshooting," to learn how to recover the ID file or password.

Basic Client Installation and Setup

After you have registered a user, you can install and configure Notes on the user's workstation. To install Notes you run InstallShield (`setup.exe`), then choose some options. InstallShield performs the actual installation. To configure Notes, you run Notes for the first time on the user's workstation, then choose some options. Notes then carries out the actual configuration.

Installing Notes

There are several ways to install Notes on a user's workstation. You can start from the AutoRun front-end or from InstallShield. You can install from the Notes distribution CD-ROM or you can copy the contents of the CD-ROM to a file server and install from there. You can do a standard install or a shared install. In a shared install, multiple users share one program folder but maintain separate data folders. Finally you can automate the installation process with a response file (see Chapter 6 for more on that subject).

What Programs Should You Install?

When you install Notes, you might also want to install other programs that are on the distribution CD-ROM. The possibilities are

- **Adobe Acrobat Reader.** Reads Adobe PDF (Portable Document Format) files. The main reason this program is on the CD-ROM is so that you, the installer, can read and print a formatted copy of the release notes (readme.pdf) before you do any installs.

- **Domino Global WorkBench.** This is for application developers only. It allows them to more easily develop multilingual applications.

- **Actioneer for Lotus Notes.** This is a small program that a Notes user can load into memory at computer startup. It enables you to add entries to your calendar, to-do list, and personal journal without running Notes. You just pop up the Actioneer window (by double-clicking its icon in the Windows tray or pressing a hotkey combination) and start typing. Actioneer parses as you type, figures out whether you are creating a calendar, to-do, or journal entry, and enters your words into the correct Notes fields. Pretty cool, really.

- **IBM ViaVoice Runtime.** At some point after R5, Actioneer for Lotus Notes will gain the Ability to respond to spoken commands. When it does, it will use IBM ViaVoice Runtime. You can, if you want, install the runtime now, so that it will be in place when the Actioneer upgrade arrives.

The combination of programs that you install on a workstation depends on what the user will be doing:

- **Most Notes users.** On most workstations, you will install Notes, probably also Actioneer for Lotus Notes, and possibly IBM ViaVoice Runtime.

- **Application developers.** You will install Domino Designer instead of Notes (both Notes and Designer will actually be installed), and possibly also Domino Global WorkBench. Also Actioneer for Lotus Notes and IBM ViaVoice Runtime.

- **Domino administrators.** You will install Domino Administrator instead of Notes (both Notes and Domino Administrator will actually be installed). Also Actioneer for Lotus Notes and IBM ViaVoice Runtime.

For some users, yourself probably included, you will want to install all three of the Notes client front-ends, that is, Lotus Notes, Domino Designer, and Domino Administrator. Remember, however, to install only what you have properly licensed.

If anyone in your organization uses SmartSuite alongside Notes R5, you should install the SSN5 Update for Notes 5 and SmartSuite. This corrects a bug that causes SmartSuite applications to run extremely slowly when Notes 5 is running. It is located in the \Apps\SmartSuite folder on the CD-ROM.

If you need to work with character sets other than the Latin character set, the CD-ROM has a set of TrueType fonts on it that support Greek, Cyrillic, Slavic, Turkish, Arabic, Hebrew, Japanese, Korean, and Simplified and Traditional Chinese character sets.

AutoRun Front-End Versus InstallShield

The primary benefits of using the AutoRun front-end that comes on the CD-ROM are esthetic. You get to see a nice, short (about 15 seconds) introductory animation, accompanied by a driving, upbeat musical riff. You get to make your initial choices in a pretty, push-button interface. Most importantly, it draws your attention to things Lotus thinks you should be aware of (such as the Guided Tours), but that you might miss if simply exploring a listing of folders.

When you finally click an Install button to install Notes, the front-end runs InstallShield for you with your front-end choices preselected in InstallShield. That way, you deal with fewer screens in InstallShield and that portion of the installation goes more quickly.

You should definitely explore the AutoRun front-end at least once. But if, after that, you prefer to skip the pretty pictures and run InstallShield directly, you can navigate in Windows Explorer to the appropriate folder and run `setup.exe` (for the Notes clients—`install.exe` or `programname.exe` for some of the other applications). InstallShield will then ask you all the things the front-end would have asked you. You'll end up in the same place, whether you run InstallShield directly or indirectly.

CD-ROM Versus Network Installation

It doesn't matter to Notes where its distribution files are located during installation. If you are installing Notes on workstations connected to a LAN, you might conclude that it is more convenient for you to access the distribution files on a file server than to tote a CD-ROM around with you. If you are installing Notes on workstations that have no access to a file server (or slow WAN access), you'll want to install from the CD-ROM.

When you copy the contents of the CD-ROM to a file server, you can copy everything, including the AutoRun front-end, or just individual folders full of distribution files. AutoRun is in a folder of that name, so copy it if you want.

The Notes 5.0 CD-ROM includes Notes clients for Intel versions of Windows (Windows 95, 98, and NT) and the Alpha version of Windows NT. Later CD-ROMs will also include a version for the Macintosh PowerPC. Each version of the client is in its own folder. All the other applications are in their own folders inside the Apps folder.

Standard Install Versus Shared Install

A standard installation of Notes puts the Notes program and data folders where you direct and puts `notes.ini` (an ASCII text initialization file) in the Notes program folder. As an alternative, you can do a shared installation (it's one of the choices you make in InstallShield). In a shared installation, multiple users share a single Notes program folder, which would typically be installed on a file server (*not* a Domino server) accessible to all of the sharing users.

Setting up a shared program directory has a couple of advantages. First, you save disk space on users' workstations. Second, and more importantly, when you want to upgrade Notes, you can upgrade numerous users by upgrading a single program folder. There are also two disadvantages. Users have to pull Notes program files across the network every time they run it. This increases network traffic and may impact the performance of Notes and many other applications. The server on which the program files reside is a single point of failure. Also, Notes upgrades often replace not only program files but database templates as well. In such an upgrade situation, you would have to install the data files on every user's workstation anyway, so the benefit of only having to install the program files once is pretty marginal.

When you choose to do a shared installation of Notes, nothing appears to change. That is, you still have to choose a program folder and a data folder, and InstallShield goes ahead and installs both the program and data files (overwriting the program files it installed before). The difference is that it installs `notes.ini` in the Windows folder instead of the Notes program folder. It can't install `notes.ini` in the program folder because each user must have in individual copy of `notes.ini`.

There are two other variations of the shared installation, as well. First, some administrators like to install users' data folders on a file server as well, usually in each user's home folder. This provides two benefits. Combined with Windows NT roaming profiles, this allows users to log on to the Windows NT domain from any computer and have his/her Notes program and data files available. Also, it's easier to arrange for backup of users' data files if they are on a file server than if they are on the users' own workstations.

Second, you can install the program files on the user's workstation and the local data files in the user's home folder on the network. This lets users run Notes locally and lets you provide backup services for user data in a central location. In addition, users can run Notes from any workstation with Notes installed on it; they just have to log in to the network as themselves first, so that they'll have access to their own home folder.

If you do this, you may want to edit the `notes.ini` file to have the cache (`cache.dsk`) file located locally. Notes will rebuild it on startup and it will give the user faster performance, because the cached design elements are local instead of on the network. It reduces traffic as well.

There are a few variations, like having the `desktop.dsk` , `notes.ini` and `user.id` in both places (on file server and local) but synchronizing them can be a challenge. NT replication can do it. A batch file arrangement can work too. You'll definitely want to tinker with it to work out the details.

To set up users so their data files reside on a file server, you have to manually copy each user's `notes.ini` file from the Windows or local Notes folder to his/her home folder on the file server. Then, you have to edit the command line of each user's shortcuts to tell Notes to look for `notes.ini` in the user's data folder. There are two ways to do this. You can edit either the Target field or the Start in field in the shortcut dialog box.

Edit the Target field as follows. The standard Notes shortcut command line (where the Notes program files are located at `p:\notes`) looks like this:

```
p:\notes\notes.exe
```

Edit it (where the user's data folder is located at `h:\notes`) so that it looks like this:

```
n:\notes\notes.exe =h:\notes\notes.ini
```

In this command line there is a space preceding the equal sign but no space following it.

Alternatively, edit the Start in field (again where the user's data folder is located at h:\notes) so that it looks like this:

```
h:\notes
```

Make sure you map the Notes data folder to a drive letter. The Windows shortcut could accept and understand a command line that uses the Windows universal naming convention (for example, \\computername\resource) instead of mapped drive letters. But notes.ini must use drive letters. In particular, the variable Directory in notes.ini points to the location of the Notes data files, and uses drive-letter notation, so the mapped drive letter must remain the same (that is, always h: in the above examples) no matter where the roaming user logs in.

Installation Procedure

Because the order in which you make decisions during the installation process is different, depending on whether you install from the AutoRun front-end or run InstallShield directly, I won't describe the installation procedure in steps, but rather in general. The choices you have to make are as follows:

- Whether to accept the license agreement.
- Whether to perform a shared installation. See the preceding discussion of this subject.
- The location of the program and data folders.
  - If Notes was never before installed on a given computer, the default folder locations are: programs in c:\lotus\notes; data files in c:\lotus\notes\data.
  - If Notes was previously installed on a given computer, InstallShield will probably offer to install it in the same folders as the previous installation occupied, whether or not the previous installation was removed. Also, you may want to make backup copies of names.nsf, desktop.dsk, notes.ini, and possibly other files before proceeding with an install that overwrites a previous installation of Notes.
  - Read the destination folders names carefully before accepting them. If you changed them, you may have made a typo. If Notes has found an old Notes installation, it may set the destination folders differently from what you want.

- What client(s) to install.

  - Choose Notes Client for your regular users.

  - Choose Domino Designer for your Notes application developers. (Both Notes and Domino Designer will install.)

  - Choose Domino Administrator for Domino administrators. (Both Notes and Domino Administrator will install.)

  - Choose All Clients for users who do both Notes development and administration.

- Whether to customize the installation. This allows you to pick and choose the files you want to install. As a general rule you should only customize an installation if you are installing on a computer with limited free disk space or you are, as an afterthought, installing some special file, such as additional help files.

- Where in the Windows menu to put the Notes shortcuts. By default, it puts them in a folder called Lotus Applications and puts one for Notes Minder in the Startup folder. Notes Minder is a memory-resident program that notifies the user when mail arrives.

Configuring Notes

To configure Notes, you simply run it for the first time. The fact that `notes.ini` is missing certain variables triggers Notes to run the Lotus Notes Client Configuration wizard. You make a series of choices in the wizard, then Notes uses that information to configure itself.

During the configuration process Notes will do the following things:

- Populate `notes.ini` with appropriate variables.

- Connect to the user's home server and retrieve certain information.

- Copy the user's ID file to the data folder if it isn't already there.

- Create a Personal Address Book database (`names.nsf`), a Notes Log database (`log.nsf`), a Headlines database (`headline.nsf`), a subscription database (`subscriptions.nsf`), and desktop and cache databases (`desktop5.dsk`, `cache.dsk`).

- Configure location documents in the Personal Address Book with information specific to the logged user.

- Add connections documents to the Personal Address Book, if necessary.

- Add Internet account documents to the Personal Address Book, if so instructed.

- Configure the user's Execution Control List.

We won't trace your progress through the Lotus Notes Client Configuration wizard here, because we already did that in Chapter 3, in the section titled "Setting Up the First User." We defined this chapter's target user as one that is located in the office and connected to a LAN and has no need to set up modem access to a server or Internet accounts. The process for setting up such a user is exactly as described in Chapter 3.

Chapter 3 also describes the problems that might arise while setting up this user. So if an error message rears its ugly head, refer to Chapter 3 to troubleshoot it.

The process for setting up users who need to connect to a server by modem is in Chapter 6. The process for setting up users who need access to Internet servers (mail, directory, news) is also in Chapter 6.

Other User Setup Issues

If you followed the procedure prescribed at the beginning of this chapter, you performed a set of preliminary user setup chores. Then, you registered the administrators who were to become recovery authorities and set up their Notes workstations. Then, you set up ID and password recovery (see the preceding section).

Now you are ready to register the rest of your users and install and configure their copies of Notes. If the total number of users you will register and set up is small, you may decide to do them the same way as described above. If you have a large number of users to set up, then you might prefer to automate these chores.

The following techniques, all detailed in Chapter 6, can automate the user registration and setup process, and may be of interest to you:

- Text-file user registration
- Registering Notes and Windows NT users simultaneously, from within either Notes or the Windows NT User Manager for Domains.
- Upgrading users from other email products
- Automating Notes installation
- Automating Notes configuration

Finally, you may have users with special needs. You may have mobile users who have to dial in to the office LAN or a Domino passthru server to reach their home servers. You may have users who need to connect to Internet mail servers, directory servers, or news servers. You may need to set up multiple Notes users on a single workstation. See the next chapter, "Advanced Client Setup," to learn how to set up all such users.

6

Advanced User Setup

IN THIS CHAPTER WE'LL CONTINUE TO EXPLORE THE process of setting up users. In Chapter 5, "User Registration and Client Setup," we covered the preliminary steps you should have taken before setting up any users and the basic user setup process. In this chapter we cover techniques that you'll love if you have a large number of users to register and set up. We also look at the setup process for users who have special needs—mobile users, users who have to communicate with Internet servers, and users who have to share a workstation.

We'll cover the following topics in this chapter:

- Registering units from a text file
- Registering Notes and Windows NT users simultaneously
- Upgrading users from other mail products and importing users from the Windows NT Security Accounts Manager
- Response file workstation setup
- Setting up mobile users
- Setting up Internet server access
- Setting up shared workstations

Advanced User Registration Techniques

If you have to register a large number of users, you will appreciate any tool that minimizes the amount of work you have to do. Domino has several such tools. First, you can enter user information once—in either the Domino user registration screen or in Windows NT's User Manager for Domains—and create both accounts simultaneously. Second, you can import user information rather than entering it at the keyboard. You can import user information from any program that can produce a delimited ASCII text file, from a variety of email programs, and from the Windows NT Security Accounts Manager.

Text File Registration

If the users you want to register are already listed in a database of some kind, and you can export the data to a delimited text file, you can save yourself the work of reentering the user information by importing the contents of the text file. The information on file doesn't have to include all the information you need to register a user. In fact, depending on the method you use, you can import as little as a single item of information—the users' last names.

You can import the text file in one of two ways:

- From within the Register Person dialog box: You can import the new users into the registration queue, then enter any missing information.

- From the menu: You can register users directly from the text file, bypassing the Register Person dialog box entirely. Choose People from File in the Configuration, Registration menu on the Configuration tab or choose Register from File on the People, People menu on the People & Groups tab. If you use this method, the text file must include users' passwords (in addition, at minimum, to their last names.

If the nonunique registration information about all users in the text file is not the same (for example, different certifier IDs, registration servers, mail servers, group membership), you should import into the registration queue. There you can speedily enter the missing information by selecting multiple users and entering information for selected users with a single field entry. If the nonunique information in the text file is the same for all users, you can use the second method.

The text file can have as many as 20 fields, in the following order:

1. **Last name** (Required)

2. **First name**

3. **Middle initial.** Use a period if your organization's naming convention requires it.

4. **User-unique organizational unit.** Use only to differentiate two users from each other who have the same name and are (or will be) certified by the same certifier ID. (For example, if there are two Mary Jane Smiths in /Acctg/ Stillwater, but one is in Accounts Receivable and the other in Accounts Payable, you could make them `Mary Jane Smith/AR/Acctg/Stillwater` and `Mary Jane Smith/AP/Acctg/Stillwater`. In this field, you would enter `AR` for the one and `AP` for the other.

5. **Password.** (Required if importing from the menu)

6. **ID file folder.** Location where the user's ID file will be saved. The folder must exist already.

7. **ID file name: If you leave this blank, Notes will generate a filename based on the user's name.**

8. **Mail server name.** Enter it in abbreviated format (for example, Osprey/Servers/Stillwater).

9. **Mail file folder.** Location under the server's data folder where the user's mail database will reside.

10 **Mail file name.** If you don't specify, the mail filename will be composed of the first letter of the user's first name and the first seven letters of the user's last name. You only need to specify a mail filename if two users whose mail files will occupy the same folder have the same first initial and last name.

11. **Location.** This entry will go into the Location field of the Person document.

12. **Comment.** This entry will go into the Comment field of the Person document.

13. **Forwarding address.** This entry will go into the Forwarding address field of the Person document.

14. **Profile name.** This entry will go into the Profile name field of the Person document.

15. **Local administrator.** This entry will go into the Local administrator field of the Person document.

16. **Internet address.** This entry will go into the Internet address field of the Person document.

17. **Short name.** If you don't specify, the user's short name will be composed of the first letter of the user's first name and the user's last name. Short names should be unique in a Domino domain, so you need to specify a short name if two users have the same first initial and last name.

18. **Alternate name.** The certifier ID should contain alternate language information.

19. **Alternate organization unit.** The certifier ID should contain alternate language information.

20. **Mail template file name: If you leave this blank, Notes will generate a filename based on the user's name.**

Domino Administrator expects the fields in the import file to be separated by semi-colons (;). However, you can use another character by adding the variable BatchRegSeparator=*character* (where *character* is the separator character) to the notes.ini of the workstation where you will import the text file. The text file can have any filename, but if you expect to use this method regularly, you can set a default text filename by adding the variable BatchRegFile=*filename* to the notes.ini file.

Importing from the Menu

When you import a file from the menu, you are prompted for the password of the default certifier ID (press Cancel to choose another certifier ID) and the location and name of the text file. Then the Register People from Text File dialog box appears. See Figure 6.1.

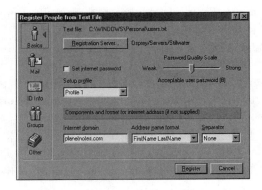

Figure 6.1 In this dialog box, you can set nonunique information for all imported users and patterns for Notes to follow when generating unique information about each user.

This dialog box looks very much like the Register Person dialog box. Here you enter the settings not otherwise defined for the imported users. If a setting duplicates a populated field for a given user in the import file, the entry in the import file overrides. When you have set all fields, choose Register.

Importing Into the Registration Queue

To import a file into the registration queue, open the Register Person dialog box. Set default entries in any fields you like (except fields that gray out (see Figure 6.2) when you select more than one user in the registration queue). Choose Import Text file. Locate and select the file, then choose Open. Domino Administrator imports the users in the file into the registration queue. Select individual users (or groups of users) in the registration queue and change any fields you like, then register them.

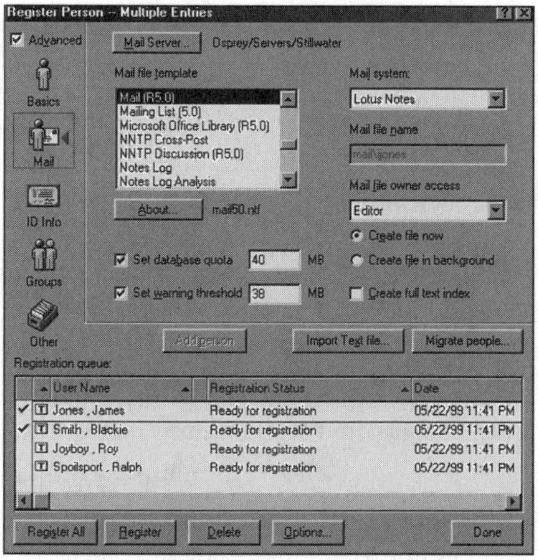

Figure 6.2   When you select more than one user in the registration queue, certain fields "gray out" and you can't edit them (for example, the Mail filename field above). Any fields that you *can* edit will change for every selected user.

Registering Windows NT Users as Notes Users

If the Notes users you have to register already exist in a Windows NT domain, you can either import them into the registration queue or register them from within Windows NT's User Manager or User Manager for Domains. Alternately, if the users don't exist in Windows NT, but you have to create them in both the Domino and Windows NT domains, you can create them once, in either place, and Domino Administrator will make sure they are created in both places.

The first technique, importing Windows NT users into the registration queue, is a function of the Microsoft Windows NT to Notes migration tool, which you can optionally install along with Domino Administrator onto a computer running Windows NT. The other techniques are functions of the Domino Directory NT Sync Services, which install automatically onto a computer running Windows NT when you install Domino Administrator.

Migrating Windows NT Users into Notes

The Microsoft Windows NT to Notes migration tool is one of several migration tools that you can install either when you install Domino Administrator or later. But you can only install and use it on a computer running Windows NT, not on a computer running Windows 9x.

To install it, you have to perform a custom installation. If you run InstallShield indirectly from the AutoRun front-end on the R5 distribution CDROM, choose Custom Install. If you run InstallShield directly (by opening setup.exe in the client subfolder), choose Customize in its fifth screen. Either will cause a screen to appear in InstallShield where you can choose the components you want to install. There, select Migration Tools. Optionally, choose Change, then deselect any of the other migration tools you know you won't use.

To use the Microsoft Windows NT to Notes migration tool, you have to be logged on as an Administrator or Account Operator of the NT domain(s) you want to import from. Follow these steps:

1. In Domino Administrator, go to People & Groups and, under Tools, People, choose Register to open the Register Users dialog box.

2. Set any defaults you want (such as a default password quality), then choose Migrate people.

3. The People and Groups Migration dialog box opens. In the Foreign directory source field, choose Windows NT Users/Groups. (If None appears, you have not installed any migration tools. Shut down Domino Administrator and perform a custom install of either Domino Administrator or all clients. During the custom install, you'll have an opportunity to choose which migration tool(s) to install.)

4. The Choose Windows NT Domain dialog box opens. In it appear the available Windows NT domains (as well as the name of the computer at which you are working if it isn't a domain controller). Select the domain from which you want to import users. Choose OK.

5. The users and groups in the selected domain appear in the Available people/groups list. Select as many as you want to add (using Control, Shift, and Control+Shift to control which entries are selected), then choose Add. Or choose Add All, then remove unwanted entries from the People/Groups to migrate list. If you choose a group in the Available people/groups list, one or more dialog boxes will appear:

    - **Existing Group '*groupname*' Migration Options.** Appears if you added a Windows NT Group having the same name as an existing Notes group. Your choices are (see Table 6.1):

Table 6.1 **Existing Group 'groupname' Migration Options**

Option	Description
Use the existing Notes group	Will add the members of the selected Windows NT group to the existing Notes group.
Create a new group—don't use the Notes group	Will add the members of the selected Windows NT group to a new Notes group.
Skip this group—do not migrate it for now	Cancels the migration of the group and its members.

- **Group Migration Options.** Appears if the Windows NT group you selected does not have the same name as an existing Notes group or, if it does, after you choose OK in the Existing Group '*groupname*' Migration Options dialog box. Your choices are (see Table 6.2):

Table 6.2   **Group Migration Options**

Option	Description
Create a new Notes group with the following settings	If you check this box, you can then enter the new Notes group's name, type, and description. The members of the selected Windows NT group will become members of the new Notes group.
Add members of this group to the existing Notes group	This box appears if, in the Existing Group '*groupname*' Migration Options dialog box, you chose Use the existing Notes group. Members of the selected Windows NT group will be added to the existing Notes group.
Add nested groups contained in this group and their members OR Add people contained in nested groups as Notes users	One of these boxes appears, depending on whether you checked either of the boxes described previously. If you check this box, Windows NT groups nested in the selected group and their members will also be added in Notes.
Use above setting for all currently selected or nested groups (don't prompt again)	If you check this box, all other selected and nested groups will get the same settings as chosen for this group.

6. You can also choose the following migration options (see Table 6.3):

Table 6.3   **Other Migration Options**

Option	Description
Generate random passwords	If you select this, new Notes users in the registration queue will have passwords that meet the chosen password quality standard. The passwords are stored in a database named `NTSynch45.nsf`.
Add full name provided to the Notes person document	The NT user's full name will become one of the secondary names in the Full name field of the user's Person document.
Allow addition of empty groups to Notes	By default the migration tool doesn't import a group if in Notes it would be empty (either because it was never populated in Windows NT or because is contained names of people who were not registered Windows NT users). Select this option to create groups in Notes even if they will be empty.

7. Optionally choose Advanced to choose how the migration tool will parse the user's Windows NT full name into Notes first name, middle initial, and last name, and also to choose whether the Windows NT user name will become the Notes short name.

8. Choose Migrate. The users become a part of the registration queue. Choose Done when you are finished migrating users to Notes.

Once the migrated users are in the queue, you can select and edit them. Choose Register when ready to register them.

Synchronizing Notes and Windows NT Users

If your Notes users typically also have user accounts in a Windows NT domain, or if you are a veteran Windows NT administrator and you live inside the Windows NT administration tools, you may find the Domino Directory NT Sync Services a very useful set of tools. They can save you keystrokes when setting up new users or making changes to existing users. They allow you to do the following things:

- In User Manager, to select existing Windows NT users and groups and set them up as Notes users or groups.

- In User Manager, when adding new Windows NT users or groups, to set up corresponding Notes users or groups as well.

- In Domino Administrator, when registering new Notes users, to add them as Windows NT users as well.

- In User Manager, when renaming a Windows NT user, to add the new name to the user's Person document in the Domino Directory as well.

- In User Manager, when deleting a Windows NT user, to delete the corresponding Notes user as well.

- In User Manager, to synchronize certain user settings with corresponding settings in Notes.

The Domino Directory NT Sync Services are installed automatically when you install Domino Administrator on a Windows NT computer (but not on a Windows 9x computer, on which they do not work). They set themselves up as an additional menu (called Notes) in the Windows NT User Manager (under Windows NT Workstation) or the Windows NT User Manager for Domains (under Windows NT Server in a Windows NT domain). You can also install the Domino Directory NT Sync Services on a computer without installing Domino Administrator, by doing a custom install and deselecting everything except Domino Directory NT Sync Services. This would install the Notes menu in that computer's copy of User Manager.

There are some problems that might arise when setting up Domino Directory NT Sync Services. First, you probably want to access Windows NT domain user accounts, not Windows NT Workstation local user accounts. But when you install Domino

Administrator or Domino Directory NT Sync Services on a computer running Windows NT Workstation, the Notes menu gets installed in User Manager, not User Manager for Domains. You could solve the problem by doing your administrative chores while sitting at a computer running Windows NT Server. But if that computer really is a server on your network, you probably don't really want to use it in this way. Rather, what you should do is the following:

1. Install Domino Directory NT Sync Services on both your domain's Primary Domain Controller and a workstation running Windows NT Workstation.

2. Install the Windows NT client-based network administration tools on the same workstation.

3. Run the client-based version of User Manager for Domains at that workstation. The Notes menu will appear there and all of its functionality will be available.

To install the Windows NT client-based network administration tools on your workstation, locate the distribution files for Windows NT Server, either on a file server on your network or on the Windows NT Server CDROM. From your workstation, run the batch program setup.bat, located in the \clients\srvtools\winnt folder of the Windows NT Server distribution CDROM. The batch file copies a series of files into the Windows NT system folders on your workstation, then informs you that you can create shortcuts for the following programs: dhcpadmn.exe, poledit.exe, rasadmin.exe, rplmgr.exe, srvmgr.exe, usrmgr.exe, and winsadmn.exe. The one we care about is usrmgr.exe (but you undoubtedly care about the others too).

The second problem that might interfere with the smooth running of Domino Directory NT Sync Services arises if your Windows NT installation involves master and resource domains. In the standard master/resource domain setup, user accounts are located in the master domain(s), services (such as Domino servers) are located in the resource domain(s), and the resource domain trusts the master domain.

In this situation, you won't be able to access user accounts in the master domain if you run User Manager for Domains on a computer in the resource domain, because the master domain doesn't trust the resource domain. The solution to this problem is to set up a two-way trust between the resource and master domains. The resource domain already trusts the master domain. Therefore, you just have to set up the master domain to trust the resource domain. For more information on this topic, see Lotus Notes Technote titled Registering Notes Users in a Windows NT Master or Multiple Master Domain Model, document #150871, in the Lotus Notes Knowledgebase, located at www.lotus.com/support.

Finally, remember that, to use the Domino Directory NT Sync Services, you must have either administrator or account operator rights in the Windows NT domain(s) where user accounts are maintained. You must also have sufficient access rights to the Domino Directory, Administration Requests, and Certification Log databases on the Domino server where changes to Notes user status will take place, and access to appropriate Notes certifier IDs if you will be creating new users.

When Domino Directory NT Sync Services are properly set up, a menu called Notes will appear in User Manager. Next you have to configure it. The first time you open the Notes menu, only one item on the menu—Notes Synchronization Options—is available to be selected. Choosing it displays the Enable Notes Synchronization Options dialog box. The choices you make there dictate which of the other menu options become available for selection. The available choices (in the dialog box) are as follows in Table 6.4:

Table 6.4 **Lotus Notes/Windows NT Synchronization Options**

Option	Description
Enable all synchronization operations Or Select synchronization operations to enable	Choose the first option to enable all synchronization options. Choose the second option to enable any of three individual synchronization options (represented by three checkboxes that become available and which are described in the following three rows).
User/Group registration	Select this to enable you to use User Manager to register existing NT users or groups as Notes users or groups of if you want to use either Notes or User Manager to create new users or groups in both Notes and Windows NT.
User/Group deletion	Select this to enable you to have users deleted in User Manager also be deleted in Notes.
User synching	Select this to enable any of the following: • When you rename a Windows NT user in User Manager, you can automatically update the Network account name field in the user's Person document in Notes. • When you change the full name of a Windows NT user in User Manager, you can automatically have the new full name appended to the User name field in the user's Person document in Notes.
Set common password on user synching	If you enable User synching (see previous item), you can synchronize a Notes user's Internet password with his Windows NT password.

Option	Description
Prompt to confirm/cancel synchronization operations	Your choices here are to be prompted always, never, or only on user/group deletions.
Name format for full name parsing	You can choose the most appropriate name format, based on your standard method of formatting Windows NT user full names in User Manager.

If you don't want to reset this dialog box every time you restart User Manager, make sure Save Settings on Exit is checked in User Manager's Options menu.

If you enable synchronization of user/group registration, the synchronization service will do any of the following three things:

- Create a Windows NT user account (and add that account to one Windows NT group) for each new Notes user you register in Domino Administrator.

- Create a Notes user or group account for each new Windows NT user or group you create in User Manager.

- Select existing Windows NT user or groups accounts and create corresponding Notes users or groups.

If you enable synchronization of user/group deletion, the synchronization service will delete the corresponding Notes user or group whenever you delete a Windows NT user or group in User Manager.

If you enable user synchronization, the synchronization service will upgrade certain fields in a Notes user's Person document whenever you change the corresponding Windows NT user name or full name.

Creating a New NT User from Within Domino Administrator

To create a new Windows NT user account from within Domino Administrator, you can simply check the Add this person to Windows NT field when adding new people to the registration queue in Domino Administrator. The Windows NT user name field will default to the Notes short name, but you can change it. You can also choose one Windows NT group in the Add person to Windows NT group field, and the new user will be added to that group.

Creating a New Notes User from Within Windows NT User Manager

To create a new Notes user from within Windows NT User Manager, you must first set registration defaults in two dialog boxes that you can open from the Notes menu. Choose Registration Setup to open the Notes Registration Setup dialog box. Choose Mail/ID Registration Options to open the Notes Mail/ID Registration Options dialog box.

In these two dialog boxes you can set a variety of options that are mostly analogous to fields in the Domino Administrator Register User dialog box. In fact, because these two dialog boxes are so similar to the Register User dialog box in Domino Administrator, I won't describe them in detail here, except for the following items in the Notes Registration Setup dialog box:

- **Internet registration only (no Notes ID or mail file created).** Check this box if you only want to create a Person document for new users. The resulting user will be able to use simple name-and-password authentication to access Domino servers from within Web browsers, LDAP clients, or news readers, but won't have Notes mail databases and won't be able to use a Notes client to access most Domino servers.

- **Use common password.** Check this box to set a common password for Windows NT, the Notes user ID, and (optionally) the Notes Internet password. If the Windows NT user already exists, his/her password will be replaced by the common password. This is of particular interest if you install the Notes single logon feature when installing Notes on computers running Windows NT Workstation (but not Windows 9x). With Notes single logon installed, a Windows NT logon is also a Notes login—you don't have to re-enter your password when you run Notes on that computer. See Chapter 10 for more information about the Notes single logon feature.

Once the defaults are in place you can create new Notes users and groups either as you create new Windows NT users or groups from selected existing users or groups. When you create a new Windows NT user or group and choose Add, a dialog box automatically appears, prompting you for Notes-related information about the new user or group. To create a Notes user or group from existing Windows NT users or groups, select them in User Manager, then choose Add Selected NT Users/Group to Notes from the Notes menu.

If you add new Notes users (by either method), the Enter Notes User Information dialog box appears. There you can confirm, change, or enter Notes name and password information for the user. When you choose OK, User Manager will confirm that it can reach the Domino servers named in the Registration Setup and Mail/ID Registration Options dialog boxes. If it cannot reach them, it will display an error message and halt the operation. If it can reach them, User Manager will display a confirming dialog box. Choose Begin Registration to complete the creation of the Notes user.

If you add new Notes groups (by either method) the Notes Group Registration Options dialog box appears. There you can confirm or change the name of the group and its Notes type (multipurpose, mail only, et al.), you can enter a description, you can alter its membership, and you can choose whether to register its members as Notes users. When you choose OK, User Manager immediately creates the group in Notes with the settings you chose.

If you chose to register the group members as Notes users, a series of additional dialog boxes will appear. First, you will be asked to confirm that you want to register the group members as Notes users. Then you will be asked if you want to be prompted for name and password information on each user individually. If you choose that option, you will see a succession of Enter Notes User Information dialog boxes. If you choose, instead, to Register users at once without additional prompts, User Manager will parse its full name field to come up with a user name for each Notes user and will generate a random password for each Notes user ID. User Manager will confirm that it can reach the Domino servers named in the Registration Setup and Mail/ID Registration Options dialog boxes. If it cannot reach them, it will display an error message and halt the operation. If it can reach them, User Manager will display a dialog box confirming the number of Notes users to be registered. Choose Begin Registration to complete the creation of the Notes users.

As the user registration process takes place, dialog boxes may appear informing you of any problems (such as existence of other users or mail files having the same name as a user to be registered. You'll have the opportunity to choose how to deal with these problems. When registration ends, a dialog box will confirm the number of successful registrations and the number of errors, if any.

In other words, the process of creating new users and groups in User Manager is essentially the same as it is in Notes. You have to supply the same basic information. You will encounter the same prompts and error messages. The primary difference between doing it in Domino Administrator and doing it in User Manager is cosmetic—different-looking dialog boxes. The one significant difference is that, in User Manager you can assign new users to as many NT groups as you like but only to one Notes group whereas, in Domino Administrator, you can assign new users to any number of Notes groups you like but only one NT group.

This feature of Notes administration has been available since Release 4.x. We can look forward to even more comprehensive integration of Notes and Windows administration when Windows 2000 and its Active Directory Manager arrive in late 1999 or early 2000.

Upgrade from Other Mail and Calendar Products

If you are upgrading users to Notes from another mail system, chances are there is a migration tool on the CDROM that will move the users from the old mail program into the Notes registration queue. Along with the Windows NT to Notes migration tool described earlier in this chapter, the Lotus Notes distribution CDROM includes tools to migrate data from the following mail and directory programs:

- Lotus cc:Mail
- Microsoft Mail
- Microsoft Exchange
- Novell Groupwise 4.x
- Novell Groupwise 5.x
- Netscape Messaging Server
- LDAP directories (via LDIF file)

All of these tools work the same way the Windows NT migration tool, described earlier in this chapter, works. You access them by choosing Migrate people in the Register Person dialog box. You choose the foreign directory source. You choose names of users and groups from the foreign directory, choose from available options (such as Generate random passwords), and choose Migrate. The migration tool then creates equivalent users in the Notes registration queue. When you register the new users (and if you choose the Convert mail option), the contents of their mailboxes in the old systems are also migrated into their new Notes mail databases—mostly intact and mostly still in the folders they occupied in the old mail system, but with potential inconsistencies depending on the source mail system. When you migrate cc:Mail users, the contents of their Organizer databases can also be migrated. When you migrate users from an LDAP directory via LDIF file, there is no option to convert mail files because, of course, LDAP is not a mail standard.

The migration tools described previously migrate public, centrally stored data from the old systems into Notes. But each of the foreign systems either allows or requires users to store at least some personal data locally. The migration tools don't have access to that information, but the migrated users do. So, Notes provides a second set of migration tools for use by migrated users that help them move their personal data from the old systems into their new Notes databases.

Lotus provides upgrade wizards for three of the systems: Lotus cc:Mail, Microsoft Mail, and Microsoft Exchange/Outlook. In those cases, after you have migrated and registered the new users, you can send an email to them with a hotspot in it that, when the user clicks it, runs the upgrade wizard. The user answers the prompts in the wizard, then the wizard migrates their personal data, including private addresses, mailing lists, and message archives to Notes.

To send the email with the wizard in it, you have to choose the Send Upgrade Notifications action in the Server/Mail Users view of the Domino Directory. From Domino Administrator, choose a server and open the People & Groups tab. In the Tasks pane, expand Domino Directories (if necessary), right-click the name of your Domino Directory, then choose Open Directory. When the directory opens, expand Server (in the Navigation pane), then choose Mail Users. Finally, choose Send Upgrade Notifications in either the Actions menu or the Action bar.

When the Upgrade Message appears, enter the names of users who will receive it, choose Send out cc:Mail/MS Mail/MS Exchange convert local information notices, choose which mail system the users are converting from, and enter the other data. Then choose Send. The users will receive a message in which the body of the message consists of the text from the Additional Information field, plus a button, Convert Local Data to Notes. When the push the button, the Lotus Notes Upgrade Services wizard runs. The users make several simple choices, then choose Finish to move their personal data from the old program into Notes.

For users of the other systems and of the calendar programs listed in the Table 6.5, Notes includes a set of databases (created by Binary Tree) for migrating personal mail and calendar information into Notes. The databases, and the mail/calendar programs from which they pull data, are as follows in Table 6.5:

Table 6.5 **Databases and Data Migration**

Database Name	Migrates Data From
C&S 1.0 for Notes 5.0	Lotus Organizer 2.1
	Lotus Organizer 97
	Microsoft Schedule+ 1.0
	Microsoft Schedule+ 7.0
	OpenText OnTime
Groupwise 5 -> Notes 1.03	Groupwise 5.x
MailPort for GW4 v1.06	Groupwise 4.1
Netscape -> Notes 1.12 final	Netscape Messenger in Netscape Navigator 3.x and 4.x and Netscape Communicator 4.x
Eudora -> Notes v1.52	Qualcomm Eudora

Each of these databases includes a complete set of instructions in its use. The short of it, though, is that you can use them in two ways. By the first method, you the administrator fill in a Settings form, then send an email to the migrated users. The email, in essence, tells the user to press one or more buttons embedded in the body of the message. The buttons trigger agents that do the actual work of moving the user's data from the old system into Notes. By the second method, a user opens the database himself, enters the proper settings, then presses the buttons that trigger the agents. This eliminates the middleman—you and your email.

Automating Notes Installation

The next aspect of user setup that you may want to automate is the installation of Notes on user workstations. You can automate this chore in two ways. First you can perform a "silent installation" in which you set up a response file that supplies the answers to some or all of the questions InstallShield normally asks when you run it. That way you can control the installation process and, conceivably, make it easy enough for (gasp!) users to do their own installs.

Second, you can arrange for the installation process to copy additional or replacement files or your choice. For example, you could add your own applications to the list of files to be installed or you could replace standard templates with ones that you have customized to meet your special needs.

A big caveat here: Before you plow into these two topics, I should warn you that, as recently as R5.0.1, both of the preceding procedures are very rough. Silent installation is not very flexible or smooth. Copying additional files, as documented by Lotus, does not work at all. Be prepared for an adventure.

Automating Client Installation

There's no really easy way to automate the installation of Notes unless you are willing to forgo installation of the other apps that come with it. In particular I'm thinking of Actioneer for Lotus Notes, which is a very nice add-on that, for one person I know, is the sole reason she was willing to upgrade to Notes 5 from her trusty Notes 4.

To fully automate the installation of Notes or Actioneer *alone* is very easy. You simply record a response file, that is, a file that supplies responses to InstallShield at its decision points. Thereafter, you invoke the response file whenever you do an install.

But to install both Notes and Actioneer automatically as the result of a single command, a batch file won't suffice. You have to write your own install script, which, though not necessarily difficult, is a whole other ball game. For one thing, you have to shell out for a copy of InstallShield Pro for $800 (or InstallShield Express for $300, but I'm not sure if InstallShield Express would be adequate to the job of scripting the silent installation of multiple independent applications). Then you have to learn how to use it and possibly how to write scripts in its language.

Creating a Response File

Writing InstallShield scripts is well beyond our scope here. We'll limit ourselves to creating and using response files. The easiest way to create a response file is to record one. Do so as follows:

1. Run setup (or whatever your InstallShield executable is called) in "recording" mode. Run it from a command line, as follows:

   ```
   setup ·r
   ```

2. Do a complete installation of the program in question. Setup records your responses to all of its options in a file called *setup.iss*, which it saves in your system directory. (iss stands for InstallShield Silent.)

Then, copy the response file (setup.iss) into the directory where the install files are located. That will be some directory on a file server, of course. You can also rename it, if you desire.

Using a Response File in an Install

To run setup so that it uses the response file (that is, in "silent" mode), use one of the following command lines:

```
setup -s
```

or

```
setup -s -f1 setup.iss
```

or

```
setup -s -f1setup.iss
```

In the first example, `setup.exe` will look for a script named `setup.iss` located in its own folder. In the second and third examples, you specify the name of the .iss file. If the .iss file is located elsewhere than in the same folder as `setup.exe`, you can specify the full pathname of the .iss file.

Notice, in the second and third examples, that you can or cannot use a space between `-f1` and `setup.iss`. The space is optional. I point this out because a little further on you'll see that a space is *not allowed* between `-f2` and `setup.log`. You can or cannot use the space (in the cause of readability) use it (in the cause of syntactic consistency).

If you plan to run setup from a location other than the folder that setup.exe and setup.iss are in, you should enter the command line using the full path name of setup.exe (and possibly setup.iss). Otherwise the command interpreter may not be able to locate the files. For example, say the setup files are located in the following location:

```
n:\clients\w32intel\
```

where n: is a mapped network drive. Your command line (from a command prompt or a batch file) should be as follows:

```
n:\clients\w32intel\setup.exe -s -f1n:\clients\w32intel\setup.iss
```

But your command line from within a shortcut file can be as follows:

```
n:\clients\w32intel\setup.exe -s -f1setup.iss
```

unless `setup.iss` is not located in the same folder as setup.exe, in which case you should specify the full path name of `setup.iss`.

Using Setup.log

When InstallShield runs silently, it produces a log file called `setup.log`. If an error occurs during installation, the installation may terminate before completion. You can determine the cause of an error condition by referring to the log. You can dictate the location and filename of the setup log by adding the following argument to the command line:

```
-f2<pathname of log file>
```

For example, we might tell InstallShield to write the log to the user's Notes folder, as follows:

```
n:\clients\w32intel\setup.exe -s -f1n:\clients\w32intel\setup.iss -
f2c:\lotus\notes\setup.log
```

As generated by InstallShield, the log file will include a variable called ResultCode, which will be equal to a numeric value. The values that a silent install might generate are in Table 6.6. These are *not* all possible result codes, only those that are relevant to a silent install.

Table 6.6   **Selected InstallShield Result Codes**

Code	Description
0	Success
–1	General error
–3	Required data not found in the setup.iss file
–4	Not enough memory available
–5	File does not exist
–8	Invalid path to the setup.iss file
–11	Unknown error
–51	Cannot create the specified folder
–52	Cannot access the specified file or folder

Creating a Shortcut That Runs a Silent Install

To run setup without having to remember a long command line like the ones shown previously, create a shortcut using the desired command line, then run setup.exe from the shortcut. To do so, follow these steps:

1. In Windows Explorer, right-click setup.exe and choose Create Shortcut. A shortcut file named Shortcut to Setup.exe will appear in the same folder.

2. Right-click Shortcut to Setup.exe and choose Properties. The Shortcut to Setup.exe Properties dialog box will appear, with the content of the Target field selected. The Target field holds the command line that runs setup.exe.

3. Move the text cursor to the right end of the command line in the Target field and enter -s -f1<filename> -f2<pathname> (where <filename> is the name of the appropriate .iss file and <pathname> is the name and location where the log file should be written). Don't include the angle brackets. Do include all of the spaces, including the one preceding -s. Type carefully. typographical errors are the bane of the computer user's existence. Using our earlier example, your command line should appear as follows:

```
h:\clients\w32intel\setup.exe -s -f1setup.iss -f2c:\lotus\notes\setup.log
```

4. Choose OK.

5. Consider renaming the shortcut file so that, weeks later, its purpose will still be obvious. For example, you could call it something like "Double-click here to install Lotus Notes for standard users."

Putting It All Together

To automate the installation of, say, Notes and Actioneer, you could generate response files for each, then create shortcut files for each. You could move the shortcut file to a folder by themselves, accessible by the appropriate users. Then you could send an email message to the users, telling them to open the shortcut folder and run first the Notes shortcut, then the Actioneer shortcut. If a user encounters a problem and calls the help desk, the log file might reveal the cause of the user's problem.

One problem with installing Notes in this way is that it is truly silent in the sense that InstallShield doesn't give you any hint about what it's doing or when it has finished. The only reason you know anything is going on is because your hard disk light flickers a lot. The only reason you know a Notes installation is finished is because that particular InstallShield script ends by starting up a Lotus product registration program. So you know Notes has been installed successfully because a screen appears asking you to register Notes.

That brings up another point: If you don't want all of your users registering their copies of Notes with Lotus and opening the junk mail floodgates, or getting tangled up while trying to register Notes, you can just rename the registration program and InstallShield won't be able to run it. Its filename is LotusProductRegistration.exe. Of course, if you rename it, your users *really* won't know when InstallShield has finished installing Notes, or whether it succeeded. So they won't know when they can start the Actioneer install. One thing you might try is to create a program that announces that Notes is installed, name it LotusProductRegistration.exe, and substitute it for the real LotusProductRegistration.exe. I can't provide a way for you to do that, however; you're on your own with that one.

The bottom line is that there is no simple and clean way to set up a fully automated Notes installation without resorting to creating your own InstallShield scripts. You can buy whole books on that topic. To learn more, visit www.installshield.com. If you want to learn how to write a response file, or if you simply want to know more about InstallShield Silent Installs, go to www.installshield.com, and find document ID Q101901, titled "How to: Creating a Silent Installation." You can also go to www.notes.net and search the R5 discussion for the word "InstallShield" to find out the latest developments on this front.

Adding Databases to the Setup Files

You can also customize the content that gets copied onto the users' computers when they install Notes. For example, you might want to install the local files of a third-party application that your company is deploying along with Notes.

You could, of course, use a setup profile to cause specific databases to be copied to the users' data folder during workstation configuration. But you might need to copy files other than databases. In addition, under certain circumstances it might make better sense to copy the files during installation, rather than replicating them from the server during user setup. An example is a user whose only connection to any Domino server is by modem. You could quickly copy files from a CDROM during installation. Or you could slowly replicate the files during user setup. Take your choice.

Unfortunately, Lotus's documented method for customizing the installation does not work. Briefly, the method advocated by Lotus is to create a list of additional files, save the list as `copyfile.txt` in the folder containing the install files, then place copies of the files listed in copyfile.txt to the same folder.

The problem with this method is that Lotus does not fully document the syntax of the list in copyfile.txt. No amount of experimentation by anyone who has contributed to the notes.net forum as succeeded in unraveling the mystery syntax. And please to Lotus and InstallShield for help have gone unanswered as I write this. My own suspicion is that Lotus never got this feature working for R5.0, and that Lotus's documenters didn't get a chance to remove the procedure from Administration Help.

However, this isn't to say that it is impossible to set up InstallShield—only that you have to find some other way to do it. InstallShield 5.5 Professional includes a utility named iscab.exe that allows you to modify the contents of InstallShield Cabinet files (which are the compressed files in which are stored the files to be installed). I understand (although I haven't tried it myself) that you can use this utility to add your own files to the CAB files provided by Lotus on the Notes installation CD-ROM. For information on how to do this, see the article titled "Q103003 HOWTO: Creating a Custom Set of Compressed Files," retrievable from support.installshield.com.

It is rumored that you can also download iscab.exe itself from support.installshield.com. However, I was unable to locate it when I looked. It may be that you have to download the evaluation version of InstallShield 5.5 Professional to get it. If you can't download it, your alternative is to buy a license for InstallShield 5.5 Professional for $800. Of course, if you're going to do that, you don't have to tinker with Lotus's installation routine; you can create your own entirely customized Notes installation routine from scratch.

With luck, Lotus will have remedied this situation by the time you read this. To find out the current status of the situation, search for "InstallShield" at the notes.net forum and in the Notes Knowledgebase, located at www.lotus.com/support.

Setting Up Users with Special Needs

Not all Notes users use Notes in the same way. Some only use it when they are in the office, connected to the office LAN. Others use it at home, in hotel rooms, everywhere. Some people only access Domino servers. Others may also access Internet servers of various kinds. Finally, not all Notes users have a computer all to themselves; they share a computer with others. In the rest of this chapter we'll learn how to set up these kinds of users.

Setting Up Mobile Users

Mobile Notes users aren't always connected to the company LAN. Sometimes they have to reach their Domino server via modem or from a LAN other than the one to which they connect when in the office. Other times they may not be able to connect to a server at all. For these users you have to set up multiple location and connection documents, and you have to set them up with local replicas of databases that they may need to access when they don't have convenient access to a Domino server. If you know at the time you are setting up Notes for such users that this will be the case, you can choose appropriate options in the Lotus Notes Client Configuration wizard, and the wizard will do the work for you. Or you can do the work yourself at a later time.

Mobile users have two special problems that office workers never have to worry about:

- Mobile users have to figure out how to establish a connection to their Domino servers. The way they do it depends on where they are located and what types of connections their servers permit and their computer can handle. If they have to use a modem, the sequence of numbers they have to dial may change from one location to the next.

- Mobile users often have to get by with a slow, modem-speed connection to their Domino servers. It can take a long time for a document delivered by a server at modem speeds to appear on a user's screen, and mobile users might refuse to use Notes if they have to endure the long wait times. At other times mobile users may not be able to connect to a server at all, but they still need to get their work done.

However, Notes is particularly adept at accommodating the needs of mobile users. Notes attacks the these problems as follows:

- **Location and Connection documents.** Notes makes it easy to connect to a server from any location because it stores all location variables in a single location document and any special connection variables in connection documents. If a user's location and connection documents are properly set up, all a user has to do to connect to a given server from any location is switch to the appropriate location document, then choose to connect.

- **Server-to-Workstation Replication.** Notes can store local copies of Notes databases and replicate all changes with the server as a background task. Mobile users don't have to endure long wait times for documents to appear on their screens because they look at locally stored copies. They don't notice the long downloads/uploads produced by slow connections because those take place while the users are busy doing something else.

- **Local short-term storage of sent mail.** When a user who is remote from his mail server chooses Send, the message is stored temporarily in an Outgoing Mail database until the user chooses to send it to the server (which transfer can then take place in the background).

As an administrator, you have to understand how a user's location and connection documents work together to make it possible for mobile users to connect to a server from anywhere without having to think about how to do it. The reason you have to understand it is because you are the one who will have to make it happen.

Take Joe Doaks, for example. When Joe is in the office, with his laptop computer connected to the office LAN, his Office location document tells Notes that the LAN port (TCP/IP) is available and that Joe's mail is located on his home server—Server1. So when Joe opens his mail database, Notes connects to Server1 via the LAN port and opens the mail database there. When he opens the sales support database, Notes connects via LAN to Server2 and opens that copy.

Joe is leaving tomorrow on a sales visit to a customer in another city. Before he leaves for the day, he places a replica copy of the sales support database on his laptop and refreshes the copy of his mail database that is already there by replicating with Server1 and Server2. To do this, all he has to do is open the Replicator page (by clicking the bookmark for it in the Bookmarks bar) and choose Start. The icons for his mail database and the sales support database appear on the page with checkmarks next to them, so Notes connects via LAN to each server in turn and replicates with it.

At home that evening, Joe turns on his laptop, plugs a phone line into his modem, starts Notes and switches to one of his Home location documents (by choosing it in the lower right corner of the screen or in the File, Mobile menu). This location document tells Notes that the only port currently available is COM1, that Joe's mail is now Local (located on his laptop), that, from this location, it should replicate every hour, and that Server3 is the default pass-thru server. So the first thing Notes does is try to replicate with Server1 and Server2. There are no connection documents telling Notes how to connect to them from this location, but there is one that says it can connect to Server3 by dialing 555-6666 on the modem attached to COM1. So Notes dials Server3 and asks it if it can pass Notes through to Server1. Server3 obliges, Notes connects to Server1 and replicates Joe's mail. Then it asks Server3 to pass it through to Server2, where it replicates the sales support database. Then Notes hangs up.

When Joe opens his mail, Notes opens the local copy of it. He reads a new message and replies to it. Because Joe's mail is currently Local, Notes puts the reply in the Outgoing Mailbox. To send the message to the server, Joe opens his Replicator page and chooses Other Actions, Send Outgoing Mail. Notes dials Server3, passes through to Server1, delivers the reply to Server1, then hangs up. Joe powers down.

The next morning, on his flight, Joe powers up, starts Notes, then switches to the Island location documents. This one tells Notes that no ports are currently available, so even if Joe tries to connect to a server he won't be able to.

That evening, in his hotel room, Joe switches to the Travel location document. A dialog pops up, asking Joe to tell Notes what number to dial to get an outside line (Joe says 8) and what the country code and area code are where he's currently staying. The Travel location document tells Notes that the TCP/IP port and COM1 ports are available.

Joe chooses Start on the Replicator page to replicate the mail and sales support databases with the servers. There are two connection documents this time. One (the same one as the night before at home) tells Notes that it can connect to Server3 via COM1 by dialing 444-555-6666. (Because of his remote location at another area code, Notes knows this time to dial long distance). The other tells Notes that it can connect to Server3 via TCP/IP by telling Windows Dial-Up Networking to dial the local CompuServe node, then using that connection to reach Server3 over the Internet. This connection document wasn't available last night at home because it specifically states that it is only available from the Travel location. Notes chooses this one because it is set to Normal usage priority and the other one is set to Low usage priority.

Notes automatically dials 8 plus the local phone number of the CompuServe node. The phone is busy. Notes tries again several times with the same result, then fails over to the other connection document. Because this one indicates a long distance call, and the location document contains the sequence of numbers for billing the call to Joe's AT&T calling card, Notes dials 8, then 1-800-CALL-ATT, then 1, then Server3's area code and phone number, then the AT&T PIN number. The connection goes through, etc.

Joe never had to think about any of this because all the details were contained in the location and connection documents. You, however, have to know how to set all this up because your Joe Doaks won't want to think about this stuff any more than mine does, and he'll expect you to set up his location and connection documents to take care of all this.

Setting Up Mobile Users When Setting Up a New Workstation

If, when setting up a new Notes workstation, you know that you are setting up a mobile user, you should let the Lotus Notes Client Configuration wizard do the work. The wizard will set up the appropriate location and connection documents for one mobile location and will make a local replica copy of the user's mail database—all worksavers for you.

At about its third screen, the wizard will present you with a screen called "How Do You Want to Connect to a Domino Server?" You will have the following options:

- **Set up a connection to a local area network (LAN).** This option is for the user who only uses Notes in the office. We covered this option in Chapter 5.

- **Set up a phone connection to a Domino or remote network.** This option is for the home user or the user in a remote office who will always connect to Domino servers by modem.

- **Set up both a LAN and phone line connection.** This option is for the laptop user who sometimes uses his computer in the office, sometimes at home, sometimes on the road. This is the true mobile user.

If you choose either the second or third option, the wizard will later (either immediately or with some intervening screens) present you with a screen called "Type of Phone Connection." Your choices are:

- **Dial directly into a Domino server.** Choose this if the user will dial up a Domino server that has one or more of its own modems. This may be either a destination server, such as the user's home server, or a pass-thru server. For more on pass-thru servers, see the next section in this chapter. For this type of connection Notes handles all dialing chores itself and you have to set all dialing parameters in Notes.

- **Dial a remote network server.** Choose this if the user will dial up a remote network server (probably a computer that does not run Domino) and connect through it to a LAN and through the LAN to one or more Domino servers. From Notes's point of view, and that of the servers to which it connects, this user is connecting via LAN. But it is a very slow LAN, because this user connects to the LAN by modem. Under this type of connection Notes relies on the remote access services of the underlying operating system (Dial-Up Networking under Windows, AppleTalk Remote Dial-Up or Macintosh PPP on a Macintosh) to control the modem, dial out, and establish a connection with the destination server, and later disconnect. Notes merely prompts the underlying OS service to establish the connection, then uses the connection as if it were using a LAN connection, then prompts the underlying OSS service to terminate the connection. Naturally, for this kind of connection to work properly, the underlying OS service must be properly configured.

- **Set up both types of phone connections.** Choose this if the user will be able to connect either way.

Depending on your choice, the wizard will next present you with a series of screens in which it will prompt you for the information necessary to set up the kind of connection you chose. If you chose the first option, the screens will be called "Dialing a Domino Server Directly." If you chose the second option, the screens will be called

"Dialing a Remote Network Server." If you chose the third option, you'll have to complete all six screens.

In the "Dialing a Domino Server Directly" screens, you will have to provide the following information:

Domino server phone number. Enter the server's complete phone number, including the area or city code, even if the user will dial locally. For example, enter 1-610-555-6666 even though the user only has to dial 555-6666.

Dialing prefix, if any. For example, if the user has to dial 9 for an outside line, enter the 9 here.

Modem type. Choose your modem from the list. If your modem doesn't appear in the list, choose a likely substitute. If no named modem in the list works, try .Auto Configure (for unlisted modems only) or Generic All-Speed Modem File (with instructions). If either of these works, you might later want to find a named modem that works because these two choices make connections at relatively slow speeds, certainly slower than the user's modem is probably capable of. If you have to troubleshoot this selection, see Chapter 3.

Modem port. Choose the COM port to which the user's modem is connected.

Modem setup. This opens the Additional Setup dialog box, in which you can adjust a whole series of modem settings and choose an acquire script, if necessary. In most situations you should be able to leave these settings alone, at least initially. (You can always go back and change them later.) But a few of the fields may warrant your attention now. Among them are the following:

Maximum port speed. The default might be set lower than the modem's maximum speed. You might want to reset this to the highest speed the modem will accept, and back it down later to a lower speed if the modem fails to connect to the server at the higher speed.

Log modem I/O. You should turn this off now and only turn it back on if you have trouble establishing a connection. Once you have solved any problems establishing a connection, turn this off again. With this turned on, every command the computer sends to the modem is recorded in the user's Notes Log, along with every response from the modem. If you leave modem I/O logging turned on needlessly, the logged information will eventually overwhelm the user's hard disk.

Log script I/O. The same goes for script I/O logging. Leave it off except when you are debugging an acquire or connect script.

Wait for dialtone before dialing. You might want to turn this off for some home-based users. Some modems don't recognize as a dial tone the stutter-tone that some premium phone services use when you go off-hook to inform you of some special condition. For example, if a user has the phone company's answering service, the stutter-tone will inform the user of missed calls. To turn off the stutter-tone the user must dial in and pick up his messages. Turning off the Wait for dialtone before dialing option allows such modems to dial out even when greeted by a stutter-tone but also makes it impossible for the modem to inform you if a no-dial-tone condition exists.

Acquire Script. You might have to select an acquire script if the user in question does not have his own modem but instead will have to acquire one from a modem pool. Presumably you will have known about this ahead of time and will have copied the necessary script file into the user's modems folder before reaching this point.

In the "Dialing a Remote Network Server" screens, you will have to provide the following information:

Phonebook entry to use. On a Windows-based Notes client, this is one of your Dial-Up Networking entries. (On a Macintosh this is different, but because the Macintosh client has not been released as I write this, I can't comment on its requirements.) All existing Dial-Up Networking entries will be available for you to choose from.

Create New Entry. If none of the available Dial-Up Networking entries is suitable to the user's needs or if none yet exist, you can press this button to run Dial-Up Networking's Make New Connection wizard. The wizard will prompt you to enter a name for the new connection, to choose an installed modem, and to enter the phone number of the destination computer. You will also have an opportunity to configure the modem. For more information about setting up Dial-Up Networking connections, see Chapter 3.

The following fields are all optional. If you leave them blank, Notes will use the information stored in the corresponding fields of the Dial-Up Networking connection chosen in the Phonebook entry to use field. If both fields are blank, Notes will prompt the user for the information each time it dials using this connection.

User name. Enter here the user name by which the destination computer knows you.

Password. Enter, then reenter the password that lets you into the destination system.

Phone number. Enter here the phone number of the destination computer.

Dialing prefix, if any. Enter here any numbers you have to dial before dialing the destination computer's phone number. Examples of prefixes include 9 to get an outside line. If you leave this field blank, Notes will use any prefix information it finds in the location profile that appears in the Dialing from field of the Dial-Up Networking connection. To find out what the settings are for that profile, choose Dial Properties in the Connect To dialog box for that Dial-Up Networking connection.

When you finally reach the end of this journey and choose Finish, the wizard creates the following objects on the user's workstation. It creates these because of the choices you made in the previously described wizard dialogs. It creates them in addition to the other things it creates as a result of other choices you made in other wizard dialogs.

- **A Notes Direct Dialup connection document to the user's home server** (if at the Type of Phone Connection screen you chose Dial directly into a Domino server). This connection enables Notes to dial up the user's home server.

- **A Network Dialup connection document to the user's home server** (if at the Type of Phone Connection screen you chose Dial a remote network server). This connection document enables Notes to direct Windows Dial-Up Networking to establish a dial up connection to a remote LAN so that Notes can use that LAN connection to connect to the user's home server.

- **A local replica of the user's mail database**, located in the user's mail sub-folder.

- **An entry for the user's mail database on the Replicator page of the Notes client.** This sets up background replication of this database.

- **An entry called "Send outgoing mail" on the Replicator page of the Notes client.** This sets up background sending of outgoing mail to the user's mail server. This entry appears on the user's Replicator page only when a location is current that has Local selected in the Mail file location field (on the Mail tab of the location document).

- **An "Outgoing Mail" database (named mail.box).** When the user is working at a location remote from a Domino server, outgoing mail is stored here when the user chooses Send. It is transferred to the user's mail server when the user chooses Start, Send & Receive Mail, or Other Actions, Send Outgoing Mail on the Replicator page. A location is remote from a Domino server if the location document has Local selected in the Mail file location field (on the Mail tab of the location document).

Setting Up Existing Users for Mobility

Had you not made the choices as described previously in the Lotus Notes Client Configuration wizard, you would have had to create all of these objects yourself. In fact, you won't always be able to anticipate a given user's future mobility. So let's turn the preceding bullet list into a checklist of things you need to do when an existing user needs to be set up for remote server access. That is, to set up an existing Notes workstation for mobile use, do the following things:

- (Optional) Create a location document. If the user has more than one home or travels a lot, the standard set of locations (Office, two Homes, Travel, Internet, and Island) might not meet all of his needs. You might have to create additional location documents to cover special situations. For example, in some hotels your users might want to bill phone calls to their room, but in others they might prefer to bill them to a credit card. You could set up two Travel location documents. One would incorporate the credit card dialing sequence. The other would not. The user would switch to whichever Travel location is appropriate for a given hotel.

- Create at least one connection document. The type of connection document depends on how the user will connect to his home server (or to the server for which you are creating the connection document).

- Create a local replica of the user's mail database. You should be sure to create the local replica in the mail subfolder on the user's workstation, because that's where the user's standard remote location documents (two Homes, Internet, Island, Travel) will look for it. Creating the local replica will also cause an entry for the user's mail database to appear on the Replication page.

- Create a local Outgoing Mail database. Notes actually creates this for you automatically the first time you switch to a location document that has Local selected in the Mail file location field. It also adds Send Outgoing Mail to the Replicator page when any such location document is current.

Location Documents

A location document contains all the variables associated with a particular working location. For example, the location document tells Notes whether to connect to a server by LAN or modem and, if by modem, whether to dial locally or long-distance. A newly set up Notes workstation includes six standard location documents:

- **Office (Network).** Assumes that you are in the office and within easy reach of your home server by LAN.

- **Home (Network Dialup).** Assumes that you are at home and that, to reach a Domino server, you have to use a remote LAN connection. That is, you have to connect to the Domino server using a LAN port, but you have to connect to the Domino server's LAN by dialing up a remote access server on that LAN or one connected to it.

- **Home (Notes Direct Dialup).** Assumes that you are at home and that, to reach a Domino server, you have to dial it up directly using a modem on a COM port.

- **Travel (Notes Direct Dialup).** Assumes you could be anywhere in the world other than at home or the office, and that, to reach a Domino server, you have to dial it up directly using a modem on a COM port.

- **Internet.** Assumes that you have a full-time LAN connection to the Internet but not necessarily to your home server.
- **Island (Disconnected).** Assumes that you cannot connect to any LAN or telephone line and that you therefore have no connection to any Domino server.

If during Notes setup you chose to create any Internet mail accounts, there may be other Location documents specific to the user's Internet mail accounts. Ignoring those for now, the above-listed set of location documents is more than enough for most pure Notes users, even very mobile users. Therefore, for most pure Notes users you will never have to do more than edit one of them. Some users might need other location documents, however. For them you can create new ones as needed. Some users, of course, will create them for themselves. But many users will rely on you to do the work. If you have to create a new location document for a user, you could do it directly on the user's workstation. Alternatively, you could do it on your own workstation, copy it to the Locations view of the Domino Directory, then have the user copy it into his/her own Personal Address Book.

To create a new location document, follow these steps:

1. Open the Personal Address Book to the Advanced, Locations view.
2. Choose Add Location in the Toolbar or choose Location in the Create menu.
3. Fill in the fields, then save and close.

A location document is large, complex document with lots of fields. In Table 6.7, I've commented on all of its fields. But the importance of many of the fields is further illuminated in other parts of the book. I've added cross-references in some cases. If you need more information about any field and there is no cross-reference, check the index.

Table 6.7 **Some Important Fields in a Location Document**

Field Name	Description
	BASICS TAB
Location type	Your choice determines what tabs appear and fields appear on the form. If you choose Local Area Network, the Phone Settings tab disappears. If you choose No Connection, the Servers, Ports, and Phone Settings tabs disappear. The assumption for Local Area Network, Network Dialup, and Custom is that you will be defining a LAN-based location. The assumption for Notes Direct Dialup is that you will be defining a modem-based location. The assumption for No Connection is that you will be defining an unconnected location.
Location name	Enter any descriptive name. In the Locations view, the location documents is listed by the name in this field.

continues

Table 6.7 **Continued**

Field Name	Description
	BASICS TAB
Internet mail address	Your return Internet address goes here. Any messages you send to Internet recipients from this location will have as its return address the address you enter here. The address can be in the form `name@domain` or `display name<name@domain>`.
Prompt for time/ date/phone	If you say Yes in this field, a dialog box prompting for time, date, and telephone information will appear whenever you switch to this location document. Set this to Yes for any location document that will be used for travel purposed, that is, from many possible locations all over the world.
Proxy	Appears only when the Location type is set to Local Area Network, Network Dialup, or Custom. Enter the host name or IP address of any proxy server you will use from this location. Or click the button to specify more than one proxy server or hosts or domains that will bypass the proxy server.
Default display name	Choices are Display primary names or Display alternate names. You choice determines lists of Notes user names will display in their primary or alternate language.
	SERVERS TAB (ON ALL LOCATION TYPES EXCEPT NO CONNECTION)
Home/Mail server	Your choice here determines what server Notes will seek out to retrieve or deliver mail. Defaults to the Home/Mail server on the logged in user's Person document in the Domino Directory. Normally you would leave this as is, but under unusual circumstances you might set another home/mail server. For example, if a user spends a lot of time in both the Los Angeles and Tokyo offices of a company, you might set up home/mail servers for the user in both offices by placing replica copies of the user's mail database on a server in each office. All servers would continue to deliver mail to this user at the mail server named in the user's Person document in the Domino Directory. But when the user picks up or reads his own mail or delivers new mail, Notes will go to the server named in this field.
Pass-thru server	If Notes can't find a path to a Domino server, it will seek out the Domino server named in this field and ask to pass through it to reach the other server. By default the logged in user's home/mail server is set as the passthru server.
Catalog/domain search server	The user will go to this server to conduct domain-wide database searches.
Domino directory server	The user will go to this server to perform name lookups in the Domino Directory or the Directory Catalog when addressing mail.

Field Name	**Description**
Ports to use	All ports enabled in this copy of Notes are listed here. Choose the ones that will be available at this location.
MAIL TAB	
Mail file location	Your choices are Local and On server. If you choose Local, Notes will assume that your mail server is not close at hand. It will open the local mail database when you click a mail bookmark. It will hold all sent mail in the local Outgoing Mail database. If you choose On server, Notes will assume your mail server *is* close at hand. It will open the server copy of your mail database when you click a mail bookmark. It will deliver all sent mail directly to the server's Outgoing Mail database.
Mail file	Enter the partial pathname of your mail database. If Mail file location is set to Local, this is the pathname of the local copy of your mail database. Otherwise it is the pathname of the server copy of your mail database. If this is not correctly set, you will not be able to create new mail by choosing Mail in the Create menu (there will be no choices), and your mail shortcuts may not work properly.
Notes mail domain	Enter your mail server's Domino domain name.
Internet domain for Notes addresses when connecting directly to the Internet	Enter your mail server's Internet domain.
Recipient name type-ahead	Determines whether Notes looks up user names as you type them and completes them for you. The normal settings would be Local then Server if your mail or directory server is near at hand, Local Only if you are remote from your mail and directory servers.
Recipient name lookup	Determines how Notes will look up addressee names. It can Stop after first match or it can Exhaustively check all address books. Stop after first match is faster. Exhaustive ensures there are no duplicate matches.
Mail addressing	This field is only available if Mail file location is set to Local. If this field is set to Local Only (the default), only local address books will be available to choose addressee names from and to resolve addressee names. Also, when you send a new message (to the local Outgoing Mail database), Notes will not check names for correctness. If you set this field to Local and Server, Notes will check all addressee names against both local and server-based address books (directories) and will require all addressee names to be resolved against a name in an address book before allowing a message to be sent. But, of course, if no server is easily, quickly accessible (in other words, accessible by LAN) you don't want to choose Local and Server, because the lookups will take forever.

continues

Table 6.7 **Continued**

Field Name	Description
	MAIL TAB
Send outgoing mail	You can send all outgoing mail through Domino Server or directly to Internet. In this case outgoing mail is mail addressed to Internet addressees. Notes can deliver such mail directly to SMTP hosts or to a Domino server (which will in turn deliver it to an SMTP host). This is mostly of interest to Notes users who use Notes as their mail reader for their non-Domino POP and/or IMAP mail accounts.
Format for messages addressed to Internet addresses	This is the default message format. You can override your choice here when sending a given message. Choose Notes Rich Text Format or MIME Format. If you choose Notes Rich Text Format, messages to Internet mail users will be converted to plain text. Otherwise it will remain in MIME format. To sign or encrypt messages stored in MIME format, you must have an X.509 certificate and key pair stored in your ID file. See Chapter 8, Mail Routing, for more information about native MIME message formatting, and Chapter 10, Security, for more information about X.509 certificates.
Transfer outgoing mail if __ messages pending	This field is only available if Mail file location is set to Local. Notes will automatically initiate the transfer of mail in Outgoing Mail to a server when the number of pending messages reaches the number in this field. The default is blank, which means Notes will never initiate message transfer except on demand or along with scheduled replications.
	INTERNET BROWSER TAB
Internet browser	Your choice here determines what browser Notes will open if you hit a Web server from within Notes. Choose Notes to user Notes's or Domino's own, internal browser. It is known as the Personal Web Navigator when Notes runs it and Server Web Navigator when Domino runs it. Choose Notes with Internet Explorer (the default) to use an OLE version of Internet Explorer running inside the Notes window. Choose Netscape Navigator or Microsoft Internet Explorer to run an instance of either of those programs in its own window. Choose Other to specify any other browser to run in its own window. (Note: The Web Navigators in Notes/Domino R5 are vastly improved over their predecessors in Notes/Domino R4. Among other improvements, they now support HTML 4.0, which includes support of frames, among other things.)

Field Name	**Description**
	INTERNET BROWSER TAB
Retrieve/open pages	If you choose Notes or Notes with Internet Explorer in the preceding field, this field appears. If you choose Notes in the preceding field, your choices here are from InterNotes server, which is a Domino server running the Server Web Navigator (and effectively acting as a proxy browser and is useful if you don't have TCP/IP at user workstations; from Notes workstation, which is Notes acting as its own browser; and no retrievals, which disables Web browsing. If you choose Notes with Internet Explorer, you choices in this field are from Notes workstation and no retrievals.
Internet browser path	If you choose Other as your browser, this button appears, which lets you select the browser's executable in the file system.
	REPLICATION TAB
Schedule	This defaults to Disabled. If you enable it, the other fields (described below) appear.
Replicate daily between	Choose a time period during which replication will automatically occur. Or choose one or more discrete times at which replication will occur.
Repeat every	If you choose a time range in the preceding field, the time range you enter in this field dictates the frequency with which Notes initiates replication.
Days of week	Specify here the days of the week that Notes will operate under the replication schedule described in the two preceding fields.
High priority replication	You can use this field to define a separate replication schedule for databases defined as high priority. The default for all new databases is medium priority. You can set a database's replication priority in the Replication Settings dialog box. Choose File, Replication, Settings in the menu, then choose Other. If you enable this field, a second set of scheduling fields becomes available.
	PHONE SETTINGS TAB (ON ALL LOCATION TYPES EXCEPT LOCAL AREA NETWORK AND NO CONNECTION)
Prefix for outside line	Enter the number (for example, 8 or 9) necessary to get an outside line.
International prefix	Enter the prefix for an international phone call.
Country code at this location	Enter this code even if you don't plan to make any international calls.

continues

Table 6.7   **Continued**

Field Name	Description
PHONE SETTINGS TAB (ON ALL LOCATION TYPES EXCEPT LOCAL AREA NETWORK AND NO CONNECTION)	
Long distance prefix	Defaults to 1. Change it if necessary.
Area code at this location	Enter this code even if you don't plan to make any long-distance calls.
Calling card access number	Enter this if you plan to bill phone calls to a credit card.
Calling card number or extension suffix	Enter this if you plan to bill phone calls to a credit card or if the location you are calling from expects you to dial additional numbers after dialing the destination phone number or the destination expects you to enter numbers after it picks up.
Dialing Rules	Press this button after setting the other fields in this section. A dialog box will appear showing the sequence of numbers that Notes will send to the modem. Use this to check the accuracy of your entries in the other fields.
ADVANCED TAB, BASICS SUBTAB	
Use operating system's timezone settings.	Defaults to Yes. If you change it, you will have to maintain Notes's time zone settings independently of the OS.
Only for user	Defaults to an asterisk, which means everyone. If you enter the names of individual users, only those users can use this location document.
UserID to switch to	You can enter the path name of an ID or choose an ID from the file system. Whenever you switch to this location document, Notes will switch to that ID as well, and its password dialog will appear.
Load images	Defaults to Always, which means that images that are part of documents will always load with the documents. If you reset this to On request, images will not load automatically but only if you want to load them.
Bookmarks filename	The filename of the Bookmarks database, which is the database that stores the bookmark settings for this copy of Notes. Defaults to `bookmark.nsf`.
Subscriptions filename	The filename of the database that stores your subscriptions and the results of them. The default name is `headline.nsf`.
Network dialup idle timeout	The number of minutes of idle time before Notes terminates the connection. Defaults to a null value, which means that Notes will never terminate a call.

Field Name	**Description**

ADVANCED TAB, SSL SUBTAB

Accept SSL site certificates	Defaults to No, which means Notes will not accept site certificates from unknown certifying authorities.
Accept expired SSL certificates	Defaults to Yes, which means Notes will not enforce expiration dates of certificates.
SSL protocol version	Defaults to Negotiated, which means that Notes will use whatever version it can agree on with an SSL-enabled server. Alternately you can specify a version of SSL.

ADVANCED TAB, WEB RETRIEVER SUBTAB

Web Navigator database	Defaults to `perweb.nsf`. This is the database that Notes will use to store retrieved HTML documents if you designate Notes as its own browser.
Concurrent retrievers	This is the maximum number of active retrievals of HTML documents that Notes can manage at one time. Defaults to 15.
Retriever log level	Specifies the verbosity of Web Retriever messages that will be recorded in the workstation's `log.nsf` database. Defaults to no logging. The other choices are Terse and Verbose.
Update cache	Determines how often Notes will update its cache of retrieved Web pages. Defaults to Once per session. This means that the first time after you restart Notes that you tell it to retrieve a Web page that it had retrieved in the past (and is therefore cached), Notes will check the Web site to determine if its cached copy is still up to date. If it is, it will deliver the cached copy; if not, it will retrieve the updated version from the Web site. The other choices are Never and Every time.

ADVANCED TAB, JAVA APPLET SECURITY SUBTAB
(SEE ALSO "USER SETUP PROFILES" IN CHAPTER 5.)

Trusted hosts	TCP/IP hosts and domains from which any Java applets received are presumed to be benign.
Network access for trusted hosts	The degree of network access that Notes will permit to a Java applet received from a trusted host.
Network access for untrusted hosts	The degree of network access that Notes will permit to a Java applet received from an untrusted host.
Trust HTTP proxy	Defaults to No. This means that Notes will *not* rely on an intervening HTTP proxy server to resolve the host name of a host from which a Java applet has been received to the host's IP address. In other words, Notes will perform the resolution itself, even if the intervening proxy server is doing the same thing.

Table 6.7 **Continued**

Field Name	Description
	ADVANCED TAB, SECONDARY SERVERS SUBTAB
Secondary TCP/IP Notes name server	Relevant only if Notes is using TCP/IP for network communications. If a user's TCP/IP-based home/mail server is unavailable, Notes will try to contact the secondary Notes name server for name lookups. If this server is also unavailable (or was never set), Notes will broadcast its presence on the network and will accept the first server that replies as its name server. Because it broadcasts using TCP/IP, only TCP/IP-based servers will reply.
Secondary TCP/IP host name or address	The host name or IP address of the secondary server.
Secondary NDS Notes name server	Relevant only if Notes is using SPX for network communications and has access to a NetWare file server of Release 4 or higher. (NetWare 3 and earlier do not use NDS.) If a user's NDS/SPX-based home/mail server is unavailable, Notes will try to contact the secondary Notes name server for name lookups. If this server is also unavailable (or was never set), Notes will broadcast its presence on the network and will accept the first server that replies as its name server. Because it broadcasts using SPX, only SPX-based servers will reply.
Secondary NDS name server address	The NDS name of the secondary server. NDS names are similar to Notes names in that they follow X.500 naming conventions. The difference between them is that under NDS the components of a name (C, O, OU, and CN) are separated by periods, not slashes.
Secondary NetBIOS Notes name server	Relevant only if Notes is using NetBIOS, NetBIOS over IP, or NetBIOS over SPX for network communications. If a user's NetBIOS-based home/mail server is unavailable, Notes will try to contact the secondary Notes name server for name lookups. If this server is also unavailable (or was never set), Notes will broadcast its presence on the network and will accept the first server that replies as its name server. Because it broadcasts using NetBIOS, only NetBIOS-based servers will reply.
	ADVANCED TAB, MIME SETTINGS SUBTAB
Outbound attachment encoding method	Defaults to Base64. The other choice is Quoted-Printable. Accept the default unless you have a specific need to use Quoted-Printable.
Outbound Macintosh attachment conversion	Defaults to BinHex 4.0. The other choice is AppleDouble (Base64 only). Accept the default unless you have a specific need to use Quoted-Printable.

Field Name	Description
	ADMINISTRATION TAB
Owner	By default holds the name of the creator of this document. The owner will be able to edit this document if he/she has at least Author access to this database.
Administrators	Enter the names of administrators who will have edit access to this document if they have at least Author access to this database.

Connection Documents

A connection document tells Notes how to connect to one or more Domino servers (but usually just one server). You can create a connection document either of two ways.

First, you can use the Connection Configuration wizard. Frequently, when you create a location document, you have to create a companion connection document at the same time, so Notes provides the Connection Configuration Wizard action right in each location document's Action Bar. The wizard will step you through the process. The resulting connection document will be of the same type (Local Area Network, Network Dialup, or Notes Direct Dialup) as that of the associated location document. Also, it will be usable only when the associated location document is current.

Second, you can create a connection document manually following these steps:

1. Open the user's Address Book.

2. Open the Advanced, Connections view. Find it in the View menu or by choosing the tools icon (the one on the right) at the bottom of the Address Book's Navigator pane.

3. Choose Add Connection in the Actions bar or Server Connection in the Create menu.

4. Fill in the fields, then save and close the new connection document.

You can create five kinds of connection documents. You make that choice in the Connection type field, which is the first field of the connection document. The choices are as follows:

- **Local Area Network.** Use this to define a connection to a server via LAN or WAN, using network protocols. You don't normally have to create this type of connection document, because Notes normally locates LAN-based servers automatically (by polling first its home server, then local name servers, then broadcasting locally). If Notes can't find a LAN-based server, it's a sign that the server may not be configured properly on the network. For example, it may not be properly listed in the local DNS database or in local hosts files. The usual reason people create this type of connection document is to force Notes to use a preferred network protocol when more than one is available.

- **Network Dialup.** Use this to define a connection to a server via a remote LAN connection. After Notes Direct Dialup connections, this is the most commonly used kind of connection. When this type of connection is in place, Notes causes remote LAN service of the underlying OS (Windows or Macintosh) to dial up a remote LAN, then uses a LAN protocol to connect to a Domino server on the remote LAN, then causes to remote LAN service to disconnect. This is the type of connection you would define for a user who connects via modem to the Internet, then by Internet to the company LAN, and finally to the company's Domino servers. As more and more people gain Internet access on their home and laptop computers, this type of connection document should become the one you most commonly create.

- **Notes Direct Dialup.** Use this to define a connection to a server in which Notes dials up the server directly via modem. This is the default choice when you create a new connection document and the most commonly created kind of connection document. The most important information this document provides is the destination server's phone number and the modem port.

- **Passthru Server.** Use this to define a connection to a server via another Domino server. You only have to create this type of connection in rare, special circumstances, because the default pass-thru server, defined in the user's location document, takes care of most pass-thru needs. See the next section of this chapter for more information about setting up pass-thru server connections.

- **Hunt Group.** Large Notes organizations may designate multiple pass-thru servers to accommodate all of its mobile users, and may combine the pass-thru servers into hunt groups to balance the load on them. Users could dial one phone number and any member server of the hunt group could answer and pass the user through to his destination server. With the emergence of the Internet as a ubiquitous, universally available WAN, use of hunt groups should wane over time. See the next section of this chapter for more information about setting up hunt groups and hunt group connections.

The fields that appear in a connection document depend on your choice in the connection type field. Therefore, we'll look at the fields in each type of connection document separately. The fields in a Local Area Network and Network Dialup connection document are identical except that the Network Dialup connection document has an additional tab that displays the dialup information. Therefore, Table 6.4 covers both kinds of connection document, but the Network Dialup section of it describes fields that are unique to Network Dialup connection documents. Table 6.8 covers the fields in a Notes Direct Dialup connection document. We'll look at pass-thru and hunt group connection document fields in the next section of this chapter.

Table 6.8 **Fields on Local Area Network Connection Documents and Network Dialup Connection Documents in the Personal Address Book**

Field Name	Description
	BASICS TAB, BASICS SECTION
Connection Type	Choose Local Area Network or Network Dialup
Use LAN port	Lists all LAN ports defined for this copy of Notes. Choose one or more LAN ports from the list.
	BASICS TAB, DESTINATION SECTION
Server name	Enter the name of the Domino server for which this document defines a connection. You can define more than one server here by listing them or with wildcards.
	NETWORK DIALUP TAB (NETWORK DIALUP CONNECTION DOCUMENTS ONLY)
Choose a service type	The choices are AppleTalk Remote Access, Microsoft Dial-Up Networking, and Macintosh PPP.
Edit Configuration	Press this button to open a dialog box displaying fields from the remote access service chosen in the Choose a service type field. These are fields of information necessary for the remote access service to make a connection to the remote access server. All of the services include fields for a remote connection name, a login name and password, and country code, area code, and phone number. Microsoft Dial-Up Networking also permits a field for a call-back phone number. In every case, only the remote connection name field is required, because the other fields merely duplicate (and, if populated, override) the information in the corresponding fields on the named remote connection document.
Other fields on this tab	Other fields that may appear on this tab depend on which choice you make in the Choose a service type field and are read-only. To edit their contents, press the Edit Configuration button.
	COMMENTS TAB
Comments	Enter here any information that will help you or your successors to recall the purpose of this document in future years. Also record special information here, such as contact information for the destination server's administrators. This is especially useful if the destination server is in another company's domain.

continues

Table 6.8 **Continued**

Field Name	Description
	ADVANCED TAB
Only from Location(s)	Use this field to define at which locations this connection will be usable. By default the field lists an asterisk, meaning this connection is usable at all locations. You can limit its use to certain locations by choosing those location documents.
Only for user	Use this field to define which users can use this connection. This defaults to the name of the user who is logged in when the document is created. If more than one user may use this copy of Notes, you may prefer to enter an asterisk to indicate that any user can use this connection.
Usage priority	Choices are Normal (the default) and Low. When trying to determine how to connect to a given server, Notes first looks for Normal priority connection documents, then polls its home server and name servers on the LAN, then broadcasts on the network for the destination server, then looks for Low priority connection documents. Thus you can use a low priority connection document to define a backup path to a server.
Destination server address	This field is optional. Ordinarily you would leave it blank, but you can use it to define the network address of the destination server. On a TCP/IP network, you could enter the server's host name or IP address. If you enter the IP address, the workstation would not have to go to a name server to learn the server's IP address.

Table 6.9 **Fields on a Notes Direct Dialup Connection Document in the Personal Address Book**

Field Name	Description
	BASICS TAB, BASICS SECTION
Connection Type	Choose Notes Direct Dialup
Always use area code	Default is No. Choose Yes if the local phone company in the destination server's area code requires the dialing of area codes for local calls.

Field Name	**Description**
	BASICS TAB, DESTINATION SECTION
Server name	Enter the name of the Domino server for which this document defines a connection. You can define more than one server here by listing them or with wildcards.
Country code	Enter the destination server's country code. Always enter the country code, even though this field is optional. If both the country code and the area code fields are completed on both the connection and location document, Notes will be able to determine whether it needs to dial the country code, the area code, or just the local phone number. If either the location document or the connection document is missing either the country code or the area code, Notes assumes that it must dial the whole number.
Area code	Enter the destination server's area code (or city code). Again, you should always enter an area code, for the reasons cited for the Country code field, even though the area code field is optional.
Phone number	Enter the destination server's local phone number.
	COMMENTS TAB
Comments	Use this field to enter any information that will help you or your successors to recall the purpose of this document in future years. Also use it to record special information, such as contact information for the destination server's administrators. This is especially useful if the destination server is in another company's domain.
	ADVANCED TAB
Only from Location(s)	Use this field to define at which locations this connection will be usable. By default the field lists an asterisk, meaning this connection is usable at all locations. You can limit its use to certain locations by choosing those location documents.
Only for user	Use this field to define which users can use this connection. This defaults to the name of the user who is logged in when the document is created. If more than one user may use this copy of Notes, you may prefer to enter an asterisk to indicate that any user can use this connection.

continues

Table 6.9 **Continued**

Field Name	Description
	ADVANCED TAB
Usage priority	Choices are Normal (the default) and Low. When trying to determine how to connect to a given server, Notes first looks for Normal priority connection documents, then polls its home server and name servers on the LAN, then broadcasts, then looks for Low priority connection documents. Thus you can use a low-priority connection document to define a backup path to a server.
Modem port(s)	Optionally choose one or more ports if more than one is available. If none is selected, Notes will try all COM ports defined for this copy of Notes.
Login script filename	If you must use a connect script to connect to the destination server, enter the filename of the connect script here. You typically have to use a connect script to connect by phone to a server hosted by a server hosting service, such as CompuServe, because you typically are really dialing up a local node of the service's X.25 network, then connecting to the server over the service's network. Because of this, you normally have to provide a user name and password to be allowed onto the service's network. A connect script feeds that information (and any other necessary information) to the host service's local node server.
Login script arguments	These are the arguments that the script will pass to the host service. Usually you have to supply two arguments—the user name and the password.
Only to servers in domain	The destination server's domain name. This is optional and defaults to an asterisk wildcard, which means that any domain name is acceptable. You can limit the use of this connection so that it allows connections only to servers named in the domains you list in this field.

Creating a Local Replica of a User's Mail Database

Mobile users almost always need a local replica copy of their mail database. You or the user can easily created it by choosing New Replica in the File, Replication menu. The one important fact to keep in mind when you create this replica is that all of the location documents expect this database to have the same filename as the server copy and to be located in a subfolder called "mail." When you make the new replica, the default filename in the dialog box will be the same as the filename of the server copy, but the default location will be the data folder. To correct this, prepend "mail\" to the filename.

For example, Joe Doaks's mail database on his mail server is named `mail\jdoaks.nsf`. When you make the new local replica, Notes will want to name it `jdoaks.nsf` but you want to edit the name so it reads `mail\jdoaks.nsf`, that is, so that it resides in the "mail" subfolder locally just as it does on the server.

If you don't name the local copy this way, the Mail, Calendar, and To Do bookmarks won't work properly when a remote location document is in force. Also, the Create, Mail menu will have no entries. To correct these conditions, you have to do one of two things. Either move the local mail database into a folder (under the data folder) named mail. Or, in every location document that has the Mail file location field set to Local, edit the Mail file field so that it just says `filename.nsf`, not `mail\filename.nsf`.

Failure to coordinate the location of the local mail database and its filename in location documents is the most common error that users commit when they set themselves up to use Notes locally. You're forewarned.

The Outgoing Mail Database

Notes automatically creates a local Outgoing Mail database the first time a user makes current a location document in which the Mail file location document is set to Local. So you don't have to create it manually. Just switch to a Home or Travel location. The filename of the database is "mail.box" and it won't appear in the list of databases when you choose File, Database, Open. But you can open it by entering its filename in the Filename field of the Open Database dialog box.

One nice thing that many users discover about using local mail instead of server-based mail is that, if they hit the Send button by mistake, they can delete the sent message from the local Outgoing Mail database. If they do the same thing using server-based mail, the message is truly sent and not retrievable. Even if the user can open the server's Outgoing Mail database before the server routes the message to its destination, the user doesn't have the right to delete the message from that database. Some users set the Mail file location field of their Office location document to Local just to gain this benefit.

The downside is that you have to remember to choose Send outgoing mail periodically, or none of the "sent" messages will leave your computer until you exit Notes (at which point Notes reminds you that outgoing messages are pending). You can overcome this problem by scheduling periodic replication in the location document.

Setting Up Server Pass-Thru

We discussed server pass-thru in regard to servers in Chapter 4. Here we discuss it again, but this time in regard to users. Server pass-thru is a feature of Notes and Domino by which Notes users and Domino servers can pass through one or more Domino servers to reach yet other Domino servers. This feature produces many benefits. It benefits mobile dialup Notes users because they only have to dial up one server, but can then pass through that server to reach other servers. Before the advent of server pass-thru, dialup users had to dial up each server separately. In addition, Domino administrators don't have to set up modems on every server, but only on designated pass-thru servers.

Yet another benefit of server pass-thru is that a pass-thru server is, in effect, an application-level proxy server. You can set it up as a firewall server between your local LAN (or Intranet) and the Internet. Any Internet user can try to hit on the pass-thru server but it will only allow authenticated Notes users and Domino servers to pass through it to the other Domino servers on the inside of the firewall.

Because of these benefits it is a common practice for Notes organizations to set up pass-thru servers to accommodate either their Internet-based users or their mobile dialup users or both. Dialup pass-thru servers typically use multi-port serial interfaces to accommodate multiple (4, 8, 16, or more) modems and incoming phone lines.

Companies with especially large armies of dialup users may also consolidate multiple pass-thru servers into "hunt groups." A hunt group is a group of Domino servers that share a set of phone lines. All users dial the same phone number but any server in the hunt group may actually pick up the line. The user passes through the hunt group to his or her destination server(s).

To set up server pass-thru, you have to enable it for the initiating users, the pass-thru servers, and the destination servers. If any member of the chain does not enable its portion of pass-thru, it will fail. Specifically you have to do all of the following things:

- **Users have to designate a default pass-thru server in the appropriate location document** (in the Passthru server field on the Servers tab). (Alternately users can create a Passthru Server connection document, which states that, to reach Server1, the user must pass through Server2. But this is less useful than designating a pass-thru server in the location document.)

- **Users have to be able to connect to the designated pass-thru server(s).** For a mobile user this means that the user must have a Notes Direct Dialup or Network Dialup connection document describing how to reach the pass-thru server.

- **The pass-thru server must allow users to pass through it and must allow them to pass through to the destinations they seek.** The server document has three fields that cover this requirement. Under Security, Passthru Use, they are Route through, Cause calling, and Destinations allowed.

- **The server the user wants to reach must permit itself to be reached via passthru.** The Access this server field in the server document covers this requirement. The field is located in the Security, Passthru Use section.

See the section in Chapter 4 on server pass-thru for more information.

Setting Up Access to Non-Domino Servers

Notes users can reach all sorts of servers other than Domino servers. These include Web, FTP, and Gopher servers, Internet mail servers, Internet news servers, and LDAP directory servers. Notes is set up by default with the capability of accessing Web servers, FTP servers, Gopher servers, and some LDAP servers. To access the other kinds of servers, you have to do some setup work.

Setting Up Access to Web, FTP, and Gopher

Notes access to Web (HTTP), FTP, and Gopher servers is in place by default, in the form of a choice of browsers, as long as Notes has access to a TCP/IP port. (There must also be Web, FTP, or Gopher servers on the net to which the TCP/IP port connects). That port could be a LAN connection to a network that has proxy server access—or (can you imagine?) direct access—to the Internet; or it could be a Network Dialup port to an ISP. By default Notes uses an OLE version of Internet Explorer, running inside the Notes window, as its browser. But you can change the browser in the Internet Browser field of your location document, and use any browser that you want, including Notes itself, which is compliant with HTML 4.0 and HTTP 1.1.

For Notes users that don't have access to a TCP/IP port, setting up access to Web, FTP, and Gopher servers involves a little work. Such users might be located on a LAN that only uses SPX or NetBIOS. For these users, you can set up a Domino server to be their InterNotes® server. An InterNotes® server is, in fact, a proxy browser. The user sends a URL to the InterNotes® server. The InterNotes® server forwards the request in its own name to the responding Web server, and receives the requested Web page. It stores the Web page in a shared database called Server Web Navigator (web.nsf) and sends the resulting Notes database document to the requesting Notes user. Because of all the processing, browsing this way is slower than browsing directly, but it beats a poke in the eye with a sharp stick.

Set up an InterNotes® server as follows:

1. Make sure the designated InterNotes® server has access to a TCP/IP port. The port should be a LAN port and it should connect to the Internet or at least to the company's Intranet.

2. On the designated InterNotes® server, run the InterNotes® Web Retriever server task. To run it manually, enter Load Web at the server console or choose Web Retriever in the Start New Task dialog box in Domino Administrator (in the Server, Status screen, choose Tools, Start. To set it to start automatically each time the server starts, add the word "web" to the servertasks variable in the server's notes.ini file, as follows:

   ```
   servertasks=...,web
   ```

When InterNotes® Web Retriever starts for the first time, it will create a database on the server called Server Web Navigator, using the filename `web.nsf`. InterNotes® Web Retriever will store all retrieved HTML documents in that database, and any users you wish will be able to browse the database.

3. In appropriate user setup profiles, enter the name of the InterNotes® server to the InterNotes® server field and choose from InterNotes® server in the Retrieve/open pages field (both on the Basics tab).

4. In users' location documents, enter the name of the InterNotes® server to the InterNotes® server field (on the Servers tab) and choose Notes in the Internet browser field and from InterNotes® server in the Retrieve/open pages field (both on the Internet Browser tab).

5. Tell the affected users that they can now use Notes to browse the Web (or at least to browse company Web servers). Tell them about the Server Web Navigator database on the InterNotes® server.

The Domino server-based InterNotes® Web Retriever is not as fast or as nice for users as having their own built-in browsers. But for users who would have no other access to the World Wide Web, it's a very nice solution. In fact, even if you have your own browser, the server-based Web browser is potentially useful, because it is a "shared" browser. It stores the pages it downloads into a shared Notes database that has some nice features, including Web Tours and a Web page rating system. Its users can benefit from each other's browsing experience. For information about tuning the InterNotes® Web Retriever and advanced features of Server Web Navigator, see Chapter 13.

Other Internet Servers

Notes can be a client to other Internet servers as well, including POP and IMAP mail servers, SMTP hosts, NNTP news servers, and LDAP directory servers. Except for a few LDAP accounts which Notes sets up automatically, you have to set up an account document in your Personal Address Book before you can use Notes to interact with POP, IMAP, SMTP, NNTP, or LDAP servers.

In addition, to interact with a POP mail server, you have to create a location document and maybe a connection document. Also, you have to designate a local mail database (which may be your Notes mail database or a separate mail database) in which to store your POP mail.

To interact with IMAP servers, you have to create a location document and maybe a connection document. Notes will create a proxy database, which you can optionally convert to a database that replicates the contents of your IMAP account on your IMAP server.

Creating Account Documents

You can create account documents either with the Lotus Notes Client Configuration wizard during Notes workstation setup, or manually on existing Notes workstations. Either way, you enter the information Notes needs to be able to converse with the foreign server later on. In either case, before you start the process of creating the account, you should have certain information in hand:

- Any phone number necessary to dial up an ISP.
- The ISP's Internet domain name (for example, isp.com).
- The fully qualified domain name of the Internet server for which you are creating the account (for example, mail.isp.com).
- The user name assigned to you by the ISP.
- The password assigned to you by the ISP.

To create account documents during Notes workstation setup, simply answer Yes to the appropriate questions when they appear. You will have the opportunity to create every kind of Internet account. If you choose to create POP or IMAP account documents, Notes will also generate the other objects necessary to use the accounts, including location documents and databases.

To create an account document on an existing Notes workstation, open the user's Personal Address Book to the Advanced, Accounts view, and choose Account in the Create menu or Add Account in the Toolbar. An Account form will appear. Depending on what kind of account you set up, the form will either have two or three tabs. No matter what kind of account you create, you will have to fill in the following fields (see Table 6.10):

Table 6.10 **Account Document Fields**

Field	Description
	ON THE BASICS TAB
Account name	Enter any descriptive name. The account will appear in the Accounts view under this name.
Account server name	Enter the fully qualified domain name (for example, mail.isp.com) or IP address of the account server.
Login name	Enter your login name for any account that requires one.
Password	Enter your password for any account that requires one.
Protocol	Choose the protocol for which you are creating this account. Your choices are IMAP Offline, IMAP Online, LDAP, NNTP, NNTP, POP, and SMTP.

continues

Table 6.10 **Continued**

Field	Description
	ON THE BASICS TAB
SSL	Choose Enabled if the server requires it. If the server makes it optional, enable it only if you need to connect to the server securely. If the server doesn't support SSL, don't enable it. For more information about SSL security, see Chapter 20.
Only from location(s)	By default the asterisk is selected, which means the account will be usable from any location. If you wish to make it usable from selected locations, deselect the asterisk and select individual location documents. If you are creating a mail account and you haven't yet created the location document you want to associate with this account, you'll have to stop, create and save the location account, then come back here and finish this document.
	ON THE ADVANCED TAB
Port number:	This defaults to the standard well-known port number for each protocol, and you shouldn't have to change it unless instructed to do so by the administrator of the account server.
	ON THE ADVANCED TAB IF (ON THE BASICS TAB) SSL IS ENABLED
Accept SSL site certificates	Choose Yes to accept site ertificates from unknown c certifying authorities, No to refuse them. If you choose No, you will have the opportunity, when such a certificate is offered, to accept or reject it.
Accept expired SSL certificates	Choose Yes to accept expired site certificates without question, No to refuse them. If you choose No, you will have the opportunity, when such a certificate is offered, to accept or reject it.
Send SSL certificates when asked (outbound connections only)	Choose Yes to send certificates without question to a server that requests them, No to refuse the request.
Verify account server name with remote server's certificate	If enabled, Notes compares the name on a server's certificate with the s Account server name field (Basics page).
SSL protocol version	Defaults to Negotiated, which means Notes will use any version (from 2.0 to 3.0) of SSL upon which it and the server can agree. Alternately you can choose the version to be used. Leave this at Negotiated unless, as a troubleshooting technique, you have to set a version to make Notes and the server talk to each other.

Fields specific to each kind of account appear in each account type's section later.

Creating POP Mail Accounts

In the early days of Internet email, host computers were on line all the time and mail was pretty much always immediately deliverable to all mail accounts. With the growth of small computers that may not be powered up and on line 24x7, a need arose for a type of server that could accept mail for a user and hold it until the user came on line and could retrieve it. The Post Office Protocol (POP) was one response to that need. Currently in version 3 (hence often referred to as POP3), POP defines a type of mail server that does exactly that—it holds one's mail until one picks it up. When a POP mail client picks up its mail, it downloads it into its own files. By default, mail readers erase the server copies of messages after downloading them, but that is optional (and the Notes default is to *not* erase them). Once downloaded, the POP client manages the messages internally.

Notes as a POP mail client downloads the messages into a standard Notes database based on a Notes mail template. You can use your Notes mail database (the one in which you receive mail from Notes users) or you can create a separate mail database to hold mail for one or more POP accounts.

To create a POP mail account, you must create an account document and a location document in your Personal Address Book. If you are not using the Internet location document for other purposes, you could use it here instead of creating a new one. You must also designate a Notes database to hold downloaded messages (and create the database if it doesn't exist). If you use a modem to connect to the Internet, you will need a Network Dialup connection document that is usable with the location document you create. If one doesn't already exist, use the Connection Configuration wizard to create one. You can access the Connection Configuration wizard from the Action Bar when the location document is open.

We learned how to create account and location documents earlier in this chapter. Here we'll review just the aspects of them that are unique to POP mail setup.

A POP mail account document has only one unique field, as follows (see Table 6.11):

Table 6.11 **The POP Mail Document Field**

Field	Description
	On the Protocol Configuration Tab
Leave mail on server	Yes means that, when you download messages from a POP server, they won't be erased from the server. No means they will be erased. Defaults to Yes. (But defaults to No on most non-Domino POP servers.)

The significant fields in a location document associated with a POP mail account are as follows in Table 6.12:

Table 6.12 **Fields in POP Mail Account Location Document**

Field	Description
	ON THE BASICS TAB
Location type	Choose Local Area Network if the connection to the ISP is constant. Choose Network Dialup if the connection to the ISP is by modem. Choose Custom if there are multiple connection types.
Location name	Enter a descriptive name, one that will inform you which ISP and protocol are involved (for example, Eagle POP Mail).
Internet mail address	Enter your return Internet address for this ISP (for example, RobK@isp.com). This will be the address to which correspondents reply to you.
On the Servers tab:	Don't enter the ISP's mail server in any of these fields. However, you can enter your Domino servers' names here.
	ON THE MAIL TAB
Mail file location	Choose On Server if the mail file that will receive messages from the Internet mail server is on a Domino server (for example, your Notes mail database). Choose this only if your mail server is accessible by LAN. Choose Local if the mail file that will receive messages from the Internet mail server is on your workstation.
Mail file	Enter the partial path name of the database that will receive messages from the POP server (for example, mail\EagleMail.nsf).
Internet domain for Notes addresses when connecting directly to the Internet	Enter the ISP's Internet domain name (for example, isp.com).
Send outgoing mail	Choose directly to Internet if you intend also to set up an SMTP account for this ISP's SMTP server. Choose through Domino Server to deliver outgoing mail to your Domino mail server.
On the Replication tab:	Optionally, set a replication schedule. Notes will pick up mail from and deliver it to your ISP on that schedule.

If you designated an existing database (for example, your mail database on your Mail server or an existing local replica of it) in the Mail file field in the location document, you are finished setting up this mail account.

If you designated the local replica of your mail database, and you have not created a local replica, you have to do that now. See "Creating a Local Replica of a User's Mail Database," earlier in this chapter.

If you designated a database that doesn't exist anywhere (for example, a database other than your mail database), you have to create it now, as follows: On your File menu, choose Database, New. The New Database dialog box appears. Fill in the fields as follows in Table 6.13:

Table 6.13 **Fields in the New Database Dialog Box**

Field	Description
Server	Choose Local if, in the Mail file location field of the location document, you chose Local. Choose your mail server (that is, the server designated in the Home/Mail server field of the location document) if, in the Mail file location field of the location document, you chose On server. Caveat: If you choose a server, you must have the right to create new databases on that server, or this process will fail.
Title	Enter any descriptive database title, up to 32 characters.
File Name	Enter the partial path name of the new database (for example, `mail\EagleMail.nsf`).
Template Server	Leave Local chosen if you chose Local in the Mail file location field of the location document. Otherwise, choose the same server as in the Server field. In either case, in the list below the Template Server button, choose Mail (R5.0).
Advanced	(Optional) Choose Allow soft deletions.

When you click OK, Notes will create the database. You have successfully set up a POP mail account. Switch to the POP mail location document to use it. But before doing so, you may have to create an SMTP account. See the next section of this chapter for details.

Creating SMTP Mail Accounts

If, when creating your POP mail location document, you chose through Domino Server in the Send outgoing mail field, you don't have to create an SMTP mail account. If, instead, you chose directly to Internet, then you should create an SMTP mail account to go with your POP mail account.

You will receive incoming mail through the POP mail server. You will send outgoing mail through the SMTP server. Every ISP that offers POP mail services also has an SMTP server. Its name may be smtp.isp.com or mail.isp.com, but you should check with the ISP to verify their SMTP server's name (or ping those host names and see if you get a positive reply).

To create an SMTP mail account, all you have to do is create an SMTP account document in your Personal Address Book. The account document has no special requirements. Just choose SMTP in the Protocol field and select your POP mail location in the Only from location(s) field. You don't have to create a location document because this account will use the same location document you created for your POP account.

The first time you send mail with the POP mail location document selected, Notes creates a database to hold outgoing SMTP mail (if one doesn't already exist) and deposits the outgoing message in it. The database is called Outgoing Mail and its filename is smtp.box. The name is confusing because the database for outgoing Notes mail is also called Outgoing Mail but has the filename mail.box. Most people rarely if ever have to open either database, but if you ever do, and you're not sure which one you are looking at, choose File, Database, Properties. The filename will appear on the Database Basics tab. While you have Database Properties open, maybe you should retitle the database. Call smtp.box Outgoing SMTP Mail and call mail.box Outgoing Notes Mail. If you have previously added these databases to a bookmark folder, you may also find that you have to rename their bookmarks. To do so, right-click on the bookmark and choose Rename.

Creating IMAP Mail Accounts

The big drawback of POP is that you have to download your mail to read and respond to it. For Notes users whose POP mail is stored on their mail servers, this isn't a big problem. But for most Internet users, this means that they can only use one computer to access their mail. IMAP was developed to address this problem.

IMAP mail resides full-time on the IMAP server, just as Notes mail does on the Domino server. Notes as an IMAP mail reader can work with the mail IMAP on-line, disconnected, or off-line modes. But Notes refers to both disconnected and off-line modes as "off-line" mode. (See Chapter 17," IMAP Mail," for a full explanation of IMAP mail.)

In online mode, users download mail headers into their mail reader. They peruse them, then choose to read individual messages, which are downloaded on demand. When a user replies to a message, the reply returns to the IMAP server, which delivers it. When the user finishes reading and writing mail, all the messages remain on the IMAP server. If the mail user wants to organize his messages into folders, the IMAP server maintains the folders. In disconnected mode, IMAP mail users can download batches of messages into their mail reader, disconnect from the mail server, work with the messages offline, then reconnect and upload local changes to the server. Finally, in offline mode, IMAP users can, if they want, download messages, then delete the originals from the server while continuing to maintain the local copies; this is how POP mail readers work.

When you set up an online IMAP account for a Notes user, Notes creates a proxy database, which it uses to store the message headers and downloaded message bodies. However, the proxy database only stores them temporarily. Notes deletes them when you terminate the session with the IMAP server.

In IMAP off-line mode, Notes permits you to download messages in either of two ways. First, you can download them into your Notes mail database. Any messages downloaded this way land in the Inbox. If they were in folders on the IMAP server, the copies in your Notes mail database lose those relationships. This is true IMAP offline mode. The benefit here is that all of your mail comes into a single inbox (your "universal inbox," as Lotus likes to call it).

Alternatively, you can replicate your IMAP account into a Notes database. Then all downloaded messages remain in the same folders they were in on the IMAP server. You can change folder relationships in either place, and Notes will replicate the changes. This is really IMAP disconnected mode. The downside of this is that you have to maintain two separate inboxes, one for your Notes mail, the other for you IMAP mail.

To create an IMAP account, you have to create an account document and a location document. Notes creates the proxy database for you when you save the account document. If you are not using the Internet location document for other purposes, you could use it here instead of creating a new one.

When you create the account document, follow the instructions in "Creating Account Documents" earlier in this chapter. In the Protocol field of the account document, choose IMAP Offline or IMAP Online. If you choose IMAP Offline, no special fields appear. If you choose IMAP Online, the Protocol Configuration tab will appear, on which you have to decide what to do with the Sent folder name and Drafts folder name fields. Their default entries are Sent and Drafts.

If folders already exist for those purposes (sent mail and drafts) on the IMAP server, you have to make sure that the names that appear in these fields on the account document match the names of those folders on the IMAP server. If the folders don't exist on the IMAP server, you can leave these fields as is, and Notes will attempts to create folders on the IMAP server called Sent and Drafts (or whatever names you enter here).

When you create the location document, follow the directions earlier in this chapter under "Creating POP Mail Accounts." If you use a modem to connect to the Internet, you will need a Network Dialup connection document that is usable with the location document you create. If one doesn't already exist, use the Connection Configuration wizard to create one. You can access the Connection Configuration wizard from the Action bar when the location document is open.

Your IMAP online or IMAP offline account is ready to be used. To use it, switch to the location document for which it is active, then access it in one of three ways:

- Click the Mail icon in the Bookmark bar.
- Choose Open Proxy, which appears in the Actions menu and on the Action bar when the IMAP mail account document is open in read mode.
- Open the proxy database. Its name is *accountname* (IMAP), where *accountname* is the name you entered in the Account name field of the IMAP mail account document.

If you created an offline IMAP account, and a location from which it is available is currently selected, the Replicator page includes two new entries: Receive Internet mail and Send outgoing Internet mail. When you click Start or Send & Receive Mail on the Replicator page, Notes will retrieve new messages from the IMAP account and put copies of them in your Notes mail inbox. Also, it will deliver any pending messages to your IMAP server.

If, instead of pulling IMAP messages into your Notes mail inbox, you prefer to maintain a local replica copy of your IMAP account, you can set one up as follows:

1. Open the IMAP proxy database.
2. Choose File, Replication, New Replica. The IMAP proxy database becomes an IMAP replica database.
3. At the Replicator page, choose Start to pull data from your IMAP account into the replica database. Later, when you make changes to the replica data, replication will push those changes to the IMAP server, in addition to pulling IMAP server changes into the replica.

Creating Internet News Accounts

Usenet newsgroups are a type of Internet-based discussion forum. Internet News servers host newsgroups, and there are many such servers on the Internet. Usually anyone can follow the discussions and contribute to them without logging in but that depends on the news server. Most ISPs host news servers for their own users; those servers may only let their own users in. News servers can carry replica copies of each other's newsgroups, so not everyone in the world has to try to access the same news server to participate in a given discussion.

Newsgroup discussions generally limit discussion to the topic for which they were created. They are named according to a hierarchical naming system that classifies and identifies their discussion topics. For example, a newsgroup where discussion about Lotus Notes system administration takes place might be named comp.groupware.lotus-notes.admin.

Users use newsreader programs to communicate with their news server. Typically a user will first browse the available discussions on the news server. If, judging from its name, a newsgroup looks potentially interesting or useful, the user can subscribe to it. Then the user can read and write newsgroup articles (as the discussion documents are called). News servers and newsreaders communicate with each other using a protocol called Network News Transport Protocol (NNTP).

Naturally, Notes can be used as a newsreader program. To do so, you have to set up an NNTP account document. You don't need to create a location document. However, when you create the NNTP account document, you might want to limit its use to locations where you have Internet access.

When creating the NNTP account document, leave the Login name and Password fields blank unless you know you have to log in to the news server. Choose NNTP as the protocol. When you do so, a field called Use Replication history when replication will appear. Leave it set to Yes. By doing so, you effectively tell Notes not to download message headers that it has previously downloaded. That speeds things up for you each time you revisit a server.

When you save the NNTP account document, Notes creates a proxy account called *accountname* (NNTP), where *accountname* is the name you entered in the Account name field of the account document. The proxy account temporarily stores downloaded article summaries and articles, but discards them when you close the database.

To access a news server, open the proxy database. Notes connects to the news server. Click on the Newsgroups button to download a list of newsgroups on the server. Subscribe to a newsgroup to download a list of article summaries. Browse the summaries, download the full text of any that you want to read more fully, and reply to them if you want.

Instead of storing article summaries and content only while on line, you can maintain a local database that holds replica copies of the article summaries and content that you download from subscribed newsgroups. Then you can read and write replies offline. Later, when you replicate, your replies are uploaded to the news server and new content from other contributors is downloaded to your replica database.

To create a replica of a news account, follow these steps:

1. Open the NNTP proxy database.

2. Subscribe to newsgroups you want to replicate.

3. Choose File, Replication, New Replica. The proxy database is converted to a replica database.

4. Click Start on the Replicator page to populate the database with articles.

Creating LDAP Directory Accounts

An LDAP directory is a directory that complies with the Lightweight Directory Access Protocol (LDAP). An LDAP directory is a list of objects. While it could list any sort of objects, most LDAP directories are directories of people, and you can use them to look up information about the people in them, such as their email addresses. In that way they are much like the Domino Directory (which is itself an LDAP-compliant directory) or a Notes user's Personal Address Book.

You may not realize it, but you already know something about LDAP. LDAP is a subset of the Directory Access Protocol (DAP), which is also known as the X.500 directory protocol. The reason you know something about it already is that the Domino Directory and naming system comply with X.500 as well as LDAP. Notes' hierarchical name system, in which users are named things like CN=Osprey/OU1=Servers/O=Stillwater/C=US, is a hallmark of both X.500 and LDAP directories. People in other LDAP directories are similarly named.

Conformance to the LDAP protocol makes it possible for anyone with an LDAP-compliant client (such as Lotus Notes) to look up information in any LDAP-compliant directory. Thus anyone with an LDAP client could theoretically look up your name in your Domino Directory (assuming you are willing to let them in), and you could use your Notes client to look up information about people in any LDAP directory.

There are a number of public-access LDAP directories on the Internet. Anyone can have their names listed in them. Account documents for the most well-known of these public directories were already in each Notes user's Personal Address Book when it was created. All you have to do is use them.

In addition, you can create account documents for any other LDAP directory. When you create such an account, choose LDAP as the protocol. Don't enter a login name or password unless you know that the server requires you to log in. LDAP account documents have a series of LDAP-specific fields on the Protocol Configuration tab. Those fields are in Table 6.14:

Table 6.14 **LDAP-Specific Fields on the Protocol Configuration Tab**

Search timeout	The amount of time in seconds that Notes will wait for the LDAP server to return the results of a search directed to it. The default is 60 seconds.
Maximum entries to return	The maximum number of directory entries to return as the result of a search. The default is 100.
Search base	If you leave this blank, searches of the directory will search the whole directory. You can limit the parts of the directory that are searched by entering limiting terms here. For example, entering c=us would limit searches to all entries that are located in the United States.
Check names when sending mail	This defaults to No. If set to Yes, Notes will look up addressee names in this directory (in addition to the Personal Address Book, the Domino Directory, and any other directories as are normally included in name lookup searches).

After you have created an LDAP account document, you can direct searches to it as follows:

1. Click the arrow to the right of the Search icon (looks like a magnifying glass) or press Alt+Shift+S. A menu of search options appears.

2. Choose Find People. The Directories dialog box appears.

3. Choose a directory. The available directories include your Personal Address Book, other local address books, and all of the LDAP directories for which you have account documents and which are available in the current location.

4. Enter search terms. You can enter names or addresses. You can choose Detailed Search to generate multiple-condition searches by choosing search terms in a series of fields.

Setting Up a Workstation for Shared Use

Some Notes users don't sit in front of a computer all day and don't even have a computer to call their own. They share a computer with one or more other users like themselves and sit down at it periodically to pick up email or update databases that they use. There are several ways to set up a Notes workstation so multiple uses can share it. Here are some ways:

- Set up multiple complete copies of Notes on the computer, one for each user.
  Pros: Easy to set up. Each user has his own identity.
  Cons: Uses lots of disk space.

- Set up one copy of Notes but multiple sets of data folders, one set for each user.
  Pros: Uses less disk space than the first scheme. Users still have their own identities.
  Cons: Still uses a lot of disk space, though not as much as the first scheme. Hardest scheme to set up. Registry entries all point to the last installed copy of Notes (other users can't double click a Notes database in Windows Explorer to run their copy of Notes).

- Set up one copy of Notes with one set of data folders that all users share. Set up a separate location document and ID file for each user, so he can use his own mail database with ease.
  Pros: Each user has own identity, own mail file. Uses relatively little disk space.
  Cons: Users must share local databases. Users must remember to clear their passwords when finished using Notes. Registry entries all point to the last installed copy of Notes (other users can't double click a Notes database in Windows Explorer to run their copy of Notes).

- Set up a single copy of Notes with a single, generically named ID file (for example, Shipping Department).

  Pros: No special setup requirements. Uses relatively little disk space. Only uses one Notes license.

  Cons: Users don't have their own identities or mail files; therefore, there is no audit trail.

To set up the first scheme, you install each copy of Notes in its own set of program and data folders, but you specify a separate folder for each set of shortcuts. If you use separate user profiles at this computer, then you don't even have to specify separate folders for shortcuts. You just have to make sure you log in as the eventual user for each Notes install.

When specifying shortcut paths in InstallShield during a Notes install, you can, if you want, specify a folder name like the following: Lotus Notes\Rob Kirkland

InstallShield will put the shortcuts for that installation of Notes in a folder called Rob Kirkland, which itself is in a folder called Lotus Notes. The Lotus Notes folder is in a folder called Programs.

To set up the second scheme, you install Notes multiple times, once for each user. Each time you specify the same program folder but a new data folder. Name the data folders after the users, so that later it will be obvious which data folder belongs to which user. After each install, move the newly installed `notes.ini` file from the program folder into the newly installed data folder. With each install, specify a new folder (named as described previously) for the shortcuts. Or, if using multiple user profiles, log on as the appropriate user for each install. Edit each set of shortcuts so that it points to the location (in the data folder) of `notes.ini`; otherwise Notes won't be able to find `notes.ini` and it won't start. For example, where the Notes program folder is c:\lotus\notes and the data folder is c:\lotus\joedoaks, the Target field of each shortcut should read as follows:

```
c:\lotus\notes\notes.exe =c:\lotus\joedoaks\notes.ini
```

The Start in field should read as follows:

```
c:\lotus\joedoaks
```

To set up the third scheme, install a single copy of Notes. But then copy the ID files of all sharing users into the data folder. Then create a series of location documents in the Personal Address Book. Name each location document for the user who will switch to it. The server fields in each location document should point to their owner's servers. The Mail file field of each location document should name its owner user's mail database. The Only for user field should contain an asterisk wildcard. Otherwise the users' location documents would disappear from the lists and be impossible to switch to. But the User ID to switch to field should contain the path name of the owner's ID file. Then, when a user switches to his location document, Notes would automatically switch to his ID file as well.

To set up the fourth scheme, create a generic user ID, then set up a standard Notes workstation using that ID file. Because you probably won't be able to positively identify the person who was using the ID file at any given time in the past, you won't be able to positively identify who did what. Therefore, you should consider giving this user relatively few database access rights.

II

Maintenance and Troubleshooting

Upgrading from Domino 4.x to Domino 5.0

7

IN GENERAL, LOTUS DID AN EXCELLENT JOB DOCUMENTING the tasks you need to perform to upgrade an existing Notes/Domino installation to R5. In fact, it may be the best documented aspect of Domino R5. By following the instructions outlined by Lotus, you should be able to upgrade your domain to R5 with very few surprises. So I won't waste your time in this chapter rehashing what Lotus has to say about upgrading to R5. Rather, I'll supplement Lotus's upgrade documentation, give you a heads-up on the few pitfalls that Lotus failed to warn you about, and in general, give you the keys to a successful upgrade.

The overall process of upgrading a Notes or Domino domain to R5 consists of the following general tasks:

- Planning and preparing for the upgrade
- Installing the new software
- Upgrading various features including directories, databases, search, and security

Lotus, of course, has provided you with an excellent book covering these topics in step-by-step detail. So, I'll just focus on the aspects that I think could stand a little extra attention.

Planning and Preparing for the Upgrade

There are three aspects of the planning and preparation process that I want to empha-size: reviewing your hardware capacity to ensure that your hardware will be able to han-dle the heavier load you're likely to put on it under R5; the value of conducting a dry run before upgrading for real; and the value of education to yourself and your users.

Hardware Review

First, you need to understand that Domino and Notes R5 do more than they did in R4. So, it should be no surprise that they use more computer resources than R4. Most organizations seem to overspec their servers anyway, so this may not be an issue for you. But if under your current version of Domino, your server is minimally config-ured, you'll definitely want to compare its specs with the R5 hardware requirements.

Even if your current servers have multiple processors, hundreds of megabytes of RAM, and terabytes of disk capacity, you should review your server's disk configura-tion at this time. R5 has a new feature called transaction logging, which enhances the integrity of your data, the speed of disk I/O, and the efficiency of the backup process. It is an optional feature, but you should definitely learn more about it and consider implementing it. However, there's a very good chance you'll want to rearrange your files on disk first, because you should locate the transaction logs on a physically differ-ent hard disk or disk array than the data files. If you only have one hard drive (or array), you'll want to add another. If you have more than one, you may want to rearrange data files so as to free one up for the transaction logs.

Dry Run

Second, I encourage you to do a dry run before upgrading for real. In fact, I urge you to do it. You'll learn a lot. You'll feel free to experiment. You won't have to panic if you make mistakes or something goes wrong. You'll have fun.

If a team of administrators will work together to upgrade your domain, then have the team do the dry run together. Pick a Saturday, preferably a cold and rainy one, and work through the whole process together. As the group progresses through the process and discovers one new R5 feature after another, you'll get really excited about R5.

Set up at least two servers and two workstations on a segregated network. You should have user IDs for users with administrative rights and users with standard rights. Set up the servers with the same versions of Domino and Notes as are currently running on your real computers, and with the same (or different but identically named) IDs and the same Public Address Book and Notes applications that reside on your real servers. (By using identically named IDs, you can just copy databases over to the test servers without having to worry about editing access control lists to reflect the fictional names you invented.)

If you don't have access to your real IDs, just create a set of fake ones in the Server Administration screen. Create an Organization certifier, OU certifiers, server IDs, and user IDs. They won't be usable in your real Notes domain, only your test domain. (That's good.) Give them filenames that make it obvious that they are for your test domain. That way if they ever get mixed up with your real IDs you won't tear out your hair trying to figure out why they don't work.

The test servers don't need to be hardware replicas of their real-life counterparts; they won't be handling the real-life loads that your real-life servers do. But they should be software replicas as much as possible, because after you upgrade them, you'll use them to test your R4 applications under R5 conditions.

When your test servers and workstations are up and running your current versions of Domino and Notes, but before you start to upgrade them, stop and consider whether you should rearrange the files on your servers' hard drives.

Why? Two possible reasons. Perhaps, in your hardware review (see the preceding section) you concluded that you'll need to rearrange the files on your hard disks to accommodate R5's transaction logging. Alternatively, even if you have researched transaction logging and concluded it's not for you, you may still want to rearrange your files. Here's why:

- Under R3 the standard software installation put all program and data files in the c:\notes folder (except under Windows, where one file, `notes.ini`, ended up in the Windows OS folder).

- Starting with R4.0, the standard software installation changed so that program files ended up in c:\notes and data files ended up in c:\notes\data. On Windows computers, `notes.ini` still went into the Windows OS folder.

- Starting with R4.6, the install program puts program files in c:\lotus\domino and data files (including the `notes.ini` file) in c:\lotus\domino\data.

- Under R5 the default is the same as under late releases of R4—program files in c:\lotus\domino and data files in c:\lotus\domino\data. Except now `notes.ini` is being installed in c:\lotus\domino on nonpartitioned servers, c:\lotus\domino\data on partitioned servers!

Which one of these ways are your servers configured? Oops, I mean, *how many* of these ways are your servers configured? Are you happy with your current server configuration(s)? If not, there's no time like dry-runtime to learn how to reconfigure your computer. You can't do any real harm.

Two "by-the-ways": First, if you don't tell Domino or Notes where to find `notes.ini` with a command line argument, it always looks for it first in the search path, then the system folder, then the installed program folder. Second, here are the places you'll have to make changes if you do decide to rearrange the files on your server(s):

- The server's `notes.ini` file. Open it in a text editor and search for all drive references.

- The shortcuts (if your servers run under Windows) or batch or cmd files or scripts that run the server. Under Windows, the shortcuts are in the "Start Menu" folder. Under Windows NT there are several "Start Menu" folders, one under each branch of the "Profiles" folder in the Windows folder.

- In Windows, the Registry. To edit it, open `regedit.exe` (or `regedt32.exe`) and search for "lotus," "notes," "domino," and so on. If you are uncomfortable editing the Windows Registry, you could skip it. If you do, you might discover that, when you run the Domino installation program, it can't find your current copy of Domino. Just tell it where the files are really located and move on. Remember, these servers are for test purposes. So, don't worry about hurting anything.

But, let's get back to your dry run. Your test servers and workstations are running. You have (or have not) rearranged the locations of the files on them. You are finally ready to upgrade the test servers and workstations. To do so, follow Lotus's step-by-step instructions. Upgrade first to the latest quarterly maintenance release/update of your current version of Domino and Notes (or to at least 4.1.x if you are running 4.0 or earlier). Then upgrade to 5.x.x (whatever is current as you read this).

As you work your way through Lotus's checklists, write notes in the margins. You will discover that, here and there, Lotus left out a step—usually the last step of restarting whatever they had you stop in the first step. You might also discover, somewhere along the way, that your server responds in some unexpected way. You'll have to figure out how to get back on track. Aren't you glad this is a dry run? Aren't you glad this isn't a midnight upgrade of the CEO's mail server?

After you've installed the first R5.x server and brought it back up, but before you upgrade any other box, use a Notes 4.x client to examine the Public Address Book on the upgraded server. You might notice that some of the documents don't format properly anymore (or Lotus might have fixed that problem between my writing and your reading this). Here's the point: Don't upgrade your real servers until you are ready to upgrade your administrators' workstations, because you can't administer R5 servers from R4 Notes clients.

Next, upgrade a workstation to Notes R5, Domino Administrator, and (optionally) Domino Designer. Then, upgrade your other server(s). Then, upgrade your other workstation(s). As with the first server, write notes in the margins of Lotus's installation checklists, because you will encounter anomalies and you want to document them and your workarounds.

When all your test servers and workstations have been upgraded, hand the workstations over to the people who manage your Notes applications. Have them run through every feature of every application to see how they work under R5. Document any problems and workarounds. (If it's still 1999 as you run these tests, try turning the clock ahead to 2000, then test again.)

As you can see, a dry run is a great opportunity for you to find out where the pitfalls are while you're still playing in the sandbox. You can experiment without risk. You will gain an amazing amount of knowledge about the upgrade process and the differences between your current installation and your future one, all without having to worry about making a fool of yourself or losing your job.

Education and Training

If you want your upgrade to R5 to be successful, be sure to educate your administrators, your designers, and your users in its new features. Don't skimp on this. The more you and your people know about R5, the smoother the transition will go. And when people discover Notes's new features, they'll get really excited about them. The transition to R5 will gain momentum. Your company will reap greater value from Notes and Domino.

Start by reading up on Domino and Notes R5. Read the first chapter of this book. Read the R5 Release Notes. Read the last several sections of the first chapter of the Lotus yellow book "Moving to Notes and Domino Release 5." The sections titled "New Domino server features," "New Domino mail features," "New Lotus Notes client features," New Domino application features," and "New Domino search features" are good, short, well-organized summaries of R5. In fact, while you are still running R4, you can pull up these (and similar) documents at www.notes.net and email them to your key people to sort of kickstart the upgrade process.

In addition, go yourself and send others on your transition team to classes on transitioning from R4 to R5. Lotus has developed a couple of good seminars on the subject. Be sure to send your Notes developers too. There are plenty of new features to whet their appetites for R5.

Also, as soon as you have the opportunity to use the Domino Administrator, push yourself to learn its features and use it to perform administrative functions. As an experienced R4 administrator, you'll be inclined to open the Domain Directory (formerly the Public Address Book) directly, work from its views, and create and edit its documents correctly. It is still possible to do that (and occasionally you actually still have to do that). But the Domino Administrator is a phenomenally great administration interface. I recommend that you get comfortable with it as soon as possible.

Finally, plan to offer comprehensive educational opportunities to your users. Offer them a range of classes, videos, self-study materials, and books on R5. In addition to this book, Macmillan USA has a whole series of books under the Sams and Que imprints for Notes users, developers, and administrators. In particular, Sams's *Teach Yourself Lotus Notes 5 in 10 Minutes* by Jane Calabria and Dorothy Burke is a good, inexpensive, and a concise step-by-step guide aimed at busy corporate users. (Full disclosure: I'm married to Jane Calabria.)

Remember, the more your users know and the more resources they have at their fingertips, the less likely they'll be to bug you and the Help Desk with dumb questions.

Installing R5 Software over R4

In the section earlier in this chapter about performing a dry run, I suggested that you use an R4 administrative Notes client to view the Public Address Book on the first R5 server after you bring it up. If you did that, you would see that you can't administer R5 servers from a Notes R4 client. It's worse than that—you can't administer *any* servers in your domain from an R4 workstation after you've upgraded one server to R5, because you can't read certain documents in the R5 Public Address Book except from an R5 workstation.

The point here is that you shouldn't upgrade any servers in your production Notes domain just for the fun of it. If you want to play with R5, set up a separate test domain just for that purpose. Don't upgrade any of your production servers until you are ready to upgrade your entire domain. Not that you have to upgrade everything all at once—you don't. But at the very least, if you upgrade any servers, you have to upgrade your administrators' workstations as well.

Upgrading a Domino server from R4 to R5 takes some time. Among other things, you have to back it up, manually rebuild some views in the Public Address Book, upgrade the designs of various databases, and generally just tweak a lot of things. Do it during off-peak hours if you can; and warn users that it will be down for at least a couple of hours. You will have to perform extra chores when upgrading the administration server for the Public Address Book and any servers running the SMTP MTA, so allot even more time for them.

When you do upgrade, you'll upgrade one server first. Lotus recommends you upgrade a hub server first. The first step will be to shut down the server. Then you'll back it up and you're on your way. One thing Lotus neglected to have you do, which will make your life easier during the upgrade, is to disable any server autostart feature that may be in place. Under Windows NT, this means to disable automatic startup under Windows NT Services. Under other operating systems it means REMming out a line in a batch or script file. If any other programs (antivirus programs, for example) automatically load on computer startup, you should disable them too.

The goal here is to minimize frustration levels during the upgrade process. You may need to reboot the computer, and the autostart feature will be a nuisance. I recommend this for all of your upgrades.

Another thing that you should do on all of your servers before you upgrade them is clean out any old junk that has accumulated on their disk drives. You may discover old, obsolete Notes databases or other, unrelated programs left over from some earlier epoch. You can reclaim a lot of disk space by removing these things. If disk space is tight, this is especially important and valuable. During the upgrade process you will be rebuilding views on your databases. If you are short of free disk space, you might encounter errors during the rebuilding process.

After you've upgraded one server, I recommend you upgrade at least one administrative workstation next. Then upgrade the rest of your servers (or as many as you intend to upgrade initially). Regarding user workstations, there is no great hurry to get them upgraded, other than the fact that your users might want to take advantage of R5 features they may have heard about. Notes R4 works perfectly well with Domino R5 servers. The one thing that might cause you a problem is if you start upgrading your applications to R5 before you have upgraded all of your R4 users. Then they might run into problems running the applications.

Upgrading Databases, Directories, and Search, Security, and Monitoring Tools

After you have upgraded your server and workstation software to R5, there are miscellaneous other upgrades you can perform, including database file format, database design, directory, search, and security upgrades. Most of these are not urgent. You can function just fine without them. But they represent great new functionality; so you don't want to put them off forever. Two upgrades you do not want to put off are of the database file formats and the mail database designs.

Database Upgrades

Existing databases still have two R4 (or even R3) characteristics—their internal file format (their "on-disk structure," which is ODS20 under R4, ODS17 under R3) and their designs. In general, you want to upgrade them to R5's internal file format (ODS41) as soon as possible. The internal structure of a database doesn't replicate, so you don't normally have to worry about incompatibilities arising from this upgrade (and if you tested your applications in a dry run, you should know if any of them cannot tolerate this upgrade.)

You can upgrade the databases' ODS by compacting them. After compacting, you can run `updall` to update their view indexes. It's not strictly necessary to update the view indexes, but if you don't, the next user to open each view will experience delay because the server will rebuild that view's index before delivering it to the user.

If you don't want to upgrade a database, you can rename it *filename*.ns4. If you need to downgrade a database back to ODS20, you can compact it with the -R switch (not -r). You can find out a database's file format in the Files page of Domino Administrator, where the file format is listed along with other statistics about the file. If you don't want to compact a server's databases during the day, you can set up a Program document to run in the middle of the night.

Update database *designs* with some caution. Users still using Notes R4 can't use R5 database features and, depending on a variety of factors, may not be able to use a database at all if you upgrade its design prematurely.

Upgrading Mail Databases

One database whose design you want to upgrade quickly is each user's mail database. You want to upgrade this as soon as possible after upgrading a user's workstation. If you don't, the user will soon call the Help Desk, because the R4 mail templates don't support all the features that the Notes R5 interface assumes they do. For example, a user will click the Inbox shortcut in Notes, then switch to another folder (or to the calendar view). Then, the user will close that window. The next time the user clicks the Inbox shortcut, if the user's mail is based on an R4 template, the other folder will appear, not the Inbox.

On the other hand, if you upgrade a user's mail while the user is still using Notes R4, you'll disable the user's access to his mail, because Notes R4 won't recognize all the features in the R5 mail template. Also, if you upgrade a mail database on an R4 server to the R5 template, the mail database will not function properly. This is mostly a problem in clustered mail servers where one server has been upgraded to R5 but another has not. Don't upgrade those mail users until both servers (and users' workstations) have been upgraded.

You have to do two things when you upgrade a user to R5. First, if you have the opportunity, warn the user that his mail interface might be a little goofy until you get a chance to upgrade the design of his mail database. Second, don't waste time getting around to upgrading user mail templates after upgrading their workstations. (Don't waste time upgrading that second clustered mail server.)

You can upgrade the design of user mail databases two ways. First, you can do each one manually through the Notes interface. You might use this method as the last step of a Notes upgrade. You could bring up Notes, have the user enter his password, then right-click the user's mail shortcut and, in the pop-up menu, choose Database, Replace Design. In the Replace Database Design dialog box, click Template Server, choose the user's mail server, then choose the Mail (R5.0) template (mail50.ntf).

Alternatively, you can upgrade whole groups of mail databases all at once using the convert utility. This is the same utility we used when we upgraded from R3 to R4, so maybe you'll remember it. You can use it to upgrade one or more mail databases simultaneously. A good way to use it is with a text list of mail filenames. If you upgrade, say, 20 users in one day, at the end of the day you could run a command something like the following:

```
load convert -f textfilepathname * mail50.ntf
```

This command takes the files in *textfilepathname* that are based on *any* mail template (*) and upgrades them to the R5 mail template (`mail50.ntf`).
A good way to create the list is to run the following command:

```
load convert -l c:\temp\masterlist.txt
```

This creates a text file that lists every *primary* mail file on the server. A primary mail file is a mail file on one's mail server. Some users might have replica mail files on other servers. The replicas are not primary mail files.

What you can do is treat `c:\temp\masterlist.txt` as a, well, master list. At the end of each day, you could open the file in a text editor, open a blank file in another text editor, then cut from the master file the filenames to be upgraded and paste them into the new file. Save and close the old file. Save the new text file under, say, `c:\temp\list.txt`. Then, run the first command above to upgrade just the users you upgraded that day.

The reason you cut and paste is that, each day, the master list will be shorter than it was the day before. You'll be able to see your progress as the master list gets shorter and shorter.

But wait! There's a little hitch here. You should stop the router before you upgrade these files (so it won't try to deliver a message in the middle of the upgrade), then restart it afterward. But, darn, it's time to go home. It'll take an hour or more to upgrade all those mail files. You don't want to wait around all that time just to restart the router. But neither do you want to leave without restarting the router.

To solve this problem, you can create a series of Program documents. The first one can shut down the router. The second one can load convert. The third one can run some hours after the first and second and restart the router. The key to getting these Program documents to work properly is in the first two fields, "Program name" and "Command line." Table 7.1 shows the entries for these two fields in all three Program documents.

Table 7.1 **Field Contents for Mail Conversion Program Documents**

Program Document	Program Name	Command Line
First Program document	nserver	–c "tell router quit"
Second Program document	nconvert	–f c:\temp\list.txt ★ mail50.ntf.
Third Program document	nrouter	Leave this field blank

Set the starting time of the second program document just one minute later than the first. Set the third Program document long enough after the second one for convert to do its work. Figure maybe five minutes per database to do the full conversion. The amount of time it will actually take depends on the speed of your computer and what other chores Domino has to perform at the same time. To arrive at a more precise number, you can convert one mail file manually and time it. If you set up these Program documents to run in the middle of the night, you don't have to shut down the router during business hours.

Generating Internet Return Addresses

If you plan to give your users email access to the Internet and you intend to use R5 Domino servers to do it (versus. R4 servers running the SMTP MTA), you really should make sure that all Person documents have a valid Internet email address in their Internet address field. Under R4 it was optional to populate that field; the SMTP MTA would use settings in a Global Domain document to cobble up a valid return address for all outgoing mail. Technically, you can still rely on the Global Domain document for that purpose. But Lotus highly recommends that you override the default and Global Domain return addresses by entering a valid address in each user's Internet address field.

In a small domain, you could do this manually. But you don't have to. Lotus has provided you with a tool that will generate valid Internet addresses and populate the Person documents with them. The tool is available in Domino Administrator under the People & Groups tab. Select the Person documents for which you want to add Internet addresses. Alternatively, don't select any Person documents—then the tool will add Internet addresses to all Person documents that don't already have them. In the Tools pane, choose People, Set Internet Address. Or, in the People menu, choose People, Set Person's Internet Address.

In the Set Internet Address dialog box, you choose a pattern for the addresses and enter the domain name. When you click OK, the tool generates addresses based on your supplied pattern, using information stored in each Person document. If your pattern would result in more than one user having the same Internet address, the tool will either use an alternate pattern that you can also supply or it will not create the duplicate address but create an error in the Notes Log instead.

Upgrading Directory Assistance and Cascading Address Books

If you use Directory Assistance (also known as. the Master Address Book) in R4, you should upgrade the design of the Directory Assistance database. You can do this in Domino Administrator under the Files tab. Select the database on any server on which it resides (but preferably one that has the right to push design changes to other servers), then open it. Choose File, Database, Replace Design. Choose the same server as Template Server, then choose Directory Assistance in the list of templates. Its filename is `da50.ntf`. Select Inherit future design changes and choose Replace.

If you use Cascading Address Books in R4, Lotus highly recommends you switch to using Directory Assistance. Lotus further recommends that you implement Directory Catalogs, a new feature in R5. See Chapter 11, "Domino Directory Services," to learn how to implement both.

Domain Search and the Database Catalog

Domain Search is a great new feature of Domino R5 that Lotus encourages you to implement early on. It is an improvement over Site Search if you are using that feature under R4. Domain Search allows you to index your whole Notes domain in a single full-text index, searchable from any Notes or Web client. You can also index selected file systems. In an improvement over Site Search, Domain Search filters all searches through appropriate access control lists so that users only find documents to which they have Reader access. (But that is not the case with file systems; don't index file systems where sensitive files are maintained.)

You set up Domain Search on a single, powerful server in your domain. Because the server has to do a lot of indexing, Lotus recommends that the Domain Search server (in Lotus's words) be "fast, powerful, and have a large amount of disk space—multiple processors, lots of RAM, and multiple high-volume drives…" The Domain Search server also sucks a lot of information in from databases and files located on other servers, so it (and your other servers) should be on a fast (100MHz or faster) LAN.

Like Site Search in R4, Domain Search builds an index on a single database—but in this case it builds the index on the Catalog database (`catalog.nsf`). This is the successor to the R4 Catalog with which you are undoubtedly already familiar. To enable Domain Search, follow these steps:

1. Open the Domain Search server's Server document (in Edit Mode) to the Server Tasks, Domain Indexer tab.

2. Set the Domain wide indexer field to Enabled.

3. Set the indexing schedule to meet your needs. (If you're not sure yet what your needs are—which is entirely understandable—accept the defaults.)

4. Optionally add server names to the Limit domain wide indexing to the following servers field. If you leave it blank, the indexer will index databases on all servers in your domain. I suggest that you limit indexing to servers that are accessible via reasonably fast and uncongested network connections.

5. Save and close the server document.

6. Run the catalog task on the Domain Search server (also known as. the "Domain Catalog" server). At the server console, enter **load catalog**.

When the catalog task loads, it discovers it is now the designated "Domain Cataloger." It discards any existing Catalog database and builds a new one.

To include a database in the index, enable the database property "Include in multi database indexing". Databases to be included in the domain index may reside on any servers included in the preceding step 4.

Be picky about what databases you include. Include only databases that add broadly useful information to the index. Otherwise you are consuming valuable computer resources with little return. For example, don't include user mail databases; nobody can see the indexed content except the mail user who owns the database.

To include file systems in the index, create one or more File System documents in the Catalog database. In general, create one File System document for each Domino server that hosts one or more file systems that you want to include.

File systems must be subfolders of the Domino server's data folder. To include file systems that are not such subfolders, create either directory links or Mapping/Redirection documents.

Create a directory link in Domino Administrator under the Files tab. Choose New Link in the Tools pane under Folder.

Create a Mapping/Redirection document as follows:

1. In Domino Administrator open the Server document for the appropriate server.

2. Choose Web in the Toolbar, then Create URL Mapping/Redirection.

Notice that URL Mapping/Redirection documents are no longer located in the Domino Configuration database. In R5 they are Responses to Server documents, residing, therefore, in the Domain Directory (formerly the Public Address Book). Same for Virtual Server documents. Notice also that you can now create File Protection and Realm documents. See Chapter 15, "Web Server Setup, Maintenance, Tuning, and Troubleshooting," for more information on all these developments, as well as others having to do with the Domino HTTP service.

To set up Notes users to search the Domain Index, you have to add the name of the Domain Search/Catalog server to their Location documents in the "Catalog/ domain search server" field under the Servers tab. Once you do, Notes users can conduct domain searches by clicking the drop-down section of the Search navigation button (upper-right corner of Notes screen), then choosing Domain Search.

Rather than update each user's Location documents one at a time at their workstations (that's *so* "R4"), add the name of the search server to the Catalog/Domain Search server field of your users' User Setup Profiles. (Oh, by the way, you can use User Setup Profiles to update existing users' workstations in R5. Refer to Chapter 5, "User Registration and Notes Client Installation," and Chapter 13, "Client Maintenance and Troubleshooting," for more information.)

To really set up Domain Search, there's a lot more you should know. You can categorize information in databases and file systems so that people can browse the Catalog for information, rather than finding it through full-text searches. You can adjust the number of indexing threads to increase indexing speed (at the expense of search speed) or increase search speed (at the expense of indexing speed). See Chapter 14, "Database Maintenance and Troubleshooting," for more information.

Before we leave the subject of Domain Search and the Catalog database, I want to suggest that, even if you've decided not to implement Domain Search just yet, you should look around in the Catalog database. It holds a lot more information about cataloged databases than earlier catalogs did, and is much more useful. You'll really like what you find there.

Upgrading Security

Lotus R5 upgrade documentation states that you can use X.509 certificates in Notes IDs, either alongside Notes certificates or instead of them. I have tried unsuccessfully to find evidence that the second option (X.509 certificates instead of Notes certificates) is true in R5.0.x. I suspect the developers pulled that feature from the Gold release of Notes at the last minute and the documenters didn't have time to update the documentation.

There's no question, however, that users can store both Notes and X.509 certificates in their IDs. Notes and Domino R5 can read, write, and store documents natively in MIME/MHTML format. Notes can use S/MIME to sign messages users send to Internet mail recipients and to decrypt messages they receive from Internet senders. Users must have an X.509 certificate to use S/MIME. See Chapter 10, "Security," for more information.

You should also be aware of limitations that arise in mixed (R3/R4/R5) Notes environments due to several changes in the R5 Notes ID file:

- ID files created under R5 aren't usable in an R3 Notes client. If you will need to continue creating R3-compatible Notes IDs, you should keep an R4 Notes administration client handy.

- If you use alternate names/languages in an R5 Notes ID, you can't use that ID with R4 or R5 Notes clients or Notes/Domino servers. see Chapter 6, "Advanced Client Setup" for more information about alternate names/ languages.

- R5 Domino Administrator can't create flat ID files. If you will need to continue creating flat Notes IDs, you should keep an R4 Notes administration client handy. (If you still haven't upgraded your organization to hierarchical IDs, call me; we need to have a serious talk!)

- Only R4.5 and later Notes clients can authenticate with servers that implement password checking. And only R4.5 and later Domino servers can perform password checking. If you use an ID to authenticate with a server that performs password checking, that ID is no longer usable with Notes releases earlier than R4.5.

- ID files that include X.509 certificates can't be used on an R3 Notes client. But, they can still be used on an R4 Notes client.

- Under R5 you can now control the tightness of Web name-and-password security. On the Server document under Security, in the Web server authentication field you can choose More name variations with lower security (which is how Web authentication worked pre-R5) and Fewer name variations with higher security. Under the second option, users have to enter more complete names than the first option permits.

Monitoring Tools

If you have used the server monitoring tools (the Reporter and Event Dispatcher; Statistic, File, and Event Monitors) under R4 or R3, you will discover that the tools you are familiar with don't work the same way under R5 as they did under R4. Unfortunately, if you don't pay close attention, R5 will stop notifying you of some of the potential problems that it warned you of under R4. So read on.

You'll notice when you upgrade your servers that Lotus has retired the Reporter. They have you remove it from the ServerTasks variable in your servers' notes.ini files. What they don't have you do is substitute the Collector for the Reporter. The reason for this is that the Reporter could only report statistics and statistic events generated by the server it was running on. So it had to run on every server.

The Collector can run on one server and collect statistics generated on other servers too, not just the one on which it runs. So you don't have to run it on every server. You can run it on one or two chosen computers. But you have to take the incentive and add "collect" to the ServerTasks variable of the notes.ini file of the server or servers that you determine should collect statistics from the other servers. Lotus unfortunately neglects to remind you to do that.

In addition, in the Statistics & Events database (events4.nsf) on the collecting server(s), you need to add one or more Server Statistic Collection documents so that the Collector will know what servers it should collect statistics from. (In Domino Administrator you can find Statistics & Events under Configuration.)

Collecting servers should not try to collect statistics from servers that they connect to over slow (for example, dialup) connections. Those servers can collect their own statistics. The Statistics Reports database (`statrep.nsf`) on all servers in the domain are replicas of each other, so those servers' statistics will eventually replicate to a server that's local to you.

If you pay attention to the Alarms and Events views of the Statistics Reports database (find it in Domino Administrator under Server, Analysis), you may also notice that Statistic Monitors no longer generate Alarm documents in R5. Also, Replication and ACL Change Monitors no longer email you when they detect replication failures and ACL changes.

If you look around in Statistics & Events, you'll also notice that what you knew in R3 and R4 as Event Monitors are now called Event Notifications.

What's going on here is that Lotus finally got around to making the functions (and names) of these documents logical. The Monitors no longer notify you of things. Only the Event Notifications do. To be notified of statistic events, replication events, and security events (which are what the Monitors always generated), you now have to create Event Notifications. The Monitors alone won't do that anymore.

What's curious about all this is that it's not clear that Lotus intended that the Monitors stop notifying you. If you read the R5 documentation on this subject, it implies that they still generate Alarms. But if they do, then my servers aren't working properly, because my Monitors don't generate Alarms or emails or anything other than events for which I have to create Event Notifications if I want to know about them. I suspect what happened here is that, in their fever to get R5 out the door without any more delays, the developers just didn't have time to keep the documenters fully informed of everything they did. Whatever the case, consider yourself notified.

Other New Features

There are many other new features that you will want to discover and implement. There just isn't any more space in this chapter to cover them.

You'll want to learn about Probes and how to implement them, so you can monitor your servers' on-going quality of service as you increase the loads on them over time. See Chapter 18, "Server Monitoring," for more information on this.

You'll want to learn about Message Tracking and Mail Reports, which can tell you all sorts of interesting things about your users' email habits. See Chapter 8, "Mail Routing Setup and Maintenance," for more information.

You'll want to learn about transaction logging, Web server clusters, directory catalogs (different from the database catalog), new Internet security features, and many more. If you skipped over Chapter 1, "Features of Lotus Notes and Domino 5.0," you might want to go back to it now for a review of a lot of the new features. I also recommend that you download the Reviewer's Guides from the Lotus Web sites (www.lotus.com and www.notes.net).

In this chapter I have assumed, more than in any other chapter, that you the reader already have extensive knowledge of Notes and Domino (because you are an R4 administrator upgrading to R5). Therefore, my goal here has been to tell you what's new in R5 and different from R4, and to alert you to potential problems, surprises, and opportunities. I skimmed over the details of actually setting up most features. You can find the details in the rest of the book and in the Lotus documentation.

8

Mail Routing Setup and Maintenance

MAIL ROUTING IS THE SINGLE MOST IMPORTANT service that Domino provides. It is also the most likely to cause trouble for the administrator. The mail router is the Domino component that transfers documents between Notes databases. (The replicator also transfers documents between Notes databases, but only between replica databases—the mail router transfers documents between all databases, replicas and non-replicas.) Domino mail routing provides the basis not only for Notes electronic mail but also for most Notes workflow applications.

It has always been important for the Domino administrator to understand how Domino mail routing works so that he could keep it running optimally. It is more important now than ever because, beginning with Release 5 (R5), mail routing has become both more powerful and more complex. It is more powerful because Lotus has incorporated SMTP mail routing capabilities right into the Domino mail router (and done away with the separate SMTP Message Transfer Agent in the process). Lotus has also given the administrator lots of new control over the mail routing process, such as anti-spam controls and the ability to put size restrictions on mail attachments. All this new control increases the complexity of the mail routing process.

This chapter addresses mail routing setup. It also addresses important issues as such shared mail setup and maintenance, routing topologies, and performance monitoring.

Planning for Mail Routing

To set up mail routing, you have to first make decisions about how and when mail should route, then you have to carry out your decisions. Over time, as circumstances change or you realize your initial decisions aren't working out as well as you hoped, you may have to change the way mail routes. The decisions that relate to mail routing are as follows:

- How many Notes domains there should be and how they should relate to each other.
- How many Notes named networks there should be and how they should relate to each other.
- How and to what extent your Notes domain(s) will transfer mail to and receive it from other mail domains, both Notes and non-Notes, and especially Internet mail domains.
- For each server, what Notes domain and Notes named networks it should be in and what role it will play, if any, in routing mail across domain and named network boundaries.
- For each server, whether and to what extent it should employ SMTP mail routing or NRPC mail routing.
- For your Notes domain(s) as a whole, and for each server, what restrictions you want to place on mail routing.
- For each server, whether or not to use shared mail.
- For your Notes domain(s) as a whole, and for each server, whether or not to use Message Tracking and other performance monitoring tools.

We have discussed most of these issues in earlier chapters. Others we'll discuss later in this chapter or in later chapters. We'll review two of them—Notes domains and Notes named networks—here briefly, as they relate to mail routing.

Notes Domains

A Notes domain is defined as a group of servers that share a Domino Directory. Every Domino server is a member of one and only one Notes domain. Users are a member of their home/mail server's domain. You decide what domain a server or user will be in when you create them. Moving a server or user to another domain is a relatively major undertaking.

For purposes of this discussion, the principal significance of the Notes domain is that servers that use NRPC mail routing cannot route mail across domain boundaries without a connection document. Also, one's domain is part of one's mail address; mail is always addressed to *addressee@domain*. (Users don't always have to address it that way. They can often address a message to just plain *addressee*. But Notes appends addressees' domains before sending a message, so that the address ends up as *addressee@domain*.)

Most organizations set up all of their Domino servers in a single domain. But, for various administrative purposes, you might decide to set up multiple domains. See Chapter 2 for a detailed discussion. You may also have multiple domains as a result of mergers or acquisitions. In that case, you have to plan how mail will route among your domains. Also, you may have to arrange mail routing between your domain(s) and others' Notes domains. Finally, you will almost certainly have to arrange mail routing between your domain(s) and Internet domains.

Notes Named Networks

Notes named networks allow you to tailor mail routing to the topology of your underlying network. Domino servers in the same Notes named network can transfer mail to each other immediately and without benefit of connection documents. Domino servers in different named networks can only transfer mail to each other if a connection document tells them how.

Domino servers can be in the same named network if they are constantly connected to each other and use the same network protocol (TCP, SPX, or NetBEUI). Servers that use different network protocols cannot be in the same named network (because they "don't speak the same language"). Servers that connect only by telephone (modem or ISDN) are not constantly connected and so cannot be in the same named network. Servers connected by a slow, expensive, or busy WAN link can be in the same named network but you might not want them to be. Also, you might have reasons unrelated to mail routing to set up multiple smaller named networks even though they could be in one large named network. See Chapter 2 for a detailed discussion.

Domino servers can run multiple protocols and can have multiple network ports (which may run the same or different protocols). Such a server can and will be in multiple named networks. We discussed the issues regarding network protocols and the techniques for adding, renaming, and removing ports in Domino servers in Chapter 3 and Chapter 4.

For each enabled port, a Domino server is in one named network. You can see the membership of named networks by looking at the Server/Networks view of the Domino Directory. You can see what ports a server has enabled and what named network each port is associated with in the Ports, Notes Network Ports tab of the server's Server document.

For a given port, you can move a server from one named network to another simply by changing the Notes Network field for that port in the server document.

When you first set up a new Domino server, it receives a default name for each enabled port. You should never accept the default names, but rather should choose your own. The problem with accepting Lotus's default network names is that you may inadvertently put servers in the same named network that aren't really candidates for membership in the same named network, with the result that you cripple mail routing.

For example, servers that only connect by telephone may end up in the same named network. They will try repeatedly and futilely to connect with each other through their non-existent network connection, only failing over to their real telephone connection after many failed tries to connect by network.

If none of your servers are remote from others, this problem may never arise. But, if you ever set up any remote servers, this pitfall may swallow you up. Protect yourself against it by always choosing your own names for named networks.

Understanding How Mail Routing Works in Domino

Through Release 4 (R4), the working of Domino mail routing was pretty straightforward. You used Domino's mail router to route mail between Notes users. The mail router used what Lotus calls NRPC or Notes RPC (Notes Remote Procedure Call) to transfer mail between servers. You used a Lotus Message Transfer Agent (MTA) or a Lotus or third-party gateway to transfer mail to non-Notes mail users or to the Internet. Okay, there was more to it than that, but not much more.

Beginning with R5, there is much more to it. Lotus has incorporated SMTP mail routing into the mail router. This complicates the mail routing setup process, because now we have to choose the degree to which (if at all) we use SMTP to route mail to Notes mail users, rather than NRPC. In Domino R5, we can do any of the following:

- Use NRPC to route mail to Notes users and SMTP to route mail to Internet mail users. This is the same as in previous releases of Domino/Notes.

- Use SMTP to route mail to all users, both Notes and non-Notes. We can only do this if all Domino servers run R5 and use TCP/IP as the underlying network protocols.

- Blend NRPC and SMTP mail routing techniques to the degree that suits us.

The third option causes much of the complexity. You could, of course, just go with the defaults, but that won't necessarily be the best choice for your Domino installation. And, as I've warned you repeatedly, accepting the default named network setting for a server can potentially bring mail routing to its knees.

To understand how you should set up mail routing in your Domino installation, you must understand how mail routing works, both Notes mail routing and SMTP mail routing. Then, you must understand how they work together in the Domino mail router. That's the tricky part.

How NRPC Mail Routing Works

NRPC mail routing works as follows:

1. A user (or a program or agent) addresses a document to one or more recipients, then sends the message. The process of sending consists of depositing the document into the Outgoing Mail database, which exists on all Domino servers that run the mail router and is traditionally named mail.box.

    - Beginning with R5, a server can have more than one Outgoing Mail database. If so, they are named mail$n$.box, where n is an integer. For example, if there are two Outgoing Mail databases on a given server, their names would be mail1.box and mail2.box.

    - A mobile user working in disconnected mode puts the document in a local Outgoing Mail database. Later, when reconnected to a server and upon the user's command, Notes transfers the message to the server's Outgoing Mail. A user is in disconnected mode if the Mail file location field in his or her current location document is set to Local.

    - When a user sends a message, Notes will, before depositing the message into Outgoing Mail, try to verify the address of any addressee name that does not include a domain name in the address. If Notes cannot find a group or person document that corresponds to the name of such an addressee, it will ask the user to correct the name or remove the addressee from the list of recipients.

2. The mail router, which is a loadable/unloadable Domino server task, monitors its local Outgoing Mail databases. When a message appears in one, the router reads the addressee names, then refers to documents in the Domino Directory to determine what to do with the message.

3. The mail router disposes of each recipient's copy of the message in one of the following ways:

    - If the recipient's mail database is on the current server, the router *delivers* the message to that database. (If shared mail is enabled, the router may move the message partially to the recipient's mail database and partially to the shared mail database. See "Shared Mail" later in this chapter.) The router may convert the message format at this time as well, either from Notes rich text format to MIME format, or vice versa, depending on a setting in the recipient's Person document. This completes the routing of that message.

    - If the recipient's mail database is on another Domino server, the mail router determines a route to that server, then *transfers* the message into the Outgoing Mail database of the first server on that route. If the message is in MIME format and the final destination server is an R4 or earlier server, the mail router will convert the message to Notes rich text format at this time. The mail router on the receiving server then repeats the routing process—it either delivers the message to the destination database (if it resides on that server) or transfers the message to the next server on the route.

■ If the destination is not in a Notes domain, the mail router determines a route to a Domino server acting as a mail gateway to the recipient's mail system, then transfers the message to the first server on that route. The gateway server transfers the message into the other mail system. The mail router can tell if mail is destined for another mail system from either the format of the recipient's address or information in the recipient's Person document, if one exists.

■ If, for some reason, the server can't move the message forward, it will try to return it to the sender, appended to a Delivery Failure Report. It may do this immediately or after 24 hours.

  • Immediate return: The router returns the message immediately if it cannot determine any route to the addressee or if the shortest route exceeds the maximum number of hops allowed.

  • Return after 24 hours: If legal routes exist but the router cannot successfully transfer the message to the first server on any such route within 24 hours, it will return the message to the sender. A route is legal if it doesn't exceed the maximum hop count. By default, the maximum hop count is 25, but for an R5 server, you can change it in the Maximum hop count field in a configuration document, under Router/SMTP, Restrictions and Controls, Transfer Controls.

■ If for some reason the server can move the message neither forward toward its recipient nor back toward the sender, it marks the message Dead and leaves it in Outgoing Mail, where an administrator must decide what to do with it. It may do this immediately or after 24 hours, using the same rules as for returning mail (see preceding bullet points).

The Role of Notes

When a Notes mail user sends a message, Notes must perform the following tasks:

■ Replace any local group names with the names of the members of the groups. Notes gets the name from the local group documents, which it may find in the Personal Address Book or other local directories. If the user used the names of groups defined on the server, Notes does not have to expand them into their membership names.

- Validate all addresses except those that include a domain component (that is, those in the form `addressee@domain`). Notes looks to the settings in the current location document to determine how to do this. It uses the following rules:

  • If the Mail file location field is set to Local and the Mail addressing field is set to Local Only, Notes will validate names that it can locate in contact documents in the Personal Address Book. If it can't validate a name, a message appears to that effect, but Notes lets the address stand as-is. If it later turns out that the server couldn't resolve an unvalidated address, the server will return that copy of the message to the user, appended to a Delivery Failure Report.

  • If either the Mail file location field is set to on Server or the Mail addressing field is set to Local and Server, Notes will check the Personal Address Book and other local directories listed in User Preferences, then server-based directories. Server-based directories that Notes will search may include the Domino Directory, the Directory Catalog, and directories listed in the Directory Assistance database. In this mode, Notes will require all addresses to be validated. If Notes can't validate an address through directory lookup, it will give the user the option of removing that addressee from the address fields or manually correcting the name.

- For each addressee, format the message as either Notes rich text or (R5 only) MIME. Notes assumes Notes rich text format for messages addressed to Notes users, MIME for messages addressed to Internet users. It determines which kind of user by the format of the recipient's address.

- If the sender chooses, sign and/or encrypt the message. Notes will use the standard Notes public and private keys to do this for recipients who are Notes users. Notes R5 will use X.509 public and private keys (if available) to do this for recipients who are Internet mail users. Also, if a recipient's public key is not available for encrypting (because the user is currently disconnected from any Domino server), Notes R5 will tag the message so that the sender's mail server will encrypt it as soon as it receives it.

- Submit the message to a mail server. If the Mail file location field in the current location document is set to on Server, Notes will try to connect to the mail server named in the Home/mail server field and deposit the message in that server's Outgoing Mail database. If the Mail file location field in the current location document is set to Local, Notes will deposit the message in the local Outgoing Mail database. Later the user will have to send it to a server. If messages still reside in Outgoing Mail when the user exits Notes or changes locations, Notes may at that time remind the user that messages still wait in Outgoing Mail and offer to transfer them to a server.

The Role of Other Mail Clients

The other mail clients that Domino supports—IMAP, POP3, and HTTP clients—perform essentially the same tasks as Notes. (Of course, a given client may not be capable of some tasks, such as encrypting or signing mail.)

The primary difference between Notes and the other clients is that Notes typically interacts with the Database Server when it deposits messages in the server's Outgoing Mail database. The other clients interact with other server tasks. IMAP and POP3 mail clients interact with the SMTP Listener task. HTTP clients interact with the HTTP task. If the appropriate task is not running on a server, it won't be able to accept mail from the corresponding kind of client.

The Role of the Domino Directory

The mail router refers to numerous documents in the Domino Directory during the routing process and can't function without it. The documents in the Domino Directory which contain information the router needs are as follows:

- **Person (if the addressee is a person), Mail-In Database (if the addressee is a database), and Resource (if the addressee is a resource, such as a conference room) documents.** To determine the location and name of the recipient's mail database. Also, if necessary, to retrieve a recipient's public key so as to encrypt an outgoing message. The fields that hold the location information include: Domain, Mail server, and Mail file. (If a person does not use Notes mail, the Person document may not have all of these fields. But it will have analogous fields appropriate to the mail system the person uses.)

- **Group documents.** If an addressee is a group, the server extracts the individual recipients' names from the group document.

- **Server documents.** To determine what servers are in what named networks.

- **Connection and Domain documents.** To determine what routes to the recipient's mail server are available.

- **Configuration documents.** To determine what mail routing rules and restrictions, if any, may be in place. Also, in R5, to determine whether to use traditional or SMTP mail routing techniques.

Domino Mail Routing Scenarios

The mail router determines each message's destination, discovers the best route to that destination, and sends the message along that route. A message's destination includes the name of the addressee's mail database, the name of the mail server on which the mail database resides, and the name of the Domino domain in which the mail server resides. All of that information comes from the addressee's Person, Mail-In Database, or Resource document, if one exists. For addressees in other Domino domains or foreign mail systems, the mail router may not have access to any such document. In those cases the mail router gets the addressee's domain from the address itself.

From the point of view of the mail router with a message to route, the following scenarios are possible:

- It must deliver the message to a database on the same server.
- It must transfer the message to another Domino server in the same named network.
- It must transfer the message to a Domino server in a different named network.
- It must transfer the message to a Domino server in an adjacent Domino domain.
- It must transfer the message to an adjacent Domino domain which will in turn transfer the message to another domain, adjacent to the second domain but non-adjacent to the first domain.
- It must transfer the message to a foreign mail system, neither Notes-based nor Internet-based.
- It must transfer the message to the Internet.

When Are Connection and Domain Documents Needed?

We'll look at each of the preceding scenarios more closely later, but we can summarize the requirements for connection and domain documents as follows:

- If the mail router needs to deliver a message to a database on the same server or transfer a message to another server in the same named network, it can do so without benefit of a connection document.
- All other scenarios require connection documents to enable mail transfer.
- Mail can be transferred to another Domino domain, either adjacent or non-adjacent, without benefit of domain documents. The only requirement is that connection documents exist defining a route to a server in the other domain. Adjacent Domain and Non-adjacent Domain documents can restrict the delivery of some messages to other domains. Non-adjacent Domain documents can assist the mail router in determining what intervening domain to route to.
- To enable mail delivery to a non-Domino domain, that is, to the Internet or to a non-Notes mail domain, both connection and domain documents must be in place.

When Does Domino Route a Message?

The time of mail routing can be either immediate or on a schedule. The factors that determine this include the destination of the message, a message's delivery priority, and the number of pending messages in Outgoing Mail. The rules are as follows:

- Mail bound for a database on the same server as the mail router is always delivered immediately. This includes messages marked delivery priority: Low.

- If the next hop is to a server in the same named network, the mail router delivers high and normal priority mail immediately. It delivers low priority mail immediately but only during low priority hours.

- Mail marked Delivery priority: High always gets immediate delivery.

- In situations where a connection document is required, mail marked Delivery priority: Normal (which is the default) gets delivered on a schedule defined in the governing connection document.

- The mail router will deliver pending normal priority messages immediately if their number reaches the number in the Route at once if ... messages pending field of the governing connection document.

- Mail marked Delivery priority: Low will be transferred to other servers only during low-priority mail delivery hours, which by default are between midnight and 6 a.m. During those hours the rules for normal mail apply to low priority mail as well.

- You can change the low priority mail delivery hours in the Low priority mail routing time range field of a configuration document. Look under either Messaging Settings or Router/SMTP, then under Restrictions and Controls, Transfer Controls.

Scenario: Delivery to a Database on the Same Server

This is the simplest and most straightforward of all mail routing scenarios. A message appears in Outgoing Mail. The mail router checks the addressee's Person, Mail-In Database, or Resource document and discovers the message should be delivered to a database on the same server. The router will deliver the message to the recipient's mail database immediately, without reference to connection or domain documents (see Figure 8.1).

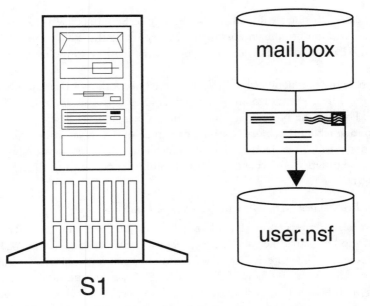

Figure 8.1 If the addressee's mail database is on the same server, the mail router delivers messages to the mail database.

Scenario: Transfer to Another Domino Server in the Same Named Network

This is second most straightforward mail routing scenario. A message is addressed to a user whose mail server is in the same named network as the routing server (see Figure 8.2).

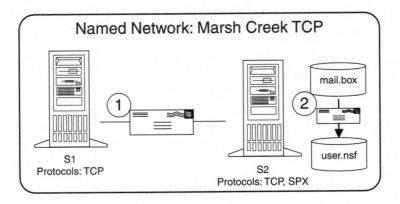

Figure 8.2 S1 has a message addressed to a user on S2. S1 immediately transfers the message to S2. No connection document necessary.

In either case, the router will transfer the message to S2 immediately, without reference to connection or domain documents, by depositing the message into S2's Outgoing Mail database. S2 will, in turn, deliver the message to the recipient's mail database.

Servers know the membership of every named network in a Domino domain because the information is stored in each server's Server document (under Ports, Notes Network Ports, in the Notes Network column). When a server first starts up, it builds a mail routing table in memory from the data in all of the server, connection, and domain documents in its Domain Directory. While running, the server updates its routing table to reflect any changes, additions, and deletions in those documents that may appear.

Scenario: Two Named Networks with a Server in Common

In this scenario, a message on S1 is addressed to an addressee whose mail database is on S3, in another named network. S1 is in named network Marsh Creek TCP. S3 is in named network Marsh Creek SPX. They cannot communicate directly because they use different transport protocols (TCP vs. SPX). S2 is a multi protocol server with both protocols installed, and it is a member of both named networks (see Figure 8.3).

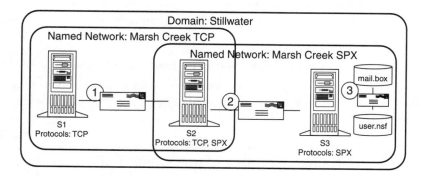

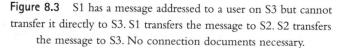

Figure 8.3 S1 has a message addressed to a user on S3 but cannot transfer it directly to S3. S1 transfers the message to S2. S2 transfers the message to S3. No connection documents necessary.

S1 will transfer the message to S2 immediately, without reference to connection or domain documents, because they are both in named network Marsh Creek TCP. S2 will, in turn ,transfer the message to S3, also immediately and without reference to a connection document because S2 and S3 are both members of named network Marsh Creek SPX. S3 will deliver the message to the recipient's mail database.

Scenario: Two Named Networks, No Server in Common

If the addressee's mail server is in a different named network from the subject server, and no server exists in both named networks, one or more connection documents must exist that define a route from the routing server's named network to the destination server's named network. In Figure 8.4, S1 and S2 are in named network Marsh Creek TCP. S3 and S4 are in named network Philly TCP.

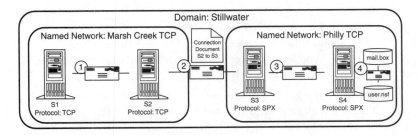

Figure 8.4 S2 needs a connection document to route mail to S3.
When the connection document is in place, both S1 and S2
will be able to route mail to either S3 or S4.

To route mail in this scenario, a connection document must set the rules. In Figure 8.4, a connection document tells S2 how to connect to S3, when to make the connection, and that it should route pending mail when it does connect. When the connection document is in place, S1 will be able route mail to S4 by transferring it to S2, which will transfer it to S3, which will transfer it to S4.

Notice, however, that, under the facts, the servers in Philly TCP cannot route mail to the servers in Marsh Creek TCP. To enable this, another connection document must be in place, telling a server in Philly TCP (probably S3) how and when to connect to a server in Marsh Creek TCP (probably S2).

Scenario: Sending Mail to Other Domino Domains

To send mail to destinations in other Domino domains, you have to set up connection documents, just as in the previous example regarding named networks. That is, for mail to route directly from domain Stillwater to domain PlanetNotes, there must be a connection document in the Stillwater directory that defines a mail routing connection from a server in Stillwater to a server in PlanetNotes. If mail is to route in the opposite direction, then a connection document in PlanetNotes's directory must define a mail routing connection from a server in PlanetNotes to a server in Stillwater. Typically, the same pair of servers would route mail to each other (see Figure 8.5).

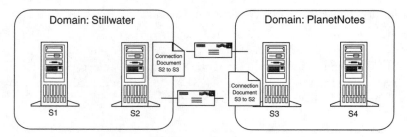

Figure 8.5 A connection document enables mail routing from
Stillwater to PlanetNotes. A second connection document
enables mail routing in the opposite direction.

Of course, where there are two Domino domains, more are bound to show up sooner
or later. That's when mail routing gets interesting. If there are three domains it is possible for a domain without connection documents to servers in the third domain to
route mail to it by routing through the second domain. For example, in Figure 8.6
there are connection documents linking domains Stillwater and PlanetNotes, and
connection documents linking domains PlanetNotes and Raptor.

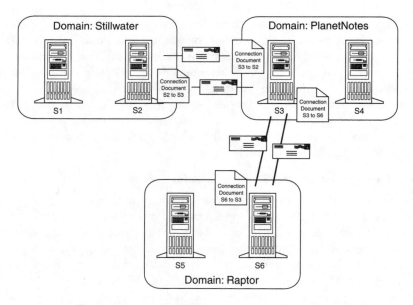

Figure 8.6 Mail sent from domain Stillwater, addressed
to a recipient in domain Raptor (or vice versa)
can route through domain PlanetNotes.

A message on S2 addressed to Joe Doaks @ Raptor is undeliverable, because no connection documents exist in domain Stillwater that define a route to Raptor. However, a message addressed to Joe Doaks @ Raptor @ PlanetNotes is deliverable because S2 can connect to S3 in PlanetNotes and S3 can connect to S7 in Raptor.

Of course, the users will never master addresses like Joe Doaks @ Raptor @ PlanetNotes, but the administrator of Stillwater can do a number of things to eliminate the necessity. For one thing, the administrator can create a Non-adjacent domain document. It will say, in essence, that any mail addressed to Raptor domain should be routed through PlanetNotes domain. When that document is in place, users at Stillwater will be able to write just Joe Doaks @ Raptor.

Second, if the three domains are related to each other (and they frequently are, in situations like this), the domains can share domain directories with each other. Using any of the three techniques, the administrators can set up their directories so that a user just has to enter Joe Doaks. The techniques are cascading address books (which you shouldn't use because it's outmoded), directory assistance, and a directory catalog. To learn how each of these techniques works and how to deploy them, see Chapter 11, "Domino Directory Services."

The fact that you can route mail to one domain through another domain can cause problems for administrators. For one thing, it costs bandwidth and the administrator in the middle domain may not appreciate others using his bandwidth for their purposes. Second, the middle domain might be paying for the privilege of sending mail into the third domain. The administrator of PlanetNotes surely won't like it if users in Stillwater are sending mail through PlanetNotes's domain into the CompuServe domain (for which connection PlanetNotes has to pay CompuServe by the minute).

To prevent that sort of thing, domain documents allow you to restrict what mail can pass through your domain into other domains. Most kinds of domain documents have two fields for this purpose:

- **Allow mail only from domains.** Domino will only allow mail originating in the listed domains to pass into the other domain.

- **Deny mail from domains.** Domino will not allow mail originating in the listed domains to pass into the other domain.

To see how this works, look at Figure 8.7. It shows that mail can route from Stillwater to PlanetNotes, from PlanetNotes to Raptor, and from Raptor to Firesign (and in the opposite direction). The administrator of PlanetNotes wants to keep users in Stillwater from routing mail through PlanetNotes to Raptor and Firesign.

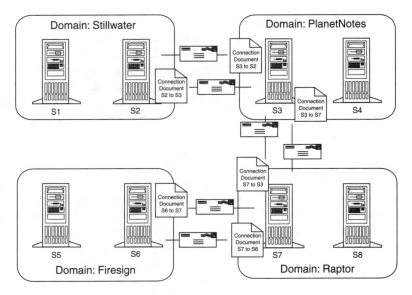

Figure 8.7 Mail originating in Domain Stillwater, addressed to Domain Firesign, can route through PlanetNotes and Raptor.

The administrator can do two things:

- If PlanetNotes has a Non-Adjacent Domain document for Firesign (which says, in effect, Route mail addressed to Firesign via Raptor), the administrator can add Stillwater to the Deny mail from domains field. This will block Stillwater mail addressed Ralph Spoilsport @ Firesign or Ralph Spoilsport @ Firesign @ PlanetNotes.

- The administrator can create an Adjacent Domain document that names Raptor as the adjacent domain and names Stillwater in the Deny mail from domains field. This will block Stillwater mail addressed to Ralph Spoilsport @ Firesign @ Raptor @ PlanetNotes. It will also block Stillwater mail addressed to Joe Doaks @ Raptor and Joe Doaks @ Raptor @ PlanetNotes.

The combination of these two techniques lets Stillwater mail into PlanetNotes but completely blocks any Stillwater mail from being forwarded to the other two domains. PlanetNotes's router will return the messages to their senders appended to a Delivery Failure Report that says, basically, no route found to domain x from domain PlanetNotes.

You might wonder why, in the first bullet point in the preceding list, the Non-Adjacent Domain document does not block Stillwater mail addressed to Ralph Spoilsport @ Firesign @ Raptor @ PlanetNotes. The reason is that this address *explicitly* names every domain in the route. Unlike the other addresses in bullet one, it doesn't rely on the Non-Adjacent Domain document to supply a missing domain name. So routers in PlanetNotes don't ever look at the Non-Adjacent Domain document with its Deny field.

Scenario: Sending Mail to a Foreign Mail System

If the addressee is in a foreign mail domain, that is, a non-Domino mail domain, at least one Domino server will be designated as a gateway computer. It will run gateway software that will enable it to send mail to the foreign mail system and receive mail from it. The documents that must be in place to enable mail transfers through the gateway will depend on the design of the gateway product. In general, the following kinds of documents will be necessary:

- A connection document must define a mail routing connection from a Domino gateway computer to a non-Domino computer that can accept mail for the user. It may be a special connection document form added to the Domino Directory by the gateway software.

- One or more domain documents must exist, in which information about the foreign domain is set forth. In particular, it will give the foreign domain a name which Notes mail users will be able to use when addressing mail to the foreign mail users. For example, you might call the Stillwater cc:Mail system Stillwater ccmail. User can then address messages to C.C. Rider @ Stillwater ccmail.

Scenario: Transferring Mail to the Internet

Because R5 Domino servers can be SMTP hosts, any R5 server can be an SMTP mail gateway for a Domino domain that uses Notes mail routing internally. Alternately, if you have an R4 server in place with the SMTP MTA running on it, you can continue to use it as is. More information on this subject is provided throughout this chapter.

Mail Routing Topologies Under NRPC Routing

In an organization with many Notes named networks or Notes domains, you may want to optimize your mail routing topology by setting up a mail routing hub. If you have four or more named networks or domains, you can minimize connection documents and hops by designating a hub mail server. If the hub is a member of one or more of the named networks, you can minimize connection documents even more. Compare Figure 8.8 with Figure 8.7. Pretend the domains are named networks—the principle is the same either way.

In Figure 8.7, the domains are arranged in an end-to-end connection scheme. There are six connections. The end domains are three hops away from each other. In Figure 8.8, the domains are arranged in a hub pattern, with PlanetNotes as the hub. There are six connections here as well, but no domain is more than two hops from any other. In Figure 8.7, you could create another pair of connections that route mail between S2 and S6. That would create a circular topology, in which there are no end domains and no more than two hops between any two domains, but there would be eight connection documents.

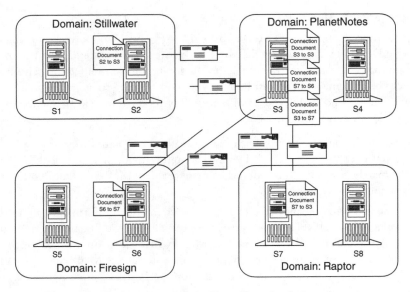

Figure 8.8   Server S3 in domain PlanetNotes is a hub mail router.
Mail routing between any of the two domains never has to pass through
more than one intervening domain. If these were Notes named
networks instead of domains, the principle would be the same.

While the difference is perhaps trivial in this example, it becomes less so as you add more domains or named networks to the mix. In any case, this kind of planning may become less necessary if you implement SMTP mail routing, which is covered next.

How SMTP Mail Routing Works

Simple Mail Transfer Protocol is the standard mail transfer protocol on the Internet and on TCP/IP networks in general. It depends on TCP to establish connections for it, so it does not work on non-TCP/IP networks. SMTP is described initially in two Request for Comments documents (RFC 821 and RFC 822) but was originally intended to be extendible and it has been extended numerous times, each extension described in yet another RFC. RFC 821 describes the way SMTP hosts will transfer messages among themselves. RFC 822 describes the format of the messages to be transferred. If you want to read any RFCs, do a lookup for RFC on any Internet search engine. Among the search results, look for RFC indexing services. Choose one and you should then be able to search that index for any RFC by number or keywords.

SMTP mail routing works as follows:

1. A mailer, which is an SMTP client, connects to a local, designated SMTP sender host, usually over port 25, and transfers one or more messages to it. The messages transferred must conform to a particular format as described in RFC 822 (as modified by later RFCs). RFC 822 describes the format of the addresses, the message header fields, and the message as a whole.

2. Message addresses are all in form *localpart@domain* or *(phrase)localpart@domain*. The SMTP sender host extracts the domain part of each addressee's mailing address, then queries the local Domain Name Server (DNS) to learn the identity of an SMTP host responsible for receiving mail addressed to that domain. DNS stores this information in the form of Mail eXchanger (MX) records.

3. If the DNS server does not have the information, it will refer the SMTP host to a more authoritative DNS server; alternately, the DNS server might itself submit the query to the more authoritative DNS server. This cycle of referrals/lookups will continue until a DNS server that holds the necessary information passes to the querying SMTP host.

4. The DNS server will pass all MX records that it has for the domain in question, and corresponding Alias (A) records as well. Each MX record includes the host name and preference level of an SMTP host that will accept mail for the domain. The corresponding A records include the SMTP hosts' IP addresses.

5. If there is more than one MX record, the querying host will choose the one with the lowest preference number. If more than one exists with that preference number, the host will choose one at random. The sending SMTP host then contacts the receiving SMTP host, establishes a session, and transfers the messages. If it cannot establish a session or transfer the messages and there were alternate MX records, the sending SMTP host will try another one. It will continue trying other ones until it succeeds in transferring the pending message or until it times out. The timeout period may be anything, but is frequently 24 hours. (If there are no MX records for the destination domain, Domino SMTP will make one, last-ditch effort and look for an A record for the domain itself (for example, for example.com, rather than hostname.example.com). If one exists, Domino SMTP will attempt to establish an SMTP session with the host at that IP address.)

6. If the receiving SMTP host is the post office server for the addressee, it will process the message, making it available to the addressee. If the receiving host is a relay host, it will repeat this process and forward the message to another SMTP host for the destination domain, but one with a lower preference number. That way, the message will eventually get to the post office server for the domain and then the addressee.

SMTP Message Format

Messages transferable by SMTP servers must have certain well-defined features (which are, as I mentioned, set forth in RFC 822 as amended). They consist of lines of plain text. They have a header and a body. The header consists of fields of information, each on its own line. Each field must meet rigid specifications. Some fields are required; others are optional. The body is basically undefined by RFC 822 but must consist of plain text in US-ASCII format.

Because people want to send more than plain text, several methods arose to allow RFC 822 messages to incorporate other character sets, formatting, and non-textual information. Eventually, the Multipart Internet Messaging Extensions (MIME) protocol (current version described in RFC 2045 et seq.) emerged as the standard method of incorporating non-ASCII content in an RFC 822 message body. MHTML (MIME-encapsulated HTML, RFC 2110) became the standard method of adding formatting and hyperlinks to an RFC 822 message body.

How SMTP Mail Routing Differs from Notes Mail Routing

SMTP routing is different from Notes RPC routing in many ways. For one, it is decentralized (as a public mail transfer system must be). It doesn't designate hubs or transfer points. Rather, every SMTP host can locate and contact any other SMTP host and transfer mail to it. In this sense, SMTP mail transfer is similar to Domino mail transfer within a Domino named network, in which each server sends mail directly to the addressee's mail server.

If you enable SMTP mail routing on a Domino server, it can participate in the system described previously. It can query DNS to locate a destination SMTP host, then contact the host and transfer messages to it. If such a Domino server can connect to the Internet and DNS has a MX record for it, it can receive mail from any other SMTP host on the Internet.

If every one of your Domino servers fits this description, you could do away with Notes mail routing altogether and rely exclusively on SMTP mail routing. However, this isn't always possible. Also, it may not be desirable.

SMTP relies on the TCP/IP suite of protocols, including DNS, for full functionality. If parts of your network use other protocols, the mail clients and servers on those segments won't be able to implement SMTP.

Also, the Internet model assumes more or less universal connectivity among SMTP hosts. But, you will want to insulate most of your Domino servers from the anarchy of the Internet by hiding them behind a firewall. Or your networks may not all connect to the Internet or, for that matter, to each other. You may have choke points through which all mail has to pass to get to another set of servers, and you will designate firewall or pass-thru or dialup servers to pass mail through those choke points. So, there's a good chance you will mix Notes and SMTP mail routing techniques in your network. To put it another way, SMTP is not an "NRPC killer." Notes mail routing is a highly configurable, highly tunable system. You can use SMTP exclusively if you want to, but don't throw out the baby with the bath water. If NRPC solves a mail routing problem for you, don't hesitate to use it.

SMTP Message Formatting in Notes Documents

Another major difference between proprietary Notes mail and SMTP mail is the format of the messages. Notes has always implemented rich text capability in its mail system. Lotus developed a proprietary technique (called Notes CD, Notes Compound Document, or just Notes Rich Text) for expressing and storing rich text (formatting, attachments, embedded objects, hyperlinks, et al.) long before any Internet standards emerged.

SMTP, on the other hand, requires messages to be in US-ASCII format. Rich text is therefore encoded as US-ASCII, using MIME and MHTML encoding methods. The MHTML component is the part that provides the equivalent of Notes rich text.

In keeping with its efforts to support Internet standards, Lotus has adopted the RFC 822 message format (including MIME and MHTML) as an alternate native format for storing email messages in Notes R5. Lotus really had to do that in order to support SMTP fully. In R4.6, Domino could store RFC 822 messages as attachments to Notes rich text fields. In R5, Domino can store the components of RFC 822 messages natively, without conversion or encapsulation, as Notes objects. Lotus refers to this as "native MIME" support (even though an RFC 822 message doesn't actually have to include any MIME at all). Not only does this enable Domino to maintain full fidelity to the SMTP standard; it also makes it possible for Domino and Notes R5 to provide much more rich support of POP3 and IMAP than in R4.6.

Domino servers can optionally transport and store messages in either Notes rich text or MIME format. Which one they use depends on settings in the mail recipient's Person or Mail-In Database document.

Domino R5 servers can convert back and forth between the two formats as needed. For example, if a Domino server receives a message in MIME format and must forward it to another Domino server that doesn't read native MIME (say, for example, an R4 server), the sending server will automatically convert the message to Notes rich text format first. Also, any Domino R5 server receiving a message for a local user will automatically convert the message to the recipient's preferred format, MIME or Notes rich text, as needed.

How Notes Mail Routing and SMTP Mail Routing Work Together in Domino

The primary goals of the designers of R5 mail routing was to afford Domino and Notes R5 with full fidelity to the Internet message transfer and message formatting standards, while simultaneously retaining full fidelity to Notes's own message transfer and formatting standards, and to permit full convertibility between them while minimizing the need to convert between them. Perhaps the key here, for our present purposes, is the minimization of the need to convert messages between Notes rich text and native MIME formats.

Both Notes and Domino R5 can convert messages freely between Notes rich text and MIME formats. But, when they do convert a message they cannot guarantee full fidelity to the original message, because Notes rich text supports certain kinds of formatting that MIME/MHTML do not. When you convert a message from Notes rich text to MIME, any such formatting has to be abandoned. When you convert the same message back to Notes rich text, the original formatting cannot be retrieved. Furthermore, as with any conversion program, there is no guarantee that formatting that was retained in the first conversion process won't be reconverted wrongly in the second conversion process. Therefore, a primary goal is to minimize the need to convert messages between Notes rich text and MIME.

A message won't need to be converted at all if the sending mail program, the routing servers, and the recipient server and mail program all support the same message format, whether that be MIME or Notes rich text. If they don't, the message will have to be converted at least once. If the sender and receiver don't both support the same format, the message will have to be converted once. If a routing server doesn't support the format, the message may have to be converted more than once.

The various programs involved in Notes mail routing, and the formats they support, are as follows:

- Notes R4 reads and writes Notes rich text only. If it receives a message that originated in MIME, the message will have been converted to Notes rich text by some server along the way.

- Domino R4 routes and stores Notes rich text only. Any server sending a MIME message to it must first convert the message to Notes rich text.

- The Domino R4 SMTP MTA sets up an SMTP router on a Domino R4 server and converts messages between Notes rich text and MIME formats.

- Notes R5 and Domino R5 can read, write, and store messages in Notes rich text or native MIME.

- The Domino R5 NRPC router can route messages in Notes rich text or native MIME formats.

- SMTP mail routers (Domino's included) can route messages in MIME format only.

- Internet mail programs can read, write, and store messages in MIME or plain text only.

In general, to help Domino route mail smoothly in a mixed NRPC and SMTP mail routing situation, you need to do the following things:

- Make sure (if possible) that your intermediate Domino mail routing servers are upgraded to R5. Do this so messages will never have to be converted more than once.

- In your users' Person documents, make sure the Format preference for incoming mail field is correctly set. This field controls the storage format—Notes rich text or MIME—for messages arriving in the user's mail database. In a mixed R4/R5 environment, Lotus recommends setting it to Prefers Notes rich text for best overall fidelity and performance. In an all-R5 environment, Lotus recommends setting it to No preference for Notes users and Prefers MIME for non-Notes users (such as, users of POP and IMAP mail readers).

Setting Up Mail Routing

To set up mail routing, you have to configure the following documents in the Domino Directory:

- For each server, its Server document.
- For each server or for named groups of servers, a Server Configuration document.
- If mail routing takes place across Notes named network or Notes domain boundaries, two or more connection documents and, optionally, domain documents.
- If mail routing takes place across boundaries with non-Notes domains, appropriate connection and foreign domain documents and, depending on the requirements of the gateway software, other documents.
- If mail routing takes place to the Internet, either entries in server and configuration documents or Foreign SMTP Domain and SMTP Connection documents, depending on whether internal servers use SMTP or NRPC to route Internet-bound mail.

Setting Up NRPC Mail Routing

To set up a server to perform NRPC mail routing, you basically don't have to do anything. NRPC mail routing is the default. The first time you start the server, the router starts. It creates a database called Outgoing Mail (mail.box), into which mail clients and other routers will deposit messages. The router monitors Outgoing Mail for the arrival of messages to be processed. In the absence of any other configurations, it will only receive and transfer mail using Notes RPC mail routing.

To make the server fit into your mail routing topology, you may have to set up the server's ports and Notes named network membership. To verify what ports are active on a server, you can view the server in Domino Administrator under the Server, Status tab. You can also create a new port or remove or rename an existing port in the same place by choosing Tools, Server, Setup Ports. For details on doing this, see Chapter 3 and Chapter 4.

You can verify a server's membership in Notes named networks in the Networks view of the Domino Directory, which isn't directly available in Domino Administrator. You have to open the Domino Directory then switch to the Networks view. You can also review and change a server's named network membership in its Server document, under the Ports, Notes Network Ports tabs.

Setting Up Mail Routing Connection Documents

You may have to set up connection documents to enable mail routing in any of the following circumstances:

- If your NRPC servers are in more than one Notes named network, you may have to create two or more connection documents to enable mail routing among them. But if any server is a member of two Notes named networks, you do not have to set up any connection documents to enable routing between those named networks. The servers in them will automatically route mail addressed to a server in the other named network via the dual-membership server.
- If you have multiple Notes domains and you want to set up mail routing among them, you have to create two or more connection documents.
- If you have servers that must connect to each other by telephone (modem or ISDN) or dial in to a network by telephone, you have to set up two or more connection documents.

Notice in each case in the list that you have to create *two* connection documents. That's because mail routing is a push–only process. Each server has to push its own mail to the receiving server. So, if you want mail to route in both directions, which you almost always do want, then you have to set up connection documents for both directions. Domino does permit you to set up a "pull-push" connection in which one server contacts another and initiates the mail routing process in both directions. But, even then you have to create two connection documents if the responding host is a Domino server (not a non-Domino SMTP host). For more information on pull-push connections, see the discussion of router types later in this chapter.

If you also have to set up replication between two servers, you can have one connection document initiate both mail routing and replication. In that way, you can eliminate one connection document. But, my own preference is to set up separate connection documents to initiate mail routing and replication. That way I find that, later on, it's easier to sort out what connections exist between pairs of servers. To learn more about setting up replication, see Chapter 9.

To create a connection document that will connect to NRPC servers for mail routing purposes, make sure a server is selected in Domino Administrator. It should be a server in the same domain as the server that will initiate the connection you are about to create. Then, in the Configuration tab, expand Messaging, and select Connections. Choose Add Connection, then complete it as set forth in Table 8.1.

Table 8.1 **Messaging-Related Fields in the Connection Form**

Field	Description
	ON THE BASICS TAB
Connection type	Choose one of the following: Local Area Network: If the initiating server will connect to the responding server over the network. Notes Direct Dialup: If the initiating server will connect to the responding server by dialing it up directly, using a modem. Network Dialup: If the initiating server will connect to the responding server's network by modem, then connect across the network to the responding server. Passthru Server: If the initiating server will connect to the responding server by passing through a third server.
Source server	The fully distinguished name of the initiating server.
Source domain	The name of the source server's Notes domain.
Use the port(s)	Click the Choose ports button and select the port you want. If you select more than one port, the source server will use the ports in the order that they appear in the field. If you leave the field blank, the server will try all of its ports until one succeeds.
Usage priority	Leave this set to Normal unless this connection is intended as a backup connection, in which case you should choose Low. When a server tries to connect to another server not in its named network, it looks for Normal priority connections first, tries the protocol stacks second, and looks for Low priority connections third.
Destination server	The fully distinguished name of the initiating server.
Destination domain	The name of the source server's Notes domain.
Optional network address	If using a TCP/IP port, enter the destination server's host name or IP address.
	ON THE REPLICATION/ROUTING TAB
Routing task	For NRPC mail routing, select Mail Routing.
Route at once if x messages pending	Defaults to 5. You don't normally need to change this. Normal priority messages usually route according to the schedule you set in the Schedule tab. However, if the number of normal priority messages you set in this field accumulates, the server won't wait for the next scheduled connection, but will instead connect immediately. You can cause all Normal priority messages to route at once by setting this to 1, but you should consider the consequences (network cost) of doing this first.

continues

Table 8.1 **Continued**

Field	Description
	ON THE REPLICATION/ROUTING TAB
Routing cost	Defaults to 1 for network connections, 5 for modem connections. You can set it to any number from 1 to 10. See the discussion following this table for more information.
Router type	Default is Push Only. In most situations, you want to accept the default. To learn about the other selections, see the discussion following this table.
	SCHEDULE
Schedule	Defaults to Enabled. If you select Disabled, the source server will not use this connection document at all.
Call at times	These are the times the server will try to connect under this document. To learn about your choices here, see the discussion following this table.
Repeat interval of x minutes	Defaults to 360—six hours. Select any number of minutes 0 or greater. To learn more about your choices here, see the discussion following this table.
Days of week	Choose the days of the week that this schedule will be active. Defaults to every day.

Save and close the connection document. If you created it on a server other than the source server, it will not become effective until it replicates to the source server. If you created it on the source server, it becomes effective immediately.

The Routing Cost Field

If a server discovers two or more routes to an ultimate destination server, it will add up the costs of all hops in each route, then use the route with the lower cost. (If there is only one route, the server ignores this field.) If two routes have the same cost, the server will use the one with fewer hops. If two routes have the same cost and the same number of hops, the server will use the route in which the next non-identical hop is to an alphabetically higher server.

If a connection fails, the server will increment the cost of that hop by 1. Repeated failures will eventually raise the cost of a route to the point at which it is no longer the lowest cost route. Then, the server will try an alternate route.

The Router Type Field

Normally, you should accept the default of Push Only. The source server will connect to the destination server, push pending mail to it, then disconnect. If you want mail to route in both directions, set up two connection documents, one for each server to push mail to the other.

Use the other routing types in the following circumstances:

- When one server cannot easily connect to the other
- When you want one server to bear the cost of all connection costs

One situation in which a server cannot easily connect to another server is where one server connects to the other by network dialup. The destination server may not have any way of connecting to the source server. Another example is where a server not constantly connected to the Internet needs to connect to an SMTP server on the Internet and tell it to send any pending mail. The other choices are as follows:

- **Pull Push.** The source server connects to the destination server, pushes mail to it, then tells the destination server to push mail to the source server, then disconnects.
- **Pull Only.** The source server connects to the destination server, tells it to push mail to the source server, then disconnects.
- **Push Wait.** The source server waits for the destination server to call it and tell it to push mail to the destination server. It pushes any pending mail, then disconnects.

When using these routing types for NRPC mail routing between two Domino servers, you have to create two connection documents: one for the initiating server; the other for the responding server.

- For the initiating server, create either a Pull Push or Pull Only connection in which you list the initiating server in the source server field, the responding server in the destination server field.
- For the responding server, create a Push Wait connection in which you list the responding server in the source server field, the initiating server in the destination server field.

When using a Pull Push or Pull Only connection to cause an SMTP-enabled Domino server not constantly connected to the Internet to call and pick up mail from an SMTP server on the Internet, you only need one connection document. (Chances are the SMTP server being contacted is not a Domino server.) But in this situation, the destination SMTP server must support the ETRN command. See the next sections for more information.

The Schedule Fields

The Call at times field can accept a single time (for example, 8:00 a.m.), a range of times (for example, 8:00 a.m.–10:00 p.m.), or a series of single times and/or time ranges (for example, 8:00 a.m.; 11:00 a.m.; 2:00 p.m.–4:30 p.m.). When a scheduled connection time arrives, the source server will try to connect to the destination server and carry out the tasks designated in the Replication/Routing fields.

If a connection is not successful, the source server waits a certain amount of time, then tries again. Repeated failures cause the source server to wait longer before each successive try. The wait time is initially short, but longer and longer. The source server uses a Randomized Exponential Backoff Algorithm to calculate wait times. This algorithm causes the server to wait approximately but not exactly twice as long after each failure as it waited after the previous failure.

If a connection resulting from a single time (for example, 8:00 a.m.) fails, the source server will continue trying to connect for 60 minutes (or until it succeeds); then, it will give up and wait for the next scheduled connection time.

If a connection resulting from a time range (for example, 8:00 a.m.–10:00 p.m.) fails, the source serve will continue trying until it succeeds or until the end time passes.

If a connection resulting from a time range succeeds, the source server will wait the amount of time in the Connection interval field, then it will try to connect again. The connection interval time count begins when a successful connection terminates. The server ignores the setting in the Connection interval field if it is connecting because of a single connection time setting (for example, 8:00 a.m.) in the connection document.

Setting Up SMTP Mail Routing

Domino servers can use SMTP mail routing in any or all three ways:

- **For receiving SMTP mail.** Use this to enable a server to receive mail through SMTP.

- **For sending mail outside the local Internet domain(s).** Use this to enable a server to use SMTP to send messages to SMTP hosts in Internet domains other than those to which your Domino servers belong or to use SMTP to forward Internet-bound mail to a relay host.

- **For sending mail within the local Internet domain(s).** Use this to enable a server to use SMTP to send messages to other SMTP-enabled Domino servers. You can enable SMTP routing either within Notes named networks or within your local family of Notes domains. You can also enable SMTP routing to a local "smart host" if some local SMTP mail users are hosted on non-Domino mail servers.

The term *local Internet domains*, as used in the bullet points, means the Internet domains set forth in Global Domain documents, if any, in the Domain Directory, otherwise, in each server's Fully qualified Internet host name field.

You have to make the three decisions for each R5 server in your domain. Unfortunately, there is no clear-cut set of rules to tell you how you should set up each server. You have to weigh a number of factors, any of which may change over time. Having weighed them, you may still find yourself with a flip of the coin. Among the factors that you should weigh, consider the following:

- SMTP assumes that all SMTP hosts are on the same network. Therefore, it makes no provision for routing from Domain A to Domain C through Domain B; rather, it will always try to route directly from Domain A to Domain C. This minimizes hops and dispenses with the need (and the ability) to predefine mail routes between hosts.

- Notes only assumes servers are directly available to each other within Notes Named Networks. Across the boundaries of named networks, domains, and mail systems, Domino does not assume two servers can connect, but looks for connection documents to tell it how to route mail across these boundaries. This means you can and must predetermine the routes mail will take across these boundaries.

- SMTP mail routing only works over TCP/IP networks. Notes mail routing works over many different protocols, including both network and dialup protocols.

- If you are upgrading your servers and users from R4 to R5, there is no need to rush the implementation of SMTP mail routing. Until you are ready to add SMTP routing, your existing Notes mail routing infrastructure will continue working as well as or better than it did under R4. If you want, you can even leave your R4 SMTP MTA server running in R4 format while upgrading the rest of your servers.

- R4 servers don't implement SMTP mail routing to route mail to other Domino servers. They must use Notes mail routing.

- SMTP mail routers use MX records, retrieved from DNS, to determine the identities and addresses of destination SMTP hosts. Any Domino mail router that uses SMTP to route mail to the world at large must have access to DNS. Servers that only route mail to other Domino SMTP hosts, a local smart host, or a relay host do not need access to DNS. Servers designated to receive SMTP mail from the world at large must have an MX record in a DNS database accessible to the world. On the other hand, you can set up internal NRPC mail routing without reference to DNS or any other non-Notes directory system.

For any given server, it may or may not be obvious whether and to what extent you should implement SMTP mail routing. However, once you make the decision to do it, it is easy to do.

Setting Up a Server to Receive Mail Through SMTP

A server set up with this option will be able to receive mail through SMTP routing. To set it up, enable the field labeled SMTP listener task in the server document under Basics, then restart the server. This causes the SMTP server task to run. You don't have to add SMTP to the ServerTasks variable of `notes.ini`; in fact, you should not do so.

The SMTP task "listens" on TCP port 25 (or whatever other port you may select in the server document) for connections from other SMTP servers. If another SMTP server connects, the listener receives the message and deposits it in mail.box. The router then processes the message.

The servers on which the SMTP Listener should be enabled are as follows:

- Any server designated to receive mail directly from external SMTP hosts. That could include servers receiving mail from the Internet or from other intranet domains or from a relay host.
- Any server enabled for internal or external SMTP mail routing.

Setting Up a Server to Use SMTP to Send Mail Outside the Local Internet Domains

Servers configured to use SMTP to send messages addressed to non-local Internet domains usually work in one of two ways. Either they send messages directly to their Internet destinations or they use SMTP to forward mail to local SMTP relay hosts. The relay host is usually a firewall server and could be non-Domino SMTP server or another Domino server enabled for sending mail outside the local Internet domain.

To set up such a server, follow these steps:

1. Create a configuration document for the server or use an existing one. If more than one configuration document exists for this server, consolidate them into one.

2. In the configuration document, under SMTP/Router, Basics, set the field named SMTP used when sending messages outside the local Internet domain to Enabled. Save the configuration document.

3. If the server will act as a relay host for R4 Domino servers or R5 Domino servers that are not SMTP-enabled, add SMTP Mail Routing to the Routing Tasks field in the Basics section of the relay host's Server document.

Setting Up a Server to Use SMTP to Send Mail Within the Local Internet Domain

A server with this option enabled will be able to use either Notes mail routing or SMTP mail routing to route mail to other Domino servers in either the local Notes named network or the local family of Notes domains.

To set up such a server, create a configuration document for it and set two fields in the configuration document. The two fields are located under SMTP/Router, Basics. They are SMTP allowed within the local Internet domain and Servers within the local domain are reachable via SMTP over TCP/IP.

The first field, SMTP allowed within the local Internet domain, offers three choices:

- **Disabled.** This is the default. The server will only use Notes routing to route mail internally.

- **MIME messages only.** Select this to enable internal SMTP mail routing but not all internal servers can accept mail through SMTP. The server will use the most appropriate routing method—NRPC or SMTP—for each message.

- **All messages.** Select this only if all internal Domino servers and all Notes mail users can accept mail through SMTP. The server will convert all Notes rich text messages to MIME format. If a destination server can't accept mail through SMTP, the transfer will fail.

The second field, Servers within the local domain are reachable through SMTP over TCPIP, offers two choices:

- **Only if in same Notes named network.** If you choose this, the server will use SMTP to route mail within its own TCP/IP Notes named network(s) to servers that will accept mail through SMTP. It will use NRPC routing to route mail to servers that cannot accept SMTP mail and across Notes named network and Notes domain boundaries.

- **Always.** If you choose this, the server will use SMTP to route mail to all Domino servers in the *local Internet domain* that are SMTP enabled. The "local domain" is the local *Internet* domain, which is defined as *all the Internet domains listed in this Notes domain's Global Domain documents.* The server will route mail through SMTP across Notes named network and Notes domain boundaries, as well as within Notes named networks.

Connecting Notes Domains to the Internet

For a given family of Notes domains, there are basically three ways to connect to the Internet:

- **Inbound/Outbound Gateway Servers.** A small group of servers can share gateway duties for the rest of the servers in your Domino installation. The gateway servers relay messages from the internal servers to the Internet and from the Internet to the internal servers. You may use as few as one gateway server but should use at least two to provide redundancy. This is a good configuration for a Domino installation in which the internal servers cannot be enabled for SMTP or you want to completely insulate the internal servers behind a firewall. Also, this is how Domino R4 domains that rely on Lotus's SMTP Message Transfer Agent relate to the Internet.

- **Inbound Gateway Servers Only.** All or most servers route mail directly to the Internet, but only a few designated servers act as inbound gateways. They receive inbound mail and forward it to the internal servers. If all or many of your Domino servers are capable of connecting to the Internet, consider letting them route their own outgoing mail to the Internet. This eliminates an outbound hop and frees up the gateway servers to concentrate on routing inbound mail.

- **No Gateway Servers.** All servers route their own mail to the Internet and receive mail from the Internet. This strategy is probably best suited to an organization that only has a few servers and is not worried about their vulnerability to Internet hackers.

When setting up connectivity between your Notes domain and the Internet, Domino servers can play three different roles:

- **Outbound Mail Router.** Receives mail from internal Domino servers then routes it to SMTP hosts on the Internet.

- **Inbound Mail Router.** Receives mail from external Internet hosts then routes it to internal Domino servers.

- **Internal Mail Router.** Only routes mail to other local Domino servers. Sends Internet-bound mail to an outbound gateway server. Receives Internet mail from an inbound gateway server. May or may not have SMTP mail routing enabled.

To set up each kind of server, see the following sections.

Setting Up the Outbound Gateway Servers

To set up an outbound gateway server, perform the following steps:

- Enable SMTP used when sending messages outside the local internet domain in a Configuration document for this server.

- Make sure the server can connect to the Internet. A LAN connection is best, but a modem or ISDN connection works too.

- If the server will act as a relay host for R4 Domino servers or R5 Domino servers that are not SMTP-enabled, add SMTP Mail Routing to the Routing Tasks field in the Basics section of the relay host's Server document.

Setting Up the Inbound Gateway Servers

To set up an inbound gateway server, perform the following steps:

- Enable the SMTP Listener task.

- Create an MX record for the server in a DNS database accessible from the Internet, either your own or your ISP's.

Setting Up the Internal Servers

Internal servers only transfer mail to other local Domino servers. They transfer Internet-bound mail to gateway servers acting as relay hosts. They need to know which server(s) to transfer their Internet-bound mail to. How they know that depends on whether they use SMTP or NRPC to route mail to the Internet. An SMTP-enabled server knows from the contents of a field in its configuration document. An NRPC server knows from any of several sources. It is easier to set this up on an SMTP-enabled server, so if you have the option of enabling a server to use SMTP to route outbound Internet mail, this may be a good reason to do so.

SMTP-Enabled Servers

To enable a Domino server to use SMTP to route Internet-bound mail to a gateway server, set up the following fields in the server's configuration document, under Router/SMTP, Basics:

- Set the field SMTP used when sending messages outside of the local Internet domain to Enabled.
- Set the field Relay host for messages leaving the local Internet domain to one of the following:

  - If there is only one outbound gateway server, enter its host name or IP address in the field. The host name is preferred (because it is less likely to change than the IP address). The internal servers will forward all outbound mail to that server.

  - If there is more than one outbound gateway server, create MX records for them in their domain's DNS database. Then, in the Relay host for messages leaving the local internet domain field, enter the name of the gateway servers' Internet domain. The internal servers will transfer mail to the gateway servers in order of their DNS priority, randomly choosing from servers with the same priority.

NRPC Servers

There are actually several ways to enable NRPC-only Domino servers to route Internet-bound mail to a gateway server. They include Lotus's officially sanctioned way and a couple others. Which method you should use depends on two factors: whether the NRPC server is in the same Notes domain as the gateway server, and how many gateway servers serve a particular gateway.

All the ways described here require you to create at least one Foreign SMTP Domain document. In addition, you may need one or more connection documents. The primary purpose of the Foreign SMTP Domain document is to tell the NRPC server which messages should be forwarded to the domain or server named in the

Foreign SMTP Domain document. In the Internet Domain field, you enter a domain name (for example, `example.com`) or a wildcard pattern (for example, `*.uk`, `*.us.example.com`, `*.*`). Whenever the NRPC server encounters an address that matches the domain name or the wildcard pattern, it forwards the message as directed by the Foreign SMTP Domain document.

With one exception, the connection documents act like any connection document—they tell the sending server what server to connect to, when to connect, and what to do when it connects. The one exception to this is in the first case listed in the next section, in which the connection document does not tell the sending NRPC server what server to route the Internet mail to. In that case, the sending server gets the identity of the destination server in an unusual way.

NRPC Server and Gateway Servers in the Same Notes Domain: Lotus's Method

If an NRPC server is in the same domain as the gateway server, you can set it up to route Internet mail using Lotus's official method. This method is harder to set up than the second method, but its benefit is that, if a gateway is manned by more than one server, the NRPC server can route Internet mail to any of them. Set up is as follows:

1. On the server document of each gateway server that the NRPC server may route Internet mail to, add SMTP Mail Routing to the Routing tasks field. This is how the NRPC server knows where to route Internet mail.

2. In Domino Administrator, under Configuration, Messaging, Domains, create a Foreign SMTP Domain document as set forth in Table 8.2.

Table 8.2   **Fields in the Foreign SMTP Domain Form**

Field	Description
	ON THE BASICS TAB
Domain Type	Choose Foreign SMTP Domain.
	ON THE ROUTING TAB
Internet Domain	Enter the name of Internet domain to which mail will route under this document. If this document enables mail routing to all Internet domains, enter `*.*`. If this document enables mail routing to a specific SMTP domain, enter the name of that domain.
Domain name	Enter the name of the domain to which mail should be routed under this document. This will be either the name of a Notes domain or a symbolic name such as "The Internet."
Internet host	Leave this field blank.

3. In Domino Administrator, under Configuration, Messaging, Connections, create an SMTP Connection document as set forth in Table 8.3.

Table 8.3   **Fields in the SMTP Connection Form**

Field	Description
	ON THE BASICS TAB
Connection type	Choose SMTP.
Source server	Enter the fully distinguished name of the NRPC server. You can use a wildcard to represent multiple servers (for example, ★/Servers/Stillwater). Caveat: If you use a wildcard here, the formula in the Choose record button (see below) may not work properly.
Source domain	Enter the name of the source server's Notes domain.
Connect via	Choose Direct connection if the source server connects to the gateway server via LAN. Choose Dial-up connection if the source server connects to the gateway server via Notes dial-up or network dial-up.
Dial using connection record	This field appears if you choose Dial-up connection in the previous field. If the source server uses network dialup to connect to the gateway server and a Network Dialup connection document already exists for that purpose, you can click the Choose record button and choose the connection record from the list. Caveat: The formula behind this button finds existing connection records in which the source server is the same as in this connection document. So, if you used a wildcard in this record, the formula will only find existing records that use the same wildcard. If the source server uses Notes direct dialup to connect to the gateway server, enter the full name of the gateway server in this field.
Destination server	In this particular case, Domino doesn't use this field, but you have to enter something in it because you can't save this document if you leave this field blank. Also, the Connections view sorts itself on the contents of this field, so you should enter something descriptive in this field. For example, if you entered ★.★ in the Internet Domain field on the companion Foreign SMTP Domain document, enter All Internet Servers. If you entered some Internet domain (for example, example.com) in the Foreign SMTP Domain document, enter Internet Servers in example.com or something similar.

continues

Table 8.3 **Continued**

Field	Description
	ON THE BASICS TAB
Destination domain	Enter the same text as you entered in the Domain name field of the companion Foreign SMTP Domain document. For example, if you entered "The Internet" there, enter it here as well. It is the presence of the same text in both of these fields that ties these two documents together. It tells the NRPC server to use this connection document to route mail addressed to the Internet domains covered by that Foreign SMTP Domain document.
Replication/Routing fields	Fill in these fields as you would on any connection document. If you want the source server to transfer only Internet mail to the gateway server, disable the Replication task and choose SMTP Mail Routing as the Routing task. If you leave Mail Routing as the Routing task, the source server will route any pending non-Internet mail along with the Internet mail.
Schedule fields	The source server will route mail under this document according to the schedule you set in these fields.

If you have more than one Internet mail gateway, you have to create the pair of documents for each one. For example, one gateway may lead to the Internet; another may lead to a private domain on your intranet; yet another may lead to all Internet domains ending in *.uk. You would create a Foreign SMTP Domain document and SMTP Connection document for each of these gateways. The first would route mail that fits the pattern *.*. The second would route mail that fits the pattern, say, example.com. The third would route mail that fits the pattern *.uk. Mail addressed to example.co.uk or to example.com would automatically use the more specific connection document rather than the less specific one (*.*).

NRPC Server and One Gateway Server in the Same Notes Domain: A Simpler Method

This method is much simpler than the one previously described, but only works if you have one gateway server for a given gateway. All you have to do is create a Foreign SMTP Domain document in which you leave the Domain name field blank and enter the name of the gateway server in the Internet host field.

All NRPC servers that can route mail to the gateway server will route Internet mail to it on the basis of this document alone. Of course, if no mail route to the gateway server exists, you would also have to create one or more standard connection documents to create one.

NRPC Servers and Gateway Servers in Different Notes Domains

If the NRPC server is not in the same Domino domain as the Internet gateway server(s), you have to set up the gateway domain as described in either of the two preceding examples, then set up an additional Foreign SMTP Domain document in the NRPC server's domain. This document would name the gateway Notes domain in the Domain name field. The NRPC server would route Internet mail to the gateway domain the same as any other mail.

Of course, we assume that it can route other mail to the gateway domain. If not, then you would have to create standard connection documents to set up the route. If you only wanted to route Internet mail to the gateway domain, and not standard Notes mail, you could choose SMTP Mail Routing in the Routing tasks field of any connection document you set up. If you want to route Internet mail using a different schedule from Notes mail, you could set up one connection document for SMTP Mail Routing and another for just Mail routing. Any such connection document could also enable replication if you want it to.

Complex Domain Relationships

When a message, addressed to, say, jdoaks@planetnotes.com, comes into a Notes domain from the Internet, the server that receives the message must figure out how to deliver it to its addressee. jdoaks could be related to the server in any of four ways:

- jdoaks@planetnotes.com could be a member of the server's own domain. The server should easily be able to find jdoaks in its Domino Directory.

- jdoaks could be a member of another, related Notes domain. The server may be able to tell which Notes domain from a Global Domain document.

- jdoaks may not be a member of any Notes domain, but planetnotes may be a local Internet domain to which the server must forward the message. The server may be able to forward the message to a non-Domino "smart host," which will know who jdoaks is and how to deliver the message.

- jdoaks and planetnotes.com may not be related to the server at all. In that case, the server will have to return the message to its sender.

The Global Domain Document

The Global Domain document tells a server how local Internet domains are related to local Notes domains. For example, if the sending server is in rockteam.com and the addressee is jdoaks@planetnotes.com, a Global Domain document will let the server know that, even though jdoaks is in a different Internet domain than the server, jdoaks is still in the same Notes domain. Alternately, a Global Domain document may tell the server that jdoaks is in a neighboring Notes domain.

You need to create a Global Domain document if you have more than one Internet domain or more than one Notes domain. A global domain document serves other purposes than correlating Notes and Internet domains, so not all of the fields in one are relevant to this problem. The relevant fields are as follows:

- **Notes domains and aliases.** Enter the names of all Notes domains that share the Internet domains listed in the two fields described below. If you list more than one Domino domain, you need to copy this Global Domain document to each of the Notes domains or create similar ones in those Domino Directories.

- **Local primary Internet domain.** Enter the name of the server's Internet domain.

- **Alternate Internet domain aliases.** Enter the names of other Internet domains whose members are also members of the Domino domains governed by this Global Domain document.

When a message comes into the domain from the Internet, the receiving server will be able to tell from this Global Domain document whether the addressee is a member of the server's Notes domain or a related Notes domain. It can forward the message accordingly.

Setting Users' Internet Addresses

Another purpose of the Global Domain document is to define a default return Internet address for Notes user who send mail to the Internet. In the R5 Person document, there is a field for an Internet return address. When you register a new user under R5, the field is automatically populated with a return address. But, under earlier releases, the Person document had no such field. Organizations upgrading from earlier releases of Notes may have many Person documents in which the Internet address field is not filled in. For those users the Global Domain document provides a formula for generating a return address.

Instead of setting up a Global Domain document for this purpose, you can populate the Internet address fields of all the Person documents in your domain. You don't have to do this manually. Domino Administrator provides a tool for this purpose: Under People & Groups, choose Tools, People, Set Internet Address.

The Set Internet Address dialog box appears. There, you can define a standard format for converting Notes names into Internet names. When you choose OK, the tools generates Internet addresses based on the rules you set and enters them in the Internet Address fields in the selected Directory. It also validates the addresses, making sure they conform to RFC 822 standards and that they are unique in the Directory.

The "Smart Host"

Many organizations aren't standardized exclusively on Notes. They have some Notes mail users and some users of other mail programs, unrelated to Notes. Yet, all the users may be members of planetnotes.com. In this case, a message could come in to our Domino server from the Internet that is in fact addressed to a user not listed in any Domino Directory. The server has to forward the message to a "smart host," that is, a non-Domino system that knows who the addressee is and how to deliver the message to the addressee.

To enable our server to forward the message to the smart host, you have to set two fields in the Basics tab of the server's configuration document (see Table 8.4).

Table 8.4   **Fields in the Configuration Form for Setting Up Forwarding to a Smart Host**

Field	Description
Local Internet domain smart host	Enter the host name of the server that hosts the directory for non-Notes mail recipients.
Smart host is used for all local Internet domain recipients	Choose Enabled or Disabled (the default). When this is enabled, the server forwards all messages to the smart host without trying to determine if they are Notes users or not. When this is disabled, the server only forwards a message to the smart host after failing to locate the addressee in any local Domino Directory.

Calendaring and Scheduling Setup

Although Notes calendaring and scheduling are not strictly mail related, they are pretty well integrated into the mail function. Users' calendars are part of their mail databases. Also, when users schedule meetings, their invitations and resource reservations go out through mail. So, we'll cover calendaring and scheduling as part of the mail function.

There is little actual administration involved in Notes calendaring and scheduling. It pretty much just runs itself. When first setting up a Domino domain, you should create a Resource Reservations database and configure it. Also, if you have multiple Notes domains and users will be inviting people from other domains to meetings, you should create Adjacent Domain and maybe Non-adjacent Domain documents to allow users to perform free-time lookups in the other domains. You can also permit free-time lookups in cc:Mail and OfficeVision domains with Foreign Domain documents. Finally, you can create holiday documents for any company events or non-standard holidays that you want your employees to be aware of. Holiday documents already exist for standard holidays.

How Notes Calendaring and Scheduling Works

Lotus Notes has a full calendaring function built into the standard mail database template. It includes the ability to create meetings, look up the free times of prospective invitees to the meetings, send invitations, and reserve resources (such as meeting rooms). Users can also import information about company holidays into their mail databases.

Domino servers run two tasks in support of these functions:

- Schedule Manager polls user mail databases and the Resource Reservations database to learn what dates and times have been scheduled. It stores that information in the Free Time database (filename `busytime.nsf` on a stand alone server, `clubusy.nsf` on a clustered server), which it creates the first time it runs. When a user looks up another user's (or a resource's) free time, the Schedule Manager retrieves the other user's busy times from `busytime.nsf`/`clubusy.nsf` and delivers them to Notes. Notes displays the busy times on a bar graph so the user doing the lookup can see what times the other user (or resource) is not busy.

- Calendar Connector. When a user needs to look up the free time of a user or resource on another mail server, Calendar Connector retrieves the information. Calendar Connector can retrieve information from mail servers in other Notes domains, cc:Mail domains, and OfficeVision domains.

Schedule Manager and Calendar Connector are by default loaded into memory whenever a server starts. They appear in each server's `notes.ini` file, as `sched` and `calconn` in the `ServerTasks` variable. You can load them manually from the server console with the commands `load sched` and `load calconn`. You can unload them from memory with the commands `tell sched quit` and `tell calconn quit`.

You can also load and unload them from within Domino Administrator. Schedule Manager also supports other `tell` commands, which you can run as console commands or from within Domino Administrator (Server, Status tab).

Schedule Manager and Calendar Connector should run on mail servers, any server maintaining a Resource Reservations database or an application that uses Notes calendaring and scheduling functions, hub servers, and servers that serve as the connectors between domains. You can safely unload the Schedule Manager and Calendar Connector from memory on any server that does not host a calendaring-and-scheduling related application and on servers that don't connect other servers or domains to each other.

The calendars of resources, such as meeting rooms and projectors, are maintained in one or more Resource Reservations databases. Each resource is represented by a document in the Resource Reservations database itself and a Resource document in the Domain Directory. The resource document in the Resource Reservations database describes the resource and organizes reservations of its time. The Resource document in the Domain Directory is a specialized Mail-In Database document that tells the router how to route reservations created in a user's mail database to the Resource Reservations database. You have to create the resource document in Resource Reservations, but if the Administration Process is properly configured, it will create the Resource document in the Domain Directory for you.

Setting Up the Resource Reservations Database

You can create one or more Resource Reservations databases, but many organizations only need one. You might want to create more than one if you have widely separate and independently managed offices or if one group of servers is connected to another group by modem connections only. If you do have more than one, they should certainly not hold duplicate records of the same resources.

You don't want to replicate a Resource Reservations database to multiple servers, because replica copies would be prone to being out of date. Besides, the Calendar Connector can reach across the network to retrieve needed information from the database.

When you create a Resource Reservations database (File Database, New), place it on a server. Base it on the Resource Reservations (5.0) design template (filename resrc50.ntf, located on the server). Name it anything you want (but everyone pretty much uses Resource Reservations). And give it any filename you want (but resource. nsf is common). There's no need to encrypt it, index it, or limit its size. But, under Advanced Database Options, you can select "Don't maintain unread marks" and "Don't overwrite Free space," if you like.

When you first create the database, open the ACL (File, Database, Access Control). Notice that you, the server on which you created the database, and LocalDomainServers are Managers. Default access is Author, which is appropriate for most users. You should add other Managers as desired. Anyone who will be permitted to create resource records should be assigned the [CreateResource] role; nobody else can create resources.

The database is organized by sites, then resources, then reservations. You must first create one or more sites. Then you can create resources, which are associated with a site. You have to be assigned the [CreateResource] role to create sites and resources. Thereafter, standard users can reserve the resources.

To create a site, navigate to any view that displays the New Site action and click it. Enter a site name and save the document. If the new site doesn't appear in a view, press F9 to refresh the view. If the message "You have insufficient access to perform this operation" appears when you click New Site, it's because the database thinks you haven't been assigned the [CreateResource] role. If you know that's not true, close the database, reopen it, and try again.

After you have created a site, you can create resources associated with it. Click the New Resource action, complete the form, and close and save it. The significant fields are as set forth in Table 8.5.

Table 8.5 **Fields in the Resource Form**

Field	Description
	ON THE TYPE TAB
Resource type	Choose Room or Other.
	ON THE RESOURCE INFORMATION TAB
Name	Enter a descriptive name for the resource, one that will immediately identify it to people familiar with it.
Site	Choose from the list the site where the resource resides.
Capacity	This field appears if you chose Room as the resource type. Enter the number of people the room can comfortably support.
Category	This field appears if you chose Other as the resource type. Initially, there won't be any categories, but as you create them they will appear in the list when you create later resources. Categories may be things like "Audio/Video equipment," "Transport," "Computer equipment," and so on.
Description	Describe the resource to the extent necessary to identify it to people who might want to reserve it.

Field	Description
	ON THE RESOURCE OWNER OPTIONS TAB
Ownership type	The choices are: None: Anyone can reserve this resource. Only owner can book resource. Others have to book it through the owner. Only select list of people can book resource. Only select list of people can book resource via autoprocessing – all others require owner approval. Temporarily disable reservations.
Owner's name	This field appears if you choose the second or fourth option in the Ownership type field. You can enter or choose one name from the list.
List of names	This field appears if you choose the third or fourth option in the Ownership type field. You can enter or choose multiple names from the list.

On the Availability Settings tab: Set the days of the week and times of the day when the resource is available to be reserved. The default is 9 a.m. to 5 p.m. weekdays.

When you save a resource document, Notes submits an Add Resource request to the Administration Process. When that request replicates to the administration server of the Domino Directory, the Administration Process running on that server will create a Resource document in the Domain Directory. This is the Mail-In Database document for the resource. People will be able to reserve the resource from within their mail databases; when they do, their reservations will be mailed to the Resource Reservations database.

Enabling Cross-Domain Group Scheduling with Domain Documents

If you have more than one domain, you can enable cross-domain free time lookups. To do so, you have to create, in each domain, appropriate domain documents. For adjacent domains, create Adjacent Domain documents. For non-adjacent domains, create Non-adjacent Domain documents. For cc:Mail and OfficeVision domains, create Foreign Domain documents.

Whichever kind of domain document you create, the one significant field in all of them for our purposes here is the variously named field in which you enter the name of a calendar server:

- In the Adjacent Domain and Foreign Domain documents, the field is called Calendar server name and you enter the name of a calendar server in the other domain.

- In the Non-adjacent Domain document, the field is called Route requests through calendar server and you enter the name of a calendar server in the "route-through" domain. The route-through domain must be adjacent to both the current domain and the non-adjacent domain for which you are creating the document. In other words, there cannot be more than one intervening domain between the current domain and the non-adjacent domain.

The calendar server in each domain must be reachable by servers in the other adjacent domains by LAN connections with reasonably fast response times. A calendar server can be any server that runs the Schedule Manager and Calendar Connector tasks.

Holiday Documents

The Holidays view of the Domino Directory stores documents describing holidays. Holiday documents already exist that describe the standard holidays in many countries of the world, as well as religious holidays. You can view existing holiday documents in Domino Administrator by choosing Configuration, Miscellaneous, Holidays.

You can also create holidays in the same view by clicking the Add Holiday action. When you create a holiday you enter its name, information about when it occurs, how many days it lasts, how frequently it repeats, and so on, and you classify the holiday by the countries and/or religions in which it is celebrated. For a company event or holiday, you could add your own classification.

Users can import holidays from the Domino Directory into their mail databases by choosing Tools, Import Holidays from their Calendar view. A dialog box will appear in which the user can select the classes of holidays (countries, religions, and so on) to import.

Free Time Database Validation

Every night at 2 a.m. the Schedule Manager validates its free time database. It also validates it when you restart the server. You can also force validation by entering the command `tell sched validate`. If validation errors appear, they almost always arise from one of two causes:

- A mail database exists for which there is no corresponding Person document. Delete the mail database.
- A Person document says there is supposed to be a mail database but their isn't. Create the database, edit the Person document, or delete the Person document.

Shared Mail Setup and Maintenance

By default, each Notes, POP, and IMAP mail user's messages are stored in a Notes database separate from everyone else's messages. There are several advantages to this form of mail storage over the storage model—one monolithic database—employed by most mail systems. For one thing, a corrupted database affects only one user. For another, you can devise more efficient backup strategies. For yet another, it is relatively easy to move a mail user from one mail server to another.

The one glaring drawback of Domino's multi-database system is the duplication of message storage that occurs. If I copy 10 people on a message, all 10 copies may be stored on the same drive but in different databases. Domino shared mail allows you to recapture the disk space lost to duplicate message storage while at the same time mitigating the disadvantages of the monolithic storage model.

In the past, many or perhaps most Domino administrators have shied away from implementing Domino shared mail for two reasons. First, implementing shared mail increases the administrative burden dramatically. Second, under R4, administrators did not trust the integrity of Notes databases, especially very large ones, enough to commit scores or hundreds of mail users' messages to a single very large database. Finally, disk space is cheap. Why sweat the disadvantages of implementing shared mail when it's easy to alleviate disk space problems by adding more?

Under R5, at least one of the disadvantages of shared mail has been largely eradicated. With the advent of transaction logging and the addition of numerous other database improvements, the integrity of Notes databases is much greater than under R4. In addition, the increasingly powerful Administration Process has mitigated many of the administrative chores that shared mail brings with it. Many Domino administrators will continue to shun shared mail because of the other two reasons. But, before you write off shared mail, maybe you should understand how it works and what the administrative burden is.

How Shared Mail Works

When shared mail is enabled, one or more shared mail databases (also known as Single Copy Object Stores or SCOSes) exist on the server. When the router delivers a message to a local mail database, it splits the message into two parts. The message header, containing the summary fields (To, From, and so on), goes into the recipient's mail database. The message body, which holds the message's content, goes into the shared mail database. The router adds pointers to the header and body, each of which points to the location of the other part. If a message is addressed to more than one recipient on the server, the body will have multiple pointers attached, one pointing back to the mail database of each recipient.

When a user opens a message, the database server retrieves the header from the user's mail database, follows the pointer to locate the body, and retrieves it from the shared mail database, then delivers the reunited message to the user. The user is never aware that the message is stored in two different places.

Exactly how this system works depends on whether Shared_Mail is set to 1 or 2. If set to 1, the message body is stored in the shared mail database only if the message is addressed to two or more recipients on the mail server. If set to 2, the message body is always stored in the shared mail database, even if addressed to only one user on the server.

That, at least, is the end result. The actual mechanics are a little more complicated. When Shared_Mail is set to 1, the router takes a message from mail.box and places a copy of it in the first addressee's mail database. If there are no more addressees, that's it. If there are additional addressees, the router puts the body of the message in the shared mail database and a copy of the header into each addressee's database, including the first addressee's. In the process, it overwrites the full copy of the message that it first placed in the first addressee's mail database.

When Shared_Mail is set to 2, the router takes a message from mail.box and places the body in the shared mail database. Then, it looks to see who the addressees are. If any addressees are resident on this mail server, the router puts a copy of the message header in each addressee's mail database. If no addressees are resident on this mail server, the router transfers the message to the appropriate other servers, then removes the message body from the shared mail database.

On the face of it, you would think the first process would be more efficient. But apparently the second one is more efficient because the second one is the default if you enable shared mail in such a way as to let the server choose which version to implement (see the next section).

The shared mail database is very secure. It is encrypted with the server's public key and has no views. The host server is the only entity listed in the ACL. It doesn't appear in the Open Database dialog box.

When each recipient deletes his copy of a message, the pointer to that recipient's header is removed from the body of the message. When all recipients have deleted their copies of a message, the body is removed entirely from the shared mail database.

You can create multiple shared mail databases. This is a good thing to do because it allows you to gain the benefit of shared mail (conservation of disk space) and retain to some extent the benefit of storing mail on numerous separate, relatively small databases (easier restores from backup, less chance of widespread data corruption). In fact, the best way to manage shared mail on a Domino server is to create multiple shared mail databases, then to rotate the currently active one among them frequently.

When you have multiple shared mail databases, one of them is "active" in the sense that it is the one the router will use to store newly arrived mail. The others are "archival" because they store older messages. The server knows which one is currently active because there is a database link file—a text file called `mailobj.nsf`—which contains a single line of text consisting of the path name of the currently active shared mail database.

When the router delivers a newly arrived message to local users, it looks in `mailobj.nsf`, discovers the location of the "real" shared mail database, then places the message body there. When you tell the router to use a different shared mail database, the router writes the name of the new database into `mailobj.nsf`, overwriting the name of the old database.

By frequently telling the router to make a different shared mail database active, you can spread the message load more or less evenly among numerous databases. If any one of them somehow becomes corrupt, the fact that it holds only some fraction of user messages softens the impact.

Of course, it is the need to do this kind of thing that has made administrators shy away from shared mail in the past. In addition, there are many other maintenance chores for the administrator to carry out. Finally, it is much more work to move a user from one mail server to another or to remove a user entirely when shared mail is in place. However, you can automate many of your maintenance chores with program documents. The increasingly powerful Administration Process will carry out the drudgery of moving and removing users, if you let it. In short, Lotus is gradually eliminating the objectionable qualities of shared mail.

Setting Up Shared Mail

You can enable shared mail by adding the variable `Shared_Mail=1` (which means Enabled for Delivery Only) or `Shared_Mail=2` (which means Enabled for Transfer and Delivery) to your `notes.ini` file. (Shared_Mail=0 or the complete absence of the variable means shared mail is disabled.) You can do so directly, by editing `notes.ini`, then restarting the server. Or you can do so indirectly, by adding the variable to a configuration document. This is the preferred method, because you don't have to restart the server.

To enable shared mail the second way, follow these steps:

1. Open a configuration document that names the server on which you want to enable shared mail. If one doesn't exist, create it.

2. Under the NOTES.INI Settings tab, choose Set/Modify Parameters.

3. In the dialog box that appears, click the small "helper" button to the right of the Item field.

4. In the Select a Standard Parameter dialog box, select SHARED_MAIL, then choose OK.

5. In the Value field, enter 1 or 2, then choose Next, then choose OK. `SHARED_MAIL=n` appears in the configuration document.

6. Save and close the document. Within a few minutes of the appearance of this document on the effected server, the server will add the variable to its `notes.ini` file and create the shared mail database (filename `mailobj1.nsf`) and begin using it.

Because the Shared_Mail variable has been added to the server's `notes.ini`, the server will work in shared mail mode each time it restarts.

You can enable shared mail two other ways as well. The server console command `tell router use` *shared.nsf* will create the named database if it didn't exist and enable shared mail if it was not already in effect. The same goes for the command `load object create` *shared.nsf*. (In these and the examples that follow, *shared.nsf* refers to a shared mail database, and *usermail.nsf* refers to a user's mail database or a mail directory.)

The benefit of using either of these methods is that you can choose the name of the shared mail database. But you don't get to choose the type of shared mail that goes into effect. The server automatically sets the variable `Shared_Mail=2` in its `notes.ini` file.

If you are considering implementing shared mail on your servers, keep the following rules of thumb in mind:

- If a server is not a mail server, don't implement shared mail. There's no benefit to be gained.

- If a server doubles as a mail server and a mail hub, or for some other reason transfers a myriad of messages to other servers, implement shared mail "for delivery only"; that is, `set Shared_Mail=1`.

- If a server is a "leaf" or "spoke" mail server that transfers relatively few messages to other servers, implement shared mail "for transfer and delivery"; that is, `set Shared_Mail=2`.

Shared Mail Maintenance Chores

The kinds of chores you have to perform when shared mail is in place on a server include:

- Creating new shared mail databases
- Rotating activity among existing shared mail databases
- Linking, unlinking, and relinking user mail files to and from shared mail databases
- Excluding files from and including files in the shared mail process
- Removing obsolete files from shared mail databases
- Moving user mail files from one mail server to another
- Removing user mail files from a server
- Deleting shared mail databases

Creating Shared Mail Databases

To create a shared mail database, use one of two commands. First, the following command:

```
load object create shared.nsf
```

The Object task will load into memory, create the new database, then drop out of memory, its job done. The new database won't be active. That is, the router won't add messages to it, because this command didn't edit the `mailobj.nsf` database link file. This command is most useful when setting up a shared mail database rotation schedule. See the next sesction for details.

Alternatively, you can create a shared mail database and make it the currently active one with the following command:

```
tell router use shared.nsf
```

The router task will create the new database, then edit the `mailobj.nsf` database link file so that it names the new database. Thereafter, the router will add all new messages to the new database.

Rotating Activity Among Shared Mail Databases

To designate a shared mail database as the active database (the one to which the router delivers newly arrived messages), use the following command:

```
tell router use shared.nsf
```

To accomplish the same thing with a program document, enter `nserver` in the Program name field and `-c 'tell router use shared.nsf'` in the Command line field. (On the actual Program document, use double quotation marks around the words `"tell router quit."`)

To use Program documents to set up a regular rotation among a set of shared mail databases, do the following:

1. Create from five to seven shared mail databases (one for each work day). Name them `mailobj1.nsf, mailobj2.nsf, mailobj3.nsf`, and so on.

2. Create from one Program document for each shared mail database. Each program document will run one day a week at 4 a.m., as follows: The Program document for `mailobj1.nsf` will run on Monday and will run the command `tell router use mailobj1.nsf`; the one for `mailobj2.nsf` will run on Tuesday and will run the command `tell router use mailobj2.nsf`; and so on.

The result is that the router adds new messages to mailobj1 on Mondays, mailobj2 on Tuesdays, mailobj3 on Wednesdays, and so on. We set up a weekly rotation schedule for the simple reason that Program documents are easy to set up that way. Another easy rotation schedule, though a busier one, would be to have each Program document run daily and set each one to run at a different hour, say, 8 a.m., 9 a.m., 10 a.m., and so on. An interesting by-product of each of these rotation schedules is that the relative sizes of the shared mail databases would show you the relative amount of mail activity that occurs from day to day each week (under the first schedule) or from hour to hour each day (under the second schedule).

Linking, Unlinking, and Relinking Databases

Probably the first command you will issue after enabling shared mail on a Domino server is

```
load object link usermail.nsf shared.nsf
```

This will cause existing messages in users' personal mail files to be split and the message bodies moved into the new shared mail database. If the server has been in service for a long time, you'll probably realize a huge reclamation of disk space when you do this. Thereafter, you will only have to run the link commands occasionally. The link commands are

- `load object link usermail.nsf shared.nsf`. Use to link a user mail file or a directory full of mail files to a shared mail file.
- `load object unlink usermail.nsf|shared.nsf`. Use to unlink a user or shared mail database from all the files to which it is linked. All message bodies are moved back into the user mail file(s). Use this command before removing a user mail file from a server and before deleting a shared mail file from a server.
- `load object link -relink usermail.nsf shared.nsf:`. Use to unlink existing links in a user mail file, then link everything in the user mail file to the named shared mail file.

Excluding and Including Databases

You can permanently exclude a user mail database (or a folder full of them) from shared mail process with the following command:

```
load object set -never usermail.nsf
```

You can re-include a previously excluded mail database (or a folder full of them) with the following command:

```
load object reset -never usermail.nsf
```

Use the set -never command before unlinking a file preparatory to moving or removing it.

You can include replicas of mail files (or a folder full of them) in shared mail with the following command:

```
load object set -always usermail.nsf shared.nsf
```

You can exclude a previously included replica mail file (or a folder full of them) from shared mail with the following command:

```
load object reset -always usermail.nsf
```

Usually, the router moves messages from mail.box into their databases; and it is the router that splits messages when shared mail is active. Therefore, if a mail database gets populated by replication instead of by the router, it doesn't ordinarily get to participate in the shared mail process. Think of it this way: If the router doesn't touch a message, the message doesn't get split up.

A mail file might be populated by replication if it is on a server other than a user's mail server. For example, Joe Doaks is based in New York and his mail server is in New York. Joe spends a lot of time working in London. He has a replica copy of his mail database on a London mail server so that he can read mail in London without constantly reconnecting to his mail server in New York.

When people send messages to Joe, the messages are routed to the New York server because it's his official mail server. Then, the messages are replicated to Joe's London database. Because the router in New York handles Joe's messages, they are split up and the message bodies are placed in the shared mail database. But, because the router in London does not handle Joe's messages, they do not get split up on the London mail server. The `set -always` command, run against Joe's London mail database, forces its inclusion in shared mail on that server even though the server would otherwise ignore it.

Removing Obsolete Files from Shared Mail Databases

The primary maintenance chore that arises under shared mail is the removal of pointers and message bodies from the shared mail databases as users delete the message headers from their personal mail databases. This takes place automatically on the active shared mail database. But, you have to make sure that it happens on the archive shared mail databases too.

You could do it manually with the following server console command:

```
load object collect shared.nsf
```

However, there is no need to do this manually. You can automate the collection task in two different ways. First, you can add the collection task to a ServerTasksAt*n* variable in the server's `notes.ini` file. That's how Lotus automated the collection of the active shared mail database.

If you look at the ServerTasksAt2 variable in any Domino server's `notes.ini` file, you'll see that one of the tasks the server performs at 2 a.m. is Object Collect `mailobj.nsf`. Remember that `mailobj.nsf` is a link file that points to the currently active shared mail database. That's what actually gets cleaned up by Object Collect. You can add other Object Collect items to `notes.ini`. Append them to the existing ServerTasksAt*n* variables or add new ones.

The second way to automate the collection task on inactive shared mail databases is with program documents. A program document will run any program you tell it to. It will run it at the time(s) of day and on the day(s) of the week that you specify. This makes a program document a little more flexible than the ServerTasksAt*n* variables, which run every day and on the hour.

To create a program document, open Domino Administrator to the Configuration tab, expand Server, and choose Programs. Choose Add Program and fill in the fields as set forth in Table 8.6.

Table 8.6 **Fields in the Program Form**

Field	Description
	ON THE BASICS TAB
Program name	Enter the filename of the program (but excluding the extension). In the example, enter "object" in this field.
Command line	Enter any command arguments. In the example, enter `collect shared.nsf`, where `shared.nsf` is the name of one of your shared mail databases.
Server to run on	Enter the full name of a Domino server.
Comments	As a general rule, always enter descriptive information in every document you create so that, a year later, you or your successor will be able to figure out why you created the document in the first place.
On the Schedule tab:	Set up the schedule on which you want this program to run.

Set up one program document for each shared mail database. Then, you can remove `object collect mailobj.nsf` from the `ServerTasksAt2` variable in `notes.ini`, because your program documents will take care of the active database as well as the archive databases. You could actually take care of all your shared mail databases with a single program document by using the command `object collect` (naming no database). Running Object Collect without naming a database causes it to collect all shared mail databases that it finds. However, you might prefer to run Object Collect on different databases at different times and on different days in order to spread the load over time. Occasionally, message bodies can get orphaned in a shared mail database. That is, they contain a pointer to a user database, but the user database no longer exists. This can happen if you delete or move a mail database from a server without first breaking the links it has to shared mail databases. The Object Collect task will not ordinarily pick up this anomaly. To remove orphaned message bodies, you have to run this command:

```
load object collect -force database.nsf
```

Another version of Object Collect is

```
load object collect -nodelete
```

Use this to see ahead of time what documents would be purged from a database and how much disk space would be reclaimed. If you're a good C++ or Java programmer, you could write a program that pre checks the impact of Object Collect, then only runs it for real if the amount of reclaimed disk space exceeds some defined number. (If you write such a program, please send me a copy; my programming skills aren't nearly that strong.)

Moving User Mail Databases from One Server to Another

On R5, servers you can tell the Administration Process to do this, and it will take care of all the details for you. If, however, you have to move a mail file manually, follow these steps:

1. Enter `load object set -never` *usermail.nsf* to stop any incoming mail from being included in the shared mail process.

2. Enter load object unlink *usermail.nsf* to move all message bodies back into the user mail database from any shared mail databases they might reside in.

3. Create a replica of the user mail database on its new mail server, then replicate all messages to the new replica.

4. Change the user's Person record in the Domino Directory to reflect the changed mail server.

5. Replicate the changed Person document to all other servers in the domain.

6. Edit the user's Location documents to reflect the move to a new mail server.

7. Replicate the two mail databases one last time to ensure that all messages are in the new copy of the database.

8. Delete the old copy of the mail database.

9. If the new mail server uses shared mail, run `load object link` *usermail.nsf* *shared.nsf* to include existing messages in the shared mail database on the new server.

Deleting User Mail Databases from a Server

On R5, servers you can tell the Administration Process to do this, and it will take care of all the details for you. If, however, you have to delete a mail file manually, follow these steps:

1. Enter `load object set -never` *usermail.nsf* to stop any incoming mail from being included in the shared mail process.

2. Enter `load object unlink` *usermail.nsf* to move all message bodies back into the user mail database from any shared mail databases they might reside in.

3. Enter a forwarding address, if one exists, in the user's Person document, so that any future mail gets redirected.

4. Replicate the changed Person document to all other servers in the domain.

5. Delete the mail database.

Deleting Shared Mail Databases

Before you delete a shared mail database, you must unlink it from other databases. Run `load object unlink` *shared.nsf.* Then delete the shared mail database.

You may have to wait awhile before deleting the database. If it stores many linked messages, it can take quite a while to move them all back into the users' mail databases. You can tell if the unlinking process is still active with the `show tasks` command. If unlinking is still proceeding, the object task will appear in the list of server tasks. If it is finished, object won't appear in the list.

Before you run this command against a large shared mail database, make sure you have plenty of free disk space on the drive occupied by the mail files of the users whose messages are linked to the database. Remember that the shared mail database's purpose is to conserve disk space by storing only one copy of message bodies that were addressed to more than one user. Unlinking them will multiply the number of stored messages.

I can't tell you how to calculate the amount of free disk space you'll need. I don't know if anyone can. But, there are a couple ways to gain some hints. First, if the Shared_Mail variable was set to 1 (Shared Mail for Delivery Only) when messages were being added to the database, unlinking it will consume more disk space than if the Shared_Mail variable was set to 2 (Shared Mail for Transfer and Delivery). That's because, under Shared Mail for Delivery Only, the only message bodies actually stored in the shared mail database would have been for messages that were addressed to more than one recipient on this server. Under Shared Mail for Transfer and Delivery, all message bodies would have been stored in the shared mail database, even though addressed to only one user. So, in the first scenario, you know that a higher percentage of messages unlinked by this process will expand the size of two or more user mail databases.

You might also be able to get a feel for the amount of disk space to be consumed by the unlinking process by running the `show stat object` command. It will display statistics about the contents of all shared mail databases. Specifically, it will display the numbers of messages in the database that are shared by different numbers of people. That is, it will show how many messages are linked to only one user's mail file, how many are linked to two, to three, and so on. You can see the same statistics in Domino Administrator under Server, Statistics. Look under Object.

You can assume (for the sake of making an estimate) that all messages are equal in size. Then, a little arithmetic (okay, maybe a lot) would give you an idea how much the size of the messages involved will expand upon unlinking. For example, say that an imaginary, drastically simplified shared mail database is 6,000 bytes in size and has six messages in it, distributed as follows:

```
3 messages shared by 1 person each
2 messages shared by 2 people each
1 message shared by 3 people
```

If each message is equal in size, then 6,000/6 is 1,000 bytes per message. When you unlink them, the three messages won't expand in size; the two messages will double in size, and the one message will triple in size. That is:

```
3 messages shared by 1 person each x 1 = 3000 bytes
2 messages shared by 2 people each x 2 = 4000 bytes
1 message shared by 3 people x 3 = 3000 bytes
```

Add this up: 3,000 + 4,000 + 3,000 = 10,000 bytes. That's a rough estimate of how much disk space the messages will occupy after unlinking.

Fine Tuning Mail Routing with Configuration Documents

Having set up your basic mail routing scheme, you can tune it. Domino provides a mind-numbing variety of tools for tuning the actions and performance of your mail routing system. They take the form, mostly, of fields in the configuration form and are pretty well organized on that form. Therefore, I'll present them here, as ordered and organized as they appear on the configuration form.

The reason Lotus put these fields on the configuration form instead of the server form is so that you could use one form to configure multiple servers. The configuration form lets you define a configuration document to cover your whole domain, a server group, or a single server.

While this can save you plenty of work, it can also cause serious problems. If you create two or more configuration documents that govern one server, Notes may not be able to reconcile any conflicting settings in them, with unpredictable results.

It's okay to create, say, a domain-level configuration document, a group-level configuration document, and a server-level configuration document, all configuring a given server. In fact, that's exactly what you should do. The settings in the more specific configuration documents will override the settings in the less specific configuration documents (with an interesting exception that we'll discuss in Chapter 11, "Domino Directory Services." But, if you create more than one configuration document at a given level, be very careful that they don't try to govern the same set of servers or, if they do, that their settings don't conflict with each other. This is potentially a big pitfall. Avoid it assiduously.

The settings in the configuration form that interest us in this chapter are located on the Router/SMTP and MIME tabs. Here we'll focus on the settings on the following tabs:

- Router/SMTP
  - Basics
  - Restrictions and Controls
  - Advanced

- MIME
  - Basics
  - Conversion Options
  - Settings by Character Set Groups
  - Advanced

We won't cover the settings on the Message Tracking tab because we cover them elsewhere. If you create a default configuration document for the whole domain, an additional tab appears named LDAP or LDAP Settings (depending on how you open the document). We'll cover the settings in that tab in Chapter 11.

Some of the fields described here occur in what you might call Allow/Deny pairs. One member of the pair allows only the entities named in the field to do a thing. The other member of the pair denies the entities named in the field the right to do the thing.

The Allow fields are restrictive; you have to be named in one to be allowed to do the thing. If an Allow field is empty, then (usually) everyone can do the thing. If the Allow field contains a single entry, then nobody else in the world can do the thing. The Deny fields are permissive; if you aren't named in a Deny field, you can do the thing (subject to restrictions in the corresponding Allow field). If the Deny field is empty, then everyone can do the thing (again subject to restrictions in the corresponding Allow field).

In general, you should enter names in only one of the two fields, not both. Use the Allow field if you only want to permit a small number of entities to do the thing. Use the Deny field if you want to permit most of the world to do the thing. If you enter names in both fields, the Deny field would only be effective to the extent that it names an entity that is also named in the Allow field; in that case, it would override the Allow field.

Router/SMTP Basics

Number of mailboxes. The default is 1 and its name is mail.box. If a mail server is very busy, with many users all sending documents simultaneously, contention for access to mail.box can be a bottleneck that slows a server's responsiveness. If you set this field to 2 or more, then restart the server, the router will create multiple mailboxes named mail1.box, mail2.box, etc., and mail users can access whichever is available at a given moment.

SMTP used when sending messages outside of the local internet domain. We discussed this field earlier in this chapter. Use it to enable or disable use of SMTP to transfer messages addressed to Internet addresses.

SMTP allowed within the local internet domain. We discussed this field earlier in this chapter. Use it to enable or disable use of SMTP to transfer messages addressed to local users.

Servers within the local Notes domain are reachable via SMTP over TCPIP. We discussed this field earlier in this chapter. Use it to allow a server to use SMTP to transfer mail to all local SMTP servers or just to ones in its own Notes named network.

Address lookup. Determines how the server matches Internet addresses to names in the Domino Directory. "Fullname" requires an exact, case-insensitive match of a message's Internet address with an Internet address in the $Users view. If it can't find one, the address is assumed to be invalid. "Local Part" only requires a match between the parts of the names to the left of the @ sign. "Fullname then Local Part" tries first for a "Fullname" match but, if it can't find one, falls back to a "Local part" match.

Exhaustive lookup. Enabling this forces the router to look up users' names in all available directories to find all possible matches. This ensures, where there are multiple directories available, that names aren't misaddressed. But, it may also increase the amount of time the lookups take.

Relay host for messages leaving the local internet domain. If a server transfers Internet mail to a relay host, enter its host name here. If a server uses a group of relay hosts, enter their domain name here. If a server can address mail directly to the addressee's domain, leave this field blank.

Local Internet domain smart host. If your local Internet domain includes mail users who are not members of your Notes domains, enter here the host name or IP address of a non–Domino SMTP host that can handle mail for those mail users.

Smart host is used for all local internet domain recipients. Use this when all mail coming in from the Internet, even mail addressed to Notes users, must pass through the smart host first for special handling.

Host name lookup. Dynamic lookup is through DNS. Local lookup is in a local hosts file.

Router/SMTP Restrictions and Controls: Restrictions

The first four fields in this section apply to mail arriving from other Notes domains and organizations. The remaining fields apply to all incoming mail.

Allow mail only from domains. This refers to other Notes domains. Mail from all other domains will be returned to the sender.

Deny mail from domains. This refers to other Notes domains. Mail from the named domains will be returned to the sender.

Allow mail only from the following organizations and organizational units (*/Acme, */Sales/Acme). Mail from all others will be returned to the sender.

Deny mail only from the following organizations and organizations units (*/Acme, */Sales/Acme). Mail from those named here will be returned to the sender.

Maximum message size. Defaults to 0 kilobytes, which means there is no restriction on message size. If this is set greater than 0, larger messages are returned to the sender with an explanation.

Send all messages as low priority if message size is between. If you enable this, two other fields appear, one in which you can enter the minimum size, the other for the maximum size of messages to be sent low priority. If you leave the second parameter set at 0, all mail above the minimum size will be sent low priority. Low priority mail is routed only between designated off-hours.

Obey database quotas during message delivery. By default, database quotas only block the saving of new documents, not the mailing in of documents. This allows you to override that default. Messages that cannot be accepted because of this are returned to the sender with an explanation.

Router/SMTP Restrictions and Controls: SMTP Inbound Relay Controls

These fields allow you to deny external hosts or domains the right to relaying mail through your domain to other external Internet or Notes domains. One reason to do this is block bulk mailers from relaying mail through your domain, which they might want to do in order to hide the true origin of their bulk mail. Another reason is simply to conserve your precious bandwidth.

In the following two fields, you can enter Internet or Notes domain names. Precede Notes domain names with a % sign. acme.com would block relays to acme.com and sales.acme.com. But "@acme.com" would block relays from acme.com only, not from sales.acme.com.

Allow messages from external internet domains to be sent only to the following internet domains. Mail will be relayed only to the named domains.

Deny messages from external internet domains to be sent to the following internet domains. Mail will not be relayed to the named domains. You can enter an asterisk (*) in this field to block all relays.

In the following two fields you can enter fully qualified domain or host names or IP addresses. If you enter acme.com, you block relays from all hosts in acme.com. Enclose IP addresses in square brackets and use asterisks to deny whole subnets. For example, "[10.0.0.*]" blocks every host with IP address beginning with the 10.0.0.

Allow messages only from the following external internet hosts to be sent to external internet domains. Only the named hosts will be allowed to use your domain as a relay.

Deny messages from the following external internet hosts to be sent to external internet domains. The named hosts will not be allowed to use your domain as a relay.

Router/SMTP Restrictions and Controls: SMTP Inbound Connection Controls

The following three fields allow you to refuse connections to hosts. Compare to the next three, which allow you to refuse to accept mail from specific senders.

Verify connecting hostname in DNS. If enabled, the server will deny a connection to any host whose name cannot be found in the DNS system.

In the following two fields, you can enter fully qualified domain or host names or IP addresses. If you enter acme.com, you block relays from all hosts in acme.com. Enclose IP addresses in square brackets and use asterisks to deny whole subnets. For example, "[10.0.0.*]" includes every host whose IP address begins with the 10.0.0.

Allow connections only from the following SMTP internet hostnames/IP addresses. Hosts not named here or not having IP addresses listed in this field will not be able to connect to this server. Therefore, they won't be able to transfer mail to this server.

Deny connections from the following SMTP internet hostnames/IP addresses. Hosts that are named here or that have IP addresses listed in this field will not be able to connect to this server. Therefore they won't be able to transfer mail to this server.

Router/SMTP Restrictions and Controls: SMTP Inbound Sender Controls

The following fields allow you to block mail on the basis of who the sender is. Compare to the previous three fields, which allowed blocking of connections to SMTP hosts.

Verify sender's domain in DNS. If enabled, the server will refuse to accept mail from any sender whose name can't be found in the DNS system.

In the following two fields, you can enter domain names or email addresses. Domains act like wildcards in that acme.com includes *.acme.com. Addresses must be an exact match. doaks@acme.com does not include jdoaks@acme.com.

Allow messages only from the following external internet addresses/domains. Messages from entities not named here will be blocked.

Deny messages from the following external internet addresses/domains. Messages from entities that are named here will be blocked.

Router/SMTP Restrictions and Controls: SMTP Inbound Intended Recipients Controls

The following two fields allow you to restrict the entities allowed to receive mail from the Internet.

Allow messages intended only for the following internet addresses. If the addressee of a message is not named in this field, the message will be blocked.

Deny messages intended for the following internet addresses. If the addressee of a message is named in this field, the message will be blocked.

Router/SMTP Restrictions and Controls: SMTP Outbound Sender Controls

The first two fields described next affect mail according to the sender's Internet address. The second two fields affect mail according to the sender's Notes address. These are local Internet and Notes addresses.

Allow messages only from the following Internet addresses to be sent to the Internet. Only the senders listed will be allowed to send mail to the Internet.

Deny messages from the following Internet addresses to be sent to the Internet. The senders listed will not be allowed to send mail to the Internet.

Allow messages only from the following Notes addresses to be sent to the Internet. Only the senders listed will be allowed to send mail to the Internet.

Deny messages from the following Notes addresses to be sent to the Internet. The senders listed will not be allowed to send mail to the Internet.

Router/SMTP Restrictions and Controls: Delivery Controls

Maximum delivery threads. By default, the router sets the number of threads, based on available memory. By setting a number here, you override the router's choice. Lotus recommends a setting between 1 and 25, depending on the server load.

Encrypt all delivered mail. If you enable this, the server encrypts all messages delivered to it. If you disable this, the server only encrypts what senders and recipients specify.

Pre-delivery agent timeout. The amount of time a predelivery agent has to complete its task. The default is 30 seconds.

Router/SMTP Restrictions and Controls: Transfer Controls

Maximum transfer threads. By default the router sets the number of threads, based on available memory. By setting a number here, you override the router's choice. Lotus recommends a setting between 1 and 25, depending on the server load.

Maximum concurrent transfer threads. The maximum number of threads Domino will devote to transferring messages to a single destination. The default is one-half of the maximum transfer threads (see the preceding field).

Maximum hop count. The maximum hops allowed before delivery failure occurs. Default is 25 hops.

Low priority mail routing time range. The default is from 12 a.m. to 6 a.m. Change it to any time range you want.

Initial transfer retry interval. The amount of time in minutes a server will wait after the first message transfer failure before trying a second time. Default is 15 minutes. The server will wait longer after each successive failure.

Expired message purge interval. How often the router checks for expired messages. Default is 15 minutes.

Router/SMTP Advanced: Inbound SMTP Commands and Extensions

Over the years since the RFC 821 and RFC 822 standards were published, they have been extended by various other RFCs. The fields that follow correspond to specific commands that Domino supports in RFC 821 and RFC 822 and the extensions. You can enable or disable each command to suit your needs.

SIZE extension. Enabled by default. The server will reject incoming messages that exceed the maximum message size set on the Router/SMTP, Restrictions and Controls, Restrictions page.

Pipelining extension. Enabled by default. Allows multiple SMTP commands to be sent in a single network packet to speed up SMTP transactions.

DSN extension. Disabled by default. If enabled, Domino will respond to requests for delivery status notification.

8 bit MIME extension. Disabled by default. When enabled, Domino will try to send 8-bit messages as is. If another router or host rejects the 8-bit transfer, Domino will fall back to 7-bit encoded transfer. This is useful if you use a language that requires multi-national characters.

HELP command. Enabled by default. When disabled, Domino will refuse to comply with HELP commands.

VRFY command. Disabled by default. Domino refuses to comply with commands to verify user names.

EXPN command. Disabled by default. Domino refuses to expand mailing lists.

ETRN command. Disabled by default. Domino doesn't accept PULL requests from other SMTP hosts. You would want to enable this on a Domino server that has to wait for another server to connect to it before it can transfer mail to the calling server.

SSL negotiated over TCP/IP port. Disabled by default. Enable this to allow secure SMTP connections.

Router/SMTP Advanced: Outbound SMTP Commands and Extensions

SIZE extension. Enabled by default. The server will refuse to transfer outgoing messages that exceed the maximum message size set on the Router/SMTP, Restrictions and Controls, Restrictions page.

Pipelining extension. Enabled by default. Allows the other server to send multiple commands in a single network packet.

DSN extension. Disabled by default. If enabled, Domino will respond to requests for delivery status notification.

8 bit MIME extension. Disabled by default. When enabled, Domino will accept 8-bit message transfers.

Router/SMTP Advanced: Controls, Miscellaneous

Logging level. Normal is the default. Other choices are minimal, informational, and verbose. Choose informational or verbose only when troubleshooting.

Router/SMTP Advanced: Controls, Advanced Transfer

Ignore message priority. When enabled, the server ignores sender message priority settings and treats all messages are as though set at Normal priority.

Dynamic cost reset interval:. The amount of time after which the router resets an incremented routing cost back to its original setting. Default is 60 minutes, meaning that, if a failed connection increased the cost of a route from 1 to 2, it will be reset to 1 after 60 minutes.

Router/SMTP Advanced: Controls, Additional (Delivery and Transfer)

Restrict name lookups to primary directory only. Disabled by default. Users can look up names in the primary directory and secondary directories as they appear in Directory Assistance. When you enable this, users will only be able to perform lookups in the primary directory, not secondary directories.

Cluster failover. This field is relevant only if your domain includes Domino server clusters. If it is enabled, mail deliveries may be proceed even when certain servers are down. The choices are Disabled, Enabled for last hop only (the default), and Enabled for all transfers in this domain. Enabled for last hop only means that, if a mail recipient's mail server is down, the message can be delivered to another server in the cluster—the user's failover mail server. Enabled for all transfers in this domain means that, if any clustered server on a mail route is down, servers can transfer messages to another server in the same cluster.

Hold undeliverable mail. Disabled by default. If enabled, undeliverable mail will be held in mail.box instead of returned to the sender.

Router/SMTP Advanced: Controls, Failure Messages

In each of these fields you can specify the path name of a text file that holds additional text that will be displayed to users along with the standard text when the listed event occurs. You can use these fields to add foreign language text, phone numbers, anything you want. You can designate a text file for the following kinds of events:

- Transfer failure
- Delivery failure
- Message expiration
- Domain failure
- Server failure
- Username failure
- Size failure
- Restriction failure

MIME in Domino and Notes

Unless this book just fell open to this page and you started reading here, you should know by now that, as part of their overall support of Internet standards, Domino and Notes R5 support Multipurpose Internet Mail Extensions (MIME) formatting of email messages as an alternative to Notes rich text formatting. The support is much deeper than it was in earlier versions of Domino and Notes. R4.6's MIME support consisted of preserving MIME formatting in messages received from Internet mail programs by extracting the textual part of it to the Notes rich text field and embedding the MIME content in one or more attachments. R5 actually recognizes, understands, and incorporates MIME formatting in its internal document formatting.

One result of this much more integrated support of MIME is that there is a whole raft of new options for tailoring the support. In Domino, those options appear mostly in the Configuration form, but with at least one option appearing in the Person form. In Notes, those options appear in the International MIME Settings form of the Personal Address Book and in the International and Mail and News pages of User Preferences. To learn about setting MIME preferences in Notes, see Chapter 13, "Client Maintenance and Troubleshooting." To learn about setting MIME preferences in Domino, keep reading.

Understanding MIME

To understand the import of the MIME settings in Domino and Notes, it may help to understand how SMTP and MIME work. So, we'll look at that for a moment.

A message that conforms to the requirements of SMTP (RFC 822) includes a header and a body. RFC 822 defines message headers in great detail and message bodies hardly at all. Message headers consist of a series of fields, each on its own line, all expressed using the US-ASCII character set. Some fields are required; others are optional. Field syntax is *fieldname*: *value*; *comment*. The comment is optional. A message header looks more or less like this (although there can be many other fields in a real message header):

```
Date   :        22 Aug 99 0932 EST
From   :        rkirk
Subject         :       Some subject
Sender          :       rkirk@example1.com
Reply-To        :       rkirk@example1.com
To     :        JDoaks@example2.com
Message-ID      :       something
```

An RFC 822 message body, on the other hand, is entirely optional and can consist of anything you want, as long as you express it using the US-ASCII character set.

Of course, people frequently need to transfer non-ASCII information, such as formatted text, text in character sets other than US-ASCII, or non-textual content. MIME (RFCs 2045-2049) provides a standardized way of doing these things. Specifically, MIME allows for the following departures from RFC 821:

- Use of character sets other than US-ASCII in RFC 822 message headers and bodies

- An extensible set of formats for non-text portions of message bodies

- Multi-part message bodies (for example, a part consisting of plain text, another part consisting of an attached file, another part consisting of an embedded picture, and so on)

The body of a MIME-compliant message includes one or more MIME body parts. If it includes more than one MIME body part, each is separated from the others by a defined boundary. The message will be flagged as being MIME-compliant by the presence in the message header of certain fields. In addition, each MIME body part may include certain fields.

The standard MIME-defined fields include the following:

- MIME-Version. Declares the version of MIME that in the message conforms with. This field must appear as MIME-Version: 1.0, and it must appear in the topmost set of header fields, not within any MIME body part.

- Content-Type. Declares what type of content appears in a MIME body part. Its syntax is `Content-Type: type/subtype; [parameter=value]`. There are currently seven defined types: text, image, audio, video, application, multipart, and message. Within each type there are one or more defined subtypes. For example, within type text there are subtypes plain and HTML, among many others. Some content-types take optional or required parameters. Two of special interest to us are

  - `charset=string`. Content-type *text* takes an optional `charset` parameter. If the parameter isn't present, the character set is presumed to be US-ASCII. Possible values under RFC 2046 (in addition to US-ASCII) include ISO-8859-X, where X is a number 1 through 10, corresponding to the character sets defined under ISO-8859 as of the publication date of RFC 2046. The ISO-8859 character sets are the officially designated Internet mail character sets.

  - `boundary=string`. Content-type *multipart* takes a mandatory `boundary` parameter, which defines the boundary string that delimits different MIME body parts from each other.

- Content-Transfer-Encoding. Declares how the content in the following MIME body part is encoded. If this field doesn't appear in a message, it is presumed to be encoded as 7bit, which is the RFC 811 standard. Other possibilities include 8bit, binary, quoted-printable, and base64.

- Content-ID. Optionally appears at the beginning of any MIME body part. Identifies the MIME body in some unique way so that it can be cross-referenced in other MIME body parts by its content-ID.

- Content-Description. Optionally appears at the beginning of any MIME body part. Provides a place to enter descriptive information about the MIME body.

In addition to these fields, the MIME standard (RFC 2045) provides for the definition of other fields. The only restriction on such later-defined fields is that their names begin with the word "Content."

MIME also allows for the use of "private" content types and subtypes and content transfer encodings. In other words, a sender and receiver can use content types or subtypes or content transfer encoding methods that don't conform to any public standard. The only requirement is that they use "x-tokens" to label these private types/subtypes/methods. For example, Stillwater and PlanetNotes might come up with a subtype of text that they call PigLatin. MIME requires that they label it "x-piglatin" in their MIME-compliant messages.

If you ever open a MIME-compliant message in a text editor (one that doesn't interpret the MIME content), it would look something like the following, which I stitched together from two examples that appear in RFC 2046:

```
From: Whomever
To: Someone
Date: Whenever
Subject: whatever
MIME-Version: 1.0
Content-type: multipart/mixed; boundary="simple boundary"

This is the preamble.  It is to be ignored, though it
is a handy place for composition agents to include an
explanatory note to non-MIME conformant readers.

—simple boundary

This is implicitly typed plain US-ASCII text.
It does NOT end with a linebreak.
—simple boundary
Content-type: text/plain; charset=us-ascii

This is explicitly typed plain US-ASCII text.
It DOES end with a linebreak.

—simple boundary—

This is the epilogue.  It is also to be ignored.
```

Notice that it has a MIME-Version field in the main header, along with a Content-Type field that defines the content that follows as multipart/mixed with the words `"simple boundary"` as the boundary between MIME body parts. Multipart/mixed means that more than one MIME body part will follow and that each one may hold content of a different type than the others. There are preamble and epilogue parts that appear outside the boundaries. They are optional aspects of the multipart content type and provide places to enter commentary and the like.

The MIME multipart parameter in the example defines a boundary string as `"simple boundary."` The boundaries surrounding the MIME body parts will consist of that string preceded by a pair of dash (-) characters. The ending boundary includes another pair of dashes following the boundary string.

MIME Settings in Domino

Notes and Domino MIME settings can be divided into two general categories: Those of interest to every Notes domain that supports mail transfers to and from the Internet, and those of interest only to organizations that support multiple languages—the International MIME settings.

The International MIME settings help Notes or Domino to determine how to convert a MIME message to Notes rich text and how to determine what character sets and fonts to use when displaying documents created in languages other than English. If your organization never receives documents or messages written in languages other than English, you need not worry about the International MIME settings. Domino will never need to refer to them.

If your organization does routinely deal in languages other than English, the International MIME settings are of great interest to you. Depending on what languages you use, the settings can become complex. We don't have sufficient space to do justice to this topic here. Luckily for you, we don't have to, because one of the primary developers of R5's MIME features, Jeff Eisen of Iris Associates, published a comprehensive article on the topic in Iris Today, the Webzine at notes.net, in July 1999. The article is titled "Worldwide Messaging: Using International MIME in R5." You can download a copy from www.notes.net. If your users work exclusively in English, it's only of academic interest; if your users work in any languages other than English, I highly recommend this article to you.

Domino MIME settings are located in the Server Configuration form. If more than one Server Configuration document exists for a given server, Domino will use the MIME settings in the most specific one. For example, if there is a default Configuration document for the whole domain, another for a server group called Mail Servers, and yet another for the server called Mail01/Servers/Stillwater, only the MIME settings in the last will have effect, because it applies most specifically to server Mail01. (If two or more Configuration documents at the same level of specificity affect a single server, either delete one of them or remove the server from one of the groups.) In addition, the International MIME setting in a Configuration document will have no affect at all if the field International MIME Settings for this document on the Basics tab is not enabled. Finally, if you make changes in MIME settings, under R5.0.x you must restart the Domino server for the changes to take effect. Lotus promises to have the changes take immediate effect in a future release. If you are using a version of Domino later than 5.0.1, look at your release notes to see how your version behaves.

The MIME settings in the Server Configuration form are described in Table 8.7. Note that I make no effort to describe some of the International settings, but refer you instead to the Jeff Eisen's article mentioned earlier.

Table 8.7 **MIME Settings in the Configuration Form**

Field	Description
	THE BASICS TAB
Primary character set group	Defaults to English. Set it to the character set group for your domain's primary language.
Secondary character set groups	Defaults to none. Set this to the character set groups for any other languages used routinely in your domain. Set as many as you want.
	MIME CONVERSION OPTIONS: GENERAL
Return receipts	Defaults to Disabled. Set to enabled if you want to use return receipts with Internet mail.
Return receipt mapping	Specify which SMTP header field to use. The default is Disposition-Notification-To. The alternative is Return-Receipt-To, which is an older, non-standard header field. Change this only if dealing with correspondents whose mail readers don't recognize Disposition-Notification-To.
	MIME CONVERSION OPTIONS: INBOUND
Line length	Defaults to 75 characters. Defines where CRLFs will be inserted when converting a MIME message to plain text. If your users are seeing Internet messages that appear as alternating long and short lines, you may be able to minimize the problem by adjusting this parameter.
	Use character set auto-detection if message has no character set informationIf you receive messages in languages other than English and they often don't include character set information (see the `charset` parameter described in "Understanding MIME" in this chapter), set this to Yes.
	MIME CONVERSION OPTIONS: OUTBOUND
Attachment encoding method	Set the preferred method. Defaults to Base64, which is the most widely used under MIME. It provides the most compact encoding. Other choices include QuotedPrintable, UUencode, and BinHex. QuotedPrintable provides less compact encoding than Base64 but is readable when encoded. UUencode is not a MIME standard encoding method but is widespread otherwise. BinHex is useful for encoding binary material.

Field	Description
	MIME CONVERSION OPTIONS: OUTBOUND
Message content	Defines how Domino converts from Notes rich text to MIME format. Default is Convert from Notes to Internet message format. Alternatively choose Create multi-part alternative including conversion and encapsulation, which both converts the message to MIME and encapsulates a Notes-formatted version of the message. This option approximately doubles the size of the outgoing message. Use it only if your users send a lot of messages to users of Notes 4.x over the Internet. Those users will receive a fully formatted message, whereas, with the first option, they would receive a plain text version of the message with a MIME attachment readable in a Web browser.
Convert tabs to spaces	Defaults to No. Set to Yes if recipients' mail readers don't recognize tabs.
Outbound line length	Defaults to 75 characters. Defines where CRLFs will be inserted when converting a Notes rich text message to plain text. If your users' Internet correspondents are seeing your users' messages as alternating long and short lines, you may be able to minimize the problem by adjusting this parameter.
	Lookup Internet address for all Notes addresses when Internet address is not defined in document All addresses on messages in MIME format must be formatted according to the rules of RFC 821, even if the addressee is another Notes user in the same Notes domain. Setting this to Enabled will cause Domino to look for a Notes user's Internet address in his/her Person document. Leaving it disabled (the default) causes Domino to form an Internet address from each user's common name and Notes domain. For example, Joe Doaks @ Stillwater in planetnotes.com would be Joe_Doaks% stillwater@planetnotes.com.

continues

Table 8.7 **Continued**

Field	Description
	MIME CONVERSION OPTIONS: OUTBOUND
Perform exhaustive lookups when converting	Notes addresses to Internet addresses Appears if the preceding field is enabled. Disabled by default, meaning that Domino will stop looking for an Internet Address when it finds a Person document that matches the addressee's name. Enabling this field causes Domino to search all available directories to find every match for the addressee's name and, if more than one match turns up, to ask the sending user to choose which one to use.
	SETTINGS BY CHARACTER SET GROUPS
MIME setting by character set group	For every character set group, you can choose the fonts, character sets, and encoding that Domino should use. Set this field to a character set group, then set the other fields on the page. Then, set this field to another character set group, and so on. As a general rule you shouldn't have to change any of these settings. However, if you use multiple languages, see Jeff Eisen's article for information on situations which might require you to change these settings.
	ADVANCED, ADVANCED INBOUND MESSAGE OPTIONS
Resent headers take precedence over original headers	Disabled by default. Under RFC 822, when a message is forwarded, resent- headers may be added to it and the original headers retained. Under MIME, forwarded messages become encapsulated in the new message in MIME body parts of content-type message. Resent-headers aren't used. Enable this only if your users receive Internet mail that uses resent-headers and replies are being addressed to the original sender by mistake, instead of to the forwarding sender.
Remove group names from headers	Disabled by default. Enabling it only if the presence of group names in the headers causes problems when sending replies. Enabling this may affect performance.
If each recipient's address does not appear in any address header, then add their address to the BCC list	Disabled by default. Enabling it only if the absence of recipient names in the headers causes problems when sending replies. Enabling this may affect performance.

Field	Description

ADVANCED, ADVANCED INBOUND MESSAGE OPTIONS

Field	Description
For non-MIME messages or MIME messages with an unknown character set, 8-bit character set is assumed to be	Defaults to Windows-1252, which includes all characters used in Western European languages. Primarily of interest if your users receive messages in languages other than English. See Jeff Eisen's article for detailed information.
Character set name aliases	Primarily of interest if your users receive messages in languages other than English. See Jeff Eisen's article for detailed information.

MIME ADVANCED OUTBOUND MESSAGE OPTIONS

Field	Description
Macintosh attachment conversion	No information available.
RFC822 phrase handling	An RFC822 phrase is an optional part of an Internet address. It can consist of any string of text appearing within parentheses and preceding the localpart@domain parts of the address. It is commonly used to permit the inclusion of people's full names in their Internet addresses. This field controls Domino's handling of the phrase part when creating Notes users' return Internet addresses. The choices are "Do not add phrase" (the default); "Use DN as phrase," which includes the sender's fully distinguished Notes name in the phrase; "Use alt. name if available - otherwise DN," which includes the sender's alternate name if possible, otherwise his distinguished name; and "Remove phrase," which removes phrases included by virtue of their inclusion in users' "Internet address" fields.
Internet Mail server sends Notes private items in messages	Disabled by default. Enable it only if sending messages under custom applications to other Notes clients.
Notes fields to be removed from headers	Add the names of any Notes fields that should not be incorporated into messages sent to Internet users.
When converting multilingual message to MIME	See Jeff Eisen's article for an explanation of this field.
Character set name aliases	See Jeff Eisen's article for an explanation of this field.

Monitoring and Troubleshooting Mail

Messaging is so central to everything that Domino does that it is very important that the messaging system works smoothly. For that reason Domino provides a large number of tools to help you monitor the health of your mail delivery system and track down the cause of problems. Your toolkit includes the following:

- Domino Administrator
- The Notes Log database
- The Outgoing Mail database
- Mail statistics collection, reporting, and monitoring tools
- The Messaging tab in Domino Administrator
- Mail probes
- Mail tracing
- Mail Tracking
- Mail Usage Reports

Some of these tools, including the Notes Log and statistics collection, reporting, and monitoring, are covered more fully in other chapters. Here, we'll look briefly at those aspects of them that touch on messaging.

Domino Administrator

Several tabs in Domino Administrator give you access to information about Domino messaging. The primary tab is Messaging, of course, where you can access most of the tools listed previously (see Figure 8.9). But, you can also reach mail-related information under the Files tab, the Server tab, and the Configuration tab.

The Notes Log

The Notes Log (`log.nsf`) is a database maintained by every Domino server and Notes client. Domino records a vast array of information there about the ongoing activities of the server. Two views are of particular interest when you have to troubleshoot mail problems. First, the Mail Routing Events view records every loggable event that takes place on the server. It is organized chronologically. You can browse the events or you can search for events containing particular keywords using the Log Analysis tool (see Figure 8.10).

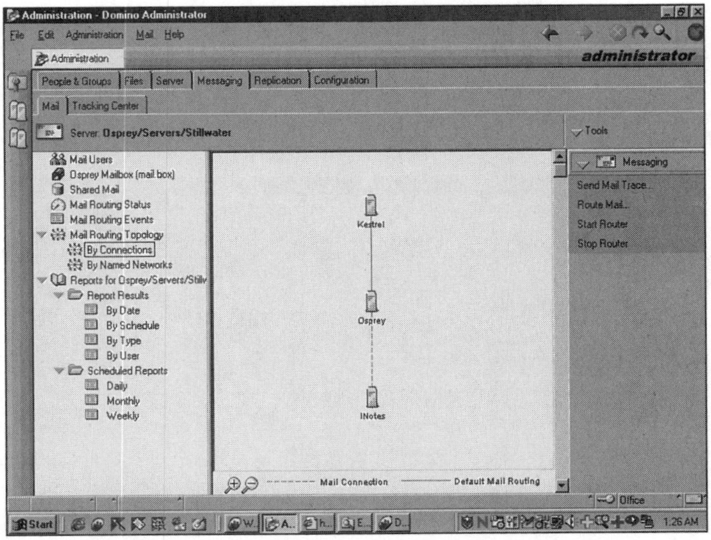

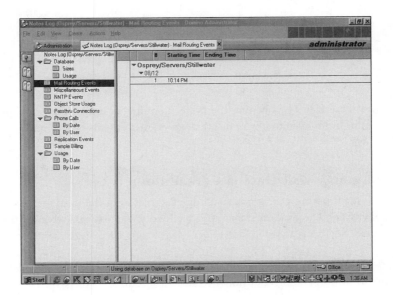

Figure 8.9 In general, the items under the Messaging tab show you the status of messages. The items under the Configuration tab let you configure messaging.

Figure 8.10 The Notes Log includes a Mail Routing Events view and an Object Store Usage view.

Second, the Object Store Usage view records information daily about the usage of the currently active shared mail database (see Figure 8.11). It shows which mail databases are linked to it, how many documents in each database it links to, and how much of its space each mail database occupies.

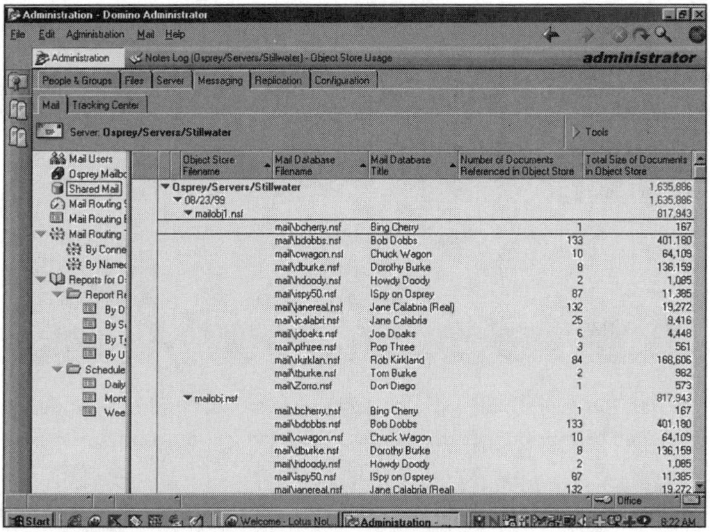

Figure 8.11   The Object Store Usage view displays vital statistics about the object store as of defined times.

You can see these views by opening the Notes Log directly, under the Messaging, Mail tab of Domino Administrator, or under the Server, Analysis tab of Domino Administrator.

The Outgoing Mail Database (mail.box)

If you have mail routing problems that cause dead messages, the dead messages collect in Outgoing Mail. The dead messages are appended to reports that set forth the reason the mail died. So, this is a good place to go when trying to analyze the cause of dead mail.

Remember that a message dies only if it can neither be forwarded to an addressee nor returned to the sender. Most undeliverable mail returns to the sender's mail file, appended to a Delivery Failure Report. If a message can't be returned to the sender, it could signify a trivial problem or a serious one. You should always investigate to determine which caused each dead message.

Most dead mail occurs either when one of your servers generates an undeliverable message or when undeliverable spam arrives in your domain. These are what I mean by "trivial" causes. They don't normally signal a serious mail routing problem. Domino servers can't receive mail normally because they don't have mail databases. So, any time a server generates undeliverable mail, the message will die. All you have to do is figure out why the server is generating mail to an invalid address and fix the problem.

Spam mail usually dies when it is addressed to someone who no longer exists in your domain. Spam mail is almost always sent from an address that won't accept reply mail. So if it is not properly addressed, it dies. If you see a lot of dead spam mail addressed to the same long-gone employee, you can block it out of your domain entirely by adding the addressee's name to the Deny messages intended for the following internet addresses field of an appropriate configuration document. The field is located under SMTP, Restrictions and Controls, SMTP Inbound Controls, Inbound Intended Recipients Controls. An "appropriate" configuration document is one that controls servers that accept mail from the Internet—inbound gateway servers.

If, on the other hand, messages generated by a Notes user or mail-in database in your own domain are dying, then you have a genuine problem. It means there is an error somewhere in the Person document or the filename of the user's mail database or a connection document. You need to track down the problem and eliminate it.

Mail Statistics Collection, Reporting, and Monitoring Tools

Domino has a whole series of tools for collecting, reporting, and monitoring statistics. These include the show statistics console command, the stats server task, the collect server task, the event server task, and mail probes. You can use most of these tools from within Domino Administrator.

The Show Statistics Console Command

The show statistics console command (which you can enter by typing `sh st`) displays a long list of current server operating statistics. Of interest to us now are `sh st mail` and `sh st mailbydest`, both of which display only mail-related statistics. You can also retrieve a single statistic by typing the full name of the statistic. For example, entering `st st mail.dead` returns the number of dead messages in the server's Outgoing Mail database. You can run console commands either at the server console itself or from the Server, Status tab of Domino Administrator, where you can click the Console button.

The Stats Server Task

The stats server task, which, by default, the server loads whenever it starts, allows you to do several things. First, you can retrieve statistics about a remote server by entering `load stats servername`. To retrieve mail statistics you could enter `load stats servername mail` or `load stats servername mailbydest`. To retrieve a single mail statistic you could enter something like `load stats servername mail.dead`.

Second, you can request statistics by mail. The stats server task creates a mail-in database and a Mail-In Database document the first time it starts. The filename of the database is `statmail.nsf` on a new R5 server or `statsxxx.nsf` (where *xxx* is a random number) on an R4 server. Its name (and mail-in name) is *servercommonname Stats/orgname* (for example, Osprey Stats/Servers/Stillwater).

Don't bother to open this database; it's just an empty mail database. The value of it is that you can send signed messages to it, and stats will send statistics back to you by email. If you don't sign the message, stats won't reply to you. If you leave the subject of your message blank, stats will send you all statistics—the same list that you can get by typing `st st` at the server console. But if you type `mail` or `mailbydest` or `mail.dead` in your subject line, stats will reply with just those statistics.

The Collect and Event Server Tasks

Then, there is the Collect server task, which reports statistics on a schedule (by default hourly) into the Statistics Reports (`statrep.nsf`) database, and the Event server task, which can notify you when statistic that you define cross thresholds that you define. Mail-related statistics are collected under the Statistics Reports\Mail & Database view. Statistics about the shared mail database are collected under the Single Copy Object Store Statistics view.

If you create a statistic monitor and an event notification in the Statistics and Events (`events4.nsf`) database, collect will generate an event if the monitored statistic crosses a defined threshold. You can set up monitors to watch the status of dead mail, pending mail, mail transfers, failed transfers, and numerous other mail related statistics. If you run the event task on the server, you can also set up event notification, so that, for example, statistic alarms can be reported to your network management software or your pager.

The collect task also populates the Monitoring and Statistics tabs in Domino Administrator. The Monitoring tab collects and displays ongoing statistics about specific server tasks and events. You can choose to have it display any mail-related statistics you want. The Statistics tab is yet another view of server statistics, similar to what you get from the Show Statistics console command and the stats server task.

Mail Probes

A mail probe is a mail trace that the ISpy server task sends out in response to a Mail Probe document created in the Statistics & Events database (`events4.nsf`). The probe measures the number of seconds it takes to traverse a mail route and generates a statistic, QOS.Mail.*RecipientName*.ResponseTime=*n*, where *n* is equal to the number of seconds. If the probe fails, the value of the statistic is -1, and the ISpy server task generates an *event* of type Mail and severity Warning (High).

If the collect task is running, it reports the statistic to the Statistics Reports database (`statrep.nsf`). If the event task is running, you can create an event notification that a probe failure will trigger.

To generate probes you have to run the ISpy server task. ISpy is written in Java, and its name is case sensitive. To load ISpy manually, enter `load runjava ISpy` at the server console. To shut it down manually, enter either `tell runjava quit` or `tell ISpy quit`. To run ISpy automatically whenever the server starts, add `runjava ISpy` to the `ServerTasks` variable in the server's `notes.ini` file.

When ISpy is running on a server, it automatically sends a probe to the server's own mail.box every 15 minutes. To test mail routes to other servers, you have to create mail probes for them. To create a mail probe in Domino Administrator, go to the Configuration tab, expand Statistics & Events, then Probes. Select Mail. The Mail Probes view of the Statistics & Events database appears. Either create a mail probe directly by choosing New Mail Probe in the action bar or let a wizard create it by choosing Setup Wizards, Probe in the Actions menu. The fields in a mail probe document are as set forth in Table 8.8.

Table 8.8 **Fields in the Mail Probe Form**

Field	Description
	ON THE BASICS TAB
All Domino servers in the domain will probe themselves	Don't check this field. A probe of that type already exists.
Recipient	Enter or select the name of a mail user on the target mail server. The probe will probe the route to that server.
Server(s)	Enter or select the name(s) of one or more servers that will generate this probe. Each server that you enter must be running ISpy.
	ON THE PROBE TAB
Send interval	The number of minutes between probes. Default is 15 minutes.
Timeout threshold	The probe must complete within the number of minutes in this field or be declared a failure. Default is one minute.
	ON THE OTHER TAB
On timeout, generate a Mail event of severity	Choose a severity level. The default is Warning (high).
Disable this probe ISpy will not generate probes	If you select this check box, under this document.

Mail Tracing

Mail tracing tells you if a mail route is valid or not. Mail traces are a useful tool if user messages to other users on your Notes system are turning up in dead mail.

You send a mail trace to a user on a given mail server. In response, the user's mail server and, optionally, intermediate servers send Trace Reports back to you. The trace reports indicate the date and times the server processed the mail trace. There will be two date/times for each server. The first one tells when the server received mail trace; the second tells when the server sent the trace report. You can use the reports not only to validate a mail route but to time it as well.

You can send mail traces in Domino Administrator under Messaging, Mail, by choosing Send Mail Trace under Tools. Make sure you are not logged in as a server, however. If you are, your Trace Reports will all end up in dead mail.

Users can also send mail traces when they send email by choosing Trace entire path under Delivery Options, Delivery Report. The difference between the two kinds of mail trace is that your mail trace never actually gets delivered to the addressee. It only triggers trace reports from the routing servers. The user's email, being a normal message, will be delivered if possible.

Mail traces and mail probes do pretty much the same thing. The differences between them are set forth in Table 8.9.

Table 8.9 **Mail Traces Versus Mail Probes**

	Mail Trace	**Mail Probe**
When sent	On demand	Periodic, automatic
How sent	email	ISpy
Format of results	email trace report	Monitorable QOS Statistics

Message/Mail Tracking

Use message tracking (also called mail tracking, depending on what you read) to find out what happened to individual messages that were previously mailed. Were they delivered? If so, did the recipient ever read them? Are they still there or were they deleted? Are they in dead mail somewhere? Are they still en route? Message tracking is different from mail tracing and mail probes. The latter two don't tell you anything about individual messages but only tell you the state of a mail route—whether it is valid and how long it takes each trace to traverse the route.

Setting Up Message Tracking

Message tracking does not take place automatically. You have to set it up on every server that should track mail. That would include all mail servers and mail hubs. It might also include servers that transfer mail to other domains. Once mail tracking is running, both administrators and users can track mail. Administrators can track all messages. Users can track their own messages.

To use message tracking, you have to enable it in a configuration document. In each appropriate configuration document, choose Router/SMTP, Message Tracking. Under Basics, set Message tracking to Enabled. While you are in edit mode, you can also set the following other fields (see Table 8.10).

Table 8.10   **Message Tracking Fields in the Configuration Form**

Field	Description
Don't track messages for	Select the names of people, databases, and groups whose messages should not be tracked. If the field is empty, all messages will be tracked. If you have set up ISpy to send out mail probes, add ISpy on *servername* to this field to avoid having the tracking database fill up with useless records of mail probes.
Log message subjects	Default is No. If you set this to Yes, the text of the Subject field of each message will be recorded in the tracking database. This allows you to track messages by their subjects. It also increases the size of the tracking records and poses a potential privacy/security issue, as administrators not otherwise privy to a mail exchange may be able to infer message content from the subject lines.
Don't log subjects for	Select the names of people, databases, and groups whose message subjects will not be logged. This field is relevant only if you set the Log message subjects field (above) to Yes.
Message tracking collection interval	Defaults to 15 minutes. This is how often the MT Collector goes out and gathers data. Setting it to a short interval may slow server performance, so be judicious.
Allowed to track messages	If this field is blank, all users can track their own messages and administrators can track all messages. If you add names to this field, only those named in this field (and the following field) will be able to track all messages. Everyone else will be able to track their own messages. If you add names to this field, be sure to add the names of servers as well; otherwise, you won't be able to track messages across multiple servers.

continues

Table 8.10 **Continued**

Field	Description
Allowed to track subjects	This field is relevant only if Log message subjects is set to Yes. If this field is blank, all users can track their own messages by subject and administrators can track all messages by subject. If you add names to this field, only those named in this field will be able to track all messages by subject. Everyone else will be able to track their own messages. If you add names to this field, be sure to add the names of servers as well; otherwise you won't be able to track messages by subject across multiple servers.

You can also load the MT Collector into memory manually, by entering `load mtc` at the server console or in Domino Administrator under the Server tab. To unload it, enter `tell mtc quit` at the server console or tell Domino Administrator to unload it.

The first time the Mail Tracking Collector runs on a server, it creates the MailTracking Store database (`mtstore.nsf`) in the mtdata subfolder. It also sets this database up to be full-text indexed.

Using Message Tracking

Administrators authorized to track all messages can do so in Domino Administrator in the Tracking Center under Messaging. Click New Tracking Request. In the New Tracking Request dialog box, enter as much information as you can to identify the message that you want to track. When you choose OK, Domino Administrator will send your request to the server specified in your request. The server will return all messages that meet your request parameters. So, the more you can narrow your request, the fewer the messages that will be returned.

The messages returned will appear in the top half of the Tracking Center screen. For each message, you will see the sender, the recipient and, if available, the delivery date and time and the subject line.

You can then select any listed message and choose Track Selected Message. Domino Administrator will then retrieve from all relevant servers the information about that message stored in the server's MailTracker Store database. In the bottom half of the screen, you can select a server on the left side (Select a server for transfer details), and the tracking details will appear in the right (Mail Transfer Details).

Users can track messages in their mail databases by selecting any message sent out by them and choosing Actions, Tools, Send Tracking Request in the menu. In the Message Tracking dialog box, the user selects the recipients whose copies of the message they want to track, and whether to learn the current status of the message or to track its entire path, then chooses OK. The tracking request goes out by email to the mail server(s) of the recipient(s) being tracked. The home server(s) and, optionally, the intermediate server(s) send the results back to the requesting user by email. The information returned will tell the user if and when the message was delivered, whether and when a recipient read the message, and whether and when the recipient has deleted the message.

The possible delivery states of a message include the following:

- **Delivered.** The message was deposited in the recipient's mail database.
- **Delivery failed.** The server was unable to deposit the message in the recipient's mail database.
- **In queue.** The router is still processing the message.
- **Transferred.** The router sent the message to the next server en route.
- **Transfer failed.** The router was unable to sent the message to the next server.
- **Group expanded.** The message was addressed to a group and this server expanded the group to its constituent membership.
- **Unknown.** The server does not know the state of the message.

If a message has been successfully delivered to a recipient, it also has a mailbox status, which can be one of the following: Read, Unread, Deleted, Unknown.

Administering Message/Mail Tracking

In general, you don't have to do anything proactive to maintain the message tracking system. The `mtstore.nsf` database is preconfigured to purge documents after 30 days; you may, if you want, shorten or lengthen the amount of time documents are retained, depending on your needs. You probably should set up the ACL of the `mtstore.nsf` database so that the Administrators group is manager. Initially the only manager, beside LocalDomainServers, is the user who enabled message tracking.

In addition, there are some optional `tell` commands that you can use at need. They include the following (see Table 8.11).

Table 8.11 **The Message Tracking *tell* Commands**

Command	Description
`tell mtc process`	Forces MT Collector to collect message delivery information immediately.
`tell mtc interval *minutes*`	Where *minutes* is a number of minutes. Changes the collection interval from that set in the configuration document.
`tell mtc compact`	Compacts the `mtstore.nsf` database.
`tell mtc reindex`	Updates the `mtstore.nsf` database's full-text index.
`tell mtc purge *days*`	Where *days* is a number of days. Purges every document older than *days* from the database.

Mail Usage Reports

Having set up message tracking (see preceding section), you can also generate mail usage reports. The Domino MailTracker Store database accumulates useful information over time and the usage reports are designed to extract this information and present it usefully. You create mail usage reports in a specially designed database called (imaginatively) Reports. There, you can create reports on demand or on a schedule. You can store the reports right in the database or have the database mail them to one or more recipients. A series of agents in the database actually create the reports. All you have to do is fill in forms describing what reports you want generated.

Setting Up Mail Usage Reporting

To set up mail usage reporting you have to set up message tracking (which we discussed in the preceding section), create the Reports database, and configure security so that the report generation process will work properly.

To create the Reports database, choose File, Database, New in the menu. Then, complete the fields in Table 8.12 and choose OK.

Table 8.12 **New Database Field Entries to Create a Reports Database**

Field	Description
Server	This database must reside on the same server whose `mtstore.nsf` database will be the source of the reports.
Title	Reports
Filename	`reports.nsf`
Template	Set the Template Server to the same server you set in the Server field, then choose Reports (`reports.ntf`).

To finish setting up the database, complete the following tasks:

1. In the ACL of Reports, make sure all administrators who will generate reports and the server itself have Manager access. By default, all other users have no access.

2. Enable all scheduled agents. In the View menu, choose Agents. Click the check boxes to the left of the scheduled reports to add checkmarks to them. Then, close the view.

3. Give all administrators who will create reports unrestricted agent access on the server. Open the server document to the Security tab. Under Agent Restrictions add the administrators' names to the Run unrestricted LotusScript/Java agents field.

Generating Mail Usage Reports

This is the easy part. Open the Reports database. Click the Run Report action. Complete the form and choose OK. In the form, you'll choose the report type, the time range that it covers, the execution interval, whether to save the report, mail it, or both, and optional special parameters.

You can create the following reports:

- Top 25 users by count
- Top 25 users by size
- Top 25 senders by count
- Top 25 senders by size
- Top 25 receivers by count
- Top 25 receivers by size
- Top 25 most popular "next hops"
- Top 25 most popular "previous hops"
- Top 25 largest messages
- Message volume summary
- Message status summary

Each kind of report can cover several time ranges, including: one day, one week, two weeks, one month, or the full range of time stored in the `mtstore.nsf` database. You can schedule the reports to run once, daily, weekly, or monthly.

9

Replication

R EPLICATION IS ONE OF DOMINO'S GREAT STRENGTHS. It is the key to Domino's
distributed architecture, in which multiple, peer copies of databases can reside on multiple Domino servers as well as on users' workstations. This makes it possible for users
to access any copy of a database that is currently handy. They can read from and write
to any copy of the database, to the extent of their access right. Over time, replication
distributes their additions, edits, or deletions—and everyone else's—to the other copies
of the database.

With each new release of Notes/Domino this original function of replication has
receded in importance. Fewer, larger servers now support greater numbers of users.
Cheaper wide-area network bandwidth has lessened the need to place servers close to
users. But, in addition to its original function, replication has turned out—almost by
accident in some instances—to be a wonderful adjunct to additional features that
Domino has picked up with each new release.

For example, replication (along with workflow) streamlines the creation, design, and
management of corporate Web applications. The application designers can update the
design of an application on one server and replicate their updates to the production
copy only when ready. Content creators throughout the organization can contribute
content to one or more production copies of the database behind the firewall.

Managers can then approve the content (using Notes workflow features) for publication to the outside world. Selective, scheduled replication then moves only approved content to one or more Web servers outside the firewall, where the public has access to it.

On balance, the importance of replication to the smooth functioning of a Notes domain has not diminished over the years. Its proper functioning is vital to almost all Domino installations. This chapter will explain in detail how it works, how to set it up, and how to keep it working smoothly and efficiently.

Understanding Replication

Many products use some sort of replication to distribute data among multiple data servers. Most of them do so in a master/slave manner, in which one copy of the database is the master copy to which all new changes are written, and all other copies are read-only slaves. Alternatively, there may be multiple master copies, but typically the masters divide up responsibility for different segments of the data, so that only one master exists for each part of the data.

Databases usually have to work this way to maintain data integrity—to avoid the occurrence of separate, independent changes in two copies of the database. Most data management systems cannot allow such changes to occur because they have no way of reconciling the resulting incompatible differences in the data.

But in this regard (as in so many other ways) Domino is different from other data processing products. Domino replicas are fundamentally peers of each other. In the absence of design restrictions, all replicas are writeable masters. This does mean that incompatible changes can occur in different copies of the data; and those changes will have to be reconciled. Domino, however, provides several built-in mechanisms for dealing with this issue. These include:

- Several methods to prevent edits of existing documents, which in turn prevent replication conflicts.
- Manual and programmatic methods of reconciling replication conflicts.

To learn more about dealing with replication conflicts, see the discussion later in this chapter.

Another regard in which Domino replication is different from replication in many other programs is the granularity of it. In Domino replication, the two replicating entities only replicate whole documents when a document is new. When they replicate changes in existing documents, they only replicate the changed fields. This results in an efficient replication process.

There are two fundamental kinds of replication in Domino/Notes—Pull replication and Push replication. In a Pull replication, the replicating entity requests new documents and the changed fields of modified documents from the Domino server with which it is replicating. In a Push replication, the replicating entity sends its own new documents and modified fields of existing documents to the Domino server with which it is replicating.

I used the word "entity" in the previous paragraph because replication can take place either between two Domino servers or between a Notes client and a Domino server. When two servers replicate with each other, the replicator service on one or both of them does the work. When Notes and Domino replicate, Notes does the work; the server's replicator does not get involved at all.

Actually, when Notes replicates with a server, it reads and writes records on the server in basically the same way as when a user works interactively with data on the server—by making read and write requests to the Database Server component of the Domino server. When you replicate, Notes just automates the process and, instead of displaying records onscreen, it writes them to its local copy of the database.

Pull and Push replications can be combined in four ways:

- **Pull-Pull.** Available only in scheduled replications between servers. The first server pulls data from the second server; the second server pulls data from the first. Both servers' replicators do part of the work. Each server logs its own replicator's activity. If replication takes place over a network connection, Server 1 pulls first, then Server 2 pulls. Over a modem connection both servers pull simultaneously (which maximizes throughput over the slow connection).

- **Pull-Push.** Available in both Domino/Domino and Notes/Domino replications. The first server (or the Notes client) pulls data from the second server, then pushes data to the second server. The first server's replicator (or the Notes client) does all the work. The first server's (or the Notes client's) log records the whole transaction.

- **Pull Only.** The first server (or the Notes client) pulls data from the second server. The first server's replicator (or the Notes client) does all the work. The first server (or the Notes client) logs the transaction.

- **Push Only.** The first server (or the Notes client) pushes data to the second server. The first server's replicator (or the Notes client) does all the work. The first server (or the Notes client) logs the transaction.

As pointed out in the preceding bulleted list, Pull-Pull replication can only take place between two servers and then only as triggered by a connection document. As a general rule, you should only use Pull-Pull replication in one circumstance—when the two servers replicate over a modem link or other slow connection. Pull-Push replication is generally preferred because the whole session is logged in only one server log. With Pull-Pull replication, each server's log records its own replicator's activities, so each log records only one-half of each session. This can be cumbersome when troubleshooting.

But when two servers perform scheduled replication by modem, you might prefer Pull-Pull, because both servers' replicators will pull from the other server simultaneously. This results in a generally more efficient use of the slow connection, therefore shorter replication times.

Speaking of scheduled replication, you should know that there are three ways to trigger replication:

- **On a schedule**: You can schedule Domino/Domino replication in a connection document. Most Domino/Domino replication takes place this way because replication between servers needs to take place frequently and regularly. You can schedule Notes/Domino replication in a location document. Most Notes/Domino replication does *not* take place this way because most users who maintain local replicas of databases don't need to replicate them with the server on any regular basis.

- **On demand**: An administrator can command a server to replicate with another server. A user can command Notes to replicate with a server. Typically, on-demand server replication takes place only under special circumstances because scheduled replication takes care of most Domino/Domino replication needs. On-demand Notes replication, on the other hand, is the norm.

- **Event driven**: Servers in a Domino cluster (see Chapter 20, "Enhancing Data Availability") also use cluster replication, in which a server immediately pushes all changes in a database to replicas (if any) on other servers in the cluster. Cluster replication is carried out by the Cluster Replicator, not the Replicator, and in some ways works quite differently from standard replication. To understand the differences, see Chapter 20.

What Happens During Replication?

A Pull-Push replication between two servers involves the following steps (the process between Notes and Domino is basically the same):

1. The Replicator on server S1 idles until it receives a command (from the console or a connection document) to begin replicating with server S2.

2. S1 establishes a connection with S2 and the two servers authenticate each other to ensure they are replicating with the "real" S1 or S2.

3. Each server builds lists of local databases to which the other server has Reader or higher access and for which replication is not disabled. S1 compares the lists, looking for databases that have the same replica ID (and are therefore replicas).

4. Starting with the first replica, S1 requests from S2 a list of documents that are new or modified since the two servers last successfully replicated. (They know when that was because their last successful replication of this database is time-stamped in each copy's replication history. If the replication history has no time-stamp, S1 retrieves a list of all documents from S2. To see a database's replication history, choose Replication, History in the File menu.)

5. In response, S2 sends a list of Universal IDs (UNIDs) to S1. As requested, it sends UNIDs for documents that are new or modified since they last replicated. But it withholds any for which S1 does not have read access. S2 also sends another time-stamp to S1, which, if this replication proves successful, S1 will store in its replication history, replacing the current time-stamp.

6. S1 then builds a similar list of UNIDs from its own copy of the database, then compares the two lists, one document at a time.

7. S1 starts pulling documents from S2 into its own copy of the database, using the following rules: If a UNID appears in S2's list but not S1's, it represents a document that is either new or newly modified on S2 but not on S1. If the ACL on S1's copy of the database indicates that S2 has sufficient rights to write the document into S1's database, S1 pulls the document from S2 and writes it into its copy of the database. (S2 needs Manager access to send a changed ACL to S1, Designer access to send changed design documents to S1, and Editor access to send changed data documents to S1.)

   - If a UNID appears in S2's list but not S1's, it represents a document that is either new or newly modified on S2 but not on S1. If the ACL on S1's copy of the database indicates that S2 has sufficient rights to write the document into S1's database, S1 pulls the document from S2 and writes it into its own copy of the database. (S2 needs Manager access to send a changed ACL to S1, Designer access to send changed design documents to S1, and Editor access to send changed data documents to S1.)

   - If a UNID appears in both S1's and S2's lists, it is a potential replication conflict. S1 performs a conflict analysis to determine if in fact there is a conflict and, if so, what to do about it. (The document might not represent a conflict if, for example, it was replicated from S2 during an earlier, aborted replication attempt.)

   - If a conflict exists, S1 will merge S2's version of the document into its own if it can. It will only do this if the form used to create the document has the "Merge Replication Conflicts" property enabled and the changed fields are different in each copy of the document. If a given field is modified in both copies of the document, S1 won't try to merge it.

   - If S1 can't merge a conflict, it will determine which version of the document has the higher sequence number or, if both sequence numbers are the same, which has a later modification time/date. It declares that version the "winner." The server on which the "loser" version exists creates a conflict document. This is a document that holds the "losing" version of the document and appears as a child of the "winning" version of the document. The conflict document appears in views with the label "<Save or Replication Conflict>" and indented beneath the "winner." However, because we are still in the "Pull" stage of the replication process, the conflict document may not yet appear in both copies of the database.

8. When S1 finishes pulling new and changed documents from S2, it sends S2 a time-stamp, which S2 stores in its replication history. If the process aborts before S1 can finish pulling, it will not send the time-stamp to S2; therefore, the next time the two servers replicate, they will start over again from where they started this time.

9. S1 repeats the preceding process (steps 4 through 8) with every other replica database.

10. When S1 finishes pulling all replica databases, it starts over again from step 4, only this time it pushes its own new and modified documents to S2.

A Pull-Pull replication session would be basically the same as described previously, with two exceptions. First, in the second run through the databases (step 10), S2 would do the work and would pull documents. Second, if the servers were connected by modem, the servers would pull from each other simultaneously, not sequentially.

A Pull Only replication would end at step 9. A Push Only would end at step 9, and steps 4 through 8 would involve pushing S1's changes to S2 instead of pulling from S2 as described previously.

Scheduled Server/Server Replication

To set up scheduled replication between two servers, you have to set up a connection document that provides for replication. One server initiates the session; the other responds. The significant fields in a server connection document that implements scheduled replication are as set forth in Table 9.1.

Table 9.1 **The Significant Fields in a Connection Document for Setting Up Scheduled Replication**

Field	Description
ON THE BASICS TAB	
Source server	Enter the name of the server that will initiate the session. In a Pull-Pull replication, this server will pull first. In a Pull-Push replication, this server will pull then push.
Destination server	Enter the name of the server that will respond. In a Pull-Pull replication, this server will pull second. You can enter a wildcard in this field to specify more than one server.
Source domain and Destination domain	Enter the source servers' respective domains. If both servers are in the same domain, you may leave these fields blank.

Field	Description
Replication task	Enabled by default.
Replicate databases of x priority	Defaults to "Low & Medium &High," which are all of the priorities. Alternatively, you can choose "Medium & High" or "High." You would normally replicate databases of all priorities. Use the others only to refine a replication schedule so that higher priority databases replicate more often.
Replication Type	Defaults to "Pull Push," which you should use most of the time. You may want to choose "Pull Pull" when the connection will be by modem. You can also choose "Pull Only" and "Push Only."
Files/Directories to Replicate	Leave this blank to replicate all databases in common. Alternatively, enter one or more database or folder names. Do not use wildcards.
Replication Time Limit	By default, replication will be allowed to take as long as it needs to complete. Under certain circumstances you may have to limit the time a given replication session will take. You can do so by entering here the maximum number of minutes replications may take under this connection document. Use caution with this field. Too short a limit can cause data to never replicate. See later in this list for further discussion.
Schedule	Is enabled by default. Disabling the schedule disables this connection entirely.
Call at times	These are the times the server will try to connect under this document. To learn about your choices here, see the discussion following this table.
Repeat interval of	Defaults to 360—six hours. Select any number of minutes 0 or greater. To learn more about your choices here, see the discussion following this table.
Days of week	Choose the days of the week that this schedule will be active. Defaults to every day.

The Call at times field can accept a single time (for example, 8:00 a.m.), a range of times (for example, 8:00 a.m.–10:00 p.m.), or a series of single times and/or time ranges (for example, 8:00 a.m.; 11:00 a.m.; 2:00 p.m.–4:30 p.m.). When a scheduled connection time arrives, the source server will try to connect to the destination server and carry out the tasks designated in the Replication/Routing fields.

If a connection is not successful, the source server will wait a certain amount of time, then try again. Repeated failures cause the source server to wait longer before each successive try. The wait time is initially short, but longer and longer. The source server uses a "Randomized Exponential Backoff Algorithm" to calculate wait times. This algorithm causes the server to wait approximately, but not exactly, twice as long after each failure as it waited after the previous failure.

If a connection resulting from a single time (for example, 8:00 a.m.) fails, the source server will continue trying to connect for 60 minutes (or until it succeeds); then it will give up and wait for the next scheduled connection time.

If a connection resulting from a time range (for example, 8:00 a.m.–10:00 p.m.) fails, the source serve will continue trying until it succeeds or until the end time passes.

If a connection resulting from a time range succeeds, the source server will wait the amount of time in the Connection interval field, then it will try to connect again. The connection interval time count begins when a successful connection terminates. The server ignores the setting in the Connection interval field if it is connecting because of a single connection time setting (for example, 8:00 a.m.) in the connection document.

Replication Connections Versus Mail Routing Connections

Replication connections and mail routing connections are different from each other in some important ways. First, you always need a connection document to schedule replication. Contrast this to mail routing, in which you only have to provide connection documents to route mail between servers that are not in the same Notes named network or Notes domain.

Second, you can schedule two-way replication with only one connection document. Two-way mail routing always requires two connection documents (when it requires any at all).

Finally, when setting up connection documents for replication, you specifically should *not* create competing connections. By that, I mean you should *not* set up two connections in which the same pair of servers is connecting to each other during the same time period to initiate two-way replication. Domino assumes that only one server in the pair will initiate replication connections during a given time period. It will actually refuse to carry out all of the scheduled replications if two servers are trying to replicate with each other on conflicting schedules, and you'll go crazy wondering why. If there is some overriding reason why two servers must share the load of initiating replications, you can either have them both run push-only or pull-only schedules or you can have them call each other at different times or on different days.

Server/Server Replication On Demand

Replication on demand occurs in response to a command issued at the server console or in Domino Administrator. The three commands are `replicate`, `pull`, and `push`.

The `replicate` command results in a pull-push replication. That is, the server to which you issue the command does all the work and logs the whole transaction. There are two forms of the replicate command:

```
replicate servername
```

and

```
replicate servername databasename
```

The first form tells the server to replicate *all databases in common* with `servername`. The second form tells the server to replicate the named database with `servername`.

When you issue the replicate command at the server console, you can abbreviate it to `rep`. Normally you should also use the responding server's fully distinguished name (for example, `rep Kestrel/Servers/Stillwater`). However, I have found that the command also works (most of the time) if I just use the responding server's common name (for example, `rep kestrel`).

The `pull` command results in a pull-only replication. The server to which you issue the command pulls data from the other server and logs the whole transaction. The `pull` command also has two forms:

```
pull servername
```

and

```
pull servername databasename
```

The `push` command results in a push-only replication. The server to which you issue the command pushes documents to the other server and logs the whole transaction.

The `push` command has the same two forms as the `replicate` and `pull` commands. You also can execute these three commands from the Server, Status tab of Domino Administrator. In Tools, choose Server, Replicate. In the dialog box, choose the name of the server with which to replicate, the replication style (Push-Pull, Push, or Pull), and choose All databases in common or select a database.

Workstation/Server Replication

Like server/server replication, replication between a Notes workstation and a Domino server also can occur on demand or as triggered by a schedule in a document (but not event driven, as in cluster replication). Replication on demand can take place in the foreground or the background. If in the foreground, you can't use Notes for any other purpose while it's taking place. If in the background, you can continue to use Notes while it's taking place.

Foreground replication takes place as follows:

1. Open a local database in Notes or right-click the database's bookmark.

2. If you opened the database, choose Replication, Replicate in the File menu. If you right-clicked the database's bookmark, choose Replication, Replicate in the pop-up menu.

3. In the dialog box, choose Replicate with options then choose OK.

4. In the second dialog box, the words "Replicate: Local with *servername*" should appear. If the words "Replicate: *servername* with *servername*" appear, you did not choose a local copy of the database, but rather the copy on the first named server. You have to cancel and start over. Otherwise, choose whether to send documents, receive them, or both. If you choose to receive documents, choose whether to receive full documents or summary documents. Choose OK.

You can start background replication several different ways. First, you can follow the preceding steps but in step 3 choose "Replicate via background Replicator." This replicates a single database.

Second, you can initiate replication from the Replicator page. Choose Replicator in the Bookmarks bar. Initiate replication of a single database by choosing it in the Replicator screen, then choosing Actions, Replicate selected database. Better yet, right-click the database, then choose Replicate Selected Database in the pop-up menu.

Initiate replication of all or selected databases by clicking the Start action at the top of the screen. The databases with checkmarks in the left column will be replicated with the home server unless a call entry appears in the list of databases telling Notes what server to call. You can actually use Start to initiate replication with multiple servers. Either you can insert Call and Hangup entries at appropriate spots in the list of databases on the Replicator page or (if one call reaches more than one server via, say, a pass-thru server) you can just check off databases whose replicas are on multiple servers.

To schedule replication from a Notes client, you have to enable it in a location document, not a connection document. On the Replication tab of each location document you can enable two replication schedules. First you can enable scheduled replication of all databases. Second, you can enable an additional (presumably more frequent) scheduled replication of high-priority databases.

To set a database as high priority, open the Replication Properties box (choose File, Replication, Settings) to the Other tab and choose Low, Medium, or High.

To set a replication schedule in a location document, set the schedule fields as set forth in Table 9.2.

Table 9.2 **The Schedule Fields in a Location Document**

Field	Description
Schedule and High priority replication	Both of these fields default to Disabled. Select Enabled in the Schedule field to reveal the fields listed later. This also reveals the High priority replication field. Select Enabled there to reveal a second set of schedule fields.
Call at times	These are the times Notes will try to carry out the checked tasks on the Replicator page. You can enter a single time (for example, 8:00 a.m.), a range of times (for example, 8:00 a.m.–10:00 p.m.), or a series of single times and/or time ranges (for example, 8:00 a.m.; 11:00 a.m.; 2:00 p.m.–4:30 p.m.). When a scheduled connection time arrives, Notes will try to carry out the tasks checked on the Replication page.
Repeat interval of x minutes	If you entered a time range in the Call at times field, this field defines how often during the time range Notes will try to carry out the tasks on the Replication page. If you entered one or more single times in the Call at times field, this field has no effect.
Days of week	Select the days of the week that this schedule will be active. Defaults to every day.

Replication Topologies

As a general rule, every Domino server in a domain must replicate regularly with the other servers in its domain—if only to replicate changes in the central shared databases, including the Domino Directory (`names.nsf`), Administration Requests (`admin4.nsf`), and possibly others, depending on what services are running. Each server doesn't have to replicate directly with all the other servers. But each server must replicate with at least one other server, which in turn must replicate with at least one other server, and so on, so that all servers receive all changes in all replica databases.

If you have deployed applications that require frequent updates of replica databases, you may want to maximize the frequency of replication among servers. On the other hand, replication is a very resource-consuming activity. It uses a lot of processor time and network bandwidth when it's taking place. So, you have to strike a balance between the competing needs of frequent updates and resource conservation. (If you need immediate updates, you should consider setting up a Domino server cluster, where cluster replication forces immediate updates. See Chapter 20.)

In other words, as you add servers to your domain, you have to decide what replicas will reside on each server, how they will replicate with each other, and how often. Initially, this is a pretty academic question. If you have only a few servers, you can probably have them replicate any old way that pleases you. Common topologies (as displayed in Figure 9.1) are

- **Hub-and-spoke.** One server, the hub, replicates with all the other servers, the spokes.
- **Peer-to-peer.** Every server replicates (either as initiator or responder) with every other server in the domain.
- **End-to-end.** Server S1 replicates with Server S2, which replicates with S3, and so on to Sn.
- **Ring.** You could close the circle on the end-to-end topology by having Sn replicate with S1.

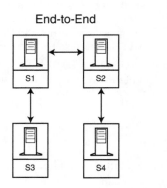
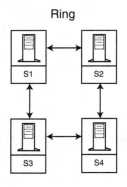
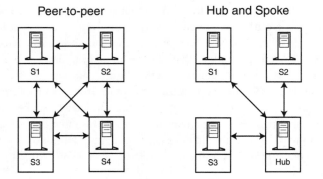

Figure 9.1 If you have as few as four servers, you need to think about replication topology—which servers replicate with which. Beyond four or five servers, hub-and-spoke (lower right) emerges as the best topology.

If you have only three to five servers, a peer-to-peer topology offers a lot of benefits. It propagates information quickly to all of your servers. It is fault-tolerant in the sense that bringing one server down does not break other servers' replication links to each other. However, as the number of servers increases, the number of necessary connection documents increases exponentially ($=(n(n-1)/2)$ and peer-to-peer becomes unworkable.

For larger numbers of servers, you will want to implement a hub-and-spoke topology. This topology minimizes the number of hops data must take to reach other servers. It also minimizes the number of connection documents you must complete. It allows you to limit the degree of access necessary to spoke servers (they can get by with Reader or Editor access in most cases). Finally, and perhaps most importantly, it centralizes all replication logs on a single server.

In fact, from the moment you have four or more servers you probably want to designate one of them as a hub server for replication purposes. If you have a lot of servers, you may want to dedicate a server to the role of replication hub, off-loading other roles—mail server, application server, directory server—to servers dedicated to those roles.

In a really large domain (Lotus recommends no more than 25 spokes per hub) or a domain that is highly dispersed, with groups of servers scattered in locations all over the world, you might want to implement a cascading-hub model (see Figure 9.2) or a peer-hub model (see Figure 9.3). In a cascading-hub model, a central hub replicates with sub-hubs or regional hubs, which in turn replicate with their spoke servers. In a peer-hub model, a few hubs replicate with each other as peers but each replicates with its spokes on the hub and spoke model. Because the hubs represent single points of failure, you might also want to implement some sort of clustering technology, probably an OS cluster, to minimize the impact of a failure of the hub.

All these topologies are subject to tweaking to meet your special needs. Nothing has to be written in stone. The more you adhere to the rules of a given topology the easier you'll find it over time to stay on top of which servers should be communicating with which other servers and why. But if a pair of spoke servers have some special, overriding reason to replicate one database between them, I say go ahead and set up the special relationship. If you want to set up a particular subset of servers differently from others, go ahead and do it. For example, in Figure 9.3, Hub1 and S1, S2, and S3 could replicate among each other on a peer model, while Hub1 replicates for all of them with the other hubs. The goals are simplicity of management, maximization of user convenience, and minimization of load on resources. Just be sure to document your design, so that your successors can figure out what you did and why.

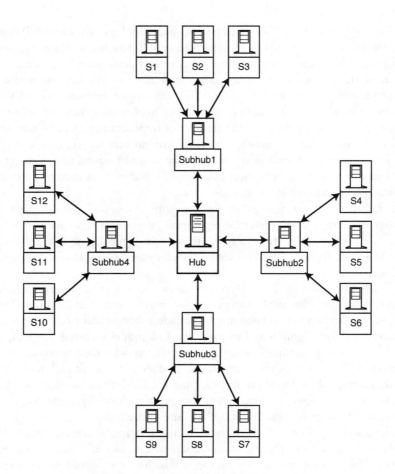

Figure 9.2 A cascading-hub replication topology. In real life there would most likely be many more spoke servers.

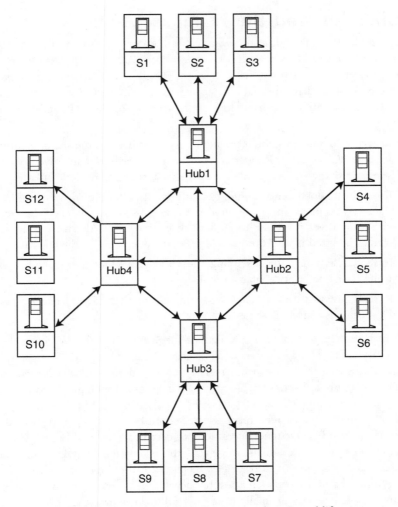

Figure 9.3 A peer–hub replication topology. In real life there would most likely be many more spoke servers.

Replication and the Database ACL

Whether replication takes place and what gets replicated depend, among other things, on the settings in the ACLs of each database on both entities (server/server or server/workstation) involved in the replication. That is, in the sending entity's ACL, the receiving entity must have the right to receive documents; and in the receiving entity's ACL, the sending entity must have the right to send documents. The specific rules are as follows:

- To receive documents, the receiving entity must have, in the sending entity's database ACLs, at least Reader access. Also, if readership of any given document is restricted, the receiving entity must be an authorized reader of that document.

- To send data documents, a sending Notes workstation must have Author or higher access in the receiving server's database ACLs. In general, if the sending entity is a server, it should have Editor or higher access. Alternatively, it would have to be listed in an Authors field on every document in the database.

- To send design elements, a sending entity must have Designer or higher access in the receiving entity's database ACLs.

- To send a revised database ACL, a sending entity must have Manager access in the receiving entity's database ACL.

Many database managers solve the problem of adequate ACL rights by giving all servers in the local domain Manager access to all databases. They usually do that by assigning Manager access to the LocalDomainServers group. In a domain in which replication is *not* set up on a hub-and-spoke topology (see "Replication Topologies," earlier in this chapter), it is pretty much a necessity to set up the database ACLs this way.

Other administrators exercise much greater control over what gets replicated by giving Manager and/or Designer access only to certain servers and Editor or Reader access to most servers in a domain. In general, this is only feasible when a hub-and-spoke replication topology is in place (see Replication Topologies later). In such a topology, only the hub servers (and possibly development servers) need Manager access to databases; spoke servers normally need only Editor or Reader access to databases. They need Editor access if their users can make contributions to a database; they need Reader access if their users only have Reader access. See Chapter 10, "Security," for more information about database ACLs and Reader and Author access to documents.

Replication Scheduling Issues

Replication schedules can be a problem in two different situations. First, if a single hub serves a large number of spokes, you have to make sure the hub doesn't skip scheduled replications on some of the servers for lack of sufficient time. Second, if a server is providing dialup services for both users and other servers, you may have to limit replication during certain time periods so that servers don't monopolize the telephone lines. The first problem arises in large domains. The second one may arise in frugal companies.

Skipped Replications

If you try to set too short a repeat interval and squeeze too many spoke servers into a replication schedule, you can cause one or more spoke servers to get skipped over during busy replication cycles. It works like this. The replicator on the hub server can carry out replication with only one other server at a time. It can queue as many as five pending replication requests. Let's say the hub has to service 20 spoke servers. Connection documents tell the hub that it must replicate with each spoke every two hours from 8 a.m. to 10.p.m. every day. The hub starts replicating with SpokeA and takes, say, five minutes to complete replication with it. Then, it moves to SpokeB and takes five minutes to replicate with it too. It moves on to SpokeC, SpokeD, and so on, taking five minutes to replicate with each one. When it completes the cycle, it is 9:40 a.m.

The replicator waits the two-hour repeat interval before it replicates with each server again. The repeat interval begins from the time replication finished with each server. So, at 10:05 a.m. the hub begins replicating with SpokeA again. At 10:10, it is scheduled to replicate with SpokeB, at 10:15 with SpokeC, and so on.

Activity in the databases has heated up with the arrival of users at work, and now it takes 10 minutes to complete replication with each server. At 10×20 that's 3 hours 20 minutes to finish the second replication cycle. SpokeA will finish at 10:15 and be ready to replicate a third time around at 12:15.

At 12:15, SpokeM will be finishing up. SpokeN through SpokeR will be waiting in the queue. SpokeS and SpokeT will still be trying to get on the queue. But SpokeA falls alphabetically before SpokeS and SpokeT, so at 12:15 the hub will let SpokeA onto the queue instead of SpokeS and SpokeT. At 12:25, it will let SpokeB on the queue instead of SpokeS and SpokeT, and so on. The last two spokes could, in extreme cases, get locked out for weeks on end.

This was a big problem in Notes R3, but nowadays it is a rare problem. Replication is much more efficient in R4 and R5 than it was in R3; so you can replicate more data in a shorter period of time. The biggest change in that respect was the advent of field-level replication with R4. In addition, R4 and R5 servers can accommodate many more users than could R3 servers; so it is much less likely that a given organization will have enough spoke servers to raise the possibility of this problem arising. Finally, Lotus has provided a panoply of tools with which you can attack the problem if it does arise. These include the following:

- **Multiple replicators.** You can load up to two instances per processor (but not more than eight total) of the replicator task. Each replicator can process one server at a time and queue up to five requests. In our example, R1 could service SpokeA while R2 services SpokeB, and so on. To have a server load multiple replicators whenever it starts, add the `Replicators=n` variable to `notes.ini`, where n is the number of replicators the server should run. Each replicator occupies about 3MB RAM when idle, so don't add replicators if you don't really need to.

- **The "Replicate databases of" field.** This field allows you to refine your replication schedule so that higher priority databases replicate more often, low priority databases less often.

- **The "Files/Directories to Replicate" field.** This field also enables you to refine your replication schedule, so that specific time-sensitive databases can replicate on a more frequent schedule than the others.

- **The "Replication Time Limit" field.** In extreme cases, you can make sure every server gets a bite of the apple by limiting the amount of time each server has to complete replication. However, use this field with care. If you limit replication times too severely, your servers may fall further and further behind, never able to complete a replication, because more changes accumulate than they can process within the time limit. This field really serves another purpose, discussed in the next section.

Monopolized Phone Lines

If you have a limited number of modems shared by both users and servers, you might want to use the Replication Time Limit field in the connection document to limit the amount of time a server can tie up a phone line for replication purposes. I had a client once who had one dialup Domino server with two modems attached. The server accommodated about 40 dialup users and several servers. Busy signals were acceptably rare most of the time. Occasionally, however, a database on one of the outside servers would receive a massive update, which would take anywhere from two to twelve hours to fully replicate to my client's server over one of the modem lines. When that happened, all other clients had to fight over one phone line and the rate of busy signals became very unsatisfactory.

The long-term solution was to add more phone lines (and an even longer-term solution was to add a T-1 connection to the Internet). But in the short term we set up a two-tier replication schedule between the offending outside server and the dialup server. One connection document provided that during day and evening hours on weekdays, the outside server could only call in to replicate a few times a day and each time could only replicate high priority databases for a maximum of 10 minutes. A second connection document provided that during night and weekend hours, the outside server could call much more often and replicate all databases, but it still could replicate for only 90 minutes per call.

We calculated that this would allow important data to replicate during the daytime calls, and the large database updates to replicate in a reasonable amount of time during off-hours. But the server could never tie up the modem for hours on end, even during hours of low demand. This worked out well, and later we implemented similar schedules for the other servers as well.

Selective Replication

Sometimes you don't want to replicate everything in a database to a given server or workstation. For example, a sales force automation application may have replicas at company headquarters and each of the local sales offices. The headquarters copy would naturally hold all data generated in the application, both at headquarters and in the field. But perhaps the copies at the local sales offices should only hold data of interest to the local sales teams. This would keep the size of each local replica much smaller than the replica at headquarters. It would shorten replication times dramatically. And it would keep confidential or distracting information away from the eyes of the sales force.

Taking this idea a step further, maybe each salesperson should only replicate to his own laptop data that concerns his sales. This would serve the same purposes—small local replica, short replication times, and focused information.

You limit what gets replicated in the Replication Setting dialog box. This is true for both Notes and Domino replication. Open Replication Settings by opening a database, then choosing Replication, Settings in the File menu. Or right-click a database's bookmark, then choose Replication, Settings in the pop-up menu. Or, if the Database Properties box is open, click the Replication Settings button on the Database Basics tab.

The Replication Settings dialog box has four screens:

- **Space Savers.** This screen provides several ways to limit the number and type of documents in the selected copy of a database. The fields in this screen are of particular interest to Notes users wanting to limit the size of a local replica.

- **Send.** This screen lets you limit what the current replica sends to other replicas. Again, this screen is mostly of interest to Notes users, not server administrators.

- **Other.** This screen lets you assign miscellaneous replication properties. You can disable replication temporarily, set the replication priority of a database, and set dates limiting the age of documents that this replica will accept from other replicas. This screen is mostly of interest to server and database administrators.

- **Advanced.** This screen allows you to refine database selection formulas. It is of most interest to server and database administrators.

The fields in the four replication settings screens are described in Table 9.3.

Table 9.3   **The Fields in the Replication Settings Dialog Box**

Field	Description
THE SPACE SAVERS SCREEN	
Remove documents not modified in the last x days	This is actually two fields; the second one serves two purposes. First, if you check the checkbox, Domino or Notes will automatically delete and purge documents not modified in the last x days from the database. On most databases this defaults to unchecked but some database templates have changed the default. Second, you can change the number of days. On most databases this defaults to 90 days but some database templates have changed this to a shorter default. The number of days field serves the additional purpose of setting the purge interval for documents deleted from the database. See the section titled "Deleted Documents, Deletion Stubs, and Purging" later in this chapter for more information.
Include	This field appears only if the database you are examining is an address book or a directory. You can choose "All Fields," "Minimal Address Book," "Minimal Address Book, Encryption," "Minimal Address Book, Person Info," or "Minimal Address Book, Encryption, Person Info." Each of the "Minimal Address Book" choices sets a predefined replication formula in the following field, which formula limits the fields and documents replicated. This field is useful if you have not enabled the Directory Catalog. It permits users to replicate a compact version of the Domino Directory to their laptops so they'll be able to look up addresses in it when disconnected from a server.
Receive summary and 40kb of rich text only	This field only appears when you examine Replication Settings for a database that resides on a server. A Notes user can check it to limit what replicates to his local copy of the database. All rich text fields are truncated at 40KB and no attachments are included. The word "Truncated" appears in the title of a truncated document. The user can retrieve the rest of the document by opening it, then choosing "Retrieve Entire Document" in the Actions menu.

Field	Description
	THE SPACE SAVERS SCREEN
Replicate a subset of documents	When you check this box, You can select one or more views or folders in the list of views and folders. Only documents in the selected views and folders will replicate to this copy of the database.
Select by formula	When you check this box, the list of views and folders is replaced by box in which you can enter and edit a selection formula. See Designer Help for information about writing selection formulas.
Fields & Functions	This button appears when you check "Select by formula." Press the button to display a list of @functions and fields. You can select one and insert it into your formula. You can also select an @function and read a help screen about what it does and how to use it.
Formula Window	This button appears when you check "Select by formula." Press the button to open a larger window in which to edit your formula.
	THE SEND SCREEN
Do not send deletions made in this replica to other replicas	A Notes user can check this box for the local copy of a database, so that he can delete documents solely to save local disk space. These deletions won't be replicated to the server version of the database.
Do not send changes in database title & catalog info to other replicas	When you check this box, changes to the local database's title and Database Catalog categories settings won't replicate to other copies of the database.
Do not send changes in local security property to other replicas	Check this to ensure that the local encryption property of a database does not replicate to another copy of the database.
	THE OTHER SCREEN
Temporarily disable replication	Check this box when you want to make sure that a database won't replicate. You would do this when you are in doubt about the integrity of this or another replica of the database and you want to prevent any problems from spreading to other replicas of the database.

continues

Table 9.3 **Continued**

Field	Description
	THE OTHER SCREEN
Scheduled replication priority	Set to "Low," "Medium," or "High." Connection documents with the "Replicate databases of priority" set to "High" or "Medium & High" use this setting to determine whether or not to replicate this database. Don't confuse this with low, normal, and high priority mail delivery settings. The two settings are unrelated.
Only replicate incoming documents saved or modified after	Only documents created or modified after the date/time in this field are replicated. The system sets this field automatically, but you can override the setting if you need to.
CD-ROM publishing date	Some databases are so large that it is more convenient to make replicas of them by CD-ROM. You copy the database from the CD-ROM to a server's data folder, then enter the CD-ROM's publication date in this field. The first time the new replica replicates with the original, they will only replicate documents created or modified after the date in this field.
	THE ADVANCED SCREEN
When computer	Choose a computer from the list. This is the destination server.
Receives from	Choose another computer from the list. This is the source server.
Replicate a subset of documents	When you check the box you can select one or more views or folders from the list below.
Select by formula	When you check this box the list of views and folders is replaced by a window in which you can enter a selection formula.
Fields & Formulas	This button appears when you check "Select by formula." Press the button to display a list of @functions and fields. You can select one and insert it into your formula. You can also select an @function and read a help screen about what it does and how to use it.
Formula Window	This button appears when you check "Select by formula." Press the button to open a larger window in which to edit your formula.

Field	Description
THE ADVANCED SCREEN	
The Replicate checkboxes	You can choose what kinds of nondocument database objects the first computer will replicate from the second.
Replicate: Forms, views, etc.	Selected by default. If the source server has Designer access to the database, it will be able to send all design documents to the destination database. Deselecting this field blocks sending of all design documents except agents.
Replicate: Agents	Selected by default. Deselecting this field blocks sending of agents.
Replicate: Replication formula	Deselected by default. Selecting it causes the source server to send the replication formula defined in the "Replicate a subset of documents" field to the destination server.
Replicate: Access control list	Selected by default. Deselecting it blocks sending of the ACL, even though the source server is a Manager in the ACL of the destination server.
Replicate: Deletions	Selected by default. If deselected, the destination server will refuse to accept deletions from the source server. This is the destination server's equivalent to the sending server's "Do not send deletions made in this replica to other replicas" field, described earlier in this table.
Replicate: Fields	Deselected by default. If selected, you can click the Define button to open the "Replicate Selected Fields" dialog box. There you can choose "All fields" (the default" or "Custom." If you choose "Custom," a checkmarked list of fields in the database appears. You can deselect the fields you do not want the destination server to accept from the source server. If the database is an address book or directory, you can also choose from the "Minimal Address Book" entries described earlier in this table.

An especially interesting aspect of the Advanced screen, described in the last subtable in Table 9.3, is that you can set different combinations of computers in the "When computer" and "Receives from" fields and define a unique selection formula for each combination. Then, if you select "Replicate: Replication formula" in the same screen, the replication formulas will replicate to each destination server. This provides you with a way to define in one place (the source replica) the replication formulas for all of the destination replicas.

There are three other very important facts about the settings in this dialog box that you should remember. First, most of these settings are specific to the replica for which you set them. With one exception they do not replicate to other copies of the database. The one exception is the replication formula, and then only if you check the "Replicate Replication formula" checkbox, and then only the formula that is relevant to the destination server replicates to it.

Second, replication formulas do not constitute security. You can set up a formula that limits what a server in, say, a field office pulls from the headquarters server. You can devise the formula on the headquarters server, then replicate it to the field office server. But you cannot stop someone who has access to the field office's server or Manager access to the database from changing the formula and replicating more than you intended. (If you need a secure way to limit replication of whole documents, you can limit document read access; this, however, is in the domain of the application developer, not that of the administrator.)

Third, you must have Designer access to a database to change its replication formula and Replication fields, and Manager access to change the other replication settings. Anyone, however, can see a database's replication settings, including (surprisingly) a user who has No Access in the ACL (if that user has access to a bookmark of the database). (Try this: Create a bookmark for a server-based database for which you have Manager access. Add a user to the ACL; set the user to No Access. Switch to that user's ID. Right-click the bookmark for the database and choose Replication, Settings.)

Replication and Save Conflicts

Because Notes is a system of distributed databases, it cannot protect against conflicting edits of the same document, so it doesn't try to do so, at least not by default. Instead, it provides tools and procedures for minimizing conflicts and for dealing with them when they arise. Two kinds of document conflicts can occur in Notes databases:

- **Save conflicts.** When two people simultaneously edit a data document on a single replica of a database, the first to save will be able to do so normally. When the second person tries to save, Notes displays the following Yes-or-No warning: "Another copy of this document was saved while you were editing it. Save your changes also as a Save Conflict document?" To avoid creating a conflict, the second user has to abandon the edit.

- **Replication conflicts.** When a document is modified on two different replicas of a database between replication sessions, a potential replication conflict arises. The next time the two databases are replicated, the replicator will have to resolve the conflict or turn one of the documents into a conflict document.

When either preceding case results in the creation of a conflict document, the conflicting document appears in views as a child of the other version of the document and has the title "[Replication or Save Conflict]." This is the "loser" and the other is the "winner" of the conflict resolution process. See Figure 9.4.

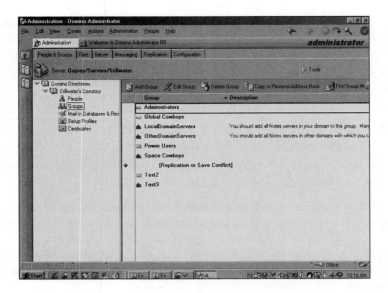

Figure 9.4   The documents titled "Space Cowboys" and "[Replication or Save Conflict]" are in conflict with each other. In official Lotus geek-speak, "Space Cowboys" is the winner and "[Replication or Save Conflict]" is the loser in the conflict resolution process.

The Conflict Resolution Rules

Domino will resolve certain save and replication conflicts. Those include the following:

- If two people edit the ACL independently, one of the edits will overwrite the other.

- If two people edit a Design document independently, one of the edits will overwrite the other.

- If one person edits a data document and another deletes the same document, one will overwrite the other.

- If two people edit a data document on two separate servers between replications, a conflict may be avoided under the following circumstances:

  - If the form property "Merge replication conflicts" is enabled for the form on which the document is based and the two editors don't edit the same fields, the Replicator will merge the two versions of the document.

  - If version control is enabled for the form on which the document is based, such that edits of an existing document create a new document (either a sibling or a child of the edited document, but not a parent of the edited document), the two editors' changes will not generate a conflict.

- If the designer of the database has created a LotusScript conflict handler (it could be an agent, for example), it may be able to resolve the conflict according to its own special rules.

Which ACL, Design, or Data document gets deleted in these cases, and which data document is declared the "winner" and which the "loser" in cases where the Replicator can't resolve a conflict? The rules are as follows:

- **The "most frequently" rule.** In a replication conflict, the version of the conflicting document that was edited more times wins.

- **The "most recently" rule.** If both versions were edited the same number of times, the version edited most recently wins.

Under the "most frequently" rule, if one copy of a document was modified, say, twice between the two replication sessions and the other copy was modified only once, then the first copy will overwrite the second copy at the second replication.

Under the "most recently" rule, if both versions of the document were modified the same number of times between replication sessions, the one with the most recent edit will overwrite the other one at the second deletion.

Resolving a Conflict Manually

If, despite all these measures, a conflict document does appear in a database, a manager of the database must resolve the conflict. To do so, the manager must do the following:

1. Examine both documents and determine where they are in conflict.

2. Optional: Copy data from one document to the other in order to bring one of them fully up to date.

3. Delete the document not updated.

If you have to resolve a conflict of this sort, the easiest resolution is to keep the winner and delete the loser. That way, all you have to do, after copying any data from the loser to the winner, is delete the loser.

If, instead, you decide to keep the loser and delete the winner, you have to first convert the loser back into a regular document. Here's how I prefer to do that:

1. Mark the winner deleted.

2. Open the losers in edit mode, save it, then close it. (Press Ctrl+E, Ctrl+S, Ctrl+W in succession—you don't have to let up off the Ctrl key between successive keystrokes.) The loser now appears in the view as a regular document, probably right below the winner, and with the same title as the winner. (But, depending on what changes occurred in it, the loser could switch places with the winner (which is why we marked the winner deleted in step 1) or change its title and perhaps move to another part of the view entirely.)

3. Press F9 to refresh the view, thus completing the deletion of the winner.

Because reconciling conflicting documents is a cumbersome procedure, you want to avoid their creation if possible. We saw earlier how the database designer could minimize replication conflicts by enabling the form property "Merge replication conflicts," enabling version control, and writing a LotusScript conflict handler. Here are some ways the database manager can minimize the occurrence of conflicts:

- Minimize the number of users who can edit existing documents in a database by giving most users Author or lower access to the database. The fewer the document editors, the fewer opportunities there are for conflicts to arise.

- Database managers should create only as many replica copies of the database as necessary. Users know when they are about to create save conflicts and can avoid them. They can't avoid replication conflicts. So the fewer replicas, the less opportunity for users to create replication conflicts. An additional benefit is that fewer replicas mean less resource-intensive replication takes place over all.

- If you set a limit in the database property "Limit entries in $Revisions field," set it to no less than 10 entries. Fewer than that and you run the risk that the replicator (which uses that field in its conflict analysis) may have to assume there is a conflict when in fact there is not.

Creating New Replicas

In the preceding bullet list, one of the recommendations was to minimize the number of replicas of a database in order to minimize the opportunity for replication conflicts and to minimize the demand that replication makes on a network. The implication of that recommendation is that replicas are bad. But that would be an unwarranted conclusion. Within reason, creating replicas of databases is a good thing. The benefits of adding new replicas of a database include the following:

- You distribute the load of a heavily used database across more servers, improving server performance in the process.

- You can localize network traffic and make data more available to remote users by putting replicas of databases on servers that are local to users.

- You can separate the production version of a database from the one the developers are redesigning.

- You can maintain database availability when a server goes down.

- You can use selective replication to provide workgroups with just the subset of data they need and to provide business partners, suppliers, customers, and the public with only that information which is approved for their consumption.

- Remote, disconnected users (for example, a user working on his notebook computer at 39,000 feet) can work in a local copy of the database.

Domino creates some replicas automatically—the Domain Directory and Administration Requests are two examples. Most replicas, however, you have to create. In R5, to create replicas on servers, you can have the Administration Process create them for you or you can create replicas manually. To create replicas on user workstation, you can use setup profiles or you can create replicas manually.

When creating replicas on servers, you usually want to use the Administration Process because it streamlines the creation process for you. It lets you request creation of multiple databases on multiple servers. Then it does the work for you. It creates replica stubs (unpopulated databases) on each server. Because the Administration Process created them, they are called "wildcat" replica stubs, meaning that any other server can populate them during replication.

You should create a replica manually, however, if you don't have access to the Administration Process of if you need to set up the new replica in some special way. For example, you may want to restrict replication in some way or encrypt a database locally.

Creating Replicas on Servers—Preliminary Considerations

Before you try to create a new replica of a database on another server, make sure you can do it. You need to provide for the following prerequisites:

- Can the source server connect to the destination server(s)? You may have to create the necessary connection documents. (You can use the "Trace Connections" tool in User Preferences, Ports to test and troubleshoot connections. See Chapter 4, "Additional Server Setup," and Chapter 6, "Advanced User Setup," for more information about Trace Connections.)

- Do you and the source server have the right to create replica databases on the destination server(s)? Check the "Create replica databases" field on the Security tab of the Server document of each target server. If necessary, populate the field with the names of groups of which you and the source server are members.

- Do you and the destination server(s) have at least Reader access to the database(s)? If not, the source server will reject your request to create a new replica.

Use the Administration Process to Create New Replicas

To create new replicas using the Administration Process, make sure you meet the preliminary conditions (see the previous section, then follow these steps:

1. Open Domino Administrator to the Files screen.
2. Select the server on which current replicas exist.
3. Select one or more databases. (Use the Shift and Control keys to select the second and subsequent databases.)

4. With the desired database(s) selected, choose Database, Create Replica(s) in the Tools pane. The Create Replica dialog box appears.

5. Select the names of the destination servers in the "Create replicas on these servers" field.

6. To edit the filenames of the database on each destination server, choose File Names. In the Edit Destination Path dialog box select each server in turn in the "Destination database and server" field, then edit the file path name in the "Destination file path" field.

7. Choose OK to close each dialog box. A message appears from the Domino Administrator telling you how many databases were processed and how many errors (if any) there were.

The Administration Process then creates the database stubs and they are populated the next time a scheduled replication takes place between the target server(s) and a server that has a fully populated copy of the database.

Create a New Replica Manually

There are two ways to manually create a replica database on a new server—and one way not to. First, you can choose Replication, New replica in the File menu. Second, you can use operating system tools to copy a database to another server. However, you can *not* make a new replica by choosing Database, New Copy in the File menu.

Two databases are replicas of each other if they share the same replica ID. Choosing New Replica copies the replica ID to the new database. Choosing New copy does not; it creates a new database with a new replica ID that, though otherwise similar to the original database, will never replicate with it. An operating system copy, because it does not alter contents of a file being copied, leaves the original replica ID intact so that the new copy is a replica copy of the original.

To create a manual new replica on an R5 server, you have to meet the same prerequisites as when requesting the Administration process to do it. The source and destination servers must be able to connect; you and the source server must have the right to create new replicas on the destination server; and you and the destination server must have at least Reader access to the database.

This is a change from the requirements under R4, and if you operate in a mixed R4/R5 environment, you need to be aware of the difference. To create a new replica on an R4 server, the source server and you must have at least Designer access to the original database or the creation of the new replica will fail on the destination R4 server.

You will succeed in creating the replica stub. But as soon as the ACL arrives in the database during the initial replication of the database, the destination server will see that either the source server or you do not have Designer access and will refuse to accept any design documents. Replication will come to a halt. You will be unable to use the database until a source server with Designer access in the destination server's ACL replicates the design documents into it.

This is actually standard behavior under standard Notes security rules. The way R5 servers work—accepting a full copy of a database from a server that may have as little as Reader access to the database—is an exception to the usual Notes security rules.

To manually create a new replica using Notes or Domino Administrator, follow these steps:

1. In the File menu, choose Replication, New replica. If a database was open on the screen when you chose New replica, the New Replica [*database title*] dialog box appears. If a database was not open, the Choose Database dialog box appears.

2. If the Choose Database dialog box appears, use it to choose the source server and database. Choose the server, then choose the database or, if it doesn't appear in the Database list, enter its filename in the Filename field. Choose Open or Select.

3. The New Replica [*database title*] dialog box appears. Choose the name of the destination server in the Server field. If you want, change the filename in the File name field.

4. Choose any other options you wish, then choose OK. The options are as follows:

   - **Create.** Choose "Immediately" or "Next scheduled replication." Choose "Next scheduled replication" if the database is large, because choosing "Immediately" will tie up your workstation until replication finishes.

   - **Encryption.** Pressing this button opens the "Encryption for [database title]" dialog box. There you can choose strong, medium, or simple encryption. The new replica will be encrypted with the destination server's ID.

   - **Size Limit.** This only applies to databases being created on R4 servers or in R4 database format. The choices are 1, 2, 3, or 4 gigabytes. (R5 databases (that is, in ODS41 format) are constrained only by the limits of the underlying OS.)

   - **Replication Settings.** This opens the Replication Settings dialog box (described fully elsewhere in this chapter). Change any settings you want and choose OK.

   - **Copy Access Control List.** If you deselect this, the new replica will have a fresh ACL listing its server and you as Manager and having otherwise default settings. (Among other things, you can use this feature to view the design of a database for which you don't have Designer access; you still don't have Designer access to the server copy of the database, but you have Manager access to your local copy.)

   - **Create full text index for searching.** The new replica will be immediately full-text indexed.

Making a New Replica on a Notes Workstation

Notice in the preceding section that, from your own workstation you can choose any database on any accessible server and make a replica of it on any other server, as long as you meet the access requirements. You can use this same technique to create a new database on a Notes workstation. However, you must actually perform the steps at the target workstation, not remotely. If you want to remotely create one or more replica databases on a user workstation, you can use a Setup Profile to do it. However, you will create the replica database(s) on every Notes workstation governed by the chosen Setup Profile.

To use a Setup Profile to create a replica on Notes workstations, follow these steps:

1. Open the database to be replicated. The copy you open will be the source from which the new replica will be created.

2. With the source database open, choose Copy As Link, Database Link from the File menu.

3. Close the source database. Open the appropriate Setup Profile in the Domain Directory. Open it in Edit mode.

4. On the Databases tab, place the text cursor in the Create As new replicas on user's machine field. Choose Paste. A database link icon appears.

5. Save and close the Setup Profile.

The next time each user to whom this Setup Profile is assigned logs into Notes, his local Dynamic Configuration program (`ndyncfg.exe`) will check the Setup Profile, discover the change, and pull the new replica database from the source server. See Chapter 13, "Client Maintenance and Troubleshooting," for more details on Setup Profiles.

Deleted Documents, Deletion Stubs, and Purging

If you haven't figured it out yet, you may be wondering what becomes of documents deleted from a database during replication. At first glance you might assume that, because a document no longer exists (it was deleted) on the replica on S1, replication should cause S2 to send a new copy of the deleted record to S1, so that they'll both have a copy. That can happen, but it does so very rarely, because certain features of Notes tend to minimize the possibility.

For example, when a user deletes a document, the document does not ordinarily disappear from the database. Rather, the data fields are deleted but a "deletion stub" remains in the database. (That's a hard deletion. If soft deletions are enabled in a database, the data fields don't actually disappear until a defined number of hours pass. But then they do disappear, and the deletion becomes "hard.")

The next time replication takes place, the deletion stub, being the most recently edited version of the document, replicates to the other server, deleting that copy of the document. That's how deletions propagate across the network.

Periodically, Notes, Domino, or Updall purges deletions stubs (and possibly some documents, depending on certain replication settings) from the database. Purging removes them entirely. After they're gone, no evidence remains in the database of their ever having been there.

Deleted documents can reappear in a replica in two different ways: either because of conflict resolution or because deletion stubs are purged before they can replicate.

If, between replications, a document is deleted on one replica but edited on another replica, the edited version might overwrite the deletion at the next replication, causing the deleted document to reappear.

Under the "most frequently" rule, if the edited version of a document was modified more times between the two replication sessions than the deleted version, then the edited document will overwrite the deleted document at the second replication. The deletion itself is considered to be an edit under this rule.

Under the "most recently" rule, if both versions of the document were modified the same number of times between replication sessions but the edit took place more recently than the deletion, the edited document will overwrite the deleted document at the second deletion.

The second way deleted documents can reappear in a replica is if their deletion stubs are purged before they are replicated to other replicas of the database. Then, under the right (well, wrong) circumstances, the undeleted versions could replicate back into the purged replica. Ordinarily this won't happen because both the replication history and the "Only replicate incoming documents saved or modified after" replication setting prevent it.

When replication occurs, the undeleted version of a document, not having been modified more recently than either of those dates, isn't a candidate for replicating. But if you clear both the replication history and the "Only replicate incoming documents saved or modified after" field, at the next replication all documents are candidates for replicating. Then the servers will discover that the deleted document exists only in one replica and will replicate it back into the other replica.

Alternately, if someone edits the undeleted copy of a document, the edited version becomes a candidate for replicating at the next replication, and will replicate back into the other replica.

The solution to this problem is to make sure that replication occurs more frequently than purging of deletion stubs. It almost always does, as scheduled replication must provide for at least weekly replication, whereas deleted documents must by default in most databases age 90 days before becoming a candidate for deletion. But under some circumstances purging can occur more frequently than replication:

- If you set the "Remove documents not modified in the last [x] days" field in Replication Settings to some low number of days, for example, three days, and replication occurs, say, every seven days, you now have document purging occurring more frequently than replication.

- If a database doesn't participate in scheduled replication for a long period of time, say, because "Temporarily disable replication" was checked, documents could be deleted and purged before you reenable replication.

- If a user makes a local replica of a database but does not get around to replicating with the server again for a long time, documents may be deleted and purged in the interim.

The replication history, the "Remove documents not modified in the last [x] days" field, and the ACL normally protect against this. But if you clear the replication history and the "Remove documents not modified in the last [x] days" field and the user who made the deletion has deletion rights in the ACL of the other copy of the database, you have a potential surprise on your hands.

To protect against inadvertent deletion/purging of documents in one copy of a database before the deletions can replicate to other copies, you should take the following precautions:

- Don't use short purge intervals on databases that have replicas on other servers. Set the "Remove documents not modified in the last [x] days" field in such a database to a number higher than the interval between scheduled replications.

- Don't clear both the replication history and the "Only replicate incoming documents saved or modified after" field except as a last resort. Many people clear these almost reflexively whenever they experience replication problems. But doing so rarely solves replication problems.

- If you do decide to clear the Replication History, only clear individual entries, not the whole history. To clear an entry, select it, choose Zoom, then choose Remove.

- Minimize the deletion rights of ordinary users in shared databases. Most users should have the right to delete only documents they created and maybe not even those. Only database editors or managers should have the right to delete documents in most databases.

Monitoring Replication

You need to watch over the replication process to make sure everything is working as intended. Not that it's unreliable or anything. But if something does go wrong and replication fails to occur as intended, it can cause all sort of real-world problems, such as users acting on false assumptions. People rely on the data in Notes databases; if replication fails, people find themselves relying on stale data. Then, they get in trouble and they stop trusting the data. Then, Notes loses its value.

Domino provides a series of tools to keep you informed of the state of replication. They include the following:

- The Notes Log
- Replication statistics

- Replication monitors and Event notifications
- Graphical monitoring tools in Domino Administrator

The Notes Log

The Replicator reports the results of its activities to the Notes Log. The information appears in the Miscellaneous Events and Replication Events views. The Replication Events view, in particular, it where you will go to determine what happened during a given replication session. Just remember to look in the Notes Log of the computer that actually did the work. The server whose replicator did the work is the one on which the information is logged.

You can view the Notes Log by opening it directly or from within Domino Administrator. From within Domino Administrator you can see all Notes Log views under the Server, Analysis tabs. To look at just the Replication Events view, look under the Replication tab.

Replication Statistics

Domino collects the following general replication statistics: Replica.Docs.Added, Replica.Docs.Deleted, Replica.Docs.Updated, Replica.Failed, and Replica.Successful. You can retrieve these statistics any number of ways. You can use the Show Statistics (sh st replica) command at the server console. In Domino Administrator, you can see them under the Server, Statistics tab, or in the Statistics Reports database, which you can see under the Server, Analysis tabs. In Statistics Reports, replication statistics appear in documents in the Statistics Reports\Mail & Database and Statistics Reports\System views.

You also can check the Replication History of a given database. Open the database, then choose Replication, History in the File menu. Or choose Replication History in the Database Properties box. Look in the Replication Settings dialog box for a given database to determine what is supposed to replicate.

Replication Monitors and Event Notifications

The Statistics and Events reporting system enables you to monitor individual databases for replication failures. You can have the system notify you in some way of a failure of the database to replicate with one or more other servers within a number of hours that you can choose.

You can set this up in the Statistics & Events database (events4.nsf), which is the configuration database for Domino's statistics collection and event dispatching systems. Access this database under Statistics & Events in the Configuration tab of Domino Administrator. You have to set up two documents:

- **A Replication Monitor.** This causes the Event Dispatcher to watch for described replication failures and generate a Replication event when they occur.

- **An Event Notification.** This tells the Event Dispatcher to notify you in some way when an event described in the Replication Monitor (or of the type and severity defined in the Replication Monitor) occurs.

You can set up a Replication monitor either by creating the document directly or by launching a wizard that will prompt you for all the necessary information then generate the monitor document itself. To create one manually, select the Monitors, Replication view in Statistics & Events, then choose New Replication Monitor in the Action Bar. Fill in the fields as set forth in Table 9.4.

Table 9.4 **Fields on the Replication Monitor Form**

Field	Description
	ON THE BASICS TAB
File name	Enter the filename of the database to be monitored. Enter a single filename only.
Server(s)	You can monitor replication failure on any subset of servers in your domain, from one of them to all of them.
Server(s) with which the database must replicate	You can monitor replication failures between the servers named in the previous field and any combination of other servers in your domain, from one of them to all of them.
Replication timeout; Timeout x hours	Defaults to 24 hours. Change it to suit your needs.
	ON THE OTHER TAB
Event: Generate a Replication event of severity	The choices are Fatal, Failure, Warning (high), Warning (low), and Normal. I recommend you choose Fatal, for reasons that I'll go into below.
Enablement: Disable this monitor	Allows you to stop the monitor from generating events without actually deleting it.

Note to R4 administrators: Under R4 you only had to create a Replication Monitor. Under R5 you have to create an Event Notification as well. Unlike the R4 Replication Monitor, the R5 Replication Monitor does not generate any notification of replication failures; it merely flags them as Replica events of x severity (as chosen by you). To be notified of the event, you have to tell the Event Dispatcher how to notify you with an Event Notification document. However, this is only a problem with the earliest versions of Domino R5. Beginning with R5.0.1, the Statistics Reports database includes by default a set of Event Notification documents that generate Event documents in the Statistics Reports database upon the occurrence of events of any type and of severity "Warning: High" or greater.

390 Chapter 9 Replication

To use a wizard to create this document, open the same view, but choose Setup Wizards, Monitor in the Actions menu. The wizard will prompt you for the information that appears in the fields listed previously.

Upon saving (or on subsequent replication of the monitor document to the affected server(s)), the Event task (if it is running) on the affected server(s) will watch for replication failures of the named database. If, for the length of time designated in the monitor document, replication never succeeds between any affected pair of servers, the Event task on the replicating server will generate an event of type Replica and severity chosen by you in your monitor document.

This is all well and good. But you want to be *notified* of the event. For that, you have to create an Event Notification document. Go to the Event Notification view. Either create one directly (by choosing New Event Notification in the Action bar) or create one indirectly, via a wizard (by choosing Setup Wizards, Event Notification in the Actions menu). Fill in the fields as set forth in Table 9.5.

Table 9.5 **Fields on the Event Notification Form**

Field	Description
ON THE BASICS TAB	
Trigger	Choose the first option if you want notification of the occurrence of a specific event and you know the message the event will generate. You will have to choose the triggering event in the Event tab. Choose the second option if you want notification of the occurrence of any of a class of events or if you don't know the message that an event will generate. You will have to choose an event type and severity in the Event tab.
Server(s) to monitor	You can be notified if a defined event occurs on any subset of servers in your domain, from one of them to all of them.
ON THE EVENT TAB	
Built-in/Add-in task event	If you chose this field on the Basics screen, you will see the following items:
Select Event	Choose this button to reveal a list of the messages an event can generate. The list is endlessly long, so if you don't know what message your event will generate, go back to the Basics tab and choose "Any event that matches a criteria."
Events can have any message	Choose this if the generic message that you chose under Select Event is specific enough for your needs.
Events must have this text [in] the event message	Choose this if you want to supply any variables for the message that you chose under Select Event.

Field	Description

ON THE EVENT TAB

Field	Description
Criteria to match	If you chose "Any event that matches a criteria" on the Basics screen, you will see the following items:
Event ... type	If you want notification of events of every type, choose "Events can be any type." If you want notification of events of a single type, choose "Events must be this type," then choose the type in the desired type. For our purposes (notification of replication failures) we would choose "Replica" as the event type.
Event ... severity	If you want notification of all severities, choose "Events can be any severity." If you want notification of less than all severities (and you almost always will), choose "Events must be one of these severities," then select the severities for which you want to receive notice. For our purposes (notification of replication failures) we would choose the same severity you chose in the Replication Monitor.
Event ... message	If you want to be notified of all events of the type and severities chosen in the preceding fields, or if you don't know what message your desired event will generate, choose "Events can have any message." If you want to be notified only of events that have certain text in their event messages, choose "Events must have this text [in] the event message," then enter the desired text. For our purposes (notification of replication failures) we would choose "filename.nsf has not replicated with." Replace filename.nsf with the actual filename. Include the quotation marks.

ON THE ACTION TAB YOU WILL HAVE TO CHOOSE A NOTIFICATION METHOD AND AN ENABLE-
MENT OPTION (ENABLE/DISABLE/ENABLED ONLY DURING THESE TIMES). THE FIELDS THAT
APPEAR DEPEND ON THE CHOICES YOU MAKE. THE NOTIFICATION METHODS ARE

Field	Description
Broadcast	You will have to choose who will receive the broadcast message.
Log to a database	You will have to specify the name of the database and the server on which it is located. It will default to statrep.nsf on the same server as the occurrence of the event.
Mail	You will have to enter the email address(es) of the administrator(s) who should receive the notice.
Log to NT Event Viewer	No options.

continues

Table 9.5 **Continued**

Field	Description
ON THE ACTION TAB YOU WILL HAVE TO CHOOSE A NOTIFICATION METHOD AND AN ENABLEMENT OPTION (ENABLE/DISABLE/ENABLED ONLY DURING THESE TIMES). THE FIELDS THAT APPEAR DEPEND ON THE CHOICES YOU MAKE. THE NOTIFICATION METHODS ARE	
Pager	You will have to enter the email address(es) of the pager(s) that should receive the notice.
Run Program	You will have to enter the name of the program, the command line arguments, and the name of the server on which it should run.
Relay to other server	You will have to enter the name of the relay server.
SNMP Trap	You will have to enter the name of the SMTP server.
Log to Unix System Log	No options.

You must be careful how you define the event for which you want to receive notice. If you define it too generally, you will receive 10 or 100 or 1,000 spurious notices for every legitimate notice. To minimize spurious notifications of replication failures, define your event in one of the two following ways:

- Choose "Failure" as the severity level in your Replication Monitor. Choose "Replica" as the event type, "Failure" as the severity level, and "Events can have any message" in your Event Notification. There are very few events that qualify as "Replica" and "Failure," so you will receive few if any spurious notifications.

- In your Event Notification, require that "*filename.nsf* has not replicated with" appear in the message text (replacing *filename.nsf* with the real filename). Then you may choose "Events can be any type" and "Events can be any severity."

Graphical Monitoring Tools

Domino Administrator provides several graphical tools to enable you to see quickly and easily the status of replication in your domain. On the Replication tab you can see each server's replication schedule and its replication topology. On the Server, Monitoring tab you can monitor the current status of the Replicator task (among other things) for selected servers.

The replication schedule is compiled from the connection documents in which the currently selected server originates replications. In R5.0.0 it does not show the status of replication under the schedule, but it probably will in later releases. R5.0.0 also includes a bug. If you include multiple individual times or time ranges in a replication document, only the first one listed appears in the replication schedule graphic.

The replication topology is also generated from connection documents, but this time it shows all connections in which the currently selected server either originates or responds to replications. If the replication topology doesn't show up for a given server, it's because the Maps server task isn't running. Enter "load maps" at the server console, and add "Maps" to the list of tasks in the ServerTasks variable in the server's notes.ini file.

Finally, on the Server, Monitoring screen, you can see the current status of the Replicator on selected servers. Various icons show if it is running, not running, or not responding, and whether any events of Warning, Failure, or Fatal severity have occurred.

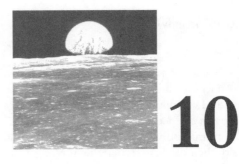

10

Security

MOST ORGANIZATIONS THAT USE NOTES SOONER or later use it to store and manage information that they consider to be either sensitive or private or to have competitive value. They want only certain people to have access to that information. Lotus knew from the beginning that its customers would use Notes this way, so they built comprehensive and granular features into the product from the ground up. Notes/Domino's security features are so pervasive and central to the product that you can't really understand how to administer a Domino/Notes installation without a thorough understanding of the security procedures.

A good starting point is to understand what the Domino server's job is. It is the custodian of the information stored in the databases. It must accept information only from entities (people, programs, and computers) that are authorized to submit information to it, and from no others. It must dispense information only to entities that are authorized to receive it, and to no others. Domino security is all about this function.

There are other security considerations as well. People who use Domino servers need to be able to verify the identity of the servers with which they trade information. People who store local copies of databases in Notes must be able to protect the data in them from unauthorized access. People need to secure and authenticate their email communications. And people need protection from viruses and worms that may hide in Notes data.

Security issues have become acute in recent years as more and more companies connect to the anarchic Internet in order to establish easy, inexpensive connections with their suppliers, business partners, customers, and the public. Lotus has provided for this by incorporating SSL and S/MIME security features in Domino and Notes.

In this chapter we'll look first at authentication features, then Domino server security, then database security, then Notes workstation security. Finally, we'll look in detail at how Domino and Notes use SSL security.

Authentication

Authentication is the process of identifying the other party to a transaction, and it's the core of Domino security. A server can't usually tell what degree of access to data to permit if it doesn't know the identity of the user. Of course, for some purposes the server doesn't need to know and doesn't bother to authenticate. Also, the degree and type of authentication depend on the kind of client a user employs.

Domino servers and their clients can use four kinds of authentication:

- **Notes proprietary.** This is how Domino servers and Notes clients normally authenticate each other. It is certificate-based and very secure.

- **Secure Sockets Layer (SSL).** This is an optional form of authentication that you can enable for non-Notes clients. Like Notes proprietary authentication, it is certificate-based and very secure. You can authenticate Domino servers this way or both Domino servers and non-Notes clients.

- **Name and password.** This is also an optional form of authentication that you can enable for non-Notes clients. It is the weakest form of true authentication. Only users can authenticate this way—not servers.

- **None.** Okay, this isn't really authentication, but rather the absence of it. Unauthenticated users are anonymous to the server. Unauthenticated servers are not anonymous to clients; rather, the clients assume they are dealing with the named server without verifying the fact. HTTP, LDAP, NNTP, SMTP, and IIOP clients are anonymous by default. You can optionally permit anonymous Notes clients. Anonymous clients are anonymous only as long as they only try to access the server in ways permitted to anonymous users. The moment a Web client, for example, tries to author a document in a database in which anonymous users are only permitted to read documents, the Web client will have to authenticate by either SSL or name and password authentication.

The available authentication combinations in transactions between the Domino server and various clients are set forth in Table 10.1. The first combination in every case is the default. For example, in the first row, a Notes client can authenticate a server only one way—using Notes proprietary authentication; the server has two options for authenticating the user—Notes proprietary authentication or no authentication. Notes proprietary authentication (the first choice in the third column) is the default.

Table 10.1 **Authentication Options**

Client Type	When Client Authenticates Server Using	Server Can Authenticate Client Using
Notes	Notes proprietary	Notes proprietary None
HTTP, IMAP, NNTP	None	None Name and password
	SSL	None Name and password SSL
POP3, IMAP	None	Name and password
	SSL	Name and password SSL
SMTP, IIOP	None or SSL	None Name and password

How Name and Password Authentication Works

This is the simplest form of authentication. Domino allows all non-Notes clients to authenticate this way. The client submits a name and password to the server, which checks one or more directories for a record with the same name and password. The password is supposedly secret; therefore, the entity submitting it is presumed to be the entity named in the server's record.

The benefit of this system (as compared with a certificate-based system) is its simplicity—the server and user agree ahead of time on a name and password for the user, who then always uses them. The problems with this system are as follows:

- The password may not really be secret. People use passwords that are easy to guess, or they write them down or share them with others.

- The name and password are passed across the network from user to server. Unless they are passed in an encrypted form, an eavesdropper can pick them up en route. But to pass them in an encrypted form, either you have to agree ahead of time on a secret encryption key, which itself may be compromised when passed between the parties, or you have to institute a certificate-based authentication system.

- There is no defense against password-guessing programs.

- The user has to register with the server ahead of time so that the server will have some record against which to compare the name and password submitted by the user.

Certificate-based authentication systems address all of these objections.

How Certificate-Based Authentication Works

Both Notes proprietary and SSL authentication are certificate-based. The idea behind certificate-based authentication is like that in which two parties to a transaction don't know each other, but they have a friend in common who vouches for them. Each trusts the other based on the assurances of his friend.

The way this works electronically is that the party to be identified presents a certificate to the other party. Think of the certificate as a letter of introduction signed by the trusted friend. The certificate says, in effect, that the public key in this certificate belongs to the entity named in this certificate. The whole thing is "signed" by a t hird party known in Notes parlance as a *certifier* and in SSL as a *certifying authority* (or just CA).

The certificate ties a public key to a name. If the receiver of the certificate trusts the certificate's signer, it believes the truth of the assurance—that the public key belongs to the named entity. All it has to do then is find out if the party who presented the certificate has the private key that corresponds to the public key in the certificate. If so, the presenter, in theory, has to be the entity named in the certificate. Voila! Positive identification!

Encryption Keys, Public Keys, and Private Keys: Encryption, Signatures, and Identification

If the preceding explanation went by a little too fast for you, it may be that you didn't understand what the "keys" are. They are encryption keys. Like a real key, they lock and unlock things. In this case, they lock and unlock information. You take information and change it with the key by doing something mathematical to it. Say, for example, that you multiply a salary in a field by an encryption key (except that what you do in real life is something a little less simple than that). The information is now scrambled. To unscramble it, you have to reverse the process that scrambled it—in our example, you would divide by the key to produce the original message.

This is, in essence, how an encryption key works—you scramble information with it and then unscramble the information with it. In order to unscramble the information, you either need to know what key scrambled it or you have to do a whole lot of work to figure out what key was used. The nature of the keys used to scramble information on computers is such that it takes a whole lot of really fast computers a lot of time to figure out what key was used. While not impossible, maybe, the effort would be very expensive and presumably either not within the financial reach of the decryptor or not worth the effort.

When you use the same key to both lock and unlock information, you are performing what is called *single-key encryption and decryption*. Authentication is based on a slightly different kind of encryption—*dual-key encryption*. As its name implies, dual-key encryption requires two keys, a unique and magical set of keys that are mathematically related to each other in such a way that each one can unlock only what the other locked. Use whichever key you want to scramble a piece of information; you must use the other key to unscramble it.

The beauty of this scheme is that it overcomes the big weakness of single-key encryption. That weakness is that, for two entities to use an encryption key to communicate with each other over a network, they must both gain possession of it. But if one creates it and sends it to the other across the network, an eavesdropper can grab a copy of it en route. The key is then no longer secret. Anything encrypted with it can be decrypted by the eavesdropper. The two parties could encrypt the key before sending it, but with what? Another encryption key? How do they both gain possession of that one? By phone? By snail mail? By FedEx? None of these erases the possibility that an interloper could snag a copy of the key en route. Besides, those modes of delivery are cumbersome and antiquated. The whole point of computerized communication is to push bits, not atoms.

But dual-key encryption solves this problem. Here's how. You can make one of the keys public and keep the other one private. You can send the public key to the second party any old way you want. If some third party gets hold of it, you don't care, because the only key that can decrypt anything with it is the one you held private. The second party can encrypt information with the public key and send it to you. Third parties can't decrypt it. In fact, even the second party can't decrypt it. Only you, the first party, can decrypt it, using the private key that never left your possession.

But that isn't the only remarkable thing about this pair of keys. Another is that you can also use them to positively identify the origin of a message and verify its integrity. Think of it—if you never let the private key out of your possession, you are the only person in the world who can encrypt something with it. If you encrypt a message with your private key and send it to the second party, the second party can use your public key (and none other) to decrypt it. If your public key can decrypt the message, it could only have been encrypted by you. In effect, what you did by encrypting the message with your private key was to sign the message. The encryption was your electronic signature.

Except, in reality you don't encrypt the whole message when you sign it; that would take too much time and effort. Rather, you run the message through a *hashing algorithm*. This is a mathematical procedure that produces a short digest of the longer message. Then you encrypt the digest. The recipient uses the same hashing algorithm as you to produce an identical digest and then decrypts your digest with your public key. If it decrypts, it must have been encrypted by you—that's your signature. If the two digests are identical, the recipient knows your message has not been altered since you hashed, er, signed it.

How did the second party get a copy of your public key? You sent it to him. If you have a long-standing relationship with each other, maybe you sent it a long time ago and the second party keeps it on file. Or maybe this is your first communication to the second party. Well, then maybe you sent the public key along with the message itself. And that brings us to the third cool thing about dual-key encryption.

Think about this. You receive a message from a total stranger. The message is signed by the stranger but includes the stranger's public key so that you can decrypt the signature and verify that the message did originate with the stranger. The stranger's name is Bill Clinton. Cool, a message from the President!

But wait! How do you know, really, that the message is from the President? On the basis of what we know so far, you don't. Anyone can generate a pair of keys. The algorithm that generates them is public. Programs that crank them out are freely available on the Internet.

Now, maybe you and I have some ongoing relationship; we've palled around since kindergarten, er, college. (Same thing, right?) In such a case I could deliver my public key to you on a floppy disk the next time we meet at the tennis club. You would accept it without hesitation. Fine. But what about those total strangers all over the world that you will never meet except electronically? How do you verify that the email that purports to be from Bill Clinton really is from that Bill Clinton and not Rob "Bill Clinton" Kirkland? This is where certificates come in.

If you and I can agree that some third party is trustworthy, we can do something like this: I'll generate a pair of keys and send the public key to the trustworthy third party. The trustworthy third party will certify that the public key I sent to it really belongs to "Rob Kirkland." That is, the trustworthy third party will issue a certificate with my name and my public key on it and, for good measure, an expiration date. The trustworthy third party will sign the certificate, attach its own public key to it, and send the whole thing back to me. Meanwhile, you can do the same thing. Or, if you don't want to go through all that trouble, you can just acquire a copy of the trustworthy party's public key.

Now when I send you a message, I'll send my certificate along with it. You can use the trustworthy—or should we start saying "trusted"—third party's public key to decrypt its signature. You recognize the key; you have a copy of it yourself. So you trust its authenticity. You compare the digest resulting from the decryption with the one you generated. They are identical. Therefore the name and public key on the certificate haven't been tampered with since the trusted third party signed it. Now you have a trustworthy statement from a trusted third party (the certifier) that the public key in the certificate belongs to "Rob Kirkland." You can use that public key to encrypt some bit of information, send that to me, ask me to decrypt it, and return the result to you. If I return the same information you encrypted, you know that I, the anonymous originator of the stream of bits coming down the wire, must really be Rob Kirkland. Voila! Positive identification!

There's another detail you should know about how this whole thing works. In order to work the way they do and still provide the same degree of security (that is, be as hard to decrypt) as a single encryption key, public and private keys must be much longer than single encryption keys—anywhere from 768 to 2048 bits, versus key sizes in the neighborhood of 56 bits and up for a single encryption key. The difference is that single encryption keys are usually based on a single large prime number. Dual encryption keys are based on the product of two large prime numbers. One result of this fact is that it takes a lot more work for your computer to encrypt and decrypt information with the public and private keys than it would with a single encryption key.

Therefore, what dual-key authentication systems typically do is carry out the initial authentication process using the public and private keys. But then one of the parties generates a random single encryption key (called a session key because it will be discarded at the end of the session between the parties) and sends it, encrypted with the recipient's public key, to the second party, which decrypts it. Now both parties have an encryption key that they know could not have been compromised in transit. They can use this shorter key, if necessary, to encrypt further transmissions. (They still have to use their private keys to sign transmissions.)

This is also how mail encryption works. The sender generates an encryption key and encrypts the body of the message with it. Then the sender encrypts this key with the recipient's public key, attaches it to the message, and mails it. The recipient uses his private key to decrypt the encryption key and then uses that key to decrypt the body of the message.

One last thing: How do you decide whether to trust a third-party certifier? In the end, you just do. You are presented with the decision and you decide either that you will trust it or you won't. Okay, but how do you decide which way to go? That depends on who the third party is.

In the proprietary Notes authentication system, the certifier is your own organization. That's an easy one. Your organization certifier certified your own public key. When someone else presents you with his or her certificate, signed by the same certifier that signed your certificate, you pretty much have to trust the signature, and you do. In Notes, it's automatic. You and I don't have any say in the matter.

In a public system such as that represented by the Secure Sockets Layer standard, the certifying authority (CA) may again be your own organization, or it might be a true third party, a company that certifies public keys for a fee. With these companies there are two measures of trustworthiness:

- The integrity of the private keys they use to sign certificates
- The procedures that CAs use to positively identify the entities to which they issue certificates and to revoke certificates that later become compromised

The integrity of the whole public/private key system depends on these things. First, a CA's root private keys must be protected at all costs from theft, unauthorized use, loss, or other compromise. If, for example, a CA's private key is stolen, certificates signed by it are no longer trustworthy, because they could be signed by the stolen copy.

Second, the CA must strive not to issue certificates to impostors. If the CA negligently issues a certificate to Rob Kirkland that says the enclosed public key is assigned to "Bill Clinton," the trustworthiness of all certificates issued by that CA is in doubt. The CA should also have procedures in place for revoking certificates issued by it that later become compromised.

Typically, commercial CAs such as Verisign (www.verisign.com), EnTrust (www.entrust.com), and Thawte (www.thawte.com) publish their procedures for issuing certificates. They also offer certificates affording varying degrees of assurance. You can pay for the degree of assurance that suits you. They also issue different kinds of certificates to different kinds of entities for differing fees. You'll get one kind of certificate for your Web servers, another kind for developers, and yet another kind for individual users.

The certificate you get for your Web server may be, say, of Class X or Class Y. Class X is based on, say, your affidavit that your server belongs to your company. Class Y, on the other hand, is based on your presenting a signed corporate resolution, posting a bond, and standing on your head. It requires more proof of identity and costs more money, but it provides more assurance of identity. Class X may be sufficient for some purposes, such as setting up an e-lemonade stand. But for your electronic bank payments clearing house, maybe a Class Y certificate is the way to go.

The preceding explanation was intended to convey the general concept of how certificate-based authentication schemes work. If you want to know more, the best source I know of to find out everything there is to know about electronic cryptography systems in general is the Web site of RSA Data Security, Incorporated (www.rsa.com). RSA holds the patent (which expires in the year 2000) on the dual-key encryption system described previously. The RSA cryptosystem forms the basis of almost every commercial dual-key-based security system in existence today, including Notes's proprietary system, the SSL standard, and the S/MIME system. The RSA Laboratories' FAQ (www.rsa.com/rsalabs/faq), which you can read online or download, includes everything you never wanted to know not only about the RSA cryptosystem but about every other publicly described encryption system extant.

How Notes Proprietary Authentication Works

Notes proprietary authentication works in general just as described in the preceding section. In particular, all Notes servers and users belong to an organization. The organization is named /*OrganizationName* and is embodied in a small, insignificant-looking binary file called the Organization Certifier ID. By default this file is named cert.id. It is encrypted with a password and contains the following items:

- The organization's name, optionally in more than one language
- The organization's private and public keys
- A self-signed certificate (that is, issued to itself by itself) in two versions: North American and International. The International version complies with U.S. export laws.

- An expiration date for the certificates. By default the certificates expire 100 years from their creation date. In R5 you can recertify an organization certifier ID; when you do, the default expiration dates for the recertification are only two years into the future. I suspect this is unintentional behavior and will be fixed in a later version.
- Optional encryption keys
- Optional comments

Access to the ID file is protected by a password. You can lock it up even tighter by requiring more than one password to open it up. Like all ID files it is protected from attempts to guess the password by a time delay that gets progressively longer after each failed attempt to enter the password. Finally, it tries to foil password-spoofing programs by generating a pattern of hieroglyphics that is unique to each password. The idea is that it would be very difficult to write a program that would mimic the pattern of hieroglyphics and the user would know something was wrong when the spoofing program failed.

When you register an organizational unit, a server, or a person with the organization ID file, Domino Administrator generates an ID file for the new entity as well as public and private keys for it. It creates a certificate signed by the private key of the organization certifier and puts that certificate, as well as a copy of the certifier's own certificate into the new ID file.

If you registered a new organizational unit (a level-one OU, or OU1), its name is /OU1name/organizationname. If you then use that organizational unit certifier ID to create a lower-level ID (another OU, a server, or a person), Domino Administrator uses *that* certifier's private key to sign the certificate of the new entity. It puts the new certificate in the new ID file, along with copies of the certifying OU's certificates and the originating organization certifier's certificate.

The point here is that an entity's (person's, server's, or organizational unit's) ID contains not only its own certificate, signed by its parent certifier, but also copies of all the certificates of its ancestors. During authentication, a user or server sends copies of all of the certificates in its ID file to the other entity. The other compares those to the certificates in its own ID file, and will trust any presented certificate whose own pedigree can be traced back to any of its own ancestor certifiers. For example, server S1 in Figure 10.1 will trust the public keys of server S2 and users U1 and U2, because all of their public keys are certified by descendants of the same ancestral certifier.

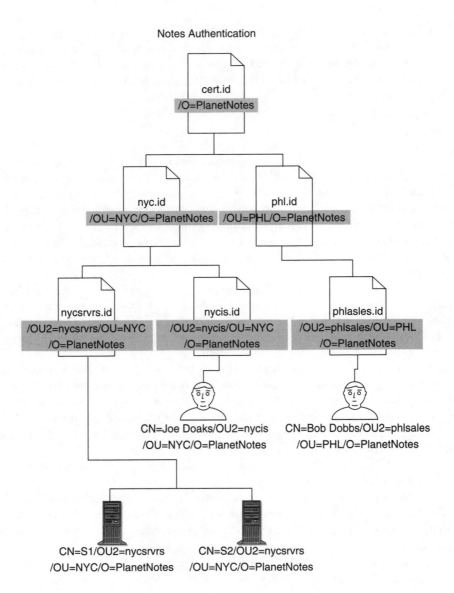

Figure 10.1 S1 and S2 can authenticate because they both descend from nycsrvrs. S1 and Joe Doaks can authenticate because they both descend from NYC. S1 and Bob Dobbs can authenticate because they both descend from PlanetNotes.

How Notes Cross-Certification Works

What's nice about basic Notes authentication is that two entities descendant from the same certifier can always present to each other certificates that the other will trust. It happens automatically. But this automatic quality disappears if two entities belong to different organizations. Because they don't descend from the same ancestral organization certifier, they can't automatically present trustable certificates to each other. So we have to find some other way for them to trust each other.

The way we do that is to have each entity issue a special certificate (which we call a cross-certificate) in favor of the other one. To authenticate each other, each needs to locate a certificate associating the other's name and public key and signed by an entity it can trust. In a cross-certificate we have just that. Only, instead of the certificate being carried around by the other entity in its ID file and presented at authentication time, the issuing party stores the cross-certificate in its own Directory. When the other party comes knocking, the issuing party already has a certificate in the other's favor—the cross-certificate—and can authenticate the other on that basis.

What's really great about cross-certificates is that the authenticating party (server or user) can issue them, or any of its ancestors can issue them. Because the authenticating party trusts its ancestors, it will trust cross-certificates issued by them. In addition, the issuer of a cross-certificate can issue it in favor of the other authenticating party (server or user) or in favor of any of its ancestors. Because the other party can trace its pedigree to an ancestor in whose favor a trusted cross-certificate exists, I can trust the other party.

To sum it up, I or any of my ancestors can issue a cross-certificate in favor of you or any of your ancestors. On the basis of that cross-certificate I can authenticate you. Likewise, if you or any of your ancestors issues a cross-certificate in favor of me or any of my ancestors, you can authenticate me. Now we've authenticated each other; let's do business.

In case I explained this so eloquently that the most important fact slid right by you, I'll point out here that, for you and me to be able to transact business, I have to authenticate you, and you have to authenticate me. If only one of us authenticates the other, we can't do business. If only one of us issues a certificate in favor of the other, we can't both authenticate each other. I or my ancestor must issue a certificate in favor of you or your ancestor; *and* you or your ancestor must issue a certificate in favor of me or my ancestor. There. I've beaten it into the ground.

The only remaining issue is: At which level in my organization should I issue the cross-certificate? And in favor of which level in yours? The general rule is that the issuer and beneficiary should be as low in their respective hierarchies as possible, consistent with meeting the objective of the cross-certification. In other words, if you can meet your objectives by having two servers cross-certify each other, don't cross-certify the server OUs or the organizations.

The consequences of cross-certification at given levels are as follows:

- If a server or user issues the cross-certificate, only that entity will honor it.

- If an O or OU certifier issues a cross-certificate, all of its descendants will honor it because they all trust its signature.

- If a cross-certificate issues in favor of a server or user, only that entity can authenticate under its authority.

- If a cross-certificate issues in favor of an O or OU certifier, all of its descendants can authenticate under the cross-certificate's authority, because the issuer of the cross-certificate trusts certificates issued by the beneficiary O or OU and its descendant OUs. If the issuer is itself an O or OU, its descendants also trust certificates issued by the beneficiary O or OU and its descendant OUs.

If these rules make sense to you, you can figure out from the circumstances of any situation at which levels in the organization a cross-certificate should be issued, and in favor of which levels of the beneficiary organization. Let's look at some examples.

Say that two organizations want to transfer email back and forth. They need two servers to authenticate and route mail to each other. The two servers are the only entities that need to authenticate across the organization boundary. So each server should issue a cross-certificate in favor of the other server. There's no need to cross-certify at any higher level in the hierarchy, so we don't do it.

Now say that a consultant, Joe Doaks/PlanetNotes, needs to authenticate with all of the servers in /Servers/Stillwater. Nobody else in /PlanetNotes needs access to Stillwater servers, and nobody in /Stillwater needs access to PlanetNotes servers. Joe Doaks should issue a cross-certificate in favor of /Servers/Stillwater, and /Servers/ Stillwater should issue in favor of Joe Doaks/PlanetNotes. Joe will trust certificates issued by /Servers/Stillwater and therefore will trust Osprey/Servers/Stillwater and Kestrel/Servers/Stillwater. Those servers, in turn, trust certificates issued by /Servers/ Stillwater and so can now trust Joe. But they don't trust Bob Dobbs/PlanetNotes, because no trusted certificate exists on his behalf. Likewise, Bob Dobbs doesn't trust them for the same reason; issuance by Joe doesn't count, because Joe isn't Bob's ancestor.

Finally, let's say that Stillwater and PlanetNotes merge with each other. Now we want all users and servers in each organization to be able to authenticate with all servers in the other organization. We can have /PlanetNotes issue a cross-certificate in favor of /Stillwater, and vice versa. Now all entities in each organization have a basis for trusting all entities in the other organization.

If you understood all of this, then all that's left to learn is how to issue cross-certificates. There are five ways:

- **By email.** The intended beneficiary of the cross-certificate emails a safe copy of its ID to someone in the other organization who can issue the cross-certificate. The safe ID contains the intended beneficiary's correct name and public key, which are just what the issuer of the cross-certificate needs to certify. The issuer extracts that information from the safe ID, issues the cross-certificate and, no longer having a need for the safe ID, discards it.

- **By courier.** The only difference between this method and the first is that the safe ID is copied to a floppy disk and hand-carried to the other organization's representative.

- **By telephone.** Administrators from each organization get on the phone with each other. They dictate the names of the beneficiaries and their public keys to each other—carefully, with no typos.

- **From a Person document.** If you have access to a Domino Directory containing Person documents of entities in another Notes organization, you can create cross-certificates on the basis of the public keys stored in people's Person documents.

- **On demand.**.Occasionally Notes will be unable to authenticate an entity—a user or a server—from another organization. When that happens, Notes will pop up the Create Cross Certificate dialog box, which offers to issue a cross-certificate in favor of that entity. If you are confident that the other entity is genuinely the one he/she/it purports to be, you can issue a cross-certificate on his/her/its behalf simply by choosing Yes or Advanced. If you are not sure of the identity of the entity, you can choose No.

Of these five methods, the most popular are by email and on demand, because they are the easiest. By phone is the least popular, because you have to enter the information manually, and because nobody is quite sure which key to dictate to the other fellow. (Hint: It's the Primary Key on the Basics screen of the ID dialog box.)

Cross-Certifying by Email

To cross-certify by email, you initiate the transaction by emailing the safe ID of the entity to be cross-certified to someone in the other organization capable of issuing the necessary cross-certificate. To generate the email, follow these steps:

1. Choose File, Tools, User ID, and then enter your password. Your own ID appears.

2. Choose Certificates. Choose Request Cross Certificate. The Choose ID by Cross-Certified dialog box appears.

3. Choose a user's, server's, or O or OU certifier's certificate, and then choose Open. The Mail Cross Certificate Request dialog box opens.

4. Enter the email address of the person who will issue the cross-certificate—for example, the administrator of the other organization. You can also choose an email address from a directory by choosing Address. Optionally, you can add text to the Subject field. Choose Send when finished. Close the dialog box for your user ID.

If you are the addressee of a message of this sort, you can issue the cross-certificate by opening the message and then choosing Cross Certify Attached ID File in the Actions menu. The Choose Certifier ID dialog box will open, where you will have to choose the ID file of the entity that will issue the cross-certificate. It can be your own ID file or that of a server or an OU or O certifier in your organization. Choose Open and enter the password of the certifying ID. The Issue Cross Certificate dialog box opens, as shown in Figure 10.2. You can complete the fields as described in Table 10.2 and then choose Cross Certify.

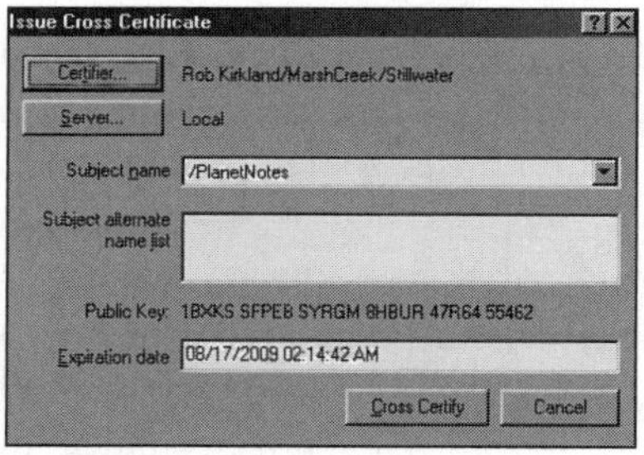

Figure 10.2   This dialog box allows you to choose which entity will issue a cross-certificate, and which entity will benefit from it.

Table 10.2   **Fields in the Issue Cross Certificate Dialog Box**

Field	Description
Certifier	Click this button if you chose the wrong ID to issue the cross-certificate. You'll have an opportunity to choose again.
Server	Here you can choose the location of the directory or address book in which the issued cross-certificate will be stored. If you are issuing the cross-certificate personally (using your own Person ID), choose Local. Otherwise, choose the name of a server in the certifier's Notes domain.
Subject name	Here you can choose to issue in favor of the entity whose safe ID you received or any of his/her/its ancestor certifiers. For example, if you received the safe ID of Joe Doaks/MarshCreek/Stillwater, you can issue in favor of Joe or /MarshCreek/Stillwater or /Stillwater.

Field	Description
Subject alternate name list	This isn't an editable field. It displays the alternate names of the subject. The cross-certificate will issue in favor of the entity under all of its names.
Expiration date	Defaults to 10 years from today's date. Change it if you want.

When you choose Cross Certify, Notes (or Domino Administrator) issues a cross-certificate and stores it in the Domino Directory of the server chosen in the Server field or in your Personal Address Book if you chose Local in the Server field.

Cross-Certifying by Courier

By "courier," I mean by physical means instead of electronic means. The party requesting the cross-certificate delivers the safe ID to be certified by floppy disk. If you are the requesting party, you initiate the transaction by creating a safe ID from the ID to be cross-certified. Do so as follows:

1. If you are requesting a cross-certificate for yourself, choose File, Tools, User ID, and then enter your password. If you are requesting for a server or an OU or O certifier, open the Configuration screen in Domino Administrator and choose ID Properties in Tools, Certification or in the menu under Configuration, Certification; then choose the ID and enter its password.

2. Choose More Options. Choose Create Safe Copy. The Enter Safe Copy ID File Name dialog box appears.

3. Choose a location for the safe copy—perhaps drive A:. Enter a filename or accept the default filename (`safe.id`). Choose Save.

4. Send the safe copy of the ID to the person in the other organization who will issue the cross-certificate.

If you receive a floppy disk that holds a safe ID to be cross-certified, you'll follow these steps:

1. Place the disk in a drive on your workstation. Start Domino Administrator, go to the Configuration screen, and choose Cross Certify under Tools, Certification (or in the menu under Configuration, Certification).

2. The Choose Certifier ID dialog box opens. Here you'll choose the ID file of the entity (yourself, a server, or an OU or O certifier) that will issue the cross-certificate. The big mistake that everyone makes here is to choose the safe ID. Read the title of the dialog box. It tells you which ID to choose—the one that will certify or the one that will be certified. Choose Open. Enter the password of the chosen certifying ID.

3. The Choose ID to be Cross-Certified dialog box opens. *Now* choose the safe ID. Choose Open.

4. The Issue Cross Certificate dialog box opens. Fill in the fields as described in Table 10.2. Then choose Cross Certify.

Notes (or Domino Administrator) now creates a cross-certificate and stores it in the Domino Directory of the server chosen in the Server field or in your Personal Address Book if you chose Local in the Server field.

Cross-Certifying by Telephone

1. The administrator requesting cross-certification opens the ID file of the entity (person, server, or OU or O certifier) to be cross-certified.

2. The administrator doing the cross-certifying opens Domino Administrator to the Configuration screen and then chooses Tools, Certification, Cross Certify Key. The Choose Certifier ID dialog box opens. The administrator chooses the certifying ID file, chooses Open, and enters the password of the chosen ID file. The Issue Cross Certificate dialog box opens.

3. The certifying administrator can change the Certifier, Server, and Expiration date fields (see Table 10.2) for an explanation. But the contents of the Subject name and Public Key fields will come over the phone from the requesting administrator.

4. The requesting administrator reads the name of the entity to be cross-certified from the Names field on the Basics screen of the User ID dialog box. The certifying administrator enters the information into the Subject name field.

5. The requesting administrator reads the public key information of the entity to be cross-certified from the Primary Key field on the Basics screen of the User ID dialog box. The certifying administrator enters the information in the Public Key field.

6. The requesting administrator closes the User ID dialog box. The certifying administrator chooses Cross Certify. Notes generates the cross-certificate.

7. The parties may now reverse roles and repeat the process.

Cross-Certifying from a Person Document

If you have access to the Person document of the person you want to cross-certify (this method doesn't work for servers or certifiers), you can open it and then choose Create Cross Certificate in the Actions menu. If the person to be cross-certified has a North American license, you will be prompted to choose between the North American and International keys. The Issue Cross Certificate dialog box will appear. You can set the fields as described in Table 10.2. Your own ID is the default Certifier. Your own address book is the default Server. When you choose Cross Certify, Notes will create the cross-certificate.

Cross-Certifying on Demand

Acting as a user, an administrator in the first organization tries to authenticate with a server in the second organization. In the process, the server sends certificates to the administrator. If the administrator doesn't yet have in his Personal Address Book a cross-certificate in favor of the server, Notes presents the Create Cross Certificate dialog box to the administrator. This dialog offers to issue the necessary cross-certificate (see Figure 10.3). Notes can issue a certificate because, due to the attempt at authentication, it has possession of the server's name and public key. This method works only for a user. The server at the other end has the user's name and public key too, but it can't make the decision whether to issue a cross-certificate, because it's only a computer. So it simply refuses to authenticate.

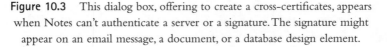

Figure 10.3 This dialog box, offering to create a cross-certificates, appears when Notes can't authenticate a server or a signature. The signature might appear on an email message, a document, or a database design element.

The message presented to the administrator by the Create Cross Certificate dialog box says, in effect: We don't have a cross-certificate in favor of Server X; may I issue one now, and store it in our Personal Address Book? (Refer to Figure 10.3.) The administrator can choose Yes, No, Advanced, or Help.

If the administrator chooses Yes, the administrator issues a cross-certificate in favor of the server's organization, not the server itself. And the cross-certificate resides in the administrator's Personal Address Book. This would be okay if the administrator wants to set up personal cross-certification of the server's organization. But this won't do if the administrator wants to set up cross-certification of just the server or by his own organization. For that, the administrator must choose Advanced.

If the administrator chooses No, a message will appear reiterating that the administrator has no cross-certificate in favor of the server, but offering to connect to the server without requiring authentication. If the administrator now chooses Yes, and the server is able to authenticate the administrator, the administrator is in business, but just for this session. The next time the administrator tries to connect to the same server, the same set of dialogs will appear. If the administrator chooses No in the second dialog, Notes refuses to open a session with the server. If the administrator chooses Yes in either the first or second mentioned dialogs, but the server can't authenticate the user, the server will refuse to open a session with the user.

If the administrator chooses Advanced, the dialog box becomes the standard Issue Cross Certificate dialog (refer to Figure 10.2). Here the administrator has complete control of the following:

- Which entity (himself, a server, or an OU or O certifier) issues the cross-certificate
- In favor of which entity (the server or any of its ancestor certifiers) the cross-certificate issues
- On which server the new cross-certificate is initially stored
- The expiration date of the cross-certificate

Refer to Table 10.2 for details about your choices in the Issue Cross Certificate dialog box.

How SSL Authentication Works

Whereas the primary purpose of Notes authentication is to provide each party with positive identification of the other party, this is only a secondary and optional purpose of SSL security. The primary goal of SSL security is to allow two parties to communicate over public networks privately and securely. Accordingly, an SSL session works differently than a Notes session. It starts when a client requests an SSL session by communicating with the server over an SSL port. The server sends its certificate and cipher preferences to the client. Cipher preferences are the types of encryption the server supports.

The client optionally accepts the certificate at face value or validates it by determining whether it can trust its signer. (If the client cannot validate the certificate, it may choose to end the session or to waive validation.) If the client accepts the certificate without validating it, the client is, in effect, not bothering to authenticate the server. The server will go ahead with the second phase of authentication and prove that it has the companion private key, but that alone does not constitute authentication.

The client next generates a master key, encrypts it with the server's public key (extracted from the certificate), and sends it to the server. The server decrypts the master key with its private key, authenticates (signs) a message with it, and sends the message to the client. The fact that the server is able to do this completes the server's authentication to the client; that is, it proves to the client that the server has the private key that corresponds to the public key it sent to the client. From this point until the end of the session, all transmissions between these parties are encrypted and authenticated with keys derived from the master key.

The next step, authentication of the client, is at the server's option. The server may not care who the client is, in which case the parties proceed with their session. If the server needs to know the client's identity, it may accept name and password credentials from the client or it may demand a certificate from the client. The way this works is that the server sends a challenge to the client. The client signs the challenge and returns it to the server along with its certificate. The server validates the certificate and uses the public key in it to verify the client's signature.

To use SSL at all, an entity (server or client program) must create a public/private key pair and submit an unsigned certificate (containing the entity's name and public key) to a certificate authority (CA) for certification. You may do this any number of ways, but at least part of the process typically involves submitting information to the CA by filling in a form on the CA's Web site. The CA signs the certificate and then returns it to the requestor by email or posting it on its Web site for the requestor to retrieve. If the certified entity is a Domino server, it retrieves the certificate and merges it into a *keyring* file (`filename.kyr`), which is analogous to the Notes ID file. If the certified entity is a person, the certificate may end up any number of places—one or more Web browsers, mail readers, or, if the person is a Notes user, in his ID file alongside his Notes certificates.

Like a Notes certificate, an SSL certificate contains the certified entity's name, a copy of the certified entity's public key, and an expiration date. It may also contain information about how the certificate can be used. For example, it may be another CA certificate, usable to certify public keys. This is analogous to creating a Notes OU certificate. Or it may be a server certificate or a developer's certificate, usable to sign programs, or an individual user's certificate, usable to authenticate with servers under SSL and/or to sign and encrypt email under the S/MIME standard. All such certificates are formatted according to the international standard known as X.509. They are therefore sometimes referred to as X.509 certificates.

Later in the chapter you can read in detail about how to administer SSL on Domino servers and in Notes workstations. But first we'll continue with our survey of Domino and Notes security features.

Server Security

If it is properly configured, Domino is one of the most secure data management platforms you can buy. But it's only as secure as the systems underlying it. You need to secure both the underlying systems and Domino itself. Securing a Domino server includes the following aspects:

- Physical security
- Network security
- Operating system security
- Domino server access controls

Physical Security, Network Security, and Operating System Security

The first three items in the preceding list are mostly things you can do outside of Domino to keep people from bypassing Domino's internal security barriers—that is, to keep people from hacking into Notes databases. There are two ways that you can bypass Domino security features on an unsecured server. First, on a Windows-based server, if you can gain physical access to the Domino server, you can use a local copy of Notes to bypass most Domino and Notes security features—all except enforcement of a uniform access control list on a database and data encryption. (You can do that on OS/2- and UNIX-based servers too, if you are willing to use an R4.5.x or older client.) Second, if you can gain access to the file system in which Domino stores its databases, you can copy the databases to a remote system and then gain local access to them there. So it is imperative that you secure your Domino servers physically, that you secure access to the network, and that you secure the operating systems of the computers they run on.

Physical security. Physical security generally means keeping your servers under lock and key. It can also mean locking or removing keyboards. It is also possible to lock the Domino console. The command `set secure` *password* makes it impossible to issue certain commands from the server's console. Those commands include `load`, `tell`, `exit`, `quit`, and `set configuration`.

Actually, you can enter the `exit` and `quit` commands by appending *password*—that is, by entering `quit` *password* or `exit` *password*. To enter the other commands you have to reenter the `set secure` *password* command to unlock the console.

You can also change the console password by entering `set secure` *oldpassword newpassword*. Finally, you can break the password as follows:

1. Open `notes.ini` in a text editor, find the SERVER_CONSOLE_PASSWORD variable, and delete it. Save and close `notes.ini`.

2. Force Domino down using whatever tools for that purpose the server operating system provides. Under Windows and OS/2 you can just hit the power switch. Under UNIX you can use the `kill` command. (Interestingly, only NetWare, which Lotus stopped supporting in R5, does not provide a way to force Domino down and bypass server console security.)

3. Restart Domino. The console is no longer secure.

Network security. Securing the network means keeping malicious people and programs off of it. You should maintain a secure firewall to keep outsiders off of your private LAN. This may include things like enabling call-back on your dialup servers. You should maintain up-to-date anti-virus software to keep malicious programs off of your LAN. You should use the standard tools that your network OS provides for maintaining tight security. These may include requirements that users use passwords and change them periodically. They may also include security auditing programs included with your network OS. You might also want to hire consultants to perform security audits for you. Finally, you should educate your users regarding the scams people might use to trick them into revealing their passwords.

If you feel a Domino server is particularly vulnerable at any of these levels, there are two things you can do at the database level to protect your data. First, you can set the advanced database access control property called Enforce a consistent Access Control List across all replicas of this database. Second, you can encrypt your data.

Enforcing a consistent ACL causes Notes to enforce the access control list against the local user. When a consistent ACL is not enforced, only Domino enforces the Access Control List of a database. Notes users accessing local databases have full, Manager-equivalent access to them. However, Enforce a consistent ACL is a problematic feature of Notes. It's not always suitable to set this property, and even when it might be, many administrators shy away from it because it causes so many problems. (See a more detailed discussion of the problems involved later in this chapter.)

The second protection, encrypt ing sensitive data on the server, is both more effective and easier to work with. There are two ways you can do this.

First, you can encrypt individual fields using encryption keys designed just for that purpose. Only users who have a copy of the appropriate encryption key can gain access to the data in an encrypted field. For this to be an effective method of hiding data, it must be designed into a database. Therefore, whether this is available to you is pretty much out of your hands as a Domino administrator.

Second, you can encrypt whole databases. This is called *local database encryption*. If you have Manager access to a database, you can encrypt it. So, if you're an administrator, this is the method for you.

Of these two kinds of encryption, the one that is really intended for our purpose (of protecting the data from hackers) is local database encryption. To apply it to a database, see the procedure later in this chapter, in the section "Local Database Encryption."

Even if you locally encrypt a database on a server, a hacker can still access the data by logging into Notes using the server's ID. To protect against this, you can do one of two things.

First, you can password-protect the server's ID. Then the hacker would have to guess the password to gain access to the private key.

Second, you can set up the database ACL so that the server ID can't be used to access it. To do this, you have to assign user type Server or Server Group to the server's ACL entry. This disables the server ID for use within Notes.

Operating system security. Securing the underlying operating system generally means two things. First, you should prohibit access via the operating system to the Domino program and data folders. Only Domino itself and the user account under which it runs, if any, should have access to Domino's folders. Standard users should be locked out of those folders whether accessing the server locally or over the network. Not all operating systems on which Domino runs can be locked from local access (for example, OS/2, Windows 9x, and Windows NT's FAT file system). But to the extent you *can* lock users out, do it.

Second, you need to limit administrative access to the Domino machine as much as possible. Only personnel who need access to the Domino machine should know the administrative password. Just as important, you need to keep the operating system as up-to-date as possible, especially when it comes to applying patches to correct security breaches. With the free availability of programs like Back Orifice that open covert administrative back doors to your servers' operating systems, you must keep a vigilant eye out for security vulnerabilities, breaches, and fixes.

Domino Server Access Controls

Domino itself provides a variety of server-level controls that limit access to the server's data. They are not designed to thwart the hacker so much as the unauthorized Notes or non-Notes client. You need to examine each control and decide whether it is appropriate for your situation. Most of the controls are settings in server, server configuration, and Web configuration documents. You can set other controls in the server's notes.ini file.

Most server access controls reside in the server document. They include the items in Table 10.3. Many of these fields take the names of servers, people, and/or groups. In general, Lotus recommends that you use group names or wildcards such as */Stillwater instead of individual server or user names. Doing so allows you to restrict users and servers by adding them to or removing them from the constituent groups rather than the server fields. The benefit is that you can make changes without having to stop and restart the server. While Domino R5 is much better than earlier versions at polling the server document for changes, Lotus has not made it clear exactly how good Domino R5 is at this. In other words, I don't know what Server document changes the server knows about without a restart. You can avoid this whole issue if you simply use group names and wildcards in the server restriction fields. Descriptions of the relevant fields follow in Table 10.3.

Table 10.3 **Server Access Control Fields in the Server Document**

Field	Description
	ON THE BASICS TAB
Administrators	Enter one or more group names, wildcards representing OUs (for example, */IT/Stillwater), or individual administrator names, separated by commas. Administrators whose names appear here can perform the following tasks on the server: Enter commands at the server's remote console; Designate this server as Administrative server for databases; Compact databases; Manage full-text indexes; Manage directory and database links.

Field	Description
ON THE SECURITY TAB, UNDER SECURITY SETTINGS	
Compare Notes public keys against those stored in Directory	Defaults to No. See the discussion following this table to learn the consequences of enabling it.
Allow anonymous Notes connections	Defaults to No. Setting it to Yes allows Notes users to visit the server without initially authenticating. (But if they try to do something in a database not permitted of anonymous users, they will then have to authenticate.) Use this field to permit public access to a Domino server. For example, you might permit people participating in a public discussion on a Web server to use either their Web browser or Notes to read and write messages.
Check passwords on Notes Ids	Disabled by default. See the discussion following this table to learn the consequences of enabling it.
ON THE SECURITY TAB, UNDER SERVER ACCESS—WHO CAN	
Only allow server access to users listed in this Directory	Defaults to No. If you enable this field, only people who have Person documents in the server's Domino Directory will be permitted access to the server. In addition, only other servers listed in the Access server field will be permitted access to the server. So if you enable this field, be sure to populate the Access server field too, in such a way that all people and servers that should have access to this server do.
Access server	If left blank, this field allows all comers to access the server. If you enter any names, only those entities will be permitted access to the server. Use group names, wildcard entries (for example, */Stillwater), and individual names, separated by commas. Note that if you change the preceding field (Only allow server access to users listed in this Directory)to Yes, you *must* populate this field, or no servers will be able to access this server for any purpose.
Not access server	Blank by default. If you enter names here, this field takes precedence over all other fields and locks out the named entities out. Create one or more groups of type Deny List only and enter their names here. When you want to lock out a formerly authorized user of your servers, add the user to one of these groups.

continues

Table 10.3   **Continued**

Field	Description
ON THE SECURITY TAB, UNDER SERVER ACCESS—WHO CAN	
Create new databases	If left blank, anyone can create new databases on the server. Most administrators prefer to maintain control over this and enter group names here. If you add names here, be sure to add server group names, such as LocalDomainServers.
Create replica databases	If left blank, nobody can create replica databases on the server. This is usually undesirable. Add group names representing servers and administrators.
Allowed / Not allowed to use monitors	The first field defaults to *, and the second field defaults to blank. This means everyone can use monitors on this server. Monitors are documents representing users' database subscriptions. When a change occurs in a subscribed database, the monitor notifies the user. Monitors reside in the Headlines database on each Notes R5 workstation. If a lot of users subscribe to databases on a server, overall server performance can suffer. You can use these fields to limit who can subscribe to databases on this server. An entry in the Allowed field locks out everyone else. An entry in the Not allowed field locks out only those named.
Administer the server from a browser	Blank (default) means nobody can. Enter names of administrator groups to permit their members to use the Domino Web Administrator (R5) (`webadmin.nsf`) database from a browser to administer this server.
ON THE SECURITY TAB, UNDER AGENT RESTRICTIONS—WHO CAN	
Run personal agents	Blank (default) means everyone can run personal agents on this server. Adding names locks out all not included.
Run restricted/unrestricted LotusScript/Java agents	These two fields are blank by default, which means nobody can run them on this server. Add wildcard entries (for example, */Stillwater), groups, and individuals. If you add any names, be sure to add server groups (for example, LocalDomainServers) as well. Entities permitted to run unrestricted agents can, by inference, run restricted agents as well, whether or not they are included in the restricted field. Restricted agents cannot manipulate system time, perform file I/O, or access the operating system. See the Designer Help database for the precise list of restricted operations.

Field	Description
Web server authentication	The default, More name variations with lower security, uses R4 Web authentication rules. Fewer name variations with higher security uses R5 Web authentication rules. Choose the second option only if all directories searched by this server use the R5 Directory template. Both options allow Web users to authenticate by entering their hierarchical name, common name, or any alias name in their Person document's User name field. The first option also allows users to enter only their first name, only their last name, their shortname, or a soundex value (sounds like).
Access this server	Blank (the default) means nobody can access this server via passthru.
Route through	Blank (the default) means nobody can pass through this server to access another.
Cause calling	Blank (the default) means nobody can cause this server to dial up another server for passthru purposes.
Destinations allowed	Blank (the default) means anyone who can pass through this server can pass through to any reachable server. If you want to restrict passthru destinations, enter the names of servers (or groups holding their names) allowed to be accessed via this server. Passthru will be denied to all other servers.
Run restricted/unrestricted Java/JavaScript	The same rules apply to these fields as to the restricted/unrestricted LotusScript/Java agents fields.

Locking Out Compromised IDs

Two of the fields in the Server document have special significance. They are Compare Notes public keys against those stored in Directory and Check passwords on Notes IDs. They warrant more discussion than the other fields.

As powerful as certificate-based authentication is, it has the weakness that private keys don't always stay private. In fact, it is pretty easy for people to get hold of IDs that belong to others and use them for unauthorized purposes. It is also not that hard in many organizations for administrators to misuse organization and organizational unit certifier IDs. In fact, if in most organizations abuses don't take place, the probable reason is because most people have honest intentions, and the dishonest ones don't realize how much damage they could do by stealing IDs.

Two fields in the Server document are there primarily to help you combat the consequences of compromised ID files. They are Compare Notes public keys against those stored in Directory and Check passwords on Notes Ids. Between them, I recommend you use the second one and ignore the first.

Compare Notes public keys against those stored in Directory. The normal behavior of a server when it authenticates another server or user is to accept and use the public key that it receives from the other entity. As long as the certificate in which the public key arrived was signed by a trusted certifier and the other entity can prove that it has the corresponding private key, the server is satisfied. But if the other entity's ID has been compromised, it may be that an impostor is authenticating. This field allows you to lock known impostors out of a server.

When you enable this field, the server does not accept the public keys in proffered certificates at face value. Instead, it compares them to the public keys that are stored in the Domino Directory. If they aren't the same public key, the server refuses to proceed further with authentication.

So, for example, if you know that a user's ID has been stolen, you can issue that user a new public key. You can put a copy of the new public key into the user's Person document. Then you can enable this field. The next time the impostor (using a copy of the ID that contains the old public key) tries to authenticate with the server, the server locks him out.

There are a couple of drawbacks to enabling this field, however. First, you don't benefit from it if you don't issue new public keys to users whose IDs have been compromised. This is a problem because, first, you may not know that a given ID has been compromised and, second, issuing a new public key is a hassle. Second, this field has the side effect of locking out of the server all potential users and servers who don't have a Person or Server document in the Domino Directory. (If that's your goal, there's a much easier way to do that—use the Access server field.)

Because of these problems, Lotus went back to the drawing board and came up with a better solution, the Check passwords on Notes IDs field.

Check passwords on Notes Ids. By enabling this field, you can accomplish the same goal—lockout of compromised IDs—much more effectively and with less bother than with the Compare Notes public keys against those stored in Directory field. When you enable the Check passwords on Notes Ids field, Notes clients (R4.5 and later) create a *digest* from the password on their ID files and send the digest to the server along with their certificates.

The server stores the password digest in the user's Person document. Each time thereafter that the user logs in, the server compares the newly received password digest with the one originally stored in the Person document. If they are the same, the server authenticates the user. If the user changes the password on the ID file, the server stores the new password digest in the user's Person document and retains the first. (The server retains the last 50 passwords, so users won't be able to reuse passwords for a long time.)

If a user ever tries to enter an old (not current) password, the server refuses to accept the password and directs the user to change the password to the current one. If the user trying to enter the old password is not the same person who changed the password to the current one, the user won't know the current password, won't be able to change it, and won't be able to authenticate. If the user who can't authenticate is an unauthorized user of that ID file, he is now out of luck. If the user is the authorized user and an unauthorized user changed the password on him, the administrator can clear the password digests from his Person document, and the user can then set a new password and then log in to the server. The unauthorized user will be blocked the next time he tries to log in.

Other nice aspects of enabling password checking on a server are that you can specify a Required change interval and a Grace period. Toward the end of the required change interval, the server will remind the user to change his password. At the end of the number of days in the required change interval, the server will lock the user out until the user changes his password. If the user does not change his password within the grace period, the user will no longer be able to get into the server, even if he does change his password; he will require administrator intervention.

There are two benefits here. First, if someone compromises an ID and you don't know about it, that person will automatically be locked out of the server after the expiration of the required change interval and grace period, if not sooner (when the legitimate user changes the password). Second, inactive users will be locked out automatically with the expiration of their grace periods.

To enable password checking, you have to enable it both in the server document of each server that should check passwords and in the Person document of each person whose passwords will be checked. To set up Person documents for password checking, select as many of them in the People view as you want. Then, in the Actions menu, choose Set Password Fields. In the dialog box that appears, set the Check password field, the Required change interval field, and the Grace period field, and then choose OK. This generates a Change User Password in Address Book request in the Administration Requests database. The Administration Server for the Domino Directory will carry out the request as soon as the request document replicates to it.

An interesting note about the Check password field in the Person document is that, in addition to setting it to Check password and Don't check password, you can also set it to Lockout ID. If you set the field to Lockout ID, that user will not be able to log in to any server in the domain that checks passwords. This is an alternate way to lock inactive users out of your servers (the other way being to add them to an Inactive Users group, which you in turn add to the Not access server field in the server document).

Lotus suggests you use this method if you are concerned about users seeing who is in the Inactive Users group. However, for two reasons, I prefer to use the Not access server field to lock users out. First, it locks users out of all servers in the domain, not just the servers that check passwords. Second, it locks out users who don't have a Person document in the Domain Directory. Finally, you can hide the Inactive Users group from the view of non-administrative users by setting it to group type Deny List only. When you do that, it will appear only in the Deny Access Groups view, which only administrators can see. (Of course, users can create personal views in which the Deny List groups would appear, but only your more knowledgeable Notes users will know how to do that.)

Database Security

After a user has passed through the server-level security barriers, he next has to pass through a series of database-level security measures. Database security includes the following aspects:

- The database access control list
- Form, view, and document security
- Section and field security
- Local database encryption

A user's broadest possible rights of access to the contents of a database are set forth in each database's access control list. The other security features listed here serve to limit a user's rights even further, not to broaden them.

The Database Access Control List

The database access control list is the linchpin of database access control in Notes. All other database access controls simply refine the limits set by the ACL. You can access the ACL of any database by opening it and then choosing Database, Access Control in the File menu. Alternatively, you can right-click a database bookmark and then choose Database, Access Control in the popup menu. The ACL, as organized in its dialog box, is divided into four parts: Basics, Roles, Log, and Advanced. Most of the action is in the Basics screen (see Figure 10.4).

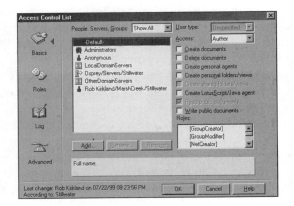

Figure 10.4   When you select a user in the list, the other fields display that user's access rights. In the figure, -Default- is selected.

The User List

The centerpiece of the Basics screen is the list of users. You can select any user in the list, and the other fields show that user's access rights. The first user in every ACL is -Default-. The rights assigned to -Default- are the rights of all users not otherwise named in the user list. The other users can be any of the following:

- **People.** Individuals can be listed by their hierarchical name, their common name if they are members of the same hierarchical organization as the server on which they are accessing the database, or their alternate name if you use them. Lotus recommends that you make a habit of using people's hierarchical or alternate names, not common names. Of course, some users (for example, Internet users) won't have full hierarchical names.

- **Servers.** Servers can be listed by their hierarchical name or their common name if they are members of the same hierarchical organization as the host server. Lotus recommends that you make a habit of using servers' hierarchical, not common, names.

- **Wildcard entries.** You can list whole organizations or organizational units by wildcarding them (for example, */Stillwater or */MarshCreek/Stillwater).

- **Groups.** You can enter the names of groups listed in the local Domino Directory or in LDAP directories that have been set up for group expansion in a Directory Assistance database. Using groups gives you great flexibility in managing ACL rights. For example, by giving a user the right to change the membership of a group that has Reader access to a database, you give that user control over what user can read the database, without actually giving the user the right to change the ACL itself.

- **Anonymous.** You can create an entry called Anonymous that covers all unauthenticated users.

- **Database replica Ids.** This permits agents in other databases to access this database to perform lookups, updates, and other activities.

When ACL Rights Conflict

It is possible for a user to appear in the ACL more than once; not only could a user be named individually, but the user could also have membership in one or more listed groups. The rules of precedence for multiply listed users are as follows:

- If a user is a member of more than one listed group, the user gets the higher set of rights, as long as the user is not a member of a group listed with No Access.

- If a user is listed individually, the rights assigned under that listing take precedence over all other rights except No Access rights assigned to a group of which the user is a member.

- If a user is a member of any group listed as having No Access to the database, the user has no access, no matter what rights the user may have under other listings.

The Seven Levels of Database Access

Each user's basic level of access rights appears in the Access field in the upper-right corner of the dialog box. There are seven possible access levels. From highest to lowest, they are Manager, Designer, Editor, Author, Reader, Depositor, and No Access. Each is described in Table 10.4. The rights at each level are, in general, cumulative; they include all rights of the lower access levels unless such rights are specifically excluded (see Reader); and they exclude rights allowed to higher access levels unless such rights are specifically included (see Editor).

Table 10.4   **Lotus Notes Database Access Rights**

Access Level	Activities Allowed
Manager	Can make changes in the ACL; encrypt the database; modify replication settings; and delete the database. Can also perform all tasks allowed at the lower levels.
Designer	Can read, create, and modify design documents; create a full-text index; and modify replication formulas. Can also perform all tasks allowed at the lower levels.
Editor	Can create new documents, read existing documents, and edit existing documents. Can be given the right to create shared views and folders, a right that is normally reserved to Designers and Managers.
Author	Can create new documents (but only if also assigned the Create document right) and read existing documents. Contrary to a widespread misconception, Authors cannot modify existing documents, even those they authored, unless they are listed in a document in a field of Authors data type either individually or by inclusion in a listed group. If they are so listed, they can edit such documents whether they authored them or not.
Reader	Can read existing documents but cannot create or modify documents, except, optionally, documents assigned the Public property.
Depositor	Can create new documents but cannot read or edit existing documents. However, Depositors can be given the rights to see elements of a database that are assigned the Public property, and to create or modify documents with forms assigned the Public property.
No Access	Generally, not allowed to open a database. However, these users, too, can be given the rights to see elements of a database that are assigned the Public property, and to create documents with forms assigned the Public property.

The Five User Types

Whenever you add a new user to a database ACL, you should also assign a user type. Doing so closes potential security holes. The five user types are Person, Server, Mixed group, Person group, and Server group. A mixed group is any group consisting of people and servers. If you leave an entry unspecified as to user type, it is possible for a user to gain higher access to the database than that to which he is entitled. The two potential problems are as follows:

- **User ID and group have the same name.** If the common name in a user ID is the same as a group name, the server could mistakenly give a user logging in with that ID the rights of the group. Assigning the group one of the group user types in the ACL prevents this from happening, because the server would then know that the ACL entry refers to a group, not a user, and would know not to give the group's rights to a user of the same name. But if the user type is unspecified, the server has no way of knowing whether an entry is supposed to be a user or a group, and so gives the rights to any entity of that name that comes along.

- **A person logs in using a server's ID file.** Servers often have very high rights in a database. If a server is listed in the ACL of a database with unspecified user type, a user could log in using the server's ID and gain the server's access rights to the database. The server would give the user the other server's ACL rights because it has no way of knowing the listing in the ACL is really a server, not a person. Assigning the server to user type Server in the ACL blocks this abuse, because now the host server knows that a user logged in with a server's ID can't really be the server, because servers don't have fingers and servers don't use Notes to communicate with other servers. Because the host server doesn't know who the user really is, it gives the user Default access to the database instead of the server's designated access.

If a database ACL already has numerous entries in it and their user types are unspecified, you can assign user types to them en masse by clicking the Look Up User Types for 'Unspecified' User button on the Advanced ACL screen. The server looks up the user type of each entry in the Domino Directory. It can't tell if a group's membership is servers, users, or both, so it assigns Mixed group to all groups.

Optional Privileges

On the right side of the Basics screen of the ACL dialog box are eight optional privileges that can be assigned to users. Which ones are assignable depends on the user's basic access level. At a given basic access level, some privileges may be automatically assigned and not removable (grayed out with a checkmark), automatically assigned but removable (not grayed out, but with a checkmark), not assigned but assignable (not grayed out, not checked), or not assignable (grayed out, not checked). The optional privileges are as follows:

- **Create documents.** This only affects users with Author access. For them it is checked by default. If you remove the checkmark, the user would not be able to create new documents but could edit existing documents if his name appeared in an Authors field on the document. The is the default access of the Domino Directory. It allows users to edit their own Person documents and no other document in the database.

- **Delete documents.** You can give this privilege to or remove it from users with Author or higher access. Managers should remove this privilege from themselves primarily to protect themselves from making wholesale deletions by mistake.

- **Create personal agents.** Agents are programs that automate database activities. They can be very powerful and useful tools. They can run on Notes workstations and Domino servers. When they run, they can occupy a lot of processor time and memory. When they aren't running, they can occupy a lot of disk space. A personal agent is an agent created for the sole use of its author. Managers and Designers automatically have the right to create both shared and personal agents. Editors, Authors, and Readers can be given the right to create personal agents. Because personal agents can consume such resources, you should use discretion when deciding who can create them.

- **Create personal folders/views.** All users with Reader or higher access to a database can create personal folders and views. Personal folders and views, along with their indexes, can occupy a lot of disk space. So, for Editors, Authors, and Readers, you have the option of unchecking this privilege. Doing so doesn't prohibit these users from creating them, but merely from storing their personal folders and views in the database itself. Instead, their personal folders and views are stored in their own workstations, in their desktop.dsk file. This can potentially save lots of disk space on the server, but the users' personal folders and views lose their portability; if the user runs Notes on another computer, his personal folders and views are unavailable to him.

- **Create shared folders/views.** This affects Editors only. Designers and Managers have this right inherently. Authors and lower cannot be given the privilege.

- **Create LotusScript/Java agent.** This affects Designers, Editors, Authors, and Readers. They all have the privilege by default but can have it removed. LotusScript and Java agents are potentially much more powerful than agents that use simple actions and formulas. They are also potentially much more demanding of computer resources. So, even more than with personal agents (just discussed), you should use discretion when deciding who can create them.

- **Read public documents.** Public documents are a special breed of document that you can allow any user to read or write, even users who are assigned No Access as their basic access right. Iris programmers conjured up this class of documents to enable group calendaring and scheduling in Notes. Each user's personal calendar information is stored in his mail database, which, by default, is accessible only to that user. But for group calendaring and scheduling to have any power at all, users have to be able to allow others some degree of access to their personal calendars. So the concept of public documents was born, so that users could give other people access to some documents (calendar entries) but not others (mail entries). This privilege only affects Depositors and those with No Access, because they are the only users who couldn't read the documents anyway.
- **Write public documents.** This privilege affects Readers, Depositors, and those with No Access.

Roles

Roles are special functions that a designer can define within a database. For example, in the Resource Reservations database (which is part of the Calendaring and Scheduling function), there is a role named [CreateResource]. Most users should only be able to reserve resources (conference room, A/V equipment, etc.). But someone has to define and manage resources. The database is designed such that only people who have been assigned the role called [CreateResource] can do so. The Sites view, the Resource form, and the actions that one would choose to create a Resource document are invisible to all but those assigned [CreateResource].

Only Managers create, rename, or remove roles. They can do so in the Roles screen of the Access Control List dialog box. In practice, however, Designers create roles during the development process, at which time they still have Manager access to the database. Role names can have up to 15 characters, including spaces, upper- and lowercase letters, and numbers. Notes automatically encloses role names in square brackets; existing roles always appear within square brackets; and any time you have to use the name of a role in a field or a formula, you must enclose it in square brackets.

After a role has been created, it appears (enclosed in square brackets, of course) in the Roles list on the Basics screen of the Access Control List dialog box. You can assign a role to a user (or unassign it) by selecting the user in the list of users and then clicking on the role name to make a checkmark appear next to it or disappear.

Roles in the Domino Directory

While most database roles are mostly of interest to database developers and managers, some (such as the [CreateResource] role in the Resource Reservations database) are of particular interest to Domino administrators. The most important of these roles are the ones that appear in the Domino Directory. There are eight of them in four pairs:

- [UserCreator] and [UserModifier]: People assigned these roles can either create or modify Person documents.

- [ServerCreator] and [ServerModifier]: People assigned these roles can either create or modify Server documents.

- [GroupCreator] and [GroupModifier]: People assigned these roles can either create or modify Group documents.

- [NetCreator] and [NetModifier]: People assigned these roles can either create or modify all other kinds of documents in the Domain Directory.

Actually, whether a person assigned these roles can perform them depends on what the person's basic level of access is. Users with Author access or higher will be able to perform these roles; Readers and lower will not.

Here's another important point: The Creator roles apply to all access levels of Author and higher; the Modifier roles apply to Authors only. Thus, to create any document in the Domino Directory, you have to be assigned Author or higher access, the Create document privilege, and the appropriate Creator role. To modify a document, you have to be Manager, Designer, or Editor, or you have to be Author with the appropriate Modifier role.

The purpose of these roles is to permit you to delegate administrative functions more effectively. For example, an administrator whose sole function is to manage existing user accounts only needs to modify existing Person and Group documents. Author access plus the [UserModifier] and [GroupModifier] roles would be sufficient access to the Domino Directory for someone to perform this function. A person with this much access would only be able to read other kinds of documents, and you wouldn't have to worry that he might poke around and make changes where he has no business.

Here's one last point: Creator roles are more of a convenience feature than a security feature, because they only stop non-Creators from using the Notes UI to create documents. One could still use, say, a LotusScript agent to create documents that the absence of a Creator role might otherwise prohibit. Modifier roles, on the other hand, do constitute security. Absence of a necessary Modifier role will completely block an ACL Author from creating the prohibited document.

The ACL Log and ACL Change Monitors

The third screen of the ACL dialog box is the ACL log. It records the date and time of all changes to a database's ACL and identifies the user who made the change and the general nature of the change made. By "general nature" I mean that it tells you what user was affected and whether the user was added, updated, or deleted, but nothing more specific than that.

Because changes in the ACLs of databases have such potentially far-reaching impact, it is important to be able to track this information. For that reason, you can also set up ACL Change Monitors in the Statistics & Events database (events4.nsf). These documents cause the Event server task to flag occurrences of ACL changes in specific databases. Such changes become Security events of a severity level defined by you in the monitor. You could then create an Event Notification document, also in Statistics & Events, that would notify you in any number of possible ways—by email, pager, or posting to a database, for example—when such an event occurs.

Advanced ACL Features

The Advanced screen of the ACL dialog box holds several tools that let you refine database access even more. These include fields for designating an Administration Server, enforcing tighter database security, defining a maximum Internet access level, and mass update of the User type field. The last we talked about earlier in this chapter; so we'll cover only the first three in the sections that follow.

Designating an Administration Server

First, you can designate an Administration Server here and define it's duties. Most Notes databases need to be assigned an Administration Server so that user name changes will be automatically updated in the database's ACL and Readers and Authors fields.

Enforcing a Consistent ACL

Second, you can select Enforce a consistent Access Control List across all replicas of this database. This is a major step you can take to tighten security in a database. It's also a problematic step, because its side effects can take you by surprise. You need to understand how it works before selecting it.

By default only Domino (the server) enforces the database ACL. Notes (the client) does not. This is a potential security failing because if a user can gain physical access to a server (Windows-based only), the user can gain direct (local) access to the database rather than going through the database server. In this way the user bypasses all server-level and most database-level access restrictions. See Figure 10.5 for an illustration of this.

Notes's nonenforcement of the ACL can also confuse users because when they access local databases, they are not restricted by the ACL as they would be if accessing a server-hosted database, and as they therefore expect to be.

The primary effect of choosing to enforce a consistent ACL across all copies of a database is to tell Notes to enforce the ACL. When Notes starts enforcing the ACL, a user running Notes on the server can no longer bypass access restrictions by bypassing the server, because now Notes also enforces the restrictions. And a user with Reader access to the database can no longer edit documents in his local copy of the database, because his copy of Notes is now enforcing his read-only access, just as the server always did and as the user expected.

The secondary effect of enforcing a consistent ACL, and the one that tends to surprise database managers, is that you can change the ACL on only one master copy of the database. If you make one change in server S1's copy of the ACL and another change in S2's copy of the ACL, the two copies are no longer consistent. As a result, the two servers will no longer replicate with each other—because their ACLs are no longer consistent. You have to manually bring the two copies of the ACL back into consistency before the two servers will replicate again. If you are not closely monitoring the servers for replication errors, you may not discover the replication failures for days or weeks, with all sorts of unpleasant consequences.

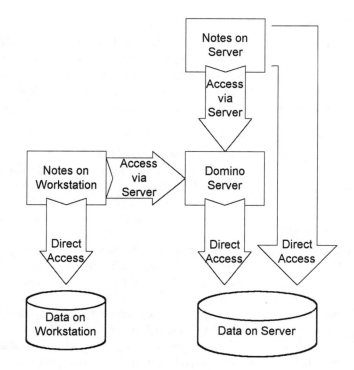

Figure 10.5 Notes running on a workstation has direct access to local databases but must go through the Domino server to gain access to server-hosted databases. Notes running on the server machine can access the server's databases either directly (because the databases are local) or through the server software.

This side effect of enforcing a consistent ACL is not well publicized in Lotus's documentation and is not well understood by a lot of administrators. They try out this feature, get all messed up, and then disable it and swear it off.

It also makes enforcement of a consistent ACL very difficult where the database will be used in multiple independent Notes domains. What happens is that the administrators of the secondary domains make replicas of the database on one of their own servers and then change the ACL to suit their own needs. In so doing, and they disable replication with the source domain's database. If you want to enforce an ACL across domains, the source domain's administrator has to be the source of all ACL changes and should add group entries that suit the needs of the other administrators. It's no mean administrative feat to pull this off.

Yet another problem with enforcing a consistent ACL is that it is potentially dangerous. It is possible to lock oneself entirely out of a database's ACL by removing all non-server managers from the ACL. If that happens, the only way around the problem is to make a new copy or replica of the database, leaving the ACL behind in the process. You have to have Reader access or better to do this. And any elements to which you don't have read access will not copy/replicate into the new database. These might include other users' personal folders, views, and agents, and documents to which you don't have read access. The bottom line is: Understand all of the consequences of enforcing consistent ACLs, and be careful.

Setting Maximum Internet Access

Finally, you can set the maximum access that a user may have when accessing the database via a Web browser and using name and password authentication. This defaults to Editor access. You can change it to any of the other access levels.

Other Ways to View and Manipulate ACL Fields

The Access Control List dialog box lets you view and manipulate the currently selected database's ACL. You can view it if you have less than Manager access and manipulate it if you have Manager access. But what if you need to see or change access rights in multiple databases?

To see the status of multiple databases, you can look in the Database Catalog (title: Catalog (5.0); filename: `catalog.nsf`). It has three views of database access control lists. You can view them sorted by database, by access level, and by user name. The only databases you cannot examine this way are those that are excluded from the catalog by a setting in their own database properties dialog boxes.

To manipulate multiple database ACLs simultaneously, you can use the Multi ACL Management tool in Domino Administrator. To use it, go to the Files tab, choose the server on which the databases in question are located, and then select the databases. Then, under Tools, Database, choose Manage ACL. This opens the Multi ACL Management dialog box. Because Domino Administrator can't assume all of the selected databases have the same current ACL entries, the current ACL settings of the selected databases don't appear. (In fact, even if you choose one database, its current settings don't appear; we hope this is an early release shortcoming.)

Here you can add users and then rename or remove the ones you added. You can specify each user's user type, access level, and access privileges. You can add, rename, and remove roles (but not assign users to them). You can modify the Administration Server settings, the Consistent ACL setting, and the Internet name and password (maximum Internet access) setting. When you choose OK, the Administration Process will update the ACLs of all selected databases (or at least the ones that you had Manager access to).

Recommendations for Setting Up Database ACLs

Notes requires that every database have at least one manager (it will not let you remove all manager access). However, Lotus recommends that you have more than one human manager. The idea is that, if one person isn't available to perform managerial duties, the other will be. Lotus also recommends that you not assign Manager access to groups but rather to individual administrators. That way you know exactly who the managers are. Most people, however, prefer to set up groups with manager access.

If you are enforcing a consistent ACL, I would especially recommend that you assign Manager access to at least one human user and one non-server group. That way, you minimize the risk of locking yourself out of the ACL by removing all human managers. As an added precaution, you might designate any server groups that have Manager access as Mixed groups. That way, you could sneak in with a server ID if you had to. But so could an unauthorized user.

In addition, keep user access levels as low as possible. The fewer Managers, Designers, and Editors there are in a database, the less chance there is of replication conflicts.

Finally, consider keeping server access levels as low as possible. To replicate a database properly, servers need (in the other server's ACL) the following access levels:

- Manager if they have to write ACL changes to destination servers
- Designer if they have to write design changes to destination servers
- Editor if they have to write data changes to destination servers
- Reader if they have to accept changes from source servers

What some organizations will do, especially if they have a hub-and-spoke server replication topology, is designate their hub server(s) as the sole non-human Manager(s) of most databases. (If you have multiple hubs or cascading hubs, you must name all of them Manager so that they can pass ACL changes to their respective spoke servers.) Any development servers will have Designer access and sometimes Manager access to databases. Spoke servers will have Editor access to databases in which their users have write access (Depositor, Author, or higher) and Reader access to read-only databases such as help databases or employee manuals.

User mail databases are an especially difficult problem because, by default (and in many existing installations), only the owner user and his mail server have any access at all to the database. Starting in R5.0 you have the option to give owner users less than Manager access to their own mail databases. Starting with R5.0.1 you have the option to add an Administrators group to new users' mail databases as an additional Manager. Depending on your company policy regarding the privacy of your users' mail, you might want to take advantage of these new options.

View Access Lists

Designers of views can restrict access to their views. They do so in View Properties, under the Security (key) tab, by setting May be used by to something less than All readers and above. This is more of a convenience feature than a security measure because any user can create a personal view that displays the same documents that a restricted-access view displays. But it is something you should be aware of.

Form Access Lists

Forms can have two different access lists: Default read access for documents created with this form and Who can create documents with this form. Both of these are available to the form designer in Form Properties under the Security (key) tab.

When a designer sets the Default read access for documents created with this form field to something less than All readers and above, Domino Designer generates an internal field in the form called $Readers. This is a Names field that contains the names of the people, servers, and groups checked off in the Default read access... field. All documents created with this form will inherit this field and its settings. Only users listed in it, and in any fields of Readers or Authors data type in the document, will be able to read the resulting documents.

If a designer sets the Who can create documents with this form field to something less than All authors and above, the form becomes unavailable to all users not selected in that field. This is how the Domino Directory restricts document creation rights to people assigned the various Creator roles—only those roles are selected in the Who can create... field of their respective forms.

Designers can tighten security around forms in other ways as well. In particular, a designer can specify that documents created with a form will not be printable, forwardable, or copyable. This removes all the easy ways for people to misuse the information in the documents created with the form.

$Readers, Readers, and Authors Fields

Designers and document authors and editors can restrict access to individual data documents in several ways. We just saw in the preceding section how one could use the Default read access... form property to restrict future readers of documents created with a given form. Document authors and editors can change document readership restrictions by manipulating the document property Who can read this document. This property inherits the setting of the Default read access... form property. To put it another way, it inherits and reflects the setting of the $Readers field (if any) the document inherited from the form. And changes users make to Who can read this document become changes in the $Readers field.

Designers can further restrict document readership with fields of Readers data type. If any such fields exist in a document, the users, servers, and groups listed in them (along with users, servers, and groups listed in the $Readers field and Authors fields) are the only ones who can read the document. If such fields exist but are empty, anyone can read the document.

Finally, Designers can restrict document editor rights with fields of Authors data type. These fields affect only users with Author access to the database. Such users can edit documents only if their names (or groups of which they are members) are listed in an Authors field of a document. Otherwise, they can only read the documents.

Restrictions on Parts of a Document

Designers can also restrict who can edit a section of a document. A section is a defined portion of a form or of a document created by a form. Anyone who can read a document can read all sections in it. But if editorship of a section is restricted, only users named in the section editors list can change fields in that section.

Finally, authors and editors can sign and/or encrypt individual fields within a document. When a user signs a field he asserts that it was he who edited the field last. The signature also assures the reader that the signed value has not changed since it was signed. It also tells the reader when the field was signed. If a field is in a section of a document, the signature affects all of the fields in the section. If a document has multiple sections, each section can be signed separately.

An author or editor who encrypts a field can do so with either one or more public keys or with specially created encryption keys. If a field is encrypted with a public key, only the owner of the companion private key can decrypt it. If a field is encrypted with an encryption key, only holders of that encryption key can decrypt the field. Different fields in a document can be encrypted with different keys. However, any one of the encryption keys can decrypt all of the fields.

Although any document author or editor can encrypt any field on an ad hoc basis, more often field encryption takes place automatically, because it was designed to do so by the database designer. In those cases, the database designer or a database manager probably created the encryption keys at design time. Then, when the database was rolled out, the designer would have transferred the encryption key(s) to the database Manager, who would in turn have distributed copies to the users who need to be able to encrypt/decrypt the fields. Those keys are stored in each user's ID file. You can see what encryption keys a user has by examining his ID file and looking on the Encryption Keys page.

Local Database Encryption

In contrast to field encryption, described previously, local database encryption encrypts the entire contents of a database. The database itself is encrypted with an encryption key, which is itself encrypted with the public key of an individual user or server (depending on the location of the database). To have any kind of access from within Notes to the contents of the database, you have to be logged in using the ID of the user or server whose private key can decrypt the encryption key. (To block non–Notes access to the contents of a locally encrypted database, you have to use either medium or strong encryption, not weak encryption. More about that later.)

The purpose of local encryption is to prevent unauthorized local access to a database located on a server or workstation. The danger on a server is that a user could use a local copy of Notes to bypass ACL security and gain Manager access to a database. The danger on a workstation is that a person could gain unauthorized read access to the database; one could open it without knowing the password to any Notes ID file.

To encrypt a database, you have to have Manager access to it. Usually users have Manager access to the databases on their workstations, so they can encrypt them themselves, using their own IDs. But if enforcement of consistent ACLs is active on a local database, the user may have to ask a database manager to encrypt the database for him. The database manager would have to switch to his own ID and then encrypt the database with the user's ID, in the process locking himself out of the local copy of the database. (Caveat: Make sure, if doing this, that the local copy is not the only copy of the database.)

To encrypt an existing database, open the Database Properties dialog box. On the Database Basics tab, choose Encryption Settings. (If it is grayed out, you don't have Manager access to the database.) The Encryption for *DatabaseName* dialog box will appear.

Choose Locally encrypt this database using and choose a level of encryption strength: strong, medium, or simple. If you accessed the database via a Domino server, the words For `servername` will appear, telling you that the server's public key will be used to encrypt the database. If you accessed the database locally (whether on a server or a workstation), the word "For" will be a button, and the name that follows it will be the one under which you are logged in; pressing the "For" button will allow you to choose another user's or server's name from a directory. If the chosen entity's public key is available in the directory from which his/her/its name was selected, Notes will encrypt with that public key, locking you and all others out of that copy of the database. Considerations for deciding what level of encryption to use are as follows:

- Use **medium encryption** most of the time. It provides relative difficulty to crack and does not unduly slow down data access times.
- Use **strong encryption** only for the most sensitive of data. It is hard to crack but slows down data access times.

- Use **simple encryption** only when security is not a high priority and if you need to retain file compressibility. It protects the data from casual snoopers only, not determined crackers.

Under simple encryption, the data isn't actually encrypted. Rather, Notes refuses to show it to anyone but the owner of the decrypting private key. One could still read the data with an API program.

You can also encrypt a database when you create it. The New Database, New Copy, and New Replica dialog boxes all include an Encryption button that, when chosen, displays the dialog box just described.

Workstation Security

Workstation security encompasses the following subjects:

- Protection from viruses, worms, and Trojan horses
- Protection of local data from unauthorized access

To protect against malicious software, Notes includes the Execution Control List. To protect against unauthorized access to local data, Notes provides a whole series of tools, including features to protect the user ID and features to protect individual databases.

The Execution Control List

Under the first bullet point in the preceding list, you might include third-party antivirus software, about which there is plenty to say. But we're interested in Notes's built-in feature, the Execution Control List (ECL). The ECL is reminiscent of a database ACL in that it limits the access that entities have to a system. Like the database ACL, it lists entities—in this case, entities that sign programs—and, for each entity, sets forth its program execution rights (see Figure 10.6). You can specify a different set of rights for each of three kinds of programs—Lotuscript/Formula Language agents, Java applets, and embedded JavaScript code.

To open the ECL on a workstation, run Notes, and then choose User Preferences in the File, Tools menu. In the User Preferences dialog box, on the Basics screen, choose Security Options. The Workstation Security: Execution Control List dialog box opens.

This dialog box has three separate screens: Workstation Security, Java applet security, and JavaScript security. Select them in the upper-right corner of the dialog box. In each screen you can add, rename, and remove signers. For each signer you can select or deselect different types of access or execution rights.

Here's a pitfall that got me a couple times before I figured out how this dialog box works: When you add a signer in one screen, Notes does *not* automatically add the signer to the other two screens. If you want the signer to appear in more than one of the screens, you have to add it separately in each.

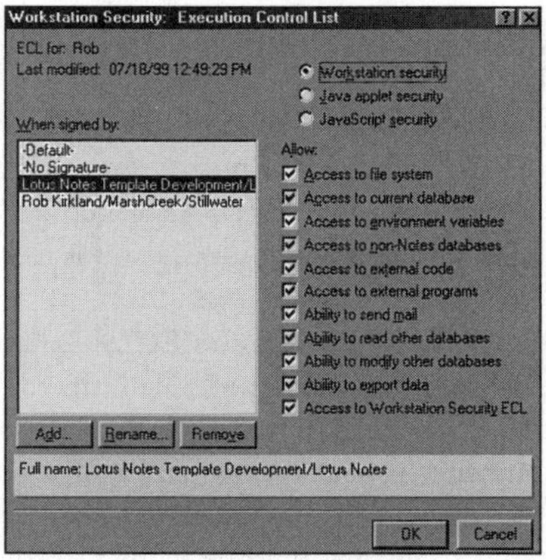

Figure 10.6 For each listed signer you can specify what kinds of access his programs may have to your system.

By default, workstation security is disabled. That is, all default signers have all execution rights. Among the default signers are -Default-, -No Signature-, Lotus Notes Template Development/Lotus, and the workstation's primary user. The upshot is that, on the default Notes system, any program running inside of Notes, signed by anyone or not signed at all, can perform any function that the language it was written in permits.

By today's standards, that is a dangerous situation. It is a scarily simple matter for someone to create an email that could, for example, wipe a recipient's hard disk clean. Or maybe it could spirit confidential information out of Notes databases and send it to a foreign system or set up a portal through which strangers could later invade the system and do what they want. Here is one way to set up such an email message, courtesy of Tom Lowery, *Configure the ECL to Thwart Trojan Horse Attacks*, Advisor Expert: Lotus Notes & Domino Administration, Premiere 1999, p.13:

1. Modify the Memo form in a Notes Mail database to auto-launch an attachment.

2. Set the Memo form property Store form in document.

3. Attach a Trojan horse program to a message created with the altered Memo form and send it.

On most systems, the only thing that prevents a program like this one from executing is the goodwill and/or ignorance of one's correspondents. But you can set up your users' systems so that Notes's ECL would also prevent it. To do so you have to set up the Administration ECL and then update your users' ECLs with its settings (users you set up later will automatically inherit the Administrative ECL at setup time, so you don't have to do anything special for them).

Setting Up the Administration ECL

The Administration ECL is located in the Domain Directory. To set up the Administration ECL, open the Domain Directory on any server. Choose Edit Administration ECL in the Actions menu. Choose a security type, and then modify the entries. Watch out for the same pitfall that I described earlier regarding the user's ECL dialog box—when you add a signer, you only add it to the current screen, not all three screens at once.

If you want to set up multiple Administration ECLs—say, different configurations for different kinds of users—you can set up multiple Directory databases and then configure each one's Administration ECL separately. Each database will be based on the Domino Directory template (`pubnames.ntf`) and will, of course, have a unique filename.

It looks like Lotus intends to enable multiple named Administration ECLs in a single Directory, but as of R5.0 they apparently have not yet done so. If in a future release Lotus does enable this feature, you would not have to create multiple Directory databases. Rather, you should be able to create multiple named ECLs in a single Directory of your choice. Watch for this development.

Refreshing Users' ECLs

To push your Administration ECL changes to the users, you have to send them an email message in which they will click a button that performs the update. You can do this as follows:

1. Create an email message addressed to users whose ECLs you want to update.

2. Add a button to the message that, when clicked, executes the following formula:

   `@RefreshECL (servername:filename; ECLName)`

3. Describe the purpose of the memo; instruct the recipient to click the button; send the memo.

In the preceding formula:

servername:filename is a text list indicating the location and name of the Administration ECL from which the formula will refresh the user's ECL. The first part is the fully distinguished name of the server, and the second part is the filename of the Domino Directory from which to refresh the user's ECL. To use the Domain Directory on the user's home server, substitute quotation marks ("") or the word NULL for the whole sequence.

ECLName is the name (if any) of an Administrative ECL from which to perform the refresh. Until Lotus enables multiple Administration ECLs in a Directory (which it hasn't as of R5.0), you should always use a pair of quotation marks ("") or the word NULL to indicate a nameless ECL.

If you want the formula to refresh from the Administration ECL in the Domain Directory (names.nsf) on the user's home server, you can enter the formula as follows:

```
@RefreshECL ( "" ; "" )
```

The first pair of quotation marks tells Notes to retrieve from names.nsf on the user's home server. The second pair of quotation marks tells Notes to retrieve the unnamed Administration ECL from that database.

If you want the formula to refresh from an Administration ECL in a special directory that you established just for this purpose, enter a formula similar to this:

```
@RefreshECL ( "Osprey/Servers/Stillwater":"ECL1.nsf" ; "" )
```

or this:

```
@RefreshECL ( "":"ECL1.nsf" ; "" )
```

In the first example, you are telling the formula which server and database to use. In the second example, you are telling the server which database to use but to look for it on the user's home server. Notice that the server's name and the database's filename are enclosed in quotation marks. This is important: the formula will fail if you leave them out.

Using the ECL Painlessly

The reason Lotus disables the default ECL is because it can drive you crazy if not set up properly. Rather than drive you crazy from the outset, Lotus prefers that you figure out how to use the ECL and then set it up to suit your needs.

Before it executes a program (any embedded formula, LotusScript, or JavaScript, or a Java applet), Notes checks the ECL to find out what it should permit the program to do. Notes looks for a signature on the program, authenticates the signature, and then looks for the signer's name in the ECL. If the signer's name doesn't appear, Notes uses the settings for -Default-. If the program isn't signed, Notes uses the settings for -No signature-.

If the program then tries to perform an action not permitted to the signer of the program, the rather daunting Execution Security Alert dialog box appears (see Figure 10.7).

This dialog box is the ECL's downfall. It is obscure and meaningless to most Notes users. Either they don't know what to do with it, so they call the Help Desk, or they figure out that they can choose Trust Signer to make it go away. But by doing so, they render the ECL progressively less and less useful, because they may be allowing all future programs signed by the same entity (or by nobody) to do things that could hurt them. If they call the Help Desk, the person on the other end of the line is tired of these calls and tells them to just click Trust Signer and move on.

Alternately, you lock down the users' ECLs so that they cannot click Trust Signer but only Abort or Execute Once. If the users have to do this too many times, they begin to hate Notes, hate you, hate their jobs, and hate life itself. To gain relief, you disable the ECL by giving all permissions to all signers.

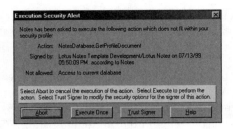

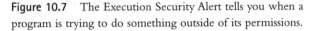

Figure 10.7   The Execution Security Alert tells you when a
program is trying to do something outside of its permissions.

Here's a better solution that works by minimizing the potential for the appearance of
the Execution Security Alert dialog box, thus rendering its appearance meaningful:

- Limit who can create new databases on your servers.

- Create a fictitious Notes user to be used for the sole purpose of signing internally developed databases. Give this user enough administrative rights to gain
access to files on Domino servers through the Domino Administrator. For
example, Lotus signs its databases and templates using an ID for a user named
Lotus Notes Template Development/Lotus Notes. They created both an organization (/Lotus Notes) and a user (Lotus Notes Template Development) for this
purpose.

- Update users' ECLs so that all potential signers of databases on your servers have
the permissions they need to do their jobs.

- Make sure every new database is signed by a recognized entity before putting it
on any of your servers. Also make sure all existing databases are signed. You can
sign the templates or the databases. Databases will inherit a signature from their
design template.

- Educate your users and Help Desk personnel on the importance and meaning of
and the proper responses to the appearance of Execution Security Alerts.

This is a lot of hard work. But it is becoming more and more necessary in our increasingly computerized and connected work world. The alternative is just to wait until
disaster strikes.

One caveat: Lotus normally signs all Notes databases and templates with an ID
called Lotus Notes Template Development/Lotus Notes. However, in their rush to get
R5.0 out the door, they failed to sign many of the databases and templates that came
with it. Before you roll out any applications based on these templates and databases, be
sure to check that they are signed and to sign them yourself if they are not. Otherwise,
your users will be faced with the choice of not using the applications or enabling
unsigned entities to perform some very invasive activities on their computers.

Signing Databases and Templates

To sign databases and templates, follow this procedure:

1. Switch to the user ID file you will use to sign the database(s) or template(s).

2. Open Domino Administrator to the Files screen. Select the server on which the database(s) or template(s) you want to sign reside.

3. Select the database(s) or template(s) you want to sign; then, under Tools, choose Database, Sign. The Sign Database dialog box appears.

4. Choose Options, and then choose OK.

The options are to sign all design documents, only documents of a particular type (selectable from a list), or only a particular document (whose Note ID you'll have to know). You can also choose only to update existing signatures.

To find the Note ID of a design document, follow this procedure:

1. Open the subject database in Domino Designer.

2. In the Bookmark pane, choose the type of document whose Note ID you need. A list of all documents in the database of that type appears.

3. Right-click the desired design document, and then choose Design Properties from the popup menu. The Design Document Properties dialog box appears.

4. Choose the Document IDs tab. It looks like a propeller beanie.

5. The Note ID is the last line of information, beginning with the letters "NT." You only need the rightmost characters, the ones following the leading zeros.

Protecting Workstation-Based Data

The other issue with workstation-based data is that workstations are often located in areas where the information on them is exposed to unauthorized access. This is particularly a problem with laptop computers carried around by a company's top executives. If you haven't heard horror stories about laptop computers containing companies' 5-year plans being stolen in airports, from hotel rooms, or right off of desks in the corporate headquarters, it's only a matter of time before you do.

Measures you can take to protect data on such computers from prying eyes include the following:

- Enabling the enforcement of consistent ACLs, which causes the local copy of Notes to enforce the ACL.

- Locally encrypting databases.

- Persuading users to lock their IDs when they leave a Notes workstation unattended.

- Setting Notes to lock IDs automatically after some period of inactivity.

- Requiring unusually strong passwords to open an ID file.
- Requiring multiple passwords to open an ID file.
- Disabling printing/forwarding/copying of documents in sensitive databases.

Enforcement of Consistent ACLs

We've already discussed enforcement of consistent ACLs. The benefit of it here is that anyone viewing the local copy of the database would only have the local user's level of access to it. But if you want to keep unauthorized users from viewing the data at all, this feature won't stop them, because the local user will always have at least Reader access to local databases.

Local Database Encryption

We've also already discussed local encryption of a database. With this kind of encryption, the whole database is encrypted with an encryption key that is, in turn, encrypted with a specific user's public key. Thereafter, you can only use the database when logged in with the same user ID, because you need the private key from that ID to decrypt the contents of the database. If you don't know the password of the ID file containing the private key, you can't open the ID or read the contents of the database. Only medium or strong encryption would be effective against someone really determined to see the data.

Locking the User ID

By default, after you enter your password, your ID file remains open until you exit Notes. However, you can lock your ID at any time. By doing so, you force yourself to re-enter your password the next time you need access to your private key (to authenticate with a server, to sign a message, or to read encrypted incoming mail). You can also set Notes to lock your ID after a period of inactivity.

You can lock your ID manually by pressing the F5 key on the keyboard or by choosing Lock ID in the File, Tools menu. You can set up timed locking by opening User Preferences (File, Preferences, User Preferences) and entering a number in the Lock ID after x minutes of inactivity field on the Basics screen.

Strong Passwords

When new users are registered or existing users are recertified, you can set a minimum password quality for them. When you do, you in effect say that their ID password must meet the minimum quality that you set. For a user, the default minimum password quality is 8, on a "password quality scale" that ranges from 0 (None required) to 16 (Extremely strong).

The password quality scale corresponds roughly to the number of characters in a password—however, not precisely. A password quality of 8 may require nine characters if the password consists of one or more dictionary words, but only six characters if the password consists of random numerals, letters (upper- and lowercase), and punctuation characters.

When setting the password of an ID that decrypts a database full of very sensitive data, you can make it more difficult to crack by making it long, using non-dictionary words, and using non-alphabetic characters. Among other things, you could use a passphrase consisting of several words separated by spaces. A passphrase is usually easier to remember than a meaningless password, as well.

Multiple Passwords

You can set up any ID file so that it requires multiple passwords to unlock it. Normally you want to use this feature only with certifier IDs or occasionally with servers. Multipassword user IDs are incompatible with password checking, so you would have to disable password checking for any user who uses multiple passwords. But if you really, really want to protect data, you can locally encrypt a database with a multipassword ID.

With multipassword IDs you can enter as many passwords as you like, and then require some subset of them to open the ID. For example, you could enter five passwords, one known to each of five people, and then require the use of any three of them to open the ID.

To set up an ID with multiple passwords, run Domino Administrator. Open the Configuration screen. Choose Tools, Certification, Edit Multiple Passwords. Select the ID to which you want to assign multiple passwords. Then have each person in turn who will know one of the passwords enter his name and a valid password in the appropriate fields, and choose Add.

Disabling Printing/Forwarding/Copying

Earlier in this chapter we saw how you can disable printing, forwarding, and copying of all documents created with a particular form. (The form designer chooses the form property Disable printing/forwarding/copying to clipboard.)

In addition to that, you can disable printing and copying of individual paragraphs of text in rich text fields. Put your text cursor in the paragraph(s) to be blocked, and then choose Text Properties in the Text menu. In the Hide When tab (which looks like a window shade), check the Printed and Copied to the clipboard boxes.

SSL Security in Domino and Notes

Domino servers employ SSL in several possible situations:

- A public Domino Web server on which you run an e-commerce application must be able to prove its authenticity to total strangers wanting to buy your products on the Web site. This server needs a certificate issued by a commercial CA. The server typically doesn't need to authenticate the buyer. (It only needs to get the buyer's money.)

- Another Domino server may permit your customers, suppliers, or business partners to use a Web browser to track the status of their accounts or various ongoing transactions with you. Depending on the details of such an application, the server may need a certificate issued by either a commercial CA or a Domino CA (that is, by you). The clients making use of this server probably need to prove their identities to the server as well. Depending on the sensitivity of the information they are accessing, the server could accept either name and password identification or certificate-based authentication, the certificate issued by you or a commercial CA.

- Another server may maintain mail accounts for employees who use POP3 or IMAP mail readers instead of Notes. Or it may maintain a private, NNTP-enabled discussion area. Or it may provide directory access to selected non-Notes clients. Or it may let selected SMTP senders contact it through the company firewall. Or it may contact a trusted LDAP server to authenticate Internet clients. All of these servers can require (or allow) their clients to contact them over an SSL-secured connection. They may require their clients to authenticate using either name and password identification or by submitting a certificate to the server. Usually a private CA, not a commercial CA, would issue the certificates to the server and clients under these arrangements.

Under the final scenario in the preceding list and possibly the second one, you need to set yourself up as a private CA, in the same sense that you are a private CA when registering Notes servers and users. As such you will issue certificates to your servers and possibly some of your employees, suppliers, business partners, or customers. Under all three scenarios, you will have to set up one or more of your servers with X.509 certificates. Finally, you may have to either issue X.509 certificates to your employees or help them obtain certificates from a commercial CA so that they can encrypt and sign mail under S/MIME.

Becoming a Certificate Authority

If you need to issue X.509 certificates to your servers, users, or third parties such as suppliers or business partners, you need to become a certificate authority. To do this, you can use the Domino Certificate Authority application, which exists on each Domino server as an advanced design template. The template is named Domino R5 Certificate Authority, and its filename is `cca50.ntf`.

Use the template to create a Domino Certificate Authority database on a Web-enabled Domino server—that is, on a Domino server with the HTTP server task running. This will become the CA server. Clients will request and retrieve certificates from you via this server's Web interface. You may name the database and file anything you want. After creating the database, you have to configure it as follows:

1. Set up the ACL of the CA database.
2. Create a CA key ring file and root certificate.
3. Complete the Certificate Authority Profile.
4. Issue a server certificate to the CA server.
5. Configure SSL on the CA server.

You may also want to deselect the Show in 'Open Database' dialog property for this database so that it doesn't appear when casual users browse the CA server.

The ACL Settings

Set up the ACL of the Certificate Authority application as follows:

- Default access: Author with Create documents selected
- Administrators who will issue certificates: At least Editor with Delete documents selected and the [CAPrivilegedUser] role assigned.

Create a CA Key Ring File and Root Certificate

The key ring file will contain the CA's root certificate and private key. Be prepared to protect it from compromise with the same degree of care that you apply to the protection of your Notes organization certifier ID.

In the CASetup navigator, which appears when you open the Certificate Authority application, choose Certificate Authority Configuration (left side of screen), and then choose Create Certificate Authority Key Ring & Certificate (center of screen). Fill in the form as described in Table 10.5.

Table 10.5 **Fields in the Create Certificate Authority Key Ring Form**

Field	Comments
Key Ring File Name	Defaults to CAKey.kyr. Notes will save it in the local Notes data folder unless you specify a different path. I recommend you save it to a secure location.
Key Ring Password and Password Verify	Lotus recommends a password of at least 12 characters in length.
Key Size	The choices are 512 or 1024 bits if you have the North American version of Notes or if you own a Verisign Global Server ID (**www.verisign.com**). Otherwise, the only choice is 512 bits (which is not very secure).
Common Name	Use a name that describes the CA, such as "Stillwater CA."
Organization	Enter your Notes organization name here, or something similar to it.
Organizational Unit	Optional. If this is a CA for an OU within your Notes organization or for a division or department within your company, enter the OU, division, or department name here.
City or Locality	Optional. The city where the CA resides.
State or Province	The fully spelled-out name of the state or province where the CA resides. This field requires a minimum of three characters.
Country	The two-letter ANSI code for the country where the CA lives (for example, US for United States, CA for Canada, UK for United Kingdom).

When ready, choose Create Certificate Authority Key Ring. Notes creates the key ring file and the CA's root certificate (issued to itself, signed by itself) and then presents you with a dialog detailing the particulars. Notice that the certificate expires in 10 years.

After closing the dialog box, if you ever want to examine the key ring file again, choose View Certificate Authority Key Ring (left side of screen) and then Display CA Key Ring (in Action Bar) in the Certificate Authority application.

The Certificate Authority Profile

The Certificate Authority Profile is a form that holds default settings that will be applied when you issue certificates. To set it up, choose Certificate Authority Configuration (left side of screen), then Configure Certificate Authority Profile (center of screen), and then complete the form as described in Table 10.6.

Table 10.6   **Fields in the Certificate Authority Profile Form**

Field	Comments
CA Key File	Defaults to the original location of the CA key ring file. If you move the key ring file, enter its new location here.
Certificate Server DNS Name	Enter the server's fully qualified domain name or an alias name registered with DNS.
Use SSL for certificate transactions?	Defaults to Yes. Turn this off only if you don't intend to secure certificate request transactions with SSL.
Certificate Server Port Number	If you leave this blank, the port number is 80. If you set the HTTP port to something other than 80 on the CA server, set this to that same port number.
Mail confirmation of signed certificate to requestor?	Sets the default behavior regarding mailing of confirmations to certificate requestors. Defaults to Yes.
Submit signed certificates to AdminP for addition to the Directory?	Sets the default behavior regarding addition of issued certificates to the Domino Directory. Defaults to Yes.
Default validity period	Sets the default number of years of validity of signed certificates. Defaults to two years.

Issue a Server Certificate to the CA Server

The Certificate Authority application assumes that entities requesting signed certificates from it will connect to the CA server using SSL security. To make this possible, the CA must issue a certificate to its own host server. It does so in this step.

In the Certificate Authority application, choose Certificate Authority Configuration (left side of screen) and then Create Server Key Ring & Certificate (center of screen). Fill in the form as described in Table 10.7.

Table 10.7   **Fields in the Create CA Server Key Ring Form**

Field	Comments
Key Ring File Name	Defaults to `keyfile.kyr`. You might want to call it `CAserver.kyr` or `servername.kyr`. Just be sure to use the `kyr` extension for the sake of naming uniformity.
Key Ring Password and Password Verify	Lotus recommends a password at least 12 characters in length.

continues

Table 10.7 **Continued**

Field	Comments
Key Size	The choices are 512 or 1024 bits if you have the North American version of Notes or if you own a Verisign Global Server ID (`www.verisign.com`). Otherwise, the only choice is 512 bits (which is not very secure).
CA Certificate Label	Enter a descriptive name for the signer of the server certificate. This is how the signer's name will appear during future examinations of the server's key ring file.
Common Name	Defaults to the server's fully qualified domain name. Some browsers won't connect if the common name on the server's certificate doesn't match the server's name as it appears in DNS. You could, of course, use any alias name for which a DNS record exists—for example, `caserver.stillwater.com`.
Organization	Enter your Notes organization name here, or something similar to it.
Organizational Unit	Optional. If this is a CA for an OU within your Notes organization or for a division or department within your company, enter the OU, division, or department name here.
City or Locality	Optional. The city where the CA resides.
State or Province	The fully spelled-out name of the state or province where the CA resides. This field requires a minimum of three characters.
Country	The two-letter ANSI code for the country where the CA lives (for example, US for United States, CA for Canada, UK for United Kingdom).

When ready, choose Create Server Key Ring. Notes will prompt you for the password of the CA key ring file so that it can use the CA private key to sign the server's certificate. Then Notes creates the server's key ring file with the server certificate in it and displays the particulars to you in a dialog box.

Take note of the path name of the key ring file. You'll have to copy it (and its "stash" file) to the CA server in the following step.

Configure SSL on the CA Server

The final configuration step is to enable and configure the SSL port for HTTP. Follow these steps:

1. Copy the CA server's key ring file (*filename*.kyr) and the corresponding stash file (*filename*.sth) from the workstation on which you created them to the server's Domino data folder.

2. Configure the CA server's SSL port for HTTP so that only the CA server must authenticate. Open the CA server's Server document in the Domino Directory. Under Ports, Internet Ports, Web, set the fields in Table 10.8.

Table 10.8 **Some Fields in the Server Form, Notes Network Ports, Web**

Field	Comments
SSL key filename	Defaults to keyfile.kyr. If you used a different filename, enter it here. If the key file isn't in the server's Domino data folder, enter its full path name here.
TCP/IP port number	Defaults to 80. This number should match the number you entered in the Certificate Authority Profile. It should also match the actual port number that Domino's HTTP service uses.
TCP/IP port status	Set to Enabled.
Name & password	Set to Yes or No. The Certificate Authority application does not need this set to Yes.
Anonymous	If users will use Internet Explorer to connect to this server, the Certificate Authority application needs this set to Yes. Otherwise you may set this to Yes or No.
SSL port number	Defaults to 443. This number should match the actual port number that Domino's HTTP SSL service uses, which would be different from 443 only if a proxy server uses that port.
SSL port status	Set to Enabled.
Client certificate	Set to Yes or No. The Certificate Authority application does *not* need this set to Yes.
Name & password	Set to Yes or No. The Certificate Authority application does *not* need this set to Yes.
Anonymous	Set to Yes. The Certificate Authority application *does* need this set to Yes.

3. Start the HTTP service on the CA server. If it was already running when you completed the previous steps, refresh it with the `tell http restart` command, run from the server console or from Domino Administrator. Also, if necessary, add `HTTP` to the list of services in the `ServerTasks` variable in the CA server's `notes.ini` variable.

4. If clients won't be using Internet Explorer 4.0 or earlier to access the Certificate Authority application, you can set the database property Web Access: Require SSL connection for the Certificate Authority application.

The last step will force users to use SSL when accessing this application. Users of Internet Explorer 4.0 and earlier can't use SSL to access this application because they can't accept site certificates from servers for which they don't have a trusted root certificate. They won't have a site certificate from this server until after they retrieve it from this application. So they have to use TCP/IP port 80; they have no choice.

When you have completed all of these steps, you need to do one more thing. People and servers will be requesting that you issue certificates to them. You need to define a security policy so that you'll be able to decide whether to issue the requested certificates. Remember that a certificate assures other entities—servers and users—that the entity named in the certificate owns the public key contained in the certificate. It also implies that you have positively identified the named entity and that you have taken reasonable steps to insure that you did not issue the certificate to an impostor. Your guidelines for issuing certificates should take all that into account. This is not a trivial undertaking.

Also remember that you are not a commercial CA. You are not in the business of certifying entities. Rather, you are probably doing this for the benefit of your fellow employees or your company's suppliers, business partners, and customers. You can turn away an applicant who doesn't fit a predefined profile of the kind of entity that should be requesting certificates from you.

Finally, you need adequate identification information from applicants. You can turn them down if they don't give it to you. They can gather the information you need and resubmit their applications.

Ongoing CA Duties

When you are finished setting up the Domino Certificate Authority application, you are ready to hang out your CA shingle. Your clients are Domino servers, Notes clients, various kinds of Internet clients, and possibly non-Domino servers of various kinds. The servers will request server certificates from you and then pick them up when they are ready. The clients will request client certificates and then pick them up. Notes clients may also submit client certificates issued by other CAs and ask you to register them (which means adding the public key to the applicant's Person document). All will submit their requests by opening the Domino Certificate Authority database in a browser. The opening browser display looks like the one in Figure 10.8.

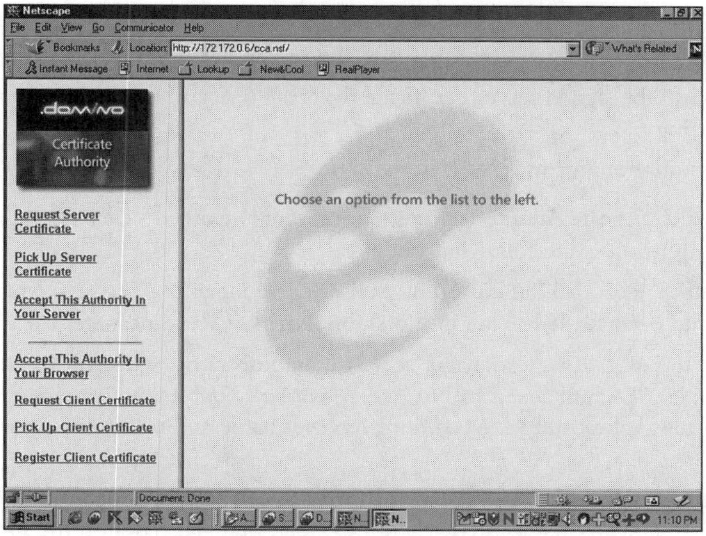

Figure 10.8   Servers can choose any of the top three items. Users can choose any of the bottom four items. The bottom-most item is really only for Notes clients.

When you receive requests for certificates, you will have to decide whether to issue them or not. That's where your policy guidelines come into play.

If you reject a certificate request, you'll have an opportunity to tell the requestor why. If you accept the request, you'll have to sign the certificate and set an expiration period. You'll have to enter the password for the CA key ring file to extract the private key.

By default, the database sends an email notification of your acceptance or rejection of each certificate request. An acceptance includes a Pickup ID. The user can then return to the database to pick up the signed certificate.

The views available to you include views of pending, accepted, and rejected server certificate requests, client certificate requests, and client registration requests. You can also examine and make changes in your CA key ring(s).

Setting Up a Domino Server to Use SSL

To use SSL on any Domino server, you have to obtain one or more SSL server certificates for the server. You also have to enable one or more SSL ports on the server. The overall process involves the following steps:

1. Run the HTTP process on the server.

2. Set up the Server Certificate Admin database on the server to be set-up for SSL.

3. Create a server key ring file, which will store the server's SSL certificate(s).

4. Request an SSL server certificate from a CA.

5. Merge the CA's own certificate into the server key ring file as a trusted root.

6. Pick up the signed server certificate from the CA, and merge it into the server key ring file.

7. Configure one or more SSL ports.

The Server Certificate Admin database (`certsrv.nsf`) exists on every Domino server. Setting it up involves the following steps:

1. From a Notes or Domino Administrator client, open the Server Certificate Admin database. If you are in Notes, bookmark it so you can get back to it easily.

2. Edit the ACL. Assign Manager access to administrators who will be responsible for it. Set Default access to No Access—nobody but administrators will need to use this application. Set Maximum Internet name and password access to No Access.

3. Optionally, deselect the database property Show in 'Open Database' dialog so that users won't see it listed when they open new databases on the server.

Create a Server Key Ring File

The server key ring file will hold the server's Internet certificates. It is analogous to the server's ID file, which stores its Notes certificates. You need to create it in a folder that the server will have constant access to, because the server will need it on an on-going basis, just as it needs access to its ID file. The problem here is that you may be running this application from a workstation. Therefore, you'll have to share the server's data folder, then map a drive to it from your workstation. This poses a potential security problem. Make sure you don't expose the server's data folders to anyone but yourself.

Setting Up Notes Users to Use SSL and S/MIME

R5 Notes users can install X.509 certificates in their ID files, alongside their Notes certificates. There are two reasons why Notes users might need X.509 certificates. First, they may need to authenticate with Internet servers using SSL. Second, they might want to use S/MIME to sign email going out to Internet correspondents and to decrypt messages coming in from Internet recipients.

Notes users can obtain X.509 certificates themselves, or you, as a Domino CA, can provide them automatically. To get their own certificates, Notes users have to apply for them from a CA, either a third-party CA or a Domino CA. If a user obtains a certificate from a third-party CA, he needs to register it with you, again in your capacity as his Domino CA. For you to provide your Notes users with X.509 certificates automatically, you also have to set yourself up as a Domino CA.

The bottom line here is that, if your Notes users are going to need to use SSL or S/MIME, you have to set yourself up as a Domino CA. Well, okay, that statement isn't strictly true; a Notes user could obtain a certificate from a third-party CA, and then manually copy the public key from it into his Person document in the Domain Directory. But if you set yourself up as a company CA, the Domino Certificate Administrator and the Administration Process can do most of the work for you and your users.

So, if only a few adventurous users want to set themselves up to use SSL and S/MIME, maybe you can let them or help them do it all manually. But if you want to provide all of your users with the ability to use SSL and/or S/MIME, you really want to set yourself up as a CA. If that is the solution for you, then you have to decide whether to set yourself up as a Domino CA, issuing certificates based on your own root certificate, or to set yourself up with a third-party CA application, issuing certificates based on a widely accepted root certificate.

The reason why you might want to set yourself up with a third-party CA application is, again, to make life a little easier for your users. Your users will present their certificates to either an SSL server during authentication or a correspondent pursuant to signing a message. The second party (server or correspondent) will then have to decide whether he/she/it can trust your user's certificate. That means the second party will have to install your CA certificate as a trusted root certificate. For mail correspondents that might not be a big deal; their mail application will ask them the first time it encounters your certificate whether they want to trust it. If they say yes, that's the end of the problem. But in all likelihood they already have a whole list of well-known commercial CA root certificates installed as trusted roots—most Internet client programs (including Notes) have them preinstalled. If your users' X.509 certificates were based on one of those, their correspondents wouldn't ever have to decisde whether to trust your users' certificates at all.

If your users are authenticating with Internet SSL servers, they may have a bigger problem. The server itself cannot make the decision whether to trust your CA root certificate. An administrator of that server will have to intervene. That administrator will have to come to your CA server and obtain your root certificate and then install it as a trusted root in his own server. Because of both the hassle and necessity to establish whether your root certificate *should* be trusted, the administrator may refuse altogether. That leaves your users with the necessity of obtaining a client certificate from a commercial CA and then registering it with you.

You can eliminate all of this hassle by somehow basing the certificates you issue on a well-known commercial CA's root certificate. To put this in terms that might be more familiar to you, you can set yourself up as, in effect, an OU certifier instead of an O certifier. Instead of self-certifying your CA root certificate, you can have a commercial CA certify it. Then you can use it to issue X.509 certificates to your users, either from a CA application supplied by the commercial CA that issued your CA certificate or in Domino Certificate Administrator itself. (I haven't tested any of this, but I can't think of a reason why it shouldn't work.)

For example, Thawte, which is one of the three largest commercial CAs (the other two being VeriSign and EnTrust, I believe), sells what it calls a "chained" CA certificate. That's their term for what you and I know as an OU certifier in Notes. Thawte offers two kinds of chained certificates. One is expensive ($100,000 the last time I checked) and allows the buyer to set itself up as a commercial CA in its own right. The other is much cheaper (around $10,000) and lets you issue limited numbers of certificates for limited purposes.

The second one is the one for you. You install that certificate in Domino Certificate Administrator and then issue certificates to your users (and servers) that, when presented to third-parties, are instantly recognized by the server or mail reader as descendants of a trusted commercial root certificate. For more information about programs offered by commercial CAs, see, for starters, www.thawte.com, www.verisign.com, and www.entrust.com.

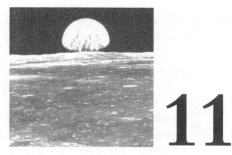

11

Domino Directory Services

DIRECTORY SERVICES—THE PUBLICATION TO USERS OF INFORMATION about entities listed in directories—have always played a central and pervasive role in Notes and Domino. In R5, Lotus has refined existing directory services and added a new one. To set up and administer an efficiently operating Notes domain, you must understand the role that each service plays and how they work together. The larger your Domino installation, the more important this is.

An exhaustive list of Domino directory services includes all the following:

- **The primary Domino directory.** This is the database called names.nsf that resides on every Domino server in a Notes domain and defines the extent of the Notes domain itself. The Domino Directory maintains information of two kinds: server configuration information that the local server uses; and directory information for the benefit of all servers and people.

- **Secondary Domino directories.** Any given server may also maintain Domino directories other than the primary one. There are two possible kinds of secondary Domino directories:

  - **Other Domains directories.** A server may host replica copies of Domino Directories that define one or more domains other than the server's own domain. A server would host another domain's directory so that users in this domain could more easily address mail to the other domain.

- **Non-domain-related directories.** You can create directories for purposes other than defining a Notes domain. For example, you can define a secondary directory to store the names of Web users who authenticate with your Domino servers. For another example, you could create a secondary directory for storing the names of people outside your Notes domain that your users correspond with frequently. The idea behind creating such directories is to avoid cluttering up your primary directory with information about people who aren't really members of your domain.

- **The Domino LDAP Service.** The Lightweight Directory Access Protocol is a set of Internet-standards defining ways to set up, manage, and access directories on TCP/IP-based networks. The Domino LDAP service permits non-Notes clients to use LDAP to access, search, and update Domino directories.

- **The Directory Catalog.** New in R5, the Directory Catalog is a highly compressed compendium of Domino Directories. It is designed to make available to your users a small but complete directory in which to do very fast address lookups when working in email or any other application in which they have to look up people's names. It is an optional feature of Domino and is most useful either to large organizations or to organizations that have users who are not always connected to their servers. Lotus recommends, if you use directory catalogs, that you actually define two:

    - The **Server Directory Catalog** for your server-connected users.

    - The **Mobile Directory Catalog** for your disconnected users.

- **Directory Assistance.** This is a service that allows your Domino servers to make secondary Domino directories and non-Domino LDAP directories available to your users for name lookup purposes.

- **Cascaded Address Books.** This is an older technique, supported in R5 solely for the purpose of backward compatibility, for giving users access to secondary Domino directories during name lookups. Directory Assistance provides more functionality. Lotus recommends that you convert to Directory Assistance if you are still using cascaded address books.

- **Directory Servers.** In Domino R5, you can designate Domino servers to provide directory services for Notes and LDAP clients. This allows you to relieve other servers of that load, so that they can provide other services more effectively. For example, if mail servers don't have to provide directory services, they can better provide mail services. In future releases, Lotus may well extend directory servers so that they also provide directory services for other Domino servers. If that comes to pass, only directory servers would host copies of the primary Domino Directory; other Domino servers would query a directory server when they need information from the Domino Directory.

Lotus Notes also provides two directory services. First, every copy of Notes has a Personal Address Book (`names.nsf`), which provides the same services to the local copy of Notes and the local Notes user that the Domino Directory (`names.nsf`) provides to the local Domino server and all of the domain's users. That is, it provides Notes with information it needs to work correctly; and it gives the local user a local directory in which to maintain personal contact information. Second, Notes has built-in LDAP client capabilities; that is, it can query LDAP directory servers.

We won't cover Notes directory services in this chapter. See Chapter 12, "User Maintenance and Troubleshooting," for that. Here we'll look at each of Domino's directory services in detail. We'll also focus on how they work together and on which services you should use.

The Domino Directory

The Domino Directory is the center of the Notes universe. Every Domino server hosts a *primary* Domino Directory with the filename `names.nsf`, which defines the membership of the local Notes domain. The Domino Directory is a Notes database. It is based on the Domain Directory template (`pubnames.ntf`).

In R4, the Domino Directory was known as the Public Address Book. In R3 and earlier ,it was known as the Public Name and Address Book. Because old habits are hard to break, many people (especially people at Lotus) still refer to it by both of those names or by acronyms such as NAB, PAB, and PNAB. But, the rest of the computing world has recently discovered the value of "directory-centric" applications. So, because Lotus wants the world to be clear about the Public Address Book's true function, its official name in R5 is the Domino Directory. In this book, we have sometimes referred to it as the *Domain* Directory to highlight its role in defining the domain and to differentiate it from secondary Domino directories.

The primary Domino Directory, the one called `names.nsf`, performs two functions. First, each server's running parameters are stored in it; Domino servers refer to it constantly while running to get their marching orders; they can't even start up if they can't locate a copy of it. It (along with a text-based configuration file named `notes.ini`) tells them what services to run, when to run them, how to run them, and when to stop running them.

It's the second function, however, that is of primary interest to us in this chapter— directory services. The primary Domain Directory stores information about every server, user, local mail recipient, group, certifier, and resource in the local domain. It stores information about how and when to route mail and replicate databases. It stores information about holidays and about neighboring domains. It is also customizable, so that you can store any information you want in the Domain Directory.

Setting Up the Primary Domino Directory

The primary Domino Directory is created automatically when you set up the first server in the domain. When you set up each additional server, it automatically receives a new replica of the Domino Directory. So, as a general rule, you don't have to create copies of the Domain Directory. (In earlier versions of Notes, users frequently did create local copies of the Public Address Book so that they could more easily address mail to people in their Notes domain. This practice is no longer necessary if you set up a mobile Directory Catalog; see the section, "Setting Up the Mobile Directory Catalog on User Workstations," later in this chapter.)

However, because the primary Domino Directory is so central to the smooth functioning of a Notes domain, there are some things you should do to set it up properly. First, you want, as a general rule, to limit access to it. Second, you want to insure frequent replication of it among your servers. Third, you want to make sure the Profile documents are properly set up. Finally, you want to monitor changes in its (ACL) and failures to replicate.

Setting Up the ACL

In general, you want to limit people's access rights to the primary Domino Directory. The Domino Directory template makes it pretty easy to do that. By default, most users have Author access to the primary Domino Directory, but cannot create or delete any documents and can only edit certain "personal information" fields in their own Person document. Beyond that, only designated users can create, edit, or delete documents. If you want to minimize the possibility of security breaches or of inexperienced people making serious mistakes, you can limit individual administrators' ability to make changes in the Domino Directory by setting their rights in the ACL as follows:

Specifically, to create a document, you have to have Author or higher access in the ACL with the "Create Documents" privilege selected and one or more of the "Creator" roles selected. (See Chapter 10, "Security," for a definition of the "Creator" and "Modifier" roles.) You can modify documents if you meet one of the following sets of conditions:

- To create only certain classes of documents (Person, Group, Server, or all others), set a person's ACL rights to Author with "Create documents" privilege and appropriate "Creator" roles selected.

- To modify only certain classes of documents, set a person's ACL rights to Author with appropriate "Modifier roles selected. If the person should be able to delete the same documents, give him the "Delete documents" privilege.

- To modify only selected documents, set a person's ACL rights to Author and add the person's name to the Administrators field of the documents to be edited. If the person should be able to delete the same documents, give him the "Delete documents" privilege.

In addition, you can limit the propagation of changes across your network by limiting the ACL rights of your servers. For example, you could give Manager access only to the hub servers and Editor access to all other servers. Then, if someone made a change in the ACL or design of the Domino Directory on a spoke server, the change would be localized because the hub(s) would refuse to accept the change from the spoke. (The only problem with doing this is you may not find out about the change as easily as if the change replicated to other servers.)

Finally, you can set up your servers so that they notify you whenever anyone makes a change in the ACL of the Domino Directory. To do this, you have to create an ACL Change Monitor and an Event Notification in the Statistics & Events database. The ACL Change monitor would cause the Event task running on selected servers to monitor changes to the ACL of the names.nsf database, and to declare the occurrence of an event of Security type whenever such a change takes place. The Event Notification would notify you in way of your choice when the defined event takes place. See Chapter 18, "Server Monitoring," for more information.

Setting Up Replication

Regarding replication of the primary Domino Directory, Lotus recommends you schedule replication of it (and the Administration Requests database) no less frequently than every 30 minutes. Because you may not want to replicate any other database that frequently, you can set up special Connection documents to replicate those two databases (or those two and any others that you *do* want replicated that frequently).

You can do that either of two ways. First, you can set up Connection documents that name these two databases (names.nsf, admin4.nsf) in the Files/Directories to Replicate field. Alternately, you can set these two databases as High Priority databases (in Replication Settings), then set up Connection documents that replicate only databases of High priority.

You also want to be notified when the Domino Directory fails to replicate for some defined amount of time. To set this up, you can create a Replication Monitor and an Event Notification in Statistics & Events. The replication monitor would cause the Event task running on selected servers to monitor replication events between selected pairs of servers. If a successful replication of names.nsf failed to occur within a defined period of time (by default, 24 hours) the Event task would declare the occurrence of a Replication event. The Event Notification document would the Event process to notify you by a method of your choice when the defined event occurred.

The Domino Directory Profile

Starting in R5, the Domino Directory uses a profile document to store certain preferences. See Figure 11.1. You should verify that the settings meet your needs. The fields are set forth in Table 11.1.

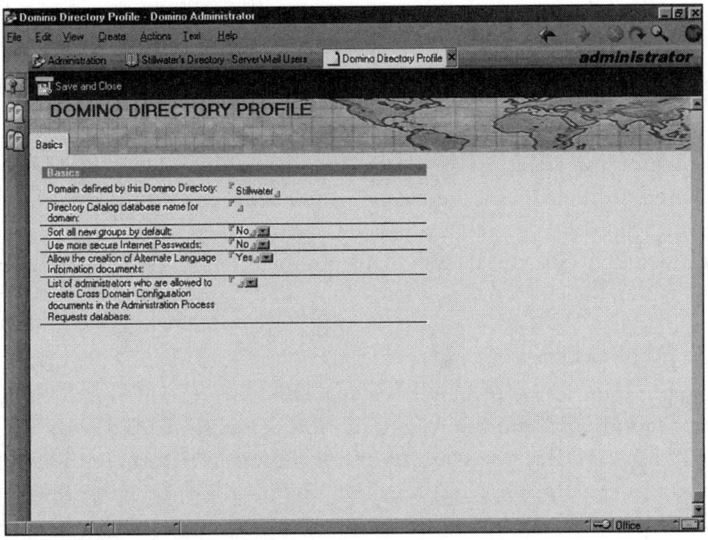

Figure 11.1 The Directory Profile holds basic settings about the Domino Directory.

Table 11.1 **The Fields in the Directory Profile**

Field	Comment
Domain defined by this Domino Directory	Leave this blank for a secondary directory that does not define a domain.
Directory Catalog database name for domain	This is the default filename of the Server Directory Catalog, if you define one. See the section on Directory Catalogs later in this chapter.
Sort all new groups by default	The default is No. If you leave the default setting, you can still sort each group by opening it in edit mode and choosing to sort it. If you prefer to sort group membership lists, set this to Yes.

Field	Comment
Use more secure Internet Passwords	Leave this set to No only if you are still running HTTP on servers running Domino 4.5.x or earlier. Otherwise, set this to Yes.
Allow the creation of Alternate Language Information documents	This is only relevant if one or more servers in the domain run LDAP. Setting this to Yes makes possible LDAP searches using alternate languages. See "LDAP Directory Services," later in this chapter, for more information.
List of administrators who are allowed to create Cross Domain Configuration documents in the Administration Process Requests database	Cross Domain Configuration documents (which you create in the Administration Requests database (`admin4.nsf`)) list requests from other Notes domains that the Administration Process will honor. List here anyone who should be able to create Cross Domain Configuration documents. People having Manager access to the Domain Directory are automatically able to create them, so you need not list them here.

Secondary Domino Directories

Administrators frequently use *secondary* Domino directories. There are two occasions for this.

First, some companies have more than one Notes domain. To make it easier for users in each domain to address mail to users in the other domains, administrators in such companies will make replicas of each domain's Directory on servers in the other domains. To learn more about this, see the sections, "The Directory Catalog" and "Directory Assistance," later in this chapter.

Second, administrators sometimes make directories that don't define any Notes domain but simply hold directory information. I have seen two circumstances for this. One is where companies have set up Web sites in which they invite people to register in order to gain special benefits. Each registered Web user has a Person document. The other circumstance typically arises in smaller companies where they may create Person documents for anyone their users frequently correspond with—suppliers, business partners, customers, family members, you name it.

In both of these scenarios, you have to create Person documents for people who aren't really members of your domain. To keep these Person documents from cluttering up the *Domain* Directory, administrators will create a secondary directory using the pubnames.ntf template and add these *special* Person documents to it. They then set up Directory Assistance or a Directory Catalog to make these people's names available to members of the domain. Again, see the sections "Directory Catalogs" and "Directory Assistance" for more information.

When you create a secondary Domino Directory, be sure to give it a unique filename (for example, `webnames.nsf` or `othernames.nsf`). You can't use `names.nsf`, which may appear by default. You should also give it a descriptive title (for example, Web Users or Other People), so you'll recognize it easily for what it is later on.

LDAP Directory Services

Beginning with R4.6, Lotus has made the Domino Directory (known in 4.6 as the Public Address Book) accessible to non-Notes clients by incorporating the Internet standard Lightweight Directory Access Protocol (LDAP) into the Domino server. Domino R4.6 supports LDAP Version 2. Domino R5 supports LDAP versions 2 and 3.

When the LDAP service is running on a Domino server, you are publishing selected contents of one or more Domino Directories to LDAP clients and other LDAP servers. This can benefit your users in a variety of ways. A few examples are the following:

- You can provide Domino directory services to your own POP3 and IMAP mail users, so that, like their Notes-using colleagues, they can look up the mail addresses of people and databases to whom they may want to send messages.

- People (otherwise unrelated to your domain) who want to send messages to people in your domain can look up your users' (and mail-in databases) mail addresses in your domain directory.

- LDAP-compliant applications can look up information in your directories.

- Third-party servers (for example, the Netscape Enterprise Web server) can use the information in your domain directory to authenticate your users. For example, the third-party server could compare a name and password or a name and certificate received from one of your users with information found in the user's Person document to verify the authenticity of the received name and password.

LDAP features supported by Domino include the following:

- **Extended searches and referrals.** When LDAP clients query a Domino server, it searches its primary Domino Directory first, then can perform extended searches on secondary Domino Directories. In addition, if the Domino server determines that the information sought by the LDAP client is probably on a third-party LDAP server, the Domino LDAP server can refer the client to that third-party server. Both of these features (known as "extended searches" and "referrals") are standard LDAP server features. To set them up, you have to enable Directory Assistance on the server. (For more information, see the section on Directory Assistance later in this chapter.)

- **Authentication options.** If you don't feel comfortable letting anonymous strangers search through your Domino Directories, you can require LDAP clients to authenticate using either name-and-password or SSL certificate-base authentication techniques. In addition, you can set up LDAP so that, when LDAP clients connect to it, they authenticate your server through SSL. Finally, Domino supports the Simple Authentication and Security Layer (SASL) protocol (RFC 2222).

- **Add, Modify, and Delete access.** You can allow LDAP clients to add, modify and delete directory entries. For example, users could change their own passwords or you could use an LDAP client to perform maintenance chores remotely.

- **Schema publishing, checking, and extension.** In simple terms, Domino's schema is a list of the documents and fields in a Domino Directory that an LDAP user is permitted to access, and whether the user may have read-only or read-write access. Schema publishing and checking allows clients to find out what information they can access, and what kind of access the can have. Schema extension allows you to change the documents and fields that you publish. You can define new forms, subforms, and fields right in your directories and, depending on how you do it, not have to worry about your changes being wiped out when you upgrade to a later release of Domino.

- **Alternate language support.** If you create Alternate Language Information documents, Domino's LDAP service can accept searches in the supported alternate languages. Alternate Language Information documents are responses to Person document and have a subset of the fields found in Person documents. The fields contain the same information as that in their Person document equivalents, but in some selected other language. Don't confuse this with alternate name/language support in user IDs. This is not the same thing. You can implement one, the other, both, or neither. One significant difference between them is that you can only assign one alternate language to a person's ID file, but you can create a many Alternate Language Information documents (each representing yet another language) as you want for each Person document.

Domino also provides some LDAP services that don't require a server to be running the LDAP service. All R5 Domino servers can provide these LDAP-related services:

- Domino servers can use third-party LDAP directories to authenticate Web users. To implement this, you have to implement Directory Assistance.

- You can use groups from third-party LDAP directories in database ACLs. To implement this, you have to implement Directory Assistance.

- Domino servers include a command-line utility (ldapsearch.exe under Windows) with which you can perform LDAP searches.

- Using the LDIF file format, you can import entries from another LDAP directory into the Domino Directory. See the section, "Migration Tools" in Chapter 6.

In addition, Lotus Notes is an LDAP client. You can set up Account documents in Lotus Notes for LDAP directories. Several such documents for commercial LDAP directories already exist at Notes setup. See Chapters 5, 6, and 13 for more information.

Understanding LDAP

The Lightweight Directory Access Protocol (LDAP), defines a set of standard techniques and rules for accessing X.500 directory services without, in the words of its authors, "incurring the resource requirements of the Directory Access Protocol (DAP)." X.500, the Directory Access Protocol, was introduced with great hope and promise in the late 80s as a standard method of implementing directory services. But, it didn't gain widespread acceptance, partially because it was costly to implement.

LDAP was introduced to reduce the overhead of implementing X.500 directory services by, among other things, making use of TCP/IP as the transport mechanism between X.500 directory services and LDAP clients. LDAP version 1 was introduced in 1993 (RFC 1487 et seq.) LDAP version 2 arrived in 1995 (RFC 1777 et seq.). The current version, version 3, arrived in 1997 (RFC 2251 et seq.)

To understand LDAP, you have to understand something about X.500 directory services. That shouldn't be too hard for yo, because Notes has complied with X.500 since R3, when it introduced hierarchical organizations and distinguished naming. X.500 requires that directories organize their membership hierarchically, and that the names of members uniquely identify them or distinguish them from other members of the directory. Notes is a good example of that, with its hierarchical system of organizing users and servers, and the mapping of that hierarchy to users' and servers' fully distinguished names. Novell's NDS is another good example. If you understand Notes's organizing and naming rules, or those of NDS, you are half-way to understanding X.500.

The other half of understanding X.500, and the tricky part, is to learn the jargon. Neither Notes nor NDS use X.500 jargon, even though both are X.500-compliant. LDAP does use X.500 jargon, so you need to translate between X.500 and Notes.

X.500 directories are technically known as *Directory Information Trees* (DITs). They contain *objects*, which are members of *object classes* and contain *attributes* defined by their object classes. The attributes of the objects contain *values*.

The Domino Directory is an X.500 DIT. In the Domino Directory, forms are the equivalent of object classes. For example, the Person form defines the class Person.

Notes documents created with the Notes forms are the actual objects that make up the membership of the class. Person documents are objects of class Person; group documents are objects of class Group; and so on.

Fields are the equivalent of attributes. The field values are what Domino delivers to LDAP clients when they ask for the attributes of all objects having some particular attribute.

Table 11.2 summarizes the relationship between LDAP and Notes objects.

Table 11.2 **Equivalencies in LDAP/DAP and Lotus Notes**

LDAP Term	Notes Term
Directory Information Tree	Domino Directory
Object class	Form
Object	Document
Attribute	Field
Attribute value	Field value

There isn't a one-to-one correspondence between every form and field and an LDAP class or attribute. Rather, in the Domino Directory, only Person, Group, Mail-In Database, and Server documents are initially mapped to object classes. Only some of the fields in those documents map to LDAP attributes. But, LDAP doesn't require that the Domino directory structure itself internally in some certain way. It only requires that Domino respond in some predictable way when presented with an LDAP-compliant query. And Domino does.

Setting UP the Domino LDAP Service

To set up a server to provide LDAP services, you must first set up the following items:

- **Install TCP/IP.** The Domino LDAP service relies on the TCP/IP protocol, so any Domino server that runs it must run TCP/IP.

- **Register with DNS.** LDAP clients will query DNS to determine an LDAP server's address, so you'll have to register your LDAP server with your local DNS server. If you expect to receive queries from clients over the Internet, you'll have to connect your LDAP server to the Internet and register it with your ISP's DNS server. You might want to use an alias name for this server, such as `ldap.planetnotes.com`.

- **Full-text index.** On the LDAP server, create a full-text index of the primary Domino Directory and any secondary Domino directories accessible to LDAP. Otherwise searches will proceed very slowly.

- **Global Domain document.** If your domain defines more than one Global Domain document, services designate one of them as the default Global Domain document. Open it in Edit Mode and set the Use as default Global Domain field to Yes.

When you have met the above conditions (and some optional ones if you like, covered a little further on), you can start the LDAP service. To start it manually, you can enter the `load ldap` command from the server console or you can choose the LDAP Server command under Server, Status, Tools, Task, Start in Domino Administrator. To shut LDAP down manually, you can enter the `tell ldap quit` command from the server console or you can select the running LDAP service under Server, Status in Domino Administrator, then choose Stop under Tools, Task. But, to get the LDAP service to run all the time, starting when Domino starts and stopping when Domino stops, you must add LDAP to the ServerTasks variable in the server's `notes.ini` file.

After you have configured and started the LDAP service you can test it, configure it, and set up client programs to access it. To test it, you can query the server with either an LDAP client program or the `ldapsearch` utility that comes with the Domino server and Domino Administrator.

ldapsearch

The `ldapsearch` utility is difficult to master at first for two reasons. First, it only works properly if you give it the right parameters. Second, Lotus misdocuments it in R5. The documented version is called `lsearch` and apparently has a filename of `?lsearch.exe`, where `?` stands for the different initial character for each server operating system. But it seems the programmers pulled a fast one on the documenters. At the last minute, they slipped a file called `ldapsearch.exe` into the Windows NT version of Domino for R5 and no utility at all into the other versions until R5.0.1, at which time they also gained utilities named `ldapsearch`.

The syntax of `ldapsearch` is

```
ldapsearch [Options] Filter [Attributes]
```

[Options]. There are over 20 options. The only one you need to know to test your server is the `-h` *hostname* option, where *hostname* is either your LDAP server's host name or alias or, if you haven't set up its host name in DNS yet, its IP address. If you want to use more than one option, you can separate them from each other with colons (:).

Filter. A filter is any search term that LDAP recognizes. It tells the directory what you are looking for. An example is `sn=`*surname* where *surname* is the last name of the person you want to search for (say, for test purposes, your own last name).

[Attributes]. is a space-delimited list of the field values you want returned. If you leave [Attributes] blank, your search will return (if successful) all fields with LDAP attributes assigned to them.

So, to test my LDAP server, I ran the command as follows:

```
ldapsearch -h osprey.planetnotes.com sn=kirkland
```

I could have run it as follows:

```
ldapsearch -h 192.168.0.6 sn=kirkland
```

Either way, when everything worked properly, it returned the following list of attribute=value pairs:

```
CN=Rob Kirkland,OU=MarshCreek,O=Stillwater
o=Stillwater
ou=MarshCreek
cn=Rob Kirkland
mail=Rob_Kirkland@planetnotes.com
objectclass=top
objectclass=person
objectclass=organizationalPerson
objectclass=inetOrgPerson
objectclass=dominoPerson
certificate=03005302 3672FE0E 1AG0162A G0020DD7 1CEDEF03 G0030200 01208600 67061
100 516725G0 024FG002 6D061100 50672500 08D31000 2B6A2585 01A07700 67061100 5167
25G0 024FG002 6D061100 50672500 08D31000 2B6A2585 4F553D4D 61727368 43726565 6B2
F4F3D 5374696C 6C776174 657
publickey=0200526F 62204B69 726B6C61 6E64G043
givenname=Rob
sn=Kirkland
fullname=CN=Rob Kirkland,OU=MarshCreek,O=Stillwater
fullname=CN=Rob Kirkland
shortname=rkirklan
maildomain=Stillwater
```

We don't have space to explore the ldapsearch command in detail. However, if, in Lotus's documentation, you substitute ldapsearch for lsearch, everything should work pretty much as documented. Formulating filters is similar to formulating searches in Notes. You can use the standard comparison operators: equals (=), approximately equals (~=), greater than (>), less than (<), greater than or equal to (>=), less than or equal to (<=), and so on. You can use the same logical operators: AND (&), OR (|), and NOT (!).

Configuring LDAP

The default settings of LDAP work just fine under many circumstances. However, there are a series of variables you can set in the default configuration document, server documents, and notes.ini, which alter the way LDAP works.

The primary settings—which are domain-wide—are in the default configuration document for the domain. If you haven't created one, do so now, as follows. In Domino Administrator, under Configuration, with a server selected, choose Server, Configurations, Add Configuration. Set the first field under Basics, "Use these settings as the default settings for all servers," to Yes. (If that field does not appear, it is because a default configuration document already exists; Domino only allows you to create one.) The LDAP tab appears. You can now set the fields that appear there.

But first, save and close this document. If you opened the Directory in Notes or under Files in Domino Administrator, you'll now see the new configuration document listed under All servers. If you created the new document in Domino Administrator, it doesn't appear in the Server, Configurations view or the Messaging, Configurations view. It only appears in the Directory, Directory Settings view, and then only the LDAP tab (labeled here LDAP Settings appears.

The items that appear under LDAP Settings, and their uses, appear in Table 11.3.

Table 11.3 **Domain-Wide LDAP Settings**

Field	Comment
Anonymous users can query	Consists of a list of fields whose values may be returned on queries by unauthenticated LDAP users. You may add or remove field names to this list.
Allow LDAP users write access	Defaults to No. Set it to Yes if you want to allow LDAP users to add, modify, and delete records.
Timeout	The number of seconds that must pass before a search automatically terminates. Defaults to 0, which means the search never automatically times out, but continues until all directories have been searched.
Maximum number of entries returned	Defaults to 0, which means there is no maximum. A search could return every record.
Minimum characters for wildcard search	Defaults to 1, which means that there must be at least one character preceding the asterisk ($\star$) wildcard in a search. In other words, sn=* would not be acceptable. In a very large directory, you might want to increase this number.
Allow Alternate Language Information processing	Allows searches on information in Alternate Language Information documents. If you set this to Yes, it automatically turns on the Optimize LDAP queries property, which in turn activates a series of hidden views in the directories.
Rules to follow when this directory is the primary directory, and there are multiple matches on the distinguished name being compared/ modified	This applies only to queries which direct Domino to modify matching entries. The default is Don't modify any. The other choices are Modify first match and Modify all matches.

You can make the settings in Table 11.3 on a domain-wide basis only. They affect all LDAP servers in the Domino domain. One of them, exceptionally, overrides settings on individual server configuration documents. By setting Allow Alternate Language Information processing to Yes, you activate the Optimize LDAP queries field on the (invisible) Basics tab of the default configuration document. This overrides the same setting in each server's configuration documents.

Setting the Optimize LDAP queries field to Yes causes the LDAP service to use four hidden views in the Directory—$LDAPS, $LDAPG, SLDAPCN, and $LDA-PHIER. The trailing letter or letters in the view names (S, G, CN, and HIER) indicate the sort order of each view. Thus, $LDAPS sorts by surname (last name); $LDAPG sorts by given name (first name); $LDAPCN sorts by common name; and $LDA-PHIER sorts by hierarchical name (fully-distinguished name to Notes cognoscenti.) These views speed up processing of LDAP queries, enable support for alternate language queries, and enable the export of objects other than people and groups.

On each server document, you can configure the LDAP ports and authentication requirements. Under the Ports, Internet Ports, Directory tabs you can enable or disable the LDAP TCP/IP port and the LDAP SSL port; you can change the port numbers; and you can specify whether and what types of authentication are required. The fields and their choices appear in Table 11.4.

Table 11.4 **LDAP Port and Authentication Fields**

Field	Comment
TCP/IP port number	Defaults to the 389, the well-known port number for LDAP over TCP/IP. If you change this, your clients will have to change it too or they won't be able to find you.
TCP/IP port status	Defaults to Enabled, which means that users can query your server without positively identifying it through SSL. You can also choose Disabled, which would cause queries on this port to fail entirely; and Redirect to SSL, which would cause the server to tell the querying client to try again on the port number set forth in the SSL port number field.
Authentication options: Name & password	Defaults to Yes, which means that LDAP clients can authenticate themselves to the server by presenting a name and password. Set to No to prevent name and password authentication.
Authentication options: Anonymous	Defaults to Yes, which means that LDAP users can send queries without first authenticating. If they try to do something prohibited to anonymous LDAP users, such as make modifications, they'll be forced to authenticate or denied the right, depending on the setting of other fields in this form.

continues

Table 11.4 **Continued**

Field	Comment
SSL port number	Defaults to the 636, the well-known port number for LDAP over SSL. If you change this, your clients will have to change it too or they won't be able to find you.
SSL port status	Defaults to Disabled, which means that users cannot authenticate your server through SSL before querying it. You can also choose Enabled. But before you do so, you must set up SSL on the server. See Chapter 10.
Authentication options: Client certificate	Defaults to No, which means that, after being authenticated itself, the server won't in turn require certificate-based authentication of the user. Set this to Yes to make possible certificate-based authentication of the user. If you enable this field and disable to two that follow, SSL clients will be required to present a trusted certificate to authenticate. If you enable this and either or both of the following fields, Domino will ask the user to present a trusted certificate; failing that, Domino will permit the user to proceed unauthenticated until the user tries to do something prohibited to anonymous users; then, the server will attempt name-and-password authentication.
Authentication options: Name & password	Defaults to No, which means that, after being authenticated itself, the server won't in turn require name-and-password authentication of the user. Set this to Yes to make possible name-and-password authentication of the user. (Whether it will be required depends on the settings of the other fields.)
Authentication options: Anonymous	Defaults to Yes, which means that, after being authenticated itself, the server will permit the user to submit a query without itself authenticating. Set this to No to require users coming in on the SSL port to authenticate by one of the two preceding methods.

Finally, in each server's `notes.ini` file, you can set the following variable:

`LDAP_Strict_RFC_Adherence=1`

This forces LDAP clients to authenticate using their fully distinguished names. Setting this variable to 0 or removing it (which is the default condition) allows LDAP clients to authenticate using any unique name that appears in the FullName or ShortName fields of their Person document.

Extending and Monitoring LDAP Services

We don't have the space to discuss the subject of extending the Domino schema here. But, for an excellent treatment of it, see *Exploring LDAP Features in Domino R5* by Kendra Bowker, published in Iris Today, www.notes.net, July 1999.

To track LDAP statistics, you can use a series of Domino console commands. For example, show tasks displays the number of currently active LDAP sessions. Show port *portname* (where *portname* is the name of the TCPIP port that LDAP uses), displays traffic and error statistics on the port. Show stat ldap displays a list of about 30 statistics about your LDAP server's performance. You can also view LDAP statistics in the Statistics Reports database and in Domino Administrator under the Server, Statistics tab.

Multiple Directories

We've already seen that a domain can have multiple secondary Domino directories in addition to its primary Domino Directory. For these directories to be useful, you have to make them available to users, servers, and programs for lookup purposes. Domino provides three different ways to do that: Directory Catalogs, Directory Assistance, and Cascaded Address Books. Directory Assistance is new in R5. Directory Assistance was introduced in R4. Cascaded Address Books are a legacy of R3 and are only supported in R5 to maintain backward compatibility. Directory Assistance and Directory Catalogs provides more functionality than Cascaded Address Books and are less resource intensive. Lotus recommends that you use either Directory Catalogs, Directory Assistance, or both as your needs dictate, and that you discontinue use of Cascaded Address Books if you are using them. I echo that recommendation.

The question remains, should you use both Directory Catalogs and Directory Assistance? The answer depends on why you have multiple directories.

To start with, unless you have a very small, simple Notes domain, you should probably use Directory Catalogs even if you only have a primary Domino Directory. The purpose of the Directory Catalog is to shrink the lookup directory to its smallest possible footprint and to speed up address lookups. It does both very well. If you are a small Notes organization, say, less than 200 users, none of them mobile users, then Directory Catalogs have little to offer you. But, the larger your organization, the more you need Directory Catalogs. And if you have mobile users, the Mobile Directory Catalog provides the best-ever solution to the problem of maintaining an up-to-date mobile address book.

Directory Assistance, on the other hand, does a couple things that Directory Catalogs don't. It can extend address lookups to LDAP entries for Notes users. It can refer LDAP clients to other LDAP directories. It allows you to authenticate Web users based on credentials stored in other LDAP directories. If you need any of those features, you have to use Directory Assistance.

Also, if you maintain secondary directories of users to whom other users won't be likely to address mail, you might consider excluding them from Directory Catalogs but including them in Directory Assistance. For example, you may maintain a secondary directory just to authenticate your Web users, who are primarily strangers to whom your regular users won't be addressing mail. There is no point in including this directory in the Directory Catalog if your purpose in creating a Directory Catalog is to accelerate address lookups and you want to keep the Directory Catalog as small as possible. But you can include it in Directory Assistance so people, such as Web application managers, can use it for address lookups if they need to.

Finally, if you are still in doubt about which service to use, there is Lotus's recommendation: Set up both Directory Catalogs and Directory Assistance. They work together to give you comprehensive directory access. If your Directory Catalog becomes unavailable for any reason, Directory Assistance backs it up 100 percent, and your users might never notice its absence (if, indeed, they ever realized it was there in the first place).

Table 11.5 compares the relative capabilities of the mobile directory catalog, the server directory catalog, and Directory Assistance.

Table 11.5 **Relative Capabilities of the Mobile Directory Catalog, the Server Directory Catalog, and Directory Assistance**

Task	Mobile Directory Catalog	Server Directory Catalog	Directory Assistance
Address lookups in secondary Domino directories for Notes mail users	Yes	Yes	Yes
Address lookups in LDAP directories for Notes mail users	No	No	Yes
Address lookups in secondary Domino directories for LDAP clients	No	Yes	Yes
Refer LDAP clients to other LDAP directories	No	No	Yes
Authenticate Web clients registered in secondary Domino directories	No	Yes	Yes
Authenticate Web clients registered in other LDAP directories	No	No	Yes

Task	Mobile Directory Catalog	Server Directory Catalog	Directory Assistance
Verify membership in groups registered in other LDAP directories	No	No	Yes
Recipient name type ahead addressing	Yes	Yes	Yes
Provide mobile Notes users with complete set of directories	Yes	No	No

Directory Search Order

If you do set up both Directory Catalogs and Directory Assistance, you might like to know the order in which they are searched. The short answer is that the Directory Catalog is searched before secondary directories listed in Directory Assistance.

But, in what order are all directories searched? The answer depends on who is doing the searching: Domino server, Notes client, or LDAP client?

A Domino server searches directories in the following order:

1. Primary Domino Directory.

2. If Cascaded Address Books are enabled, the other directories listed in the names variable in the server's `notes.ini` file. (But, if Cascaded Address Books are enabled, you can't enable the other directory services and the search ends here.)

3. If it uses a Directory Catalog, the Directory Catalog.

4. If it finds the entry that it seeks in the Directory Catalog, but can't find the item of information in that entry, it searches the secondary directory from which the entry in the Directory Catalog was drawn.

5. If Directory Assistance is enabled, it searches the secondary directories listed there.

   a. If the searching server knows the distinguished name of the entry for which it is searching, it looks for a rule in the Directory Assistance database to tell it which secondary directory or directories to search in.

   b. If the searching server only knows the common name of the entry for which it is searching or if it does not find a rule telling it which secondary directory to search, it searches the secondary directories in their enumerated search order. If any directories have the same search order, it searches them in alphabetic order.

A Notes user searches directories in the following order:

1. Local directories in the order in which they appear in the Local address books field in User Preferences, Mail and News. If Notes is set up in a standard way, this would mean, first, the user's Personal Address Book (names.nsf) and, second, if it exists on the workstation, the Mobile Directory Catalog.

2. If, in the user's selected Location document, the Mail file location field is set to Local and the Recipient name type-ahead field is set to Disabled or Local only, Notes searches no further.

3. If, alternately, the Mail file location field is set to Local and the Recipient name type-ahead field is set to Local then Server, Notes searches the directories available on its directory or mail server, but only after the user presses F9 or chooses Send.

4. If the Mail file location field is set to on Server, Notes immediately continues the search on its directory or mail server.

5. If, in the user's Location document, the Recipient name lookup field is set to Exhaustively check all address books, the search continues until all directories have been searched. If the field is set to Stop on first match, Notes stops searching as soon as it locates a match.

6. If Notes searches server-based directories, it searches them in the same order as a Domino server does. See that search order above.

The LDAP service searches directories on behalf of LDAP clients in the following order:

1. The primary Domino Directory on the LDAP server.

2. The Server Directory Catalog, if the LDAP server uses one.

3. The secondary directories listed in Directory Assistance, if the LDAP server uses it. It searches these in the same order as servers do, for example, first by rule, if it can, then in the directories' search order.

   - If the search order calls for a search of a secondary Domino directory, the LDAP service performs the search.

   - If the search order calls for a search of a listed LDAP directory, the LDAP service refers the LDAP client to that directory so that it can search it itself.

Non-Notes clients, such as POP3 and IMAP mail clients, can only search Domino directories if they have LDAP client capabilities.

The Directory Catalog

The Directory Catalog is a new feature in Domino R5. It is a highly compressed compilation of the most looked-up information from one or more Domino directories. It occupies dramatically less space than a standard Domino Directory and offers much faster lookups. If you have many users (more than 200) or if you have mobile users, you should use Directory Catalogs.

There are two kinds of Directory Catalogs: the Server Directory Catalog and the Mobile Directory Catalog. The Server Directory Catalog resides on servers and provides lookups for the servers themselves and for network-connected Notes users. The Mobile Directory Catalog resides on mobile users' computers and provides lookups for them when they are not connected to the network.

Lotus recommends you create both kinds of Directory Catalog, although they don't really say why. The reason turns out to be that you are likely to want to include different fields in each. For example, depending on how you use the Server Directory Catalog, you may need to add fields to it that you don't need in the Mobile Directory Catalog. Even if the two catalogs are identical when you first set them up, you should create separate catalogs. The day may come that you need to add fields to the Server Directory Catalog. On that day, if you already have two catalogs, you can just add the fields to the appropriate one. If you only have one catalog doing double duty, you'll have to create a whole new catalog and reconfigure your domain to reflect the fact that now there are two catalogs where before there was only one. You can save yourself a lot of work later by using two separate catalogs from the outset.

Setting Up Directory Catalogs

To set up Directory Catalogs, you designate a single server in your domain to build the source directory catalogs. Then you replicate the Server Directory Catalog to other servers in the domain. You can replicate the Mobile Directory Catalog either directly to mobile users' workstations or to intermediate servers and from them to users' workstations. The point here is that only one server builds the catalogs. Different servers can build each catalog; but only one server should build each catalog.

The overall process is as follows:

1. Designate a server to build the directory catalogs.
2. Replicate secondary Domino Directories that will be included in the directory catalogs to the designated "build" server.
3. Schedule regular future replication of the secondary Domain Directories.
4. Create and configure the source directory catalogs.
5. Build the source directory catalogs.
6. Make replicas of the source directory catalogs on the appropriate production servers and/or workstations.
7. Schedule regular future replication of the directory catalogs.

Continue reading to learn the details of each step.

Designating and Preparing the "Build" Server

The server that should build the catalogs should preferably be a hub server or a directory server. If you use a hub server, it can disseminate changes to spoke servers quickly. A directory server is a Domino server dedicated to the task of providing directory services. You only need to dedicate such servers in the largest domains. If you have one or more directory servers you can build the Directory Catalogs on one, replicate them to the other directory servers, and possibly replicate them to mail servers in case a directory server goes down.

If you are building Directory Catalogs for more than one domain, you can build them for all domains on a single server in one of the domains, then replicate them to the other domains. Alternately, each domain could build its own Directory Catalogs for the exclusive use of its own users (even though it includes directories from the other domains). Which way you go depends on several factors, including whether the domains need to aggregate the same set of directories or different ones and whether the administrators can cooperate closely enough for one of them to aggregate directories for all of them.

On the server designated to build the Directory Catalogs, follow these steps to prepare it:

1. On the "build" server, make replicas of all secondary Domino directories that will be included in the Directory Catalogs. Name them such that you will recognize them by their filenames. Consider naming them on the pattern ???names.nsf, where ??? are any characters that tell you which directory this is and "names" tells you that the file is a directory. Also, while it is possible for the server to build the Directory Catalogs from directories that it accesses on other servers, this is not a great idea because it slows the process, depends on the availability of the network, and consumes network bandwidth unnecessarily.

2. Set up Connection documents to schedule replication of the secondary Domino directories with their source replicas. You want on-going updates in those directories to appear in the Directory Catalogs in a timely manner.

3. Create two source directory catalogs—one for the Server Directory Catalog and the other for the Mobile Directory Catalog. To create each, choose File, Database, New. In the Server field, choose the "build" server. In the Title field, enter any title. I'd suggest titles that tell you the purpose of each catalog, say, "Server Directory Catalog" and "Mobile Directory Catalog." In the File Name field, enter any filename. Lotus suggests sdc.nsf and mdc.nsf—simple, short, sweet. Choose Create full text index for searching. For Template Server, choose the build server. Choose the Directory Catalog template (dircat5.ntf). Do not select the Catalog (5.0) template. Click OK.

4. Make desired changes to the ACLs. Leave default access set to Reader. Consider adding an Administrators group as Manager. Consider setting LocalDomainServers and OtherDomainServers to something lower than Designer. No servers other than the "build" server and hub servers need higher than Reader access to these databases. The hub servers need Manager access so they can forward all updates to other servers.

5. Create a Configuration document in each source directory catalog. See the next section for the details of doing this.

Configuring the Source Directory Catalogs

Open each directory catalog (the Server Directory Catalog and the Mobile Directory Catalog) in turn. In each, create a Configuration document. Choose Create, Configuration in the menu. In it, the fields that you should edit at this time are Directories to include, Additional fields to include, Restrict aggregation to this server, Send Directory Catalog reports to, and Comments. These fields are described in Table 11.6.

Table 11.6 **Fields Which You Must Complete in a Directory Catalog Configuration Document**

Field	Comment
	ON THE BASICS TAB
Directories to include	Enter the filenames of directories to include in the Directory Catalog. Include the primary Domino Directory in the Mobile Directory Catalog. You may exclude the primary Domino Directory from the Server Directory Catalog if it will be used only in your domain. If it will be used in other domains, include your primary Domino Directory. The reason you may exclude it is because servers and connected users always search the primary Domino Directory before searching the Directory Catalog anyway, so including the primary Domino Directory in the Server Directory Catalog is redundant if it will only be used on servers in your domain. If (despite the warning above) you will include secondary directories that are not replicated to the "build" server, you can refer to them either by mapped path name or by the following syntax: `portname!!!servername!!filename` where `portname` is the port the "build" server should use to reach the database's host server, `servername` is the host servers' fully distinguished Notes name, and `filename` is the relative path name of the database on the host server.

continues

Table 11.6 **Continued**

Field	Comment
	ON THE BASICS TAB
Additional fields to include	You may leave this field as is, if you want. If you decide to edit this field, Lotus makes several recommendations:

- Don't remove the default set of fields; they are the fields most often sought in directory lookups.

- Don't go overboard when adding fields because each new field increases the size of the Directory Catalog, and the amount of time replication will take.

- Add fields only from the Person, Group, Mail-In Database, and Resource forms.

- Directory Server Catalog: Add the `AltFullName` and `AltFullNameLanguage` fields.

- Directory Server Catalog: Add the Members field if users will use the Server Directory Catalog for free time lookups (only useful if doing lookups on users in other domains).

- Directory Server Catalog: Add the `HTTPPassword` field if using the Server Directory Catalog to authenticate Web users.

- Mobile Directory Catalog: Add the AltFullName and `AltFullNameLanguage` fields, but only if you have enabled alternate names in user ID files.

- Mobile Directory Catalog: Add the `Members` field, but only if users want to do free time lookups while disconnected from the network and only if you can afford the disk space and additional replication time that adding this field will incur.

Field	Comment
	ON THE BASICS TAB
Restrict aggregation to this server	Enter the "build" server's name in this field. This will prevent someone inadvertently running the dircat server task on another server and making a hash of the Directory Catalog as a result.
Send Directory Catalog reports to	Enter at least your own name here, and maybe the names of other people responsible for the healthy operation of the Directory Catalog. If you do list names in this field, then when you save and close the configuration document, Notes will present you with a dialog box asking you to select the server on which "this agent" will run. The agent Notes is referring to is the Directory Catalog Status Report agent. Choose the "build" server. The agent is scheduled to run Sunday mornings at 2 a.m.. You can change the schedule if you want by choosing Agents in the View menu when the database is open on your screen.
Comments	As usual, I recommend liberal commenting to benefit your successors. Among other things, state whether this is a server directory catalog or a mobile directory catalog. State, also, your reasons for including or excluding specific directories and/or fields.

The other fields in the Configuration document include some default settings on the Basics tab and some performance optimization parameters on the Advanced tab. You can leave these fields as they are or you can change them now or at some later time. There is one reason why you might want to change the other fields now; if you change certain ones later, Domino will have to reconfigure the whole Directory Catalog, which will force a complete replication of the database at that time. If the database is large and replicates over dialup connections, this can take a long time. If you can take the time to determine now the best configuration of the directory catalogs, you can avoid that penalty. The fields on the Basics tab include the following (see Table 11.7).

Table 11.7   **Other (Optional) Fields on the Basics Tab of the Directory Catalog Configuration Document**

Field	Comment
Sort by	Defaults to sorting by distinguished name, which is to say by first name then last name. This is the default because most people enter names in email address fields first name first. If your users tend to enter names last name first, change the sort order to Last Name. If your users have alternate names and use them when addressing mail, choose Alternate Fullname.
Use Soundex	Soundex allows people to search on phonetic spellings. Defaults to Yes. If you change it to No, you can save about four bytes per directory entry in the final Directory Catalog.
Remove duplicate users	Defaults to Yes, which means that the directory will choose the first instance if there are duplicate entries of a user. Setting this to No causes the directory to prompt the user to select an instance from the duplicates.
Group types	Mail and Multi-purpose is the default. You should normally not change this because Mail and Multi-purpose groups are the only ones that can be used in mail address fields.

The fields on the Advanced tab control the compilation parameters of the Directory Catalog. In general, you should leave them as is until you get some feedback on the performance of the Directory Catalog. To learn how they affect the performance of the Directory Cataloger, see the section, "Optimizing the Performance of the Directory Catalog" later in this chapter.

Running the Directory Cataloger

When you have finished configuring a source directory catalog (see the preceding section), you can populate it with data from the included directories by running the Directory Cataloger on the "build" server. The Directory Cataloger will pull data from member directories into the Directory Catalog. It will aggregate the contents of up to 255 documents from the member directories into each document in the Directory Catalog. It will do this in such a way that each aggregate document will contain the fields listed in the configuration document, and each field will include the data from the corresponding field in up to 255 source documents.

You can initiate this process either on a schedule or manually. You'll want to schedule the process so that updates will occur on-going without your intervention. The steps for setting up a Directory Cataloging schedule are as follows:

1. Open the "build" server's Server document in Edit Mode, preferably the copy on the "build" server itself.

2. In the Server document, under Server Tasks, Directory Cataloger, complete the fields set forth in Table 11.8.

Table 11.8 **Fields Under the Server Tasks, Directory Cataloger Tab of the Server Document**

Field	Comment
Directory Catalog filenames:	Enter the filenames of the directory catalogs that this server will aggregate, separated by commas or semi-colons. For example: `sdc.nsf`, `mdc.nsf`
Schedule:	Set to Enabled.
Other fields:	Lotus recommends that you accept the default schedule. But of course you can set whatever schedule suits your needs.

3. Save and close the document

If the server detects this change during scheduled hours, it will run the Directory Cataloger immediately. Otherwise, it will run the Directory Cataloger at the next scheduled time.

You can also build or update the directory catalogs manually, either by entering a command at the server console or by choosing it from a list in Domino Administrator.

Before you run the directory Cataloger manually, make sure it isn't already running. If two instances of it get in memory at the same time, the results are unpredictable. Look for Directory Cataloger in the list of running services in Domino Administrator, Servers, Status. Or enter the `show tasks` command at the server console and look for Directory Cataloger. If it appears, shut it down by selecting it in Domino Administrator and choosing Stop under Tools, Task. Or enter the `tell dircat quit` command at the server console.

To run the directory cataloger from the server console, enter the following command:

```
load dircat dc.nsf
```

where `dc.nsf` is the filename of the directory catalog to be aggregated.

The initial build of a directory catalog may take some time. Lotus predicts that, on a 200mhz Pentium system the Directory Cataloger should be able to process about 75,000 directory entries per hour. Updates should take much less time.

When the directory catalog is fully populated, you can disseminate it to production servers and/or user workstations.

Setting Up the Server Directory Catalog for Production Use

To set up a fully built Server Directory Catalog on production servers, follow these steps:

1. Make replicas of the Server Directory Catalog on other servers that will use it. If all replication takes place with hub servers, create replicas on the hubs as well. Lotus recommends using the same filename on all servers. When you create the replicas, Domino automatically full-text indexes them.

2. Perform one or both of the following steps. Lotus (in a sort of "belt-and-suspenders" mood) recommends you perform both.

   - Add the Directory Catalog's filename to your primary Domino Directory's Directory Profile. (With the Domino Directory open on-screen, choose Actions, Edit Directory Profile. Enter the filename in the Directory Catalog database name for domain field.)

   - Add the Directory Catalog's filename to the Server document of each server that will use it. (Enter the filename in the Directory Catalog database name on this server field under Basics.) If the filename on a given server is different from the name listed in the Directory Profile, you must perform this step on that server.

3. If the Directory Catalog is for use on servers in other domains as well, the administrators of those domains should perform step 2 as well.

4. Check replication schedules and topologies to make sure all working copies of the Directory Catalog receive updates from the source copy in a timely manner.

Setting Up the Mobile Directory Catalog on User Workstations

To set up a fully built Mobile Directory Catalog on Notes R5 user workstations (it doesn't work on any other workstations), you have to perform two tasks: First, you must create a replica copy of the Mobile Directory Catalog on each mobile user's Notes workstation. Second, you must add its filename to the Local address books field in the Mail screen of User Preferences. (This, in turn, appends the filename to the Names variable in the user's notes.ini file.)

You can do all this manually or you can automate it with User Setup Profiles. To do it using User Setup Profiles, follow these steps:

1. Create replicas of the Mobile Directory Catalog on servers to which your mobile users have access—their mail servers or directory servers. The more servers that have replicas, the more flexibility your users will have replicating it to their workstations.

2. Open any replica copy of the Mobile Directory Catalog, then choose Edit, Copy As Link, Database Link. This puts a link to the Mobile Directory Catalog into the Windows Clipboard.

3. Paste the database link into the Mobile directory catalogs field (under Databases) in the User Setup Profile(s) assigned to your mobile users. If such a profile already exists, open it in Edit Mode. If such a profile doesn't exist yet, create it. If you have assigned different profiles to different users, open each one in succession and paste the database link into it. If you create one or more new User Setup Profiles, fill in other fields as needed. Save and close each profile when finished editing it.

4. If you created one or more new User Setup Profiles, enter its/their name(s) into the Setup profile(s) field (under Administration) of the Person documents of the users for which you created them. If you have to do this for a large number of users, you can create an agent that will automate the process. See the instructions for creating such an agent under "Using an Agent to Update the 'Setup Profile(s)' Field."

The edited (or new) User Setup Profile(s) and the edited Person documents (if any) now have to replicate to the affected users' mail servers. After they have done so, the next time each affected user logs into his/her mail server, they will automatically receive a replica stub for the Mobile Directory Catalog. It will have a replication schedule enabled, so that their workstations will try to update the local replica on a regular basis. Also, as mentioned earlier, the filename of each user's local replica will automatically appear in the Local address books field of User Preferences.

A program on the Notes R5 workstation, Notes Dynamic Configuration (`ndyncfg.exe`), takes care of all this. It is possible to disable this program on a workstation. If it has been disabled, you'll either have to perform all the preceding tasks manually or reenable ndyncfg.exe.

If users in other domains will also be using this Mobile Directory Catalog, you will have to replicate it to one or more servers in the other domains. Then, the administrators of those domains should carry out the previous steps.

Using an Agent to Update the "Setup Profile(s)" Field

To create an agent that will automate the assignment of a User Setup Profile to multiple users, follow these steps:

1. In Domino Administrator, under the People & Groups tab, with a server selected so that the names of the people against whom you will run the agent are displayed, choose Agent in the Create menu. A window for an untitled agent will appear. See Figure 11.2. (The figure shows the fields as filled in, not as they appear initially.)

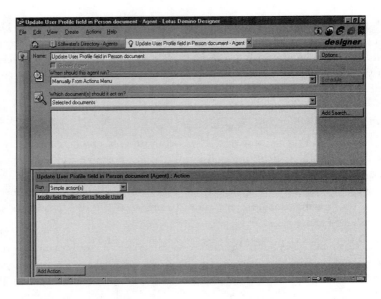

Figure 11.2 You can click the Add Search button to define search criteria by which the agent can select the documents to update.

2. In the Name field, enter a descriptive name for this agent. When you save the agent, this name will appear in the Actions menu when the current directory is open.

3. Leave the When should this agent run? field set to Manually From Actions Menu.

4. Leave the Which document(s) should it act on? field set to Selected documents.

5. Leave the Run field set to Simple action(s).

6. Choose Add Action to display the Add Action dialog box. There, complete the fields as follows:

   - **Action.** Set to Modify Field.
   - **Field.** Set to Profiles.
   - **Value.** Set to the name of a User Setup Profile. Don't include quotation marks.
   - Choose Replace value or Append value as suits your needs.

7. Click OK to add the action to the agent. Save and close the agent. Notice that your agent now appears in the Actions menu of Domino Administrator.

8. Manually select the Person documents against which you want to run this agent. Click the column to the left of each Person document to place a check mark there.

9. Run the agent by choosing it in the Actions menu. After it runs, verify that it ran correctly by viewing the Setup profile(s) field of a Person document against which you ran the agent. If the name of the User Setup Profile that you specified in the agent appears there, you were successful.

10. If you need to assign other User Setup Profiles to other users, you can edit the agent, then run it again. To edit the agent, open the Domino Directory in Domino Designer, select the Agents view, then open your agent. To edit your simple action, double-click it and edit the Value field.

The agent described previously is simple to create and straightforward in operation. Its drawback, if any, is that you have to manually select the Person documents against which you want to run it. In a large domain, that in itself can be a tedious chore. It may be possible for you to write your agent so that it will automatically search through the People view and correctly select the Person documents that need to be changed.

The trick to setting up an agent to do this is to determine what is unique about the Person documents to which you want to assign a particular User Setup Profile. If you can determine some such characteristic, you can choose Add Search in the agent window and define a search that will find the documents that meet your search criteria. In that case, you may prefer to set the Which document(s) should it act on? field to All documents in view. The search will search all documents; the simple action will change only those documents that meet the search criteria.

You can also, if you have some knowledge of the Notes Formula Language, use a formula in your agent instead of a simple action. Then you could use an @If statement to test each document and assign the appropriate User Setup Profile, depending on the test results. We don't have the space here to go into the details of setting up such an agent. But any good Notes programming book can give you the necessary knowledge to create such an agent.

One caveat before we leave the subject of creating agents: If you are going to have the agent search through a view an decide programmatically which documents should be updated, test your search criteria and make sure they select the correct documents before including the search in an agent that will update documents. If you erroneously update documents, there is only one way to roll back to the preupdated state; that is to restore a backup copy of the database. There is no Undo button when updating documents with an agent.

There are two ways to test your search criteria. First, you can use your proposed search criteria to conduct manual searches of the People view. To do this, choose the Search icon in the upper-right corner of the Domino Administrator screen. When the Search bar appears, choose More, then choose any of the Conditions buttons to define your search. See Figure 11.3.

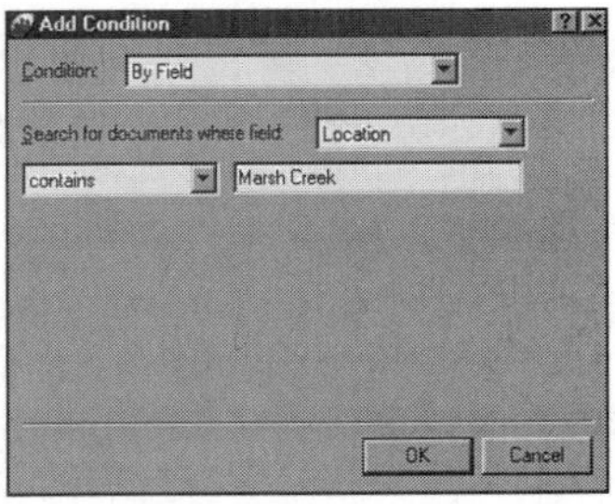

Figure 11.3 The Add Condition dialog box appears when you choose any of the buttons to the right of Conditions on the expanded Search Bar, which appears just above the dialog box. You can open the Search Bar by clicking the Search icon (looks like a magnifying glass) in the upper-right corner of the screen.

Second, if you are using a formula instead of a simple action, you can test your selection criteria by choosing Select documents in view in the lower-right corner of the agent window. See Figure 11.4. If the agent successfully selects the Person documents you expected it to, you can later change from Select documents in view to Modify documents.

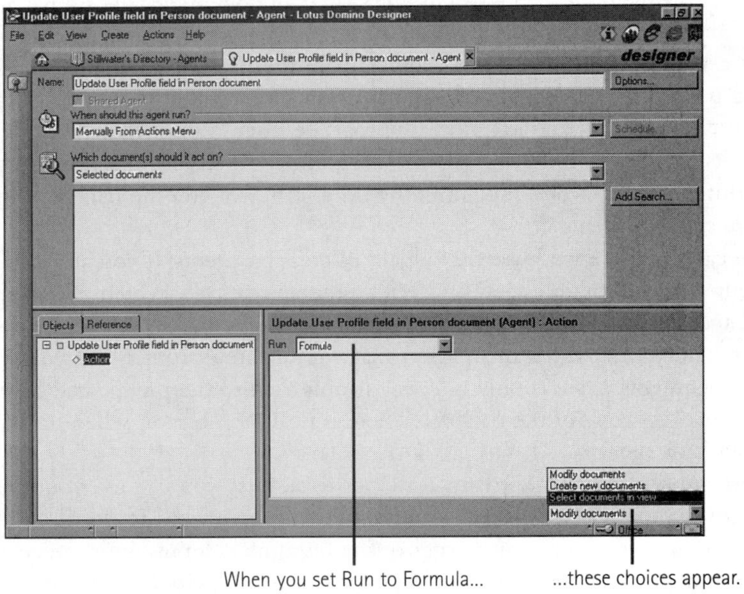

When you set Run to Formula...   ...these choices appear.

Figure 11.4 The choices in the lower-right corner appear when you choose Formula in the Run field. Choose Select documents in view to test your selection criteria. When you are satisfied they are correct, choose Modify documents.

Optimizing the Performance of the Server Directory Catalog

You might discover that certain searches performed on your Server Directory Catalog are unacceptably slow. If this problem arises, it will involve searches that search the Directory Catalog's full-text index. You can speed up those searches by editing one or more of the fields on the Advanced tab of the Directory Catalog Configuration document. These fields control the compilation parameters of the Directory Catalog. The three fields are Packing density, Incremental fields, and Merge factor.

To understand how these fields can affect search performance, you have to understand how the Directory Catalogs are structured. By default, the Directory Cataloger aggregates data from 255 documents in a single document in the Directory Catalog. It does this by listing the data from one field in each document in a single field in the aggregate document. In other words, Field1 in the aggregate document consists of a list of the entries from Field1 in each of the constituent documents; Field2 in the aggregate document consists of a list of the entries from field2 in each of the constituent documents; and so on for all included fields.

Two issues can arise as a result of this structure. First, certain searches (those which use the Directory Catalog's full-text index) may be slower than you like. If you experience slow searches, you can try setting a lower number in the Packing density field. This will cause the Directory Cataloger to aggregate fewer member documents in each aggregate document. This will speed up full-text searches but will also increase the size of the Directory Catalog. (By the way, increasing the packing density to more than 255 documents will slow down full-text searches, but will not appreciably decrease the size of the Directory Catalog; so don't do it.)

The second issue has to do with replication. Because each field in a document in the Directory Catalog contains information from up to 255 documents in the member directories, there is much greater chance than with most databases that a given field in an aggregate document may experience some change between replications. Under normal replication rules, when a change occurs in a field, the whole changed field replicates to other copies of the database at the next replication. If the Database Catalog worked this way, it would replicate the content of Field1 from up to 255 documents when Field1 in any one of them changes. This is an awful lot of unchanged data to replicate.

To avoid this result, the Directory Catalog initially stores changes received from the member databases not in the permanent fields in the aggregate documents, but in incremental fields designed just for this purpose. By default, it merges the contents of the incremental fields with the permanent fields when the amount of data in the incremental fields reach 5 percent of that in the permanent fields. This dramatically reduces the amount of data transferred during replication, but also slows down searches, because the search engine has to sort out the contents of both fields each time it searches the database.

You can marginally improve search performance either by disabling use of the incremental fields altogether (set Incremental fields to No) or by reducing the merge factor below 5 percent (set the Merge factor field to something less than 5). Disabling use of the incremental fields will result in large increases in the amount of data replicated, which is probably not acceptable if your Directory Catalog is large. However, its impact may be negligible if a Directory Catalog is small.

If your Directory Catalog contains thousands or tens of thousands of entries, it is better to reduce the merge factor, which will result in smaller increases in the amount of data replicated. If you reduce the merge factor by one percentage point at a time and monitor the resulting changes in the amount of data replicated and in search times, you may find a happy medium.

Monitoring Directory Catalogs

You can monitor directory catalogs in two ways. First, you can add the variable Log_DirCat=1 to the "build" server's notes.ini file. This will cause the dircat task to log its start and end times and the names of the directories it works on to the Notes log. Second, you can receive reports of its activities from the Directory Catalog by email each week. If you followed the preceding directions, you set this up as part of the overall setup of the Directory Catalogs. If you did not follow the preceding directions, you can set this up by adding your name to the Send Directory Catalog reports to field in each source Directory Catalog's configuration document. The report will include links to the Directory Catalog and its member databases and various statistics about the constituent databases.

Directory Assistance

Directory Assistance is a service by which Domino makes multiple directories easily available to both Notes and LDAP users for lookup purposes. Some, but not all, of the benefits it provides are duplicated by directory catalogs. So, whether you need to enable Directory Assistance or not depends on why you need it. Although we discussed the relative merits of Directory Assistance and Directory Catalogs earlier in this chapter, I'll reiterate the benefits that only Directory Assistance provides:

- It provides address lookups in third-party LDAP directories for Notes clients.
- It provides referrals to third-party LDAP directories for LDAP clients.
- It allows Domino Web servers to authenticate Web users using credentials stored in third-party LDAP directories.
- It expands groups located in third-party LDAP directories.

To set up Directory Assistance, you have to perform the following tasks:

1. Set up a Directory Assistance database using the Directory Assistance template (da50.ntf) and replicate it to servers that will use it.

2. Identify the Directory Assistance database to the servers that will use it by entering its filename in the Directory Assistance database name field in those Server documents.

3. Decide what secondary Domino Directories to include in Directory Assistance and where replicas of them will be located, then, in the Directory Assistance database, create a Directory Assistance document for each such directory.

4. Decide what LDAP directories to include in Directory Assistance, establish access to them, and, in the Directory Assistance database, create a Directory Assistance document for each such LDAP directory.

This looks easy enough, yes? And, mostly it is. The tricky part, if any, is in setting up the Directory Assistance documents.

Setting Up, Replicating, and Identifying the Directory Assistance Database

Most commonly, administrators create one Directory Assistance database to serve a single Notes domain—to give users in that domain (both Notes and LDAP clients) access to resources outside the domain, including the directories of other Notes domains and third-party LDAP directories. Alternately, you can create multiple Directory Assistance databases, each serving a subset of servers in the local Notes domain.

Under R4, you could create a Directory Assistance database for multiple domains. That is, servers in more than one domain could share a Directory Assistance database. But in R5 it appears that it is no longer legal to create a Directory Assistance document for your primary Domain Directory. While Lotus's documentation isn't 100 percent clear about this, it does at least imply that this is the case. If that is true, each Notes domain must have its own Directory Assistance database in which other domains are listed, but not the local domain.

Create the Directory Assistance Database

Create a Directory Assistance database on a server that will use it. Choose File, Database, New. In the New Database dialog box, choose the items set forth in Table 11.9.

Table 11.9 **New Database Field Settings For a Directory Assistance Database**

Field	Comment
Server	Choose the name of a server that will use this Directory Assistance database.
Title	Choose any title. If you will create just one Directory Assistance database, you could get really creative and call it "Directory Assistance."
File Name	Choose any filename, such as `da.nsf`. To make your life a little bit easier, choose a name that is available on all servers that will use this database, if possible.
Template Server	Choose the name of an R5 server, preferably the one you chose in the Server field. Then, choose the Directory Assistance template (da50.ntf).
Inherit future design changes	Make sure this is selected.

Choose OK to close the dialog box and create the database.

Set Up the ACL of the Directory Assistance Database

Next, set up the ACL. Add an Administrators group with Manager access. Replication hub servers and the server on which you will create Directory Assistance documents should have Manager access to the database. All other servers can have Reader access. Default access should remain set to Reader.

Replicate the Directory Assistance Database to Other Servers

Next replicate the database to each server that will use it. This might include just mail servers or directory servers. If all replication passes through hubs, you should place replicas on the hubs too, even if they won't themselves use Directory Assistance. To create new replicas on all necessary servers quickly, follow these steps:

1. Open Domino Administrator to the Files tab.
2. Choose the server on which the Directory Assistance database resides.
3. Choose the Directory Assistance database in the list of databases.
4. Choose Create Replica(s) under Tools, Database.
5. Choose or enter the names of the servers on which you want to create the new replicas.
6. Optionally, edit the filenames of the database on each destination server.
7. Click OK. The Administration Process will create replica stubs. Scheduled replication will populate the stubs with documents over time.

Verify Ongoing Replication

For Directory Assistance to work properly, all copies of the Directory Assistance database must be kept up-to-date. To ensure that they are, review replication schedules and topologies to satisfy yourself that all replicas of the database will receive updates in a timely manner.

Identify the Directory Assistance Database to the Servers That Will Use It

Finally, identify the Directory Assistance database to each server that will use it. You can use the Administrative Process to do this to multiple servers at once; or you can do it manually on the servers one-at-a-time.

To use the Administration Process to identify the Directory Assistance database to multiple servers, follow these steps:

1. Open Domino Administrator to the Configuration tab.

2. If Domino Administrator is showing you local data, choose a server in the Server pane.

3. In the Tasks pane, expand Server, then choose All Server Documents.

4. Select all servers to which you replicated the Directory Assistance database. If you gave it different filenames on different servers, select only servers on which it has an identical name. Click the empty column to the left of each server you want to select. A check mark will appear.

5. When check marks appear to the left of all desired servers, choose Set Directory Assistance Information in the Actions menu.

6. In the Directory Assistance Information dialog box, enter the filename of the Directory Assistance database. Click OK. This submits a request to the Administration Process to update the Directory Assistance database name field on the selected servers.

7. Repeat this process for other servers, if necessary, until all desired servers have been updated.

If you need to update any server manually, open its Server document in Edit Mode. Then, in the Directory Assistance database name: field (on the Basics tab), enter the filename of the copy of the Directory Assistance database on that server. Save and close the Server document.

You are ready to create Directory Assistance documents.

Setting Up Directory Assistance for Secondary Domino Directories

A Directory Assistance document sets forth information about a Notes domain and its Domain Directory or about an LDAP directory that servers using Directory Assistance need in order to perform lookups on those directories. You set them up differently, depending on whether they are for a Notes domain or an LDAP directory.

Before creating any Directory Assistance documents for Notes domains, you need to decide where to locate the Domino Directories that the Directory Assistance documents will point to. You need to enter at least one such location (but preferably more than one) in the Directory Assistance document for each domain. Here are some relevant considerations:

- The servers that use Directory Assistance do not have to maintain replicas of the secondary Domino Directories. In many cases, they should not; but some server to which they have constant, fast access should maintain such replicas.

- If the WAN links between servers in the local Notes domain and servers in the secondary Notes domain are slow, unreliable, or congested, you should create replicas of the secondary Domino Directory on local servers.

- If the WAN links between domains are fast and reliable, you may not need local replicas of the secondary Domino Directory at all.

- If you have designated one or more Directory Servers, you should create replicas on them.

- If you intend also to use Directory Catalogs, the server which maintains them will probably have copies of the secondary Domino Directories that are included in the Directory Catalogs.

Another thing you need to do is full-text index any secondary Domino directory that will be available for LDAP lookups. That is, you have to full-text index the copy of such a database that will be listed in a Replica field in a Directory Assistance document.

When you have decided where replica copies of secondary Domino Directories should reside, create the replicas in those locations if they don't already exist. Full-text index the replicas if necessary. When you've done all that, you can create Directory Assistance documents for each secondary Domino Directory.

To set up a Directory Assistance document for a secondary Domino Directory, open the Directory Assistance database on a server that has at least Editor access to the database. (The server on which you create documents must be able to replicate them to other servers, so don't do your work on a server that has Reader access.) Click Add Directory Assistance in the Toolbar. A new Directory Assistance document appears. Fill in the fields and save the document. When replication propagates the new document out to the other servers, the new document will be fully functional.

Directory Assistance documents for Domino directories have three tabs:

- Basics. Here you will enter miscellaneous information about the domain which the Domino Directory represents (if any).

- Rules. Here you will enter patterns of distinguished names that can be found in the secondary directory. These patterns will enable Domino to determine in which directory it is likely to find a particular name. It also tells Domino if it can use credentials found in that directory to authenticate a user whose name matches a given pattern.

- Replicas. Here, you will enter either links to the secondary directories or their names and locations.

The Basics Tab

The fields on the Basics tab are set forth in Table 11.10.

Table 11.10   **The Fields on the Basics Tab of the Domino Directory Assistance Document**

Field	Comment
Domain type	Choose Notes
Domain name	If the secondary Domino directory represents a Notes domain, enter the Notes domain here. If the secondary directory does not represent any domain (for example, it holds the names of Web users registered with one or more of your Domino Web servers), enter a fictitious domain name here. Do not enter your actual local domain name in this field.
Company name	Enter the name of the company associated with the domain named in the previous field.
Search order	Enter a search order here. Servers will first try to use the rules (set forth on the Rules tab) to determine in which directory to search for information. If they can't find an applicable rule, they search throughout all available directories in the order entered in this field. The lower the number, the earlier a directory will be searched. If two directories have the same number, they are searched in alphabetical order.
Enabled	Defaults to Yes. Set to No to temporarily remove a directory from eligibility for searching.

The Rules Tab

The Rules tab consists of fields in which you can enter up to five naming rules for a directory. Each naming rule permits you to enter eligible names at each level of the Notes naming hierarchy—OU4, OU3, OU2, OU1, O, and C. You can also enable/disable each rule separately. You can also indicate whether users whose fully distinguished names match a pattern can be authenticated from credentials in the secondary directory. This is only relevant for authenticating Web users; Notes users can always authenticate if a cross-certificate covers them.

The first rule always consists of asterisks (*) at all levels of the hierarchy. That makes the directory available for searches where the only known information about the entity to be located is its common name. The first rule is always preentered and enabled, as well.

For each of the other rules, you should enter the hierarchical components of names that can be found in the subject secondary directory. For example, if the directory holds entries for people who are members of the /PlanetNotes organization, you could enter /PlanetNotes in the Organization field and asterisks in all the other fields. That would tell the searching server that it should look in this directory if it is looking for an entity whose name includes /PlanetNotes as the O component.

In a large company, there might be a single organization (for example, /PlanetNotes) but multiple domains, one for each business unit. Each business unit might, in addition, be represented by a unique OU1 name. For example, the Variable Annuities unit might have exclusive use of the name /VA/PlanetNotes, whereas the Funds unit might have exclusive use of the name /Funds/PlanetNotes. One rule under VA's Rules tab would include OU1=VA and O=PlanetNotes, while the corresponding rule for Funds would be OU1=Funds and O=PlanetNotes. A searching server would that knows that much information about a sought entity would be able to tell from these rules which directory should list the user.

The Replicas Tab

Here you enter information about the locations of one or more replicas of the subject directory. Making more than one replica available provides failover protection should a given replica be unavailable. (Note that, if you designate a replica on a clustered server, automatic failover to another server in the cluster will not occur; you must explicitly enter each cluster replica that you want to make available.

You can enter either database links to each replica in the Database links field or the server name and directory file name for each replica. The searching server will attempt to search the replicas in the order in which they appear. You can temporarily disable access to a particular replica as well. This is useful if you have to bring a particular server or replica offline for some extended period of time.

If you enter both a database link and a server and filename, the Replica fields take precedence.

Setting Up Directory Assistance for LDAP Directories

Setting up a Directory Assistance document for an LDAP directory is a little different from setting up one for Domino directories. You don't normally have to concern yourself with replicas of the LDAP directory; rather, you connect to it wherever it is located. Instead of the Replicas tab, you have the LDAP tab, on which you enter LDAP-specific information.

The Basics Tab

The fields on the Basics tab are set forth in Table 11.11.

Table 11.11   The Fields on the Basics Tab of the LDAP Directory Assistance Document

Field	Comment
Domain type	Choose LDAP.
Domain name	Enter any descriptive name. It must be unique.
Company name	Enter the name of the company that owns the LDAP server covered by this document.
Search order	Enter a search order here. Servers will first try to use the rules (set forth on the Rules tab) to determine in which directory to search for information. If they can't find an applicable rule, they search throughout all available directories in the order entered in this field. The lower the number, the earlier a directory will be searched. If two directories have the same number, they are searched in alphabetical order.
Group expansion	Enter Yes or No. Enter Yes only if you want to be able to retrieve the names of members of groups defined on the LDAP server in question. You can enable this field for one LDAP directory only.
Enabled	Defaults to Yes. Set to No to temporarily remove a directory from eligibility for searching.

The Rules Tab

As with the rules for secondary Domino directories, you enter here the hierarchical components of names that can be found in the subject secondary directory. This enables the searching server to zero in quickly on the database most likely to contain the information in question.

You can use the Trusted for Credentials field in each rule to enable authentication from the subject LDAP directory. A Yes in that field tells Domino that, if a Web user tries to authenticate and the user's name fits the pattern of the rule, Domino can use credentials (certificate or password digest) located in this LDAP directory to authenticate the Web user.

The LDAP Tab

The LDAP tab contains fields the information in which enables the Domino server to connect to and query the LDAP server. The fields are described in Table 11.12

Table 11.12 **The Fields on the LDAP Tab of the LDAP Directory Assistance Document**

Field	Comment
Hostname	Enter the host name or IP address of the LDAP server.
Base DN for search	Some LDAP servers (large, commercial ones, for example) require you to submit a search base, which tells the server what part of its tree you want to search. A search base is the rightmost portion of a distinguished name (for example, O=planetnotes, C=US).
Perform LDAP search for	The choices are Notes Clients/Web Authentication and LDAP clients. Choose one or both.
Channel encryption	Choose SSL or None. Lotus strongly recommends choosing SSL if you will rely on a third-party LDAP server for credentials when authenticating Web users.
Port	Defaults to 389 if the preceding field is set to None; 636 if the preceding field is set to SSL. Change this only if the LDAP server actually uses some other port number.
Accept expired SSL certificates	Choose Yes to ignore certificate expiration dates. Choose No to enforce certificate expiration dates.
SSL protocol version	Choose Negotiated or a specific version. Choose one of the others only if Negotiated won't work.
Verify server name with remote server's certificate	Lotus strongly recommends enabling this if you trust the LDAP server for authentication purposes. Requires the LDAP server's host name to be included in the Subject line of the server's certificate.

Field	Comment
Timeout	Enter the number of seconds that a search may take before it times out. Defaults to 60 seconds.
Maximum number of entries returned	Enter the maximum number of entries a single search will return. Defaults to 100.

Directory Servers

If you administer a large domain with thousands of mail users, you may want to dedicate one or more directory servers. A directory server is dedicated to the provision of directory services such as doing directory lookups. Normally, a user's mail service provides these services. If you can off-load lookup services to a different server, the mail server is free to concentrate on providing mail services. It should therefore be able to accommodate more mail users.

A directory server would typically have copies of the Server Directory Catalog on it and maybe the Mobile Directory Catalog. It would also have a copy of the Directory Assistance database and copies of all secondary Domino directories. In addition to providing lookups in all these directories, it might also be the "build" server that compiles the Directory Catalogs. Finally, it might also run the LDAP service so that LDAP clients could do lookups on it.

To set up a directory server, you have to do one thing (in addition to setting up the appropriate directory services on it). You have to set up users so that they'll direct searches to it and not to their mail servers (which they do by default).

The best way to set up users to use a new directory server is to set it up in their User Setup Profiles. Enter the name of the directory server in the Directory server field under Basics in the User Setup Profile. After the change replicates to a user's mail server, the next time the user logs in to that server Notes will discover the change in the profile document and update the user's Location document.

If you need to set up a user manually to use the directory server, add the directory server's name to the Domino directory server field of the appropriate Location document(s).

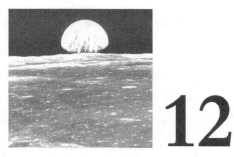

12

User Maintenance and Troubleshooting

LIFE WOULD BE SO MUCH EASIER IF WE DIDN'T HAVE to upset our perfectly running system. But users come and go, change their names, or move around the company, forcing us to update records or to migrate their databases to other servers. Occasionally, a user might even forget his password, requiring us to use Password Recovery to get him on his feet again!

Most of the changes that we'll be covering in this chapter can be accomplished through the Domino Administrator client, through actions in the Domino Directory, using the Web Administrator or using the NT User Administration program. We will concentrate on using the Administrator client because this has the most features and is easiest to use, but we will also look at the other ways, when using them would be appropriate.

In this chapter, we will examine the process used when modifying or deleting a single user, but in almost all cases, we could have just as well selected multiple users and updated or deleted them all at once. The exception is of course changing a user's name. We have to do that on a one-up request basis.

The term "renaming users" usually means changing the person's name in his person document. But in Notes, the certifiers used to create the person's ID also become part of his Notes name. So, if we want to move a user from the Sales department to Marketing, we might only be recertifying or renaming him with the Marketing certifier. On the other hand, when we move a person from one server to another, we really are moving his mail file to a different home server.

Renaming Users

There are three actions that are considered renaming a user. They are

- **Upgrade to Hierarchical.** You would use this to upgrade any users that were created using a flat certificate.
- **Change Common Name.** This is the option you'll use to change a user's common name when his/her marital status changes, or if a mistake was made when creating his/her ID.
- **Request Move to New Certifier.** While this is conceptually a move, you are really renaming the person using a new certifier, possibly one denoting a different department or location.

All these changes are accomplished through the Administration Process (AdminP) except in one case of changing the person's common name, but we'll cover that when we look at ways to request changes.

Why isn't renaming as simple as changing the person's name on the person document or issuing a new ID? The person's public key is used to sign fields and documents, the person's name may be stored in Reader or Author Names fields on documents. The person's name may be in ACLs and at the very least is in several groups in the Domino Directory. To find and change all these instances would take an administrator days or weeks. Multiply this by only a few requests and you would soon start looking at an interesting job. Luckily AdminP will do most, if not all these tasks, and will make sure that they are completed in the correct order. Imagine changing the person's name in his person document, and changing his name in every database and ACL where it appears, but the person never accepts the change. The ID contains the original name and he wouldn't be able to access any of his databases, probably not even any servers. AdminP makes sure that that condition and other errors won't keep the user from accessing his databases.

The first step in performing a user name change is to initiate a rename request. This creates a document in the Administration Requests database which AdminP will act on (see Figure 12.1). Let's follow a request through the process to understand what happens following our request. Then we'll learn how to initiate the request for the various renaming actions.

AdminP Steps in Renaming a Person

The steps involved in the rename process are

1. Change request creates an Initiate rename in Address Book request in the Administration Requests database. AdminP interval process on server, which is the Administration Server for the Domino Directory, acts on request and adds new name, certificate, and change requests to a user's person document.

2. User authenticates with server. The server sees that a change request has been initiated and asks the user to accept the change. If the authentication server is not the server that processes AdminP requests for the Domino Directory, the directory must replicate to the user's server for the acceptance request to be presented to the user.

3. User accepts change. Name on ID is changed immediately. Request is created in Administration Request database to "Rename person in Address Book." If the user does not accept the change within the time specified on the request, the request will be marked Obsolete and will be deleted the next time the Delete Obsolete Change Requests administration request is run.

4. AdminP interval process on Administration Server acts on "Rename person in Address Book" and creates the rest of the new requests:

   - **Rename in Person documents.** Performed by the directory administration server according to the AdminP "Execute once a day requests" setting.

   - **Rename person in Unread Lists.** Performed by each server according to the AdminP "Execute once a day requests" setting.

   - **Rename in Access Control List.** Performed by each server according to the AdminP "Execute once a day requests" setting.

   - **Rename Person in Free Time Database.** Performed immediately on the person's home server.

   - **Rename Person in Calendar Entries and Profiles in Mail File.** Performed immediately on the person's home server.

   - **Rename in Reader/Author Fields.** Performed on each server according to the AdminP "Delayed Request" setting.

Should any of the requests fail, they will be marked with an icon picturing a red X. Open the request and check the Action Message to see why the request failed. After fixing the problem, click the Run Request Again checkbox to have AdminP rerun the request. You may have to submit the request again if, for example, you entered the wrong name in a change name request, causing it to fail.

There may also be requests that have been processed, but don't have an icon at all. Perhaps the request was to change all Reader/Author names in databases on the server, but the server isn't the Administration Server for any of the databases on it in which case the Action message in the request will state so.

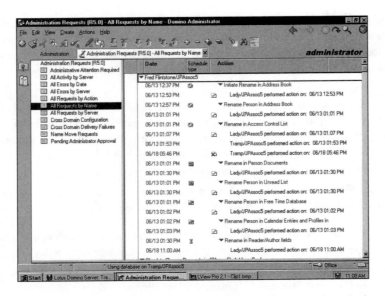

Figure 12.1 Using the All Requests by Name view shows all requests for a single person.

Now that we've taken a look at what happens after we submit the request, let's look at the different types of user maintenance requests and how those requests can be initiated.

Upgrade to Hierarchical

There are advantages to upgrading to hierarchical naming if your organization hasn't yet done this. These include:

- People with the same name can be differentiated by their organization units.
- Use Release 5 features including the Administration Process which simplifies user administration.
- Cross-certification, which simplifies access between your organization and others.

Having Problems Performing Changes?

To perform these changes you need to meet the "Prerequisites for the Registrar" outlined in Chapter 5, "User Registration and Client Setup."

To perform this change when in the Domino Directory, open the People view, select the people to upgrade and choose Actions, Rename selected people, and then click the Upgrade to Hierarchical button. If you are in the Domino Administrator, click the People and Groups tab, choose the People task, select the people to upgrade in the Results pane. Open the People tool and click Rename. The Rename Selected Entries dialog box opens (see Figure 12.2).

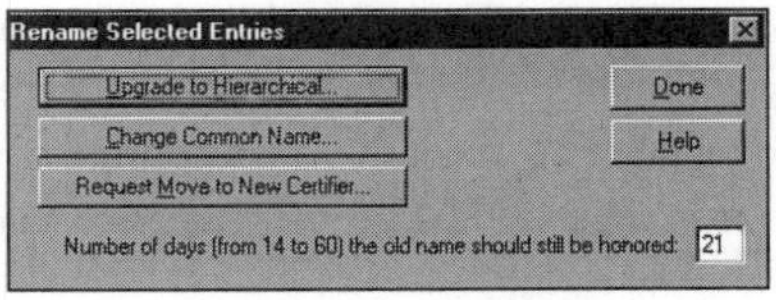

Figure 12.2   The default number of days to honor a rename request is 21.

You can change the number of days that Notes will wait for a user to accept the change before deleting the request from the Administration Requests database.

Change Common Name

Occasionally someone will need the name changed on his ID. Usually the user will contact the helpdesk or you, the administrator, directly and ask to have his name changed. You can then kick off the rename process yourself. However, there are a few ways that the person can request a name change using Notes, so let's look at them first.

User-Initiated Requests

Users can initiate some requests themselves from the More Options tab of the User ID dialog box (choose File, Tools, UserID). See Figure 12.3.

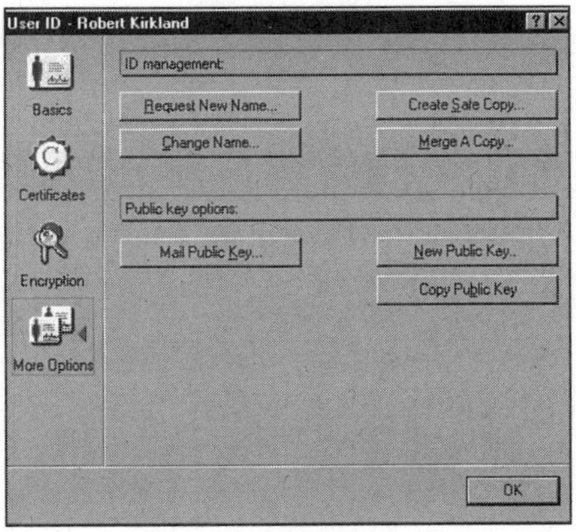

Figure 12.3   Users can initiate name change requests using built-in Notes features.

User initiated requests appear in your Inbox. The subject of the mail message instructs you how to recertify and return the ID from your Inbox. Using the Actions, Certify Attached ID file menu choice will prompt you for the name of the certifier ID. Choose the same certifier used to originally create the ID. Another dialog box appears allowing you to change the length of the password, the expiration date, or to add an alternate language name for the user. The password length defaults to zero, so be sure to reset it to the minimum length of the password used at your organization. Click Certify. Another dialog box will appear asking you specify the new name. The name entries will already be filled in with the name requested by the user. Change any entries if needed and click OK. The ID will be recertified and attached to a message already addressed to the requesting user. The message also contains instructions to the user on how to accept the new name.

Be aware, if the user gets out of Notes between requesting the name change and receiving the recertified ID, they will get an error as shown in Figure 12.4 when attempting to authenticate the next time they log in. Have the user click OK to bypass this message. This error occurs because the user's public key has been changed in the Domino Directory, but has not yet been changed in his ID file. The user will continue to receive the error until he accesses his mail file, opens the message containing his updated ID and merges the contents into his local ID file. See Technote #147165 titled, "Error Updating Local ID File...Required Parameter in a Subroutine Call..." in the Lotus Notes Knowledgebase (http://www.lotus.com/support) for more information on this error.

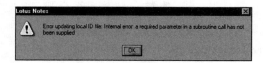

Figure 12.4   This error message will occur when a user accesses a
server before merging his new name into his local ID file.

While this will effectively change the user's name, it does not initiate a name change using the Administration Process. Therefore the user's name is not changed in ACLs, Group documents, or in Reader/Author fields. You might want to ignore the request in your mail, but create your own request using one of the methods described next so that all the benefits of the Administration Process are realized (and to save you work down the road).

Administrator-Initiated Name Change Requests in Notes

If the user has called the helpdesk or you directly, you can kick off the name change process a number of ways.

- In the Domino Directory, highlight the user's name and use the action, Rename selected people.
- Using the Domino Administrator opened to the organization's directory, select the People & Groups tab, highlight the person and choose Rename from the People tool.

Either way, you will be presented with the Rename Selected Entries dialog box as shown in Figure 12.2. Choose Change Common Name. Follow these steps to initiate the name change process.

1. Choose the certifier from the Choose Certifier ID dialog box, entering the password when prompted.

2. In the Rename Selected User dialog box, make the necessary changes to the user's name, changing the expiration date of the ID or adding a Qualifying Organization Unit if needed. If you have set up Synchronizing Notes and Windows NT Users as described in Chapter 6, you can check the Rename NT User Account checkbox to automatically rename the user's NT account.

3. Click Rename and then check the Administration Requests database to see the new request.

Administrator-Initiated Change in NT User Admin

Using the NT User Administration program is not suggested for making changes to the full name of a Notes user. When synching the changes, the new full name is just appended to the fullname field in the user's Person document.

If the user's username is changed in NT, when we synch the user with Notes, we will update the Network Account Name field in the person document and can optionally set the person's Domino Internet password and NT password the same.

"Unsyncable" Molly Brown

If the user was created in Notes before NT User Synchronization was set up, the user may not have a Network Account Name in his person document. Notes will not sync the changed name if there isn't a network account name to use for synchronization. Fortunately, if you have set up the NT User Administration to sync users, you can place the person's NT User Name in the account name field by choosing Notes, Sync Selected NT Users with Notes from the NT User Administration program. If NT can't find the user in Notes, an error message will appear and an event written to the NT Event Log.

Request Move to New Certifier

The third type of "rename" is when we want to change the organization unit or even possibly the organization on a person's ID.

For example, the certifier /Marshcreek/Stillwater was used to certify the person Bob Dobbs. His ID and his Notes name both are built using the certifier name. Suppose Bob moved up the road to the Philly location. To move Bob to the new location/department (organization unit), we'll rename him using a different certifier.

To initiate the rename to the new org unit, highlight Bob's name in the Domino Directory, or if you are in the Domino Administrator, choose the People & Groups tab and select the name there. In the directory, choose Actions, Rename Selected People. In the Administrator, use the Rename action in the People tools. In either case, choose Request Move to New Certifier from the Rename Select People dialog box, then follow these steps:

1. Choose the certifier ID that was used to originally certify this user and enter the password when prompted.

2. In the Request Move for Selected Entries dialog box, type in the name of the new certifier. In this case we'll use the /Philly/Stillwater certificate to move Bob to the new organization unit (see Figure 12.5).

3. Click Submit Request and check the Administration Requests database to make sure the request has been submitted.

4. Look occasionally in the Administration Requests database to see if there are any errors. The process won't begin until the user accepts the new name as stated in the AdminP steps in renaming a person section earlier in this chapter.

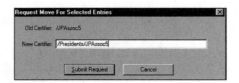

Figure 12.5   Type the new organization certifier in the box. If you make a mistake typing the certifier name, an error box will tell you that you specified an illegal certifier name.

Moving Users

In contrast to the move to new certifier process that we just discussed, moving users to a new server actually does involve moving something. Because a user can authenticate with any of our servers, as long as they have access, there is no real concept of home server except as it applies to our mail files. In fact, it is entirely possible that a user logs in or authenticates with a passthru server, but his mail file resides on a server elsewhere.

Let's say that in our previous example, besides renaming Bob Dobbs with the Philly certifier, we need to move his mail file to the server in our Philly office, "Harrier." We could just move the file, but Bob wouldn't know that it had been moved. There are a number of steps that we could take to make the move easier for poor Bob, after all, he is moving to a new location, the last thing he needs is to have his email stop.

If we were to do this manually, we would have to do the following:

- Place a replica of the mail file on the new server.
- Change the Mail Server and Mail File entries in the person document.
- Shut down the mail routers and replicate the Domino Directory to all the servers so mail won't bounce for this user. Restart the routers after replicating.
- Delete the current icon from the user's desktop and create a new one pointing to the new mail file.
- If the user moved from one domain to another, we need to copy the user's person document and paste it in the new domain. Then we need to update the mail locations in the new document.
- Delete the original mail file (making sure to replicate it one last time).

Notes makes this so much easier for us by having AdminP do most of the work. All we have to do is create the request and later, approve the deletion of the original mail file. Well, almost. In order for AdminP to perform these steps for us, we need to make sure that our servers have the rights to create replicas on each other. You should have placed the group LocalDomainServers in the Can Create Replicas field of each server document.

Like the process used to rename people, AdminP has several steps that are performed to accomplish the mail file move:

1. Our Move Mail File request creates a Check Mail Server's Access request in the Administration Requests database. This request checks to make sure that the original server can create replicas on the new server. This check is done while we are creating our request, so if the original server cannot make replicas, we will be notified immediately and can take steps to rectify the problem.

2. If the Check Mail Server's Access completes successfully, a request to Create new mail replica is created. The replica is created immediately and an Add new mail file fields request is created.

3. The Add new mail file fields request creates two new fields on the user's person document. These fields are New Mail Server and New Mail File. This request also creates the next request, Monitor new mail file fields.

4. The Monitor new mail file fields request is carried out at the next AdminP interval on the new mail server. This request checks to be sure that the person document has replicated to the new server and that mail can route to the new mail file. A Replace mail file fields request is then created.

5. The Replace mail file fields request is carried out on the administration server for the Domino Directory. This creates two new fields, Old mail server and Old mail file and populates them with the information from the original mail location. The request also populates the regular mail location fields with the information from the new location fields created in step 3. Finally the request sets a flag in the person document to indicate that the client needs to be updated.

6. Once the user authenticates with his new mail server, two things occur. The first is that the person's location document in his personal name and address book is updated with the name of his new mail server and the new location of his mail file. Second, a Push changes to new mail server request is created. This request causes the home mail server to push changes from the original mail database to the new one for the last time and creates a Get Information for Deletion request.

7. The Get Information for Deletion request runs on the old mail server and is the beginning of the end for the original mail file. This request gets the replica ID of the mail file and creates the Approve file deletion request.

8. Now it's our turn to actually do something. We need to periodically look in the Administration Requests database to see if there are any pending requests for us. The easiest way to do this is to open the Pending Administrator Approval view in the Administration Requests database. Once the request to delete the mail file appears here, we need to approve it. Place the document in edit mode and press the Approve File Deletion action button. A confirmation box will pop up allowing you to back out if you want. Press Yes to delete the mail file. A verification box opens, press OK to continue.

9. When you pressed the approval button, the document disappeared from the Pending Administrator Approval view and a Request File Deletion request was created. This request is carried out according to the AdminP interval setting on the original mail server and creates a new request, Delete Mail File.

10. The Delete Mail File request is completed on the original mail server according to the AdminP interval setting. Finally, the old mail file is deleted!

11. If the original mail file used shared mail, the Delete Mail File request would have created another request to Delete unlinked mail file. This would have allowed the Object Collect Task to purge any messages from the Single Copy Object Store before actually deleting the mail file. The mail file would be deleted according to the setting Interval between purging mail files and deleting when using object store in the Administration Process section of the server document.

As you can see from all the activity that goes on during a mail file move, and the critical timing needed to have it happen smoothly, we're lucky to have this task automated by the AdminP process. This task cannot be initiated using the NT User Administration program.

Removing Users

The flotsam and jetsam of long gone users clogs our systems with names in groups, ACLs, Reader/Author fields, roles, mail files (sometimes with Full Text Indices), and private views, folders, and agents in databases. We can let AdminP clean up this mess for us by initiating a Delete Person request. There are several ways to do this:

- From the Domino Directory, by highlighting user and choosing Delete Person from the action bar or action menu.
- From the Domino Administrator, by highlighting the person on the People & Groups tab and choosing Delete from the People Tools.
- From the Web Administrator, by opening the person document and choosing Delete Person on the action bar.
- Using the NT User Manager.

All these actions will initiate the Delete Person request, but with a couple of notes. You cannot choose to immediately delete a user (described next) when initiating from the Web or NT User Manager.

Initiating a Delete Person Request

To initiate a Delete Person request, perform one of the actions described previously. If you use the method in the Domino Directory or the Domino Administrator, a dialog box will appear asking for verification to delete the selected user or users. Click Yes, another dialog box will open as shown in Figure 12.6. Your options are

- Delete Mail file options

  Don't delete mail file. Choose this to leave the person's mail file on the server.

  Delete just the mail file specified in Person record. Choose this to remove only the mail file on the person's mail server. Unless you have created replicas of people's mail files on other servers, choose this option.

  Delete the mail file specified in Person record and all replicas. Choose this if you have created replicas of the mail files on other servers, perhaps for failover in case of a server crash. Choosing this option will create additional requests in the Administration database to have *all* servers look for a replica for deletion. You do not have to specify which servers to look on.

- **Add to group.** Type or select the name of the group, usually a Deny Access group, to which you would like this person added.
- **Delete NT user account.** Click the Yes radio button to also delete the person's NT account.

> **Warning**
>
> There is nothing to stop us from just deleting a user's person Document in the Domino Directory. However, we will not remove the user's name from groups, ACLs, and so on and could have a security problem if the server allows Anonymous Notes connections. The only time that it is appropriate to delete the person document is if the document is only used for Web access and is not associated with a Notes ID.

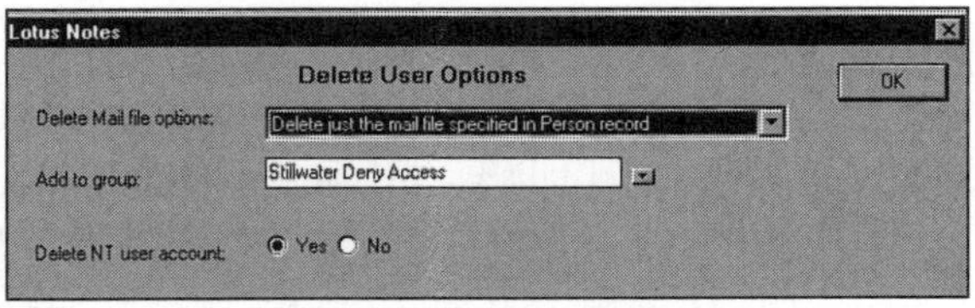

![Lotus Notes Delete User Options dialog box. Delete Mail file options: "Delete just the mail file specified in Person record". Add to group: "Stillwater Deny Access". Delete NT user account: Yes (selected) / No.](dialog)

Figure 12.6   This dialog is box presented if deleting a
person through the Domino Directory or Domino Administrator.

Click OK. Another dialog box will open as shown in Figure 12.7. You have a choice
of three options:

1. Yes - Choose this to have Notes immediately delete the user's person document
   from the Domino Directory. The agent will then search all Person Documents
   in the Domino Directory to remove the deleted person's name from any Owner
   or Administrator fields. After the agent has run, a Delete in Access Control List
   request will be created in the Administration Requests database.

2. No - Choose this to initiate a delete request in the Administration Requests
   database.

3. Cancel – Choose this to cancel the deletion process.

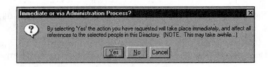

Figure 12.7   Choosing Yes (or immediately) will perform the tasks that
would normally be done by Delete Person and Remove from Person
Documents requests. This action is not offered when initiating a
request from the Web Administrator or NT User Manager.

The deletion process is quite involved. But, there are two steps that require our attention. One is to approve the deletion of the user's mail file, the other is to approve the
deletion of Private Design Elements, such as private folders or agents in applications.
The steps that the AdminP process carries out are

1. **Delete Person in Address Book** request is created anytime we indicate we
   want to delete the person, except when we choose to perform the deletion
   immediately, in which case the document is deleted from the Domino Directory
   as we wait. This request is performed according to the AdminP interval setting.

2. **Delete in Person Documents** request looks for the user's name in other
   users' Person Documents in the Domino Directory and deletes any references.
   This request is done automatically when we request to delete the person immediately, otherwise it is carried out according to the Execute once a day requests
   setting in the AdminP section of the server document.

3. **Delete in Access Control List** request removes the user's name from the ACL of any database in which the name appears if the server on which the request is being carried out is the administration server of that database. This is done according to the AdminP interval setting.

4. **Delete in Reader/Author fields** request removes the user's name from Reader and Author Names fields in all databases where the server performing the request is the administration server for that database. This request is carried out according to the Delayed Request setting for the Administration Process in the server document.

5. **Get information for deletion** is executed immediately and gets the replica ID of the user's mail file for deletion.

6. **Approve file deletion** is one request that we need to approve. Open the request and press the Approve File Deletion action button. Make sure to period-ically check the Administration Requests database to see if there are any requests awaiting approval and to check for errors.

7. **Request file deletion** request is created immediately after we approve the file deletion request.

8. **Delete mail file** request is carried out according to the AdminP interval set-ting. If the mail file is linked to the object store, the AdminP process purges the mail file of links to the object store, disables replication and then creates a Delete unlinked mail file request.

9. **Delete unlinked mail file** request is performed according to the Interval between purging mail file and deleting when using object store. This is done to allow the Object Collect task to purge old messages from the object store.

10. **Approve deletion of Private Design Elements** is the second request that we need to approve. Open the request and click the Approve Deletion of Private Design Elements action button.

11. **Request to delete Private Design Elements** is created when we approve the previous request.

12. **Delete Private Design Elements** actually performs the deletion of private views, folders, and agents that are stored in the database.

Why Aren't Agents Running Anymore?

If after deleting a user from the Domino Directory you start receiving calls that agents no longer run, have the developer check to see if any of the agents were created be the now missing user. This can be done by anyone that has rights to view the agents. Select the offending agent and bring up properties by choosing the Properties SmartIcon. If the Modified By value is the deleted user, have a developer with rights to run agents on the server open the agent and resave it, which will sign it now with her name. Consider creating an ID just for this purpose so you don't have to go through this again when another developer leaves.

Troubleshooting

There really isn't too much to worry about with users. Usually their problems have to do with their ID file becoming corrupted or they've forgotten their password. In earlier releases of Notes, all you could do was find an old copy of their ID and hope that someone had a password that worked.

Now Notes gives you the option to store password recovery information with the ID file. To do this, however, you must set up the certifier ID to create IDs with this information or you will have to recertify all the IDs after setting up your certifier. Adding Recovery Information to Certifier IDs in Chapter 5 shows how to set up the certifiers to allow Password Recovery of ID files.

Recovering Lost Passwords

If a user calls to say he has forgotten his password, we can now provide a way to recover the ID, allowing the user to enter a new password into the ID. Have the user follow these steps:

1. Save his ID from his data directory, usually /Lotus/Notes/Data/user.id to a floppy disk.

2. Now he should take the disk to an associate's workstation that is running Notes, and choose File, Tools, Recover ID.

3. A dialog box will open. There is an area on the dialog box listing authorized users. It also mentions the number of passwords that need to be used to recover the ID. The user needs to contact people on the list and have them extract their recovery password, explained next.

4. After entering the required number of passwords, the user will be prompted to enter a new password and then confirm that password.

5. The user should then take the recovered ID back to his workstation, and copy the new ID over the old one.

Each administrator that is contacted to extract recovery information needs to perform the following steps.

1. Obtain a copy of the ID that needs to be recovered. This can be a copy from the user, or one that has been detached from the central mail/mail-in database that holds backup IDs. This is the location that you specified when you created the recovery information in the certifier.

2. Open the Domino Administrator, click the Configuration tab, and choose Extract Recovery Password from the Certification Tool.

3. A file dialog box will open. Choose the ID file to recover and click Open.

4. A dialog box will open showing when the Recovery Information was created, when it was accepted and the recovery password.

5. Give the recovery password to the user.

If the user still can't open the ID, it is probably corrupted. You will have to make a copy and give it to the user to use when following the steps to recover his ID.

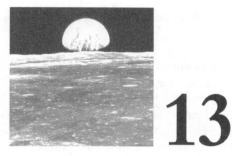

13

Client Maintenance and Troubleshooting

Introduction

The Notes client for Release 5 introduces many new features and places a new face on others. The administrator is frequently required to provide end-user technical support. Usually, this means being both a troubleshooter and tutor.

This chapter provides an overview of the Notes client for the administrator. Many of the new features are touched on. However, discussion is limited mostly to items of interest to an administrator. When dealing with a user's questions and problems, the administrator is expected to know something about everything in Notes. In this chapter, we also start by covering a few of the tools available from Lotus to help you keep your users working.

Client Troubleshooting Tools

When called on to troubleshoot a problem with the Notes client, administrators frequently become involved in aspects of network communications. To successfully connect the client to a server, we need a way to ascertain what is happening between the client workstation and the server.

Some of the R5 client enhancements require an administrator to add new tools to his troubleshooting kit. For example, a user may choose to display Web content on his Welcome page. When a user is unable to connect to a Web page from within Notes, the administrator needs a way to check connectivity between a Notes client and a specific service or task on a Domino server. This adds a new wrinkle to a familiar situation for a Notes administrator.

When a Notes user cannot successfully establish communications with a Domino server, an error message similar to "Server not responding" is displayed. Shortly afterward the Notes administrator's phone rings. After quickly checking that the server is responding from his own workstation, the administrator may want to make a house call at the user's workstation. Sure enough, the workstation and server cannot communicate. Is it a Notes problem, the protocol stack, the network?

Assuming that this client previously has successfully connected to the server, he sets out to discover what has changed. There are two commonly used methods to establish whether network communications are functioning correctly on a Windows 95, 98 or NT client computer. A third method is the result of the emphasis on Web connectivity in R5. This addition requires a way to test for the availability of various Internet services.

- The first method is a generic check of IP connectivity between the workstation and target server using the PING utility.

- The second involves tracing a connection to the target server from within the Notes client.

- The third method uses a utility available from Lotus, called NotesCONNECT, which checks the availability of specific services, via default ports, on a target server.

Services refers to some functionality provided by a network server, such as HTTP, NNTP, or FTP. Every service uses a numbered port assigned by a governing body. The section on NotesCONNECT, later in this chapter, provides additional details.

Why Three Methods to Check for One Connection?

Each of the three methods discussed tests for a different component of a workstation's connection with a target server. The progression in network troubleshooting is usually from general to specific. The methods in this chapter follow this trend.

Testing IP connectivity determines whether a network connection exists from a client to the server.

Testing Notes connectivity from within the client provides connectivity information only for Notes' native protocol (NRPC).

NotesCONNECT provides information about the availability of multiple services on a target server. This utility is similar to the TCP probe available in the R5 Statistics & Events database. NotesCONNECT works from the client to check availability on a server.

To begin, the administrator needs to know some basic configuration information, such as the IP address, DNS alias of the workstation and the server. If DNS is not used on the network, check for a local *hosts* or *lmhosts* file. These ASCII files are used for numeric address to name resolution.

Checking for IP Connectivity

The PING utility is the traditional method used to find out if a client workstation can communicate with the rest of the network. Most administrators are familiar with this utility, so I will only briefly describe the process. There are numerous books, Web sites, and classes that cover it in more detail.

1. PING the network adapter's loopback address of 127.0.0.1. If this is successful, the adapter is responding properly. If this fails, check the network adapter card for problems.

2. PING the network address of the workstation. This establishes that TCP/IP is configured correctly. It also indicates if there is another computer on the network configured with the same network address. This may be the cause of the case of intermittent connection problems, because the first machine that connects has rights to that address.

3. PING the numeric IP address of the server you want to reach. A successful reply means that IP–level connectivity is available between this client and the intended server.

4. PING the fully qualified domain name of the Domino server (for example, PING orion.lotus.com) you are trying to reach. The Notes client communicates with the Domino server by name, as opposed to numeric IP address. Success here verifies that the workstation can resolve the server name.

5. PING the Alias name of the Domino server (for example, OrionDomino). An Alias would be used if the fully qualified domain name is different from that of the Domino server. This establishes that the Alias is entered correctly in the DNS or hosts file. Failure here indicates that the Alias is missing or incorrect in the DNS or hosts file.

Finding the IP Address of a Server or Workstation

To quickly find the numeric IP-address of a workstation, either check the Network Settings in the Control Panel or open a command prompt and type (in Windows 9x or Windows NT):

```
ipconfig
```

As the name implies, ipconfig shows the IP configuration information for the host. The ipconfig /all command shows not only TCP/IP configuration, but also DNS, WINS, DHCP, and NetBIOS information.

If the administrator successfully completes the preceding routine and the Notes workstation still cannot connect to the server, he may consider whether the client is configured correctly. Having established that IP connectivity exists, the next step is to trace the connection from within the Notes client. It is possible that a change was made to the client configuration or even to a network router since the user last connected successfully. Tracing the connection from the client will help to pinpoint the problem.

Testing Connectivity From Within the R5 Notes Client

Checking for connectivity from within the Notes client after establishing IP connectivity exists may expose client-specific communications problems. For example, an incorrect entry in a Location document may cause a Notes connection to fail although network connectivity exists.

As discussed later, it is even possible that the problem is caused by values in a hidden field in the client's Location document. In such cases, the user may receive an error similar to "Unable to find path to server." In other instances, it is possible that a change in a network router filter can stop Notes traffic while allowing other traffic through. This situation may become evident when attempt connections via the Internet through a corporate firewall.

By tracing the connection from within the Notes client, you can see the point at which NRPC connectivity fails. In the case of a change in a router filter, the connection may traverse several devices before failing in an attempt to move across networks through a router. By testing from the Notes client, you established that the client is functioning correctly and identified the device that is causing the error. Using the PING utility first established that a connection was possible. Testing from within Notes isolates a specific type of network traffic. In previous versions of Notes, resolving problems exposed through these first two methods usually allowed resolution of most client connectivity problems.

To trace the connection from a workstation to a Domino server, navigate to the Ports section within User Preferences. Click the Trace button. Notes attempts to establish a connection to the specified server.

If this client has connected to the server previously, Notes will use the IP address stored in the client's Personal Address Book. The address is stored in the client's Location document in a hidden field named $SavedAddresses. Notes always attempts to connect to the server using the address stored in this field; this is called caching. Caching the address is meant to save time when connecting to a server. This setting may create problems if the server's address has changed.

For example, suppose that the IP address of the server EagleMountain/Eagle was changed from 169.254.90.26 to 169.254.90.12. The appropriate changes have been made to the DNS table. I know that I have connected to EagleMountain/Eagle in the past. Now, if I try to establish a connection, I get the error message "Unable to find path to server." When I PING the server by name, or use NotesCONNECT (discussed in the next section of this chapter) both report that the server is available. The Notes client, however, cannot connect. By tracing the connection from within the

Notes client, I learn that Notes is still using 169.254.90.26 when attempting to connect. If you were to look at the Properties of the Location document used to connect to the target server, the value of the $SavedAddresses field would show the old IP address.

To fix this problem, I could delete the current Location document from my Personal Address Book and create a new one. This forces a new lookup of the address. Alternatively, I could place the parameter dont_use_remembered_addresses=1 in the client's notes.ini file. The exercise shows a practical example of a problem experienced by users. With the right tools, you can save the day!

NotesCONNECT

Lotus has created a tool for checking TCP/IP connections through a separate utility that uses its own GUI interface instead of either the command line or Notes client methods described previously. When used to check availability of service on Notes default port (1352), NotesCONNECT uses API calls to verify that a TCP/IP connection can be established from one computer to another. Unlike the method used to trace a connection to a server from within the Notes client, NotesCONNECT may be used to check for the availability of several other service types besides Notes.

Because NotesCONNECT uses the client API, and not the Notes client interface itself, it enables you to distinguish whether the cause of the connectivity problem is the network or the Notes client. NotesCONNECT does not use information in the client's Personal Name & Address Book, the Domino Directory, or Notes address resolution logic.

NotesCONNECT is similar to the PING utility, but uses a different methodology. PING generates IP packets and involves one of the TCP/IP suite of applications called ICMP (Internet Control Message Protocol). NotesCONNECT checks for the availability of a given service on a specific or "well known port." NotesCONNECT establishes a connection more akin to a native Domino connection.

Use NotesPeek to Expose Hidden Fields In the Location Document

There are actually four fields involved in the preceding scenario. These fields cache information about the servers that the client has connected to in the past to improve performance on future connections. To view these fields, look at the Document Properties for a Location document in the Personal Address Book. The $SavedAddresses field contains only one entry per Location document. The other fields are multivalue fields. However, only the first entry in each is visible through the Document Properties. Use NotesPeek, discussed later in this chapter, to view the additional entries.

$SavedAddresses. May contain the target server's DNS name, numeric IP address, or Alias.

$SavedPorts. Saves the port over which connections were established with each server stored in $SavedServers.

$SavedDate. Saves the date of the last connection for each server in the $SavedServer field.

$SavedServers. Saves the names of servers to which the client has connected.

One limitation of the utility is that it only allows testing of named services on default, predefined port numbers. Default port numbers are assigned by the Internet Assigned Number Authority. By assigning default port numbers for common services, it is unlikely that another application will use the same port to communicate, thus causing a conflict.

For example, Domino servers use NRPC (Notes Remote Procedure Calls) to communicate with the Notes client. By default, this service is configured on port 1352. Although not usually changed, it is configurable. When configuring partitioned servers, it may be desirable to configure specific ports on which to listen for NRPC calls. Review the Notes Administration manuals for instructions.

A more common example involves the HTTP service. By default, HTTP communicates using port 80. This would be problematic if multiple Web servers are configured on the same computer. In such instances, only one Web server would respond to calls using port 80, while another may use port 8080. Even given this limitation, NotesCONNECT is a valuable tool that deserves attention. For additional information regarding default port numbering, look at RFC1340.

A workaround to the predefined port issue described previously is provided by the inclusion of "Other" in the Service List field of the NotesCONNECT GUI (see Figure 13.1). If you know the port number of the service you want to check on a given server, for example, 8080, select "Other" in the Service List field on the GUI and enter a valid port number in the Target Port Number field. NotesCONNECT will check for availability of the requested port, but the reply does not indicate which service is actually present.

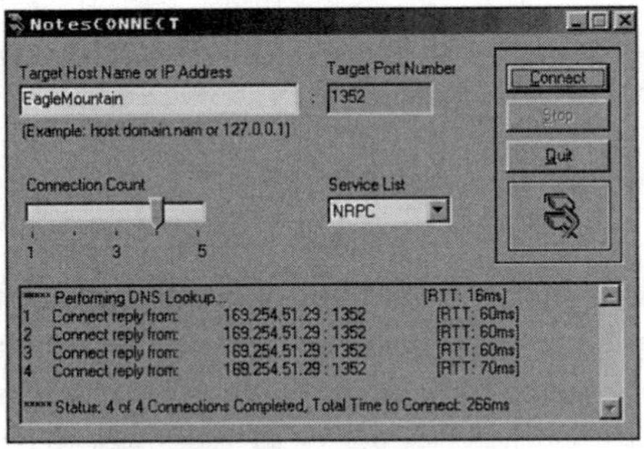

Figure 13.1 NotesCONNECT successfully established a connection with Domino server EagleMountain using NRPC on port 1352.

Either a server name or IP address may be entered into the Target Host Name or IP Address field (refer to Figure 13.1). If a server name is entered, NotesCONNECT will use DNS to resolve the name to an IP address. If the target server's name is not entered into the DNS tables or if a DNS error is suspected, the server's IP address may be entered.

NotesCONNECT can check if the following services are available on the target computer. Because Domino R5 servers support all of these protocols, administrators may find this tool increasingly useful.

- NRPC
- DIIOP
- FTP
- HTTP
- HTTPS
- IMAP
- LDAP
- NNTP
- POP
- SMTP
- SOCKS Proxy

Lotus does not officially market or support NotesCONNECT. However, it is available for download on Notes.Net. Go to http://notes.net/sandbox.nsf and check it out. There is an explanatory article available on Notes.Net in the Webzine section. Search for: Testing TCP/IP Connections with NotesCONNECT.

NotesPeek

Another "unofficial" utility available from Lotus allows users to look inside of a Notes database. Like NotesCONNECT, NotesPeek utilizes a separate GUI and provides information about almost everything that Notes can see inside of a database.

Imagine being able to see how many deletion stubs there are, or see the design elements, replication ID or, more pertinent to R5, the DBIID used for transaction logging. This spiffy utility is available for Release 4 and Release 5 on the Notes.Net Web site. Go to http://www.notes.net/sandbox.nsf to download a copy. There is an explanatory article available in the Webzine section as well. Search for: NotesPeek: X-ray Vision Into Notes Databases.

With NotesPeek, you can view information available to the API in any database on any server that you can connect to with a Notes client. After starting NotesPeek, the user is prompted for his Notes password. NotesPeek's developer ensured security by using Notes program files to view database information. Because NotesPeek enforces database ACLs, a user is not able to use this utility to access information that is unavailable to him from within his Notes client. For an administrator, NotesPeek can be an invaluable tool. Developers will use NotesPeek for the detailed information it provides as well. The level of detail provided through NotesPeek is far greater than the average user will require.

For example, Figure 13.2 shows the level of detail available when looking at a standard mail file. While it may be possible for a user to read the text of a mail message, the magnitude of additional information presented through this utility makes it improbable that anyone would use it in place of the Notes client.

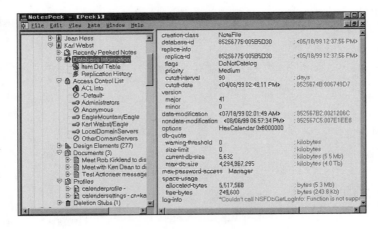

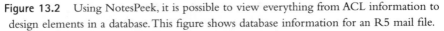

Figure 13.2   Using NotesPeek, it is possible to view everything from ACL information to design elements in a database. This figure shows database information for an R5 mail file.

Once inside, it is easy to open multiple windows, search, and manipulate the ways information is presented. If you have to support the Notes client, you can use NotesPeek. As mentioned earlier in this chapter, NotesPeek may be used to view hidden values in a user's Location document. Administrators may also use NotesPeek to check the number of deletion stubs in a database or to check the DBIID when troubleshooting a problem using the transaction log to roll back a database. Additional uses will become evident with use.

NotesPeek was probably created with database developers in mind, however administrators can definitely use much of the information provided as well. Development tools usually carry a hefty price tag, which frequently precludes their purchase for Notes administrators.

Into the GUI

Now that we have some tools to troubleshoot connectivity and look into the innards of a database, we can survey the interface and its components.

The Welcome Page

The most obvious difference between Notes R4.x and R5 is the addition of a new user interface that Lotus calls the Welcome page. Many users, especially those used to previous versions of the Notes client, look at this addition with skepticism.

The Welcome page puts an experienced user on unfamiliar ground. Many dislike having to learn a completely new interface to a product they may have used for a decade or more. In the following sections, I will discuss some of the strengths and weaknesses of the new interface. It is possible to change or abandon the Welcome page. The needs of the corporation or individual users, depending on their environment, may dictate the way R5 is rolled out to end-users. This section provides the information to implement each possibility.

Implemented out of the box, this interface may be configured by each user to fit their own needs and desires. Allowing corporate users to have their needs and desires met can be quite disconcerting to management and confusing to the users. I like to look at it from both sides of the fence. Some users will want to customize this Welcome page to streamline their daily work and become more productive as a result. Some, however, will use the customization features to ensure that their favorite recreational Web sites are always on their desktop. Still others will want to banish it to the underworld, never to be seen again. You, as the Notes administrator, are asked what can be done to either control the options available to the user or to possibly even remove the Welcome page altogether. Following are some answers.

How to Edit the Welcome Page

When the Notes client is first opened the Basics Welcome page is displayed. In the upper-right corner is a pull-down menu. Changing the default Welcome screen is actually quite easy, even for novice users.

Note that the Options button that allows users to change screen layouts does not appear on the Basics Welcome page. The user must first switch to another of the available page choices before seeing the Options button.

1. Click the down arrow and select one of the available page layout choices, for example Basics Plus. The Options button (shown in Figure 13.3) is displayed to the right of the drop-down menu.

2. Click the Options button to display a tabbed interface that lets the user change the layout and number of visible panes as well as their content.

3. You may choose to alter the layout selection for this page or save your selections under another name which is then selectable from the drop-down menu. The user may choose to display from three to five panes on the desktop. Each of the choices has default content associated with it.

4. Click the Content tab (as shown in Figure 13.4) to view the defaults for the selected layout. Users may also change the contents of all or any of the displayed panes from this interface.

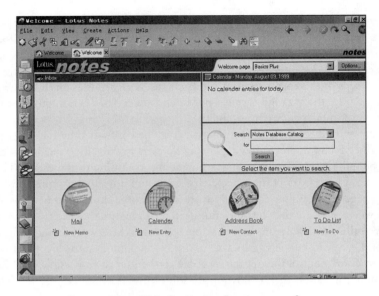

Figure 13.3 Click the Options button to configure the appearance of the user Welcome page.

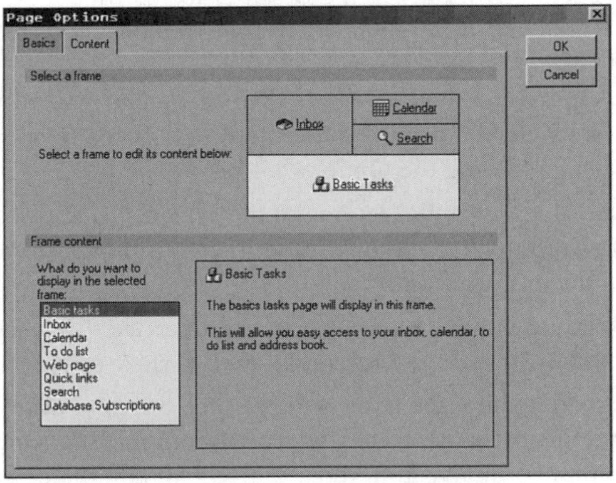

Figure 13.4 Select the frame you want to change by clicking its representation in the top half of the Page Options screen.

5. Select new content for the frame from the list under Frame content. Selecting Web Page allows you to either select from a preprogrammed list of URLs or enter a custom URL. A similar option is available by selecting Quick Links. Here you enter a name, which is displayed onscreen, and associate a URL that is displayed when the user clicks the link name.

6. When the page content is displayed to your liking, click OK and the Welcome page changes to reflect your choices.

For example, users can combine Notes features and Web pages offering them shortcuts to the things they require to do their work. A user may configure one pane to display shortcuts to his Mail, Calendar, Address Book, and To Do list; one showing the company Web page; and yet another with search options for the Notes Database Catalog, LDAP directories, and Web search engines. Another user may decide to change the content of one or more panes and display databases or Web pages that he is developing.

Controlling the Welcome Screen

This all seems rather reasonable to some people. However, in certain companies and situations user control may not be desirable. Some organizations closely monitor, or even block, Internet access. The methods for controlling what is displayed are available through a combination of administrative controls and modification of the bookmark.ntf template database.

To control the Welcome page displayed to Notes users, modify the bookmark.ntf file and then include the modified template in your company client install kits. After the initial implementation, it is possible to push changes out to users through User Setup Profiles.

This topic will be covered in detail in articles and upcoming R5 programming books. The point of including an overview in this chapter is to explain the process so you have an idea of the steps to make it possible.

Replace the Welcome Page with Any Bookmarked Item

Users may select a bookmarked database, document, or Web page and choose to use it to replace their default Welcome page. Here is how to do it:

1. Right-click the desired bookmark.

2. Select "Set Bookmark as Home Page."

You can use this method to set the R4 workspace as the default Home page. To allow users to easily toggle between the R5 style workspace and the new R5 Welcome page, drag both the Workspace and Welcome icons onto the Bookmark Bar. Either bookmark, or any other, can be selected as the default Home page. Users can now easily click to either environment.

The basic steps are as follows:

1. Create a new database. For this example, give it a title of Corporate Frameset dB and save it with the filename CorpFramesetdB.nsf.

2. Inside the new database, create a frameset displaying the information your company wants end-users to see on their Welcome page. For our example, save this new frameset as NewCorpFrameset. Close CorpFramesetdB.nsf.

3. Open the template for the Bookmark database (bookmark.ntf) with the Design client.

4. Create a new frameset and set it to load the NewCorpFrameset from CorpFramesetdB.nsf. Save this frameset as, for example, NewCorpWelcome.

5. On the new frameset in the bookmark.ntf file, enable the property to "Prohibit design replace/refresh to modify."

6. Run the "(Toggle Advanced Configuration Editor)" agent in the bookmark.ntf database. Note: This agent activates the Advanced Configuration Mode allowing you to modify layout profiles and their properties. (Running it a second time turns this mode off.)

7. Return to the frameset view. Highlight the -Welcome- frameset and preview it in Notes. This displays the current default Welcome page.

8. Select Create new page style from the drop-down menu on the Welcome page. This action displays a tabbed interface very similar to the one allowing users to customize their Welcome page. There is now an additional tab titled Advanced Properties. Click this tab.(See Figure 13.5.)

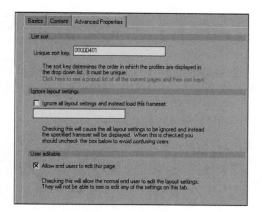

Figure 13.5 The Advanced Properties tab that appears after the (Toggle Advanced Configuration Editor) agent is run.

9. Uncheck the Allow end users to edit this page option.

10. Check the Ignore all layout settings and instead load this frameset option. Enter the name of the customized frameset into the field below.

11. In the Unique sort key field, enter 00000000. The default sort key for the Basics page is 00000001, so a sort key of all zeros will display your new page before the Basics page in the drop-down menu.

12. Click OK and the customized Welcome page is displayed.

13. Remove the framesets you do not want displayed from the template file. This may be all framesets except the customized one you just created.

14. Set appropriate ACL levels to be inherited when refreshing the design of the production bookmark.nsf. Remember to include [Anonymous].

15. Including the modified bookmark.ntf in your company's client install kit builds the user's Welcome page using the customized design instead of the default Basics page.

Using a combination of Notes, HTML, and Java a developer can create a leading-edge interface. Where there once was a bunch of square database icons whose biggest customization feature was a 3D button effect, there is now be an intricate Web style interface.

Many corporations have scripted the installation of the Notes client in their environment. By customizing the bookmark.nsf and desktop5.dsk files, a company can distribute and control the look and feel of the Notes client.

Both Domino and Notes are installed using InstallShield's Silent Install method. For more information on customizing the client installation process refer to Notes documentation. At least one Technote (#170629) describing the process is available through Lotus' Customer Support Web site. InstallShield documentation is available through the company or on its Web site at http://www.installshield.com.

Replacing the Welcome Screen

Change is not always welcome. Requiring experienced Notes users to learn the new interface may take prompting. Experienced users, and corporations alike, bemoan the loss of time necessary to learn how to use the Welcome page. If you want to ease users into the idea, it is possible to present the R4 style workspace instead. Be aware, however that Lotus has not guaranteed the inclusion of the R4 style interface in subsequent releases of the Notes client.

One interesting aspect of the Notes R5 client interface is that it was redesigned to appeal to new users instead of experienced users. As a result, many users of previous versions do not welcome the change. Frequently, the first question an administrator hears is, "How do I get my old desktop back?" Actually, it is there, but you have to know where to look.

The capability to switch back to the R4 style interface is found in the Bookmark Bar on the left side of the user's screen. The Bookmark Bar remains on the screen even when using the R4 style interface. The top half of the Bookmark Bar contains bookmarks, similar to Windows icons, to the user's Mail, Calendar, Address Book, and To Do List.

The bottom half of the Bookmark Bar contains folders that hold additional icons. The interface should be intuitive to every Windows user.

Using the R4 Style Workspace with R5

The Notes R5 client introduces the Bookmark Bar that sits on the left side of the workspace screen. The Bookmark Bar holds shortcut icons, similar to the database icons in the R4 style workspace. Folders, like those in the Windows interface, are available to store related icons.

The Workspace icon, which invokes the R4 style interface, is stored in the Databases icon folder on Bookmark Bar. A user can select it from the folder each time or drag it out of the folder onto the frame under the bookmark folders. Now the user can click back to the familiar surroundings of the R4 style Workspace.

Using that familiar workspace, in conjunction with the R5 Welcome screen and bookmarks, does have its own set of caveats. For example, the icons on the classic workspace pages and those in the bookmarks list are only synchronized at installation or upgrade. This means that additions or deletions of either bookmarks or database icons are not mirrored in the other interface. Lotus has indicated that this may become possible in later releases of the Notes client. A similar issue occurs when a user renames a page in the R4 workspace, expecting his bookmarks to reflect the change. Again, these are not synchronized. Lotus developed R5 thinking that users would use either the Web style bookmarks or the R4 client—not both. Lotus has not guaranteed that the classic Notes desktop will continue to exist in future releases.

Bookmark Bar Functionality

Like database icons in previous versions, bookmark icons have actions associated with them. The type of actions depends upon the bookmark chosen. Some of these choices were also available in previous versions of Notes, while others are new to R5. For example, by right-clicking the Mail, Calendar, Address Book, or To Do bookmarks, you see the following choices:

- Open
- Open Replica
- Open in New Window
- Open in Designer

Other choices lead to additional menu choices. These also should look familiar from previous versions:

- Database
- Replication
- Create

The following are available on all bookmark icons by right-clicking either a bookmark icon or folder on the Bookmark Bar:

- Open the folder
- Create a new folder
- Remove the folder
- Rename the folder
- Change the folder's icon

These choices also are stored in the bookmark.nsf file. An adventurous user might accidentally delete the Workspace icon or perhaps the Databases icon folder, where the Workspace icon is stored by default. In the current release of the Notes client, the quickest way to retrieve the Workspace icon is to rename or delete the bookmark.nsf database and restart the R5 client.

Users of previous versions will notice that Bookmark icons do not stack the way that Database icons do on the classic Notes workspace. If a user bookmarks multiple copies of the same database on several servers, one bookmark will appear for each database copy in the designated folder. For an administrator who may track Domino Directories on multiple servers, this can make life difficult. Besides being hard to manage, there is no apparent way to tell which icon is associated with which server. Notice that as you move the cursor over a Database icon, the path to the database is shown in the status bar at the bottom of the workspace screen. It is easy to miss if you are looking at the bookmark expecting a pop up display.

Problems Displaying the Welcome Page on Low Resolution Monitors

The lowest screen resolution supported by the Notes R5 client is 800 × 600. A client using a lower screen resolution can enable the horizontal scroll bar via the usual menu choices but because there is no vertical scroll bar, the bottom of the screen is not visible. Lotus has followed the trend of designing for higher resolution graphics. Most corporate users have mid- to high-end equipment on their desks, so this should not be a major inconvenience for the majority of users. Developers may have to resize their navigators in application databases to correctly fit the screen under R5, however.

User Preferences

In this section, we take a look at the user preferences in the R5 Notes client. User preferences give the end-user some control over the way that items are displayed or features implemented. Although often overlooked, there are important choices that deserve attention from the administrator.

One of the more important settings in the User Preferences section concerns the Security Settings. Most administrators do not change the default Execution Control List (ECL) and may be putting their systems at risk consequently. Read the chapter on security for more details on the ECL.

Another area the administrators should consider is the implementation of Web-related settings such as the activation of ActiveX in the Notes browser. See Chapter 15, "Web Server Setup, Maintenance, Tuning, and Troubleshooting," for additional information on the Notes browser.

Users may also notice that the button to select a Startup Database is no longer present. The R5 equivalent is to select a database, right-click, and choose "Set bookmark as Home Page." The selected database opens when the user enters the Notes client. Some of the Advanced settings available in previous versions of Notes no longer appear. The following are no longer available:

- **Typewriter fonts only.** This option forced Notes to use monospaced fonts only.
- **Large fonts.** This option forced Notes to display text in a font that was slightly larger and darker.
- **Keep workspace in back when maximized.** This option forced the maximized Workspace window to stay behind other open windows. Using this option, each time the user closed a window Notes returned to the last window that was current instead of to the workspace.
- **Monochrome display.** This option forced Notes to display in various shades of gray when using a color monitor.
- **Keep all windows within main Notes window (MD).** This option allowed the user to show each Notes window independently of the main Notes window. Each window had its own menu and SmartIcon bar.

Some new user preferences administrators may want to be aware of include:

- **Icon color scheme.** This affects the way that Bookmark icons display.
- **Bookmark size.** Choices are Small, Medium, and Large. Keep this in mind for your users with vision problems.
- **Default fonts.** In R5, users may notice that some of the fonts they used no longer appear in the available font list. For example, Helv/Helvetica is gone. Some fonts in previous versions were virtual, that is, the operating system mapped to another sans serif font. In R5, you can select default Sans Serif, Serif, Monospace, and Default fonts in User Preferences.

- **New mail sound.** The sound that Notes plays when new mail is received is now selectable through a button instead of editing the `notes.ini` file. Unfortunately, there is no facility for previewing the sounds before selecting one.

Dynamic User Setup Profiles

Notes R5 offers the administrator a way to control the items displayed on the user's workspace. In previous versions, once the Notes client was deployed there was no centralized method to make changes or force desktop standardization. With R5, administrators may add databases or change certain items of their users' desktops after the Notes client has been installed. This is accomplished by making changes to the User Setup Profile(s) in the Domino Directory. In R4 versions of Notes, User Setup Profiles were used to populate specific fields during client setup. Beginning with R5, User Setup Profiles can be used to dynamically change these fields when the client authenticates with the Home Server specified in their Location document. Changes are made by editing the Setup Profile using the Administration client and propagated through the Administration Process.

By making changes to the User Setup Profiles, administrators can update settings for the following items on the Notes client:

- Browser Information
- Passthru Server
- Domain Search Servers
- Secondary Server Information
- Proxy Server
- Java Applet Security
- Catalog Domain Search Server
- Optional Customer Designated Fields

To do this, both the client and his Home Server must be running at R5 code levels. Note however that administrators can only add or change settings, deletions cannot be pushed out to the Notes client. Users also may disable changes to their profile by selecting the Actions, Advanced, Set Update Flag from their menu with their Location document in edit mode. If users are not receiving profile updates, check this setting.

Using the Administrator's ID on a Server

If the administrator uses his ID locally on the server, you should disable dynamic client configuration by adding this line to the server's `notes.ini`:

`DisableDynConfigClient=1`

Changes in the Mail Service

The most popular computer application today is generally acknowledged to be email. The Notes client has always provided secure and convenient email service. R5 has introduced some changes with which administrators should be familiar.

Mail Rules

The Notes R5 client introduces Mail Rules. Users may now specify criteria that automatically trigger actions by Notes such as moving a document with specified content to a folder. By creating rules, users can manipulate incoming messages. Administrators will need to be familiar with Mail Rules. Users are likely to require some assistance setting rules and troubleshooting problems that may be associated with rules that have been created. The Mail Rules interface is shown in Figure 13.6. Clicking the Rules folder in the user's mail file accesses Mail Rules.

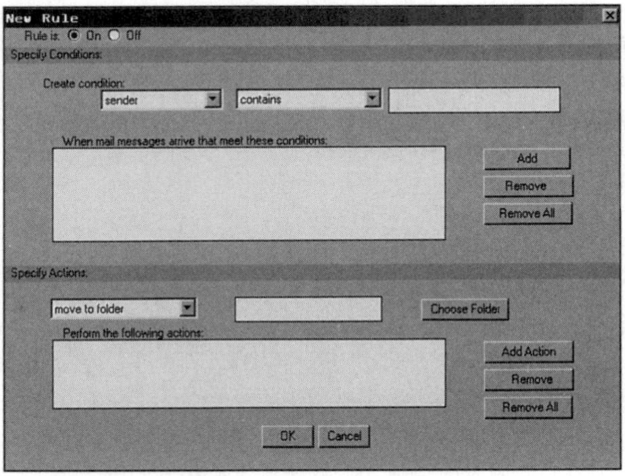

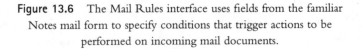

Figure 13.6 The Mail Rules interface uses fields from the familiar Notes mail form to specify conditions that trigger actions to be performed on incoming mail documents.

The following Notes mail fields may be used to specify conditions in Mail Rules:

- Sender
- Subject
- Body
- Importance
- Delivery Priority
- Address fields (To, CC, BCC, To or CC)
- Size in bytes

The following actions are available for items meeting these criteria:

- Move to another folder
- Copy to a folder
- Change importance
- Delete

Figure 13.7 shows a completed Mail Rule form. When a message arrives from Jean Hess, the value in the Importance field is changed to High. Using another rule, in which trigger is memos and the Importance field contains a value of High, I could move this message to a separate folder, which I read first, when opening my mail.

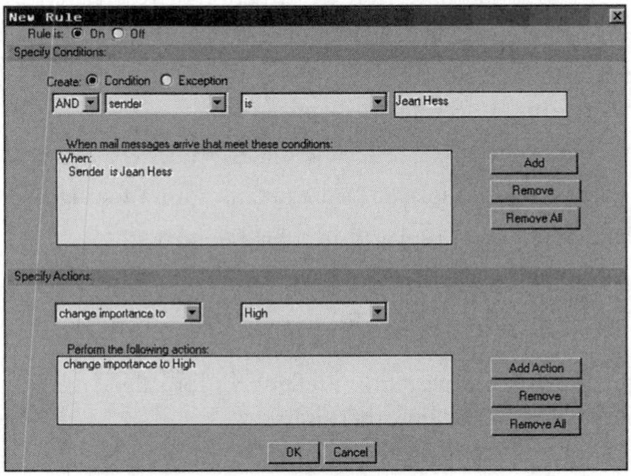

Figure 13.7 This Mail Rule changes the value of the Importance field of the memo to High.

Mail Rules can be turned on and off by editing the rule in the user's mail file. The rules use a similar interface to that found in the Agent Builder window but offer less functionality than Agents.

Rules continue to work, even if the client's workstation is turned off or not running the Notes Client at the moment. Rules are server-based so that they function provided that the mail server is online.

Auto Spell Check

In corporations, people are image conscious. The way we communicate is subjectively used to judge things like intelligence and understanding of a situation. Memos full of misspelled words detract from the impact of the message. Beginning with Notes R5, spelling can be automatically checked before a memo is delivered. Spell checking can be enabled on individual memos by selecting Auto Spell Check on the Basics tab of the Delivery Options. To enable spell checking for all messages, select Automatically check mail messages for misspellings before sending by selecting Tools, Preferences in the user's mail file.

Additional Settings for Mail, Calendar, and Delegation

R5 introduces additional mail-related features that are set in the Preferences dialog box as well. Administrators should become familiar with settings for:

- **Signature files.** Users may append plain text, (for example, "Eagle Mountain Computing" along with an address and contact number), the contents of a text file, or an image in either HTML or bitmap format to the bottom of their mail messages. As long as the message is sent to another Notes user it should appear as it does on the Memo form. Messages sent to Internet users may create attachments for appended image files instead of displaying them with the message.

- **Calendar Options.** Users may set options for:
  - Times when the user is available for meetings, appointments, and such.
  - When alarms are displayed and a default sound for alarms.
  - Default time range displayed in their calendar.
  - Auto-processing and delegation of meeting invitations
  - Displaying the day's To Do list in their daily calendar.

- **Delegation Options.** Delegation preferences for calendaring and mail allow the mail file's owner to assign other users:
  - Who can read mail, calendar, and To Do items in this database.
  - Who can read calendar To Do items, and both read and send mail on the owner's behalf.
  - Who can read, send, and edit any mail, calendar, and To Do documents
  - Who can delete mail, calendar, and To Do documents.

Additional Utilities Available on the Notes CD: Notes Minder

Notes Minder is a new feature in R5. This program checks for mail and monitors calendar alarms even when Notes is not running. After the program is started, a small version of the icon appears in the Windows System Tray. If Notes Minder detects new mail or a calendar alarm, the envelope on the icon will turn red and blink. Holding your mouse over the icon in the System Tray causes Notes Minder to display a text box containing mail status or the time that you last checked for new mail.

Place a shortcut to Notes Minder in a user's Start menu to allow him to monitor mail and alarms automatically. This has the extra benefit of giving users a shortcut to start Notes from the System Tray. By clicking the icon, Notes Minder starts the Notes client. Otherwise, start Notes Minder from the Lotus Applications folder.

Additional Utilities Available on the Notes CD: Actioneer

Actioneer is an add-in program available in the APPS subdirectory on the Notes CD. This program enables users to enter information into the Notes client calendar, even when Notes is not running.

Because Actioneer has access to the user's calendar, the user is prompted for the Notes password even if he is already logged in. After the program is active a small version of the icon appears in the Windows System Tray. Open Actioneer by clicking the icon.

Click the To Do, Appointment, or Journal Entry icon and enter text. Actioneer attempts to populate fields such as the date, beginning times, and end times based on the text a user enters.

After saving the item, Actioneer enters the item into the appropriate place in the user's calendar. Figure 13.8 shows the input window. Figure 13.9 shows the appointment that the program placed into the user's calendar.

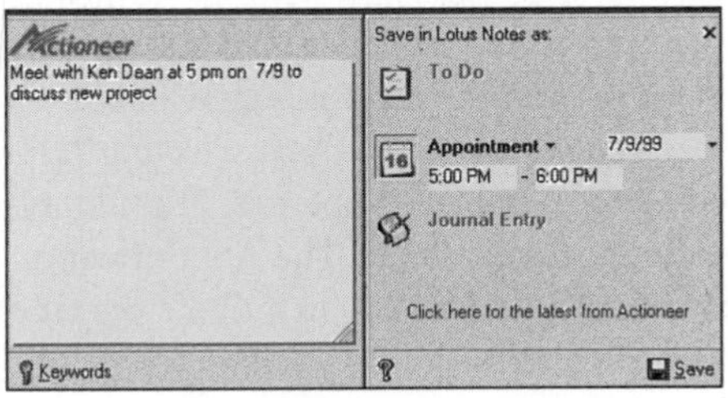

Figure 13.8   Enter text into Actioneer and the program attempts to convert keywords into a calendar entry.

Figure 13.9 The appointment entry in the user's calendar.

HC Subscriptions

The Notes R5 client enables users to set up subscriptions that advise them of specific changes to a database. Users may choose to be advised of all new or modified documents in a database or just those meeting specific criteria. The criteria can be based on a selection formula or by selecting from Author, Subject, and/or Size.

Possible performance issues exist for databases having large numbers of users subscribing. Because Notes will automatically check for new messages matching the criteria of the user's subscription, each subscription adds overhead to the system. By default, the Notes client checks subscriptions at startup and each time the client checks for new mail. These choices are selectable in User Preferences. The increased bandwidth used and server activity generated by several hundred users checking for and retrieving new documents in the Domino Directory every 10 minutes, for example, should give an administrator pause. The resulting overhead could significantly slow access to the system.

Administrators may want to limit the databases to which users may subscribe. Disable user's ability to subscribe to individual databases by selecting "Don't allow headline monitoring" on the Advanced tab of Database Properties. The administrator may also change this setting through the Administration client. The Administration Client has the advantage of allowing changes to multiple databases in a single operation.

Managing Notes System Files

So far in this chapter, we have discussed client changes that may be noticeable to endusers. Notes Architects and Administrators tasked with implementing R5 on the network also face decisions regarding resource management, similar to those faced on network servers. Notes, as any other application consumes resources, which require management. The next section covers ways to manage the impact of the R5 client on user's workstations.

R4 users may notice a sizable increase in the file size reported when they look at the properties of the classic workspace in R5. This is due to the addition of the graphical elements of the Welcome page. For example, an R4 desktop may report a size of 4MB. Under R5 users may see a 100 percent (or higher) increase, depending on their choices in the Welcome page.

The size reported on the Advanced tab of the Workspace Properties box is actually the combined size of the desktop5.dsk and cache.dsk files. This was also true in previous versions of Notes. When users choose to compact their workspace it actually compresses both files.

The desktop5.dsk file stores the user's icons, a cached copy of his unread marks, plus some additional information. The cache.dsk stores design elements from recently used server-based database forms, a log of unread marks called the Unread Journal, plus additional information. These files can grow to be quite large. The size of files in user directories on a file server is increasingly becoming an issue in many corporations. For example, companies that perform centralized backups of the user's files have a limited period in which to complete these backups without affecting user productivity. Methods of managing the size of user files can become quite heated.

There are two issues, besides backup, that the administrator should be concerned with when managing these files. These are *size* and *location*. Of the two files, the cache.dsk is considerably larger. The Workspace Properties may report a file size of 5MB, for example. The desktop5.dsk would probably consume approximately 1MB and the cache.dsk accounts for the remainder.

Disk space consumption is an issue on many networks, workstations, and laptops. Managing the size of large files can save money and increase disk space available to users. Consider a network with 1,000 users, each consuming 5MB of space with these two files. Now consider that 5MB is actually a small instance. Average users will consume between 5MB and 50MB of disk space combining these files.

There are a few ways to manage the size of the cache.dsk file. For example, the administrator can programmatically delete it and let it rebuild each session, or by specify a value for it on the Advanced tab of the Workspace Properties dialog box. By deleting the cache.dsk, the tracking of unread marks may be affected. Setting a maximum size at the workspace level can also be difficult because users can readily change it.

Duplicate Entry in Remove Programs/Software Under Windows

After upgrading a client workstation from one of the R4 versions to R5, you will notice that there are duplicate entries for Lotus Notes in the Add/Remove Programs utility in the Windows Control Panel. There is no apparent way to tell the two entries apart.

If the user tries to uninstall one in an attempt to fix what may appear to be a corruption, they will either uninstall Notes R5 or receive an error message about not being able to remove HKEY_LOCAL_MACHINE\software\Lotus\Notes\4.0 (product information from the Registry).

This occurs because the R5 installation program does not clean up the Registry entry from R4. Lotus is supposed to correct this situation in future releases of R5, but until then, upgraded workstations may show the duplicate entry.

It is possible to use RegEdit32 to remove the R4 Registry entry, however, there does not appear to be any issues if you leave it intact. Frustratingly though, the R4 Registry entry will remain even if R5 is uninstalled.

Changing settings in the notes.ini file may specify the location of the desktop5.dsk and cache.dsk. Using the CACHE parameter in the notes.ini file enables the administrator to specify the location of the cache. This allows administrators the option of storing the cache.dsk file on a larger network drive or on the user's local hard disk. Storing the cache.dsk, desktop5.dsk locally will increase user performance because this frequently used information is not required to be retrieved from and written to a network drive. Locating the cache.dsk onto the user's workstation may also help to motivate the user to periodically compact the workspace to regain disk space.

System Time Zone Settings

By default, the R5 Notes client synchronizes its time zone and daylight savings time settings with that of the operating system. These settings are stored in the user's current location document. If the computer's time zone, daylight savings time, and Greenwich Mean Time settings are either not set or incorrectly set, Notes will display the time incorrectly.

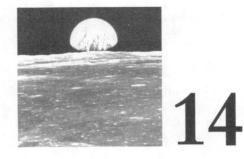

14

Database Maintenance and Troubleshooting

IN THIS CHAPTER, WE DISCUSS THE PROPER CARE AND FEEDING of your Domino databases—how to keep them up and running and performing their best for your users. One part of this is maintenance and repair, which includes troubleshooting problems. The other part is management, which is maximizing or optimizing your databases so they reach their full potential while you control their growth and development.

This chapter also defines the roles of the administrator and the database manager/owner, that are not necessarily assigned to the same person or group. The database designer or developer also has some impact on the performance of the database. Whoever occupies these roles must be aware of this interaction and know the areas of responsibility for each.

Rolling Out an Application

A database or a group of databases make up an application, which is designed to perform a task or series of related tasks, act as a forum for exchanging ideas, store important data or documents, gather and/or disseminate information, or monitor business procedures or projects.

Building and deploying an application involves several steps:

1. **Planning the application.** This involves a combination of the client (the user population or their representatives) and the application developer(s) who define what they want to accomplish with the application and in general how they want the application to work. The application developer or designer makes a plan for the application based on this information and then checks it with the client for final clarification.

2. **Creating the database file and the design elements needed to achieve the purpose of the application.** The application developer puts together the components necessary to build the database(s)—fields, forms, views, agents, actions, navigators, pages, framesets, and so forth.

3. **Develop and implement security for the application.** Based on client input about which users should be able to do what in the application, the developer implements some security while building the elements of the application. The administrator should have input about parts of the application which impact the server, such as agents, and give general support on security matters throughout the creation process. The access control list (ACL) for each database is ultimately the responsibility of the administrator, although the ACL may be originally specified by the developer. The administrator should be assigned Manager access. For more information on database security, see Chapter 10, "Security."

4. **Rollout of the application to a small pilot group that tests the application.** When the application is ready to be tested by a select group of users, the administrator oversees adding the application database(s) to the server.

5. **Incorporate feedback into the application.** The pilot test group uses the application as fully as possible to explore all its elements for possible errors and suggest corrections or improvements that may be needed. The application developer incorporates any agreed upon improvements and corrects any design flaws. The administrator monitors the application to be sure no problems occur on the server and that server performance is not impacted.

6. **Make the application available to the general user population.** Although the application developer may do some tweaking of the application after this point, most of the design work is complete. Either the developer or the administrator creates the original full text index. A copy (not a replica of the original test database) is put on the server, and a database template should be created for making later design changes (see the "Adding a New Database to the Server" section in this chapter). The database and template are signed for purposes of workstation security (see the "Signing for Security" section in this chapter for more details). The administrator defines the final access control list, creates any necessary groups, and informs users that the application is available.

At this rollout point, the administrator is responsible for setting up replication of the application database(s) between servers (as discussed in Chapter 9, "Replication"), and establishing limits on database size. Thereafter, the administrator must make sure that the database continues to replicate, maintain and update the ACL, and resolve any user problems with the database(s).

Resolving the daily application issues is the role of the database manager. Although the administrator also can be the database manager, a power user may fill this role. This person would have Manager access to the database(s), and would be responsible for maintaining the ACL or informing the administrator of needed changes. Members of groups in the ACL also have to be updated for new or terminated users, and this is another responsibility of the database manager (at least to inform someone with the proper access to the Domino Directory to modify group membership). Database managers typically resolve replication and save conflicts, check the data in the database to see if it's correctly entered, and act as a help desk on how the application works.

Now that we have established what roles are involved in building, deploying, and maintaining the database(s) in an application, we will examine how you as the administrator and/or database manager accomplish the necessary tasks to manage and maintain the databases in your care.

Adding a New Database to the Server

Before deploying the new database(s) on the server, you need to prepare the server to work with the new application. For example, you need to be sure that any users or other servers involved have appropriate access to the server. You may have to create a mail-in database document for any database to which mail is going to be routed. Permission for agents to run on the server might also be required, particularly LotusScript and Java agents.

Tracking Application Life

Applications come and go. Those designed for specific projects are no longer needed after the project is complete. Others die a quiet death as users find other methods of doing things. Meanwhile, the number of databases grow as users increasingly see Notes and Domino as the solution to their problems and demand databases as the answer. After a while, fewer people know what the different databases on the server do, who asked to have them created, and if they are still needed. Although the Database Catalog provides some information on every database on the server, it isn't tracking the usefulness of the databases. In the IBM Redbook *Secrets to Running Lotus Notes: The Decisions No One Tells You How to Make*, authors Marion Hawker, Amita Greenfield, Helen Rowan, and Andrew Wainwright suggest creating a Notes Application Registry database. This database maintains information on who asked to create the application, what its purpose is, what application a database is part of, and information to help users find the database(s) they need. This book, along with other Redbooks about Lotus Notes and Domino, is available from the IBM Web site: http://www.redbooks.ibm.com/solutions/lotus.

You also have to consider your directory structure on the server. Putting a set of related databases in one subdirectory of the root makes it more manageable for replication purposes (set the Connection document to replicate by directory), easier for users to find "their" applications, and more controllable from a security perspective.

Finally, make sure you have Manager access in the database ACL before you add the database to the server and that you have access to create new databases on the server.

To copy the database to the server:

1. Right-click the database bookmark and choose Database, New Copy.

2. In the Copy Database dialog box, select the Server on which you want to put the copy.

3. Make any changes to the title that you want to appear as the bookmark name for the server copy.

4. In File Name, enter the path and filename of the database. Although your operating system supports long filenames, Domino works best with eight-character filenames, plus the .nsf extension.

5. Select Database design and documents to copy all the database design elements as well as any existing documents, or choose Database design only to avoid copying any documents created during development.

6. *(Optional)* Select Access Control List to include the current ACL with the database if there are roles and access levels already assigned in the ACL and you want to keep them—just make sure you are assigned Manager access. If you want to begin with a clean ACL, don't select the option. The new copy will automatically list you as Manager, and you get to assign the levels instead of inheriting them.

7. *(Optional)* Select Create Full Text index to create a full-text index for the new database copy. A full-text index is needed for database searches, but it can be created later.

8. *(Optional)* Click Encryption to encrypt the new database copy, which means that any users would need a specified ID to gain access to the database. Encryption can be simple (protection from casual snooping), medium (good security but still speedy access to documents), or strong (most secure, but documents take longer to open). Although encrypted databases are sometimes used to protect workstation copies or replicas, especially laptops, encryption is rarely applied to server copies or replicas.

9. *(Optional)* Click Size Limit and select the maximum size for the database—1GB, 2GB, 3GB, or 4GB. This option only applies to R4 databases using the .ns4 filename extension or to databases hosted on servers that haven't been upgraded to R5 yet. The size limit for R5 databases is 64GB on Windows or UNIX platforms, or 32GB on OS/2.

10. Click OK.

Initially Setting Database Properties

After the database is on the server, open the Database Properties box for the database (right-click the bookmark and choose Database, Properties). On the Design tab of the Properties box, select the option Show in Open Database dialog box so users may access the database by choosing File, Database, Open from the menu.

If, as recommended, you or the application developer created a design template for the database, you need to add the name of the template to the database properties. On the Design tab of the Database Properties box, select Inherit design from template and then enter the Template name. You'll also have to place a copy of the design template on the server. You want to encourage application developers to use design templates because they can test future changes to the database without touching the current documents. When the modifications are ready for production, you just refresh the database design.

To allow users to recover documents that they deleted from the database, select Allow soft deletions on the Advanced tab of the Database Properties box. In $Undelete Expire Time, enter the amount of time you'll allow users to recover their deleted documents (in hours). For users to be able to take advantage of the soft delete feature, the database must also have a view to display the deleted documents. You or the application developer can make this view. It requires that you set the view type as Shared, contains deleted documents. The user opens the view, selects the document to restore, and undeletes it.

To learn more about the options on the Advanced tab of the Database Properties box, see the "Improving Database Performance" section in this chapter.

On the Database Basics tab of the Database Properties box are two properties that also affect database performance:

- **Allow use of stored forms in this database.** If you aren't mailing or copying documents to individuals or other databases, you probably don't need this option selected. By deselecting it, you reduce the size of the database and improve database performance.

- **Display images after loading.** By selecting this option, you improve performance because the database doesn't have to bring up each image as it's loading. However, you won't save anything in database size. You might want to check with the application developer to be that images were stored as image resources instead of individually pasted or imported onto pages and forms. Using image resources stores each image only once in the database and saves space.

Managing Databases from the Administrator Files Tab

The Domino Administrator gives you one central location for monitoring, maintaining, and managing your databases. You select a server from the Server Pane and then click the Files tab (see Figure 14.1). The View Pane then displays the file structure for Domino and Notes on that server. The contents of the Files Pane depend on the folder you select. Click the button to the right of "Show me" to close the View Pane and display all files in the Domino folder.

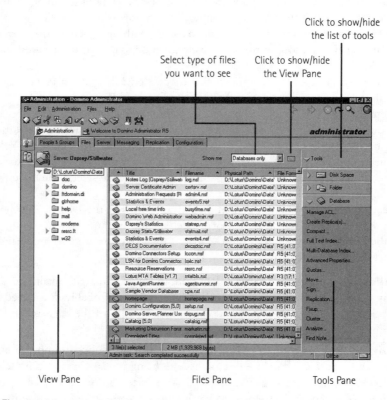

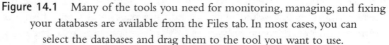

Figure 14.1   Many of the tools you need for monitoring, managing, and fixing your databases are available from the Files tab. In most cases, you can select the databases and drag them to the tool you want to use.

From the Show me drop-down list, select the type of files you want to view in the Files Pane: Databases only, Templates only, Mail Boxes only, All database types, All files, Database links only, or Custom.

The Files Pane displays the type of files you specified in the Show me drop-down list. By default, the columns you see include the Title, File Name, Physical Path, File Format, Size, Max Size, Quota, Warning, Created, Last Fixup, and Is Logged. To eliminate or reorder the columns displayed in the Files Pane, choose File, Preferences, Administration Preferences and then click the Files icon. Select the column name in the Use these Columns box and click the left arrow to remove a column; click the up and down Reorder columns buttons to change the order of the columns. Click OK after you have the columns you want displayed showing in the Use this Column box, in the order you want.

To open a specific database or template, select it and then double-click on it in the Files Pane.

The Tools Pane shows three options:

- Disk Space displays the disk size and free disk space for the hard disks on the selected server. The display includes a pie for each disk that represents the free space remaining.

- Folder lists options for managing folders and database links: New to create new folders, New Link to create a new Folder or Database link, Update Link to update existing links, and Delete to delete selected files. For details on the use of this tool, see the "Directory and Database Links" section in this chapter.

- Database contains a set of database tools to be used on the selected database(s) in the Files Pane (or drag selected database(s) to the tool. Some of the Database Tools are discussed in the next section, and others are scattered through the rest of the chapter.

Using Database Tools

Lotus recommends that you perform certain database maintenance tasks on a regular basis. Table 14.1 lists these tasks by the recommended frequency:

Table 14.1 **Regularly Performed Database Maintenance Tasks**

Frequency	Task
Daily	Monitor replication for databases that replicate
Daily (by default at 1:00 a.m.)	Keep databases that inherit design from master templates in sync with the templates by running the Designer task
Daily (by default at 2:00 a.m.)	Update all views and full-text indexes by running the Updall task
Daily for large active databases; Weekly for other databases	Check for and consolidate replication or save conflicts

continues

Table 14.1 **Continued**

Frequency	Task
Occasionally	Monitor the database cache
Weekly	Monitor database activity
Weekly	Monitor database size
Weekly or Monthly for R5 databases; Weekly in off hours for R4 databases	Run Compact
As needed	All others

Many of the tools you need for database maintenance are available in the Files tab of the Domino Administrator. Select the server that stores the databases on which you want to work and then click on the Files tab. In the Files Pane, select the database(s) on which you want to work, and then click Database in the Tools Pane. Click the tool you need for the current activity.

Managing Database ACLs

Instead of opening the ACL for each database, use this tool to update the ACL for all selected databases. Before using this tool, make sure you have Manager access in the ACLs for all the selected databases.

Setting access levels for several databases doesn't differ significantly from setting them for the ACL of a single database. Click Add to enter or select groups or individuals that you want to add to the ACLs. Acceptable names include user, server, and group names, database replica IDs, the "Anonymous" name for Internet users and anonymous Notes users, Internet clients' user and group names, and alternate names. Names should be entered in hierarchical format, although you can use a wildcard such as */Sales/ABC Corp to include everyone in an organization unit or organization.

Unless you grant access to "Anonymous" for Internet users, Internet clients must authenticate using name and password or SSL client authentication. Internet clients must be listed by the first name that appears in the User name field of the Person document (both the Default and Anonymous entries must be assigned No Access).

Assign an access level to the individuals, servers, groups of people, or server groups. Be sure to assign an access level to Default that you want to use for all users or servers not specifically assigned a level. For information on access levels, refer to Chapter 10.

There should be at least two people responsible for the database, so when one person isn't available the other can perform any necessary tasks. Both should be assigned Manager access.

Don't assign access levels higher than a person or group currently needs. Avoid replication and save conflicts by assigning Author access wherever possible instead of Editor.

Assign roles if necessary, on the Roles page. If you add roles to the ACL(s), the Roles window will only display changes to be applied. Existing role information does not appear. Therefore, when you want to rename an existing role you must click Rename and then enter the role name in the From box exactly as it appears in the ACL (including brackets and capitalization). To remove an existing role, click Remove and then type the name of the role to be deleted (you don't need to include the brackets).

On the Advanced page, you should assign an Administration Server to the database(s) in order to have the Administration Process update and manage names in the ACL and in Readers and Authors fields.

Creating Replicas for Multiple Databases

The Create Replica(s) tool lets you create replicas on servers in the same Notes domain or in another Notes domain. Connections should exist between the source and destination servers (not strictly necessary within the same cluster), and permission to create replicas on the destination server should be in place for you and the source server. You must have at least Reader access to the database from which you are creating the replica. The source server must be running the Administration Process.

If the destination server is in another domain, make sure that

- You set up cross-certification if the servers don't share a common certifier.

- An outbound Cross Domain Configuration document exists in the Administration Requests database on the source server. This allows the Administration Process to export Create Replica requests to the destination server.

- An inbound Cross Domain Configuration document exists in the Administration Requests database on the destination server. This allows the Administration Process to import Create Replica requests from the source server's domain.

- Connection documents enabled for mail routing are set up to allow the source server to send mal to at least one server in the destination server's domain.

Open the Domino Administrator to the Files tab for the source server (refer to Figure 14.1). From the Files Pane, select the database(s) for which you want to create the replica(s). Click Database on the Tools Pane and select Create Replica(s), or drag the selected database(s) to the Create Replica(s) tool.

Select the destination server(s) for the replicas (if the current domain includes a cluster, click Show only cluster members to see only the servers in the cluster as destination servers). Choose Other to specify servers not listed.

To choose a custom file path on the destination server, click File Names, choose the file path, and click OK. Repeat this for each destination server, if you want. If you don't specify a custom file path, the database is stored on the same location on the destination server that it had on the source server. To put the replica in a folder below the Domino data folder, enter the folder name, a backslash, and the filename, such as Projects\Tradeshow. Domino creates the folder if it doesn't already exist.

After you click OK, a dialog box displays the number of databases processes and shows if any errors occurred.

The quick method for making replicas in the Files tab is to use *drag and drop*. This will store all the replicas in the same folder on the destination server, and that folder must already exist. From the Files Pane, select the databases from which you'll make replicas. Then drag the selected databases to the destination server in the Server Pane. When the dialog box appears, select Create replica and then choose the folder on the destination server in which to store the replica(s). Click OK.

Compacting to Recover Unused Space

As documents are deleted and file attachments removed from a database, unused space is left in the database. Although Domino attempts to reuse the space, fragmentation may make it impossible to fully reuse it. To eliminate the unused space, you need to compact the database.

To see the amount of used space in a database, check the Database, Sizes view of the server log file, the File Statistic reports generating by the Statistics Collector server task, or the Info tab of the Database Properties box. However, these aren't necessarily accurate indicators of used space. Don't base a decision to compact solely on this information.

Although compacting databases is used primarily to recover unused space, you also need to compact databases to enable or disable certain database properties, to run the archiving tool on server databases, and to fix corrupted databases.

There are three styles of compacting:

- **In-place compacting with space recovery (-b).** This doesn't reduce the size of the database file, but does recover unused space. The relationship between the compacted databases and the transaction log remains intact. During compacting, users and server can access and edit databases. This is useful for databases that you expect to remain the same size or grow.

- **In-place compacting with space recovery and reduction in file size (-B).** This the default style of compacting when you run compact without specifying options on R5 databases that aren't enabled for transactional logging. It both reduces the size of the database file and recovers unused space. It's a little slower than in-place compacting with space recovery only. If you use it on logged databases and have an R5-certified backup utility, make a full backup of databases soon after compacting. Users and servers can continue to access and edit the database during compacting. Optimize disk space by running this style of compacting at least once a week.

- **Copy-style compacting.** This requires extra disk space because it creates a copy of the database and then deletes the original database after compacting is completed. Copy-style compacting is used by default when you use an option with compact to enable a database property that requires a structural change to a database ("Document table bitmap optimization" or "Don't support specialized response hierarchy"). It's also the default when you run Compact on a database that has a structural change pending which was initiated from the Database Properties box. Compacting an R4 database also uses copy-style formatting. Users and servers can't edit databases during copy-style compacting and can only read documents if the -L option is employed.

There are several ways to run compacting in Domino:

- On a single database, run Compact without options from the Database Properties box.
- On the server, run Compact using the Task, Start tool in the Domino Administrator. This method compacts all the databases on the server without using options. You'll be able to use the Domino Administrator while compacting the database(s).
- From the console, run the Compact command using command options directly on the server.
- Run Compact by using a Program document, which allows you to schedule Compact to run at specified times.
- From the Files tab of the Domino Administrator, use the Compact tool to compact one or more databases. You won't be able to use the Domino Administrator until compacting finishes.

To compact databases using the Database, Compact tool, start by selecting the server on the Server Pane (if you don't select a server, Compact runs on the databases stored locally). Click the Files tab and then select the database(s) that you want to compact from the Files Pane. Then select Database in the Tools Pane and choose Compact, or drag the selected database(s) to the Compact tool. Select the options to set how Compact runs, and then click OK.

There are a number of options available for Compact to specify how it runs on the database(s). These are explained in Table 14.2.

Table 14.2 **Compact Options**

Option	Console Command Equivalent (Case-Sensitive)	Description
Compact only if unused spaced is greater than *n*%	-S *percent*	Compact all databases that have the specified *n*% of unused space. Compaction is recommended at 10 percent or greater unused space.
Discard any build view indexes	-D	Discards built view indexes. Does copy-style compacting. Use before storing database on tape.
Set maximum size of database to 4GB	-M	Use only on R4 databases. Sets a maximum database size of 4GB and compacts the database. Does copy-style compacting.
Keep or revert database back to R4 format	-R	Compacts an R4 database without converting it to R5 file format or reverts R5 databases back to R4 file format. This options uses copy-style compacting.
Archive database	-A	Archives and deletes documents from a database and without compacting the database.
In-place (recommended)	-b	Recover unused spaces without reducing the file size.
In-place with file size reduction	-B	Recover unused spaces and reduces file size. Do full database backups after compacting completes if you use transaction logging.
Copy Style: Allow access while compacting	-L	Users can continue to access databases during compacting, but if a user edits a database during compacting, compacting is cancelled.
Copy Style: Ignore errors during compaction	-i	Compacting continues even if errors are encountered, such as document corruption.

Option	Console Command Equivalent (Case-Sensitive)	Description
	NOT AVAILABLE FROM THE COMPACT TOOL BUT COMPACT IN COMBINATION WITH OTHER TOOLS	
	-f	Disables "Document table bitmap optimization" database property. Does copy-style compaction.
	-F	Enables "Document table bitmap optimization" database property. Does copy-style compaction.
	-h	Disables "Don't support specialized response hierarchy" database property. Does copy-style compaction.
	-H	Enables "Don't support specialized response hierarchy" database property. Does copy-style compaction.
	-T	Enables transaction logging.
	-t	Disables transaction logging.
	-u	Disables "Don't maintain unread marks" database property.
	-U	Enables "Don't maintain unread marks" database property.
	-a	Archives and deletes documents from a database and then compacts the database.

Improving Database Performance

The Advanced tab of the Database Properties box has several options that, when selected, improve the performance of the database (see Figure 14.2). When users complain about reduced or poor database performance, consider enabling some of these properties. A description of these options appears in Table 14.3.

Figure 14.2 Many of the options on the Advanced tab of the Database Properties box will improve the performance of the database when selected. However, you may sacrifice functionality by selecting some, such as "Don't overwrite free space" (you reduce your database security).

Table 14.3 Advanced Database Properties to Improve Database Performance

Option	Description
Don't maintain unread marks	Maintaining information on which documents have been read and which have not slows database performance. Where this information isn't necessary, select this option to improve performance.
Document table bitmap optimization	Notes maintains tables of document information to which it refers when updating views. When you enable this option, it associates the tables with the forms used by the documents in the table. Thereafter, Notes restricts its searches to tables for views that contain forms used by documents in the view being updated. A slight performance cost results from maintaining this association, but enabling this option does speed up updates of small views in large databases. You must compact the database to enable this option.
Don't overwrite free space	Notes automatically overwrites deleted data in databases as a security measure. This can reduce database performance. When the database is physically secure, the deleted space is quickly reallocated in the database, or security isn't an issue, you should consider enabling this option to improve performance.

Option	Description
Maintain LastAccessed property	Selecting this option may reduce the performance of the database. By default, a database stores the date when a document was last modified. When this option is enabled, the date when the document was last read is also recorded. Use this option only when you need to track when the document was last read for purposes of deleting or archiving documents without activity during a specified time.
Disable transaction logging	Selecting this option turns off logging of all transactions for Domino API functions. You lose the benefits of full database integrity and high-speed transaction roll forward/rollback from transaction logs, and support for backup and recovery APIs. Any improvement in the performance of the database has to be weighed against the loss of these benefits before selecting this option.
Allow soft deletions	Allows users to recover documents that they deleted from the database. This requires a special view for the deleted documents (see the section "Initially Setting Database Properties" earlier in this chapter).
Don't support specialized response hierarchy	For databases that don't use response and response-to-response documents or display response hierarchies in views, there is no need to use the @AllChildren or @AllDescendents functions. In such databases, enabling this option improves database performance.
Don't allow headline monitoring	Users can subscribe to databases and have headlines that display any items of interest found. The searching of the databases by many users slows database performance. Select this option to prevent the database from being monitored.

continues

Table 14.3 **Continued**

Option	Description
Allow more fields in database (on Database Properties box Advanced tab only)	After selecting this option, you can add up to 64,000 fields to your database. However, by allowing more fields, you may reduce the performance of the database.
Limit entries in $UpdatedBy fields	Any changes to a document by a user or server is stored in the $UpdatedBy field. Maintaining this history consumes disk space and slows updates and replication. Entering a number for this option, limits the number of changes that the document tracks. When the limit is reached, the oldest entry is removed and replaced by the new edit information.
Limit entries in $Revisions fields	Each document stores the date and time of each saved modification in the $Revisions field. This information is used in resolving save and replication conflicts. By default, up to 500 entries are stored in $Revisions. Entering a number in this option reduces the number of stored entries (allow at least 10 entries for conflict resolution) and improves database performance. When the limit is reached, the oldest entry is replaced by the new edit data. Selecting this option should be considered for databases with many documents, that replicate often or have no replicas, or that contain documents which are rarely changed.
Undelete Expire Time	Enter the amount of time (in hours) you'll allow users to recover their deleted documents (if Allow Soft Deletions is enabled).

Instead of setting these options individually for each database on each Database Properties box, use the Advanced Properties tool. You must have Designer or Manager access to the databases.

To set the Advanced Properties, open the Domino Administrator, choose the server from the Server Pane, click the Files tab, and select the databases from the Files Pane for which you want to set properties. From the Tools Pane, select Database and then Advanced Properties (see Figure 14.3). Click Select for each database property you want to enable or disable, and then select the property to enable it or deselect it to disable it. Click OK.

Figure 14.3   The same properties that are available for an individual database in the Database Properties box can be applied to selected databases using this dialog box.

For three of the properties, you must compact the database in order for the property to take effect:

- Don't maintain unread marks
- Document table bitmap optimization
- Don't support specialized response hierarchy

With the appropriate Compact command line, these properties can be enabled during compaction (see the "Compacting to Recover Unused Space" section for more details).

Using Quotas to Maintain Database Size

Databases on Windows and Unix can be as large as 64GB, and on OS/2, they can be 32GB (R4 databases have a maximum size of 1, 2, 3, or 4GB). If you have the disk space to store databases of this size, you aren't interested in setting quotas. Quotas are a tool for Administrators who want to control database size, for both performance and space considerations. A quota specifies the maximum size a database can attain.

When a database exceeds its quota, a message appears to users attempting to open the database: `Cannot allocate database object - database will exceed its disk` quota. The same message appears in the Miscellaneous Events view of the Log file. Users may be able to add documents to the database even if the quota is met, if there is unused space available in the database resulting from deleted documents.

The most likely result of the exceeded quota message is an immediate (and probably irate) call to you from the user, especially if the database is the user's mail database. In a mail file, the Router can still deliver mail even after the quota is reached and users can still update the mail views and read their mail. Users just can't add new documents or views to the mail file. There is a router configuration option that can make quotas be more strictly enforced for mail ("Obey database quotas during message delivery"). It helps, when setting quotas, to also set a threshold for the database. A threshold is a specified size that is lower than the quota. When the threshold is reached in a database, the user sees this message: `Warning, database has exceeded its size warning threshold`. The same message appears in the Log file in the Miscellaneous Events view.

When the irate user calls you about the threshold message, you are able to assure the user that new documents can still be added to the database, but that the maximum size will soon be reached. This is a good time to introduce the subject of deleting or archiving mail.

For databases other than mail, you want the threshold warning to alert you that it's time to do something to reduce the size of the database. This can include archiving old files, deleting inactive files, changing database performance properties to reduce database size, limiting size of replicas using Replication Settings, decreasing purge intervals to remove deletion stubs more frequently, or compacting. You might move the database to another drive or server where there is more room.

To set quotas and thresholds for databases, open the Domino Administrator and select the server from the Server Pane. Click the Files tab, and select the files from the Files Pane for which you want to set quotas. Click Database and then Quotas on the Tools Pane, or drag the selected databases to the Quota tool.

Click More Info to see the absolute maximum size (in MB), current database size (in MB), current database quota, or current warning threshold for each of the selected databases. Click OK to return to the Set Quotas dialog box.

Select Set database quota to and enter the number of megabytes for the quota. To add a threshold warning, click Set warning threshold to and enter the number of megabytes. Click OK. The same quota and threshold warning are applied to each of the selected databases.

Archiving Database Documents

Archiving documents in a database is much simpler in R5. You no longer have to write an agent to do this. Instead archiving is available from the Database Properties box, on the Database Basics tab. Click the Archive Settings button and then select the options to determine which documents to archive and when to archive them. The archive database is automatically created for you, by default as `archive\a_databasename.nsf`. Not only can you set this up to automatically archive a database on the server, but you can log the archive activity. By default, the archive log is stored as `archive\l_databasename.nsf`.

Moving Database(s) to New Server

There are times when it's necessary to move a database from one server to another. You can do it manually, with the Move tool in the Domino Administrator, or by drag and drop to the destination server. Whatever you do, don't do this to a mail file. There is a procedure for moving mail files, and it requires working with the Administration Process. Also, you might consider creating a database or directory link, especially if you move the database outside the Domino data directory (see the section "Directory and Database Links" in this chapter).

Moving the Database Manually

You move the database manually by either using the operating system or by creating a replica on the new server and then deleting the original database. We don't recommend this, but you may have to if you're putting the database on a server outside your Notes domain or where you don't have access to the Domino Administrator.

If the database you moved receives mail, you must make changes to the Mail-In Database document in the Domino Directory to specify the new location. You also have to adjust the ACL of the database to remove the name of the previous server and add the new server name. Make sure that your Connection documents for replication are set correctly for the new server (unless your servers are clustered).

You must also notify users of the new location. One way to do this is to create a new database in the old location that has the same title and filename. Then create a form in that database that lists the title of the original database, its original filename and path, the date of the move, the reason for moving the database, the name of the new server, and the new filename and path. To be even more helpful, you might include a button on the form that opens the database at its new location. Try using the `@Command([FileOpenDBRepID]; "replicaIDnumber"; "newServerName")` for the button.

Using the Move Tool

When you don't need to use the manual method, use the Move tool in the Domino Administrator to make the move, working with the Administration Process. Be sure before you do that both the source and the destination servers are running the Administration Process. You should also have Create Database access in the Server document of the destination server and Manager with "Delete Documents" access in the source server. Also, the source server or another server (one that replicates with the source and has a replica of the database) must have Create Replica access to the destination server. The destination server must have at least Reader access in the ACL of the replica on the source server.

Open the Domino Administrator, select the source server from the Server Pane, click the Files tab, select the database(s) to move from the Files Pane, and then click Database, Move in the Tools Pane (or drag the selected databases to the Move tool). Select one or more destination servers (click Show me only cluster members if the current domain includes a cluster and then select the destination server). If the server you want isn't listed, click Other and specify the hierarchical server name.

To set a customer file path on the destination server for the database you're moving, click File Names and specify the path and filename where you want to store the database. Otherwise, the database is stored in the same location as on the source server. To put the database in a folder below the data folder, type the folder name, a backslash, and the name of the file (such as Planning\Tradeshow). If the folder doesn't exist, Domino creates it.

When you click OK, a dialog box displays the number of databases processed and shows how many errors occurred.

If the source server is not in a cluster, you have more work to do. You have to approve the deletion of each original source database after the Administration Process completes the Non Cluster Move Replica request that creates the new replica on the destination server. You must have at least Editor access to the Administration Requests database to do this. Open the Administration Requests database and then open the Pending Administrator Approval View. For each source database moved, open the Approve Deletion of Moved Replica request in edit mode. Click Approve File Deletion, select Yes, and then click Save and Close.

Now, notify the users that you've moved the database, just as you did when you moved databases manually.

Using Drag and Drop

We saved the easiest for last. In this method, you store all the databases in a folder (that you create in advance) on the destination server. This method uses the Administration Process, so you can't use it to move databases to another domain.

In the Domino Administrator, select the source server on the Server Pane, click the Files tab, and select the database(s) you want to move from the Files Pane. Drag the selected databases to the destination server in the Server Pane. When the dialog box appears, select Move database, choose the folder on the destination server where you want the database(s) stored, and then click OK.

Signing for Security

By signing a database or template, you add a signature that can be used for workstation data security. Signing databases and templates developed by your organization adds the associated name to the Administration Execution Control List (ECL). If a database is created based on a signed template, the database inherits the signature. In the workstation ECL, a user can determine how much of the workstation can be accessed by databases that are signed by an organization or person, or more especially by unsigned databases.

It's possible to sign only a specific design document or design element in a document, but that requires its Note ID. The Note ID is on the Document IDs tab of the Document Properties box, and begins with NT.... Omit any zeroes between NT and the number when you write down the Note ID.

Before you begin, make sure the currently active ID file is the one you want to use to sign the database or template files. In the Domino Administrator, select the server storing the database(s) or template(s) you want to sign. Click the Files tab, and then select the files to be signed. Click Database and then Sign in the Tools Pane.

Select one of these options:

- **All design documents.** Signs every design element.
- **All documents of type.** Signs the selected type of design element (Policy, Form, View, Icon, Design Note, ACL, Help Index, Help, Agent, Shared Field, Repl Formula). If you choose Design Note, the signing process might take some time, especially if you choose multiple databases or templates.
- **This specific Note ID.** Signs a specific design element (see the section "Find Note to Identify Documents from Log" later in this chapter to learn how to find Note IDs).

If you select Update existing signatures only (faster), only existing signatures will be updated. This option is meant for changing the signatures on elements.

When you click OK, a dialog box displays the number of databases processes and the number of errors that occurred. The details are stored in the Notes Log.

To learn more about how the Administrative ECL interacts with signed databases, see Chapter 10.

Temporarily Disabling Replication

A problem with replication of a database might need some time to troubleshoot. You don't want it to continue to replicate in the meantime because it might pass whatever problem the database is having on to another server. In the Replication Settings (File, Replication, Settings) for a database, you disable replication by selecting Temporarily Disable Replication on the Other page. When the problem has been resolved, you deselect that option to enable replication again.

Use the Replication tool in the Files tab of the Domino Administrator when you need to disable or enable replication of more than one database. Select the server where the databases are stored from the Server Pane, click the Files tab, and then choose the databases from the Files Pane. In the Tools Pane, click Database, and then select Replication, or drag the selected databases to the Replication tool. Click Disable and then click OK.

To enable the replication again, perform the same steps, but select Enable in the Replication dialog box.

Fixing Corrupted Databases with Fixup

Occasionally, you will have corrupted databases in R5, although that doesn't happen often because of transaction logging (for information on transaction logging, see the section "Transaction Logging" in this chapter). Database corruption is more common with R4 databases. Corruption can be the result of a power failure, system failure, disk failure, or an API program improperly accessing a database.

The Notes Log displays messages when corruption is detected, such as `Document NT000082NC in database Projects.nsf is damaged` where the number beginning with NT is the document number. The document number is the last 10 digits of the document ID displayed in the Document Properties box. The message is followed by a line that describes the cause, such as "Document is damaged or obsolete (unrecognized field)." If the problem is with a view that Domino is attempting to rebuild, is in the process of rebuilding, or was unable to build, the message might be `Page format is incorrect,` "`Invalid CNO vector - position == 0`, or `Container integrity has been lost - rebuild`.

To fix corrupted databases, there are several possible solutions:

- Running the Updall server task to fix corrupted views and full-text indexes (see the section "Maintaining Database Indexes" in this chapter)
- Running the Fixup server task to fix corrupted views and documents
- Running Compact with the –C option
- Rebuilding views using Shift+F9 for one view and Ctrl+Shift+F9 for all views in the database (see the section "Maintaining Database Indexes" in this chapter)
- Creating a replica of the database.

Usually you run Updall first, if views are corrupted, and then Fixup. The Fixup server task can be run several ways:

- Using the Task, Start tool from the Server, Status tab of the Domino Administrator. Specify options to customize how Fixup runs (similar to command line options). Use this method when you want to run Fixup on unlogged databases.

- Using the Console Command Load fixup *options*. This is useful when you are working directly on the server and need to enter a command at the console. Specify a database file and/or path to fixup a particular database or run fixup on all the databases in a specified folder.

- Making a Program document to schedule Fixup to run at specified times. The Program should be named Fixup and the command line options should appear in the Command line field.

- Using the Fixup tool from the Files tab in Domino Administrator. Works best on one or a few databases.

To use the Fixup tool, select the server on which the database resides from the Server Pane of the Domino Administrator. Click the Files tab and select the databases in the Files Pane on which you want to run Fixup. In the Tools Pane, click Database and then Fixup. Select any options to specify how Fixup runs and then click OK. Table 14.4 describes the Fixup options and what they do. The Fixup Options column lists the options as they appear in the Fixup tool or the Task, Start tool; the Command Line Option is the option you add to the console command or to a program document.

Table 14.4 **Fixup Options**

Fixup Options	Command Line Option	Description
Report all processed databases to log file	-L	Logs each database Fixup opens and checks for corruption. If this option isn't used, Fixup logs only actual problems encountered.
Exclude view (faster)	-V	Fixup won't run on views, so the time needed to run Fixup is reduced. Use only if view corruption isn't an issue.
Perform quick fixup	-Q	Fixup checks documents more quickly but not as thoroughly. Deselect to have Fixup check documents thoroughly.
Scan only since last fixup	-i	When running on a specific database, Fixup only checks documents modified since Fixup last ran. When you deselect this option, Fixup checks all documents.

continues

Table 14.4 **Continued**

Fixup Options	Command Line Option	Description
Scan all documents (option in Task, Start)	–F	Checks all documents in the databases when you run Fixup on all databases. Fixup checks only documents modified since it last ran if you don't select this option.
Optimize user unread lists	–U	Reverts ID tables in a database to the previous release format. Only use if Customer Support recommends it.
Don't purge corrupted documents	–N	Fixup won't purge corrupted documents. Then the next time a user opens the database or the next time Fixup is run, Fixup must check the database again. Only use this option when you need to salvage data in documents where corruption is minor or where no replica of the database exists.
Fixup transaction-logged databases	–J	Fixup runs on R5 databases that are enabled for transaction logging. When this option isn't selected, Fixup doesn't run on logged databases. When you use an R5-certified backup utility, you need to schedule a full backup of the database as soon as possible after Fixup runs.

The Quick Fix

If the corruption is limited to one or two documents, the quick-and-dirty fix may be the best solution. It only works if you have a replica of the database on another server (you might want to temporarily disable replication, then, on the corrupted database until you fix it). Delete the corrupted documents in the database on the current server. Then, open the replica and copy the same documents to the Clipboard. Close the replica and open the corrupted database. Paste the documents into the database.

If the corruption is more widely spread, you should restore the database from your backup copy. However, you might lose any new documents or changes that occurred since the last backup.

Identifying Documents from the Log

When the Log file reports a problem with a document, it refers to the document by the Note ID. The Note ID of a document can be found on the Document IDs tab of the Document Properties box, and begins with NT...

In order to find out more about the document reported in the log, you have to find it first based on its Note ID (or the Universal Note ID, or UNID). The easiest method for doing this is to copy the Note ID of the document from the Log to the Clipboard (the alternative is writing it down). Then open the Domino Administrator, select the server on which the reported database resides. Click the Files tab, and then select the database from the Files Pane. In the Tools Pane, click Database and then Find Note.

Select either by Note ID or by Universal Note ID (UNID) and then paste or enter the appropriate ID into the ID box. Click Find. The document details and properties appear in the Fields and Properties boxes. Click Done to the close the dialog box.

Armed with information about the document and the Log report, you are able to take action to correct the problem.

Note ID

A note ID is an eight-character combination of letters and numbers that uniquely represents the location of a document within a specific database file. Documents which are replicas of one another generally have different Note IDs.

Universal Note ID

The Universal Note ID (UNID) is a 32-character combination of letters and numbers that is unique. It identifies a document across all replicas of a database. Documents that share the same UNID are replicas of each other.

Directory and Database Links

Databases on the Domino server are stored in the Domino data directory by default. To group related databases, you usually create a subdirectory under the data directory. Databases can be stored outside the Domino directory, however, in a directory folder that's linked to the Domino data directory. By specifying who can access the directory folder and at what level, you add security to the databases stored in the directory folder. Another reason to use a directory folder is take advantage of disk space on other servers.

Start by creating the directory folder where you want to store the databases. Open the Domino Administrator and select the server where you want to create the folder. Click the Files tab. In the Tools Pane, click Folder and then New. Enter the name of the new folder in the Name box and then click OK. If you want to be sure the folder was created, click Refresh.

Next, move databases to the new folder (see the section "Moving Database(s) to New Server" in this chapter for ,more details on moving databases). Then create either a directory or a database link. The links are text files that appear in the Domino data directory with folder or database icons, but they are actually pointers to the folder where the databases are stored or the location of a single database.

Directory link. A directory link resides in the data directory and points to the directory folder. When users see the data directory in the Open Database dialog box, for example, they see the name of the directory link (a text file with a `.Dir` file extension that points to the actual directory). Whether or not the users can access the directory depends on the access settings.

Database link. When you're working with a single database that's stored outside the data directory, but not necessarily in a directory folder, create a link to it from the Domino data directory. When creating the link, you must include the full path and filename of the database. Domino automatically adds `.nsf` to the end of the link name.

To create a link, open the Domino Administrator, select the server on which you are creating the link from the Server Pane, and then click the Files tab. In the Tools Pane, select Folder and then click New Link. Enter a name for the link in the Link name box. This is the name that the users will see in the data directory.

Choose the type of link you want to create. Select Folder for a directory link or Database for a database link. Enter the complete path to the directory or database (include the database filename, too, for a database link).

If you want to restrict who can access the database or directory, enter or select the specific users to whom you grant access (they should also have access rights in the database ACLs). Create an "anonymous" entry if you want Web browser users to access the database(s). Add an entry "`DominoNoDirLinks=1`" to the `notes.ini` file to prevent Web users from using directory links.

Click OK. Refresh to see that the link was created.

You might want to reconsider using a directory link on an OS/2 server because it may slow performance.

You should update the link if you make changes to the contents of the directory folder. Select the link in the Files Pane and then click Update Link in the Tools Pane. To delete a link, go to the Files tab of the Domino Administrator. Select the directory or database link and then choose Folder, Delete in the Tools Pane. Click Yes to confirm deletion.

Monitoring and Analyzing Database Activity

Users are complaining about database performance problems. What do you do? If activity is high, you might enable the performance database properties, create a replica of the database on another server (especially when the servers are clustered), or move the database to a more powerful server or a less heavily used disk.

Using Statlog to Monitor Activity

How do you know activity is high? The Statlog task is daily monitoring database activity. Run by default once a day at 5 a.m., the Statlog task reports database activity for the server's databases in Database Activity Log entries that you can open from the Database - Usage and Database - Sizes views of the Log (Log.nsf). Statlog also sends reports of database activity to the User Activity dialog box of each database. By checking this information, you will know what's happening in the database.

- In both the Database Activity Log entries and the User Activity dialog box, Statlog reports the total number of times users and servers accessed, read, and wrote to a database in the past 24 hours, past week, past month, and since the creation of the database. The activities of anonymous and authenticated Internet clients are included in this information.

- The Database Activity Log entries display inactive views (the size is 0).

- The User Activity dialog box displays the names of users and servers who read and wrote documents, all sorted by date.

To use the Log file (Log.nsf), open the Domino Administrator, select the server, click the Server tab, and then click the Analysis tab (see Figure 14.4). Select either Notes Log, Database, Sizes or Notes Log, Database, Usage, depending on the statistics you want to view. Then double-click on a Database Activity Log entry to open it.

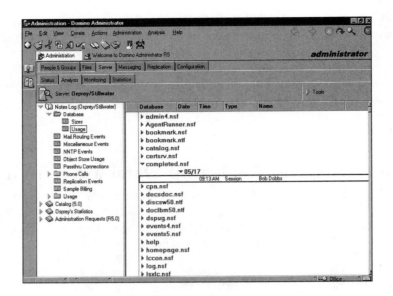

Figure 14.4 Although you can open the Log.nsf file to check log entries, the information is also available through the Domino Administrator. Double-click an entry to open it.

To use the User Activity dialog box, open the database you want to research and choose File, Database, Properties from the menu. In the Database Properties box, click the Info tab, and then click User Detail. This displays only the current information. If you want to track this data over a time period, copy it to the Clipboard and then paste it into a document you use to track usage statistics.

Unless you specify otherwise, the Statlog task reports database activity to all databases' User Activity dialog boxes. A user can disable User Activity reporting for a database, but Statlog enables recording in the dialog box again the next time it runs.

To keep Statlog from automatically recording activity in the User Activity dialog boxes, add a line in the Notes.ini file: No_Force_Activity_Logging=1. Disabling automatic recording does save disk space on the server, because recording activity adds 64K to the size of each database. However, Statlog still reports activity to the Log file.

With all automatic recording disabled, you will have to enable reporting for specific databases that you need to track. You can only do this if you have Designer or Manager access in the database ACL. Open the database for which you want to enable recording and choose File, Database, Properties from the menu. In the Database Properties box, click the Info tab, and then click User Detail. Select Record Activity (deselecting this option disables activity recording for that database). Select Activity is Confidential to only allow users with at least Designer access in the ACL to view activity. Click OK.

Database Analysis

To collect information about one or more databases, run a database analysis. The information collected includes replication history; user reads and writes; document creations, edits and deletions; design changes; replication additions, updates, and deletions; and mail messages delivered by the mail router. This information comes from various sources besides the database itself, such as the replication history, the User Activity dialog box, and the Notes Log.

The data collected by the analysis is stored in a results database that you have to create before you run the first analysis. You create the database based on the Database Analysis template (DBA4.ntf). Lotus recommends that you create the database on a local client or make sure that when several people generate results on the server that they each use different names for their results databases. Each time you do the analysis, you either overwrite the contents of the database or append new results to the contents.

Each analysis document in the database describes a specific event, collecting data in these fields:

- **Date.** The date of the event.
- **Time.** The time of the event.
- **Source of Event Information.** Either the analyzed database or its replicas or the Log file (Log.nsf).
- **Source Database.** Name of the database that contained the documents that were read or from which information was pulled about replication events.
- **Source.** Name of server that stores the source database.
- **Destination.** Name of a database on which documents were updated or to which information were replicated.
- **Destination Machine.** Name of the server where the Destination database is stored.
- **Description.** Description of the event.

The events described in the analysis documents includes the following:

- **Activity.** Number of user or server reads and writes generated by the Statlog task (see the section "Monitoring Database Activity" later in this chapter).
- **+Activity.** Number of user reads and writes as noted in the database and in the log file.
- **Mail Router.** Number of documents delivered to the database.
- **Data Note.** Document creations, edits, and deletions.
- **Design Note.** Changes to the database ACL and design.
- **Replicator.** Replication history.
- **+Replicator.** Number of replication additions, updates, and deletions, as reported in Log.nsf.

To run the database analysis, use the Analyze tool in the Domino Administrator. Select the server that stores the databases you want to analyze from the Server Pane. Click the Files tab and select the databases to analyze from the Files Pane. In the Tools Pane, click Database and then Analyze.

Select as many of the options as meet your needs:

- **Changes in: Data documents.** Shows details of document additions, edits, and deletions.
- **Changes in: Design documents.** Collects data on changes to the database ACL and any design elements.
- **User Activity: User reads.** Returns the total times users opened documents in the database and the total times servers read documents.
- **User Activity: User writes.** Returns the total times users and servers created, modified, or deleted documents and the total number of mail messages delivered to the database.
- **Replication: Find replicas on other servers.** Collects data on other replicas of the database.
- **Replication: Replication history.** Reports the successful replications of a database.
- **In logfile: Miscellaneous Events view.** Lists the events relating to the database, as recorded in the Log's Miscellaneous Events view.
- **In logfile: Database usage view.** Reports database activity recorded in the Usage-By User view of the Log file.

Enter a number (n) in the Analyze last n days of activity field for the number of days of information you want reported. Although you can enter any number up to 99, the more days you enter the longer it will take to generate the results.

Click Results. Specify the server, title, and filename of the database that will store your results. If the database already exists, click Overwrite database to write over existing documents or Append to this database to add the results of this analysis to previous ones. Then, click OK.

Click OK to run the analysis. Then open the database to see the results and choose one of the available views. Open the Database Analysis Results documents to read the analysis details.

Transaction Logging

Transaction logging is a powerful new tool that's included with R5. When it's enabled, changes to databases (such as opening a new document, adding text, saving a document) are captured and written to the transaction log. Then, if a system or disk failure occurs, the transaction log and a third-party backup utility can recover your databases.

Transaction logging defers database updates to disk during periods of high server activity, which saves processing time. Instead of recording database updates to random, nonsequential parts of a disk, transactions are logged sequentially in the log files—that also saves processing time. With the transactions already recorded, Domino can safety handle Domino can wait to do the database updates until the server activity is lower.

With transaction logging enabled, you won't have to run the Fixup task to recover databases after system failure. This means your server startups will be faster. Fixup has to check every document in every database, but transaction log recovery applies or undoes only the transactions not written to disk at the time of the failure.

Daily backups are easier, too, when transaction logging is enabled. You need to use a third-party backup utility that supports R5 and transaction logging. The backup utility performs daily incremental backups of the transaction logs instead of performing full database backups (backup utilities are available from BEI, Cheyenne/CAI, CommVault, EMC Corporation, IBM, Legato Systems, Seagate Software, and VERITAS Software).

Transaction logging only works with R5 databases. To see which databases are R5 formatted, open the Files tab of the Domino Administrator. For R4 databases, you must still use Fixup.

Setting Up Transaction Logging

The databases to be logged must reside in the Domino data directory or in one of its subdirectories.

To set up transaction logging, open the Domino Administrator. Select the Configuration tab and choose the name of server from the Use Directory on drop-down list. Click Current Server Document to open the document. Then, click the Transactional Logging tab in the Server document (see Figure 14.5). If you don't see Transactional Logging, click the right arrow on the right side of the screen to display additional tabs.

Click Edit Server and complete the information required and click OK to save the document.

- **Transactional logging.** Choose Enabled to turn on transaction logging; Disabled is the default.

- **Log path.** Path name for the location of the transaction log. Although the default is \Logdir in the Domino data directory, you shouldn't store the log file in the data directory. Instead, store it on a separate mirrored device. For example, if you have one, it's a good idea to use a Redundant Array of Independent Disks (RAID) level 0 or 1 device with a dedicated controller. If the sole purpose for this independent device is the transaction log, set Use all available space on log device to Yes.

- **Use all available space on log device.** Select Yes to use all the available space (you should have the log on a separate device if you do). In that case, you don't have to enter a value for Maximum log space. Choose No to use the default size or a specified size in Maximum log space.

- **Maximum log space.** The maximum size (in MB) the transaction file can attain. The default is 192MB, and the maximum is 4GB. Depending on how much log space you allocate, Domino formats between 3 and 64 log files.

- **Automatic fixup of corrupt databases.** Select Enabled to automatically run the Fixup task if the database is corrupt and Domino can't use the transaction log to recover it. Domino also assigns a DBIID (unique database instance ID) and notifies the Administrator to backup the database as soon as possible. Choose Disabled to not run Fixup automatically. In this case, Domino notifies the Administrator to run the Fixup task with the -J parameter on corrupt logged databases.

- **Runtime/Restart performance.** Domino evaluates each active logged database to determine how many transactions are necessary to recover each database after a system failure. When the evaluation is complete, Domino creates a recovery checkpoint record in the transaction log that lists every open database and the starting point transaction needed for recovery. Domino also forces database changes to be saved to disk if they haven't already. The creation of the recovery checkpoints affects server performance. Select Standard to have checkpoints occur regularly (this is the default, and is recommended by Lotus). Choose Favor runtime to have Domino record fewer checkpoints, thus freeing up some system resources and improving server runtime performance. Select Favor restart recover time to have Domino record more checkpoints. This option improves restart recovery time because fewer transactions are required for recovery.

- **Logging style.** Choose Circular to continuous reuse the log files and overwrite old transactions (this is the default). This option limits you to restoring only the transactions stored in the transaction log. Select Archive to not reuse the log files until they are archived. This option is recommended by Lotus. Because transactions can be archived when the log is inactive, the log file won't have any transactions necessary for restart recovery. A third-party backup utility can copy and archive the existing log. Domino increments the log filename when it starts using the existing file again. However, if all log files become inactive and aren't archived, Domino creates additional log files.

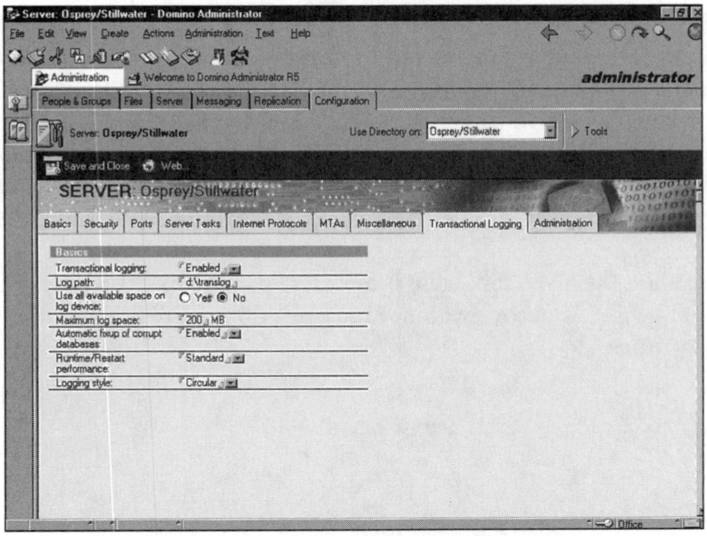

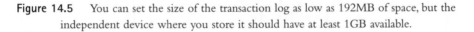

Figure 14.5 You can set the size of the transaction log as low as 192MB of space, but the independent device where you store it should have at least 1GB available.

If you need to change any of the transactional logging options, do a full backup of all the databases first. Then, open the Server document and change the fields on the Transactional Logging tab.

Disable Transaction Logging for One Database

We don't recommend that you disable transaction logging of any database because you'll have to use Fixup to recover the database in the future following any system failure. However, if you do need to disable it for a single database, do one of the following:

- For a database you're creating, choose Disable transaction logging on the Advanced Databases Options dialog box.
- For an existing database, select Disable transaction logging on the Advanced tab of the Database Properties box.
- On the Files tab of the Domino Administrator, select a database and choose Database, Advanced Properties from the Tools Pane. Choose Disable transaction logging.
- Use the Compact task with the -t parameter (using the -T parameter reenables it).

Make sure that all users have closed the database. Then use the dbcache command with the flush parameter to close the database in the database cache (see the section "Managing the Database Cache" later in this chapter). Open the database.

Deselecting the Disable transaction logging option reenables transaction logging.

Recovery from System Failure/Media Failure

When a system failure occurs, the server stops and you have to restart the server. Automatically during restart, Domino performs database recovery. For databases that were open during the system failure, the system uses the transaction logs to apply or undo database transactions not flushed to disk. The Fixup task is run on databases with pre-R5 file formats, databases that have transaction logging disabled, or corrupt databases (provided you have enabled Auto fixup of corrupt databases in the Server document).

A media failure (such as a disk failure) can cause damage to a database, or the database could be lost. To recover you need to use a third-party backup utility to restore the databases.

Transaction Log Problems

The server console displays error messages that indicate invalid log path, databases requiring media recovery or fixup, and a panic. Check the log path in the Server document to be sure that it is correct. If yes, then check to see if the server has access to that log path. If the log path is correct and the device is good, restart the server and the problem should be fixed. However, if the log path is correct and the device isn't good, you have to replace the device on the log path and then restart the server. In that case, the server creates new log files and a control file, and assigns new DBIIDs to all R5 databases. The Fixup task also runs, if "Automatic fixup of corrupt databases" is set to "Yes" in the Server document. As soon as possible after Fixup runs, perform a full database backup.

The server console displays error messages that indicate the log is damaged, databases requiring media recovery or fixup, and a panic. Restart the server and, if the problem disappears, the log wasn't damaged. It may only have been a failed read of or write to the log. Stop the server again to shut it down cleanly, perform full database backup, and restart.

If the damaged log error continues, the transaction log may be damaged or corrupt. In that case you'll have to delete the damaged transaction log file and control file. When you restart the server, new log files and a new control file are created and new DBIIDs are assigned to all the R5 databases. Fixup runs if "Automatic fixup of corrupt databases" is set to "Yes" in the Server document. As soon as possible after Fixup runs, perform a full database backup.

A media recover problem that continues to occur may involve a corrupted archive log file. Restart the server and then stop and shut it down cleanly. Before starting the server again, use a third-party backup utility to recover files. Allow the database backups to be restored if the archived log still cannot be used. Perform full database backups and then restart the server.

Maintaining Database Indexes

The database indexes are the view indexes and the full-text indexes. The view indexes are internal filing systems used to build the list of documents in a view or folder. Full-text indexes index the text within the databases documents for purposes of searching for text strings.

Full Text Indexing for Database Searches

You can't search for words or phrases throughout a database unless the database has a full text index. A full text index can be created when a database or a new replica is created, from the Search Bar in the database, or from the Full Text tab of the Database Properties box. Each of these methods works for only the current database. The Full Text Index tool gives you the ability to create or update full text indexes for more than one database at a time.

To create a full text index using the Full Text Index tool, you must have at least Designer access to the database(s) involved.

Start by selecting the server on which the database(s) reside from the Server Pane of the Domino Administration. Then, click the Files tab and select the databases you want to index from the Files Pane. Select Database and then Full Text Index from the Tools Pane. Click Create. Customize the index by choosing options, and then click OK.

The options for the full text index define how accurately and/or quickly text searches will occur. Some choices affect the size of the database because they increase the size of the index, which is stored in the database.

- **Index attached files with found text.** Choose this option to index the ASCII text of any attachments in the database. This produces faster searches but is less comprehensive than using file filters. Adding the attachments to the index does increase the size of the database file. How significant that increase is depends on the number and size of attachments in the database.

- **Index attached files with file filters.** Choose this option to index the full binary content of attachments. Although slower than "with found text," this option produces a more comprehensive (and by the way larger) index.

- **Index encrypted fields.** Depending on the amount of text in the encrypted fields, this increases the index size. More importantly, it may cause security problems. Any user can search for a word or phrase that is contained in an encrypted field and see a list of documents that contain that word or phrase even if the encrypted field can't be read. Further, a full text index is unencrypted plain text that can be read by anyone with access to the server, meaning a user may be able to read text that originally was encrypted. Because the encryption key is part of the server ID, it's active for all databases on the server. So, if you select "Index encrypted fields" for other databases, you compromise any fields using that encryption key.

- **Index sentence and paragraph breaks.** The index includes sentence and paragraph breaks in addition to word breaks, which increases the size of the index.

- **Enable case sensitive searches.** Choosing this option makes the full text index larger because it must index all cases for the same word.

- **Index update frequency.** Daily updates the index when Updall task runs on the server at 2 a.m. (by default). Scheduled updates based on the Program document for the Updall server task (you must schedule a Program document for Updall in the Domino Directory). Hourly updates every hour. Immediate updates as soon as possible after you close the database. The setting you select does affect server processing. For hourly or immediate frequency settings, monitor database and server performance. If the performance slows, reduce the frequency.

The Full Text Index tool can also update or delete the full text index for one or more database(s) that you selected from the Files Pane. Click either Update or Delete and then choose OK.

Using Update

The Update task loads when the server starts up and runs continually thereafter. Its purpose is to keep view indexes current. As views or folders change, any changes requiring updating are added to the Update work queue. After about 15 minutes, Update updates all the database indexes. Then it updates all databases that have full-text indexes that are set for immediate or hourly updates.

Whenever Update comes across a corrupted view or full-text index, it deletes the view index or full-text index and then rebuilds it.

If your server has the power to manage it, you can run multiple Update tasks. Generally, you wouldn't do this unless you had a multiprocessor machines. In that case, you might enable one Update task per processor.

To enable multiple Update tasks, create a Configuration document. Click the Configuration tab in the Domino Administrator, and select the server from the Use Directory on drop-down list. Select Server and then Configurations. If a Configuration document for the server already exists, select it and click Edit Configuration. Click Add Configuration to start a new document.

Select the NOTES.INI Settings tab and click the Set/Modify Parameters button. In the Item box, select Updaters. Enter the number of Update tasks to run in the Value box. Click OK and then click Save and Close. Restart the server to have the setting take effect.

Running Updall

Updall rebuilds all corrupted view indexes and full-text indexes that it finds. Updall doesn't run continuously, but by default, it does run daily at 2 a.m. Updall also purges deletion stubs and discards unused view indexes (if unused for 45 days). To change the time criteria for discarding unused indexes reset the `notes.ini` setting `Default_Index_Lifetime_Days`.

Although it runs daily, Updall can be run on demand when you need to clear up a corrupted index. There are three methods for running Updall:

- **Use the Task, Start tool.** In the Domino Administrator, select the server on which you want Updall to run. Click the Server tab and then the Status tab. In the Tools Pane, select Task and then Start. From the list of tasks, select Update all. Select Show advanced options to customize how Updall runs (*optional*). Click Start Task.

- **Use the console command.** Enter the `Load Updall` *path options* command directly at the server console, or, from the Domino Administrator, select the server, click the Server tab, click the Status tab, then click Console, enter the command, and press Enter. The command line options for Updall are listed in Table 14.5.

- **Use a Program document.** Click the Configuration tab in the Domino Administrator. Select the server with a replica of the Domino Directory that you want to modify from the Use Directory on drop-down list. Click Server to expand the category, select Programs, and then click Add Program. On the Basics tab, enter the Program name (Updall), the Command line (any applicable options), and the Server to run on. Click the Schedule tab and complete the scheduling information. Click Save and Close.

Table 14.5 **Updall Command-Line Options**

Option	Description
database –C	Rebuilds unused views and a full-text index in a database. You must specify the database.
database path	Updates only the specified database To specify databases in a folder, specify the database path relative to the Domino data directory.
database –T *viewtitle*	Updates a specific view in a database.
–F	Updates full-text indexes and doesn't update views.
–H	Updates any full-text indexes that have "Immediate" assigned as an update frequency.

continues

Table 14.5 **Continued**

Option	Description
–L	Updates full-text indexes assigned "Immediate," "Hourly," or "Daily" as an update frequency.
–M	Updates full-text indexes assigned "Immediate" or "Hourly" as the update frequency.
–R	Rebuilds full-text indexes and all used views. This is a resource-retentive option and should be used as a last-resort to solve corruption problems.
–V	Updates build views and doesn't update full-text indexes
–X	Rebuilds full-text indexes and doesn't rebuild views. Use to rebuild full text indexes that are computed.

Keyboard Methods

Update and Updall work for updating and rebuilding server databases, but what does a user do when a view won't open or opens with the wrong documents? There are three keyboard shortcuts a user can try to clear up a view (by the way, they also work on the server).

- F9 updates the current view and is the refresh key. Use to view document changes to the view since you opened the view.
- Shift+F9 rebuilds the current view to fix any view problems.
- Ctrl+Shift+F9 rebuilds all the views in a database that are not built and updates all the other views. Use this option if you can't run Updall.

Administering the Database Catalog

A database catalog is a database that is a centralized list of all the organization's databases, except the mail databases. The views in the catalog list all the databases by category, manager, replica ID, server, and title. Each database has a document that contains the server name, filename, replica ID, and the names of any servers, groups, or users with Manager access to the database. There is also information from the About This Database document of the database. Each document also has a set of buttons that let users look through the database or open it and add it to their bookmarks.

The Catalog task runs daily at 1 a.m. by default on every server to create or update a database catalog. Therefore, if any database moves to another server, the database entry in the catalog is updated with the new location within 24 hours.

By entering the command Load Catalog at the server console, you can populate the catalog. View the documents in the catalog by opening the catalog database from your bookmarks, the Domino Administrator, or the Web Administrator tool.

Creating a Database Catalog

When you create the database catalog, you automatically are assigned Manager access to the database. After creating it, you need to assign the appropriate access levels to administrators, users and groups. Assign categories to the databases to control how they appear in the database catalog. Replicate the catalog to as many servers as necessary. You should also monitor the size of the catalog.

To create the database catalog, choose File, Database, New from the menu. Select the name of the Server where you want to store the database catalog, give it a Title, and enter a File Name. Select Show Advanced Templates. Click the Template Server button if "Local" appears next to it, and choose the server that stores the database templates. Choose the Database Catalog template (CATALOG.NTF) from the list of templates and click OK.

Setting Up the ACL

Right-click the bookmark for the database catalog and choose Database, Access Control. In the ACL for the database catalog, assign Manager access to yourself (should already be done) and any people who need to control the ACL, such as the database manager. Also assign Manager access to any servers that will store the database catalog or its replicas. Set the Default level as Reader.

Assign Categories

One or more categories can be assigned to each database in the database catalog. The categories determine how the Databases by Category view is grouped (see Figure 14.6). Unless you specify categories the Databases by Category view is blank.

Anyone assigning categories must have at least Designer access to the database. Categories are assigned on a database-by-database basis. Open the Database Properties box for a database by right-clicking the bookmark and selecting Database, Properties. On the Design tab of the Database Properties box, select List in Database Category. In the Categories box, list all the categories for that database, separating them with commas.

Do the same for each database in the catalog. Try to keep track of the category names, so you use the same ones for similar databases. That way, the Databases by Category view will properly group similar databases.

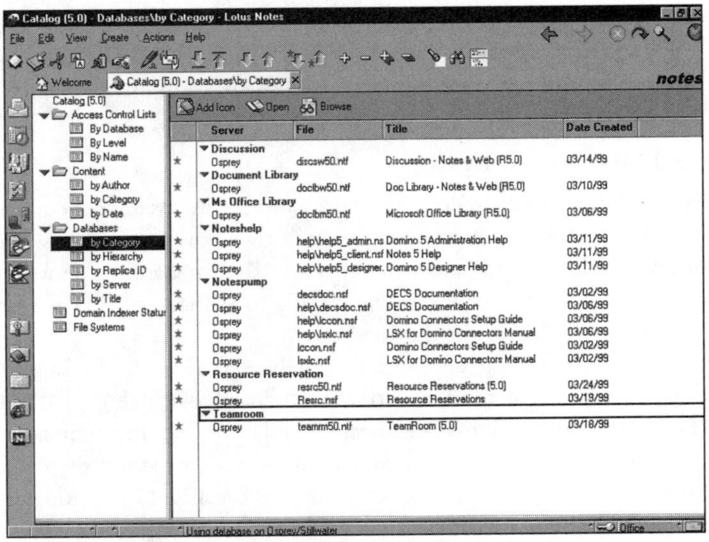

Figure 14.6 The categories shown here are the default categories for the databases.

Reducing the Size of the Database Catalog

The database catalog can grow to quite a large size, if left uncontrolled. That's especially true if it replicates to other servers. It may even become necessary to create a separate database catalog for each server, if the catalog causes a disk space problem for the server.

One way to reduce the size of the catalog is to exclude any databases that don't really need to be included.

Another reducer is the -P parameter of the Catalog command. This option excludes the listing of Policy documents in the catalog. Because the catalog program runs daily, you can change the Notes.ini file setting to read `ServerTasksAt1=Catalog -P`. Unfortunately, this doesn't affect any pre-existing Policy documents. You have to delete the current catalog and recreate it by using the console command `Load Catalog -P`.

Excluding Databases from the Database Catalog

Although databases are listed in the catalog automatically, you can exclude a database by deselecting the List in Database Catalog property on the Design tab of the Database Properties box.

You must have at least Designer access to set that property.

Domain Search

Traditionally, users have been able to search databases that have full-text indexes to find documents containing data they need. The Domain Search extends that ability across many databases, encompassing an entire domain.

Setting up domain searching involves several pieces: It starts with the Domain Catalog Server, which handles the centralized administration of domain searching. The Domain Catalog controls which databases and file systems to index, and results are filtered to users based on their access to the databases and file systems. The Domain Indexer builds a central index against which all queries are run.

The Domain Catalog Server

Handling the load of creating indexes and user queries uses quite a few resources. The Domain Catalog Server must be capable of carrying the burden. It should be fast and powerful, and have plenty of available disk space.

For a Domain Catalog Server running Microsoft Windows NT, for example, Lotus recommends at minimum an Intel Pentium II 266MHz processor, 256MB RAM, and available disk space equal to approximately 75 percent of the size of the domain being indexed. Multiple processors, lots of RAM, and multiple high-volume drives will increase efficiency and capability of the searches.

If you have six or more Domino servers in your domain, you might want to consider having a server dedicated to domain indexing and searching. Or consider clustering Domain Catalog servers for greater reliability, fault-tolerance, and balancing of the load from user queries.

To set up the Domain Catalog Server:

1. Select the server in the Domain Administrator Server Pane that you want to use as the Domain Catalog Server.

2. Click the Configuration tab.

3. In the View Pane, expand the Server section and select All Server Documents.

4. Select the Server document for the Domain Catalog Server. Choose Edit Server.

5. Click the Server Tasks tab and then select the Domain Indexer tab.

6. Choose Enabled in the Domain wide indexer field.

7. Enter or choose schedule options to set up a schedule for indexing. If you set up the schedule to frequently index, you'll have more up-to-date indexes but the indexing will consume greater resources. Experiment with different frequencies after you have the indexing running for a while. You might want to start with the default 60 minute setting.

8. In the Limit domain wide searching to the following servers field, select the servers you want to include in the index. If the field is blank, all servers are indexed. Use wildcards if needed, such as */Servers/Stillwater, to specify several servers.

9. Click Save and Close.

10. Enter `Load Catalog` at the server console and press Enter to start the Domain catalog process and have the Domain Indexer run according to its next scheduled time.

The Domain Catalog

Based on the Catalog.ntf database template (as is the database catalog), the Domain Catalog stores records that show which databases and file systems the server should index and which forms to use to search the index. It resides on the Domain Catalog Server.

The Domain Catalog is created when the `Load Catalog` console command is entered on the server, provided that you already set up the Domain Indexer.

Setting Up the File System Indexing

To specify which file systems to include in the Domain Search, create a file system document for each server in the domain. Any file system can be indexed provided that the file system services of the operating system on which the Domino server runs can access the file system. The Domain Catalog Server must be set up as a Domino Web server, so the server can return links to documents in the file systems as query responses from both Notes and Web clients.

If you plan to include a directory that isn't part of the Domino data directory, create a directory link or a mapping/redirection document (in Web Server Configurations).

Thread Tuning

Each indexing thread indexes one repository at a time. By increasing the number of threads, the Domain Catalog Server would be able to simultaneously index more repositories. However, that requires more CPU utilization and response to queries may slow.

With fewer threads, the search speeds up. There are more resources available. The downside is that changes may not be as quickly reflected in the index.

The default number of indexing threads is two per CPU.

To upgrade the number of threads, changes the notes.ini setting FT_DOMAIN_IDXTHDS= to a higher number, but don't exceed eight threads per server or you'll degrade server performance even on two CPU servers.

To set up the file system list, do the following:

1. From the Domino Administrator or Notes client, choose File, Database, Open from the menu.
2. Select the name of the Domain Catalog Server in the Server box and click Open.
3. Choose File, Create System.
4. Select a server name and click Set/Modify File System List.
5. In File system, enter the physical location of a file system (include the entire path, except where the path is relative to the Domino data directory, or URL path).
6. Click Next to add it to the list of file systems.
7. Repeat steps 3 through 5 to add other file systems.
8. Click OK when the list is complete, and then click Save and Close.
9. Restart the server.

Include a Database in the Domain Index

Using the Multi-Database Index tool is an important part of building the Domain Search Index.

You must have Manager access in the database ACL for each database you want to enable for multi-database indexing. To enable multi-database indexing for an individual database, you select Include in multi database indexing on the Design tab of the Database Properties box.

To enable multi-database indexing for several databases, go to the Domino Administrator. Select the server on which the databases reside from the Server Pane. Click the Files tab and select the databases to be indexed from the Files Pane. Select Database and then Multi-Database Index from the Tools Pane. Choose Enable and click OK.

The Domain Indexer runs on the schedule you set in the Server document. It looks in the Domain Catalog for new databases that have Include in multi-database indexing enabled. It looks for documents and files in existing databases and file systems that are new or modified since the last time the indexer ran and adds them to the Domain Index.

Database Libraries

Database libraries help groups of users find databases that are useful to or relate to their work without having to scan the Open Database dialog box for them. Databases of interest are published to a library, and the main view of a library includes an alphabetical list of these databases along with a brief abstract. Each database document in the library includes the title, abstract, and replica ID of the database, plus the name of the database manager. There are also buttons that let users browse the database, open it, or add it to their bookmarks.

Libraries are located on the server (although you can create a local library for your own use), and a server may have more than one library. When the user accesses one of the databases in a library, Domino locates it by its replica ID and opens it for the user. Domino looks for it first on the user's workstation, then his home server, and finally in the database catalog on the home server to find a path to a replica.

By creating a library, you become the librarian and have Manager access in the ACL. The default access is Author. Users with Author access can publish databases in the library. If a user with Reader access attempts to publish a database, Domino sends email to the librarian with the user's request. The librarian then publishes the database.

Create the Library

You must have Create New Databases access to the server before you can create a library there.

1. In the Notes client, choose File, Database, New from the menu.
2. In the Server box, select the name of the server on which you want to create your library.
3. Enter a title and filename for the library.
4. Click Show Advanced Templates.
5. From the list of templates, select the Database Library template (DBLIB4.NTF). If you don't see the template, click the Template Server button and choose the server that has the advanced templates.
6. Click OK.

Assign Librarians

You need at least Editor access in the library ACL to assign librarians. The librarians you are assigning must have at least Author access.

1. Select the database library from your bookmarks.
2. Choose View, Go To, Librarians.
3. Open the Librarians document in edit mode.

4. Enter the names of the users who will be librarians. A semicolon is automatically added between names when you save the document.

5. Close and save the document.

Publishing a Database

When you add a database to a library, you publish it. You must have at least Author access to the library in order to publish databases.

1. Select the database icon of the database in your bookmarks.

2. Select File, Database, Publish.

3. From the Available libraries list, select the library title you want to use. Click OK.

4. In the Abstract field, type a short description of the database. This serves as the title that appears in the view.

5. In the Long Description field, type a more complete description of the database contents.

6. Close and save the document.

Managing the Database Cache

Each server maintains a database cache. A closed database is put in the cache when no users or processes are using the database. That makes closing it quicker. It remains in the cache until it's opened or for 15 to 20 minutes, whichever comes first.

The number of databases that can be stored simultaneously in the cache is the greater of 25 or the value of the NSF_Buffer_Pool_Size setting in the Notes.ini file divided by 300K. To change the number of database the cache holds, increase the value of the NSF_DbCache_Maxentries= setting in the Notes.ini. The other alternative is to add to the physical memory.

If you want to see the databases in the cache, enter the dbcache show server console command. Close the databases in the cache with the dbcache flush console command.

To disable the cache, enter the Notes.ini setting NSF_DbCache_Disable=1.

How do you know when to change these settings or enter these console commands? You need to monitor the database cache by looking at the cache statistics. You can enter the console command show stat database.dbcache.* or view the Database Statistics (see Figure 14.7).

- **CurrentEntries.** The number of databases currently in the cache. If this number frequently approaches the MaxEntries value, consider increasing the number of databases the cache can hold.

- **HighWaterMark.** The maximum number of databases in the cache during this running of the server program. This isn't a genuine indicator of cache performance because it may be artificially high due to startup activity.

- **Hits.** The number of times an InitialDbOpen finds the database in the cache. The cache is working effectively if the ratio of hits to opens is high. If it isn't, you may need to increase the number of databases the cache can hold.

- **InitialDbOpens.** The number of times a user or server opened a database that wasn't already being used by another user or server.

- **Lookups.** The number of lookups to the database cache. A high ratio of hits to lookups means the database cache is effective. A low ratio indicates that the number of databases the cache can hold should be increased.

- **MaxEntries.** The number of databases the server can hold in the cache at once.

- **OvercrowdingRejections.** The number of times a database couldn't be placed in the cache because the CurrentEntries equaled or exceeded the MaxEntries times 1.5. Normally, this number is low. If it increases, increase the number of databases the cache can hold.

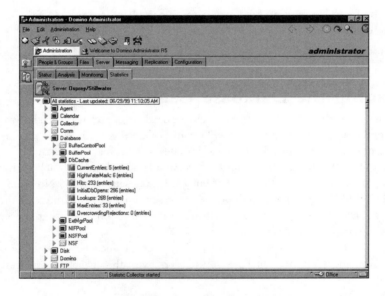

Figure 14.7   To see the Database Cache Statistics, select the server, click the Server tab, click the Statistics tab, and then expand the Database category. Expand DbCache to see the statistics for the cache.

Although many troubleshooting issues can be handled by the tools covered in this chapter, there are always new ones cropping up. Check the current ones at http://www.support.lotus.com. Other sites that may be useful include http://www.notes.net, http://www.lotus411.com (this is currently a programming tip site, but they will be adding a newsletter of system administration tips), or http://www.iris.com.

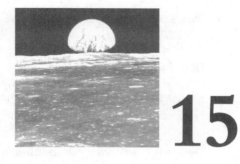

15

Web Server Setup, Maintenance, Tuning, and Troubleshooting

As you know, the Domino server is unparalleled as a messaging server, and it also excels as an application server platform. What you may not know is that it also makes a robust, flexible, secure, scaleable and extensible Web server. Although the HTTP server for Domino was only introduced in Notes 4.5, it has been continually improved and is now one of the most powerful and flexible HTTP server platforms on the market. In this chapter, we'll examine exactly what it takes to install, configure, optimize, administrate and troubleshoot the Domino http server.

What's New in the Domino R5 HTTP Server?

- **Improved HTTP stack.** The HTTP service sports many enhancements including improved performance, file system security, and better servlet support.

- **Access control for Domino file system.** You can now configure access control lists (ACLs) for files (HTML, WAVs, GIFs, and so on) served up by Domino from the file system.

- **Automatic HTTP server optimization.** Domino can now configure various server settings automatically based on the types of Web applications you are running.

- **Byte range serving.** R5 allows Web clients to download a file in sections rather than in one huge hunk, making downloads faster and more fault-tolerant. In layman's terms, this means that if a connection to the server is lost, the user can resume downloading the file where it stopped, rather than downloading the entire file again.

- **Determine browser capabilities.** You can use the formula language function @BrowserInfo to easily determine what Web browser is in use on the server-side, making it easier to tailor Web applications to specific browsers. Before R5, you had to do this using either CGI variables or client side scripting.

- **Simple URLs.** Domino R5 allows a page to be named uniquely, eliminating the need to know the unique ID. This results in simple URLs. For example, `www.definiti.com/hatter.nsf/VoteGOP?OpenPage` where `VoteGOP` is the name of the page. If the name is unambiguous, you can simplify the URL further, to `www.acme.com/News.nsf/VoteGOP`.

- **CORBA/IIOP support.** R5 supports Common Object Request Broker Architecture & Internet InterORB Protocol (CORBA/IIOP).

- **Domino for Microsoft IIS.** Microsoft Internet Information Server (IIS) can now be used as the HTTP server when serving up Domino content. This enables IIS customers to leverage their existing investment and skill sets while also capitalizing on Domino's impressive features.

- **Internet Cluster Manager.** Clustering, load balancing, and fail over capabilities now apply to Web browsers accessing a Domino Web server.

- **HTTP session authentication.** R5 provides for authentication using HTTP sessions and encrypted cookies. This makes it easy to "log in" and "log out" of a Domino served site.

- **Virtual servers SSL and key ring support.** A unique key ring can be specified for each virtual server, enabling each virtual server to use SSL. Additionally, port security settings can be specified for each virtual server.

- **Upgraded servlet support.** The Domino Web server now supports the JSDK 2.0.

- **Better log file control.** In R5, the length of time for which a log file is used: daily, weekly, or monthly, can be set.

- **Last-modified HTTP header.** Domino R5 now sends a last-modified header with most Domino responses.

- **Domino Web server API (DSAPI).** Domino now supports a server API that allows you to create your own Web server extensions (For all you hard-core programming geeks).

- **Enterprise Integration.** Domino Enterprise Connection Services (DECS) is a visual tool and high performance server environment that allows you to create Web applications with live, native access to enterprise data and applications.

Domino HTTP Stack Overview

The previous section gave a brief glimpse of the many new features that help make an already outstanding product even better. This section explains how the Domino HTTP server can help you and provide a brief overview of how it works.

Why Use Domino as an HTTP Server?

Domino has a long-standing, industry-wide reputation as a robust, secure and scalable messaging, and groupware platform. With its many enhanced features in R5, Domino is now building a similar reputation as a very powerful and secure Web application server.

One of the main reasons that Domino makes such an excellent platform for Web applications is that it can work as a conventional HTTP server, serving up static HTML files from the Domino server's file system, or, more importantly, it can dynamically convert the contents of Notes databases into Web pages!

This capability to dynamically translate the contents of a Notes database into HTML means that hybrid Intra/Extra/Internet applications can quickly and easily be built to run in either a Notes client or Web browser. Web applications also can take advantage of the many potent features of the Notes/Domino environment, such as

- Extensive and granular security, including: X.509 certificates, SSL, Basic Authentication, Database ACLs, Maximum Internet Access, Anonymous Access and many other features. For more information on Notes/Domino security, see Chapter 10, "Security," or the Domino Administration Help File (`help5_admin.nsf`).

- Vast support for industry standard protocols, including TCP/IP, SMTP, NNTP, CORBA/IIOP, LDAP, X.509, SSL and S/MIME. For more information on protocols supported by Domino, see the Domino Administration Help File (`help5_admin.nsf`).

- Rapid Application Development, including: LotusScripted agents to dynamically generate pages and perform CGI style tasks through WebQueryOpen and WebQuerySave events, integrated support for JavaScript, Formula language support, Java agents, Java applets and servlets, standard CGI support through the CGI-BIN directory, and a host of RAD tools such as the form, page and outline designer. For more information on these topics, see the Domino Designer Help File (`help5_designer.nsf`).

- Domino is a cross-platform development environment that enables companies to leverage existing skills and investments.

- Pass-thru HTML, giving you the capability to embed HTML in native Domino design elements, further enhancing your application's features and functionality.

- Excellent database integration, including Native Notes object store (.nsf files), ODBC connectivity, NotesPump, DECS, and other tools to link to legacy systems. (`help5_designer.nsf`).

- Integrated support for workflow applications. Notes/Domino has always supported mail-enabled forms and document routing and this is no different for Web enabled applications. For more information on these topics, see the Domino Designer Help File (`help5_designer.nsf`).

- Server clustering, server partitioning, virtual servers, and other advanced features that help to ensure that your mission critical applications are online when your customers need them. For more information on Advanced Domino features, the Domino Administration Help File (`help5_admin.nsf`).

- Extensive full-text search capability. Domino supports single database, multidatabase and domain full text search capability.

How Domino Works

When a Web browser requests a page from a Domino server, Domino will determine if the request is for a file in the file system or a request for content in a Domino database. If the request is for a static HTML page in the file system, Domino will serve up the file to the user if they are authorized to access the file. If the file has been secured, the user will be required to authenticate with the Domino server (this is a handy new feature of R5) before the file will be served up.

The following is a sample URL that illustrates a request for a static HTML file in the Domino file system:

```
http://www.definiti.com/html/index.html
```

If the browser makes a request for content in a Domino database and the user has access to the requested information (authentication may be required), Domino will translate the native Domino element into a Web page, or Java applet (depending on how the developer has built the application) and serve it up to the browser. Any of the Domino elements in the following list can be served up to a browser—either individually, or in conjunction with other Domino elements—to create powerful, robust, interactive Web applications:

About

Agents (the output from a LotusScript, Formula, or Java agent)

Applets

Pages

Documents

Folders

Forms

Framesets

Navigators

Outlines

Using

Views

The following is a sample URL that illustrates a request for content in a Domino database:

```
http://www.definiti.com//external/test.nsf/All+Docs?OpenView&StartKey=Hatter
```

Figure 15.1 illustrates the process of getting a page (used here loosely to indicate any element served up by a Domino server) from a Domino server.

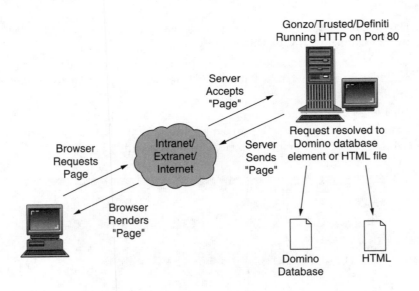

Figure 15.1   Domino Server functionality.

What this means is that virtually any Domino application can easily become a Web application! However, you need to keep in mind that not all the Notes client functionality will translate seamlessly (if at all) into browser functionality, so you need to become acquainted with the Domino features that will convert to HTML. For more information on building Domino applications, see the *Lotus Notes and Domino Essential Reference Guide,* from New Riders Publishing or the Notes Designer Help database (help5_designer.nsf).

HTTP Setup

Since the early days of Notes, Lotus has made big strides in the installation and configuration of a Notes/Domino server, and it's safe to say that configuring a Domino server has *never* been easier than it is now. The good news for you is that the same holds true for Domino's HTTP server.

The following sections explain how to configure the HTTP server on a Domino server that is already in production and how to install the HTTP when installing a new Domino server.

Installing HTTP on an Existing Domino Server

To install and configure the HTTP server on an existing Domino server, there are a few things you'll need to do:

1. Have a good grasp of the TCP/IP protocol and have TCP/IP configured and working properly on your Domino server.

2. Open the Domino Administrator, select the Configuration tab, choose Server, and then open the Server document for Domino server on which you intend to install HTTP.

3. Click the Ports\Internet Ports tab. If you do not force all connections to this server to use SSL, make sure Enabled is selected in the TCP/IP port status or SSL port status field on the Web tab. This is illustrated in Figure 15.2.

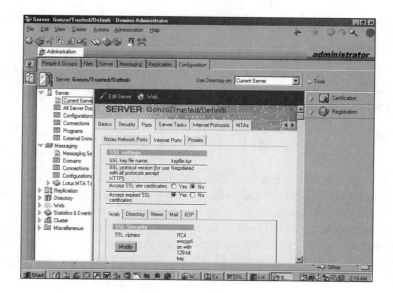

Figure 15.2   The Ports section of the server document.

4. Save the updated server document.

5. Start the Domino server and start the HTTP task. You can start the server task in two ways. First, select the Server\Status tab. Then, choose the Task, Start and choose HTTP Web server from the Start New Task dialog box. Then, click the Start Task button. This is shown in Figure 15.3.

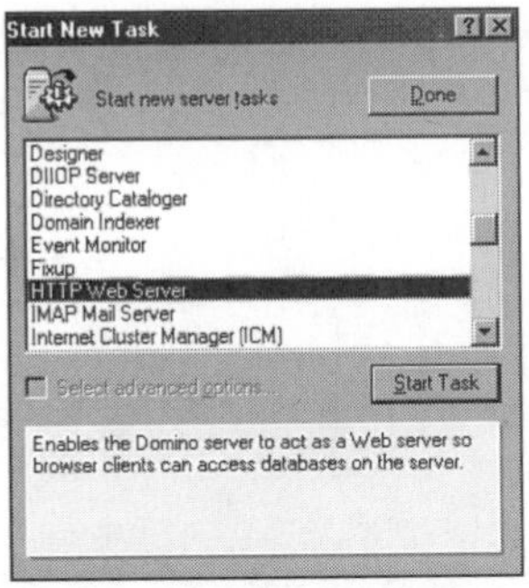

Figure 15.3   The Start New Task dialog box.

Alternatively, you can switch to the remote console mode (or at the server console on the server) and type load http. This is shown in Figure 15.4.

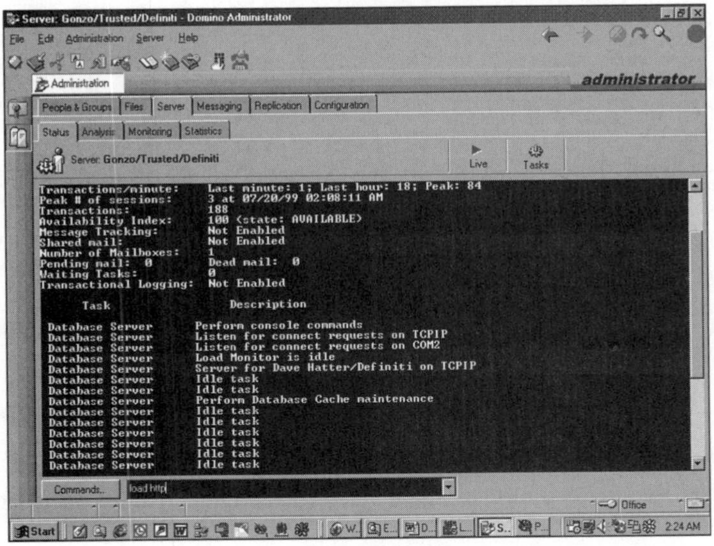

Figure 15.4   The R5 remote server console.

6. Be sure that the HTTP server is operating correctly and listening for requests. You can do this by starting your browser and entering either the IP Address or DNS name for your new Domino Web server. If everything is functioning correctly, the Domino server should respond. After you have followed the steps listed previously, the HTTP server should work correctly. The remainder of this section covers what configuration options are available to you for the HTTP server through the Port\Internet Ports\Web tab and the Internet Protocols\HTTP and Internet Protocols\Domino Web Engine tabs of a Domino server document.

Port Settings

The port settings tab enables you to control which ports are active and how they are configured. Port settings are important because they are directly related to connectivity. You should become familiar with this tab, shown in Figure 15.5.

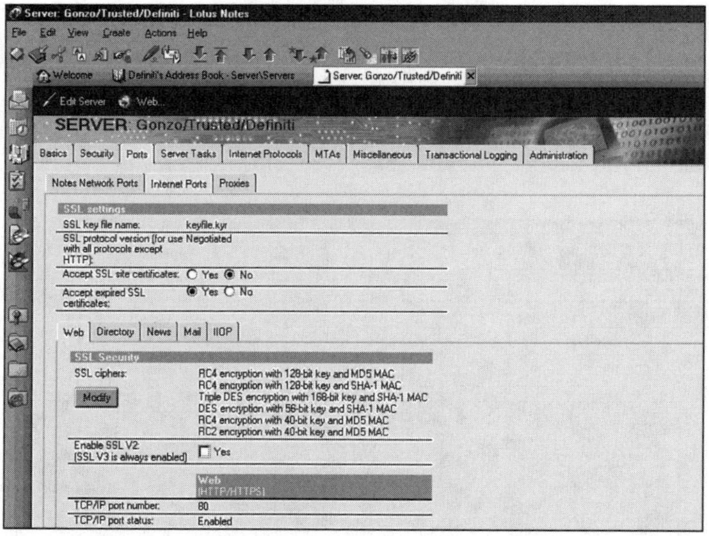

Figure 15.5   The Internet Ports tab.

SSL Section

The SSL section allows you to configure several important Secure Sockets Layer (SSL) settings:

- **SSL key filename.** The name of the keyring file containing your certificates for the Domino server. The default is keyfile.kyr. Be sure to enter only the filename and not the path. Additionally, the file you specify must have the .kyr extension.

- **SSL protocol version....** Choose the version of SSL you want to implement. Negotiated is the default. For more information on SSL, see Chapter 10.

- **Accept SSL site certificates.** If you want to allow access to users who do not share a common SSL certificate, but use SSL, select Yes. Otherwise, select No to disallow connections using site certificates. The default is No.

- **Accept expired SSL certificates.** If you want SSL certificate expiration dates enforced, choose No (the default) otherwise, choose Yes to allow users with expired certificates access. The default is Yes.

SSL Security Section

The SSL Security section allows you to configure certain SSL security options.

- **SSL ciphers.** This field allows you to select which types of encryption you want to support for your site. Click the Modify button to edit the list.

- **Enable SSL V2....** By default, SSL V3 is enabled. If you would like to enable SSL V2, check this box.

Web (HTTP/HTPS) Section

The Web section allows you to specify the port settings for the HTTP server task.

- **TCP/IP port number.** Enter the port number that the HTTP server should listen for HTTP requests on. The default value is 80, but any valid port number above 1,024 can be used.

- **TCP/IP port status.** If you want the server to listen to the port specified in the TCP/IP port number field, choose Yes. Otherwise, choose No to disable the port specified in TCP/IP port number.

- **Authentication Options\Name & Password.** If you want to allow authentication using a Notes User name and Internet password combination (basic authentication), choose Yes. Choose No to disable basic authentication.

- **Authentication Options\Anonymous.** Choose Yes to allow anonymous access for HTTP requests. Choose No to disallow anonymous Web access.

- **SSL port number.** Enter the port number that the HTTP server should listen on for HTTP connections using SSL on. The default value is 443.

Port 80

Remember that if you use a port other than 80 (the default), users will be required to include the port number in the URL when requesting resources from the server. For example:

```
http://www.definiti.com:8080/welcome.nsf
```

- **SSL port status.** If you want the server to listen to the port specified in the SSL port number field, choose Yes. Otherwise, choose No to disable the SSL port specified in SSL port number.

- **Authentication Options\Client certificate.** If you want to use X.509 certificates for authentication, choose Yes. To disallow X.509 certificates for authentication, choose No.

- **Authentication Options\Name & password.** If you want to allow authentication using a User name and Internet password combination over SSL, choose Yes. Choose No to disable Name & password authentication over SSL.

- **Authentication Options\Anonymous.** Choose Yes to allow anonymous access over SSL. Choose No to disallow anonymous access over SSL.

HTTP Settings

The HTTP tab allows you to configure a large number of options regarding how requests are served up by Domino. This section will examine each section of the HTTP tab. Figure 15.6 shows the contents of the HTTP tab.

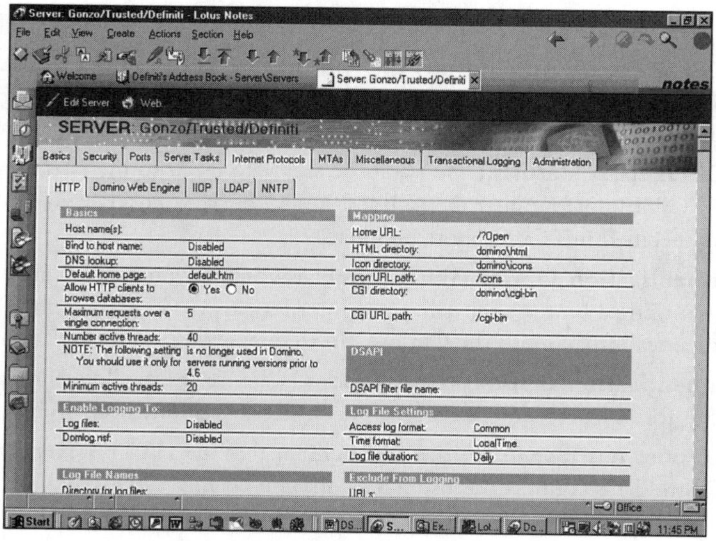

Figure 15.6 The HTTP tab.

Basics Section

The following fields are found in the basics section:

- **Host name.** Use this field to specify up to 32 host names for the current Domino server. If left blank, the default, Domino will determine the hostname based on the server's TCP/IP stack.

- **Bind to host name.** If you want to enter aliases in the Host name(s) field, enable this setting. The default is Disabled.

- **DNS lookup.** When enabled, this setting causes Domino to search DNS to attempt to determine a requesting client's hostname.

- **Default home page.** Enter the filename of an HTML to file to use as the server's home page. For this to work properly, the Home URL field must be empty and the specified file must be in the Domino HTML directory.

- Allow HTTP clients to browse databases. enabling this setting allows the server to return a list of databases on the server (similar to the File Open dialog box in a Notes client). When a user opens the site, the server implicitly or explicitly issues a URL using the ?OpenServer command this setting will be checked. The default is No.

- **Maximum requests over a single connection.** This field defines how many requests a single browser can make. The default is 5. For more information on this setting, see the "Tuning" section later in this chapter.

- **Number of active threads.** This field specifies the number of threads a Domino server can have open at one time. If the server hits this limit, new requests are queued until threads are freed up. There will be more information on this later in this chapter.

- **Minimum active threads.** This setting is no longer used and remains only for backward compatibility.

DNS Lookups

Enabling DNS lookups means that client hostnames will be logged rather than IP addresses. However, this will negatively affect server performance. If you don't need hostnames logged, or, (especially) if you are not logging, disable this setting.

Disable Database Browsing

For the sake of security, this setting should always remain turned off for all servers with Internet access to prevent hackers from snooping around.

Mapping

The following fields are found in the mappings section.

- **Home URL.** Use this field to specify a Domino design element to open when a user enters a URL with an explicit action. If this field is blank and the Default home page fields are blank, the server will do a ?OpenServer, which if database browsing is disabled, will generate an error. If a default home page is specified (using an HTML file for the home page), leave this field blank.

- **HTML directory.** Specify where the Domino server should look to find HTML files in the file system. The default is Domino\HTML and is relative to the data directory unless otherwise specified.

- **Icon directory.** Specify where the Domino server should look to find images in the file system. The default is Domino\icons and is relative to the data directory unless otherwise specified.

- **Icon URL path.** Specify the URL path for images.

- **CGI directory.** Specify where the Domino server should look to find CGI programs. The default is Domino\cgi-bin and is relative to the data directory unless otherwise specified.

- **CGI URL path.** Specify the URL path to CGI programs.

DSAPI

The following field can be found in the DSAPi section.

DSAPI filter filename. If you are using DSAPI filters, use this field to specify the filename for the filter.

Enable Logging To

The following fields are found in the Enable Logging To section. They control the format of Domino logging.

- **Log files.** If you want Domino to log Web requests to text files in the file system, set this field to enabled.

- **Domlog.nsf.** If you want Domino to log Web requests to a Domino database, set this field to enabled.

Log File Settings

The following fields are found in the Log File Settings section and are used to control how and when log entries are added.

- **Access log file.** This field allows you to specify the format to use for logging site accesses. You can use the common format, or the extended common format.

- **Time format.** Specify the time format for Web server logging. You can use either the local time format (the default) or Greenwich Mean Time format.

- **Log file duration.** This field allows you to specify for how long you want to keep information in your logs before they are overwritten. You have four choices: Daily, Weekly, Monthly, or Never.

Log Filenames

The following fields are found in the Log File Names section. They define the files in which Domino should log.

- **Directory for log files.** If logging is enabled, specify to which directory you'd like the log files written.

- **Access log.** Enter the name you'd like to use for the text file used to store Web access information. The default is access-log.

- **Agent log.** Enter the name you want to use for the text file used to store agent run information. The default is agent-log.

- **Referrer log.** Enter the name you want to use for the text file used to store URL referrer information. The default is referrer-log.

- **Error log.** Enter the name you want to use for the text file used to store internal Web server error information. The default is error-log.

- **CGI error log.** Enter the name you'd like to use for the text file used to error information generated by CGI programs. The default is cgi-error-log.

Exclude From Logging

The following list of fields is found in the Exclude From Logging section. They control what information is not included in the Domino logs.

- **URLs.** Use this field to specify any URLs that should be excluded from logging when requested. For example, entering `http://www.definti.com?openServer` would tell the server not to log requests for that URL.

- **Methods.** Use this field to specify any HTTP methods that should be excluded from logging. For example, POST.

- **MIME types.** Use this field to specify any MIME types that should be excluded from logging when requested. For example, images/jpg.

- **User agents.** Use this field to specify any agents that should be excluded from logging when requested. For example, entering `HelloWorld` would tell the server not to log requests for that agent.

- **Return Codes.** Use this field to specify any server return codes that should be excluded from logging. For example, everyone's favorite, 404.

- **Hosts and Domains.** Use this field to specify any hosts or domains that should be excluded from logging when requested. For example, entering `definti.com` would tell the server not to log any requests for that domain.

Timeouts

The following list of fields is found in the Timeouts section. They control how much time can elapse for certain functions before the server drops the connection.

- **Input timeout.** Use this field to specify the amount of time that can elapse between a client's connection to the server and a request for information. The default is 2 minutes. If this time is exceeded, the connection is dropped.

- **Output timeout.** Use this field to specify the amount of time that can elapse between a client's request for resources and the server's response. The default is 20 minutes. If this time is exceeded, the connection is dropped.

- **CGI timeout.** Use this field to specify the amount of time that can elapse from the time a CGI program is started and its completion. The default is 5 minutes. If this time is exceeded, the server warns the program. If after another 5 minutes it still has not competed, it's terminated.

- **Idle thread timeout.** This field specifies the number of minutes the server will keep an idle thread open. If a time is specified here, when the number of idle and active threads exceeds the value specified for Minimum Idle threads, the idle threads are cancelled. The default is 0, meaning that idle threads will not be terminated.

Web Agents

The fields are found in the Web Agents section. They control certain aspects of how agents run when called to be a Web client.

- **Run Web agents concurrently.** This field allows you to specify if agents launched by a Web browser can run simultaneously. The default is enabled. Unless your machine is underpowered, leave this enabled.

- **Web agent timeout.** Use this field to specify a number (in seconds) that an agent can run before the server terminates it. The default is 300.

Keep Performance in Mind

These settings can have an impact on performance and are covered in the "Tuning" section later in this chapter.

Web Agent Tuning

These settings are covered in more detail in the "Tuning" section later in this chapter.

Domino Web Engine Settings

The Domino Web Engine settings control various aspects about how the Domino HTTP server will run. These settings are discussed in the sections that follow. (See Figure 15.7.)

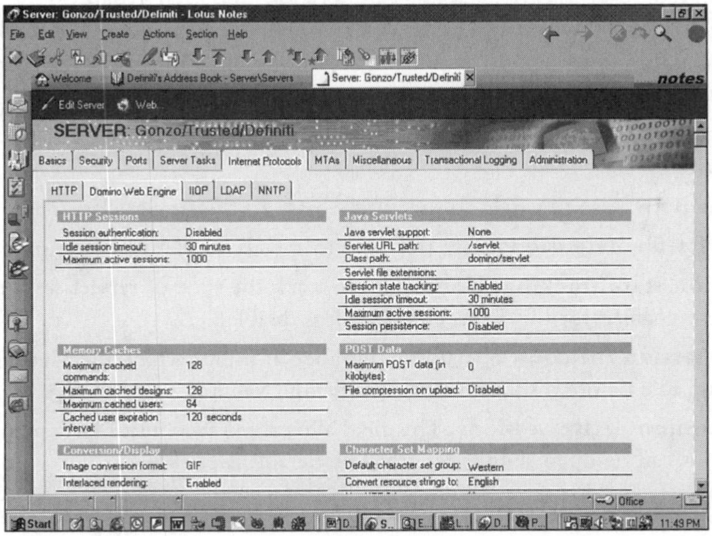

Figure 15.7   The Domino Web Engine tab.

HTTP Sessions

The following fields are found in the HTTP Sessions section:

- **Session authentication.** Use this field to specify if Domino should authenticate Web sessions. The default is disabled.

- **Idle session timeout.** This field is used to specify a time (in minutes) that a session can remain open but inactive before it is terminated. The default is 30 minutes.

- **Maximum active sessions.** This field specifies the maximum number of sessions that can be opened with the HTTP server at any one time. The default is 1,000. If your server has ample resources, increasing this number can improve the number of users that can be serviced.

Java Servlets

The following fields are found in the Java Servlets section. They control how Java Servlets interact with the Domino HTTP engine.

- **Java servlet support.** This field is used to specify if, and how, Java servlets are supported. If set to None, Java servlets are not supported. If set to Domino servlet manager, Domino handles the management of servlets. The final option, Third-part servlet support requires that you install a third party manager. The default value is None.

- **Servlet URL path.** Specify the URL path to the servlet files. The default is /servlet.

- **Class path.** Use this field to specify the path to the servlet class files.

- **Servlet file extensions.** Use this field to specify servlet file extensions.

- **Session state tracking.** If you want to track the state of servlet sessions, choose enabled for this field. The default is disabled.

- **Idle session timeout.** Specify the number of minutes that a servlet session can remain idle before it's terminated. The default value is 30 minutes.

- **Maximum active sessions.** This field allows you to control how many servlet sessions can be open simultaneously. The default is 1,000.

- **Session persistence.** Set this field to enabled to allow session persistence.

Memory Caches

The following fields are found in the Memory Caches section and control the HTTP servers memory caching. These settings can go a long way toward increasing your HTTP server's performance.

- **Maximum cached commands.** This field is used to specify the maximum number of URL requests that resolve to Domino commands (that is, OpenView, openPage) that should be cached. The default is 128.

- **Maximum cached designs.** This field is used to specify the maximum number of Domino design elements that should be cached. The default is 128.

- **Maximum cached users.** This field is used to specify the maximum number of Web users that that should be cached. The default is 128.

- **Cached user expiration interval.** Use this field to specify a time in minutes, after which, the user cache is deleted.

POST Data

The following fields are found in POST data section and are used to control how much data can be sent to the HTTP server:

- **Maximum POST data.** This field can be used to set a limit of the size of data being sent to the server in a POST operation. The default is 0, meaning that no limit is imposed. If you want to restrict the amount of information uploaded with a POST operation, enter a number here in kilobytes.

- **File compression on upload.** If you want to have files that are uploaded from a browser using Notes compression, select Enabled. Keep in mind that compressed files cannot be downloaded using byte-range serving, but they will save space.

Conversion/Display

The following fields are found in the Conversion/Display section and dictate how certain data translations occur and how data is formatted before it's sent to the Web client.

- **Image conversion format.** This field is used to specify how images pasted into Notes are converted. You have two choices, JPG and GIF. GIF is the default.

- **Interlaced rendering.** If GIF file conversion is selected, interlaced rendering can be used to make images appear to load faster in the browser. Choose Enabled to turn this feature on.

- **Progressive rendering.** If JPG file conversion is selected, progressive rendering can be used to make images appear to load faster in the browser. Choose Enabled to turn this feature on.

- **Default lines per view page.** This field allows you to specify how many rows of a view will be shown when a view is opened in a browser and when the count parameter has not be specified. The default is 30 and 0 means no limit.

- **Maximum lines per view page.** This field specifies the maximum number of rows that can be displayed in a view opened by a browser. The default is 1,000, while specifying 0 indicates that there should be no limit.

- **Default search results limit.** This field allows you to specify how many results will be shown as the result of a search in a browser. The default is 250.

- **Maximum search result limit.** This field specifies the maximum number of results from a search executed from a browser that can be displayed. The default is 1,000, while specifying 0 indicates that there should be no limit.

- **Make this site accessible to Web search site crawlers.** Use this field to make the Domino content accessible to external search engines. It converts the Domino syntax "?" to "!" when enabled.

- **Redirect to resolve external links.**

Character Set Mapping

The following fields are found in the Character Set Mapping section and are used to control and manipulate character sets used for Domino. These settings could be especially important for multinational and/or global sites.

- **Default character set group.** Use this field to select the default character set to use when sending text to a browser. The default is western.

- **Convert resource strings to.** Use this field to specify to what language resource strings should be converted. English is the default.

- **Use UTF-8 for output.** UTF-8 is a superset of ASCII that breaks Unicode values into 8-bit sequences. If you are using Unicode, you can set this field to Yes to enable the conversion.

- **Use auto-detection if database has no language information.** Use this field to specify that Domino should try to automatically detect what language is in use if no language information is specified.

- **Western.** Choose the character set mapping to use for the Western character set. The default is ISO-8859-1.

- **Central European.** Choose the character set mapping to use for the Central European character set. The default is ISO-8859-2.

- **Japanese.** Choose the character set mapping to use for the Japanese character set. The default is SJIS.

- **Traditional Chinese.** Choose the character set mapping to use for the Traditional Chinese character set. The default is Big5.

- **Simplified Chinese.** Choose the character set mapping to use for the Simplified Chinese character set. The default is GB.

- **Korean.** Choose the character set mapping to use for the Korean character set. The default is KSC5601(EUC).

- **Cyrillic.** Choose the character set mapping to use for the Cyrillic character set. The default is K018-R.

- **Greek.** Choose the character set mapping to use for the Greek character set. The default is ISO-8859-7.

- **Turkish.** Choose the character set mapping to use for the Turkish character set. The default is ISO-8859-9.

- **Thai.** Choose the character set mapping to use for the Thai character set. The default is Windows-874.

- **Baltic.** Choose the character set mapping to use for the Baltic character set. The default is Windows-1257.

- **Arabic.** Choose the character set mapping to use for the Arabic character set. The default is Windows-1256.

- **Hebrew.** Choose the character set mapping to use for the Hebrew character set. The default is ISO–8859–8.

- **Vietnamese.** Choose the character set mapping to use for the Vietnamese character set. The default is Windows–1258.

- **Character set in header.** If you want to have the server send information about the character set in use in the HTTP header, enable this option.

- **Meta character set.** This setting works closely with the preceding setting. If you want to have the server send information about the character set in use as a META tag the HTTP header, enable this option.

Disk Cache for Images and Files

The following fields are found in the Disk Cache for Images and Files section. They are no longer used in R5 and remain only for backward compatibility.

- **Cache directory.** Use this field to enter the name of a directory in which to store cache files. The default is domino\cache.

- **Maximum cache size.** Specify the maximum size in megabytes for the cache. The default is 50MB.

- **Delete cache on shutdown.** if you would like the cache cleared when the server is shutdown, set this field to enabled. The default is disabled.

- **Garbage collection.** This field can be used to tell the Domino server to automatically "clean" the cache by deleting infrequently used files. Set this field to Enabled to clean "collect the garbage."

- **Garbage collection interval.** If garbage collection is enabled, you can specify a time in minutes after which the "garbage is collected from the cache." The default is 60 minutes.

Virtual Server Settings Override Server Settings

It's very important to remember that the settings specified in a Virtual Server document take precedence over the corresponding settings in the Server document.

Virtual Server Documents

Domino R5 makes it easy to host multiple sites through the use of Virtual Server documents. For each site that you want to host, you create another Virtual Server document and associate a static IP address with the site. To create a Virtual Server document, open the Domino administrator and select the server to which you'd like to add the virtual server (see Figure 15.8.). Then, follow these steps:

1. Click the Web button and select Create Virtual Server.

2. Select Virtual Server in the Virtual Document Type prompt.

3. On the Basics tab, enter the following requested information:

    -   **IP address.** Enter the IP address of the virtual server; remember that this should be a static IP.

    -   **Hostname.** Enter a home host name for the virtual server (*optional*).

    -   **Default home page.** Enter the filename of the HTML file to display when the virtual server is accessed. This setting is optional and will only apply when the Home URL field is blank.

4. Click the Mapping tab and enter the URL to launch when a user accesses the virtual server in the Home URL field. Remember that the Home URL field overrides the Default home page field. The remaining fields on this tab in most cases can be left at the defaults unless you need to define specific directories for each virtual server. If so, enter the appropriate information here.

5. Click the Security tab and enter the requested information. In most cases, the default settings will suffice.

6. Save the new Virtual Server document.

7. After you have saved the document, you'll need to restart the HTTP server before the virtual server will be available. You can either go to the server console, or use the remote console in the Domino Administrator to enter the `tell http restart`.

Virtual Server Settings

If the virtual server is going to share files with other servers, you can leave these settings at the default.

Security Risk

Keep in mind that is directory browsing is enabled, the `/?Open` URL command will display databases for all virtual servers because Domino shares the data directory with all virtual servers. It's a good idea to disable this feature!

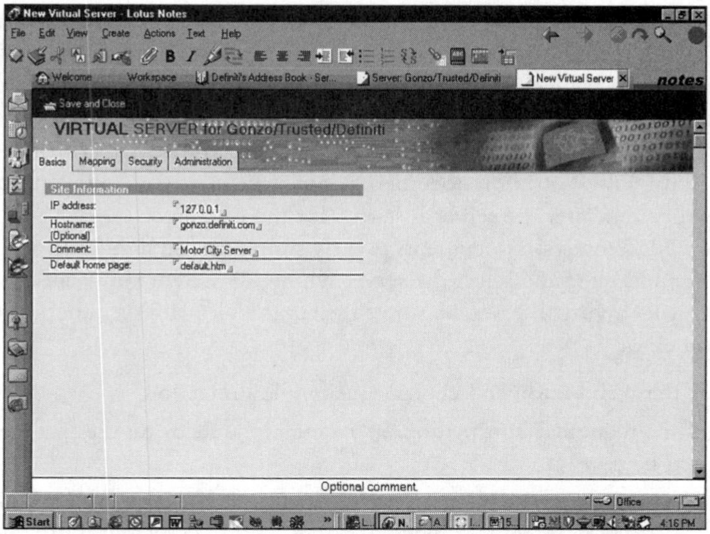

Figure 15.8   A Virtual server document.

Using File Protection Documents

Another great new feature of Domino R5 is the capability to have Domino secure your server's file system. This is easily accomplished by creating File Protection documents. File Protection documents are used to control what access users using a Web client have to the file system on your server. For example, you might not allow Anonymous users to open any JPEG files.

File Protection documents can be configured for an entire directory or for an individual file and as you can probably guess, the default path is the Domino data directory, but you can create File Protection documents for other directories. Lotus recommends that File Protection documents are defined for all directories accessible to Web users.

While this is a really cool and useful new feature, there are some caveats to the use of File Protection documents that you should carefully note. First is that while File system protection applies to any file that accesses other files—for example, HTML files that open image files, they will not be enforced for files opened by CGI Programs, servlets and agents that open other files.

For example, you can create a file protection document that only allows the group "Definiti Developers" to run a CGI script called "Test". However, if "Test" opens other files, the File Protection document is not checked for access to those files. The same is not true for files opened by other files. For example, if an HTML file references a JPEG image, the image file will not be opened if protected and the user has not been granted access.

When a Domino R5 server starts for the first time, a File Protection document is created in the Domino Directory for the domino\adm-bin directory. This File Protection document gives administrators (the list of admins is garnered from Administrators field in the Server document) the Write/Read/Execute access to the directory and gives all other users No Access. You need to remember that the administrator list in the File Protection document is not updated if you add names to the Administrators field after the server is started for the first time.

Creating File Protection documents is fairly simple and straightforward. Open the Domino Administrator and select the server whose file system you want to secure. If you are securing a virtual server, be sure to select the virtual server. the just follow the steps listed below:

1. Click the Web button and choose Create File Protection.

2. Enter the requested information on each tab; the fields on the first tab, Basics are defined here:

    - **Applies to.** The name of the server (or virtual server) for which the File Protection document will be created. This field is display only, you cannot change it.

    - **IP Address.** The IP address of the server to which the file protection applies. This field appears only if you are creating a File Protection document for a virtual server.

    - **Path.** The drive, directory, or file that you want to restrict. The path is relative to the Domino data directory.

3. Click the Access Control tab, complete this field, and save the document:

    - **Current access control list.** Select the users and groups that can access the files or directories you specified and the type of access they are allowed. This works much like a database ACL. Users not listed in the access list receive the default access level of "No Access." To add users to this list, click Set/Modify Access Control List button and user or group from the Domino Directory or type a name in the Name field and select "Read/Execute access (GET method)," or "Write/Read/Execute access (POST and GET methods)," or "No Access." After you have finished selecting users, click Next to add this entry to the access list. To remove an entry from the list, select it and click Clear. If Anonymous users will be allowed to access files, enter Anonymous in the Name field and assign the appropriate access.

Recommended by Lotus

Lotus recommends that File Protection documents are defined for all directories accessible to Web users and users have access to all other files and directories on the server until you create a File Protection documents to block them out.

4. Save the new File Protection document.

5. After you have saved the document, you'll need to restart the HTTP server before the file protections will apply. You can either go to the server console, or use the remote console in the Domino Administrator to enter the `tell http restart`.

The File Protection document is shown in Figure 15.9

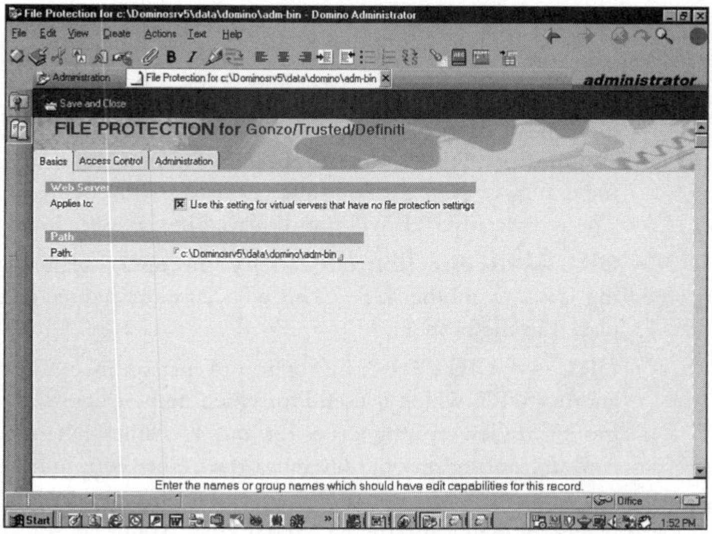

Figure 15.9 File Protection document.

Using Mapping/Redirection Documents

Domino R5 now makes it easy to map resource locations and provide redirection through Mapping/Redirection documents. Using this technique, you can keep database files, HTML files, image files, CGI scripts, and other related Web files in numerous locations, and/or move them to new locations without breaking URL links or changing Server and Virtual Server documents. When you redirect a URL, the URL is displayed in the location. Mapping a URL, on the other hand, hides the new URL from the user.

Understanding Access Types

GET lets the user open files and start programs in the directory. POST is typically used to send data to a CGI program; therefore, POST access should only be given to directories that contain CGI programs. No Access denies access to the specified user or group.

For example, if you want to move a database named home.nsf from gonzo.definiti. com to borg.definiti.com, you create a Mapping/Redirection document that will redirect uses from gonzo.definiti.com to borg.definiti.com.

To create a Mapping/Redirection document, follow the steps listed here:

1. From the Domino Administrator select the Server document for the server on which you want to redirect or remap a URL or directory.

2. Click Web and choose Create URL Mapping/Redirection.

3. Click the Basics tab, enter the information in the field here:

    ▪ **What do you want to setup.** You have three choices for this field that are defined as follows:

        • **URL —>Directory.** Select this option to map a URL to a different directory. This can be helpful if you want to rename directories, move files, or store files on different drives without confusing users. The redirected URL will not displayed in the user's location box.

        • **URL —>Redirection URL.** Select this option to map an incoming URL to another URL. This will cause the redirected to be displayed in the browser.

        • **URL —> URL.** Select this option to map an incoming URL to another URL which is useful for when doing things such as moving groups of files, creating aliases for long filenames, renaming directories, and storing files on different drives. Keep in mind that you cannot map pages stored in a Domino database to a different URL. This technique will cause the redirected URL to not be displayed in the user's location box.

4. If you are creating the mapping for a virtual server, click the Site Information tab and enter the IP address of the virtual server in the IP Address Field. This is only required for virtual servers.

5. Click the Mapping tab, and enter the requested information. The fields on the Mappings tab are defined here:

    ▪ **First URL path.** Enter the incoming URL path that you want redirected to a different directory or URL

    ▪ **Second URL path.** Enter the full path name of the directory or the URL the user should be redirected. Bear in mind that if you have set this Mapping/Redirection document to "URL —> URL" or "URL —> Directory," you must enter a location on the same server as the directory specified by the URL path.

6. Click the Access tab, and select the type of access users should have in the Access field. The following list explains what each of the choices in the Access field means.

- If you selected URL —> Directory, specify the type of access you want users to have to the directory. Read allows browsers to read files in the directory. Execute allows browsers to execute programs from this directory.

- Set Read access for any directories that contain content files, such as HTML files and images. Do not set Execute access for these directories.

- Set Execute access only for directories that contain CGI scripts and other files that browsers can run. Do not set Read access for these directories; users don't need to see what these directories contain.

7. Save the document.

8. After you have saved the document, enter the `tell http restart` command at server console, or through the remote server console to make the new Mapping/Redirection document take effect.

A Mapping/Redirection document is shown in Figure 15.10.

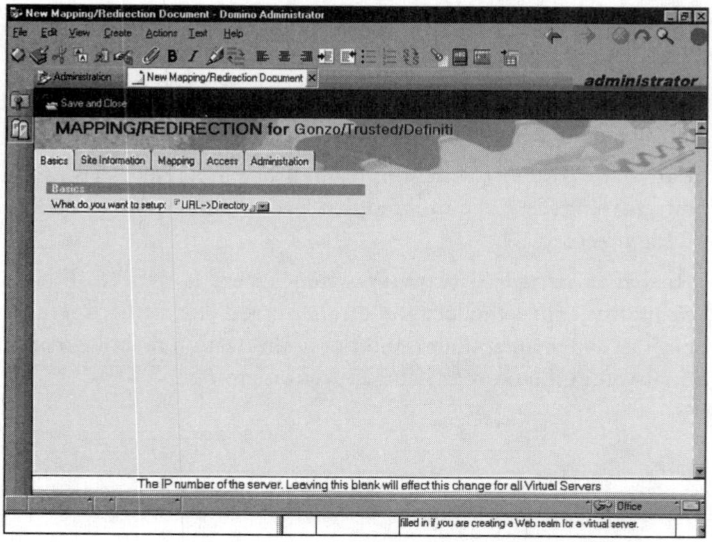

Figure 15.10   A Mapping/Redirection document.

Using Web Realms

Domino R5 now provides the capability to create Web realms controls authentication over specified drives, directories, and/or files on a Domino server. When a user attempts to access one of these resources, a string of text specified in a Web Realm document will be displayed in the authentication dialog box. After the user submits their credentials, the browser uses the realm to determine which credentials to send with the URL for subsequent requests, and credentials for different realms are cached so that prompting the user again for the same credentials is avoided.

Additionally, the realm string applies to all subdirectories of a mapped path unless the subdirectory has its own realm document. For example, the realm string specified for D:\NOTES\DATA applies to any subdirectories that do not have a specific realm defined. It's important to Notes that in a realm that is not specified for a path, Domino will use the path itself as the realm string.

Creating a Web realm document is simple. Follow the steps listed here:

1. From the Domino Administrator, select the server or virtual server on which you want to create a Web realm.

2. Open the server of virtual server document and Click the Web button.

3. Choose Create realm.

4. Enter the requested information. The fields are explained in the list that follows. The Web realm document is shown in Figure 15.11.

   - **IP Address.** The IP address of the virtual server. You only need to enter an IP address where the server is a virtual server.

   - **Path.** The path for which this realm is being defined. This can be a drive, directory, or file. Keep in mind that the path is relative to the Domino Data directory.

   - **Realm returned to browser when access is denied.** Enter a text string that names the location on the server. This string is returned to the browser when an authentication or authorization failure occurs and is it displayed in the browser's authentication prompt.

Save the New Web Realm Document

After you have saved the document, You need to restart the HTTP server before the Web realm will apply. You can either go to the server console, or use the remote console in the Domino Administrator to enter the `tell http restart`.

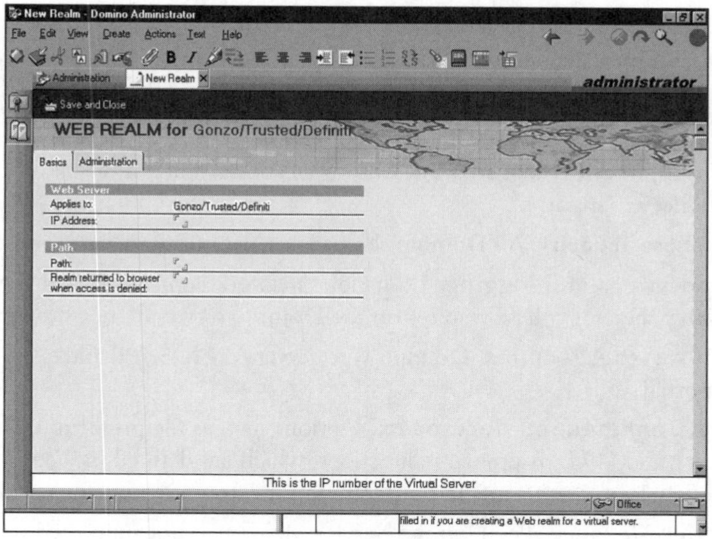

Figure 15.11 Web Realm document.

Using the Microsoft IIS HTTP Stack

One of the most useful (and coolest) new features of Domino R5 is the capability to use Microsoft IIS to serve up requests for Domino content. There are two major advantages to using this model. First, it allows you to leverage existing infrastructure and skill sets. Second, the IIS and Domino security models work together when users interact with Domino applications ensuring a high level of security for data stored in Domino databases.

When using Domino for IIS, the IIS server passes thru all URL requests that contain .NSF (the default extension for a Domino database) to Domino, while any other requests are handled by IIS.

Disable the HTTP Server Task When Using Domino for IIS

To use Domino for IIS, the Domino server must be running while the Domino ISAPI extension is loaded. Under this model, all Domino server tasks except the HTTP task can be run (this would conflict with the Domino ISAPI extension), which allows the Domino server to serve Notes clients, and perform other Domino functions such as mail routing, NNTP, and replication.

Features Supported by Domino for IIS

Domino for IIS provides access to the majority of the features that the native Domino HTTP service provides. This section will give you a brief overview of exactly what native Domino features are supported when using Domino for IIS.

- **Web application features.** All Web application features available in Domino Designer as supported.

- **Database security.** All Domino database security features are supported.

- **Connections and logging.** IIS handles network connection and server request logging; therefore, these features on the Domino server are not supported.

- **Web server API filters.** Domino Web server API (DSAPI) filters are not supported.

- **Web Configuration documents.** Options such as file protection, virtual servers, and URL mappings/redirections, which are defined in Web Configuration documents in the Domino Directory are not supported.

- **Servlet Manager.** The Domino Servlet Manager is not supported under Domino for IIS. If you require this type of functionality, a third-party product, such as IBM WebSphere Application Server, can be used.

- **Internet Cluster Manager.** The Domino Internet Cluster Manager (ICM) is not supported. Instead, you can use Microsoft's cluster manager.

- **Server document options.** Domino for IIS does not support all of the options and settings available to the native HTTP task through the Server document. Those features that are supported are listed in Table 15.1.

Some Modifications Might be Necessary to Use Domino for IIS
Applications that access resources other than Domino databases such as HTML, CGI scripts, and Java servlets, for example, might require modification to when used with Domino for IIS.

NT File System Security Can Be Used
You can protect system files using NT file permissions.

Table 15.1   **Supported Server Document Options**

Location	Option
Security Tab	Internet server Authentication
Ports\Internet Ports\Web	TCP/IP port status
	Authentication options
	Name & password
	Anonymous
Internet Protocols\HTTP	Allow HTTP clients to browse databases
Internet Protocols\ Domino Web Engine	\<HTTP Sessions settings\>
	\<POST Data settings\>
	\<Memory Caches settings\>
	\<Character Set Mapping settings\>
	Default lines per view page
	Maximum lines per view page
	Default search results limit
	Maximum search results limit
	Make this site accessible to crawlers

As you have seen, the Domino for IIS feature is quite powerful and extensive. If your organization is already using Microsoft IIS and you would like to use it to serve up Domino content, you must configure Domino for Microsoft IIS first. The remainder of this section describes the procedures you must follow to configure Domino for IIS.

Minimum Requirements for Domino for IIS

Before you begin, you need to ensure that you meet the minimum requirements to run Domino for IIS. They are as follows:

- Microsoft Windows NT 4.0 with Service Pack 4 (both the Intel and DEC Alpha platforms are supported).
- Microsoft Internet Information Server (IIS) 4.0.
- A good understanding of Microsoft Management Console (MMC). MMC is the tool that enables you to configure IIS. You can learn more about MMC in the Windows NT documentation or at `http://www.microsoft.com/NTServer/ management/Techdetails/ProdArchitect/mmc.asp`.
- A working Domino R5 server.
- A `notes.ini` file located either in the Domino program directory, or in a directory specified on the server's PATH setting. Alternatively, you can include a fully qualified path to the server ID file in the ServerKeyFilename setting of the `notes.ini` file.

- A server ID file that is not configured to use a password as you cannot enter a password when IIS starts the Domino ISAPI extension.

- "Change" file permissions in NT for the Domino directory and all subdirectories for all user accounts that will use Domino for IIS.

Configuring IIS to Support Domino for IIS

If you have met all of the minimum requirements, you are ready to configure Domino for IIS. You should start by configuring the Domino ISAPI extension for IIS so that when requests are made using a Domino style URL (contains .NSF), IIS will know how to handle it. This is accomplished through the MMC. The following steps walk you through this process:

1. Start the MMC, and open the MMC on your the Web site. This is illustrated in Figure 15.12.

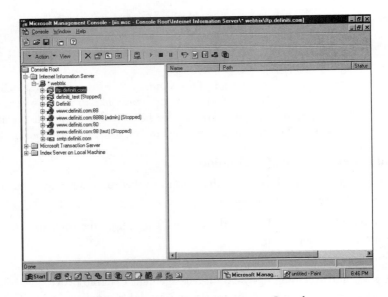

Figure 15.12　Microsoft Management Console.

2. Right-click the IIS Web site, and select Properties. This is shown in Figure 15.13.

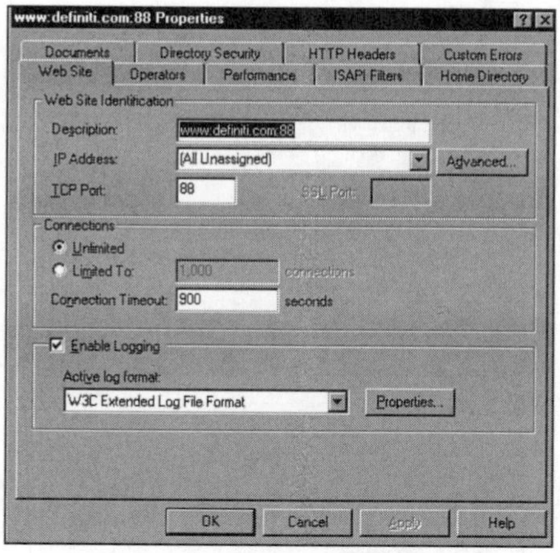

Figure 15.13 IIS Web Site Properties.

3. Select the Home Directory tab, which is illustrated in Figure 15.14.

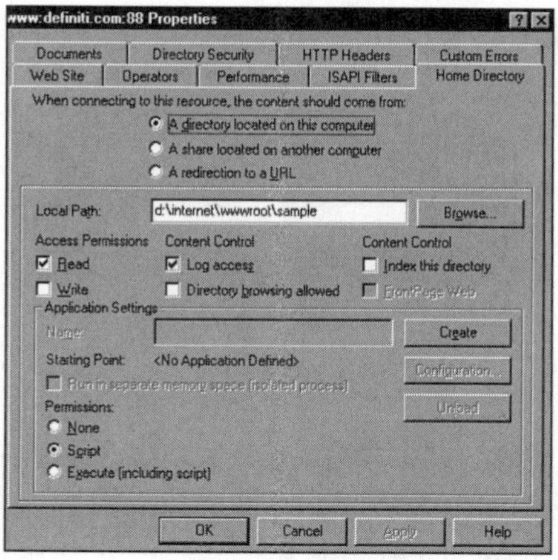

Figure 15.14 The IIS Home Directory Properties dialog box.

4. Click the Configuration button, which opens the Application Configuration dialog box (see Figure 15.15).

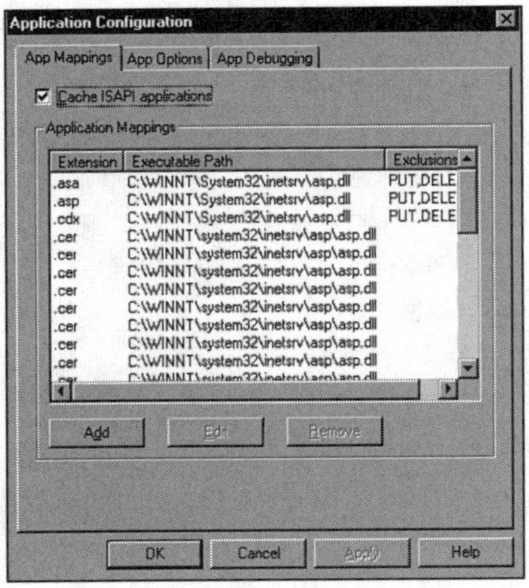

Figure 15.15   The IIS Home Directory Properties dialog box.

5. Click the Add button, which displays the Add/Edit Application Extension Mapping dialog box, shown in Figure 15.16.

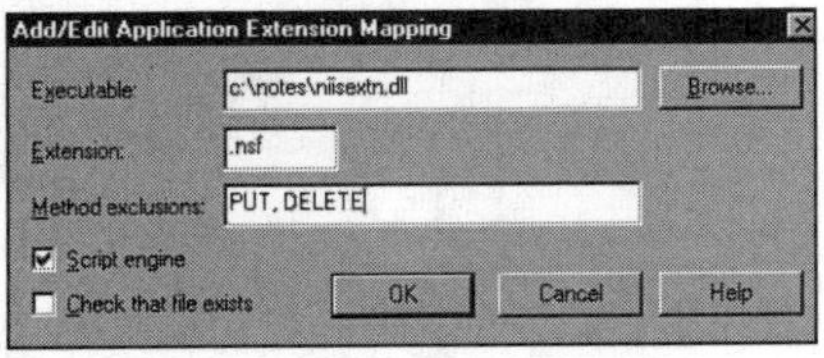

Figure 15.16   The Add/Edit Application Extension Mapping dialog box.

6. In the Executable field, enter the full path name of the ISAPI extension file, which is in the Domino directory and is named NIISEXTN.DLL for the Intel platform. For the Alpha platform, it is named AIISEXTN.DLL.

7. In the Extension field, enter .NSF, the default Domino database file extension. This indicates to the IIS server that a Domino resource has been requested.

8. Enter the HTTP methods that Domino for IIS does not support, namely PUT and DELETE, in the Methods Exclusions field.

9. Select Script Engine and deselect Check that the File Exists.

10. When finished, click OK to save your changes.

Additionally, you'll need to configure the IIS extension filter to ensure that users can be authenticated properly by Domino and to enable the Domino /?OpenServer command (as there is no .NSF embedded in the URL for this command) if you want the user to be able to browse databases. As noted earlier in this chapter, this feature is not recommended, as it makes it easy for hackers to view the databases on your site.

11. Start the MMC, and open the MMC console file for the Web site. Refer Figure 15.12 for an example of what this looks like.

12. Right-click the IIS Web site, and select Properties. Refer to Figure 15.13.

13. Select the ISAPI Filters tab shown in Figure 15.17.

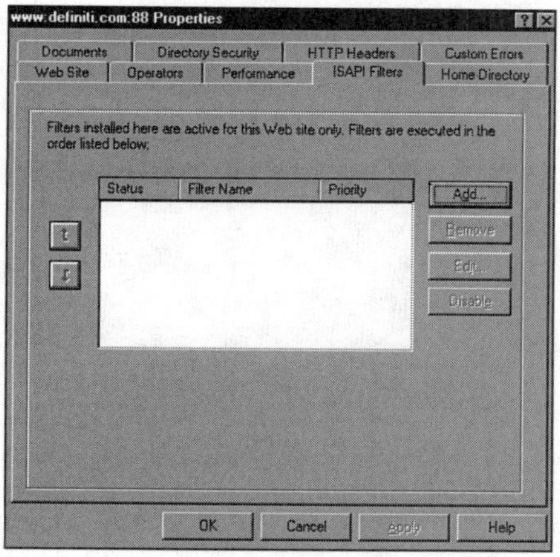

Figure 15.17   The ISAPI Filters tab.

14. Click the Add button, which opens the Filter properties dialog box shown in Figure 15.18.

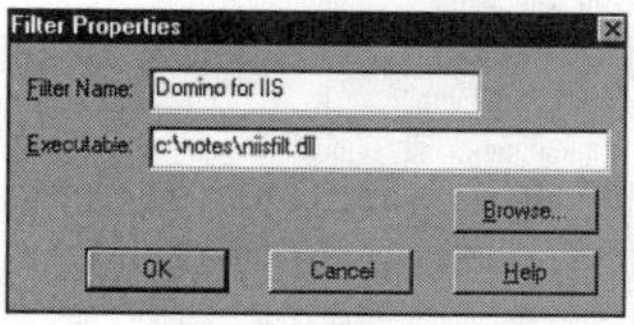

Figure 15.18   The Filter Properties dialog box.

15. In the Filter Name field, enter any text you want to describe the IIS filter.

16. In the Executable field, enter the full path name of the filter file. The file is located in the Domino directory and is named NIISFILT.DLL for the Intel platform or AIISFILT.DLL for the Alpha platform.

17. When finished, click OK to save your changes.

In order for Domino to load Java applets and icons correctly, you need to specify their location. You can accomplish this by following the procedures listed here:

1. Start the MMC, and open the MMC the Web site. Refer to Figure 15.12.

2. Right-click the IIS Web site, then choose New\Virtual Directory, which opens the New Virtual Directory Wizard, shown in Figure 15.19.

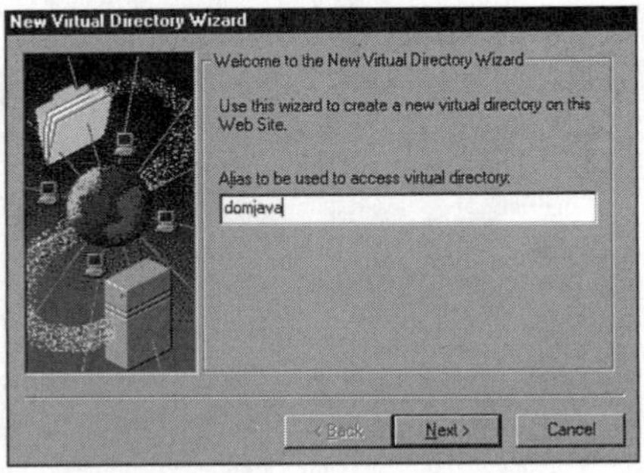

Figure 15.19 The New Virtual Directory Wizard dialog box.

3. Enter domjava in the Virtual Directory Alias field. Then, click Next, which will then prompt you for the file path, as shown in Figure 15.20.

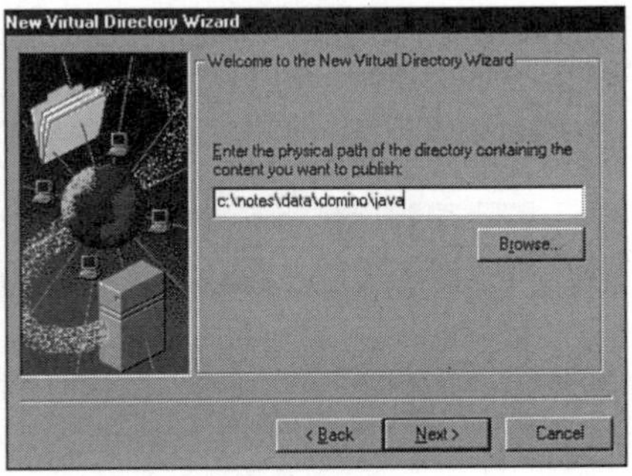

Figure 15.20 Enter the file path in this dialog box.

4. Enter the full path to the Domino applet directory (normally c:\notes\data\domino\java).

5. Click Finish. You are not required to change the default permission settings.

6. Repeat steps 2 through 5 but enter icons as the alias name and specify the full path to the icons directory (normally c:\notes\data\domino\icons).

After you have configured Domino for IIS, you are ready for IIS to start serving up Domino content. You can do so by following the procedures listed here:

1. Start the Domino server.

2. Open the MMC and start IIS. The Domino extensions for IIS will automatically be loaded the first time a Domino URL is requested.

If at any point you want to stop the Domino for IIS Service, you can open the MMC and stop IIS.

Security for Domino for IIS Overview

The final piece of the Domino for IIS puzzle is configuring security to ensure that your Domino content remains secure. Domino for IIS uses two levels of security: IIS security and Domino security (which can be really handy). IIS first attempts to validate a user based on the Windows NT directory. If IIS successfully validates that user, his credentials are passed along to the Domino server for further validation using the Domino security model.

Because Domino security is covered in detail in Chapter 10, we'll only examine IIS security features and configuration in this section.

At the time of this writing, IIS supports four methods of user authentication:

- **Anonymous access.** A user name and password are not required to access resources.

- **Basic Authentication.** The user enters a name and password and is authenticated against the Security Account Manager.

- **Windows NT Challenge/Response.** A Microsoft protocol supported only between Microsoft Internet Explorer and IIS/NT. This will not work with other browsers.

- **Secure Sockets Layer (SSL).**

Domino's Native HTTTP Tasks Conflicts with IIS

Do not load the native Domino HTTP task while Domino for IIS is running as IIS processes Domino HTTP requests and this causes conflicts between the Domino HTTP server task and IIS.

To control access to resources managed and served by IIS, user authentication is required. If a user requests Domino resources, IIS passes user's credentials onto Domino, where the user is validated using the same procedures as the native HTTP task.

Exactly what information is passed to Domino depends on what authentication methods are enabled in IIS. Each of the IIS-supported authentication methods are briefly explained in the next sections and you will need to understand them thoroughly to implement this correctly:

Using Anonymous Access

When IIS is configured to Allow Anonymous Access, Web users can access the site without supplying any credentials until they attempt to access a secured Domino resource. At this point, the Domino server will require the user to present his credentials so that authentication can be performed and access will be granted or denied based on standard Domino authentication.

If you configure to IIS to use only Allow Anonymous Access, be aware of the following caveats:

- The Web user does not need to have a Windows NT user account.
- A Web user accessing secured Domino resources will need to have a Domino user account (Person document in the Directory) and an Internet password.
- The GCI variables AUTH_TYPE and REMOTE_USER will not be available to applications because IIS see these users an anonymous.

Using Basic Authentication

If IIS is configured to use Basic Authentication, a user's credentials are validated against the NT security account manager. If a valid account is found, and that account has access to the requested resource, access is granted. Otherwise, access is not granted. If Basic Authentication is the only enabled IIS authentication method, IIS requires all Web users to present valid credentials (meaning that anonymous access disallowed). For user's who are authenticated, IIS passes the user name to Domino, which then authenticates the user using the same process as the native Domino HTTP service.

Many Directory Options

All the directory options available for the native HTTP task, such as LDAP Directories and multiple Domino Directories, are also available for Domino for IIS.

Internet Password Is Not Used During Basic Authentication Under Domino for IIS

If Basic Authentication is the only authentication method enabled for IIS, a user's password is validated based on the user's NT account, not the user's Internet password sorted in the Domino Directory.

If you configure to IIS to use only Basic Authentication, be aware of the following caveats:

- Anonymous access is not allowed.
- The Web user must have a Windows NT user account and a Domino user account.
- Domino will ignore the user's Internet password.

Using Both Anonymous Access and Basic Authentication

If you want to allow anonymous users to access only public resources, but still provide protection for secured resources, you can enable both Allow Anonymous Access and Basic Authentication. Under this model, any user can access any nonsecured resource without being authenticated. However, any user attempting to access a secured resource will be required to authenticate.

If you configure IIS to use both Allow Anonymous Access and Basic Authentication, be aware of the following caveats:

- Anonymous access is permitted for public (nonsecure) IIS and Domino resources.
- If the user attempts to access secured resources, they will be required to provide credentials and both IIS and Domino will authenticate the user using Basic Authentication.

Using Windows NT Challenge/Response

Windows NT Challenge/Response is a Microsoft-specific protocol currently supported only by Internet Explorer (IE). When a Web user makes a request to the site, IE, automatically the user's current NT logon account name to sends to IIS. IIS verifies the name against the NT security account manager on the IIS server. When a user makes a Domino request, IIS passes the user's NT name through to Domino, which validates the name using the same process as the native HTTP service.

If you configure to IIS to use only Basic Authentication, be aware of the following:

- All browsers except IE will be excluded from accessing the site.
- All Web users must have a valid NT user account to access any resources on the site.
- Each user's NT account name must be added to their Person document in the Domino Directory as an alias.
- IE automatically sends the user's NT account name on every request, making Anonymous access impossible.
- Domino ignores the Internet password, passing only the NT account name to Domino. Domino trusts IIS to validate the user's identity.

Using Windows NT Challenge/Response and Basic Authentication

If you enable both NT Challenge/Response and Basic Authentication, you can expect the following:

- Internet Explorer users are authenticated using NT Challenge/Response.
- All other browsers will be authenticated using Basic Authentication making this a secure option.

Using Allow Anonymous Access, Basic Authentication, and Windows NT Challenge/Response

If you enable all three of these methods, you can expect the following:

- Anonymous access is allowed for nonsecure requests.
- Internet Explorer users are authenticated using NT Challenge/Response.
- All other browsers will be authenticated using Basic Authentication.

Using SSL

When SSL is enabled on an IIS server, IIS handles the actual SSL connection. If a Web user provides a client certificate, IIS passes the certificate to Domino and Domino uses the certificate to authenticate the user. For more information on SSL and Domino, see Chapter 10.

Security for Domino for IIS Overview

To configure IIS security, follow the steps listed here:

1. Start the MMC, and open the Web site. This is illustrated earlier in Figure 15.12.
2. Right-click the IIS Web site and select Properties. This is also shown earlier in Figure 15.13
3. Click the Directory Security tab, which is shown in Figure 15.21.
4. Click the Edit button to launch the authentication Methods dialog box, where you can enable the authentication methods you want to use. This is shown in Figure 15.22.

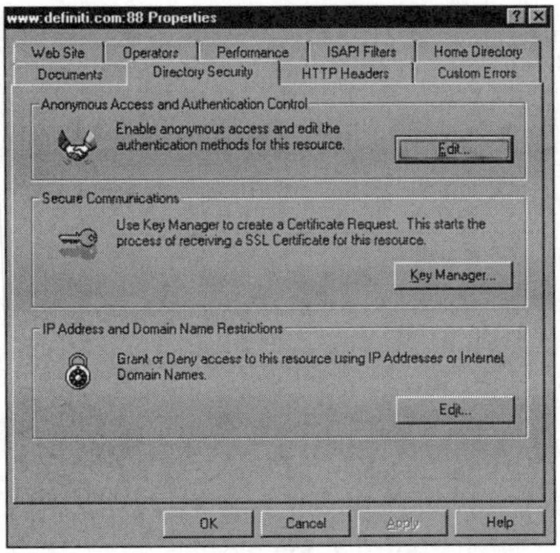

Figure 15.21 The Directory Security tab.

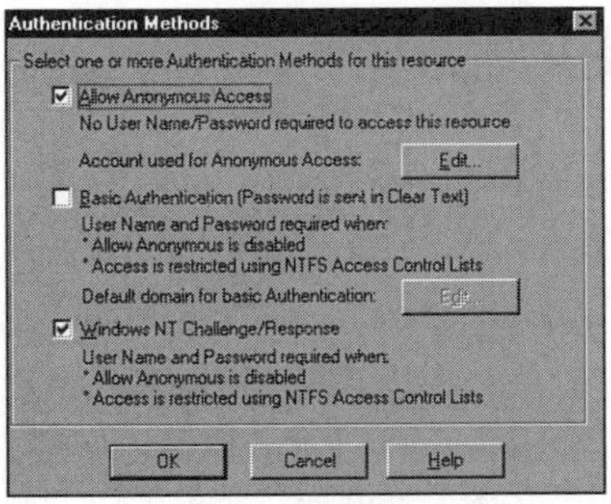

Figure 15.22 The Authentication Methods dialog box.

5. Choose one or more of the authentication options. If you need to control exactly how either the anonymous Access or Basic Authentication methods work, click its Edit button and make the necessary changes.

6. Click OK on the Authentication Methods dialog box.

Tuning

After you have you Domino server up and running, you'll want to monitor its performance. Domino R5 sports a plethora of new server monitoring tools that will let you monitor and tweak virtually all aspects of a Domino server. This section will focus solely on tuning the Domino HTTP task. For more information on general Domino optimization and tuning and performance monitoring, see Chapter 18, "Server

Monitoring," and Chapter 19, "Performance Tuning." Additionally, you might want to check the Domino Administration Help file (`help5_admin.nsf`); `www.notes.net` is an excellent reference as well.

There is a number of HTTP related or HTTP specific things you can do to improve server performance and response time as follows:

- Disable HTTP server logging
- Optimize HTTP performance based on activity
- Create a Domino Web server cluster
- Tweak the memory cache
- Tweak network time-outs
- Manage the number of server threads
- Enable byte-range serving for file downloads
- Specify Redirect URL command method
- Restrict the amount of data sent to the server
- Use progressive rendering for JPEGs
- Limit number of rows displayed for a view
- Limit number of results displayed for a search

Disable HTTP Server Logging

Although it will seriously curtail, if not completely eliminate, your ability to track and analyze hits to your site, you can disable HTTP logging to derive a relatively large performance boost for your server if you are receiving a large number of hits and are experiencing performance problems.

To disable HTTP logging, follow the steps listed:

1. Open your Domino Directory and select the Servers view.
2. Select the server you want to configure.
3. Open the Server document and click the Internet Protocols tab.
4. Select the HTTP tab to manage the configuration of the native HTTP task.
5. In the Enable Logging To section, set the Log Files and the Domlog.nsf fields to Disabled.
6. Click the Save and Close button on the Action bar.

Optimize HTTP Performance Based on Activity

If your Domino server is going to perform only certain tasks, for example, just mail routing, You can use configure the Optimize HTTP performance based on the following primary activity setting in the Basics tab of the server document to improve Domino's performance.

To configure this setting, do the following:

1. Open your Domino Directory and select the Servers view.

2. Select the server you want to configure.

3. Open the Server document, which defaults to the basics tab.

4. Go to the Optimize HTTP performance based on the following primary activity field and select from the following four choices: Web Mail, Web Applications, Both Mail and Web, and Advanced (Custom settings), the one that best matches your requirements.

5. Click the Save and Close button on the Action bar.

Create a Domino Web Server Cluster

You can gain significant performance improvements by installing a cluster of Domino servers, which will provide load balancing and fail over for Web users. This is a fairly complex topic and is covered in detail in Chapter 20 "Enhancing Data Availability."

Tweak the Memory Cache

Domino uses a memory cache, also known as the command cache, to provide optimal response times. This cache stores information about HTTP commands, databases, and users, so that they can quickly be retrieved from memory. Domino R5 currently supports the following memory cache settings:

- **Maximum cached commands.** This setting specifies the maximum number of HTTP server commands to cache for anonymous users. The conversion process of Domino elements to HTML takes time. This setting controls how many commands (that require conversion) can be stored in memory, making the request immediately available when it is reissued. The default is 128 commands.

- **Maximum cached designs.** This setting specifies the maximum number of database design elements to cache. When a database is opened, Domino maps each design element's name to an identification number. This setting specifies how many elements to store in memory, making them immediately available on subsequent requests. The default is 128 elements.

- **Maximum cached users.** The number of users to cache. After a user successfully authenticates, Domino caches the user's name, password, and the users group memberships. Use this setting to control the number of users cached by Domino. The default is 64 users.

- **Cached user expiration interval.** This setting specifies the time interval in seconds during which Domino removes user names, passwords, and group memberships from the user cache. This should be done periodically to ensure that users are required to authenticate against the Domino Directory. The default is 120 seconds.

To configure the memory cache settings, do the following:

1. Open your Domino Directory and select the Servers view.
2. Select the server you want to configure.
3. Open the Server document and click the Internet Protocols tab.
4. Click the Domino Web Engine tab, shown in Figure 15.23.

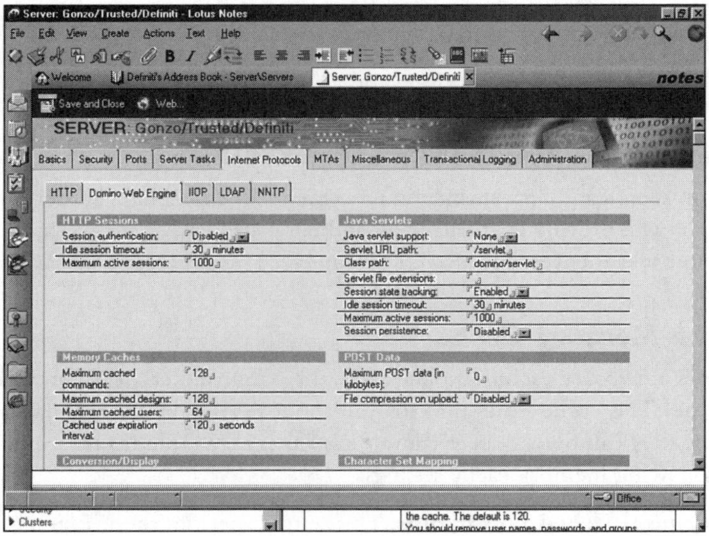

Figure 15.23   The Domino Web Engine Tab of a server document.

5. Go to the Memory Caches section and change the settings as appropriate.
6. Click Save and Close to save your changes.

Monitoring Cache Settings

To monitor the effect the memory cache settings have on the Domino server, check the Domino.Cache statistics through the Domino Administration client.

Tweak Network Time-Outs

Inactive sessions hog server resources and can lead to a denial of services. Domino provides the capability to specify time limits for most activities, which increases server performance and helps to ensure that the server will be available. Domino R5 supports the following timeout settings:

- **Input timeout.** This setting allows you to specify the number of minutes a Web browser has to send a request after the initial server connection. The server uses this field if a browser is not sending "keep alive headers" to the server within the amount of time specified. Most current browsers send "keep alive headers" make this setting unnecessary. If you are supporting older browsers, you should be sure to set this option. The default is 2 minutes.

- **Output timeout.** This setting specifies the maximum time, in minutes, that the server has to send output back to a browser before the connection is dropped. This setting applies all requests other than GGI programs. The default is 20 minutes.

- **CGI timeout.** The maximum number of minutes that a CGI program started by the server has to run. When the time specified in this setting expires, the server sends a message to the CGI program. After 5 minutes, the server shuts down the program. The default is 5 minutes.

- **Idle thread timeout.** This setting is no longer used in Domino R5 and remains only for backward compatibility

- **Run Web Agents Concurrently.** This setting specifies how many agents started by a Web user can be run at the same time. The default is 1. If your server has plenty of resources, increasing this number can improve server performance.

- **Web Agent Timeout.** This setting specifies the time, in seconds, that an agent started by a Web user can run before the agent manager stops the agent. The default is 120. If you are running agents from the browser, be sure to use this setting to keep an agent from hogging system resources.

To configure the HTTP server's timeout options, follow these steps:

1. Open your Domino Directory and select the Servers view.
2. Select the server you want to configure.
3. Open the Server document and click the Internet Protocols tab.
4. Click the HTTP tab.
5. Go to the Timeouts section and/or the Web Agents section and change the settings as appropriate.
6. Click Save and Close to save your changes.

Manage the Number of Server Threads

The number of threads specified basically dictates the number of users who can access the server simultaneously. When the number of active threads is reached, new requests are queued until current requests finish and threads become available.

Increasing the number of threads can significantly improve performance.

Domino R5 supports the following server thread control settings:

- **Maximum requests over a single connection.** This setting controls the maximum number of simultaneous requests that will be accepted by the server from a single browser. This setting only affects browsers compatible with HTTP 1.1 or later. The default is 1. Increasing this number can improve performance.

- **Number active threads.** This setting controls the maximum number of threads that can be active on the server simultaneously. The default is 40. If you have ample resources, increasing this number can improve performance.

- **Minimum active threads.** This setting only remains for backward compatibility.

To configure the HTTP server's thread options, follow these steps:

1. Open your Domino Directory and select the Servers view.
2. Select the server you want to configure.
3. Open the Server document and click the Internet Protocols tab.
4. Click the HTTP tab.
5. Go to the Timeouts section and/or the Web Agents section and change the settings as appropriate.
6. Click Save and Close to save your changes.

Byte-Range Serving for File Downloads

Domino R5 supports byte-range serving for file downloads (downloading the file in sections) for Web browsers that support HTTP 1.1 or higher. When byte-range serving is enabled, the browser tracks the progress of file downloads and, if interrupted during transmission, the browser can resume the download at the point of failure. If this feature is not enabled, the user must download the entire file again!

For byte-range serving to work, attached files cannot be compressed with the native Notes compression (you must deselect the Compress option when attaching a file).

> **Byte-Range Serving**
>
> Domino will automatically use byte-range serving for downloads if the Web client supports this feature. Unfortunately, at the time of this writing, there were only a handful of products that support this cool new feature. One product is Adobe Acrobat Reader 3.01.

Specify Redirect URL Method

To control how much time is taken to resolve links to other servers, you can change the Redirect to resolve external links option. You should enable this option on servers running the domain search and on servers for which you want to resolve links to other servers. Your choices for this option are as follows:

- **Disabled (default).** This prevents the server from accepting Redirect URL commands and stops the server from generating Redirect URL commands when a domain search is performed.

- **By Server.** Specify this setting to look up the server name in a URL in the server's copy of the Domino Directory. When this is enabled, the server will search the Host names field and the Fully qualified Internet host name field.

- **By Database.** This is the slowest option as the search will be conducted against all available servers. Domino will attempt to locate the database in the server's local catalog and then the domain catalog.

To configure the Redirect to resolve external links option, follow the steps below:

1. Open your Domino Directory and select the Servers view.
2. Select the server you want to configure.
3. Open the Server document and click the Internet Protocols tab.
4. Click the Domino Web Engine tab.
5. Go to the Conversion/Display section and change the settings as appropriate.
6. Click Save and Close to save your changes

Restrict the Amount of Data Sent to the Server

As any of you Web developers know, the HTTP POST command provides a method for Web browsers to send data to a Web server. Domino R5 allows you to specify how much data a browser can to send the server. Additionally, you can specify if files uploaded to the server are compressed. You can use the two following options to prevent users from sending inordinately large amounts of data to the server.

- **Maximum POST data.** This setting specifies the maximum amount of (in KB) that a browser can send to the server. If the browser sends more data than the specified amount, an error message will be returned. The default value is 0KB, which means there is no restriction placed on the amount of data a browser can send.

- **File compression on upload.** This setting specifies if uploaded files should be compressed before saving them in a database. The default is disabled.

Byte-Range Serving

Remember that if users are using a browser that supports byte-range serving, this feature must be disabled. Compressed files cannot be downloaded using Domino byte-range serving.

To configure the Post Data options, follow these steps:

1. Open your Domino Directory and select the Servers view.
2. Select the server you want to configure.
3. Open the Server document and click the Internet Protocols tab.
4. Click the Domino Web Engine tab.
5. Go to the Post Data section and change the settings as appropriate.
6. Click Save and Close to save your changes

Use Interlaced/Progressive Rendering for Images

If you are using images in your Web applications, you can make it appear to the user that images display more quickly by enabling interlaced rendering for GIF files and progressive rendering of JPEGs.

To enable these features, follow the steps listed below:

1. Open your Domino Directory and select the Servers view.
2. Select the server you want to configure.
3. Open the Server document and click the Internet Protocols tab.
4. Click the Domino Web Engine tab.
5. Go to the Display Conversion section and select Enabled for both the Interlaced Rendering and the Progressive Rendering options.
6. Click Save and Close to save your changes

Limit Number of Rows Displayed for a View

Domino R5 enables you to control how many rows will be displayed to Web users who access a view. The two settings that control the number or rows are explained here:

- **Default lines per page.** This setting determines how many rows to display when the count parameter is not specified in a URL. Specify a number from 1 to the number specified for "Maximum lines per view page." The default is 30.
- **Maximum lines per page.** This setting determines the maximum number of rows to display if a view a count is not specified in a URL. If you want no limit placed on the number of rows in a view, enter 0 (the number of rows is then determined by the browser's capacity). The default is 1,000. A good number is probably 100.

To configure the Rows per view options, follow the steps below.

1. Open your Domino Directory and select the Servers view.
2. Select the server you want to configure.
3. Open the Server document and click the Internet Protocols tab.
4. Click the Domino Web Engine tab.
5. Go to the Display Conversion section and change the settings as appropriate.
6. Click Save and Close to save your changes.

These two settings work hand-in-hand and can have a major impact on the performance of your server. If set too low, users will have to constantly request more data from the server to find the documents they are looking for. If set too high, the server will have to work hard to serve up the data and the users may experience long delays while the data is transferred to the browser.

Limit Number of Results Displayed for a Search

Much like defining the number of rows to display in a view, you can specify the number of documents to display as a result of performing a search. There are two settings that work together to define the number of documents to display. They are as follows:

- **Default search result limit.** This setting specifies the number of documents to display when the SearchMax parameter is not specified in the URL. The default is 250, but you can enter 0 if you want no limit imposed, or any number between 1 and Maximum search result limit.

- **Maximum search result limit.** This setting specifies the maximum number of documents to display when SearchMax is not specified in a URL. Enter 0 to impose no limit on the number of documents displayed. The default is 1000. It is not a good idea to set this to 0, as it could bring your server to its knees.

To configure the Search result limits, follow these steps:

1. Open your Domino Directory and select the Servers view.
2. Select the server you want to configure.
3. Open the Server document and click the Internet Protocols tab.
4. Click the Domino Web Engine tab.
5. Go to the Display Conversion section and change the settings as appropriate.
6. Click Save and Close to save your changes.

Specify the Size of the Result Set

Users can specify the number of documents they would like to see in the result set by using the SearchMax parameter with the SearchSite and SearchView commands.

Troubleshooting

Domino is a complex product and when problems occur, there are usually many factors that can come into play. This section explains some common problems you might have with the HTTP server, some tools that you can use to aid your diagnoses of problems and some other resources you can turn to get help.

(HTTP) Access Problems

The following sections describe some of the most common Domino access problems.

Anonymous Users Cannot Access Resources

The following are some common reasons why Anonymous users may not be able to access resources:

- The Server document has the Allow anonymous HTTP connections field in the server document set to No, requiring all users to authenticate immediately.

- The database being accessed has its ACL configured to disallow anonymous access. If the Default and the Anonymous entries are set to No Access in the ACL, every user must authenticate.

- The resources being accessed have been secured at the form, view, or document level and anonymous users have not been granted access.

Authenticated Users Cannot Access Resources

The following are some common reasons why Anonymous users may not be able to access resources:

- A database is configured to allow a Maximum Internet name & password access of No Access. This will prevent any browser access. Check the Advanced tab of the database ACL.

- The ACL for the resource (database, view, form, document) is configured incorrectly or the user in question is not named explicitly or in a group in the database ACL.

- The user is not entering the proper name and password pair. Users accessing Domino resources through a browser must enter a password matching the value for Internet password in their person document.

Users Are Required to Authenticate More Than Once at the Same Site

The Domino HTTP server adheres to the industry standard HTTP authentication model. When a user accesses a secured resource, they are immediately prompted for their credentials, which are then cached based on the realm that the Domino server sends to the browser.

After a user has authenticated with a particular realm, he can access all resources within the realm, including lower-level realms. However, if he attempts to access resources in peer realms, or higher realms, he will need to be authenticated for those realms.

The following example will help to illustrate this concept. If you access `www.defin-iti.com` , `www.definiti.com` is the top-level realm. Other branches of the site, such as Services (`www.definiti.com/services`), Products (`www.definiti.com/products`) and Opportunities (`www.definiti.com/jobs`), are lower-level realms.

If a user authenticates when accessing the home page for `www.definiti.com`, they are also authenticated for all lower-level realms, meaning that they will not need to reauthenticate for any resources within the site.

However, if the authenticates with the `www.definiti.com/products` realm first, and then accesses `www.definiti.com/jobs`, they will be required to authenticate again. This occurs because the browser examines the list of realms for which the user has been authenticated and finds that the user has not been authenticated for this realm or its parent.

To prevent multiple authentication prompts, ensure that the user is authenticated at the highest-level realm.

The Domino Server Stops Using Domino for IIS

If you are using Domino for IIS and the server will start then stop immediately, check the server's ID for a password. The server ID used with Domino for IIS cannot be password protected.

Realms

A *realm* is a string (usually the URL path) sent by the server that indicates the location for which the user has been authenticated.

Authentication

Bear in mind that the user may be required to authenticate again if they follow links to other sites.

Users Cannot Access the Web Server

Any number of reasons could cause users to be unable to connect to a Domino server. The following are some of the most common reasons.

TCP/IP Issues

TCP/IP issues can be broken down into two basic categories for the depth of coverage we can provide in this book (As you probably know, there are entire books written about TCP/IP): User configuration problems and Server configuration problems.

User TCP/IP Issues

The TCP/IP stack on a users workstation may not be configured properly, preventing them from accessing the server. While configuring the TCP/IP stack for a user's workstation is well beyond the scope of this book, there are a few basic things you can do to confirm that the problem is at the user's workstation.

- Check the network cable and ensure that it is plugged in at each end.
- Ensure that the network card senses the connection (usually a green light).
- Check the network settings for the Operation System on the workstation.
- On Windows based workstations, open a DOS window and type `PING 127.0.0.1` (a loop back address for the local machine, also known as localhost). If the message "Request timed out" is returned, the TCP/IP protocol is misconfigured.
- On Windows based workstations, if you can ping 127.0.0.1 open a DOS window and try to ping the Domino server. For example, you could try `PING www.definiti.com` (you could also try the IP address). If the message "Request timed out" is returned, the TCP/IP protocol is misconfigured.

If you cannot ping a remote site by its name (`www.definiti.com`, for example) try its IP address, which will confirm that the problem might lie in DNS.

If the server can be pinged then the problem is most likely related to the browser configuration, or the Domino server is not configured properly.

User TCP/IP Issues

The following list describes some common TCP/IP issues:

- Check the network cable and ensure that it is plugged in at each end.
- Ensure that the network card sense the connection (usually a green light).
- Check the network settings for the Operating System on the server.
- On Windows based servers, open a DOS window and type `PING 127.0.0.1` (a loop back address for the local machine, also know as localhost). If the message "Request timed out" is returned, the TCP/IP protocol is misconfigured.

- On Windows based servers, if you can ping 127.0.0.1 open a DOS window and try to ping other servers. For example, you could try PING www.definiti.com (you could also try the IP address). If the message "Request timed out" is returned, the TCP/IP protocol is misconfigured.

- Ensure that the Domino server is running.

- Ensure that the HTTP server is running. At the server console, or using the remote console in the Domino Administrator, type sh ta and look for the HTTP server task.

- Check the server document in the Domino Directory and ensure that the HTTP port number is configured and is enabled.

- Ensure that there is not a conflict with the port number specified. Many services such as FTP user specific ports (20 and 21 for FTP) be sure that if you don't use port 80, it is not conflicting with another service.

- Check the server document in the Domino Directory and ensure the appropriate security settings have been made so that your target audience can access the server.

- Start a browser on the server and attempt to access the server.

If all of the above check out, the problem is most likely in the network (firewalls, routers, bridges, and so on), or the user's browser/OS is not configured correctly.

Browser Configuration Issues

If a user cannot get to the Domino server, if may be because their browser is configured incorrectly. Determine if the user needs to access a proxy server first and if so, then determine the address and protocols for the proxy. You can then get into the browsers connection properties and configuring it correctly. Sometimes, the converse is true as well. The browser is configured to use proxy, but one if not needed.

Explicit Port Numbers

Remember that if you've specified a port for HTTP other than 80 (the default), you need to tell users so that they can enter the port number in their URLs. For example, http://www.definiti.com:8080.

Troubleshooting Tools

Domino provides several tools to help you troubleshoot problems. This section focuses primarily on tools that can help you troubleshoot problems with the Domino HTTP server and. Most of the tools are available through the Domino Administrator.

The Domino Administrator

The Domino Administrator is a powerful new tool that provides you with a one-stop-shopping interface to administrate and troubleshoot problems with Domino. When attempting to troubleshoot problems with the HTTP server, there are two features that will be especially helpful. The first is the Server\Status tab, which displays the status of the tasks running on the server. It is shown below in Figure 15.24.

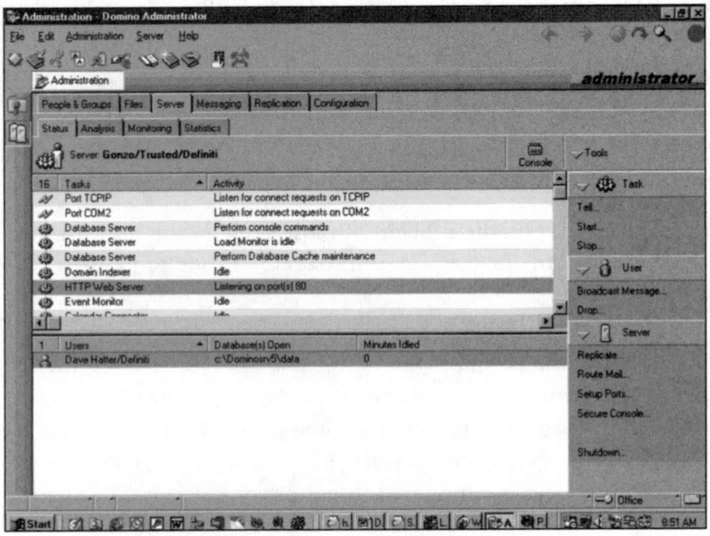

Figure 15.24   The Server Status tab of the Domino Administrator.

The second is the Server\Statistic tab, which displays a number of useful statistics about the Domino server, such as, the number of requests the HTTP server is handling (or if it is getting any requests). It is shown in Figure 15.25.

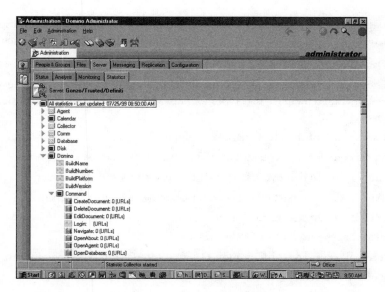

Figure 15.25   The Server Statistics tab of the Domino Administrator.

Domino Server Log File

Every Domino server has a log file, the Notes Log (LOG.NSF) that tracks server activity and provides detailed information about databases and users on the server. But, each Domino server can be configured to log HTTP server related information to either a Notes database, or to text files in the file system. Keep in mind that on very busy sites, or on sites that you want to use 3rd part log analysis tools such as Webtrends, you should log to text files.

Activity Logging

You cannot turn on the capability of the HTTP server to log activity. This is a configurable setting. Open the Domino Directory and find your server document in the Servers view. Open the server document and click the Internet Protocols tab. On the HTTP tab, ensure that one or both methods of logging (to DOM-LOG.NSF or text files) has been enabled.

After logging has been enabled, the log files provide you with a plethora of useful information about what's happening on your site. The information logged includes:

- Date and time the request was made.
- User's IP address or the DNS name if DNS lookup is enabled in the Server document. Remember that DNS lookups will negatively affect server performance.
- User's name (if the credentials were supplied).
- Status code for the request. This indicates if the request was successful.
- Amount of data, in bytes, sent from the server to satisfy the request.
- Type of data accessed by the user, for example, text/html or image/jpg.
- HTTP request sent to the server.
- Browser type used to make the request.
- Internal server and/or Common Gateway Interface (CGI) program errors.
- Referring URL.
- Server's IP address or DNS name.
- Amount of time, in milliseconds, to process the request.

Figure 15.26 illustrates the Domino Web Server log.

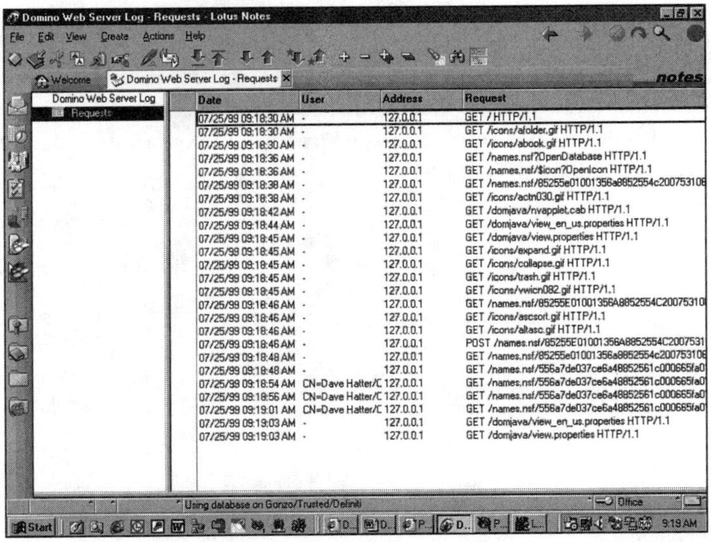

Figure 15.26 The Requests view of the Domino Web Server Log.

PING Utility

Most operating systems that include a TCP/IP stack come with the Packet Internet Grouper (PING) utility. This application allows you to test TCP/IP connectivity and can be a useful tool for determining where a problem lies. For example, if you can't ping the server from one workstation, but you can from another, the problem is certainly not in the server and most likely is in the workstation, or the network segment to which it's connected.

On a Windows based system (95, 98, NT) you can open DOS window and type PING <someaddress> where <someaddress> is the IP address or hostname of the server that you want to test. Figure 15.27 shows the PING utility. If you need help with using PING, simply start it with no parameters, (type PING) and it will display all the parameters that it accepts and what they mean.

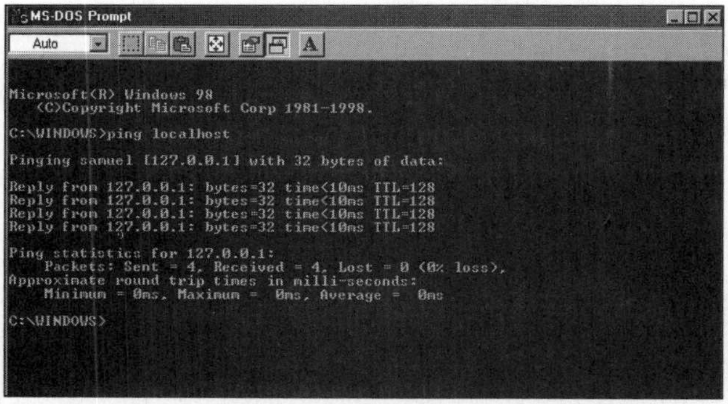

Figure 15.27 The PING utility.

If you can PING the server, then you know that there are no network connectivity issues.

Telnet

Like PING, most operating systems that support TCP/IP come with Telnet, a program that allows you to connect to a remote host over TCP/IP. You can use Telnet to determine if your Domino server is listening for HTTP requests on port 80 (or the port you have specified) by telneting to the host and specifying a port. To run Telnet on a Windows based system (95, 98, NT) open a DOS window and type Telnet. Choose Connect, then when prompted, enter the IP address or host name of the remote host and the port. You can then type in something (anything) and you should get a response from the HTTP server if it's running. Figure 15.28 illustrates the response from Domino's HTTP server.

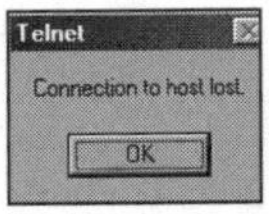

Figure 15.28 Domino's response to Telnet.

Telnet is installed on all Windows operating systems by default and can help you determine if the server is listening on the designated port. If you can Telnet to the HTTP port, but can't access the server with a browser, the browser is probably not configured properly.

Trace Route (tracert)

Like Telnet and PING, most TCP/IP enabled operating systems also include trace route (tracert). This can often help pinpoint the exactly where in your network problems are occurring. On a Windows based system, you can drop to a DOS window and type `tracert <someaddress>` where `<someaddress>` is a TCP/IP address or host name. Figure 15.29 shows a trace to www.definiti.com. If you need help, type `tracert` with no parameter to get the list of supported options.

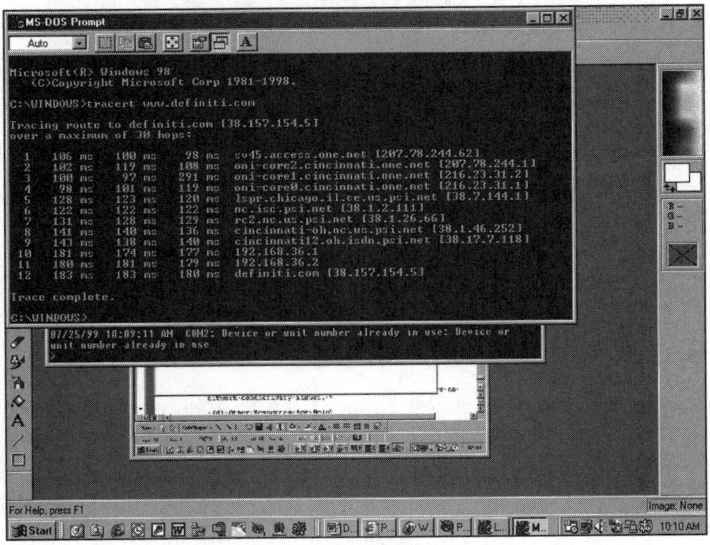

Figure 15.29 A trace to Definiti.

Other Resources for Help

The following resources can often be invaluable when you are having trouble with Domino:

- The Domino 5 Administration Help Database (`help5_admin.nsf`).
- The Notes Knowledge Base database (`kbnv11.nsf`)
- The Business Partner Technical Forum database (`bptech98.nsf`). You must be a Lotus Business Partner to get this database.

If you still haven't solved your problem after reading this section and using the resources, you will probably want to call Lotus Customer support directly for help with troubleshooting your problem.

Other Notes/Domino Resources

You can get much of the information found in the notes Knowledge Base and the Business Partner Technical Forum databases from these Lotus and Notes Net Web sites:

- http://www.lotus.com
- http://www.notes.net
- http://www.dominoedge.com
- http://www.dominohive.com
- http://www.dominopower.com

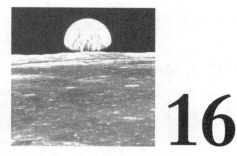

16

POP3 Mail Service

DOMINO IS OPTIONALLY A POP3 (Post Office Protocol, version 3) mail server. As a POP3 server, it can receive and store mail for users of POP3 mail client programs, then send the held mail to the POP3 clients on request. It monitors TCP port 110. When a POP3 client wants to pick up mail, it connects to that port and the client and server exchange commands and responses, in the process transferring waiting mail to the client.

POP3 does not provide a method for users to send mail, only to receive it. POP3 clients typically use SMTP (Simple Mail Transfer Protocol) to send mail, connecting to an SMTP relay host to do so. The SMTP relay host may be the same computer as runs POP3 or a different one. Because the Domino router uses SMTP, Domino can provide the outgoing mail service for its POP3 mail clients.

POP3 is an Internet mail protocol that was developed to enable Internet mail users to manage their personal mail off-line. Development of Post Office Protocol began in 1984, a time when it was becoming clear that, with the spread of personal computers, it was less and less likely that users' computers would be connected full-time to the Internet. Previously users logged onto larger computers that typically remained on all the time and were continuously connected to the network. They could only access their mail accounts on those computers while logged on.

POP Mail and Domino

A user with a POP account on a Domino server has a Person document in the Domino Directory and a mail database on the server. The mail database is a standard Notes mail database. The Domino router deposits mail addressed to the person into his mail database in the same way it deposits mail into any user's database. Because the user is a POP3 user, the router converts the message to MIME format. To pick up his mail, a user authenticates with the Domino server, so that the server knows who the user is and which mail file belongs to the user. POP users can authenticate using either basic name and password authentication or SSL authentication.

When a POP user picks up his mail from a Domino POP server, he optionally deletes the mail from the server or leaves a copy of it there.

Virtually all Internet mail programs support POP3, including the following, which are the most widely used on Windows-based computers:

- Microsoft Outlook Express
- Netscape Messenger
- Eudora Pro Mail
- Lotus Notes Mail (4.6 and later)

POP Mail Versus IMAP Mail

The limitation of POP3 mail is that the user can only download and read his mail locally. POP3 does not provide for reading or working with mail on the mail server. Because of that failing, POP3 is gradually being supplanted by IMAP (Internet Message Access Protocol), which Domino also supports (see Chapter 17, "IMAP Mail Service"). An IMAP mail user can either work with his mail on the mail server or download it into his local mail program.

Domino POP mail users can partially overcome this limitation. They can use a Web browser to access their mail and interact with it directly on the server (by entering a URL something like this: `http://mailservername/mail/mailfilename.nsf`). However, any mail that they delete from the server when downloading it to their mail reader is permanently lost from the server. Also, there is no connection between their mail reader and their mail database on the Domino server. So, if a user creates a folder in either place (locally using the mail reader or on the server using their Web browser) and moves mail into the folder, the change is not recognized in the other place.

Therefore, if you have to choose between standardizing on POP mail or IMAP mail for your Internet users, and all other things are equal, you would normally prefer IMAP mail over POP mail. In general, if you already have a large population of POP3 mail users and you want to transfer them to Domino servers in the least painful way, Domino POP3 is the way to go. If you need to support mail users who can only use POP3 mail readers, POP3 is also the way to go. In all other cases, you should go with IMAP.

You can, of course, support both POP *and* IMAP mail on a Domino server, thus meeting everyone's needs. I would, if I needed to.

Setting Up POP Mail on Domino Servers

To set up POP mail on a Domino server you have to perform the following steps:

1. Set up and configure TCP/IP on the Domino server and in the underlying operating system.
2. Configure the POP3 server.
3. Run the POP3 server task.
4. To provide outgoing mail service, set up an SMTP server. You can set up SMTP on the POP3 server, another Domino server, or a non-Domino server.
5. Register POP mail users in the Domino Directory.
6. Set up user mail software on user workstations.

The procedure for setting up SMTP on a Domino server is in Chapter 8, "Mail Routing Setup and Maintenance." The other procedures appear in the next sections, at least in part.

Configuring TCP/IP

To set up a Domino server to use TCP/IP, you have to first install it correctly in the server's operating system. Then you can enable a TCP/IP port on the Domino server, using the methods described in Chapter 3, "First Server Installation and Setup."

You also have to make sure your POP3 mail users can connect to their mail server. In most installations, this means that the Domino server must be listed properly in the local domain name server. If the Domino server name is different from the IP host name of the box on which it is running, the name server should hold records for both names. That is, there should be an A (Address) record that ties the host name to an IP address and a CNAME (Canonical Name) record that lists the Domino server's common name as an alias for the computer's host name. If users will be accessing the mail server from the Internet, it should have a constant connection to the Internet and use a registered IP address.

So, for example, your POP3 server is called `Mail01/PlanetNotes`. The computer on which it resides has host name `domsrv01.planetnotes.com`. Its assigned IP address is `10.0.0.10`. You would need an A record in DNS stating that `domsrv01.planetnotes.com` is assigned IP address `10.0.0.10`. If you want your mail users to be able to reach its Domino common name, Mail01, you need a CNAME record in DNS stating that `mail01.planetnotes.com` is really `domsrv01.planetnotes.com`. If your mail users are connecting from the Internet, Mail01 needs a constant connection (via router to T-1, for example) to your ISP; it needs a permanent, registered IP address (assigned by your ISP); and the preceding records need to be set up in your ISP's DNS database.

Configuring POP3

You can configure a Domino POP server in its server document in the Domain Directory. In Domino Administrator, open the Server document in the Configuration screen. Then choose Ports, Internet Ports, and Mail. Set up the fields in the Mail (POP) column as follows in Table 16.1.

Table 16.1   **Setup of the Fields in the Mail (POP) Column**

Field Name	Description
TCP/IP port number	Normally, you should leave this at the default setting, 110, which is the standard port used by all POP mail servers. You may have to change it, however, if you have more than one POP3 mail server running on one computer, as you might if you run multiple Domino partitions on one box.
TCP/IP port status	Set this to Enabled to use standard POP mail. Set it to Disabled if you want to force POP mail users to use the SSL port instead.
Authentication options: Name & password	This is a computed field that automatically sets to Yes if you enable the TCP/IP port, No if you disable it.
Authentication options: Anonymous	This is not an option because Domino must always authenticate mail users or it could not tell which mail database to use.
SSL port number	Normally, you should leave this set to 995, the standard port for POP over SSL. You may have to change it, however, if you have more than one POP3 mail server running on one computer, as you might if you run multiple Domino partitions on one box.
SSL port status	This is disabled by default. Enable it to give Domino the option to use SSL to authenticate POP mail users. If you want to force users to authenticate using SSL, you should also disable the TCP/IP port. If you disable both ports, you disable POP3 mail service entirely.
Authentication options: Client certificate	Defaults to No. Set it to Yes if you want POP mail clients to present an X.509 certificate to authenticate with the server.
Authentication options: Name & password	Defaults to Yes. Set it to No to require POP mail users to present a certificate during authentication.

You can configure POP mail three different ways:

- Using the TCP/IP port (110) only
- Using the SSL port (995) only
- Using both ports

If you enable both ports, users can use either one to access their mail—their choice. If you enable the SSL port, you can enable SSL authentication three different ways:

- Client required to present a certificate. (Client certificate = Yes; Name & password = No)

- Client required to enter a name and password (Client certificate = No; Name & password = Yes)

- Client may present a certificate or enter a name and password (Client certificate = Yes; Name & password = Yes). Domino will attempt certificate-based authentication of the user; if that fails (probably because the user has no certificates that the server trusts), Domino will demand a name and password, which it will compare with Person documents in the Domino Directory to find a match.

If you enable the SSL port, Domino will not let you save the server document if you set both SSL Authentication options to No.

Additional Configuration Required on a Partitioned Server

If the POP mail server is a partitioned Domino server, you have to add the following variable to its `notes.ini` file, which is located in the partitioned server's data folder:

```
POP3Address=IP Address
```

or

```
POP3Address=Fully Qualified Domain Name
```

where `IP Address` is the server's IP address (for example, 192.168.1.12) and `Fully Qualified Domain Name` (FQDN) is the computer's full host name, not its Domino name. Which version of this variable you should use depends on your assessment of which is likely to change more often, the server's IP address or its FQDN. Our server, Mail01, might have either of the following variables set:

```
POP3Address=10.0.0.10
```

or

```
POP3Address=domsrv01.planetnotes.com
```

Running the POP3 Server Task

You can start (and stop) the POP3 server task manually or you can have it start automatically whenever the Domino server starts. You of course want it to start automatically and run all the time, so you don't have to remember to start it each time you restart the server.

To set up Domino to start POP3 automatically, append `POP3` to the end of the `ServerTasks` variable in the server's `notes.ini` file. For example, if the `ServerTasks` variable is set as follows:

```
ServerTasks=Router,Replica,Update,Amgr,AdminP,HTTP
```

Change it so that it reads:

```
ServerTasks=Router,Replica,Update,Amgr,AdminP,HTTP,POP3
```

The `notes.ini` file may be located in the Domino server program folder, or (in partitioned servers) the Domino server's data folder, or (in Windows-based servers upgraded from R4.x) in the Windows folder. You can edit the file directly in a text editor or indirectly either by entering a command at the server console or by adding the `ServerTasks` variable setting to a server configuration document.

To set the `ServerTasks` variable at the server console, first determine the current value of ServerTasks with the following command:

```
Show Config ServerTasks
```

Then, assuming the value of ServerTasks is the same as in the previous example, enter the following command:

```
Set Config ServerTasks=Router,Replica,Update,Amgr,AdminP,HTTP,POP3
```

If you use this method, type very carefully. A typographical error here could sink your server the next time it restarts. Proofread your command before and after entering it.

To use a server configuration document to set the `ServerTasks` variable, open Domino Administrator to the Configuration screen and either open an existing server configuration document or create a new one. In the NOTES.INI Setting screen, choose Set/Modify Parameters. Enter `ServerTasks` in the Item field and the full, comma-delimited string of server tasks in the Value field, then click Next, then OK. Then, save and close the document.

Again, carefully proofread your entry before and after you enter it. In fact, to minimize the chance of making an error, consider cutting and pasting the values from the server's `notes.ini` file to these fields. That way you do a minimum of actual typing.

To start and stop the POP3 server task manually, either enter commands at the server console or use Domino Administrator to start and stop it. The command to start POP3 is

```
load POP3
```

The command to stop POP3 is

```
tell pop3 quit
```

or

```
tell pop3 exit
```

To use Domino Administrator to start POP3, open the Server, Status screen. In the Tasks pane, choose Start, then choose POP3 Mail Server in the dialog box. When it starts, it will appear in the Results pane. To stop POP3 this way, select any instance of POP3 Server in the Results pane, then choose Stop in the Tasks pane.

Registering POP3 Mail Users

A POP3 mail user does not need a Notes ID unless he is also a Notes user. Therefore, you can register a POP3 mail user manually, if you want to, by simply creating a Person document and a mail database for him, and by adding him to any groups he should belong to. On the other hand, if you register a POP3 user in the Register User dialog box, Domino Administrator will do all of that work for you. You just have to pay special attention to a couple of the fields in the dialog box.

To register a POP3 mail user manually, follow these steps:

1. Create a Person document. In Domino Administrator, choose the People & Groups tab, choose the POP3 Domino server (or another server in the same domain as the POP3 server), open the People view, and then choose Add Person. Complete the following fields in Table 16.2.

Table 16.2 **Setup of Fields in the Add Person Box**

Field Name	Description
	ON THE BASICS TAB
First name	Complete all three fields. The User name
Last name	field should be a combination of the First
User name	name and Last name fields.
Internet password	The password that the user will enter to access the mail server. Do not leave this field blank.
	ON THE MAIL TAB
Mail system	Choose "POP or IMAP"
Domain	The name of the mail server's Domino domain
Mail server	The fully distinguished Notes name of the user's POP3 mail server
Mail file	The partial pathname (beginning at the Domino data folder) of the user's mail database (for example, data\filename). You can leave the .nsf extension off of the filename if you like.

continues

Table 16.2 **Continued**

Field Name	Description
Forwarding address	Leave blank
Internet address	Enter a valid Internet address for the user. The same address should appear in the user's POP3 client.
Format preference for incoming mail	Choose "Prefers MIME."
Encrypt incoming mail	Choose "No."

2. Add the user to whatever groups he should belong.

3. Create a mail file on the POP3 server. Base it on the Mail(R5.0) template.

4. In the access control list of the new mail file, set the default access to No access and the user and the mail server to Manager with Delete documents access. Remove all other entries from the ACL, including yourself.

If you register a POP mail user in the Register Person dialog box, choose Advanced in the upper left-hand corner of the dialog box, then fill in the fields as usual, with the following exceptions (see Table 16.3).

Table 16.3 **Setup of Fields in the Register Person Dialog Box**

Field	Description
	ON THE MAIL PANE
Mail system	Choose "POP"
	ON THE ID INFO PANE
Location for storing user ID	Deselect both choices ("In Domino directory" and "In file"). This will prevent the creation of an ID file, which this user has no use for anyway.

Configuring User Mail Software

Exactly how you configure each POP mail client program depends on the design of that program, of course. However, each such program will need the following information from you:

- The POP3 mail server's fully qualified domain name (for example, osprey. planetnotes.com).

- The SMTP server's fully qualified domain name.

- The user's account name, which is the user's name in the Person document you created.

- Whether it should direct the POP mail server to delete messages from the server after downloading them. If you expect a user to access his mail on the server (using Notes, an IMAP client, or a Web browser) as well as locally in his POP mail client, the user should choose not to delete downloaded messages from the server.

Other options that a user may have to choose depend entirely on the features of the mail program itself. Some Internet mail programs have many features and options to choose from. Others are small and lean and offer very few options.

Tuning the POP3 Service

There are a series of notes.ini variables that you can set to refine the way the POP3 mail service works. They are as defined in Table 16.4:

Table 16.4 *notes.ini* **Variables**

Variable	Description
POP3DNSLookup=*value*	Set to 1 to enable reverse DNS lookups of client host names. Defaults to 0, which disables reverse DNS lookups.
POP3ExactSize=*value*	Set to 1 to cause POP3 to return the exact size of waiting messages. Defaults to 0, which permits POP3 to return an estimated message size.
	If POP3ExactSize is enabled, the PASS command may timeout. This is because all messages must be converted to compute the exact size for the STAT command. This conversion can take a long time, especially if there are numerous or large messages. Set this variable only if POP3 mail clients require exact message sizes.
	Alternatively, you can set the "POP3 server returns exact size of message" in a Configuration document to either "Enabled" or "Disabled". If you set this variable both in the Configuration document and in notes.ini, the setting in the Configuration document will take precedence.

continues

Table 16.4 **Continued**

Variable	Description
POP3NotesPort=*portnumber*	You can use this variable instead of the "TCP/IP port number" field in the server document to set the port number (other than 110) that the POP mail service should monitor.
	Administration Help for Domino Administrator 5.0a states that you must set this variable on a partitioned server, but in fact you do not.
POP3_Config_Update_Interval=*minutes*	Defaults to 2 minutes. Determines how frequently the POP3 service will update its configuration information.
POP3_Disable_Cache=*value*	Set to 1 to enable message caching for users. Defaults to 0, message caching disabled.
POP3_Domain=*domainname*	Sets a server-level default return address for POP3 mail users. The server will use the entry in the "Internet address" field of a POP3 user's Person document, if it is not blank. If it is blank, the server will use the entry in this variable. If neither is available, the server will use the value in the "Local primary Internet domain" field of the default Global Domain document, if any. If none, the server will use the domain name in its own TCP/IP stack. And if that is unavailable, the POP3 service will generate an initialization error.
POP3_MarkRead=*value*	Set to 1 to have the server mark messages as read upon downloading. Default is 0, messages not marked as read.
POP3_Messag_Stat_Cache_NumPerUser=*number*	Sets the maximum number of messages for which statistics will be cached for each user. Cached statistics include UNIDs and saved message sizes. Cache entries are computationally expensive, because the server must calculate the message size of each cache entry. They also consume RAM. Defaults to 50. Set a lower number if server performance is low.

Monitoring the Quality of POP3 Service

To ensure that the POP3 service is maintained at a high level of quality, consider defining one or more TCP Server probes. Specifically you want to probe the POP3 service. You can create a probe in Domino Administrator, in the Configuration screen. Choose Statistics & Events, Probes, TCP Server in the Tasks pane. Then choose New TCP Server Probe in the Action Bar over the Results pane. If one doesn't already exist, create a probe in which you choose "All Domino servers in the domain will probe their own configured ports". In addition, create at least one probe in which one server is probing another.

If the Event task is running on each probing server, creating this probe will cause the server to generate quality of service statistics on each running Internet service. It will also cause Alarms to appear in the Statistics Reports database if a timeout occurs before the probe returns a response from the probed service.

You can view statistics in the Statistics pane of the Server screen in Domino Administrator, and optionally in the Monitor pane as well. If the Collector service on any server is collecting statistics from the server in question, statistics reports will also accumulate in the Statistics Reports database. To learn more about these features of Domino, see Chapter 18, "Server Monitoring."

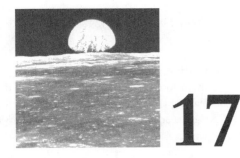

17

IMAP Mail Service

D OMINO IS OPTIONALLY AN IMAP (Internet Message Access Protocol, version 4, rev. 1) mail server. As an IMAP server, it can receive and store mail for users of IMAP mail client programs, then interact with the IMAP clients on request. It monitors TCP port 143.

IMAP does not provide a method for users to send mail, only to receive it. IMAP clients typically use SMTP (Simple Mail Transfer Protocol) to send mail, connecting to an SMTP relay host to do so. The SMTP relay host may be the same computer as runs IMAP or a different one. Because the Domino router uses SMTP, Domino can provide the outgoing mail service for its IMAP mail clients.

The IMAP paradigm defines three basic modes of access to a remote message store, that is, to one's messages waiting on a mail server:

- **Online.** The mail client reads messages one-at-a-time from the mail server, manipulates them in memory (for example, moves to a folder, edits, deletes), then stores the results back to the mail server. This is how Notes users work with their mail when the "Mail file location" field in their current Location document is set to "on Server."

- **Offline.** The mail client reads messages in a batch from the mail server, stores them locally, then (optionally but by default) deletes them from the mail server, leaving the copies on the mail client as the only remaining copies. The mail user then reads, edits, deletes, and moves to folders all locally. This is how POP mail works.

- **Disconnected.** The mail client reads messages in a batch from the mail server and stores "cache" copies locally. The mail user manipulates the cache copies in memory and saves the changes back to the local cache. At any later time the user can reconnect to the mail server and synchronize the changed cache copies with the originals still stored on the server. It is similar to the way Notes users work when the "Mail file location" field on their current Location document is set to "Local."

Support of all these modes means IMAP affords users great versatility. They can access their mail from any available workstation and work on it online, disconnected or, if they want, offline in the POP mode. Their messages aren't "trapped" on a specific workstation as they are under POP3. Rather, the "master" copy of each message remains on the mail server.

In addition, IMAP version 4 supports shared folders, which enables it to support Notes-like discussions and collaboration. It supports hierarchical folders. It supports the MIME protocol and can determine the internal structure of a MIME message remotely, then download only individual parts of the message, such as message summaries; this promotes efficient data transfer, and is especially nice when one connects to the server by modem.

Because IMAP is such a versatile mail protocol, support for it in mail clients is fast becoming universal. The most recent versions of many mail client programs support it, including the following, which are the most widely used on Windows-based computers:

- Microsoft Outlook Express, a component of Internet Explorer 4 and later.
- Netscape Messenger, a component of Netscape Communicator 4.0 and later.
- Eudora Pro Mail 3.1
- PC-Pine 3.0
- Simeon 4.1
- Lotus Notes (4.6 and later)

IMAP Mail Versus POP Mail

IMAP and POP mail were developed to serve different purposes. POP mail was intended to enable mail users to work offline. A POP mail client downloads messages from a POP mail server, then typically (though optionally) deletes the copies on the server. In the end, the only copies of the messages reside on the client computer. In a sense, a POP mail server used in this way is just a relay host—a place to hold mail temporarily until the user can pick it up.

IMAP, on the other hand, provides users the capability to work with their mail from more than one computer. Because the primary copy of every IMAP mail message is maintained on the IMAP server, even if one downloads copies to an IMAP client, users can work with the mail from another client on another computer.

More and more people are finding that the IMAP model serves them better than the POP model. They have one computer at work, another at home, and possibly a laptop computer for their travels. As a result, IMAP is fast supplanting POP as the dominant kind of Internet mail service.

On the other hand, many people have multiple mail accounts with different mail providers—say, one at work, another with AOL, and another with Yahoo. With so many Internet portal services offering free mail accounts, it's easy to accumulate multiple mail accounts. Some people actually manage their mail this way. For example, they may give out one email address to business contacts, another to personal acquaintances, and a third to commercial Web sites with which they register. That way they can separate business from pleasure and segregate junk mail from the rest of their mail. For a person such as this, having to manage multiple IMAP mail accounts might be a hassle. They might prefer POP mail accounts, so they can download messages from multiple sources into a single program.

From the mail service provider's point of view, POP mail puts a relatively lighter burden on server resources than does IMAP mail. Under POP, the mail arrives; The user connects and removes the mail. Unless a user doesn't pick up his mail or elects not to delete it after download, the mail doesn't accumulate on the server.

IMAP mail, on the other hand, accumulates on the server over time, just as Notes mail does. In addition, the IMAP server has to do a lot more processing than the POP server, as IMAP users create and remove folders and move messages from one folder to another. Finally, on a Domino server at least, setting up IMAP involves the extra step of enabling IMAP features in the user's Notes mail database. You don't have to do anything of the kind when setting up a POP mail user.

If you have to choose between supporting POP and IMAP, IMAP is probably the better choice. It's a functional superset of POP, so mail users could use it like a POP mail account if they like. But, on a Domino server, there's really not much reason to choose between them. If you have non-Notes mail users, support whichever meets your and your users' needs, and don't hesitate to support both.

IMAP Mail and Domino

A user with an IMAP account on a Domino server has a Person document in the Domino Directory and a mail database on the server. The mail database is a slightly modified Notes mail database. The Domino router deposits mail addressed to the person into his mail database in the same way it deposits mail into any user's database. Because the user is an IMAP user, the router converts the message to MIME format.

To work with his mail, a user authenticates with the Domino server, so that the server knows who the user is and which mail file belongs to the user. IMAP users can authenticate using either basic name and password authentication or SSL authentication. SSL is an Internet standard authentication scheme that, like Notes authentication, is certificate-based and therefore more secure than name-and-password authentication. See Chapter 10, "Security," to learn more about authentication.

Setting Up IMAP Mail on Domino Servers

To set up IMAP mail on a Domino server you have to perform the following steps:

1. Set up and configure TCP/IP on the Domino server and in the underlying operating system.
2. Configure the IMAP server.
3. Run the IMAP server task.
4. To provide outgoing mail service, set up an SMTP server. You can set up SMTP on the IMAP server, another Domino server, or a non-Domino server.
5. Register IMAP mail users in the Domino Directory.
6. Enable IMAP mail users' mail files for IMAP access.
7. Optionally full-text index IMAP mail users' mail files.
8. Set up user mail software on user workstations.

The procedure for setting up SMTP on a Domino server is in Chapter 8. The other procedures appear in the sections that follow, at least in part.

Configuring TCP/IP

To set up a Domino server to use TCP/IP, you have to install it correctly in the server's operating system first. Then you can enable a TCP/IP port on the Domino server, using the methods described in Chapter 3, "First Server Installation and Setup."

You also have to make sure your IMAP mail users can connect to the mail server. In most installations this means that the Domino server must be listed properly in the local domain name server. If the Domino server name is different from the IP host name of the box on which it is running, the name server should hold records for both names. That is, there should be an A (Address) record that ties the host name to an IP address and a CNAME (Canonical Name) record that lists the Domino server's common name as an alias for the computer's host name. If users will be accessing the mail server from the Internet, it should have a constant connection to the Internet and use a registered IP address.

Configuring IMAP

You can configure a Domino IMAP server in its server document in the Domain Directory. In Domino Administrator, open the server document in the Configuration screen. Then choose Ports, Internet Ports, and Mail. Set up the fields in the Mail (IMAP) column as follows in Table 17.1:

Table 17.1 **Field Setup in the Mail (IMAP) Column**

Field Name	Description
TCP/IP port number	Normally you should leave this at the default setting, 143, which is the standard port used by all IMAP mail servers.
TCP/IP port status	Set this to Enabled to use standard IMAP mail. Set it to Disabled if you want to force IMAP mail users to use the SSL port instead.
Authentication options: Name & password	This is a computed field that automatically sets to Yes if you enable the TCP/IP port, No if you disable it.
Authentication options: Anonymous	This is not an option because Domino must always authenticate mail users or it could not tell which mail database to use.
SSL port number	Normally you should leave this set to 993, the standard port for IMAP over SSL.
SSL port status	This is disabled by default. Enable it to give Domino the option to use SSL to authenticate IMAP mail users. If you want to force users to authenticate using SSL, you should also disable the TCP/IP port. If you disable both ports, you disable IMAP mail service entirely.
Authentication options: Client certificate	Defaults to No. Set it to Yes if you want IMAP mail clients to present an X.509 certificate to authenticate with the server.
Authentication options: Name & password	Defaults to Yes. Set it to No to require IMAP mail users to present a certificate during authentication.

You can configure IMAP mail three different ways:

- Using the TCP/IP port (143) only
- Using the SSL port (993) only
- Using both ports

If you enable both ports, users can use either one to access their mail—user's choice. If you enable the SSL port, you can enable SSL authentication three different ways:

- Client required to present a certificate. (Client certificate = Yes; Name & password = No)
- Client required to enter a name and password (Client certificate = No; Name & password = Yes)
- Client may present a certificate or enter a name and password (Client certificate = Yes; Name & password = Yes). Domino will attempt certificate-based authentication of the user; if that fails (probably because the user has no certificates that the server trusts), Domino will demand a name and password, which it will compare with Person documents in the Domino Directory to find a match.

If you enable the SSL port, Domino will not let you save the server document if you set both SSL Authentication options to No.

Additional Configuration Required on a Partitioned Server

If the IMAP mail server is a partitioned Domino server, you have to add one variable to its notes.ini file, which is located in the partitioned server's data folder. The variable is

```
IMAPAddress=IP Address
```

or

```
IMAPAddress=Fully Qualified Domain Name
```

where `IP Address` is the server's IP address (for example, `192.168.1.12`) and `Fully Qualified Domain Name` is the computer's full host name, not its Domino name (that is, `osprey.planetnotes.com`, not `Osprey/Servers/Stillwater`). Which version of this variable you should use depends on your assessment of which is likely to change more often, the server's IP address or its FQDN.

Running the IMAP Server Task

You can start (and stop) the IMAP server task manually or you can have it start automatically whenever the Domino server starts. You of course want it to start automatically and run all the time.

To set up Domino to start IMAP automatically, append `IMAP` to the end of the `ServerTasks` variable in the server's `notes.ini` file. For example, if the `ServerTasks` variable is set as follows:

```
ServerTasks=Router,Replica,Update,Amgr,AdminP,HTTP
```

change it so that it reads:

```
ServerTasks=Router,Replica,Update,Amgr,AdminP,HTTP,IMAP
```

The `notes.ini` file may be located in the Domino server program folder, or (in partitioned servers) the Domino server's data folder, or (in servers upgraded from R4.x) in the Windows folder. You can edit the file directly in a text editor or indirectly either by entering a command at the server console or by adding the ServerTasks variable setting to a server configuration document.

To set the `ServerTasks` variable at the server console, first determine the current value of `ServerTasks` with the following command:

```
Show Config ServerTasks
```

Then, assuming the value of ServerTasks is the same as in the previous example, enter the following command:

```
Set Config ServerTasks=Router,Replica,Update,Amgr,AdminP,HTTP,IMAP
```

If you use this method, type very carefully. A typographical error here could sink your server the next time it restarts. Proofread your command before and after entering it.

To use a server configuration document to set the ServerTasks variable, open Domino Administrator to the Configuration screen and either open an existing server configuration document or create a new one. In the NOTES.INI Setting screen, choose Set/Modify Parameters. Enter ServerTasks in the Item field and the full, comma-delimited string of server tasks in the Value field, then choose Next, then OK. Then save and close the document.

Again, carefully proofread your entry before and after you enter it. In fact, to minimize the chance of making an error, you might consider cutting and pasting the values from the server's `notes.ini` file to these fields. That way you do a minimum of actual typing.

To start and stop the IMAP server task manually, either enter commands at the server console or use Domino Administrator to start and stop it. The command to start IMAP is:

```
load IMAP
```

The command to stop IMAP is:

```
tell IMAP quit
```

or

```
tell IMAP exit
```

To use Domino Administrator to start IMAP, open the Server, Status screen. In the Tasks pane, choose Start, then choose IMAP Mail Server in the dialog box. When it starts it will appear in the Results pane. To stop IMAP this way, select any instance of IMAP Server in the Results pane, then choose Stop in the Tasks pane.

Registering IMAP Mail Users

An IMAP mail user does not need a Notes ID unless he is also a Notes user. Therefore, you can register an IMAP mail user manually, if you want to, by simply creating a Person document and a mail database for him, and by adding him to any groups he should belong to. On the other hand, if you register an IMAP user in the Register User dialog, Domino Administrator will do all of that work for you. You just have to pay special attention to a couple of the fields in the dialog box.

To register an IMAP mail user manually, follow these steps:

1. Create a Person document. In Domino Administrator, choose the People & Groups tab, choose the IMAP Domino server (or another server in the same domain as the IMAP server), open the People view, and then choose Add Person. Complete the following fields (see Table 17.2):

Table 17.2 **Field Setup for Add Person**

Field Name	Description
ON THE BASICS TAB:	
First name	Complete all three fields. The User name
Last name	field should be a combination of the First
User name	name and Last name fields.
Internet password	The password that the user will enter to access the mail server. Do not leave this field blank.
ON THE MAIL TAB:	
Mail system	Choose "POP or IMAP"
Domain	The name of the mail server's Domino domain
Mail server	The fully distinguished Notes name of the user's IMAP mail server
Mail file	The partial pathname (beginning at the Domino data folder) of the user's mail database (for example, `data\filename`). You can leave the `.nsf` extension off of the filename if you like.
Forwarding address	Leave blank
Internet address	Enter a valid Internet address for the user. The same address should also appear in the user's IMAP client.

Field Name	Description
Format preference for incoming mail	Choose "Prefers MIME."
Encrypt incoming mail	Choose "No."

2. Add the user to whatever groups he should belong.
3. Create a mail file on the IMAP server. Base it on the "Mail(R5.0)" template. Optionally create a full-text index for it, so the IMAP user can conduct searches.
4. In the access control list of the new mail file, set the default access to No access and the user and the mail server to Manager with Delete documents access. Remove all other entries from the ACL, including yourself.

If you register an IMAP mail user in the Register Person dialog box, choose Advanced in the upper-left corner of the dialog box, then fill in the fields as usual, with the following exceptions (see Table 17.3):

Table 17.3 **Field Setup in Advanced**

Field Name	Description
ON THE MAIL PANE:	
Mail system	Choose "IMAP."
Create full text index	Consider selecting this, because IMAP client programs can take advantage of it.
ON THE ID INFO PANE:	
Location for storing user ID	Deselect both choices ("In Domino directory" and "In file"). This will prevent the creation of an ID file, which this user has no use for anyway.

Enabling Notes Mail Databases for IMAP Access

Although Notes mail and IMAP mail do analogous things, they are different enough that a Notes mail database is not inherently IMAP-compliant. To make it so, you have to run a conversion program on it—the same conversion program you would run to convert R4 Notes mail to R5 Notes mail, but this time with the -m switch included. At the server console, enter a command using the following syntax:

```
load convert -m MailFilePathName
```

where *MailFilePathName* is the partial path name, relative to the Domino data folder, of a mail file or mail folder. For example, to enable IMAP features of Joe Doaks's mail database, located in the mail folder, enter the following command:

```
load convert -m mail\jdoaks.nsf
```

To enable IMAP features in every mail database in the mail folder, enter the following command:

```
load convert -m mail\*.nsf
```

Finally, if you did not enable full-text indexing of the mail database when you created it, consider doing so now. Unlike POP3 clients, IMAP clients can conduct full-text searches of Domino mail databases. To enable full-text indexing of an existing mail database, select it in the Files screen of Domino Administrator, then choose Full Text Index in the Database section of the Tools pane.

Configuring User Mail Software

Exactly how you configure each IMAP mail client program depends on its design, of course. However, each such program will need the following information from you:

- The IMAP mail server's fully qualified domain name—its host name (for example, `osprey.planetnotes.com`).
- The SMTP server's fully qualified domain name.
- The user's account name, which is the user's name in the Person document you created.
- Folder prefixes, which are root folder paths.

Domino doesn't use folder prefixes but many IMAP servers do. When configuring an IMAP client, you can usually leave blank the field(s) where you would enter that information. For example, in Outlook Express, leave blank the field called Root folder path. In Netscape Messenger, leave blank the field called IMAP server directory. In Simeon 4.1, leave blank the fields called Folder Prefix and "Folder Location."

Some IMAP clients may not let you leave folder prefix settings blank. In such a program, just enter the fully qualified domain name of the Domino IMAP server. For example, PC-Pine expects you to put something in the INBOX-PATH and Folder collections fields. If your IMAP server's FQDN is `osprey.planetnotes.com`, you can enter `INBOX-PATH{osprey.planetnotes.com}INBOX` and `Folder collections {osprey.planetnotes.com}`.

Tuning the IMAP Service

There are a series of `notes.ini` variables that you can set to refine the way the IMAP mail service works. They are described in Table 17.4:

Table 17.4   *notes.ini* **Variables**

Variable	Description
IMAILExactSize=*value*	Set to 1 to cause IMAP to return the exact size of MIME messages. Defaults to 0, which permits IMAP to return an estimated message size. It is much easier for Domino to estimate the sizes of messages than to determine their exact sizes, so its setting will affect the server's performance. Set this variable only if IMAP mail clients require exact message sizes. Alternatively, you can set the "IMAP server returns exact size of message" in a Configuration document to either "Enabled" or "Disabled." If you set this variable both in the Configuration document and in notes.ini, the setting in the Configuration document will take precedence.
IMAPGreeting=*greeting*	Sets the greeting that the IMAP server sends to connecting clients. If you don't set this, Domino sends the following informative but not so friendly greeting: `* OK Domino IMAP4 Server V.5.0 ready Mon, 10 May 1999 17:57:13 -0500`
IMAPRedirectSSLGreeting=*message*	Sets the message that the IMAP server sends to clients being redirected from the TCP/IP port to the SSL port.
IMAPSSLGreeting=*greeting*	Sets the greeting that the IMAP server sends to clients connecting via SSL. If you don't set this, Domino sends the following greeting: `* OK Domino IMAP4 Server V.4.6 ready Mon, 12 May 1997 17:57:13 -0500`
IMAP_Config_Update_Interval=*minutes*	Sets how frequently the IMAP server checks for changes made to its configuration. If this variable is absent, the server checks every two minutes.

continues

Table 17.4 **Continued**

Variable	Description
IMAP_Session_Timeout=*minutes*	Sets the period after which the IMAP server will drop an idle client session. If this variable is not present, the server will drop idle sessions after 30 minutes. Lotus recommends setting it to no less than 10 minutes, because many IMAP clients poll for new mail every 10 minutes. The overhead of supporting an idle IMAP session is less than that of breaking one down a session, then setting up a new one.

Monitoring the Quality of IMAP Service

To ensure that the IMAP service is maintained at a high level of quality, consider defining one or more TCP Server probes. Specifically you want to probe the IMAP service. You can create a probe in Domino Administrator, in the Configuration screen. Choose Statistics & Events, Probes, TCP Server in the Tasks pane. Then choose New TCP Server Probe in the Action Bar over the Results pane. If one doesn't already exist, create a probe in which you choose "All Domino servers in the domain will probe their own configured ports." In addition, create at least one probe in which one server is probing another.

If the Event task is running on each probing server, creating this probe will cause the server to generate quality of service statistics on each running Internet service. It will also cause Alarms to appear in the Statistics Reports database if a timeout occurs before the probe returns a response from the probed service.

You can view statistics in the Statistics pane of the Server screen in Domino Administrator, and optionally in the Monitor pane as well. If the Collector service on any server is collecting statistics from the server in question, statistics reports will also accumulate in the Statistics Reports database. To learn more about these features of Domino, see Chapter 18, "Server Monitoring."

III

Server Optimization

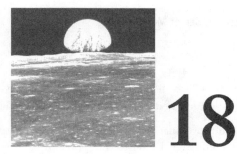

18

Server Monitoring

THIS CHAPTER EXPLORES THE TOOLS AND METHODOLOGY of collecting performance statistics for the purpose of identifying, tracking, and analyzing systemic trends. Use it in conjunction with Chapter 19, "Performance Tuning." Together, the two chapters can help point you in the direction of providing better performance to end-users. As corporate investments increase, so do expectations of increased service levels and return on investment. The advent of e-commerce means that Domino server performance can be a profit center instead of a cost center.

Why System Monitoring Matters

Monitoring is a valuable tool that provides the administrator with valuable information concerning the overall health of the system and its components.

- The information obtained by monitoring overall system function is the first step in providing reliable service to end-users.

- Monitoring the functions of strategic system components provides hard data instead of relying on perceived performance when modifying server hardware, software, or network systems.

- Investing in system monitoring up front saves money and helps to avoid downtime and crisis-mode decision making.

- Monitoring systemic trends alerts you to problems and upgrade requirements before applications and users overwhelm the system.

- Increased system reliability translates into increased profits.

One particular series of events should stick in the minds of administrators involved in e-commerce. I refer to the problems experienced by the eBay (www.ebay.com) auction site. A string of system outages greatly upset users and investors alike. Usually, a corporation's system failures do not get aired in public. However, the current media spotlight on e-commerce made eBay the exception to the rule.

The official reports say "infrastructure problems" were to blame. Since the first crash, the site has experienced subsequent problems forcing the system offline for days, costing the corporation money and its reputation. There probably were warning signs of trouble ahead. Servers rarely die spontaneously. There are usually cries for help. At the basic level, monitoring system health involves listening for those cries.

For information about the eBay crashes and the public reasons given, start by searching on "ebay" using your favorite Internet search engine. What you will find may be quite informative for those contemplating running a for-profit site.

As in Chapter 19, the discussions here are not limited to Lotus software. Domino runs atop network servers connected through interface cards and protocol stacks to networks and the world. Therefore, monitoring the functions and interaction of these systems is in the Domino administrator's best interests. In this chapter, I refer to the Domino *system*, not just the server. In addition, because the majority of current Domino systems run on Windows NT, I will concentrate on that platform. However, Domino is available on multiple platforms; therefore, it is probable that the Domino administrator or consultant needs to know something about how the software behaves on platforms other than NT.

Identifying Tools

The following paragraphs are pointers to resources for monitoring. Lotus presentations on system monitoring also focus on NT with a brief mention of some UNIX and AS/400 tools. Here is a quick summary of what they are and where to get more information:

- **SAR – system activity reporter.** Counters exist for CPU utilization, buffer usage, disk and tape I/O activity, TTY device activity, switching and system-call activity, file access, queue activity, interprocess communications, and paging.

- **VMSTAT – used to report virtual memory statistics.** On UNIX systems, memory-related activity occurs when real memory is exhausted and the kernel utilizes virtual memory. VMSTAT command syntax is as follows:

```
vmstat [ -{options} [ disks ] [ interval [ count ] ]
```

The `interval` and `count` arguments may be used to specify time in seconds and the number of intervals to report. This allows interactive monitoring of the memory workload.

- **IOStat – used to report hard disk and I/O device statistics as well as CPU utilization.** IOStat helps to determine where input/output bottlenecks exists on a system. The `iostat` command can be used to display the amount of data moving between the system and a disk or terminal device.

- **NetStat – shows network status.** NetStat is used to report a variety of network information, such as the amount of kernel memory utilization. Kernel memory buffers (or mbufs) are used to provide fast transfer of incoming network data to the kernel. Insufficient mbufs can cause network throughput to slow significantly. Allocating more mbufs is most safely performed by adding additional memory; however, on some UNIX operating systems the amount of memory dedicated to mbufs is configurable.

- **Perfmeter – displays system performance values in multiple dials or strip charts on SUN systems.** Perfmeter measures processor utilization, Ethernet traffic and collisions, paging, swapping, device interrupts, and load.

Information on performance-monitoring UNIX systems is available on vendor Web sites, but there are a few other sites that can be beneficial. Good places to start are the UNIX Guru Universe at `www.ugu.com` and the UNIX System Administration Independent Learning (USAIL) at `www.uwsg.edu`.

IBM and Lotus have been extolling the virtues of Domino running on the high-end AS/400 platform. The AS/400's built-in performance monitor is used to gather information on memory, disk, controller data, and network data. Because the environment is specialized, IBM has realized that there is a market seeking configuration and performance information for Domino on the AS/400. Visit these sites:

- `www.as400.ibm.com/developer/domino/perform` for performance information and fixes for known problems

- `http://www.as400.ibm.com/lotus_notes/notes.htm` for general Domino R5 on AS/400

- `http://www.as400.ibm.com/lotus_notes/nnfaq_1b.htm` for a Domino R5 on AS/400 FAQ list

IBM is working on at least four Redbooks for Domino 5 on AS/400. These should be published by the time this book is released. Topics will include implementation, administration, performance tuning, and partitioning of Domino servers. R5 Redbooks are available for most Domino platforms at `www.redbooks.ibm.com`.

Another tool that bears further investigation (but that is outside the scope of this chapter) for monitoring events and automating responses is the Tivoli Manager, marketed by IBM. Tivoli enables the reboot of a failed server and consistent management across the network. While on IBM's Redbook site, look at "Managing Domino/Notes with Tivoli Manager, Enterprise Edition, Version 1.5, SG24-2104" for more information.

The primary tools used in monitoring a Domino system on NT are

- Windows NT Diagnostics
- Task Manager
- Performance Monitor
- Domino Server Console
- Domino Log
- Domino Log Analysis
- Collect, Event, MTC, and ISpy server tasks
- Statistics and Events Database
- Reports Database
- Domino Server Monitor

With the exception of Windows NT Diagnostics, Task Manager, and Performance Monitor, all of the items in the preceding list are available on the other Domino platforms. We also will explore a few utilities that augment the major tools in the sections of this chapter discussing Domino monitoring tools.

The Environment

The major subsystems (processor, memory, hard disk, and network) are utilized differently depending on the system's role. These differences should be addressed during configuration and monitoring. Apply this concept at the operating-system level as well as the Domino-server level. An NT system may function as a file server, application server, or domain server in any given organization.

Domino servers are generally considered to be application servers because they are accessed by users in a client/server environment via a front-end application. As such, memory and processor functions are utilized most. That is not to imply that the hard disk and network subsystems are not contributors to attainment of expected service levels or that they can be ignored.

Next, consider the server's functions in the Domino system. Domino Hubs, Mail, and Application servers provide different services, so Domino configuration and monitoring needs to target areas most likely to generate bottlenecks in that particular system type.

Tracking Utilization

When Domino is run on a server, each process and selected server tasks utilize one or more server subsystems. Identifying which subsystems are utilized by each loaded task provides clues on what to monitor and where to look for bottlenecks. For example, Mail servers will utilize resources differently than Hub servers. While both rely heavily on the disk subsystem, there can be significant differences in other functions. Mail servers are accessed directly by users and may be serving Internet mail types in addition to Shared or standard Notes mail. The operating system, network interfaces, Domino, and client software all function together as a system. No subsystem may be modified without affecting other system components.

Monitoring and tuning are symbiotic. Monitoring provides information and performance tuning and uses that information to adjust one or more subsystems. Those adjustments need to be monitored and provide additional results, suggesting that a change can increase performance. One day, you realize that the system is in perfect harmony! Data is flowing, users are happy, and you can sit back and relax. Just about then, the alarm goes off, and it is time to go to work and use everything you know to get home in time for dinner.

Establish a Baseline

A baseline is a starting point that is used for comparison. This is an important concept, because it establishes a reference point against which to judge the information that you gather while monitoring the system. A baseline should be established when bringing a server online, or before upgrading. This makes it possible to monitor the effects of users, programs, processes, and configuration changes such as new disks or memory from a known point.

Include measurements of memory, processor, disk, and network objects, as well as Notes counters in the baseline. As usage ramps up on the server, it will then be possible to estimate system response and act accordingly. Refer to the tables in this chapter for guidelines on specific objects and counters to include. The best case would be to generate baseline information for production and nonproduction hours so that you can investigate deviations from the norm.

System monitoring, analysis, and tuning require organized record-keeping. The remainder of the chapter explores the tools for monitoring Domino on Windows NT.

Chain Reaction Rule of Performance Tuning

One rule of thumb is that the method used to clear a bottleneck in one subsystem will usually cause one in another subsystem. Monitoring allows you to track those changes in system functions whether caused by users, overtaxed components, or tuning.

Windows NT Monitoring Tools

The following sections explore monitoring tools available through Microsoft's Windows NT operating system. Many of the tools discussed are available natively, and others are included with the NT Resource Kit and its supplements. Review Windows NT Server, Workstation and Resource Kit documentation in addition to the information provided here:

- NT Diagnostics (`winmsd.exe`)
- Task Manager (`taskman.exe`)
- Performance Monitor (`perfmon.exe`)
- Data Logging Service (`datalog.exe`)
- Monitor Utility (`monitor.exe`)
- WinAT Task Scheduler (`winat.exe`)
- Performance Data Log Service (`perflog.exe`)

NT Diagnostics

This utility provides information about the network and the computer. The administrator can view, save to file, or print a report providing information including protocols, mapped devices, services, OS and patch level, drivers, IRQs, and ports. Keeping a copy of this report with server documentation is a good idea and provides some baseline information. Updated reports may be printed after system configuration changes, such as adding additional hard disks, have been made. Figure 18.1 shows the utility's opening screen.

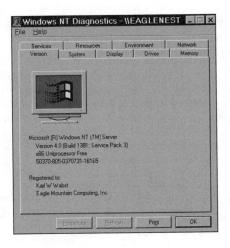

Figure 18.1   Click on the appropriate tab in the NT Diagnostics utility to view information onscreen or print a report to store with system documentation.

Task Manager

The Task Manager is usually the first stop a Domino administrator makes when a performance problem is suspected. This utility shows a subset of the information collected by the Performance Manager.

The Applications tab provides information on programs currently loaded on the system. A quick glance indicates whether a particular program is either running or not responding. By right-clicking on an application task, you can jump to the associated process on the Processes tab instead of scrolling down what can be a long list to identify the corresponding task.

The Processes tab (see Figure 18.2) shows each process currently running. By default, there are three columns displayed. Choose View, Select Columns in the menu for a listing of additional information available for each process. By right-clicking on an individual process, you can set the priority for that process. Choices are High, Normal, Low, and Realtime.

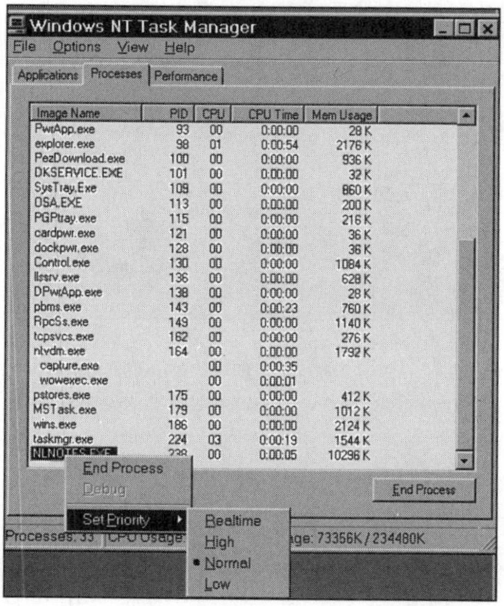

Figure 18.2   The priority of a process is usually set in its code. Use Task Manager to change the priority of the process during the current session.

Real-Time Consequences

A word of caution:

By selecting Realtime, you will place this process above the executive services that monitor and respond to keyboard input. Only use this option for a process-intensive program that has a definite end point. Selecting it for nserver.exe, for example, may force you to reboot the server to regain control of the system.

The system will process requests from processes in priority order. Additionally, a lower-level process may be interrupted when a request is received from a process with a higher=level process. Changes made to the priority of a running process are effective only for the current session. The next time the process is started, it reverts to its original priority setting.

The Task Manager Performance tab provides current information for situational use (see Figure 18.3). For monitoring system information over a period of time, the NT Performance Monitor is integrated and relatively easy to use.

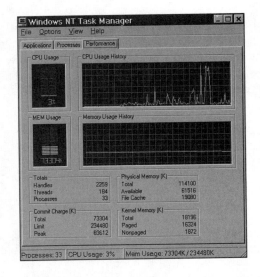

Figure 18.3   Information regarding current memory and
CPU usage can be viewed on the Performance tab.

NT Performance Monitor

NT Performance Monitor allows tracking, analysis, and reporting of various aspects of the NT system, including processors, memory, hard disks, and network resources. NT services provide ways to automate the process, allowing administrators to capture performance information at regular intervals regardless of schedule or time of day. Running Performance Monitor on new and upgraded systems establishes the baseline against which to measure future performance.

Terms

First, we will take a moment to define a few terms found throughout the Performance Monitor utility and the literature discussing performance monitoring. While many Domino administrators are familiar with monitoring tools in Notes, not all of us are necessarily NT administrators as well.

Core Objects

Objects represent system resources such as physical (installed) devices, threads, processes, and sections of shared memory. Core Objects describe the list of Objects that are included, by default, in Performance Monitor. Objects appear only for installed components, so additional objects may be created as programs or services are added. Table 18.1 lists NT's Core Objects. Some Objects are installed automatically, and others must be installed separately. For example, some of the TCP/IP counters are not available until SNMP is started, and the Notes Object (and associated instances) is not available until installed from the Domino installation routine.

Table 18.1 **NT Performance Monitor Core Objects**

Object	Description
System	Counters that apply to all system hardware and software.
Memory	Random Access Memory.
Cache	An area of memory that holds recently used data.
Paging File	File(s) used to back up virtual memory allocations.
Processor	Physical processor(s) installed in the computer.
Thread	The part of a process that utilizes the processor.
Physical Disk	Installed hard disks and/or RAID devices.
Logical Disk	Hard disk partitions.
Redirector	File system that diverts requests to network servers.
Objects	System software objects.

Instance

Instance is a subset of Objects. For example, if working on a server with multiple processors, the Processor Object would show three instances, one for each processor (0 and 1) and an additional instance for the Total. Select 0 or 1 to set counters for either processor. Select Total to set counters for both processors.

Counter

Counters provide definitions for the type of data available for the Object type selected. Counters report on things such as activity, demand, and space used by Objects. When any counter is selected, all counters for the selected object are activated, but only data for the selected counter is displayed. By clicking on the Explain button in the Add to Chart box, you can see a definition of the selected counter.

Performance Monitor contains three types of counters:

- **Averaging.** Shows an average value.
- **Instantaneous.** Shows the most recent value.
- **Difference.** Shows the difference between the most recent value and the previous value. Negative values are displayed as 0. There are no difference Counters in the basic set of Counters in Performance Monitor.

Overhead

For our purposes, this is the amount of system resources that is consumed by running a monitoring tool. Because every task consumes resources, running Performance Monitor on the system that is being tested affects the results. Overhead includes the hardware and network resources necessary to calculate, store, and display results.

The use of Performance Monitor offers the capability to centralize statistics collection for multiple servers. Note that using Performance Monitor in this way increases network traffic. Collecting information locally and transferring it to a central location at off-peak times may be a better choice. Administrators need to balance the costs and benefits of local versus network-gathered statistics.

Which Counter Should I Choose?

The most important counter is automatically highlighted when selecting an Object in Performance Monitor.

Issues to Be Aware of When Running Performance Monitor on a Domino Server

Be aware of documented instances of Domino 4.x server crashes while running Performance Monitor remotely. According to Lotus, the crashes no longer occur under NT 4.0, with Service Pack 2 or higher installed. However, it would be wise to implement monitoring in a test environment prior to relying on it for your production environment. Refer to Technotes #142687 and 172380 for information. Before upgrading to Domino R5, ensure that the server has any recommended Service Packs installed. There have also been problems running Performance Monitor on the same machine as Compaq's Insight Manager Agent monitoring tool.

Performance Monitor logs are dynamic. They grow larger depending on the options selected and the length of time the utility runs. These logs should be collected on drives with plenty of free space. These files will also affect system statistics. When using Performance Monitor to gather statistics for longer periods, ensure that there is adequate disk space available on the target drive. Modify the Update Time interval. Longer intervals will reduce file size and system overhead. The default Update Interval is 1 minute in many cases.

Bottleneck

A bottleneck is an area of poor performance. The object of system monitoring is to identify bottlenecks and take appropriate actions to improve functioning. Frequently a problem in one area can cause other system components to function poorly. Therefore, when monitoring any system, we need to be aware of the whole and not focus solely on components.

If, for example, a server is low on physical memory, the system will begin to rely on paged memory. As the paging rate goes up, so does the workload on the hard disk and processor. As the situation worsens, the result may be a reduction in performance to the end user. While a bigger hard disk or faster processor would help, adding memory would address the real problem.

Adding the Domino Object and Counters

Performance Monitor has the capability to display data from add–in programs, such as Domino. By collecting Domino statistics through Performance Monitor, the administrator has a convenient place to collect system information in a single program using a common interface. Other advantages are the capability to correlate operating system statistics with Domino statistics, and the chart or report contain excellent content for reports to management.

In order to add the Lotus Notes object and counters for Domino, you must select Notes Performance Monitor either during Domino installation or by rerunning installation and selecting only the Notes Performance Monitor option. This places the `notesreg.bat` file in the Domino program subdirectory.

The batch file is executed from the command line, with an added parameter indicating the full path to the Domino server's program directory. `Notesreg.bat` updates the NT Registry and makes the Domino monitors available through Performance Monitor. After installing the Notes counters, restart the server.

In this example, the server's program directory is located in D:\Lotus\Domino. Open a command prompt and type:

```
notesreg.bat D:\Lotus\Domino
```

The next time Performance Monitor is opened, the Lotus Notes object will be available. The instances available through Performance Monitor will look familiar to any administrator who has used the `show stat` command at the Domino server command line.

Native Domino monitoring tools should also be configured, because they provide more detailed information about Domino activities. Also, Performance Monitor is not always running in most cases. Domino statistics are collected as long as Domino is running.

Starting Performance Monitor

Performance Monitor may be started manually or automatically. Opening Performance Monitor manually is useful to spot-check server performance. Use the automatic method to monitor servers at consistent intervals or during off-hours. Settings files allow you to customize the monitored counters in a given session. A *settings file* is a collected set of Objects and Counters customized for a specific purpose. This is particularly useful when starting monitoring automatically to create tracking reports for server management.

Manually

Performance Monitor can be started from the Windows NT menu, under Administrative Tools or by typing `PERFMON` at a command prompt. When starting Performance Monitor from the command line, you may specify a settings file. The file extension indicates the Performance Monitor view that the settings are for (see Table 18.2).

Table 18.2 **File Extensions Used When Creating Settings Files**

Settings File Extension	Performance Monitor View
.pma	Alert
.pmc	Chart
.pml	Log
.pmr	Report
.pmw	Workspace

Force Domino to Populate Performance Monitor Counters

After installing the Domino counters into Performance Monitor, open the Domino server console and enter the **show statistic** command. Counters will not appear in Performance Monitor until the associated program updates the statistics. The `show statistic` command forces this to happen.

Automatically

Collecting Performance Monitor statistics can be automated. It is preferable to automate system monitoring so that information is collected at consistent intervals as opposed to relying on the administrator's memory and availability. Automating the process allows for collection on multiple servers during the same intervals, as well as during off-hours.

In order to automate Performance Monitor, first ensure that the Scheduling Service is running on each server. The actual automation method uses the AT command set to start and stop monitoring. The AT commands are relatively easy to learn if you are not already familiar with them.

For example, to enable monitoring on the server *Eagle* on weekdays between the hours of 10 a.m. and 11 a.m., use the following commands:

```
at \\Eagle 10:00 /date:M,T,W,Th,F "monitor Start"
at \\Eagle 11:00 /date:M,T,W,Th,F "monitor Stop"
```

Additional information regarding AT commands is available in Windows NT documentation.

Monitoring Disk Activity

Information on disk usage is an important component of system monitoring. Tracking behavior of physical and logical disks is useful for troubleshooting and Domino performance. Disk counters are not enabled by default in Performance Monitor. Table 18.3 lists the available options for enabling disk performance counters with Performance Monitor.

Table 18.3   **Optional Flags to Control Monitoring of Disk Usage**

Command	Description
diskperf -Y	Enables disk performance counters on the local computer.
diskperf -YE	The additional parameter E is necessary when measuring disks that are in a striped disk set.
diskperf -Y[E] \\<servername>	Enables disk performance counters on a remote computer.
diskperf -N	Disables collection of disk statistics.

Then target computer must be restarted to enable any of the options in Table 18.3.

Another way to enable disk performance counters is through the Windows NT Control Panel:

1. Open the Control Panel

2. Open the Devices icon.

3. Highlight Diskperf and change the Startup option to Boot.

4. Restart the server.

Monitoring the Network Interface and IP

To enable monitoring of the server network interface and IP protocols, it is necessary to start the SNMP service on a Windows NT server. Enabling the SNMP service adds the appropriate counters to Performance Monitor.

Performance Monitor Views

Performance Monitor views provide ways to monitor real-time or historical data, as well as to set threshold alarms. There are four views:

- Chart
- Report
- Log
- Alert

These are described in the sections that follow.

Chart

Chart view enables you to monitor real-time information for Objects, counters, and their instances. Multiple counters may be charted simultaneously. Charts may be customized for quick start-up when monitoring a specific application or subsystem.

Report

The Report view provides a report based on the values of one or many counters. Values are recorded at user-defined intervals. Values for averaged counters show the average value during the interval. Values for instantaneous counters show the value at the end of the interval.

Log

In this view, counters are recorded in a file for future analysis. Performance Monitor data may be exported to a spreadsheet to create monthly reports or trending. Points of interest during logging may be bookmarked for later reference.

Alert

As in Domino, administrators may set threshold values for a counter. Performance Monitor can send an alert message to a user or run a specific program once, or each time, the threshold is crossed. This may be useful to run ncompact, for example, when available disk space drops below a desired level on the Domino data disk.

Summary Tables of Objects and Pertinent Counters

Table 18.4 (and the tables that follow) summarizes NT system components, associated subsystems, and counters of interest for Domino systems.

Table 18.4 **The Performance Monitor Components Recommended to Monitor an NT Server Running Domino**

System Component	Monitored Subsystem	Primary Counters of Interest
Hardware	Processor	% Processor Time % Privileged Time % User Time Interrupts/Sec System: Processor Queue Length Server Work Queues: Queue Length
	Memory	Pages/Sec Available Bytes Committed Bytes Pool Nonpaged Bytes Cache Faults per Second
	Disk	Disk Queue Length % Disk Time Avg. Disk/Bytes Transfer Avg. Disk/sec Transfer Disk Bytes/sec % Disk Read Time % Disk Write Time
	Network	Network Interface: Bytes Total/sec Network Interface: Bytes Sent/sec Network Interface: Output Queue Length Server: Bytes Total/sec TCP Segments per Second TCP Segments Retranslates per Second UDP Datagrams per Second

continues

Table 18.4 **Continued**

System Component	Monitored Subsystem	Primary Counters of Interest
Lotus Notes		Mem.Allocated
		NET.TCPIP.Bytes.Received
		NET.TCPIP.Bytes.Sent
		NET.TCPIP.Sessions Established.Incoming
		NET.TCPIP.Sessions Established.Outgoing
		ServerAvailabilityIndex
		Server.Sessions.Dropped
		Server.Transactions.PerMinute
		Server.Transactions.PerMinute.Peak
		Server.Users

The tables that follow describe the function of each counter in Table 18.4.

Processor Subsystem

Table 18.5 describes specific Performance Monitor counters recommended to monitor processor activity on an NT server running Domino.

Table 18.5 **Counters Used to Monitor Installed Processors**

Counter	Description
% Processor Time	The percentage of time that the processor is not running the idle thread. Values below 80% (per CPU) are preferable.
% Privileged Time	The percentage of time that the processor is executing NT system services.
% User Time	The percentage of time that the processor is performing user services.
Interrupts/Sec	The number of interrupts that the processor is handling from applications or hardware services. Lower values are preferable.
System: Processor Queue Length	The depth of requests in the processor queue. All processes use this queue in which threads wait for processor cycles. Lower values are preferred.
Server Work Queues: Queue Length	The depth of requests in the queue for the selected processor.

Memory Subsystem

Table 18.6 describes specific Performance Monitor counters recommended to monitor server memory on an NT server running Domino.

Table 18.6 **Counters Used to Monitor Server Memory**

Counter	Description
Pages/Sec	Pages read from or written to disk to satisfy references to pages that are not in real memory. Values lower than 20 are preferred.
Available Bytes	Amount of available real memory—memory that is not committed. High values are preferable.
Committed Bytes	Memory, including pagefile space, that has been committed. Lower values are preferred. Should not exceed 70% of physical memory.
Pool Nonpaged Bytes	Real memory in the system kernel.
Cache Faults per Second	Rate at which the system must access the disk because requested data is not in the cache.

Disk Subsystem

Table 18.7 describes specific NT Performance Monitor counters recommended to monitor disk activity for an NT server running Domino.

Table 18.7 **Counters Used to Monitor Disk Activity**

Counter	Description
Disk Queue Length	Number of I/O requests waiting for service from the disk.
% Disk Time	Percentage of time the disk drive is busy. Lower values are preferable. Frequent values of 70% or more may indicate a subsystem bottleneck.
Avg. Disk/Bytes Transfer	Average size of data transferred to or from the disk.
Avg. Disk/sec Transfer	Average time to transfer data to or from the disk. Lower values are preferable.
Disk Bytes/sec	Transfer rate to and from the disk.
% Disk Read Time	Percentage of time that the disk is busy with read requests.
% Disk Write Time	Percentage of time that the disk is busy with write requests.

Enabling Monitoring of IP Protocols

Reminder: If you want to monitor the network interface and IP protocols, you will have to install and start the SNMP task on your NT server. Remember to reapply any NT service packs afterward.

Network Subsystem

Table 18.8 describes specific NT Performance Monitor counters recommended to monitor the network interface of an NT server running Domino.

Table 18.8 **Counters Used to Monitor the Server's Network Interface**

Counter	Description
Network Interface: Bytes Total/sec	Total number of bytes sent and received using this network adapter. Consistently high values may indicate a bottleneck. Compare to your baseline.
Network Interface: Bytes Sent/sec	Number of bytes sent using this network adapter.
Network Interface: Output Queue Length	Queue depth of the network packet queue.
Server: Bytes Total/sec	Total number of bytes sent and received by the server over the network.
TCP Segments per Second	Number of TCP segments sent and received. Compare against baseline.
TCP Segments Retranslates per Second	Number of TCP segments that are retranslated.
UDP Datagrams per Second	Total number of datagrams sent and received. Higher values indicate higher connectionless traffic rates.

Lotus Notes Subsystem

Table 18.9 describes specific NT Performance Monitor counters recommended to monitor Notes and Domino activities on a Windows NT server (see Figure 18.4).

Table 18.9 **Counters Used to Monitor the Domino System**

Counter	Description
Mem.Allocated	Number of bytes allocated for the Domino server.
NET.TCPIP.Bytes. Received	Number of bytes received on a specific network port. One instance for each defined Notes network port.
NET.TCPIP.Bytes.Sent	Number of bytes sent on a specific network port. One instance for each defined Notes network port.

Counter	Description
NET.TCPIP.Sessions. Established.Incoming	Number of incoming sessions established on a specific port. One instance for each defined Notes network port.
NET.TCPIP.Sessions. Established.Outgoing	Number of outgoing sessions established on a specific port. One instance for each defined Notes network port.
ServerAvailability Index	Index of how busy the Domino server was at a given point. High values are preferable.
Server.Sessions. Dropped	Number of sessions dropped, usually due to inactivity. Low values are preferable. A low Server_SessionTimeout value may cause this metric to rise.
Server.Transactions. PerMinute	Average number of Domino server transactions.
Server.Transactions.PerMinute.Peak	Peak number of Domino server transactions.
Server.Users	Number of users connected to the server.

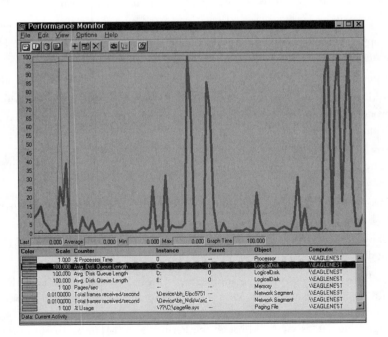

Figure 18.4 The Chart View of the NT Performance Monitor enables monitoring of various system counters.

An Alternative from the NT Resource Kit

While Performance Monitor provides administrators with valuable information, the drawbacks in disk space, network bandwidth, and processing power make some think twice. Fortunately there are alternatives to running full-blown Performance Monitor. Three tools available on the Windows NT Server 4.0 Resource Kit offer the capability to collect statistics without nearly as much overhead. Those three tools are

- The Datalog Service
- Monitor
- PerfLog

The Datalog (Data Logging) Service enables you to run Performance Monitor as a service. The second of the three programs, Monitor, controls the Datalog Service. Information is stored in Performance Monitor format, which provides continuity with previous reporting mechanisms. Microsoft claims that the Datalog Service adds less than .6 percent of overhead to the system. The savings is available because the service does not run the Performance Monitor GUI. The collected information is stored locally in a `.log` file. Because Datalog runs as a service, the administrator does not have to be logged into the server to collect data. To configure Datalog on the target server, do the foloowing:

1. Copy `datalog.exe` and `monitor.exe` from the Resource Kit CD to the NT system32 subdirectory on the target server (or workstation).
2. Open Performance Monitor to the Log view.
3. Add Objects you want to monitor to the Log. At the minimum, select memory, processor, system, physical disk, paging file, logical disk, network interface, and Lotus Notes.
4. From the Options menu, select Log. Adjust the Periodic Update setting to a value between 15 and 30 minutes. Remember that the field is measured in seconds.
5. Save the Workspace file with a meaningful name, such as `baseline.pmw`, on the local computer.
6. Copy the Workspace file (`baseline.pmw`) to the target server's system32 subdirectory.

To control the Datalog service, the administrator uses the Monitor utility, which also ships with the NT Resource Kit. Monitor utility commands are used to dictate the functions of the Datalog service.

The resulting data is viewed through the Performance Monitor. To automate statistics collection through the Datalog Service, you may create batch files containing the desired commands and run the batch files with AT commands, as described earlier in this chapter.

Valid Monitor commands are shown in Table 18.10.

Table 18.10 Monitor Utility Commands Are Entered at the Command Line to Control the Datalog Service

Command	Description
monitor setup	Initiates Datalog on the target server.
monitor filename.pmw	Specifies the Workspace file that Datalog uses to specify statistics to collect.
monitor start	Starts Datalog collection.
monitor stop	Stops Datalog collection.
monitor pause	Pauses Datalog collection.
monitor continue	Resumes collection after pause.
monitor automatic	Starts the Datalog service when the system boots.
monitor manual	Sets the Datalog Service to start manually.
monitor disable	Disables the Datalog Service.

To automate statistics collection through the Datalog Service, you may create batch files containing the desired commands and execute the batch file using the WinAT Scheduling utility.

The third monitoring-related program available on the Resource Kit CD is the Performance Data Log Service. This service is started by executing `PerfLog.exe`. This program is similar to DataLog Service, except that it saves collected data in .csv or .tsv formats that can be easily imported into a spreadsheet program for analysis. The Perflog utility will not be included on the NT Resource Kit after Supplement Three. Evidently, there were problems monitoring some of the Microsoft Exchange objects using the service. More information may become available on Microsoft's Support Web site (`http://www.microsoft.com/technet/support/default.htm`).

Use WinAT to Automate NT Tasks

A GUI-based command scheduler named WinAT on the NT Server 4.0 Resource Kit provides an easy way to schedule programs like PerfLog and Performance Monitor. With WinAT you can schedule programs on your local or networked computers. Additional information is available on the Resource Kit CD or through the Microsoft Technical Support Web site.

Domino Monitoring Tools

Domino has always provided its own rich set of monitoring tools. R5 adds additional tools, including probes and a graphical interface called Domino Server Monitor. Statistic and event monitor wizards make configuring system monitoring easier than in previous releases.

All the Lotus Notes indices in Performance Monitor are available through Domino by entering commands at the server console, Statistics Reports, and the Domino Administration Client. Additional information such as Domino server uptime is only available through Domino. While the metrics available from the operating system are valuable, they clearly do not replace the information an administrator gathers from within Domino itself. One major advantage of the statistics gathered within Domino is that the Domino server is constantly updating its information. Unlike Performance Monitor, which has to be started separately, the Domino server updates statistics by default whenever the server is running.

The most basic server monitoring is done by entering commands either at the console or through a remote session from a Notes client. The `show statistic` command generates an up-to-the-moment listing, including all the counters available in Performance Monitor, plus a few additional ones.

The server log provides the administrator with an unfiltered list of Domino events over time. Searching server logs to find specific text would be tedious if not for the Log Analysis tool. Statistics and Event Reports are more available than before in allowing administrators to find real-time and historical information quickly.

Domino Server Console

Picking out meaningful text on the Domino server console screen can be challenging. First, there is no guarantee that the information you need will be onscreen while you are looking. Second, if the server is busy processing requests, the onscreen display may be moving by very quickly.

The `show statistic` command allows for viewing statistics at the console. This command provides more information than Performance Monitor, but in text format.

If there is a particular statistic you are interested in, you can specify its name as a parameter in the `show statistic` command. For example, to view all statistics for the database cache, you would type the following:

```
sh stat Database.DbCache.*
```

Two other commands provide subsets of the information. Use `show tasks` and `show server` for a quick check of users, tasks, and server information.

The `show server` command generally provides most of the nonuser information an administrator needs at the server console. Table 18.11 summarizes the output of the `show server` command. The Administration Client provides a more convenient place to view server statistics. Console commands are helpful when the Domino Administration client is unavailable.

Table 18.11 **Summary of Output from the** *show server* **Command**

Output	Description
Version information	Shows the Domino software version, platform, license, current time, and date.
Server name	Server's name given at setup.
Server directory	Path to the Domino data directory.
Elapsed time	Number of days, hours, minutes, and seconds since the server was last started.
Transactions	Total number of transactions performed since the server was last started. These include databases opened, closed, read from, and written to, and mail routed to a database.
Availability Index	Calculation of clustered server workload.
Message tracking	Displays whether this feature is enabled or disabled.
Shared Mail	Displays whether this feature is enabled or disabled.
Number of mailboxes	The number of mailboxes on the server.
Pending mail	The number of mail documents waiting to be routed.
Dead mail	The number of undeliverable mail documents that have been returned to the server.
Waiting Tasks	The number of pending tasks on the server.
Transactional Logging	Displays whether this feature is enabled or disabled.

Enabling and Configuring Reporting

While statistics are constantly gathered by the log, statistics and event reporting are enabled separately under R5 by running one or more Domino server tasks. Each task is responsible for reporting different types of information. These server tasks can be loaded at the console or added to the `notes.ini` file, causing them to start each time the server is restarted.

- Event Monitor (Event)
- Statistics Collector (Collect)

- ISpy (RunJava ISpy)
- Mail Tracking Collector (MTC)

Most collected information is stored in the Statistics Reporting database (`statrep5.nsf`). Experienced administrators are used to looking in this database. In R5, it still provides a convenient way to view detailed information from a user workstation when the Domino Administration client is unavailable. An additional database, Report (`report.nsf`), is used to view mail-tracking information.

As in previous releases, statistic and event threshold settings are configured in the Statistics and Events database (`events4.nsf`). While documents still may be configured manually, Lotus has added new configuration wizards to R5 that make setting up monitoring easier than with Performance Monitor.

Server Tasks

Lotus has made notable changes to the Server Tasks used to monitor Notes and Domino activity. Both new and experienced administrators should review the following section to properly configure monitoring on an R5 system.

Event Monitor

This task monitors events on the Domino server. The Event Monitor task must be run on all servers you wish to monitor in the R5 environment. Place Event into the `ServerTask` line of the `notes.ini` file, if it is not already there. Event automatically creates the Statistics and Events database. If not started automatically from `notes.ini`, type `Load Event` at the server console.

Performance Monitor and Domino Monitoring Tools Complement Each Other

Use Performance Monitor to gather detailed information about the system as a whole, but use the Notes-based tools when you need in-depth focus quickly on Domino server activity.

Be Aware of These Issues

During installation of Domino 5.0, the Collect task is not added to the `ServerTasks=` line of the `notes.ini` file even when both Events & Statistics were selected in the setup. Therefore, statistics are not placed into the Statistics Reporting database (`statrep5.nsf`). The Event task is correctly placed into `notes.ini`, so events are reported correctly. Lotus will remedy the situation in a later release, but you may want to check the `ServerTasks` after installation.

If you have upgraded from a previous version of Domino to R5, note that the Report task no longer exists. The Collect task now collects statistics from all servers. Remove the Report task reference from the `ServerTasks` line of `notes.ini` to avoid a task load error on Domino R5 startup.

Statistics Collector

The Collect task is responsible for gathering statistical information about the server(s) being monitored. This task needs to be run on only one server in the domain. This server will then monitor statistics on all or designated servers in the domain, depending upon choices in the Server Statistic Collection document, in the Statistics & Events database.

As noted in the discussion of Performance Monitor, central collection of statistics will consume additional network resources. The additional load depends on the Collection report interval specified in the Server Statistic Collection document(s). In geographically dispersed environments (an international corporation, for example), administrators might want to reduce network traffic generated by sending data to a central database. One way to accomplish this is to create a replica copy of the Statistics Reporting database on a second server but disable replication between the two. Distribute reporting of statistics to the closest replica. The two replicas can be merged for summary analysis if desired.

ISpy

This task is used to send server and mail probes. Results are recorded as events in the Statistics Reporting database. To enable ISpy from the console command line, enter `RunJava ISpy`. Note that this command is case-sensitive. The first time the task is started, a mail-in database record is created in the Domino Directory through the Administration Process. Probes are a new feature in R5. Mail probes are used to check the route to a specified user's mail server. TCP server probes provide a check for availability of TCP services on a specified port.

Mail Tracking Collector

This task reads log files and produces summary reports of message traffic on the server. These reports are stored in the Reports database (`reports.nsf`). To enable Mail Tracking Collector from the console command line, enter `load mtc`. When the `mtc` task is loaded, it creates the Message Store Database. The default path for this database is `<NotesDataDirectory>\mtdata`. If the path does not already exist, the initialization of message tracking will fail.

Statistics Reporting Database

This database (`statrep5.nsf`) collects and organizes statistics and alarm and event information generated by each of the three server tasks.

Statistics Reports, which show only the most frequently viewed statistics, are stored in this database. Reports are generated for the categories in Table 18.12.

Table 18.12 **Summary of Statistics Reported**

Reported Component	Statistics Covered
Calendaring & Scheduling	Reservations and appointments
Clusters	Cluster server and replication
Communications	XPC or dial-up communications
Mail & Database	Gateways, replication, mail
Network	Network
Single copy object store	Shared mail
System	Agents, disk, memory, load
Web Server & Retriever	Web server and navigator

There are four other views available in the Statistics Reporting database. These are retained from previous releases. Additional information on alarms and events is provided in the following views:

- Alarms provide information on alarms generated when a monitored threshold is crossed. Alarms are configured in the Statistics & Events database (`events4.nsf`).
- Events show Probe results and other monitored events.
- Spreadsheet Export provides a summary system report.
- Graphs is a cascaded view. The three views underneath provide the same information found in the Spreadsheet Export view. The view shows a bar graph representation for each column. There are views showing System Loads, Resources, and Statistics. The format of the information provided is anemic compared with the more robust Administration Client. Administrators rarely use these.

Database Statistics Not Reported Correctly

There is a known problem with the Statistics Reporting database in R5.0. According to Lotus Technote #172443, the Database Statistics section inside the Statistics Reports does not populate due to a mismatch between the field name on the form and that being passed to the database.

For example, the field labeled `Buffer pool maximum` is defined as Database.BufferPool.Maximum on the Statistics Report form. The field name would have to be Database.Database.BufferPool.Maximum to correlate to the data being passed. In order to implement this workaround, however, you must first figure out a way to save a field name with more than 32 characters.

Lotus reports that this problem is fixed in version 5.01 of the product. The number of fixes included in Lotus's Quarterly Releases makes it preferable to fix this particular problem by upgrading instead of trying to write code to correct it.

Message Store Database

This database is created the first time that the MTC server task is loaded onto a server. It is not meant to be accessed by users directly. This database holds summary information such as sender's name, recipient, arrival time, and status. The information is used by the Reports database to generate reports on routing patterns, message volume, and top mail users. It is also used by the message-tracking tool to track messages sent to or from the server.

Reports Database

This database is used to create reports about mail usage, routing patterns, message volume, and top mail users on the server. Reports may be executed immediately or scheduled for daily, weekly, or monthly execution. With this database, you can generate these different reports:

- Top 25 Users By Count or Size
- Top 25 Senders By Count or Size
- Top 25 Receivers By Count or Size
- Most Popular Next or Previous Hops
- Top 25 Largest Messages
- Message Volume Summary
- Message Status Summary

The Statistics & Events Database

The Domino server is always generating statistics. Statistics reflect the health of the operating system and specific functions of Domino and Notes. Administrators are generally too busy to watch statistics counters roll by on a server. The Events task performs a filtering process, generating notifications when a statistic crosses a specified threshold. The Statistics & Events database is where statistics threshold alarms are configured. The events that are monitored in any implementation reflect a combination of general system operations and specific problem areas or devices. Generating alarms for every event would generate so much information that it would quickly become useless and create a bottleneck. Take time to review the default statistics listed in the Statistics & Events database to identify those that make sense for the environment. Thresholds and other information of key statistics may be edited for specific environments. Usually default values are fine, but this exercise familiarizes administrators with the myriad choices available. Too often administrators do not exploit this area of Notes and then buy add-in products that do the same thing.

Events

Events have two main components: type and severity. Notes event reporting breaks events down into subsystems, just as the NT Performance Monitor separates the processor, memory, hard disk, and network subsystems. Events types are categorized by the functional area to which each belongs. The event types native to Domino are

- Add-in
- AdminP
- Agent
- Client
- Comm/Net
- Compiler
- Database
- Directory (LDAP)
- FTP
- Mail
- Misc
- Network
- News (NNTP)
- Replica
- Resource
- Router
- Security
- Server
- Statistic
- Unknown
- Update
- Web (HTTP/HTTPS)

Every event is assigned a default severity level. *Severity* defines how important that event is to Domino system function. Because Domino is an application sitting on a network server, what warrants a high-level severity may be a lesser event on the system level. For example, a monitored hard disk with less than 10MB of free space is assigned a severity of Warning (high) in Notes. Event severity levels may be changed to suit your environment.

Available severity levels are

- **Normal.** Informational message.
- **Warning (Low).** May cause some performance degradation.
- **Warning (High).** Intervention probably required.
- **Failure.** Severe failure in the associated component.
- **Fatal.** System crash is probable.

When a monitored event occurs, Notes can act on behalf of the system. Actions range from notification to triggering a program to automatically fix the problem. Following is a list of the actions that are available:

- Broadcast a message to specified or all server users.
- Mail a notification to an administrator, user, group, or another database.
- Log the event to a local database or one on a remote server, usually the Statistics Reporting database.
- Report the event to the Windows NT Event Viewer or the UNIX System log.
- Send a pager message with a modified description of the event.
- Generate an SNMP trap.
- Run a program, either on the local or reporting server, in an attempt to correct the problem automatically.
- Relay the event to another server in the domain running a common protocol.

Other options are available if server management programs such as NotesView or HPOpenview are installed on the system.

Monitors

Monitors differ from Events because they do not have any actions associated with them. After a statistical threshold has been crossed, monitors trigger an Event, which in turn performs an associated Action.

There are two types of monitors: *database* and *server statistic* monitors. Database monitors are used to watch for

- Database inactivity
- Unused file space
- ACL changes
- Replication failure

Statistic monitors are used to monitor a specific statistic on the Domino system. Statistic monitors are configured by completing the choices on a Statistic Monitor document. After the monitored statistic crosses the threshold specified, an Alarm document is generated in the Statistics database (`statrep.nsf`). Review a list of all available statistics in the Statistic & Events database views Statistics Names or Statistics Names by Description.

- The first field on the Statistic Monitor document allows the administrator to specify either a single server to monitor or all servers in the domain.
- Next, designate the statistic to be monitored by clicking on the Change button. This produces a list of all available statistics. Depending on the statistic chosen, there may be additional parameters to specify, such as the unit of measurement reported.
- The administrator then specifies the desired threshold that, once crossed, generates the Alarm document.
- The severity of this event may be specified. Severity choices were described earlier in the "Events" section of this chapter.

To receive notification when an Alarm document is generated, the administrator can configure an Event Notification document, as described in the "Events" section of this chapter.

Probes

While monitors are passive, probes actively check for availability of the specified resource in a designated timeframe. If the resource takes too long to respond, an Event is generated and the associated Action performed. The three types of probes in Domino R5 are summarized in Table 18.13.

Table 18.13   **Summary of Probes Available in R5**

Probe Type	Function
Domino server probe	Tests for the availability of a target server. Optionally, you may check for the capability to access the server and open a specific database. The port used to contact the target server can also be specified. Any network configured on the testing server may be specified.
TCP server probe	Tests for the availability of the target server on a specific port. The probe measures response time, in milliseconds. Services that may be monitored are: DNS FTP HTTP IMAP LDAP NNTP POP3 SMTP

Probe Type	Function
Mail Probe	A test message is sent to a user on the target server. This message generates a confirmation from the recipient. Completion of these events within a specified number of minutes signifies successful completion. Probe intervals and timeouts are configurable.

Upon opening the Statistics & Events database (see Figure 18.5), you notice that there are now buttons allowing the setup of Event Notification, Monitors, Probes, and Troubleshooting Wizards. This approach is meant to make event notification configuration less ominous for new administrators. It is still possible to create the necessary documents manually. The same choices are presented using either method. Two exceptions: Troubleshooting documents cannot be configured manually, and Server Statistic Collection documents cannot be created via a Wizard.

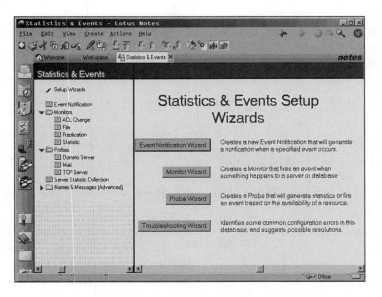

Figure 18.5 The opening screen of the Statistics & Events database.

A single Server Statistic Collection document can be configured to monitor all servers in a domain or some subset of servers. If additional Collection documents are not configured, only the server running the Collect task will be monitored.

Configuring the choices in a Statistic Collection Document is straightforward. The choices are summarized in Table 18.14.

Table 18.14 **Summary of Fields on the Server Statistic Collection Document**

Option	Description
Collecting Server	Enter the name of a server running the Collect task.
All servers in this domain	Collects statistics from all of the servers in the domain.
All servers that are not explicitly listed to be collected	Collects statistics from servers in the domain on which statistics are not currently collected.
From the following servers	Choose specific servers from which to collect.
Database to receive reports	Select this option to enable statistics logging to a specific database
Database to receive reports	Normally statrep5.nsf, the Statistics Reporting database
Collection report interval	The number of minutes between generation of statistics reports. The minimum value is 15 minutes.
Collection alarm interval	The number of minutes between generation of alarms. The minimum value is every 15 minutes.

Event Notification

The options in an Event Notification document are summarized in Table 18.15.

Table 18.15 **Summary of the Fields on the Event Notification Document**

Option	Description
Notification trigger	Choices are A built in or add-in task event. The choice determines what is displayed on the Event and Action tabs.
Servers to monitor	Select Notify of the event on any server in the domain or choose Notify of the event only in the following servers: to specify servers running the Event task you want to monitor.
Built in/Add-in Task event	These choices appear on the Event tab when A built in or add-in task event is the selected notification trigger.

Option	Description
Select Event button	Opens a list of available error messages and their type from which to choose.
Choose either `Events can have any message` or `Events must have this text in the event message.`	Generate an event response to any error of this type or specify the database, server, user name, and so on that must be embedded in the message.
Actions taken in response to an event are selected. Additionally, choose to enable or disable monitoring of this action. Action monitoring may also be enabled for a time period.	A summary of the available actions are summarized earlier in the section.
Criteria to match	These choices appear on the Event tab when `Any event that matches a criteria` is the selected notification trigger.
Choose either `Events can be any type` or `Events must be this type` to specify an event type.	Refer to the Domino documentation for Event types. Additional types may be available with add-in software packages.
Choose `Event can be any severity` or `Events must be one of these severities` to specify a severity level.	Severity can be Fatal, Failure, Warning (high and low), orNormal.
Choose either `Events can have any message` or `Events must have this text in the event message.`	Generate an event response to any error of this type or specify the database, server, user name, and so on that must be embedded in the message.

Troubleshooting Wizard

The Troubleshooting Wizard analyzes documents within the Statistics & Events database and attempts to identify common configuration errors. The Wizard will generate a report containing any problems it found and suggest solutions. The documents searched are selectable. Through the Wizard, Notes will check paths and filenames entered in Statistics & Events configuration documents. For example, if you created a

Replication monitor that checked that the database `sales.nsf` located on Server *x* replicated at least once every 24 hours, the Troubleshooting Wizard would attempt to verify that the path and filename in the Monitor document were valid. If not, the Wizard would show that it could find that database on Server *x*. This would suggest that you should check connection records and network settings.

Monitoring Domino from the Administration Client

Up to this point, we have looked mostly at the traditional tools of Domino server monitoring. It is still important to pay attention to the basics, although new features are alluring. The information available through the new Administration Client requires the correct set upof the databases, monitors, and probes discussed in the preceding sections.

The Administration client provides the support staff with a convenient graphical presentation of important reports and statistics. Before we delve into the information available through the Administration Client, there are a few configuration choices to be aware of. The next section explores the choices available in the Administration Preferences dialog box.

Administration Preferences

Preferences for server monitoring can be set through the Administration Preferences dialog box, located under the File menu. Select the Monitoring button in the Administration Preferences dialog box to do the following:

- Choose which Domino Domains are to be monitored. The servers in an added domain do not appear in the Server Monitor. After adding a new entry to the list of domains to be monitored, it is necessary to choose Administration, Refresh, Server List, All Domains in the Administration Client.
- Limit the amount of virtual memory reserved for monitoring. Valid choices are between 4 and 99MB.
- Automatically monitor all new servers.
- Specify where statistics are collected for any of the user's locations. Choices include the current computer or a remote server running the Collect server task.
- Specify the polling interval of monitored servers.
- Specify whether servers are monitored when the Administrator Client is started.

Shortcut to Administration Preferences
There is a shortcut to reach the Administration Preferences dialog box. From the Administration Client, right-click on the server icon located on the icon bar and select Preferences.

Server Properties

Earlier in the chapter we noted that server monitoring involves detailed record keeping. Gathering baseline information from Domino is just as important as when dealing with the operating system. In R5, you can retrieve information about a specific server by viewing its properties, just like with a database.

Server properties are viewable through the Domino Administration Client by right clicking on an individual server icon. If SmartIcons are displayed, you can select the server and click the Properties SmartIcon. The information reported is categorized into five tabs (see Table 18.16).

Table 18.16 **Summary of the Server Properties Interface**

Tab	Properties
Basics	Shows the Domino software version, platform, license, current time, and date. This is similar to the information returned from the `show tasks` command at the server console.
Disks	Displays information about the hard disks installed in the server. Displays information by drive letters, % free, free (MB), and size.
Cluster	Displays cluster information if the server is in a cluster. Statistics include cluster name, availability threshold, availability index, cluster network port, probe time-out, count values, and cluster members.
Ports	Provides access to the port configuration dialog box.
Advanced	Displays statistics including total transactions, peak transactions, and number of transactions in the last hour and minute. User statistics include the number of current users, peak number, and the date and time that peak occurred. Memory statistics included are availability, allocated memory, and available memory.

Information on the Status Tab

The Status tab provides a quick inventory of the tasks, ports, and users currently on this server (see Figure 18.6). The first screen is divided into two parts. The top half displays the total number of tasks, configured ports, and current activity. The bottom half of the screen displays information about users and session activity. The information displayed is equivalent to the output returned by entering the `show task` command at a server console.

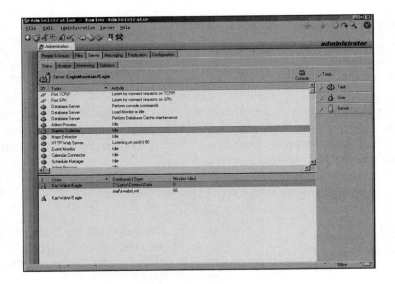

Figure 18.6 The Status tab provides information
on system tasks, ports, and current users.

Administrators will be pleased to find that there is much more functionality available on this tab than first meets the eye. Again, the tasks and information are available from other places in Domino and Notes. The Administration Client merges many administrative monitoring functions making the day-to-day life of an administrator easier.

The following commands are available from the menu, but most administrators want to know the shortcuts.

Right-clicking on a server task provides options to do the following:

- Issue a `tell` command with selectable options for the specified task. For example, choices for the `tell` command when the AdminP task is highlighted allows the administrator to process all requests or to specify types of AdminP tasks by selecting them from a dialog box. The dialog box also provides an explanation of each available option.

- Stop the task.

- Start a new task.

- By right-clicking on a configured port, you can stop that port.

Viewing Responses to Remote Server Commands

There is no response shown in the Administration Client when issuing a `tell` command that produces a response from the console. To view the response, you must either look at the actual server console or click the Console button and start a Live console session before issuing the `tell` command. You can then switch back to the console view to see the response.

When you right-click on a user name, the following options are available:

- Broadcast a message to all or specific users. Unfortunately, if you want to send a message to a specific user the user, name must be typed in manually.
- Drop the selected user's session.

Clicking the Console button on the Status tab will open the remote console screen. Commands can be entered just as in previous versions of Notes. There is a button to start a Live console session to view real-time information on the selected server. To switch to another server, select the icon from the available choices on the icon bar. The Tasks button will switch back to the Tasks view.

Information on the Analysis Tab

The Analysis tab allows the administrator to open the server (see Figure 18.7):

- Log (log.nsf)
- Catalog
- Statistics Reports view of the Statistics & Events database
- Administration Requests

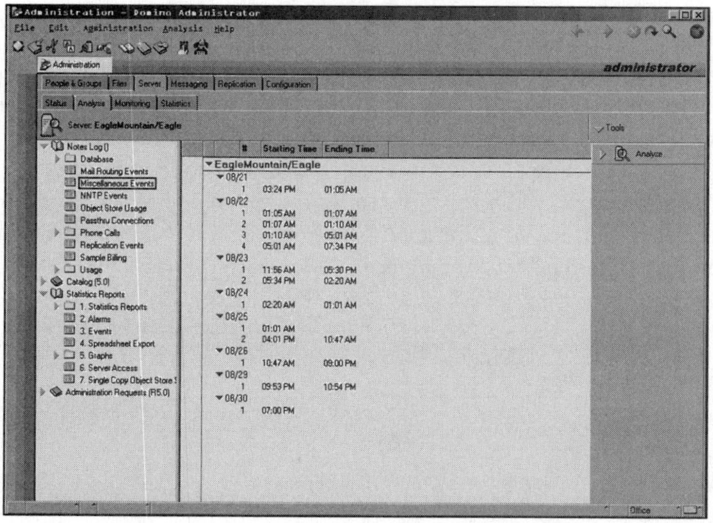

Figure 18.7 The Analysis tab provides convenient access to the Server Log, Statistics Reports, Administration Requests, and Catalog databases.

Each database is opened within a window on the Analysis tab, similar to the Portfolio type of database in previous releases.

The Log Analysis and Decommission Server tools are also available from this tab. Only the Log Analysis tool is used in server monitoring.

Log Analysis

Log analysis is accessed through the Server-Analysis tab in the Domino Administration Client. This tool provides a mechanism to search for specific character strings. It may be preferable to specify that Notes create the Results database on a local workstation, instead of on the server. This reduces the likelihood of another administrator overwriting your search results. Choose to either overwrite or append new results to the database. Unfortunately, searching multiple servers with a single query is not supported. To simulate this, specify the same character string on each of the target servers and append the results instead of overwriting the Results database each time. The log may also be searched using the Web Administrator.

Information on the Monitoring Tab

Most of the monitoring information is accessed through the Monitoring tab in the Administration Client.

Domino Server Monitor

A quick glance at the Domino Server Monitor is meant to speak a thousand words (see Figure 18.8). Task information is using one of six symbols to indicate the status of the task on monitored servers. Monitored statistics display a value. At the top of the display of the By Timeline view is a user-adjustable time scale indicating the update interval. The administrator uses this scale to set the frequency of status updates. Valid choices are between 1 and 60 minutes. As the frequency of the updates decreases, the summarization of the reported data increases. Monitoring can be initiated by clicking on the Start button or through Administration Preferences.

Limitation of the Log Analysis Utility
The Log Analysis utility searches only the Miscellaneous Events view of the Domino log. No other views or logs can be searched.

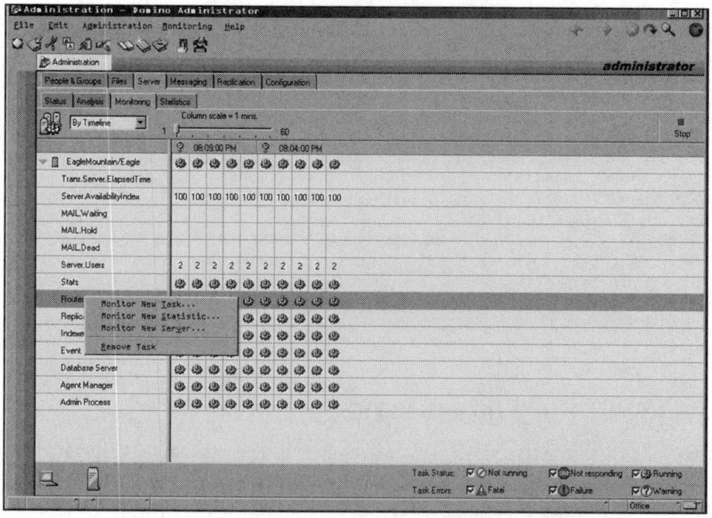

Figure 18.8 The Monitoring tab provides a convenient,
graphical status of server operations at specified intervals.

By clicking on a server name, the administrator can see the status of any monitored task or statistic on the server. Additional tasks, statistics, or servers can be added or deleted on individual servers through the Monitoring menu or by right-clicking. Additional tasks or statistics for all servers can be added or deleted by right-clicking on the Server-Monitoring tab and choosing from the list. This view provides a great overview appropriate for most help desks. It lacks the capability to drill down further to discover more information for tasks displaying an error.

The second view, By State, uses the same symbolic reporting presentation, but the server information is not collapsed, which makes detailed viewing a bit easier. Table 18.17 summarizes the status icons on the Monitoring tab.

Navigation Problem

In R5.0 there is a known bug. Using the Page Up and Page Down keys may cause server names and statistics to become unaligned. The server tasks scroll, but the server names do not. This is not a problem unless there are more than 10 servers on the screen. Lotus will issue a fix in upcoming releases of R5.

R5 Required for Icons to Function Properly

For the indicator icons to function properly, the monitored tasks must be running Domino R5, with the Event server task enabled.

Table 18.17 **Status Icons on the Monitoring Tab**

Task Status Indicator	Meaning
Fatal	Fatal errors are being generated but the task is running.
Failure	Failure errors are being generated but the task is running.
Warning	Warning errors are being generated but the task is running.
Not responding	The task is responding slowly.
Not running	The task has not been running since the server monitor was started.
Running	The task is running properly.

Information on the Statistics Tab

The Statistics tab displays the same output that a Show statistic command entered at the server console would (see Figure 18.9). The advantage to viewing the statistics in the Administration Client is that they are formatted and presented graphically. The statistics are categorized by type. Right-clicking gives the option of either expanding or collapsing all of the categories or copying the selected information.

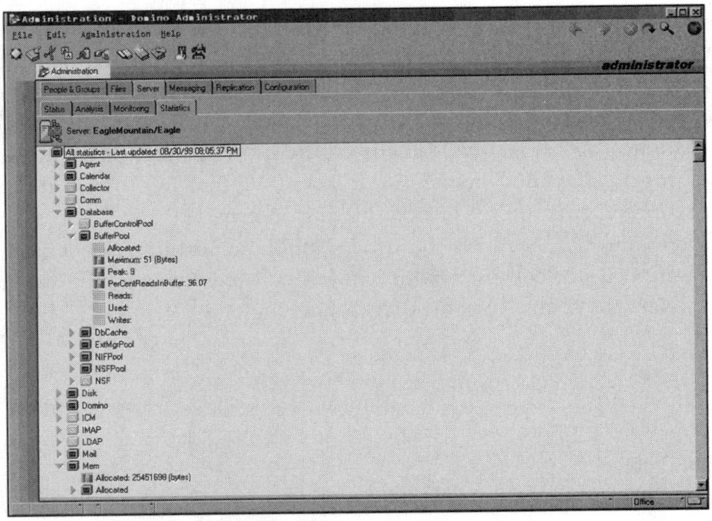

Figure 18.9 The Statistics tab provides a graphical display of the current server statistics.

Web Administrator

The Domino Web Administrator provides many of the functions available from the Administration Client via an http session using a browser. The first time that the http task is loaded onto a server, Domino creates the Web Administrator database (webadmin.nsf). The user must be listed in the Administrators field in the Domino Directory to access the database.

Setting Up Web Administrator

Setting up the Web Administrator is fairly simple. Naturally, the target server must be running the http task to be accessed by a browser. Next ensure that the user name is entered into these three fields in the Server Document:

- Administrators
- Run Unrestricted LotusScript and Java agents on the server
- Administer the server from a browser

The Web Administration database is automatically set up the first time that the http task is loaded on the server. Default database security should be acceptable for most sites. Check the roles assigned to each user to ensure that no group has inappropriate access for your environment. Access can be granted via either the usual name and password dialog box or through SSL authentication.

Using Web Administrator

To access the Web Administrator with a browser, enter the URL in this format:
`http://hostname/webadmin.nsf`

The first screen displayed when opening the Web Administrator from a Web browser is an informational display of the server name and the name of the host computer (see Figure 18.10). Operating system, Domino release, and build information are also displayed.

Through the Web Administrator menu, the following types of actions can be performed (see Table 18.18):

Table 18.18 **Summary of the Options Available Through the Web Administrator**

Web Administrator Menu	Functions
Console	Enter commands into a remote server console.
Databases	Create: Create new databases.
	Usage: View database usage statistics from the server log.
	Tools: Perform various database activities such as run Compact, create a full-text index, delete databases, replicate, create a new copy, or view and set size quotas.
	Catalog: View the database catalog.
	Access Control: Manage database ACL. You must have Manager access to the database.
	Sizes: View the database By size view in the server log. Note that database size does not include that of the full-text index. Full-text indices should be monitored manually.

continues

Table 18.18   **Continued**

Web Administrator Menu	Functions
Directories	People: Create new person records and edit existing records. Groups: Create new group documents and edit existing records. Deny Access Groups: Add or edit Deny Access Groups in the Domino Directory. Alternative Language Information: View alternate language information, if it is configured on the server.
Replication	Replication Events: View the Replication Events view in the server log.
Messaging	Routing Status: View a graphical display of message routing status. Two dial graphics indicate the number of dead and pending mail. Large amounts of dead or pending mail can consume considerable disk space and may also indicate routing or network problems. Routing Events: View the Mail Routing Events view in the server log. Mail Reports: If mail tracking is enabled on the server, you may run or view mail reports in the Reports database. Mail Users: View the Mail Users view in the Domino Directory or add a person document. Message Tracking: Track messages sent or received Today, Yesterday, Over the last week or two, or as long as information is available. Shared Mail: View Shared Mail information.
Analysis	Logfile: View the server log. Memory: View Memory information in a pie chart. Statistics: View Statistic Reports. Diskspace: View disk space information in a pie chart. Administration Requests: View Administration Requests. Statistics & Events: View the Statistics & Events database. Alerts: View system alerts by severity. Time period is selectable; default is 24 hours. Results are summarized by colored indicator "lights." Green means Normal, Yellow means Warning, and Red means Investigate. Web Statistics: View Web statistics in a bar chart showing Web requests since the server was last started.

Web Administrator Menu	Functions
Configuration	Servers: View, Edit, or Add a server record in the Domino Directory.
	Web Configuration: Access the Web Configuration view in the Domino Directory.
	Clusters: Manage cluster information.
	Connections: Access the Connections view in the Domino Directory.
	Domains: Access the Domains view in the Domino Directory.
	Programs: Access the Programs view in the Domino Directory.
	Configurations: Access the Server Configurations view in the Domino Directory.
	System Files: View or Edit text files in the Domino Data directory or one of its subdirectories.
Preferences	Edit Domino Web Administrator interface preferences.
Help	Displays the Notes Administration Help database.

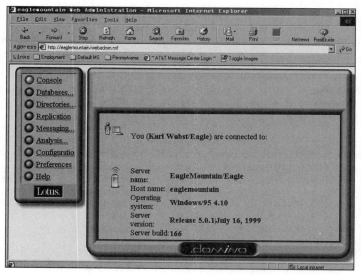

Figure 18.10 The Web Administration functionality in Domino R5 allows administrators to configure and monitor servers through a browser.

The Web Administrator accesses information in files and databases on the Domino server. If the database is not present on the server, that information is not displayed. The following databases are utilized to display information:

- Administration Requests
- Database Catalog
- Domino Directory
- Log
- Notes Administration Help
- Statistics
- Statistics & Events
- Web Server Log

Through the Web Administrator, the administrator is capable of performing most of the same functions as with the Domino Administration Client. Monitor security if you enable this feature. The benefits are obvious, but the system exposure means that you want to get this one right. Check your work; there may be a test!

The Mean Time Between Failure Utility from Iris

This add-in is an unsupported tool from the labs at Iris. IBM and Iris both use it, but it is not an official product. This is another tool that became available as a result of its widespread use at the manufacturer. Chapter 19, "Performance Tuning," contains discussions about others.

MTBF will scan your Notes log for startup and shutdown messages. When MTBF finds a server startup message that is not preceded by a shutdown message, a Server Crash document is created in the database. MTBF makes a second pass through the log and pulls out the last message that appears in the log before the crash. Administrators can then annotate the Server Crash document to track information about the crash.

MTBF is not R5-specific. It works with R4 and later English-language versions of Notes.

MTBF can be used to gather version information along with highlighting possible crash situations. As discussed in this chapter, Notes generates large amounts of statistical and event-related data. Putting it in one easily accessible location is helpful for creating crash reports with new and test lab implementations. Download MTBF from Notes.Net's Sandbox.

Monitoring Communications Between the Domino Server and Notes Client

When faced with slow response times in an application, or when benchmarking performance, understanding the components of communications between the client and server would be helpful. Do you know what processes are executed in the background after the user initiates a Notes or Domino command? The following section shows how to expose these processes and use them to better comprehend exactly what you propose to monitor.

Understanding what goes on between the Notes client and Domino server can help you understand more about Notes and Domino. There are debug parameters that will report details regarding NRPC activity. Usually, these are placed into the notes.ini file to produce additional output to assist the troubleshooters at Lotus when you call in with a problem. Some can cause problems if used inappropriately. The one that follows will fill up your hard disk before causing any major problems.

Notes.ini Parameters

To output to the screen:
```
Client_Clock=1
Debug_Console=1
```

To output to a file:
```
Client_Clock=1
Debug_Outfile=<path\filename>
```

Any one user function, such as opening a database, is actually comprised of multiple NRPCs. It is interesting and informative to combine these results with those of additional tools. Following is an example of how the output from these debug parameters can be combined and correlated with experiential and log data to benefit system function.

For our example, suppose your task was to obtain meaningful data regarding the impact, to your users, of implementing the Notes R5 client on your production network. The challenge is to capture verifiable data from various points on the network in as unbiased a manner as possible.

First, it is necessary to collect information from clients using current code levels. You could, for example, go to various workstations with a stopwatch and time various activities. The problem with this approach is that it only yields a gross calculation and there is little evidence showing the chain of events leading to the collected result. This method produces only start and finish times from which we derive elapsed time.

By placing debug parameters into the client's notes.ini file, you can capture communications between the server and client. Now, output obtained by repeating the same activity on different machines produces a comparative baseline for the network using the current client. This method has the added bonus of creating hard data for your application developers about the execution times of specific processes between workstation and server.

Start by measuring a given activity, such as opening the current Notes client. Next, install the R5 client and repeat the test. Change the output filename so you can distinguish between the two results. By comparing the results from the baseline with those after introducing the R5 client, you can make an educated guess regarding the impact of the new client. To take this a step further, after making pertinent configuration changes to the client, repeat the test and compare the new results with the original R5 test result.

While this methodology is preferable to visiting each workstation with a stopwatch, there are flaws built into the process. For example, after repeating any process a number of times, the person executing that process will become more efficient. Therefore, the time necessary for the tester to complete the designated task will vary. This has the effect of biasing the results.

By using an additional scripting tool such as ProActive Load, we can consistently test actions of Notes/Domino with variances of

- Time of day
- Location on the network
- Class of machine

The following output was obtained by adding these parameters to `notes.ini` on a workstation:

```
Client_clock=1
Debug_Outfile=c:\ln50data\performance.txt
```

The `Debug_Outfile` line allows you to specify a file (`performance.txt` is used in this example) to capture the results. This data was produced by opening the Notes R5 client and then closing it. No database functions were performed.

```
(1-23 [1]) OPEN_DB: (Connect to EagleMountain/SERVERS/Eagle: 0 ms) (Exch names: 0
ms)(Authenticate: 30 ms.)
(OPEN_SESSION: 10 ms)
20 ms. [126+290=416]
(2-23 [2]) GET_DBINFOFLAGS: 10 ms. [14+16=30]
(3-23 [3]) FINDDESIGN_NOTES: 0 ms. [38+16=54]
(4-23 [4]) OPEN_COLLECTION: 10 ms. [32+34=66]
(5-23 [5]) FOLDER_GETMODTIME_RQST: 0 ms. [78+60=138]
(6-23 [6]) GET_NAMED_OBJECT_ID: 0 ms. [96+24=120] (Special database object cannot
be located)
(7-23 [7]) FIND_BY_KEY: 0 ms. [48+26=74] (Entry not found in index)
(8-23 [8]) CLOSE_COLLECTION: 0 ms. [12+0=12]
0 ms. [12+0=12] (Session Closed)
```

How to Interpret the Output

Here's a sample line from the preceding output:

```
(2-23 [2]) GET_DBINFOFLAGS: 10 ms. [14+16=30]
```

This output is dissected in Table 18.19 showing each component and an accompanying description. Use this table as a legend to understand output produced by using the preceding debug parameters. Extrapolating from this single line of output, you can begin to understand what is transpiring between the Notes client and server. Once the process is understood, it can be used to obtain useful information, as described previously.

Table 18.19 **Detail of the Sample Output from** `performance.txt`

Output	Description
`(2-23 [2])`	Just a sequential number
`GET_DBINFOFLAGS:`	Task being performed
`10 ms.`	Amount of time spent on this task
`14`	Data sent
`16`	Data received
`30`	Total amount of data in bytes

Use information contained in the server log files during the testing period to augment your client findings. Combine use of the tools discussed in this chapter with this server-client communication to obtain an end-to-end accounting of R5 application behavior. For example, the output of the `show statistics` command would provide details regarding server and network load during the described client testing.

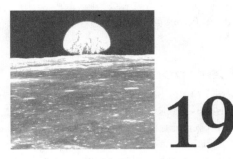

19

Performance Tuning

WHEN WE TALK ABOUT SERVER PERFORMANCE, we are really talking about the interaction between server hardware, the network, local operating system, Notes, and third-party software package configurations. How these elements are combined forges our user's and management's perception of how well the implementation does the job expected of it. A Domino server is capable of moving thousands of messages across the network in a split second, supporting discussions that can reshape the way your company does business, support e-commerce, or just help employees make lunch plans. Administrators, users and management alike, prefer low-hassle ways to make servers run faster and more reliably. In this chapter, we discuss ways to get more out of your Notes server. For tips on the Web components, read Chapter 15, "Web Server Setup, Maintenance, Tuning, and Troubleshooting." For further resources on server performance, check out the following Web sites:

```
http://www.redbooks.ibm.com/

http://www.lotus.com/performance

http://www.notes.net/today.nsf

http://www.compaq.com/activeanswers/about/lobby.html

http://microsoft.com/support

http://www.mcp.com/personal

http://www.innergy.com/

http://www.rs6000.ibm.com/
```

Components

Part I of this book helped you get the server up and running. Now, after examining the server logs and listening to users, you decide there are areas that could stand improvement. What you do depends on where the issues exist.

The first task when performance tuning any system is to become aware of the configuration of the components with which you work. You should know what you have before you start changing anything. If you haven't already done so, take an inventory of the system configuration. (Sounds like a great subject for a Notes database!) The system does not stop at the interface between the network and the server hardware. Performance tuning involves everything from the server through data delivery to the user's desktop.

The second task when performance tuning is to monitor the components of the system consistently, if not continually. This gives you a solid baseline from which to start. Without good performance monitoring, you cannot say where you started from, where you are going, or where you have been. So then, how will you know when you have arrived? If you haven't already done so, read Chapter 18, "Server Monitoring," and establish a monitoring plan.

In this chapter, I make the assumption that you have a functional server and are familiar with the general operations of Notes/Domino. As I've stated, the candidates for performance tuning are not limited to the server hardware. Server manufacturers understand this and thus do not limit their testing environment tweaks to hardware alone. Performance is rated by completing a task from start to finish. As Notes administrators, we may think of performance only as it relates to the piece for which we are responsible, but every layer of the process either adds or detracts from how our users see performance. The major components of a system are listed below. These are only the starting point.

- Hardware
- Operating systems
- Notes/Domino software
- Third-party products
- Network

Hardware

All hardware is not created equal. I am sure that this is no surprise to any of you. Hardware vendors are even more keenly aware of this truth than most of us. The manufacturers make their livings by combining the available technology into a salable product. As a result, server manufacturers have taken to quoting performance numbers in their advertisements. Server vendors claim to run tens of thousands of users on whatever particular server line they happen to be hawking in a given ad.

This is not to say that manufacturers would deliberately misrepresent the facts. Simply put, each vendor wants to show his product in the best light possible.

Before you start drooling over the performance numbers any manufacturer espouses, understand what they really mean. For example, are these performance numbers the result of accepted, standardized tests? Are they based on an unrealistic lab environment or from real-world implementations?

It is not uncommon to see advertisements for servers quoting NotesBench reports claiming to support ten thousand or more concurrent users. Do you know what sort of work the users were doing in this test? What type of activity was being measured? How was the machine configured? Does the ad mention quantities of RAM, disk configuration, the number of processors or network adapters installed? All these components can be manipulated to produce performance gains. If you work for a corporation and are making a large purchase, consider asking the vendor if he has a customer with such a configuration who wouldn't mind you stopping by for a quick visit to marvel at their achievements. These intercorporate visits happen more than you might imagine.

Later in this chapter, there are descriptions of the current NotesBench workloads. After examining the differences between the dozen or so workloads available, you may start asking your vendor the questions that can save your company money for more important things—like your salary.

General rules from previous Notes implementations continue to apply in Release 5 (R5). The following list describes some of the ways that vendors squeeze the performance out of a server to generate those amazing NotesBench numbers. If you've been around Notes for a few years, you probably have seen some of them before.

Due to budget and time constraints, most production sites elect not to make all these changes. Prioritize the items and implement them as you can. Each of them are viable methods to increase server performance. Another thing that will help is to examine the NotesBench reports that correspond to the types of servers you have or plan to implement. Valuable information can be gleaned from your manufacturers testing.

- Use the fastest drives you can afford (10,000 rpm +). Multiple, moderately sized drives are better than one large, logically partitioned drive. Consider using multiple disk controllers as well.

- Spread databases and programs across physical disks. Having more read/write heads allows data to be read or written more quickly. This can be accomplished using RAID or file pointers.

- Check for BIOS upgrades from your server manufacturer.

- Put paging files on separate physical drives whenever possible. If you do not have a spare drive in the system, place the paging file on the application drive as opposed to the data drive. Keep the operating system and paging files on separate physical or logical drives.

- Do not put the paging file, or anything else if you can help it, on the drive with the transaction log files. The transaction log writes to the hard disk sequentially. This places the drive into a different mode than for random access. Constantly switching between modes on the same drive increases overhead.

- Screen savers can use large amounts of processor resource. Assuming that your server is in a secure location, behind a locked door, disable the screen saver. If you require a screen saver for security reasons, use one that only blanks the screen. Generating the elaborate graphics in some screen savers can use up to 100 percent of the processor.

- Plan for 200–300KB of server memory per active user. Previous releases of Notes used 300-400KB per active user.

- Databases are I/O intensive, consider increasing the stripe size on RAID disks to 8 or 16 bits. Also, use hardware RAID instead of software RAID. It's faster and consumes less CPU overhead.

- Switch to PCI adapters (disk controllers or network interface cards) instead of EISA or EISA/PCI.

- Use servers with multiple high-speed processors. R5 is better able than previous versions to work with multiple processors. Interestingly, though, too many CPUs can actually degrade performance due to the overhead of managing the workload among processors. Four processors is the current, generally accepted high-end with NT 4.0 servers.

- Consider partitioning your Notes servers. As a general rule, though, plan for one processor per partition. The AS/400 platform is a notable exception to the rule. The AS/400 can isolate partitions logically, allowing others to stay up when one fails.

- Better performance can be achieved by using one network interface card (NIC) per partition instead of assigning multiple addresses on a single NIC.

- Avoid verbose logging to the server log (log.nsf) or debug parameters in the notes.ini unless necessary for troubleshooting a specific problem. Log to text files when you have a choice.

- If your server is running NT 4.0, check disk fragmentation while you have the server offline for maintenance. NT 4 doesn't have a built-in defragmentation utility, so you will need to research the available third-party products. (Windows 2000 is supposed to have a built-in defragmentation utility.)

- Do not use NT disk compression on system, paging, transaction logging, or database drives. Customers have reported system crashes, server hangs, and data corruption when using disk compression. Lotus does not support configurations with this option enabled.

- Use NT's Registry Editor to set the value of `HKEY_LOCAL_MACHINE\SYSTEM\ CurrentControlSet\Control\Session Manager\Memory Management\ LargeSystemCache` to 0 (zero). This causes NT to perform as an application server instead of using the default setting as a file server. Restart the system for this change to be incorporated.

- Eliminate single point of failure in configurations. If possible, use high-availability features to reduce stress on heavily used servers and provide failover. High-availability features include clustering, (consider both Domino and hardware or software options), HACMP, or shared disk arrays.

Operating Systems

All modern operating systems provide some capability to monitor overall health of server and network operations. In fact, today's sophisticated implementations of Windows NT and the various UNIX platforms provide excellent utilities to monitor and report potential problems or bottlenecks. See Chapter 18 for information on how to install a counter in the NT Performance Monitor to chart a multitude of Domino server statistics.

If planning a new Domino implementation, factor in new features offered by your operating system vendor, such as the new features in Windows 2000, when Microsoft eventually makes it available. There is an informative White Paper available from Microsoft titled "Planning Windows NT Server 4.0 Deployment with Windows 2000 Server in Mind." The paper is available at `http://www.microsoft.com/TechNet/ deploy/nt4tont5/nt4tont5.htm`.

Operating system performance monitoring capabilities are available either on-demand, utilized in a specific instance to gather information about a particular system or subsystem, or on a continuous basis as a background task. Most administrators use the on-demand method, but in a high-profile, production environment, you may want to use some form of continuous monitoring. While Notes provides probes to check on mail performance, and SNMP agents are available to check for connectivity, operating systems provide native tools that will continuously chart performance statistics.

IBM provides information regarding AIX performance tuning on its Web site. Start reading at `http://www.rs6000.ibm.com/doc_link/en_US/a_doc_lib/aixbman/prftungd/ contperfmon.htm` for a discussion on continuous monitoring under AIX. All the manufacturers of the major operating systems also provide suggestions to better monitor and tune system performance. Today's Notes administrator should be informed about the operating system(s) their servers run. It can be frustrating, chasing down a network administrator to ask why something is happening. With Domino's Web presence, it is also helpful for the Notes/Domino administrator to have a background in networking and security.

Special Considerations on UNIX Systems

This section covers some parameters that apply to Domino servers on UNIX platforms. Some of the same concepts are applicable to the AS/400 platform as well. Parameters set in the notes.ini are applicable on UNIX platforms, however, Domino servers on these platforms can further benefit from configuration changes at the operating system level. Parameters affecting memory usage and process prioritization are good examples of such issues.

Notes_SHARED_DPOOLSIZE

Notes_SHARED_DPOOLSIZE is a shell environment variable which determines the size of System V or memory-mapped (mmap) files. These are used to share data among server tasks. If a Domino server is unable to allocate additional shared memory, increase this variable to provide additional resources. Consult your operating system documentation for information on defaults and limitations. Both values depend on the platform.

AIX and HP-UX use System V shared memory. To obtain a list of shared memory segments used by Notes/Domino, run the ipcs -a command. The maximum segment size in use by a Domino process is the default value of Notes_SHARED_DPOOLSIZE for that platform.

Solaris systems use Memory-mapped files by default, but also support System V shared memory. Run the ls -al/tmp command and note resulting entries starting with .NOTESMEM. The default value for the Notes_SHARED_DPOOLSIZE will be the same as the largest file returned by the above command.

Prioritization of Tasks

UNIX system performance can benefit from changes to the priority assigned to tasks on a Domino server. You may use this method to grant more processing time to specific tasks. This is easiest when Domino is the only application running on that server. However, it is also possible to negatively impact performance if low-priority tasks tie up resources needed by high-priority tasks. Ensure that you can recover from changes you make if monitoring results show a degradation in performance.

Solaris-based Domino system response times can benefit from changes in Time Sharing task class. Information is contained in the NotesBench reports published by SUN.

Topics, such as task prioritization, are well-covered by the operating system vendors. Mention of operating system tweaks in this chapter is meant to provide a starting place only. For a thorough examination, contact the system vendor to ensure that you implement these concepts correctly.

Implementing Domino on SUN Servers

For additional information on tuning SUN servers for Domino, read the paper "Implementing Lotus Domino on SUN – Including Sizing Guidelines and Architectural Examples." You can obtain a copy at http://www.sun.com/servers/workgroup/solutions/lotus.html.

For Domino systems on AIX, use the `renice` and `/usrs/samples/kernel/schedtune` commands to set the priorities of different processes. Adjusting the priority of specific Notes tasks can improve performance. Check system documentation for more information.

Notes/Domino Software

There are several settings in the `notes.ini` affecting performance in the configuration of Notes and Domino after setup. Note that topics touched on here may be covered in more detail in other chapters. This chapter attempts to establish pointers for further investigation. Some of the changes are general and others are made in response to specific situations. The sections that follow discuss changes to existing, and perhaps additional, parameters in the server's `notes.ini` file.

Tweaking the `notes.ini` can produce dramatic changes in the way the server operates and responds to user requests. The following few sections discuss ways to effect these settings. Most of the settings below can be made through the Notes client instead of editing the `notes.ini` directly. If you do edit the `notes.ini` with a text editor, save a working copy (with a different name) beforehand so you can revert to it in an emergency. Some of these changes are made in specific fields in appropriate sections of the server document. Others can be made by navigating to the Configuration tab of the Server document. Open the Administration client and select the name of the server you want to configure. Next select Configurations - Add Configuration (Select Edit, Configuration, if one already exists). The Configuration Settings screen is presented. Click the `NOTES.INI` Settings tab to get to the screen shown in Figure 19.1.

Click the Set/Modify Parameters button and the Server Configuration Parameters screen appears. Then, click the down arrow to the right of the Item box to see the list of all available parameters you can change in the `notes.ini` file (see Figure 19.2).

Online AIX Command Reference

For a valuable reference to AIX commands and performance issues visit `http://www.rs6000.ibm.com/doc_link/en_US/a_doc_lib/aixgen/wbinfnav/CmdsRefTop.htm`.

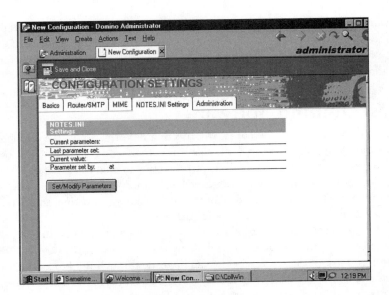

Figure 19.1 Instead of editing the notes.ini file directly, you can use the Configuration Settings interface in the Domino Directory.

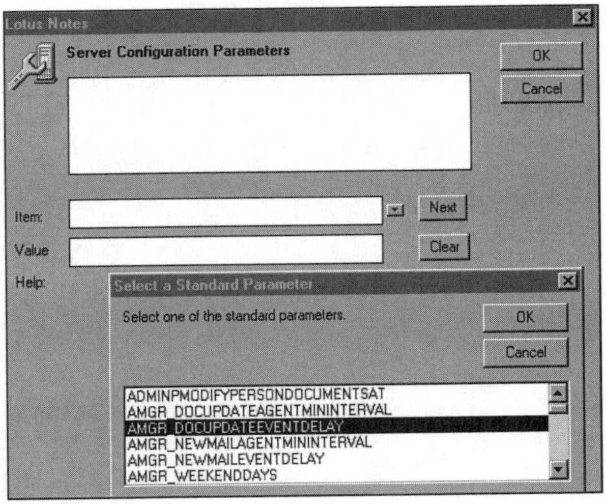

Figure 19.2 Select the notes.ini parameter you want to set and specify the desired value.

Resist the temptation to change multiple parameters simultaneously. Doing so can make it difficult to judge results, good or bad. It is important to monitor the logs, performance monitors, and whatever additional tools you rely on to judge whether your efforts have helped or hindered operations. Again, I will stress that you should put monitoring in place to provide a good baseline against which to judge the results of your changes. Charting performance numbers help you make good decisions, and come in handy when you plead your case to management for additional hardware. Lastly, if you do anything that can put data at risk, a complete backup can be invaluable!

Notes.ini Settings Affecting Performance

The following section details specific notes.ini parameters that affect Domino server performance. It is possible to specify values for each of these parameters by directly editing the notes.ini file or by using the Configuration Settings interface described in the preceding section of this chapter. After making changes to the notes.ini file, it is a good practice to monitor the log files for any expected (and unexpected) changes to system operations.

- **Settings to control when the agent manager runs event-triggered agents.** When an event-triggered agent is created, Domino schedules it to run immediately. After that, the following settings allow you to regulate how often the agents execute. If agents on your system are executing, but not in the time-frame you expected, look at these settings. Many administrators expect to eliminate any delay in the execution of triggered agents by changing the settings for Amgr_DocUpdateAgentMininterval, Amgr_DocUpdateEventDelay, Amgr_NewMailAgentMininterval and Amgr_NewMailEventDelay to 0. System overhead alone can account for delays of approximately two minutes. Naturally, providing more resources to the Agent Manager will decrease available resources for other operations.

  - **Amgr_DocUpdateAgentMininterval.** Specifies the number of minutes that must pass between each execution of the same document-triggered agent. The default is 30 minutes.

  - **Amgr_DocUpdateEventDelay.** Specifies the number of minutes that must pass between a document update event and the execution of the update-triggered agent. Any other document updates received during the delay will process as well. The default is 5 minutes.

  - **Amgr_NewMailAgentMininterval.** Specifies the number of minutes that must pass between each execution of the same new mail-triggered agent. The default is 0 minutes.

- **Amgr_NewMailEventDelay.** Specifies the number of minutes that must pass, between delivery of new mail and the execution of the new mail-triggered agent. The default is 1 minute.

- **DominoAsynchronizeAgents.** Specifies whether agents executed by Web clients may execute simultaneously or serially. The default is 0, which forces agents to run serially. Change the setting to 1 to allow multiple Web-triggered agents to run.

- **Settings to control agent queuing.** The following settings allow you some control over how often the Agent Manager checks for new agents to process.

  - **Amgr_SchedulingInterval.** Specifies the number of minutes between execution of the Agent Manager's scheduler. The default is 1 minute, but you can use a range of 1 to 60 minutes.

  - **Amgr_UntriggeredMaulInterval.** Specifies the number of minutes between the Agent Manager's checks for untriggered mail. The default is 60 minutes, with entries between 1 and 1,440 being valid.

- **Concurrent agents setting in the Server Document.** You can specify the number of agents, as many as 10, that your system is able to run at the same time. On servers running a large number of agents, allowing more agents to run concurrently will speed the processing of data along. Navigate to the Server Tasks – Agent Manager tab in the server document for the server you want to modify (see Figure 19.3.).

  Depending on the tasks performed by a particular server, you may find that agents are being queued by the server. Examine your logs and determine if agents are queuing before making any changes. Defaults are 1 during the day-time and 2 during the evenings. Increment the setting, allowing one or two additional agents to run and reexamine the logs to measure the results.

Changes to Agent Settings in R5

Previous versions of Notes included a parameter (Max % busy before delay) in the Server document that controlled the queuing of agents in relation to the activity level of the server. When the server utilization was above the percentage noted in this field, the server stopped processing agents until the server freed some resources. Beginning with R5, this setting is no longer valid.

Starting with R5, if agents are queued due to lack of resources, an entry AMgr: Agent scheduling is paused will appear in the log. Look for this new entry in the Notes log if agents seem to take longer than expected to process.

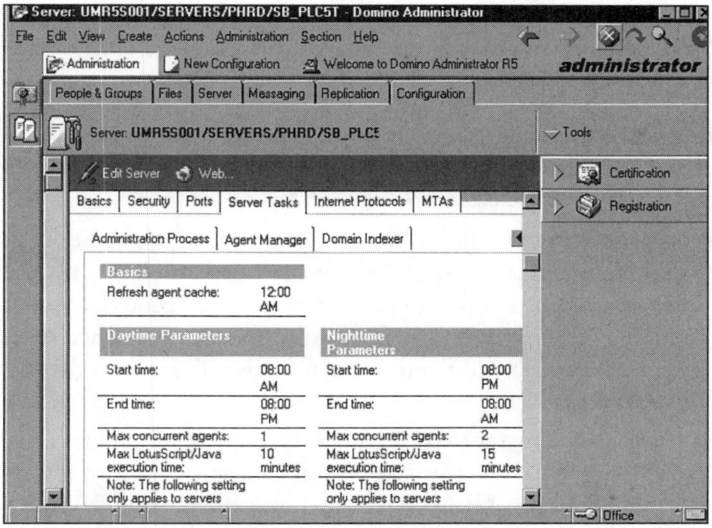

Figure 19.3 Specify the maximum number of concurrent agents you want to run. Set the number higher during off hours when agents are likely to process larger numbers of documents. Note also that the Start and End times of Daytime and Nighttime are configurable.

- **Settings Effecting Performance on Clustered and Partitioned Servers.** Although the Domino code handles resources fairly well on its own, multiple servers can require manual intervention because there is no facility to manage resources across clusters or partitions. Another item that is included in this category would be the `NSF_Buffer_Pool` parameter, which is covered later in this chapter.

  - **Server_Availability_Threshold.** This setting affects load balancing in a clustered environment. Setting the value (0–100 is acceptable) too low will inhibit failover for clients who may benefit from working on another, less used cluster member. Setting the value too high will result in unnecessary failover. The default value is 0.

  - **Server_Max_Concurrent_Trans.** This setting allows you to limit the number of concurrently scheduled transactions on a server. If using this setting on a partitioned server, Lotus recommends that the total combined value be 20 or less. For example, if running two partitions on a single computer, limit this setting to 10 (or less) on each partition. There is no default value for this setting.

On UNIX and AS/400 platforms, setting this parameter to −1 allows the operating system's kernel to control job scheduling. This has been found to be more efficient and improves performance on these platforms.

- **Setting Limits on the Number of Users and Connection Time.** It might not make you popular, but you can set limits on the number of users and the time they can stay connected.
  - **Server_MaxUsers.** Allows you to set the maximum number of users allowed to access a server. When the specified number of users is reached, the server stops accepting new Database-Open requests. By limiting the number of active users, you can ensure better performance. A setting of 0 signifies an unlimited number if active users. There is no default value for this setting.
  - **Server_Session_Timeout.** Specifies the number of minutes of inactivity allowed before the server automatically terminates network and mobile communication with a connection. Lotus recommends a value of no lower than 15 minutes. A lower setting forces the server to reopen server sessions too often which slows server performance. The default is 4 hours. Note that mobile connections usually have a shorter time-out set through the Notes client. The shorter XPC timeout takes precedence over the server setting. XPC is used by dial-up and ISDN modem connections.

Server Tasks

As time goes by, a server's role in the organization may change. For example, a server that was a mail server may become a gateway, or perhaps you decide to upgrade it to a hub. Even a new server installation is a candidate for the removal of unnecessary tasks. A fairly typical Domino default installation will place approximately 16 server tasks into the notes.ini file.

Every task running on a server consumes system resources. Examine the ServerTasks line in the notes.ini and delete any tasks that are unnecessary. This reduces the number of tasks running in memory and frees resources for the server. If you are unfamiliar with the function of particular server tasks, review the list in Appendix G of the *Administering the Domino System* book that shipped with your server software. The same list also is available in the Administration Help database or on Lotus' Notes.Net Web site.

Open the notes.ini file in a text editor and find the ServerTasks line. Compare the tasks on this line with your current needs. If, for example, you do not charge users for Notes services, the billing task could be removed. This also frees the disk space that is used by the billing database. Choose carefully to ensure that you aren't removing something you need.

Transaction Logging, a new Server Task introduced in R5 also can affect server performance. Changes to a database are recorded into the Transaction Log before the changes are committed to disk. Lotus envisions transaction logging as the way to virtually eliminate the need to run the Fixup Server Task to correct database corruption and also to enable new backup functionality. Lotus has claimed that enabling transaction logging can improve server performance by as much as 10 percent.

Some administrators are dubious regarding transaction logging, however, because the recommended configuration requires changes to controller and disk configurations. It should also be mentioned that the programs designed to take advantage of data backup using transaction logging were not released with R5. IBM has projected a 1999 year-end release for their new R5-compliant ADSM backup agent. In theory, transaction logging is a great idea; however, you may want to perform tests in your environment before relying on it.

Translog_Status

`Translog_Status` enables or disables transaction logging for all R5 databases on the server. (Transaction logging can be disabled at the database level if enabled at the server level.) The default setting is 0 (disabled). View the Transaction Logging tab in the Server document for this and other settings effecting transaction logging. You cannot change the setting for `Translog_Status` on the Server Configuration tab. It is set in the `notes.ini` through your selections on the Transaction Logging tab in the server document. Transaction logging is an important new feature introduced in R5. For information on transaction logging, review the chapter on server setup and the R5 documentation.

Multiple Replicator and Mail Router Tasks

You may improve performance on heavily loaded servers by configuring the system to run multiple replicator and mail router tasks.

The mail router (mail.box) is locked by any process either reading from or writing to the router, therefore multiple mail routers will allow Notes to process more messages. Monitor both messaging queues as well as overall system load for any error messages or significant performance degradation before and after adding additional routers. Mail hubs would be good candidates for additional routers while application servers or replication hubs may see higher performance gains from additional replicators.

On most systems, adding more than one additional router yields only marginally increased results. Lotus's general rule suggests using one mail router for the first 200 mail users, adding a second for systems supporting as many as 1,000, and adding routers incrementally, as many as 10, for systems with over 1,000 users.

Normally, a system runs one replicator for each processor in the server. Replication hubs that are not accessed regularly by users can gain increased performance by configuring additional replicator tasks. In addition, if a server conducts multiple, overlapping replication sessions, you may increase performance by adding additional replicators. Each instance of the replicator task handles one replication session at a time.

Examine the replication events in the log and connection documents to better time replications with spoke servers. If sessions on a particular port take longer than others, decrease the frequency of replication or move connections to a faster port, for example. Multiple replicators allow you to balance schedules and actually shorten replication cycles.

Settings to Improve Database and Directory Performance

Notes.ini parameters are available to adjust the way that memory is allocated on the server. As a rule, administrators do not have to set these parameters; however, there are exceptions to every rule.

NSF_Buffer_Pool

The NSF_Buffer_Pool is a section of memory that governs buffering I/O transfers between the NIF indexing functions and disk storage. On a single instance Domino server, setting a value for this parameter is unnecessary and could even hamper system performance. The default value is automatically determined by the server software. If the server has been upgraded from a previous (R4) release, check the notes.ini for this parameter. Lotus recommends removing it before upgrading single instance servers.

If running partitioned servers, this setting should be used to enhance performance because Domino cannot dynamically manage the memory across multiple partitions. If there is a high occurrence of swapping and paging on a partitioned server, setting this value below the default (one-third of system memory) will improve performance. This setting is especially useful on UNIX platforms.

The maximum setting for this parameter is 256MB for most Notes/Domino platforms. The exceptions are on the Macintosh and Windows 16-bit platforms where the maximum is 16MB. Lotus's recommendation is to use the formula:

(system RAM/number of partitions)/4

NSF_DbCache_Maxentries

The NSF_DbCache_Maxentries setting determines the number of databases a server can hold in its database cache. Opening a database from cache is much faster than retrieving it from disk. The minimum number is 25, while the maximum number is somewhere around 2,000 (platform dependent). Increasing this setting will improve system performance, at the cost of available memory. Adding physical memory also increases the number of databases Domino can hold in the database cache. The default value, also set in the `notes.ini`, is the greater of the following:

25

or

the value of the `NSF_BUFFER_POOL` (if set in the `notes.ini`) divided by 300

Advanced Database Properties Affecting Performance

The following database properties can be accessed by selecting a database icon, clicking File, Database, Properties and then selecting the Propeller Beanie tab (see Figure 19.4.) It is important to note that selecting or deselecting some of these fields will have an effect on transaction logging. A full backup of the database may be required to maintain data integrity.

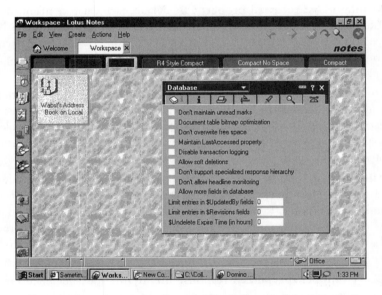

Figure 19.4   The Advanced Properties tab for a database. Several of these properties can affect database and server performance.

- **Don't maintain unread marks.** Beginning with R5, you have the option of choosing whether to maintain unread marks in each database. Maintaining unread marks slows performance. If a particular database doesn't benefit from maintenance of unread marks, as may be the case with system databases such as the log or the Domino Directory, select this option in database properties dialog box, on the Propeller Beanie tab.

- **Document table bitmap optimization.** When Notes updates a view it refers to document information tables to determine which documents to display in that view. Selecting Document table bitmap optimization causes Notes to associate tables with forms used by each document. Domino then searches only the tables associated with the forms used by documents in the view that is being updated. The result is faster view updates. After selecting (or deselecting) this property, you must compact the database for the change to take effect. If transaction logging is enabled for this database, Lotus recommends a full backup as soon as possible after making this change.

- **Don't overwrite free space.** To preserve data security, Notes overwrites deleted data on the hard drive to prevent access to the old data. This generates extra disk I/O which can slow database performance. If you are sure that the server is in a secure environment, or if the data is unimportant by nature, consider selecting this option. Remember that you are exposing your data to a risk if the data or the server's secure status changes.

- **Maintain LastAccessed property.** By default, each database maintains the date of the last change to every document. Selecting this option causes Notes to record reads of a document and changes. The option is usually only necessary if you also set document deletion based on document inactivity. Selecting the option negatively affects performance.

- **Disable transaction logging.** Selecting this option turns off transaction logging for this database. Transaction logging speeds up restart of the server because database Fixup is not necessary at startup. Transaction logging also enables backup and recovery APIs to track the database. Lotus reports performance gains of approximately 10 percent with transaction logging turned on.

- **Allow soft deletions.** This option enables/disables soft deletions inside of the database. In previous releases of Notes, after a document was deleted, it was gone. The only ways to get it back were through a restore from backup media or by replicating with another database that still had the document. R5 provides the capability to place deleted documents in a "Recycling Bin" akin to Windows 9x and NT.

- **Don't support specialized response hierarchy.** Notes documents track information about their child and response documents. This information is used only when the @functions @AllChildren and @AllDescendents are used in view selection formulas. If these @functions aren't used, select the "Don't support specialized response hierarchy" option. If transaction logging is enabled for this database, Lotus recommends a full backup as soon as possible after enabling or disabling this option.

- **Don't allow headline monitoring.** Notes 5 allows users to customize the headlines on their workstations by searching databases on servers for items of interest. The larger the number of users monitoring a database, the more performance will be effected. Headline monitoring can be enabled or disabled on the Propeller Beanie tab of the database properties dialog box. To effect multiple databases, use the Administrator Client. Consider selecting this option on large system databases.

- **Allow more fields in database.** This option allows a database, in R5 format, to contain as many as 64,000 fields. The limit, using R4.x versions of Notes, was 64KB, which equated to roughly 3,000 fields. This option can cause problems in other areas, however. Full text indexes will experience problems, and recalculation of forms with large numbers of fields takes longer.

Looking at the Propeller Beanie tab, you will notice three additional items that allow for numeric entries instead of the checkboxes above. Following is an explanation of each:

- **Limit the size of $UpdatedBy fields.** By default, the name of each user or server that edits a document in Notes is tracked in the $UpdatedBy field contained in every Notes document. Place a numeric value in this field to limit the size, and therefore the number, of edits tracked by documents in the database. When the $UpdatedBy field reaches the limit entered here, the oldest entry is removed to make room for the latest.

- **Limit the size of $Revisions fields.** By default each document in Notes includes a $Revisions field used to track edits to that document. The $Revisions field tracks the date and time of each edit. The entries in this field are used to resolve replication or save conflicts. By default, Notes will track as many as 500 edits per document. Each entry consumes 8 bytes of disk storage. By reducing the number of revisions that are tracked, especially in large databases, you save disk space. Conversely, you may also increase the number of replication and save conflicts that occur. This option is most useful in databases that are not replicated or edited very often.

- **$Undelete Expire Time (in hours).** If the Allow soft deletions property is selected on the Propeller Beanie tab, this entry specifies the number of hours for which a deleted document may be undeleted. If the document is not undeleted before the undeletion time expires, the document is permanently deleted from the database.

Performance Tools That Ship with Notes Release 5

Most of this chapter deals with ways to tune the performance of a system that is already in place. The following section discusses tools you can use to determine the best configuration for a new server or to tune an existing server.

Server.Load

Similar to NotesBench, this tool uses scripts that simulate different workloads to generate server capacity metrics. Unlike NotesBench, an administrator can create a custom script to simulate a desired workload.

Server.Load is available on the Domino installation CD. This tool contains workloads simulating Idle Usage, Simple Mail Transfer Protocol Routing, Web, IMAP, and Shared Discussion Database. To install and run Server.Load do the following:

1. Navigate to Apps\Srvload on the installation CD. There is no menu choice for Server.Load via the main installation screen.

2. Decompress the single file (sload.exe) to the Notes program directory.

3. To run Server.Load, double-click the executable file. Figure 19.5 shows the Server.Load interface.

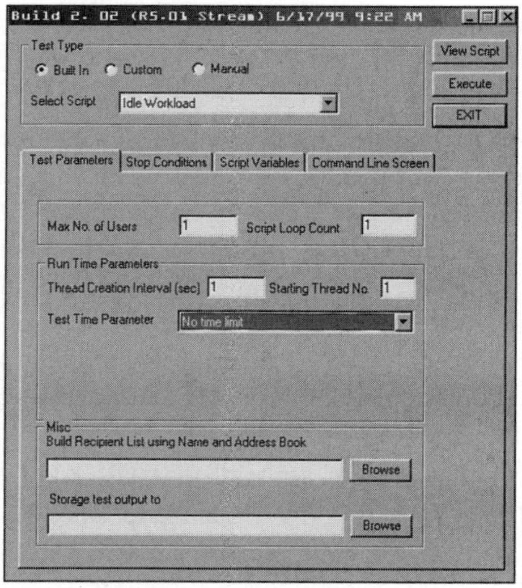

Figure 19.5 The Server.Load interface provides a tool to simulate user loads under various conditions.

For a general description of these workloads, see the section in this chapter on NotesBench, or go to `http://www.notesbench.org` for a more detailed discussion.

Server.Planner

Domino Server.Planner is a tool to help administrators gather information regarding capacity planning for new servers. This tool allows you to evaluate servers using vendor's benchmark data. You have the opportunity to enter specific information about your expected workload. This allows you to take a step toward customizing the vendor information to your environment. Use Server.Planner to point you in the direction of valid server specifications, but remember to account for the unique situation in your environment. Datasets for Server.Planner are said to be available on the NotesBench site. Unfortunately, most of the time, there are few from which to choose.

NotesBench

While NotesBench was devised by Lotus, it does not ship on the Notes CD. The reports are usually generated by vendors in their own performance laboratories. NotesBench gives hardware vendors a standardized method of reporting the behavior of Lotus Notes/Domino under a given type of load. Performance information is collected by running specific tasks on various hardware configurations.

The scripts are executed on a separate machine, called a *driver*, which presents the workload to the server being tested. To ensure consistency, the scripts cannot be edited by the testing party. Each simulated user is represented by a thread on the driver. So, for example, if you wanted to run a script simulating 500 users, there would be 500 threads executing the script against the server.

Because various types of activities place differing demands on a server, there are several models (or workloads) in use. As Notes/Domino and understanding of its use by customers evolves, additional workloads are developed. Each NotesBench workload uses a script to simulate user activity. In reality, our users exhibit combinations of these behaviors, so it may be difficult to correlate user behavior to a single script.

Read the activities performed in each workload and approximate, as closely as possible, which one is closest to the type of server you need to purchase. Manufacturers post results on their Web sites, put flattering highlights in their ads, and some even post reports on the NotesBench Web site.

NotesBench tests yield a number of results, or *metrics*, by which to judge the performance of servers under test. Table 19.1 lists the metrics that system administrators should pay attention to.

Table 19.1   **Significant Metrics**

NotesBench Metric	Description
Maximum Users Supported	The maximum number of simulated users (threads) connected to the server during the simulation.
NotesMark	Measures the cumulative number of Notes transactions per minute (tpm). The number of transactions does not map on a 1:1 basis to a user's actions. For example, opening a database may account for multiple NotesMark transactions.
Average Response Time	This measures the average response times of the server to simulated users during the test. It roughly equates to the response a user would experience under the same server load.

Description of Current Workloads

To their credit, the NotesBench consortium (which is an independent organization) publishes a description of the workloads available for testing at `http://www.notes-bench.org`. Check this site for more details and additional workload descriptions as they become available. You also can find out about becoming certified to perform NotesBench tests for your organization. At worst, you will be a better consumer. Table 19.2 provides some workload descriptions.

The NotesBench User's Guide

More detailed descriptions of each workload are available in the "NotesBench User's Guide." This guide is a Notes database that you can download from the NotesBench site. While on the NotesBench site, you should also download a copy of the paper, "What Every Performance Minded Administrator Should Know About NotesBench Reports."

The minimum amount of effort you should put into the subject is to read "What to Look for In Performance Reports." This one-page article is available in the Technical Library on Lotus' Performance Zone at `http://www.lotus.com/performance`.

Table 19.2   **Workload Descriptions**

Workload	User Activity
Calendar and Scheduling	Invitations are sent to multiple recipients.
Cluster Mail	Simulated users on a multi-node Domino cluster read, write, submit, and retrieve messages.
Cluster Mail and Shared Database	Simulated users on a three-way cluster of identical servers. Each user sends mail and adds documents to a shared database.
Cluster Topology Impact	A standalone mail/discussion database server joins a cluster, then fails-over. The simulated users work inside their mail and a shared database.
Groupware B	Simulated, experienced users send 532KB mail messages, add documents to shared databases, perform full-text searches and even replicate from their workstations to the server.
Idle Usage	Here, simulated users simply establish a session with the server. No transactions are carried out.
Mail Only	Simulated users read messages and send mail, plus carry out a few miscellaneous actions.
Mail and Shared Database	Simulated users read mail and update a shared database.
Mail Routing Hub	Simulates a server, with no users which acts as a mail router. Messages are pushed to this system and delivered to destination servers.
Online Users	These simulated users are sending large mail messages, plus file attachments.
POP3	Here, simulated users are using the POP3 protocol to send and receive messages.
Replication Hub	Simulates a single replication hub in a hub-and-spoke topology. No simulated users here.
Shared Discussion Database	Simulated users give this server a workout by reading, composing, and updating documents in a shared database.
SMTP POP3	Simulated users send and receive mail using the POP3 and SMTP protocols.
Web Buyer	Simulated Web users shop online by browsing product information, filling out order forms and processing orders.
Web Walker	Simulated Web users browse a home page and explore all the links.

Components of a NotesBench Report

Because NotesBench is a standardized test, it follows that the reports published by the testing parties must follow a standard format. If you have never actually read a NotesBench report, I encourage you to take the time to at least browse one generated by the manufacturer of your current server. There may be gold to be mined, even if you aren't currently looking for a new server.

Elements of A NotesBench Report

Next, we look at the various sections contained in a NotesBench Report. In discussions with Notes administrators, I've found that most have never read a NotesBench report. This is a waste of an important source of information. Manufacturer-tested, audited hardware, and software configurations are highlighted, as well as valid performance enhancements. Granted, you will not reach the performance numbers obtainable in a lab setting. It is also unlikely that you will get a salesman to discuss server configuration at this level of detail either. I hope that by including the report outline, more administrators and managers will realize the potential to gain valuable information and take the time to read them.

- **Executive Summary.** This section provides an overview of the test. It should contain:
  - The completion date of the tests
  - Name of the testing organization
  - Model and manufacturer of the server
  - A sentence or two outlining the server configuration and test methodology

  In addition, there is usually a table summarizing the outcome of the tests. This lets the reader quickly decide whether this report is pertinent to his needs.

- **Objectives.** In this section, the vendor explains what its objective was in preparing this test. Usually, the objective is to demonstrate that a new feature or configuration provides added value to your organization.

- **Test Methodologies.** This section is a description of how the tests were carried out. Read carefully to understand what was done and extract the information that you can apply in your own environment to boost performance. From this section, another engineer should be able to configure a network and reproduce the tests. Specifically, the testing organization should outline:
  - The configuration of the computers involved in the tests. These normally include the system under test, the driver machines, and the destination systems used.
  - The network type and protocol configuration.

- Changes made to the Notes or system parameters that deviate from default settings.

- Additional devices, programs or techniques used.

■ **Data.** This section presents the results of the tests. Graphical summaries of the results achieved for each workload that was tested plus information on timings, system responsiveness, and such. Look for the specifics regarding the maximum number of users supported, NotesMark (tpm) and average response times.

■ **Analysis.** This section provides a description of the results. Information is provided about specific machine behavior at various points in the test.

■ **Conclusions.** This is a customer-focused section. The vendor usually puts forth recommendations about the ways in which this server configuration can be used by an organization.

■ **Statement by Auditor.** This is a statement from the auditing organization that the tests and resulting report conform to NotesBench consortium standards.

■ **Appendix A – Overall Test Setup and Software Versions.** This section contains a graphic version of the network connections, as well as any devices or techniques used in the tests. This is a good place to find new configuration ideas for your network.

■ **Appendix B – System Configurations.** This section presents a table summarizing the configuration of the systems used and their functions in the tests.

■ **Appendix C – Operating System Parameters.** This section lists any system patches and configuration parameters that deviate from default settings. Scan this area for changes to incorporate in your environment.

■ **Appendix D – Notes Parameters.** Any Notes or Domino system parameters that were used are documented here. There should be a complete copy of the notes.ini from the server being tested.

■ **Appendix E – Network Configuration File(s).** This is where to find a listing of the protocols and associated vendor used. Any server or client parameters that deviate from default settings should be reported.

■ **Appendix F – Guidelines for Information Usage.** Usually a generic statement regarding how the information presented in the report may be used. It is usually something like "The information may be copied and distributed as long as the complete report remains intact."

■ **Appendix G – Pricing.** This section contains information about the pricing for the server and software tested. There are rules covering what is reported, which prices and applicable discounts were obtained by the tester. This section will give you a general idea of what it would cost to buy one similarly configured server.

- **Appendix H – Additional Vendor Defined Information (Optional).**
  Here, the vendor may provide additional information about services or products they provide. Note that the information in this section is not verified and not certified by the auditor.

Additional Third-Party Resources

An ever-growing number of companies are marketing products directed at the Notes/Domino market. The ones I mention here are involved in performance tuning on Domino servers and Notes applications. This list is not meant to be inclusive, only a sample of the innovative ways vendors have found to make your job easier. Keep in mind, though, that any product that analyzes performance also consumes resources and, as such, requires you to monitor the monitoring product for any negative impact. For other performance-related products for Notes and Domino, visit the Notes Performance Zone on the Internet at http://www.lotus.com/performance.

ProActive Assistant from G2 Associates

This tool enables you to use workstations to generate end-to-end performance testing, monitoring, and analysis of a Domino system. With ProActive Assistant, you can obtain realistic information regarding your server, network, and Notes applications. This product simulates user loads from a local workstation using customizable scripts. You can analyze the results through standard and customized reports generated by the software. For additional information, go to http://www.g2sys.com.

GroupSizr Pro, WebSizr, and MailSizr from Technovations

These tools are used to generate performance and sizing information for your HTTP, Notes/Domino, and mail environments. The GroupSize product generates simulated user loads against both Domino and non-Domino servers. The software generates result reports for analysis. WebSizr is used to analyze Web-based systems and provide metrics on sizing and HTTP-specific transactions. MailSizr provides sizing and performance information for mail hosts. For additional information, go to http://www.technovations.com.

IntelliWatch Pinnacle from Candle

These tools provide an automated approach to Notes/Domino system performance monitoring. Using parameters from its Performance Manager component, the IntelliWatch Monitor detects and corrects some common performance problems before they become bigger problems. The Tracer component provides real-time, end-to-end diagnostics of Notes client-server activity. Finally, the Analyzer component tracks historical performance data from the Monitor component. For additional information, go to http://candle.com.

Network Performance

As every administrator knows, the server's network interface can be a major performance bottleneck. Paying attention to the network side of Notes and Domino yields great benefits. Chapter 18 covers the methodology of measuring the network performance of the server. Two common areas affecting server performance revolve around the network protocol and network interface cards.

Protocol

If you are not doing so already, consider using TCP/IP as the primary protocol stack in your system. All Notes/Domino's high-availability features are configured to take advantage of TCP/IP.

Network Interface Cards

Switch to 100 Mbps network cards for user-facing ports. If your company doesn't want to toss the older 10 Mbps cards, consider using them on a network dedicated to replication or clustering. Isolating network traffic can significantly boost performance in heavy usage environments. If partitioning your Notes servers, plan for a 100 Mbps network per partition.

On networks with particularly heavy traffic or sites requiring high-availability, consider using multiport network interface cards. These cards allow for multiple physical connections to the network. Additionally, some allow for port aggregation, (the combination of two ports for higher bandwidth), network failover, or traffic segregation.

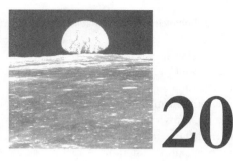

20

Enhancing Data Availability

SOME OF THE MAIN TOPICS in this chapter are

- Domino server clusters
- Domino server partitions
- Billing and auditing services
- New R5 advanced services

For enterprises to build and deploy high-value business applications targeted toward both local and global users, they must know that Domino servers are highly available, scalable, and reliable. Messaging is worthless if the messaging system is unreliable or unavailable. The most sophisticated workflow applications are worthless if they are not available or can't handle the load. A killer Web site adds no value (and negatively impacts business) if the site is too slow for the Web client to access or is currently unavailable.

Domino 5.0 has made vast improvements in the areas of performance, scalability, reliability, and availability. Notably, Domino 5.0 now offers Web browser failover and load balancing. With the extensive integration with the Web, it only makes sense that the scalability and reliability previously available to Domino clients now be available to Web applications and Web clients through the Domino Internet Cluster Manager (ICM). Similarly, messaging features, such as calendaring, scheduling, and synchronous mail agents, now also support failover and load balancing. This allows users to continue to schedule appointments with other team members and process newly delivered mail, even if their mail server is currently down. Unread marks are synchronized between the backup server and the primary server, type ahead, and addressing are supported even if the primary server is out of service. In addition, Domino 5.0 can integrate with operating system level application clusters. For example, when running on Windows NT, Domino R5 integrates with the Microsoft Cluster Server (MSCS), this will be described in detail later in this chapter.

There are several reasons why the advancements in clustering and partition capabilities are important to the system administrator and organization as a whole. As a result of new enhancements to Domino features and a new On Disk Structure (ODS), Domino 5.0 brings significant improvements in performance. Specifically, the response time of the Domino server has improved by as much as 75 percent, the I/O utilization performs 10–20 percent better, and memory requirements have been reduced by approximately 30 percent.

Despite these advancements, clustering further improves performance and provides the capability to maintain performance when the size of the enterprise increases. Also, the opportunity to exploit the clustering and partitioning features provide financial benefits, minimizing administrative costs and total cost of ownership in addition to benefits in performance, scalability, and reliability. It is a constant challenge to provide and maintain optimal system performance while minimizing the IT expense. With Domino 5.0, the ability to provide maximum performance while fully utilizing the investment in hardware is significantly easier to achieve.

For larger organizations that are running Domino servers and experiencing heavy traffic and usage, using Domino partitioned servers and clustering can help to better scale the demands on each respective server. Dividing the user load and demands on each server will not only improve performance (and provide transparent failover security) but will also help to fully exploit powerful, high-end server hardware configurations. When using Advanced services such as clustering partitioned servers, it is important to understand what role each server plays with one another and how to efficiently setup the Domino servers to maximize performance. These items, such as tweaking the notes.ini file or configuring server tasks, will be explained in this chapter.

Domino Server Clusters

The following sections describe clusters within the Domino environment and how they work. Relative topics such as failover, load balancing, availability, the Cluster Manager, the Cluster Administrator, the Cluster Database Directory, and other server tasks are presented. The "Planning, Installation, and Setup" section guide you through every step from understanding requirements to planning, preparation, and installation. The administration section will outline, in detail, the steps involved in creating, adding, and removing servers from clusters. The statistics section will instruct you how to monitor and manage the clusters and optimize their performance. Also, integration with the Microsoft cluster server is described and the steps for installing and configuring Domino servers are provided.

Description

Clustering can be defined as a coordinated set of systems and applications providing increased resource availability, scalability, and efficiency than would be provided from a single system or application. Domino clustering, more accurately defined by Lotus as "application clustering," provides high availability and scalability to enterprise applications in messaging, groupware, and the Internet. In addition, the failover and clustering functions provided with Domino clustering are based on content (requested by the user) and are often termed as "content-based routing."

The Domino clustering architecture is made available through the use of the following components:

- The Cluster Manager
- The Cluster Database Directory (CLDBDIR.NSF)
- The Cluster Database Directory Manager Task (CLDBDIR)
- The Cluster Administrator
- The Cluster Replicator Task (CLRREPL)
- The Internet Cluster Manager (ICM)

With Domino clustering, all the servers in the cluster continually communicate information regarding server availability and continually synchronize the databases replicas. Cluster replication between the replica databases on the servers ensure that all the databases are constantly in synch with one another. Based on availability on settings for load balancing, the Domino Cluster Manager maintains information on all the servers and database replicas and routes users to the optimal servers. A Domino cluster consists of two to six servers providing seamless, uninterrupted access to enterprise data.

The capability to incorporate clustering is not new to Domino. Clustering was first made available in Release 4 as "Notes for Public Networks" working with telecommunication and Internet service providers. If the application server was unavailable, the user was redirected to another Domino server that hosted the same application. However, with Domino R5, clustering ships the with Enterprise Server.

A new capability of clustering and load balancing for Internet applications and Web clients is now available via the Internet Cluster Manager (ICM), one of the new Server Tasks available to Domino 5.0. When the ICM is loaded, this tasks acts an intermediary between the Web client and the servers in the cluster, accepting the database request from the Web client and determining the best server to handle the request. Cluster replication ensures that all the databases are synchronized while the ICM factors the server availability and server.

In addition to the ICM, other new clustering features available with Domino 5.0 are

- Failover and balancing for calendaring and scheduling (using the new CLUBUSY.NSF database)
- Synchronous "New Mail Agents" that will process a user's mail even if their mail server is out of service
- Continued directory type ahead and addressing support if the primary server is out of service
- Synchronized Unread Marks between the backup server and primary server when out of service (note that Unread Marks can now be disabled as well)

Consistent with the cross-platform availability of Domino, the Domino clustering capability is available across various hardware and operating systems. Namely, the platforms supporting clustering are

- NT/Intel
- NT/Alpha
- Win95/98
- OS/2
- NLM
- AIX
- HP-UX
- Solaris/Intel
- Solaris/Sparc

Domino real-time replication and other newly added 5.0 features ensure that the enterprise applications remain synchronized. As evident throughout this book, an important feature of Domino 5.0 is the newly designed Administration client. Consequently, the capability to administer and monitor the clustering features and performance, capacity, and throughput thresholds have been greatly improved with Domino 5.0.

The benefits of using Domino clusters are

- High availability to Domino databases using failover
- Workload balancing/performance
- Scalability
- Data synchronization
- Workload analysis
- Easier maintenance for hardware and software without interruption
- Easy database backups

Failover

With Domino 5.0, the clustering capability has been extended beyond messaging and applications to support Internet failover and load balancing as well. If the Domino 5.0 server experiences software/hardware problems, network failure, is out of service, or if the database has been marked "out of service" or "pending delete," the cluster will redirect requests to the failover Domino server to continue processing mail client, Notes client, and Web client requests.

The following list of events illustrate what action could trigger failover within the cluster:

- Opening a database (`@Command([FileOpenDatabase])`), LotusScript using `OpenWithFailover`, or Java using `OpenDatabase` method of the `lotus.domino.DbDirectory` class)
- Opening a document link, view link, or database link
- Attempting to replicate with a database in the cluster that is not reachable
- Composing mail
- Name Lookups to the Domino Directory (and the type-ahead feature)
- Routing of mail messages within the Domain
- Agents that process mail acting on new mail documents
- Calendaring features such as meeting invitations and free-time lookups
- Lookups to servers
- Clicking on a Open URL icon, a URL hotspot, or accessing a URL with the Web browser

A list of potential reasons why failover would occur are listed here:

- **Server access problems**
  - Server down
  - Network connectivity problems
  - Maximum number of users has been reached (`Server_Maxusers` setting in the `notes.ini`)
  - Server is restricted (`Server_Restricted` setting in `notes.ini`)
  - Server is at BUSY state because maximum load allowed has been reached

- **Database access problems**
  - Database is marked "out-of-service" in Cluster Database Directory (`CLDBDIR.NSF`)
  - Database is marked "Pending Delete" in Cluster Database Directory (`CLDBDIR.NSF`)

Unfortunately, there are scenarios when failover will not occur and the user cannot access the requested server, database, or URL. Some of the actions that failover will not correct are

- The server becomes unavailable after the user has originally opened the database.
- The user opens a database from the pull-down menu (File, Database, Open) or attempt to view the database properties (File, Database, Properties).
- The router attempts to deliver mail but the "MailClusterFailover" setting in the notes.ini is set to "0".
- Creating new databases
- Agents (except for the mail predelivery agent).
- Replicating with an available server even if it the maximum usage or maximum number of users have been met or the database has been marked "Out of service." Theses parameters to not affect replication.

You can intentionally cause failover so that a server becomes inaccessible by clients and requests are redirected to another database replica on another server in the cluster. You may want to have this happen if you are upgrading the server hardware, software, operating system, or replacing the server altogether.

To place a server in a RESTRICTED state, add/modify the following line in the notes.ini, where *x* indicates the type of RESTRICTED state to set:

```
Server_restricted=x
```

If *x* is set to 1, the server is RESTRICTED for the current state and this setting will be cleared when the server is restarted. If *x* is set to 2, the server is RESTRICTED persistently, even if the server is restarted. Set *x* back to 0 to disable the RESTRICTED state. Unlike the BUSY state, which will accept requests if no other servers are available, RESTRICTED will deny requests even if there are no failover servers available to accept the request.

Load Balancing

Load balancing is available to provide administrators the capability to define threshold values to redirect users in order to distribute the load so that no servers become overloaded. When a server reaches its availability threshold (the Cluster Manager marks the database BUSY) or if the server reaches its maximum users limit, subsequent requests to the database will be redirected to another database replica within the cluster. The Cluster Manager uses the Cluster Manager Database Directory to determine the location and availability of the database replicas prior to redirection. If there are no other database replicas within the cluster or all the other servers have a BUSY status, the original database is opened. The availability threshold does not affect replication, therefore, replication will occur even if the database is currently in a BUSY state.

The availability index is periodically determined by the server (approximately once per minute) based on the average response time of a request the server recently processed. The availability index is computed as an integer from 0 (indicating heavy load) to 100 (indicating light load). The longer the response time, the lower the availability index. The value of the availability index is computed by dividing the response time for a function under the current load with the optimum response time for the same function under a light load and then subtracting the result from 100. Keep in mind that the server response time typically makes up a small fraction of the response time experienced from the user's perspective. If the availability index is less than the availability threshold, the server is marked as BUSY. While the server is marked BUSY, requests will be redirected to another database replica on another server within the cluster.

To set the server availability threshold, add/modify the following line to the notes.ini file, where *x* is a number from 0–100:

```
Server_availability_threshold=x
```

The higher the value of *x*, the less workload that can be carried by the server before going into a BUSY state. Entering 100, places the server in a constant BUSY state while entering 0, disables workload balancing (0 is the default value).

Managing the maximum number of users that can access a server at one time also can control the server workload. When the count of users reach this limit, the server goes into the MAXUSERS state, rejecting any additional requests and redirecting users to another database replica on a server within the cluster until the count of users falls below the maximum users limit.

To set the server to the maximum number of users, add/modify the following line to the notes.ini file, where *x* is the maximum number of users who can access the server simultaneously:

```
Server_MaxUsers=x
```

This setting does not affect replication. Therefore, replication will still occur even if the maximum users have been reached.

This setting also will work with servers that are not in a cluster. Servers not in a cluster that reach this maximum users limit will not be redirected to another server. Instead, they are denied access to the server.

Database Availability

There are three settings for managing databases availability (see Figure 20.1), namely:

- Out of Service
- In Service
- Pending Delete

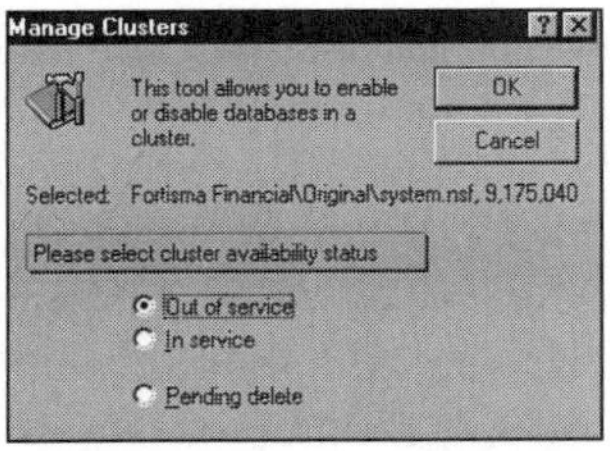

Figure 20.1 Database availability.

Database availability (used to manage the cluster availability status) can be modified:

1. Open the Domino Administrator on an existing Domino server.
2. Click the Files tab.
3. Expand the Directory to locate the database and select the database in the results pane.
4. Select Cluster in the Tools pane or right-mouse click the database and select Cluster.
5. Select the appropriate availability status from the Manage Clusters dialog box (refer to Figure 20.1).

Marking a database "out of service" will force users to failover to another replica database. This may be done because you are temporarily performing maintenance on the database. Users who where already accessing the database prior to marking the database out of service will continue to have access to the database. Also, the database continues to replicate changes and receive replication changes.

After a database has been marked out of service, you must mark the database "in service" to restore access to the database.

Marking a database as "pending delete" flags the database for deletion, but waits for every active user to finish using the database prior to deletion. Once marked pending delete, the database will no longer accept requests, therefore, users will be redirected to other databases within the cluster.

The Cluster Manager

The job of the Cluster Manager is to monitor the status, availability, and workload of the other servers in the cluster. When the Cluster Manager determines that a user should be redirected to different replica, it uses the Cluster Database Directory to determine which other cluster servers contain a database replica of the original database (using the replica ID) and then redirects the user request to the respective replica. If more than one replica database exists on the server, the Cluster Manager assumes that selective replication is used to replicate the databases. The Cluster Manager will attempt to failover to the replica that is in the same directory as the original database.

The Domino Cluster Manager automatically runs on every server within the cluster. In fact, when a server is added to the cluster, the Cluster Manager automatically starts when the server starts. Once started, the Cluster Manager uses the Domino Directory to determine which servers belong to the cluster, storing this information in memory (in the Cluster Name Cache). This information is exchanged with other Cluster Managers, communicating with one another by exchanging probes. Information received from the other Cluster Managers within the cluster also is stored in the Cluster Name Cache. The information collected is used by the Cluster Manager to perform the failover and load balancing tasks. An example of the information monitored by the Cluster Manager is displayed below (see Figure 20.2). This can viewed by typing **show cluster** at the command prompt of the server console.

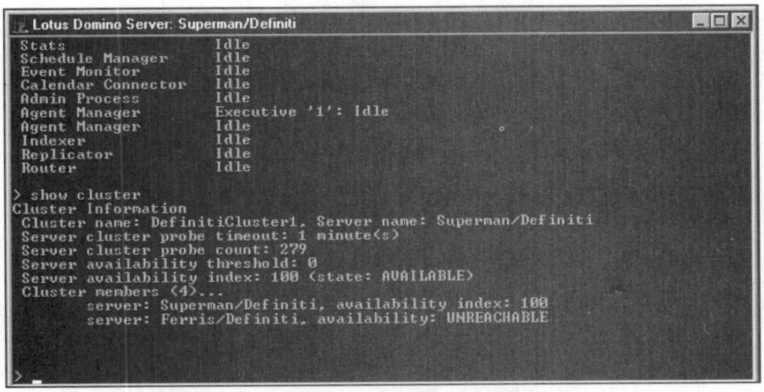

Figure 20.2   Cluster Manager Information.

The tasks performed by the Cluster Manager are

- Monitor the Domino Directory to determine which servers belong to the cluster (this is determined by the Cluster Name field in the Server document and the cluster membership list).

- Monitor which servers are currently available and monitor the workload.

- Communicate with other Cluster Managers about availability.

- Provide failover, redirecting client requests to database replicas within the cluster.

- Provide load balancing, balancing the server workload within the cluster.

- Log failover and load balancing events to the server log file.

The Cluster Database Directory (CLDBDIR.NSF)

The Cluster Database Directory (CLDBDIR.NSF) is used by the Cluster Manager to manager information about each database and replica in the cluster (see Figure 20.3). This database exists on every server within the cluster (if it doesn't already exist, it is automatically created by the Cluster Database Directory Manager task when the server starts). This database is used by the cluster components to determine where to redirect the users for failover, the Access Control for each database, which events to replicate and where the other database replicas exist. A Notes document is automatically created for each database by the Cluster Database Directory Manager task when the database is added to the server, the information contained about each database is

- Database name
- Server
- Filepath
- Replica ID
- Replication information
- Access information

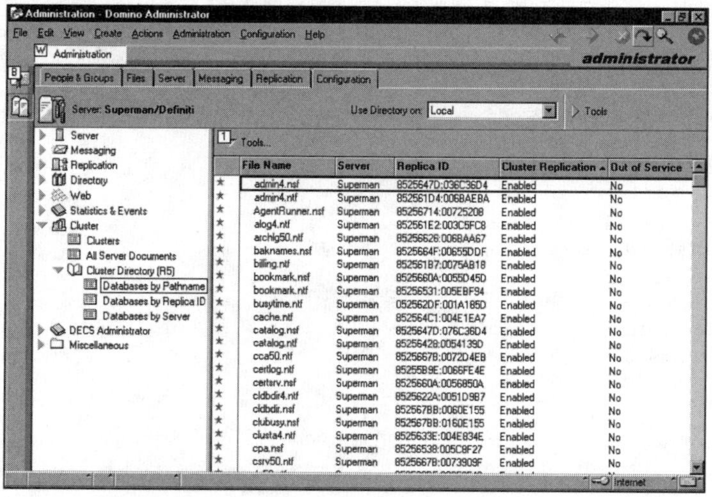

Figure 20.3   Cluster Directory database.

The Cluster Replicator ensures that any changes to the Cluster Database Directory database are immediately replicated to all other Cluster Database Directories on each server within the cluster, therefore guaranteeing that all the servers cluster components are using current information.

The Cluster Database Directory Manager Task (CLDBDIR)

The Cluster Database Directory Manager task (CLDBDIR) runs on every server on the cluster. Its job is to keep the Cluster Database Directory up to date. When a new server is added to the cluster, this task will check for the Cluster Database Directory, and if it does not exist, will create it. When databases are added to the server, the Cluster Database Directory Manager task creates a new document in the Cluster Database Directory containing all the information needed by the cluster components. Similarly, when databases are deleted from the server, the Cluster Database Directory Manager task deletes the document from the Cluster Database Directory. Finally, the Cluster Database Directory Manager task also monitors the status of the databases on the server (checking to see if they are marked out of service or pending delete).

The Cluster Administrator

The Cluster Administrator manages the cluster components. The functions of the Cluster Administrator are

- Starting the Cluster Database Directory Manager and Cluster Replicator when new servers are added to the cluster.
- Adding CLDBDIR and CLREPL tasks to the ServerTasks setting in the notes.ini file.
- Starting the Administrator Process if it is not already running.
- If a server is removed from a cluster, the CLDBDIR and CLREPL tasks are stopped and removed from the notes.ini ServerTasks setting, the Cluster Database Directory is deleted, and updates the Cluster Database Directories in all the other servers in the cluster.

The Cluster Replicator Task (CLRREPL)

The Cluster Replicator task (CLRREPL) is in charge of keeping the database replicas within the cluster synchronized with one another, thus ensuring that clients are viewing up-to-date information. When changes are made to a database in the cluster, the Cluster Replicator pushes the change to all the other replicas in the cluster. Therefore, the Cluster Replicator is "event driven" rather than "schedule driven" as in traditional replication. One instantiation of the Cluster Replicator is automatically run for each server in the cluster. However, you can run more that one Cluster Replicator to improve performance.

The Cluster Replicator uses the Cluster Database Directory to determine which databases have replicas on other servers that need to replicate. This information is stored in memory and updated is the Cluster Database Directory is modified. Similarly, if there is a backlog of replication events, they are queued in memory until they can be pushed to other cluster servers. If another change occurs in a database which is already waiting to replicate, the changes are pooled together so that the changes can be sent together to improve performance. If the destination server is unavailable, the replication event is maintained in memory until the destination server becomes available and an awaiting retry entry is logged in the Replication Log.

The Cluster Replicator Task only replicates (push/pull) between database replicas within the cluster and ignores replication formulas and all settings in the "Advanced Panel" of the replications settings dialog box (and will replicate all documents). Also, private folders are replicated to other replicas within the cluster, but their security is still preserved. Replication events created by the Cluster Replicator are not logged in the replication history, but are store, in memory. The history information is transferred to the databases approximately once an hour.

When a server is added to the cluster, the Cluster Replicator task (CLREPL) is automatically added to the ServerTasks setting in the `notes.ini` file. Nevertheless, enter the following command to start the Cluster Replicator tasks at the server console:

```
> load clrepl
```

If the Cluster Replicator is overloaded, you can enable multiple cluster replicators on a server. They work in tandem, sharing the replication workload. To enable multiple Cluster Replicators, append an additional CLREPL task to the ServerTasks setting in the `notes.ini` file. Or you can enable an additional CLREPL by typing **load CLREPL** at the server console.

Standard replication (using the REPLICA tasks) is required to replicate to database replicas outside of the cluster. In addition, even though cluster replication is enabled for the cluster, it is important to perform standard replication on a regular basis within the cluster to ensure that all the databases are up to date. Therefore, schedule replication hourly or daily (at least).

The Internet Cluster Manager (ICM)

The Internet Cluster Manager (ICM) is described in detail in the "New R5 Advanced Services" later in this chapter.

If the Server Crashes...

Always force replication within the cluster after the server crashes!

Planning, Installation, and Setup

To use Domino clustering, the following requirements must be met:

- All servers in the cluster must be running the Enterprise Server license for release 4.62 - 5.0 or the Advanced Services license for release 4.5 - 4.6 (only Release 5.0 servers can use the new clustering features such as the Internet Cluster Manager).

- Each server can only be a member of one cluster.

- All servers must be connected through a high-speed LAN. They must all support TCP/IP, use a common set of network protocols, and be on the same Notes name network.

- All the servers must be in the same Domino domain and use the same Domino directory.

- The administrative server for the Domino directory must be specified in the domain that contains the cluster. Otherwise, the Administration Process (`AdminP`) cannot modify the cluster management. However, the administrative server does not have to be a member of the cluster or be registered as a Enterprise Server.

- Every server in the cluster must have a hierarchical server ID (therefore, any flat IDs must be converted to hierarchical IDs).

- Notes clients must be running Notes release 4.5 or higher to exploit cluster failover and be running TCP/IP.

Other considerations when setting up clustering are

- Allow for servers in the cluster to consume additional disk space than nonclustered servers. Unlike nonclustered servers, clustered servers will typically contain more database replicas.

- Clustered servers require additional memory and processing capability than nonclustered servers.

Once the requirements have been met, the next steps to setting up the cluster are

- Determine if Domino clustering is required and the physical resources exist to support it.

- Determine the number of servers (and which servers) to include in the cluster.

- Determine which databases to create replicas of and how many replicas to create of each database and which on which servers they should reside.

- Determine how to distribute the database amongst the servers throughout the cluster.

Cluster Limitation
The maximum number of servers within a single cluster is six.

- Determine if a private LAN should be created for the cluster traffic.
- Configure the cluster.
- Set up scheduled replication between the clustered servers.
- Modify the cluster settings and thresholds.

After you have determined that your organization requires the use of clustering, the next step in planning your organization's cluster strategy is to determine how many servers to include in the cluster. A Domino cluster can contain between two and six servers. Increasing the number of servers within the cluster increases the clusters capability to balance the workload, availability, and performance. However, additional servers should only be added if it makes sense to provide additional capacity or redundancy because increasing the number of servers requires additional disk space and could decrease performance as a result of the demands on the CPU and increased network traffic.

Some factors to consider when determining the number of servers to include in the cluster are

- The more servers and database replicas created, the greater the need for server processor power and disk space.
- The Cluster Database Directory (CLDBDIR.NSF) requires 2MB of disk space. Add 1MB for every 2,000 databases in the cluster.
- The more server tasks running on the server, the greater the processing power required for the server.
- The more CPU intensive the applications are that are running on the server, the greater the processing power required for the server.
- The more users that are going to be handled on the server, the greater the processing power required and more memory required for the server. When determining the amount of memory required, expect to use 64MB + 1MB for every three current users.
- The more Cluster Replicators running on the server, the greater the need for memory. Add 2MB of memory for each Cluster Replicator used.
- With all these factors, do not only consider the current database demands but the demands that will be placed on the server if clients are redirected to the server as a result of failover or load balancing.

After you have determined the server configuration for the cluster, the next step is to determine the number of replicas that are required for each database in the cluster. You are not required to create a replica for each database on each server in the cluster. In fact, this would be unwise and waste system resources. For some databases, you will not have to create any replicas, thereby excluding these databases from being clustered at all. For databases that require high availability or may be handling a heavy load, consider placing a replica on every server in the cluster (limiting the number to three or less). For databases that will require limited usage or contain data that doesn't require high availability, you may only need to make one replica of the database in the cluster (if at all). Determining the number of replicas to use in the cluster begins with a simple algorithm, the greater the need for availability and load balancing, the more replicas you should create. However, most administrators know that rich object store capabilities of Domino databases can consume hard drive space quickly. But with the low cost of drive space, the need for availability easily supersedes the cost incurred with drive space. Nevertheless, the use the following list to help determine the number of database replicas to create:

- **The database size.** For larger databases, you may want to create fewer replicas.
- **The number/location of expected users.** For larger audiences, they will probably experience greater performance if the usage is dispersed among multiple replicas.
- **Server capacity.** If the Domino servers are running on high-end servers, they will better handle additional replicas.
- **Bandwidth.** If there are limitations or concerns in bandwidth, you will want to minimize replication between databases.
- **The database usage.** If you expect a high usage/utilization, additional replicas will probably improve performance.
- **The volume of data.** If the number of documents and the size of the data contained in the documents is expected to be large, creating multiple replicas can decrease performance. You will have to factor the server performance and LAN configuration to determine if bandwidth is a concern.

Use common sense when determining the number of replicas to create within the cluster. Creating more than three replicas is probably overkill. The law of diminishing returns is applicable here. Certainly, the first additional replica goes a long way to ensuring high availability. For most applications, one replica is probably sufficient. However, for more mission critical information that must always be available, create a second or third replica. Additional replicas add little value past that point and begin to negatively affect the cluster resources.

In addition, distribute the busiest databases to various servers so that they share the workload. If the servers have various processing power, be sure to include the busiest databases on the servers with the most processing capabilities and memory. Place the busiest database on servers running limited tasks, including Domino tasks and operating system processes/tasks. Again, common sense dictates that a server that is under-utilized is wasting corporate resources while an over-utilized server affects performance.

A good place to start with database distribution is with Lotus Notes mail files. In fact, if you intend on using clustering at all, the mail files would be the place to start. They grow large quickly and users demand high availability and performance when accessing their mail. Your enterprise usually depends on it. When setting up clustering for mail files, you should distribute the database replicas even among the servers in the cluster. You may want to consider setting up a dedicated mail cluster. Because all the databases are the same database type, this ensures an even distribution of the load in the event that a server becomes unavailable. Nevertheless, failover should be the focus for mail databases, not workload balancing, because only the mail owner will be accessing their respective database. You can manage all the databases and their respective replicas by using the Cluster Database Directory (CLDBDIR.NSF).

After you have configured the mail files for clustering, you will probably want to add application databases to the cluster and focus more on load balancing and failover. Consider creating additional replicas of more mission critical applications and place those applications on servers with the most processing power.

You may want to begin creating one replica for most of the databases that require clustering. Then, monitor the cluster statistics to determine if additional replicas are required. Do not create replicas for databases that where availability and workload balancing are not a concern. This will only diminish the effectiveness of the cluster.

You can further increase performance among the cluster by creating a private network. Simply install a network interface card (NIC) in each server within the cluster and connect the servers through a private hub or switch. The additional traffic created by the cluster as a result of the cluster replication and passing of nodes amongst servers could create a bottleneck on the primary LAN. Creating a private network among the cluster eliminates the concern for creating additional traffic. You could also create a private network in addition to having the servers connected over the primary LAN. This helps to ensure that the servers remain connected, even if one of the LAN segments fails.

For more information regarding the procedure to setup a private LAN for a cluster, refer to the Domino Administrative online help database.

To allow mobile users to exploit the benefits of clustering, they will need to access the cluster through a passthru server. The passthru server can then handle redirecting the user to available servers within the cluster. Otherwise, the user's will be forced to dial into each server directly to make a connection and clustering can't be utilized (unless multiple replicator items are created on the user's replicator page to each database replica on each server in the cluster).

If your organization is using the Server Web Navigator, each Web database on each server in the cluster must be a replica database of one another. Therefore, replica databases of the original Web database (web.nsf) must be created on the servers within the cluster before the Server Web Navigator is started. Otherwise, a new Web Database will automatically be created on each server and, because they will not be replicas of one another, they will not failover to one another.

Administration

The following sections will guide you through creating new clusters, adding servers to clusters, and removing servers from clusters. The steps required for each action are outlined in detail. In addition, the effects of these actions on the clustered servers are described.

Creating Clusters

For best results, use the Administration server to create new clusters. You must have at least Author access and Delete Documents access in the Domino Directory and at least Author access in the Administration Requests database to create a cluster (see Figure 20.4).

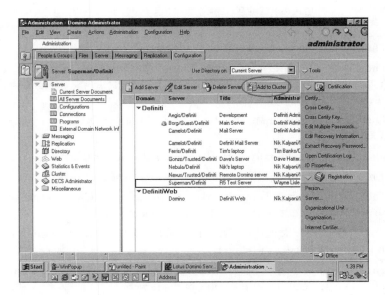

Figure 20.4   Creating a cluster.

The steps to creating a new cluster are

1. Open the Domino Administrator on an existing Domino server.

2. Click the Configuration tab.

3. Expand the Server section and click All Server Documents.

4. Select the server(s) to add to the cluster from the results pane.

5. Click Add to Cluster.

6. Select Yes when prompted to continue.

7. Select Choose New Cluster rather than selecting an existing cluster to add the servers to.

8. Enter the name for the new cluster.

9. Select Yes to add the servers to the cluster immediately or No to submit a request using the Administration Process. Selecting Yes is the fastest method, but can lead to replication conflicts. If the server is part of the cluster, it is immediately replicated to the other cluster servers. If the server is not part of the cluster, replicate the changes to one of the servers added to the cluster.

Selecting No submits a request for the Administration Process to add the servers to the cluster. This process runs immediately, adding the cluster name to the server documents. This will then be replicated to all the servers in the cluster. If you are not using the Administration server, force replication between the current server and the Administration server, then force replication between the Administration server and all other servers in the cluster.

As a result of creating a new cluster, the following activities occur on each clustered server:

- The Cluster Administrator and Cluster Manager start.
- The Cluster Administrator adds the Cluster Database Directory Manager tasks (CLDBDIR) and Cluster Replicator task (CLREPL) to the ServerTasks setting in the notes.ini.
- The Cluster Administrator starts the Cluster Database Directory Manager (CLDBDIR).
- The Cluster Administrator starts the Cluster Replicator (CLREPL).
- If not already running, the Administration Process starts.
- The Cluster Database Directory Manager modifies the Cluster Database Directory to include documents for each database on the server.
- The replicator replicates the Cluster Database Directory and Domino Directory to all other servers in the cluster.
- The clustered servers begin to send probes to other servers in the cluster, informing one another of the status of the servers.

Adding Servers to Clusters

For best results, use the Administration server to add new servers to clusters. You must have at least Author access and Delete Documents access in the Domino Directory and at least Author access in the Administration Requests database to add a server to a cluster.

The steps to adding a new server to a cluster are

1. Open the Domino Administrator on an existing Domino server.
2. Click the Configuration tab.
3. Expand the Server section and click All Server Documents.

4. Select the server to add to the cluster from the results pane.

5. Click Add to Cluster.

6. Select Yes when prompted to continue.

7. Select the name of the cluster you want to add the server to, then click OK (see Figure 20.5).

8. Select Yes to add the servers to the cluster immediately or No to submit a request using the Administration Process.

   Selecting Yes is the fastest method, but can lead to replication conflicts. If the server is part of the cluster, it is immediately replicated to the other cluster servers. If the server is not part of the cluster, replicate the changes to one of the servers added to the cluster.

   Selecting No submits a request for the Administration Process to add the servers to the cluster. Force replication between the Administration server and all other servers in the cluster.

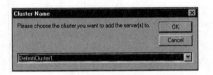

Figure 20.5   Adding servers to clusters.

As a result of creating a new server to the cluster, the following activities occur on each clustered server:

- The Cluster Administrator and Cluster Manager start.

- The Cluster Administrator adds the Cluster Database Directory Manager tasks (CLDBDIR) and Cluster Replicator task (CLREPL) to the ServerTasks setting in the notes.ini.

- The Cluster Administrator starts the Cluster Database Directory Manager (CLDBDIR).

- The Cluster Administrator starts the Cluster Replicator (CLREPL).

- If not already running, the Administration Process starts.

- The Cluster Database Directory Manager creates the Cluster Database Directory (CLDBDIR.NSF).

- The Cluster Database Directory Manager adds a document to the Cluster Database Directory for each database on the new cluster member.

- The replicator replicates the Cluster Database Directory and Domino Directory to all other servers in the cluster.

- The added server begins to send probes to other servers in the cluster, informing one another of the status of the servers.

To move a server from one cluster to another cluster, add the server to the new cluster. The Domino server automatically removes the server from the previous cluster.

Removing Servers from Clusters

For best results, use the Administration server to remove servers from a cluster. You must have at least Author access and Delete Documents access in the Domino Directory and at least Author access in the Administration Requests database to remove a server from a cluster.

The steps to removing a server from a cluster are

1. Open the Domino Administrator on an existing Domino server.
2. Click the Configuration tab.
3. Expand Cluster and click Clusters.
4. Select the document representing the server to remove from the cluster in the results pane.
5. Click Remove from Cluster (see Figure 20.6).
6. Select Yes to remove the server from the cluster immediately or No to submit a request using the Administration Process.

   Selecting No submits a request for the Administration Process to remove the server from the cluster.

Figure 20.6 Removing servers from a cluster.

As a result of removing a server from the cluster, the following activities occur on each clustered server:

- The Cluster Administration Process starts.
- The Cluster Replicator task stops.
- The Cluster Database Directory Manager stops.
- All occurrences of the CLREPL and CLDBDIR tasks are removed from the "ServerTasks" setting in the notes.ini file.
- The Cluster Database Directory (CLDBDIR.NSF) is removed from the server.
- The server database documents are removed from the Cluster Database Directory of an available cluster member. Theses changes will then replicate to the other members of the cluster.

Do not shut down the server until the Cluster Administration Process has completed its tasks. If the system is shutdown early or locks up, load the CLADMIN tasks from the server console to restart the Cluster Administrator.

Using Clusters

After the clusters have been setup and configured, you will want to monitor the efficiency of the failover, workload balancing, cluster replication, and server performance. You may need to modify some of the settings and availability thresholds, add/remove database replicas, move database replicas to other servers, and/or add or remove servers from the cluster.

Statistics

The clusters can be analyzed in four categories:

- The Cluster Analysis report
- The Cluster Manager statistics
- The Cluster Replicator statistics
- Internet Cluster Manager statistics

The Cluster Analysis generates reports providing information about the cluster configuration and helps to ensure that the cluster was properly setup. With the Cluster Analysis, you can specify the type of test to run (that is, for servers, databases, or the Server Web Navigator) and the details to report against. The results are saved in the Cluster Analysis database (CLUSTA4.NSF) or other specified database. These reports can take several hours to complete so status messages are displayed in the status bar at the bottom of the screen. After the report is complete, open the Cluster Analysis database to view the results. Three views exist (by default) to view the information:

By Cluster, By Date, and By Test. Use the views to navigate to a results document and open the document to view the report details.

For information regarding the Cluster Analysis, refer to the Domino Administration Help database.

To view information about the cluster, its members, and their statuses, type one of the following commands from the server console (see Table 20.1).

Table 20.1   **Commands to View Information about the Cluster**

Commands	Information
show cluster	Displays the names of the cluster servers, their respective availability index, and the probe count
show stat server	Displays the availability index and availability threshold of a server
show stat server.cluster.*	Display other cluster statistics, listed below (see Figure 20.7)

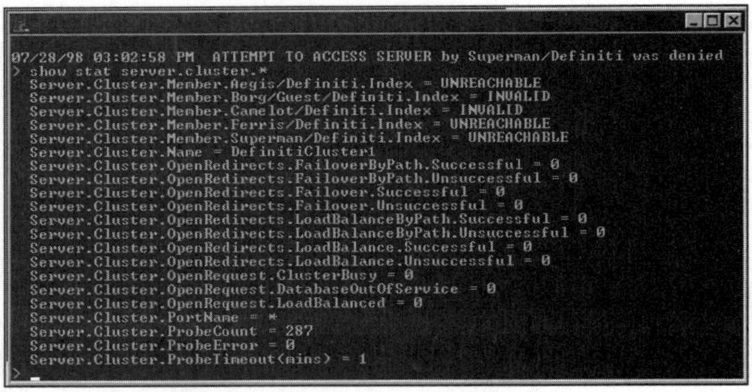

Figure 20.7   Cluster Manager statistics.

Table 20.2 lists and describes the Cluster Manager statistics.

Table 20.2   **Cluster Manager Statistics**

Server.Cluster.PortName	Default port for cluster network traffic (or enter a "*" for no default port so that any available port will be used).
Server.AvailabilityIndex	The integer value from 0 to 100 indicating the server's availability (0 indicates no resources are available, 100 indicates complete server availability).

Server.AvailabilityThreshold	The server's current availability threshold.
Server.Cluster.OpenRedirects.Failover.Successful	The total number of times the server successfully redirects a client to another cluster member after the Web client fails to open the database by the replica ID.
Server.Cluster.OpenRedirects.Failover.Usnsuccessful	The total number of times the server unsuccessfully redirects a client to another cluster member after the Web client fails to open the database by the replica ID.
Server.Cluster.OpenRedirects.FailoverByPath.Successful	The total number of times the server successfully redirects a client to another cluster member after the Web client fails to open the database by pathname.
Server.Cluster.OpenRedirects.FailoverByPath.Unsuccessful	The total number of times the server unsuccessfully redirects a client to another cluster member after the Web client fails to open the database by pathname.
Server.Cluster.OpenRedirects.LoadBalance.Successful	The total number of times the server successfully redirects a client to another cluster member after the Web client attempts to open the database by replica ID when the server is busy.
Server.Cluster.OpenRedirects.LoadBalance.Unsuccessful	The total number of times the server unsuccessfully redirects a client to another cluster member after the Web client attempts to open the database by replica ID when the server is busy.
Server.Cluster.OpenRedirects.LoadBalanceByPath.Successful	The total number of times the server successfully redirects a client to another cluster member after the Web client attempts to open the database by pathname when the server is busy.
Server.Cluster.OpenRedirects.LoadBalanceByPath.Unsuccessful	The total number of times the server unsuccessfully redirects a client to another cluster member after the Web client attempts to open the database by pathname when the server is busy.
Server.Cluster.OpenRequest.ClusterBusy	The total client requests when all the servers are busy.
Server.Cluster.DatabaseOutOfService	The total count of attempts to open a database that was marked out of service on the server.

continues

Table 20.2 **Continued**

Server.Cluster.LoadBalanced	The total count of attempts to open a database when the server was busy.
Server.Cluster.ProbeCount	The total count of attempts that the server completed a probe of other cluster members.
Server.Cluster.ProbeError	The total count of errors received when the server attempted a probe of other cluster members.
Server.Cluster.ProbeTimeout(mins)	The interval at which the intracluster probe occurs. You can view this by typing **show stat** at the server console.

Table 20.3 lists and describes the Cluster Replicator statistics.

Table 20.3 **Cluster Replicator Statistics**

Replica.Cluster.Servers	The total count of servers receiving replications from the current server
Replica.Cluster.Successful	The total count of successful replications since the server was started
Replica.Cluster.Failed	The total count of failed replications since the server was started
Replica.Cluster.Docs.Added	The total count of documents added by the cluster replicator
Replica.Cluster.Docs.Updated	The total count of documents updated by the cluster replicator
Replica.Cluster.Docs.Deleted	The total count of documents deleted by the cluster replicator
Replica.Cluster.Files.Local	The total count of databases on the current server in which there are replicas on other servers within the cluster
Replica.Cluster.Files.Remote	The total count of databases on other servers that the cluster replicator pushes changes
Replica.Cluster.Retry.Skipped	The total number of times the cluster replicator did not attempt to replicate a database (if the destination server is unreachable)
Replica.Cluster.Retry.Waiting	The total count of replicas that are waiting for retry attempts
Replica.Cluster.SecondsonQueue	The total time (in seconds) the last replicated database spent waiting in the work queue
Replica.Cluster.SecondsOnQueue.Avg	The average time (in seconds) that a database spent on the work queue
Replica.Cluster.SecondsOnQueue.Max	The maximum time (in seconds) that a database spent on the work queue

Replica.Cluster.SessionBytes.In	The total count of bytes received during cluster replication
Replica.Cluster.SessionBytes.Out	The total count of bytes sent during cluster replication
Replica.Cluster.WorkQueueDepth	The total count of databases awaiting replication by the cluster replicator
Replica.Cluster.WorkQueueDepth.Avg	The average work queue depth since the server was last started
Replica.Cluster.WorkQueueDepth.Max	The maximum work queue depth since the server was last started

To view information about the cluster members individually from the Domino Administrator, perform the following steps:

1. Open the Domino Administrator on an existing Domino server.
2. Select the server to monitor from the Server pane.
3. Click the Server tab.
4. Click the Statistics tab.
5. In the All Statistics list, click Server to view the availability index and threshold information. Click Server, Cluster to see other cluster statistics (see Figure 20.8).

Or

1. Right-click the server to monitor from the Server pane and select Properties.
2. Click the Cluster tab in the Server properties box.

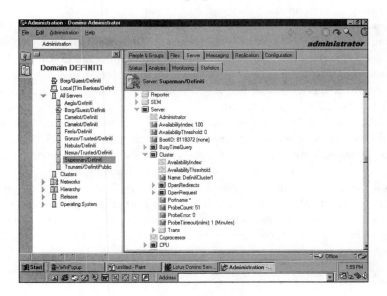

Figure 20.8   Cluster Member statistics.

If the Statistic Collector task is loaded on the Domino server, Cluster Manager statistics will be saved in the Statistics Reporting database (STATREP.NSF). Open the "Clusters" view in this database to view cluster statistics information.

Also, you can view events from contained in the Notes log, in the Miscellaneous Events view.

Rather than waiting for the Cluster Replicator to generate a log document, you can generate a log document by typing the following command at the server console:

```
> tell clrepl log
```

To enable logging of the cluster replication events, modify the notes.ini file by adding/modifying the following line:

```
RTR_logging=1
```

To disable logging of the cluster replication events, modify the notes.ini file by adding/modifying the following line:

```
RTR_logging=0
```

For information regarding the Internet Cluster Manager statistics, refer to the New R5 Advanced Services, Internet Cluster Manager(ICM) section.

For more information regarding clusters, potential problems and error messages, and fixes, refer to the Domino Administrative online help database and http://www.notes.net.

Using Microsoft Cluster Server

When the Domino 5.0 server is running on Microsoft NT, Domino clustering can be used with or without Microsoft Cluster Server (Microsoft's High Availability solution). Even though Microsoft Cluster Server (MSCS) and Domino 5.0 perform clustering in a significantly different manner, they will coexist with one another.

As described earlier in this chapter in the Domino Server Clusters section, Domino clustering is a type of *application clustering*, providing high availability and scalability to enterprise applications in messaging, groupware, and the Internet. Failover and workload balancing functions provided with Domino clustering are based on content (requested by the user), often termed as "content-based routing," using parameters and database replicas configured by the user.

The Microsoft Cluster Server uses *operating system clustering*, providing high availability (load balancing is currently not supported). Currently, the Microsoft Cluster Server supports hardware failover for two NT servers, or nodes, in a cluster sharing the same common disk device. It is important to note that this cluster capability of the Microsoft Cluster servers differs significantly from the application clustering provided by Domino 5.0. The Microsoft Cluster Server allows for fail-over protection so that if two NT servers running Domino are set up for failover and one servers (nodes) becomes unavailable, the second server (node) will come up and utilizes the shared disk subsystem, restarts the respective applications, and continues with its processes. It will use the same disk where the Domino data resides and use the same IP address that the Domino server is using. Therefore, the failover function is transparent to the clients. Unlike Domino clustering, the Microsoft Cluster Server only provides failover protection and does not allow the addition of cluster nodes for scalability and load balancing.

Organizations can implement the Microsoft Cluster Server in an Active/Passive or Active/Active configuration.

In an Active/Passive configuration, only one node provides services to the clients at a time. The passive node is reserved for failover if the active node fails. The Domino directory is installed on both nodes so that the passive node can take over if the active node fails. However, they still share the same Domino data so the data directory and files must be installed on a shared disk resource.

In an Active/Active configuration, both nodes provide services to the clients. If one node fails, the other node takes over for the failed node, servicing the users of both nodes. Each node has the capability to run two Domino servers, one for each node. Therefore, you have to install two partitioned servers on each node. However, they still share the same Domino data, so the data directory and files must be installed on a shared disk resource.

The following are the requirements for running Domino on a Microsoft Cluster Server:

- Only support by Domino release 4.6.2 or more recent.
- Domino virtual servers (a feature of the Domino Web Server) are not supported by MSCS.
- The Domino servers and clients must be configured to use TCP/IP or NetBIOS over TCP/IP.
- If configuring an Active/Active setup, the Domino servers must be installed as partitioned servers.
- The Domino program files must be installed on a local, nonshared drive for each node in the MSCS cluster.
- The path of the Domino program files must be the same for both nodes in the cluster.
- The Domino data directory must be installed in a shared drive (in an Active/Active configuration, each data directory must be in its own drive).
- Each Domino server must be assigned a static TCP/IP address, distinct from the address of the cluster nodes.

- If the Domino server is using NetBIOS over TCP/IP connections, the server's network address must be different from the network name of either cluster node (the network address is usually the name of the Domino server).

- The server ID cannot have a password or the Domino server restart or failover will not complete because the Domino server will wait for a password prior initializing and processing client requests. When the server ID is created, set the password length to zero.

The following groups/resources must be created prior to completing the MSCS configuration. The entries are nonhierarchical and should still accurately represent the type of resource and the application or group to which they belong.

- Domino Server Resource Group(s)
- IP Address Resource(s)
- Network Name Resources(s)
- Assign the physical disk resource to the Domino resource group
- Domino Server Resources(s)

For more information regarding the creation of MSCS Resource Groups and enabling the network name as the computer name, refer to the Domino Administrative online help database.

Installing the Domino server in the Microsoft Cluster Server environment involves three steps:

1. Install Domino on the first node.

2. Install Domino on the second node.

3. Configure the Domino server(s).

Installing Domino on the First Node

When creating Active/Passive configurations, you need to install only a single Domino server. When creating Active/Active configurations, you need to install two Domino partitioned servers (each Domino program directories are installed on each node's nonshared drive while the data directories are placed on a shared drive).

The following steps outline how to install Domino on the first node:

1. Use the MSCS Cluster Administrator to move the group(s) containing the shared drives to be used for the Domino data directory to the first node.

2. Launch the Domino Server installation program, click Next through the welcome screen, accept the license terms, and validate the registration information.

3. For Active/Active configurations, select Partitioned Server Installation and select a different shared drive for the Domino data directory for the second partition.

4. Specify the destination folder for the program directory as a private, nonshared drive (see Figure 20.9).

5. Select Customize when selecting the type of Domino server and enable Domino as an NT service (this also can be modified after the installation).

6. Specify the destination folder for the data directory as one of the shared drives of the cluster.

7. Select the program folders to which to add the new installation.

8. Complete the installation program.

9. If you have not set up Domino as a partitioned server, move the `notes.ini` file from the Domino program directory to the Domino data directory of the server. You may need to modify shortcuts to the Domino server and Domino Administrator by adding a space, an equal sign, and the path to the `notes.ini` file (for example, "c:\notes\data = c:\notes\data\notes.ini").

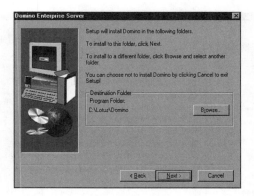

Figure 20.9 Installing Domino on the first node.

Installing Domino on the Second Node

Follow the same steps outlined for "Installing Domino on the First Node." Specify the same directory for the program files and data directories.

Configure the Domino Server(s)

Steps to configure the Domino server(s):

1. Open the Domino Administrator on an existing Domino server.

2. Click the Configuration tab.

3. If this is not the first server in the domain, register the Domino server by clicking Registration, Server in the Tools pane. The server name must be the same as the network name resource defined in MSCS. Enter the password length of zero so that the password is not manually required when the server is started (see Figure 20.10).

4. On the second cluster node, start the Domino server, which will launch the configuration program.

5. Complete the Domino configuration (TCP/IP or NetBIOS over TCP/IP must be configured for the server).

6. Exit and restart Domino. This launches the server.

7. For an Active/Active configuration, configure the server to use a specific IP address assigned to the server.

8. Repeat steps 1–7 for the second partitioned server.

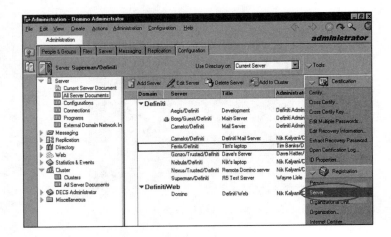

Figure 20.10   Configuring the Domino server.

Now, the Domino servers are ready to run under MSCS. From the Cluster Administrator, right-click the Domino server group, and select Bring Online. You can stop Domino by using the Cluster Administrator. Right-click the Domino server group, and select Take Offline. When the Domino server is running with MSCS, the Notes clients must be configured with TCP/IP or NetBIOS over TCP/IP.

Domino Server Partitions

The following sections describe Domino Server Partitions and how they work. The Planning, Installation, and Setup section will guide you through the process of planning and configuring partitioned servers. Multiple configurations are described, such as servers with a single IP address, servers with a unique IP address, and setting up and removing partitioned servers as Windows NT services. In addition, the using in a Domino Cluster section will describe using partitioned servers in a cluster and how to maintain, monitor, and uninstall partitioned servers.

Description

Domino server partitions enable multiple Domino servers to run on the same physical machine. Partitioning allows your organization to maximize resource utilization, minimize cost, and still provide reliable, high-performance Domino access. Because the partitioned servers run in their own memory space, if one server crashes, the other server(s) remain unaffected, thus, improving reliability. Also, you can maximize your existing hardware investment by upsizing. That is, consolidating a collection of small, lower usage Domino servers on to one physical machine. This also lowers administrative costs and time by only having one machine to administer!

The partitioned servers can share the same NIC and are supported for all protocols supported by Domino. However, when using TCP/IP, port mapping is required to allow the partitioned servers to use the same IP address for communications, therefore each uses its own port number. In addition, when Domino is running Windows NT, you can define multiple IP addresses on one physical network adapter card. This is explained later in this chapter.

Planning, Installation, and Setup

There are several ways to approach the concept of setting up partitioned servers. One way is to combine multiple Domino servers that are using different domains on one physical machine to minimize administrative costs and fully utilize the current hardware investment. Another concept is to create multiple servers even when using the same domain to improve performance. Some of the benefits of this configuration are

- The load will be better balanced because the Domino databases will be dispersed on multiple servers rather than just one.
- Better distribution of process that works against all the databases.
- The Domino server tasks can be divided among the multiple servers.
- More efficient process of requests to the Domino server (especially when the server is a symmetrical multiprocessor machine).
- More parallel task/request execution.
- Smaller mail delivery lists and smaller mail.box views.

The installation of partitioned servers is like setting up a single server. In fact, the partitioned servers share the same program files and directory. However, they each maintain their own data directory. While this saves on hard drive space, this places a significant demand on the system's resources. Because the multiple partitioned servers will be sharing resources from the same machine, when one server is running CPU intensive processes, this negatively affects the performance of the other partitioned servers. More importantly, the tasks running and when they are scheduled on each partitioned server have to take into consideration the tasks that are running on the other servers and how they will affect performance.

The steps to installing the Domino server are

1. Launch the Domino Server installation program, click Next through the Welcome screen, accept the license terms, and validate the registration information.

2. Select the checkbox for Partitioned Server Installation (see Figure 20.11).

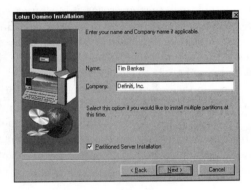

Figure 20.11 Partitioned server installation.

3. Specify the program directory, which will store all the program files that will be used by all the partitioned servers.

4. Specify the components to install for a custom installation.

5. Specify each partitioned server's data directory (see Figure 20.12). Because each partitioned server has its own data directory, you may want to name each respective directory with a meaningful name (like the server name) that delineates which partitioned server it belongs to. If you do not specify a unique directory name, by default the first data directory will be named \notes\data and all subsequent data directories will append a count to the data subdirectory (\notes\data2). Each data directory for each server partition will contain the required template files, batch files, notes.ini file, etc.

Keep in mind, that you can still use Directory (.dir) files on the file system to redirect the virtual data directory to other directories or servers but doing so may contradict the logic of setting up the partition.

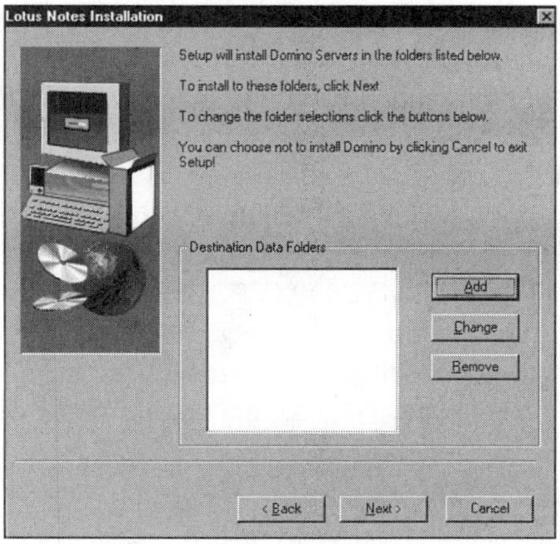

Figure 20.12 Specifying directories for partitioned servers.

6. Select the program folders to which to add the new installation.

7. Finish the installation process.

Configuration

Partitioned servers running TCP/IP can be configured in one of two ways:

- Configuring servers with a single IP address

or

- Configuring servers with unique IP addresses

Configuring Servers with a Single IP Address

One configuration option is to assign a single IP address to all the partitioned servers and set up port mapping so that each partitioned server has its own port. All the partitioned servers will run the same IP network. When setting up port mapping, one of the partitioned servers is designated as the port-mapping server that redirects the Notes or http requests to the other partitioned servers on the computer. This occurs every time a client requests a new session on a server. While this is a logical option when there is a limited number of available IP addresses, the downside is that if the port-mapping server becomes unavailable, Notes and http clients cannot establish a connection to the other partitioned servers. You may want to dedicate a server partition to handle the port mapping and remove many unneeded server tasks. Also, all the partitioned servers have to be on the same IP network. Finally, even if the processor power and memory for the machine is high powered, there may be a bottleneck, hence a performance loss, because all the partitioned servers are sharing the same NIC.

The port mapper can be modified by editing the `notes.ini` file on the server (if you modify the `notes.ini`, you will have to reboot the machine for the changes to take effect). The `notes.ini` file contains the server names, IP addresses, and port number for each partitioned server. The port-mapping server assigned by default is TCP port 1352. You can view the registered port numbers in the SERVICES file, typically located in the \WINNT\SYSTEM32\DRIVERS\ETC directory. This file represents the port number that cannot be used. Lotus recommends using port numbers 13520 through 13524 to assign to the additional partitioned servers.

The following lines need to be added to the `notes.ini` file of the port-mapping server's data directory:

```
TCPIP TcpAddress=0, IpAddress:1352
TCPIP PortMapping00=CN=ServerName1/O=Org,IpAddress:13520
TCPIP PortMapping01=CN=ServerName1/O=Org,IpAddress:13521
TCPIP PortMapping02=CN=ServerName1/O=Org,IpAddress:13522
TCPIP PortMapping03=CN=ServerName1/O=Org,IpAddress:13523
TCPIP PortMapping04=CN=ServerName1/O=Org,IpAddress:13524
```

The following line will have to be added in the `notes.ini` of all the other partitioned servers (being referenced by the port-mapping server):

```
TCPIP TcpAddress=0, IpAddress:port
```

The prefix of `TCPIP` is the port name on the `Port=` lines in the `notes.ini`. If the port name is modified or configured for multiple TCP/IP ports, you will have to change the value respectively. The values following the PortMapping variable must be listed in ascending order, beginning with 00 and ending with a maximum value of 04. Any break in the sequence or error in numbering will cause in the subsequent lines to be ignored. The *ServerNameX* and *Org* represent the actual canonicalized names of the partitioned servers. The *IpAddress* represents the IP address assigned to the actual machine. The last value in each line represents the port number assigned to each partitioned server.

If running Windows NT, you can define multiple IP addresses on one physical network adapter card. Therefore, you can dedicate an IP address for each server and not have to set up a port-mapping server to redirect to the other partitioned servers. Another option is to install multiple network adapters and run one IP address per adapter.

There are some additional steps required when running Internet services (http, POP3, NNTP, LDAP, and IMAP) on the partitioned servers. Because you are using port mapping, the host name value can be left blank in the HTTP Server section of the server document. The server will use the name determined in the operating system network (Windows NT) setup. A unique TCP port must be assigned to each service. Edit the server document, modifying the Internet Port and Security Configuration section for each partitioned server, setting a unique port address for each partitioned server. Because each internet server will be listening on a TCP port of its own, the clients must explicitly connect that port (for example, "http://ferris.definiti.com:8080/home.nsf").

Configuring Servers with Unique IP Address

Another configuration option is to assign a separate IP address to each partitioned server and use a separate NIC for each server. You can use the same NIC, but there may be some performance ramifications if multiple servers are sharing the same NIC. If you have enough IP addresses to assign one to each partitioned server, this is the best option. Because each server will use a separate NIC, this maximizes throughput. The clients access the partitioned server without having to go through the port-mapping server, so access to actual partitioned server is more likely (higher availability). Another advantage to assigning separate IP addresses is that the partitioned servers can be on different networks.

To assign IP addresses to the partitioned servers, add the following line to the `notes.ini` file (if you modify the `notes.ini`, you will have to reboot the machine for the changes to take effect):

```
TCPIP TcpAddress=0, IpAddress:port
```

The prefix of `TCPIP` if the port name on the `Port=` lines in the `notes.ini`. If the port name is modified or configured for multiple TCP/IP ports, you will have to change the value respectively. The `IpAddress` represents the IP address assigned to the actual machine. The last value in each line represents the port number assigned to the partitioned server. This should be set to 0 for the default Domino port, 1352. Setting this port number to any value other than 0 or 1352, will restrict clients from connecting to the server.

There are some additional steps required when running Internet services (http, POP3, NNTP, LDAP, and IMAP) on the partitioned servers. Because you are using a unique IP for each server, you will have to bind the hostname with the HTTP server. If this is not done, all the HTTP servers would attempt to use the same hostname, creating a conflict. Edit the server document, modifying the "Host name" value contained in the HTTP Server section of the server document. To configure the other internet services, you will have to modify the `notes.ini` file for each partitioned server. The following table illustrates the `notes.ini` modifications for each service:

Service	Setting in the *notes.ini*
POP3 server	POP3Address=*hostname*
IMAP server	IMAPAddress=*hostname*
NNTP server	NNTPAddress=*hostname*
LDAP server	LDAPAddress=*hostname*

Starting Partitioned Servers as Windows NT Services

There are several benefits to installing Domino servers as Windows NT services. Namely, you can use Windows NT's native tools to remotely shut down and restart your Domino server and if the NT server gets restarted (as a result of a power failure or system restart), the Domino server will restart without the need to log on to NT. You will need to have administrative access to the Windows NT Server on which you want to make Domino a service.

When installing the Domino server, only one Windows NT service is installed in the Control Panel, Services Applet. This requires a user to log on and start each additional partitioned server, or run the batch file. If the system crashes, only one partitioned server would automatically start! The solution is to install new services manually using the NT Resource Kit.

1. From the command prompt, launch the NT Resource Kit (`ntreskit`) file.

2. Enter the following command to add the Windows NT service for the first Domino partitioned server. Replace `ServerName` with the name of the partitioned server to add a Windows NT service. `C:` is the drive letter where the Domino program files are located and `notes\nSERVICE.EXE` is the directory path to the nSERVICE file.

   ```
   instsrv "Domino Server ServerName" c:\notes\nSERVICE.EXE
   ```

   Continue adding Windows NT services for all the Domino partitioned servers, specifying the respective `ServerName` for each Domino server.

3. Run the Windows NT Registry Editor. Open the folder for the current Domino server.

   ```
   HKEY_LOCAL_MACHINE\SYSTEM\CurrentControlSet\Services\Domino Server ServerName
   ```

   Add the full path of the `notes.ini` file in the ImagePath parameter and the number of Domino instances at the end of the command. For example:

   ```
   C:\notes\nService.EXE c:\notes\MyServer\notes.ini 2
   ```

   Continue this step for all other services created.

4. Open the Control Panel and launch the Services applet.

5. Select the installed service for the first Domino server.

6. Click the Startup button. In the service window, set the Startup Type to Automatic. Running Domino as an automatic service will cause the Domino service to automatically start when Windows NT restarts. Select the option to enable the service to interact with the desktop, otherwise, the Domino server console will not be able to start.

Removing Domino as a Windows NT Service

You can remove Domino as an NT service by opening the command prompt, changing to the root Domino directory, and typing:

```
ntsvinst -d
```

Using Partitioned Servers in a Domino Cluster

You can exploit the advantages of clustering by including the partitioned servers in a cluster. You can cluster partitioned servers with individual servers and/or partitioned servers on different computers but should not include partitioned servers running on the same computer in the same cluster (this introduces a single point of failure and contradicts the essence of clustering). Similarly, if you setup port mapping, you should not include more than one port-mapping server in the cluster. If you include a partitioned server in a cluster, you do not have to include all the partitioned servers running on that machine in the cluster. Also, do not include more than one port-mapping server in the same cluster. This creates a risk that all the partitioned servers could become unavailable even if they are not in the same cluster as the port-mapping server.

Therefore, if you have set up partitioned servers and want to take advantage of the clustering (availability, reliability, and scalability) you should cluster all or some of the servers on the partition with another machine also running partitioned servers.

Maintenance and Monitoring

The maintenance and monitoring of the partitioned servers is done in the same manner as an individual server. Because running multiple partitioned servers places a significant demand on the system's resources, it is important to use the system's performance monitor to manage the resources appropriately. Even though each partitioned server has its own data directory, they are still sharing system resources (or potentially denying system resources) with the other partitioned servers. If there is a need to improve performance, consider the following options to increase the system performance.

1. Modify the `Server_Max_Concurrent_Trans` in the `notes.ini` file to set the maximum number of concurrent transaction on each server. The optimal number of concurrent users on NT is around 20 (refer to Figure 20.12). If you have two partitioned servers on the same system, set each value to 10. Continue modifying this value dependant on the number of partitioned servers running on the same system (if you modify the `notes.ini`, you will have to reboot the machine for the changes to take effect).

2. Modify the `Server_MaxUsers` in the `notes.ini` to limit the number of users who can access a partitioned server at one time. When this threshold is reached, additional user requests to access the server are denied (if you modify the `notes.ini`, you will have to reboot the machine for the changes to take effect) See Figure 20.13.

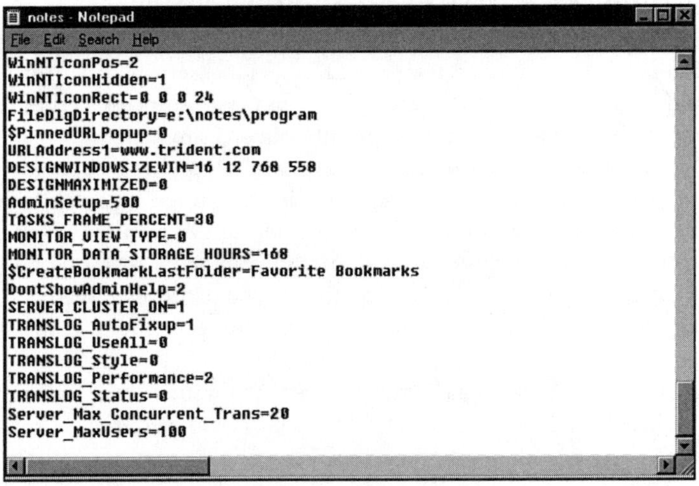

```
🗎 notes - Notepad                                                   _ □ ✕
File Edit Search Help
WinNTIconPos=2
WinNTIconHidden=1
WinNTIconRect=0 0 0 24
FileDlgDirectory=e:\notes\program
$PinnedURLPopup=0
URLAddress1=www.trident.com
DESIGNWINDOWSIZEWIN=16 12 768 558
DESIGNMAXIMIZED=0
AdminSetup=500
TASKS_FRAME_PERCENT=30
MONITOR_VIEW_TYPE=0
MONITOR_DATA_STORAGE_HOURS=168
$CreateBookmarkLastFolder=Favorite Bookmarks
DontShowAdminHelp=2
SERVER_CLUSTER_ON=1
TRANSLOG_AutoFixup=1
TRANSLOG_UseAll=0
TRANSLOG_Style=0
TRANSLOG_Performance=2
TRANSLOG_Status=0
Server_Max_Concurrent_Trans=20
Server_MaxUsers=100
```

Figure 20.13 `Notes.ini` modifications to increase performance.

3. If a specific partitioned server is using a significant amount of system resources, you may want to consider moving the server to a different system or improving the hardware specifications on that system. If there is a problem with slow disk access, you may want to move the Domino date directories to separate disk drives.

4. Monitor the Domino server log (log.nsf) to help determine bottlenecks and areas for improvement.

5. Monitor the Domino statistics on each server to determine which partitioned server is consuming most of the resources, keeping in mind that if one partitioned server is consuming system resources and impacting performance, this may affect the other partitioned servers. Therefore, you will want to compare the statistics of each of the respective partitioned servers.

Each partitioned server has its own administration client. However, when running on Windows NT, only one administration client can be run at one time. When running UNIX, you can run multiple administration clients at one time. If you are having problems setting up the partitioned servers and are receiving errors, here are some suggestions to troubleshooting some common errors:

Error:	Server Not Responding
Potential Problem:	The port-mapper server is not running.
	The destination server is sharing the same NIC with the port-mapper server.
	The port-mapping entries in the `notes.ini` are incorrect. They either reference other partitioned servers on the machine or they are not listed in numerical order (if you modify the `notes.ini`, you will have to reboot the machine for the changes to take effect).
	Check the `notes.ini` on the port-mapper server. Ensure that the port number(s) for each destination partitioned server's IP address match the port number in the `notes.ini` of the partitioned server. Also ensure that the Server name(s) and organizations are listed properly.
Error:	Server's Name changed
Potential Problem:	The port mapping entries in the `notes.ini` are incorrect. They may be referencing other partitioned servers on the (if you modify the `notes.ini`, you will have to reboot the machine for the changes to take effect).
Error:	NOTESPARTITION=x In Use
Potential Problem:	You have attempted to start more than one Domino server in the same namespace. Edit the nserve.bat for each server to ensure that each batch file refers to a unique NOTESPARTITION value.

Uninstalling

Your organization may determine that is no longer necessary to use partitioned servers and, consequently, may want to remove one or more of the partitioned servers. Currently, you can only remove the last partitioned server installed or all the partitioned servers. Removing all the partitioned servers is the same as uninstalling the software using an uninstall program. This process is the same as removing a nonpartitioned server.

You can also remove the most recently partitioned server (you cannot select which server partition to remove). The steps to uninstalling the most recent partitioned server are

1. Delete the Domino data directory for the partitioned server you wish to uninstall.

2. If the partitioned server was using a unique IP address, disable the address. Do not disable this IP address if the partitioned server was using the computer host name as the Domino server name. This should only be done is the IP address was added when the partitioned server was set up.

3. If this was a port-mapping server, set up another server as the port-mapping server. If this server was used in port-mapping, modify the `notes.ini` file so the port-mapping server no longer references the removed server.

4. If using Windows NT, make the following modifications to the registry using the Windows NT Registry Editor:
   - In the folder HKEY_LOCAL_MACHINE\SOFTWARE\Lotus\Notes\VSERVER, select INSTANCE and reduce the value for instance count by one.
   - In the folder HKEY_LOCAL_MACHINE\SOFTWARE\Lotus\Notes\VSERVER\CLIENT*n*, delete the entry for the client install path (*n*) for the partitioned server bring removed.
   - In the folder HKEY_LOCAL_MACHINE\SOFTWARE\Lotus\Notes\VSERVER\CLIENT, ensure that the values for the clients (CLIENT*n*) are listed in consecutive order.

5. Update the `nclient.bat` and `nserve.bat` files in the data directories. Theses files include the server and client instance number. An example of this is illustrated below:

   Set NOTESPARTITION=1
   start c:\notes\notes.exe =d:\notes\data1\`notes.ini`

   These files cannot have different values for the same partitioned server. Similarly, partitioned servers on the same machine cannot share a common NOTESPARTITION value (refer to Figure 20.4).

Billing and Auditing Services

The following sections describe how Billing and Auditing Services work, the steps for planning and setting up billing services, and how the BILLING.NSF database works.

Description

Billing information can be used to collect information about the activity within your organization for the use of charging users for using the Domino Server. Billing information allows you to

- Charge users for their usage
- Monitor usage trends
- Conduct resource planning
- Help determine if clustering would improve efficiency and system performance

There are seven classes of billing information that can be collected. The `notes.ini` file setting determines the type of billing to collect.

The seven classes of billing are

- **Agent.** Tracks if users and servers run agents and the duration of the agent.
- **Database.** Tracks if users and servers open and close databases and the duration of use.
- **Document.** Tracks read/write activity for specified documents.
- **HTTPrequest.** Tracks Web server requests.
- **Mail.** Tracks when the mail router transfers messages to another Domino server.
- **Replication.** Tracks when a billing server initiates replication with another server or client.
- **Session.** Tracks when users and servers start and end sessions with a billing server and when other creation and editing functions occur.

Planning and Setup

To enable billing do the following:

1. Modify the `notes.ini` file by adding the Billing task to the Server Tasks setting.
2. Add the following line to the `notes.ini` file to specify which billing tasks to track:

   ```
   BillingClass=listofclasestotrack
   ```

   The options for the *listofclasestotrack* are Agent, Database, Document, HTTPRequest, Mail, Replication, and Session.

3. Add the following line to the notes.ini file to specify where to store billing information:

   ```
   BillingAddinOutput=n
   ```

The options for the *n* are

1 - Store the records in a Domino database.

2 - Display the records on the server console.

8 -Store the records in a binary file.

9 - Store the records in both a Domino database and a binary file.

Using Billing

The Domino server will collect information about the client and server activity and place this information in a billing message queue. A billing task periodically polls this message queue to move the billing information to a Domino database and/or a binary file. If you choose to record billing in a Domino database, Domino automatically creates a Billing database (BILLING.NSF). The billing task then transfers the billing information from the message queue documents to the Billing database. If you choose to record the billing information to a binary file, Domino automatically creates a BILLING.NBF file. The billing tasks then transfers the billing records from the message queue to the BILLING.NSF in stream format. Each record begins with the length and structure type, so external programs can parse the data contained within the file. You can then write an application to use this information to create billing reports (for example, a Domino API program or third party program to manipulate the information).

New R5 Advanced Services

The following sections describe some of the new advanced services and features introduced in Domino R5.

Internet Cluster Manager (ICM)

One of the more useful tasks introduced in Domino R5 is the Internet Cluster Manager (ICM). The ICM will be described in detail, as well as how it works, how it can be best maintained, and how it can be monitored.

Description

As described earlier in this chapter, Domino 5.0 provides a new capability of clustering and load balancing for Internet applications and Web clients using the ICM tasks (both http and https protocols are supported). Prior to Domino 5.0, high availability using failover and load balancing was not support for Web clients and Web applications. The ICM acts as an intermediary between the Web clients and Web servers. The ICM tasks performs the following functions:

- Monitors the availability of the Domino servers in the Domino cluster
- Maintains information about the distribution of databases on servers in the Domino cluster
- Monitors the availability of the Domino HTTP Web service.
- Disallows new http connections to Domino servers that are out of service
- Provides failover to http clients to the optimal Domino server
- Provides load balancing for the Domino servers in the cluster (based on thresholds settings)
- Supports virtual IP addressing and map ports
- Provides content routing to http clients
- Preserves SSL encryption and decryption
- Supports the existing Domino security model

Fortunately, the ICM does not require any additional hardware or software because it comes with the Domino enterprise installation. Similarly, it is supported on all operating systems and platforms supported by the Domino server. The connection between the client and the ICM must use TCP/IP but the connection between the ICM and the Domino servers in the cluster can use any supported Domino protocol. Also, the ICM only manages HTTP and HTTPS requests. Therefore, is your server demands require clustering and load balancing for FTP, SMTP, or UDP protocols, you will have to employ a third party software product. The overhead for running the ICM is minimal, however, the benefit from running the ICM could be significant.

How the ICM Works

The http client submits a request to the Domino Web server in the cluster. The server reads the Server document, locates the host name of the ICM, and then generates an URL that refers to the ICM.

The following lists the URLs (http commands) supported by the ICM:

- Open servers, databases, views, navigators, forms, and agents
- Open, edit, and delete documents by UNID and open documents by name from a view
- Open image files, attachments, and OLE objects
- Create search queries

After the ICM receives the request, it uses information gathered from the Cluster Database Directory to determine which servers are contained within the cluster. Then, the ICM locates the most available server that contains the requested database, determines if the server is configured for HTTP or HTTPS, and redirects the client to the respective server.

Some of the steps the ICM uses to determine where to redirect the Web client are

- Determines where the database replicas reside
- Determines if the databases are marked out of service or pending delete
- Determines the availability index of each server which contains a replica of the database
- Determines the availability of the server by pinging the http/https port
- Eliminates any servers that were not reached, RESTRICTED, BUSY, or MAXUSERS
- If there are servers remaining, the ICM selects a server with the lightest current workload.
- If there are no servers remaining, the ICM will select a server that is RESTRICTED, BUSY, or MAXUSERS, if available.

The ICM does not handle the Domino security itself and does not participate in the authentication process. It merely redirects the http requests at the protocol level, sending the redirection response code and target server back to the http client. The session with the ICM is closed and the http client then sends a request to the target Domino server at which point, the native Domino security is implemented. At this point, the authentication process would take affect and the Web client would be forced to authenticate (unless Anonymous access is allowed). Once authenticated, the user ID and password are passed in the HTML header for all subsequent http requests for the current session with the current Domino server. The client's state information is preserved because subsequent requests are made to the same Domino server. If the current Web page contains links to other databases on the same server or within the same cluster, the Domino Web server will include the host name of the ICM in the URL to the databases. Thus, ensuring that clients are still using the ICM to access other databases within the cluster.

All these steps may be visible by the client in the URL address. The host name, path, and database name may change depending on where the client is redirected by the ICM. The ICM does not provide security against unauthorized users, so it would be wise to implement security on top of the Domino security model, such as a firewall. The ICM supports SSL and can be configured to require SSL sessions.

The ICM maintains information about the availability and status of the servers within the cluster by sending probes to the Domino Web servers within the cluster.

There are some scenarios where the ICM may not perform as expected, as in the following situations:

- When the URL includes a file path, the ICM may have difficulty resolving the URL to a single database if multiple servers contain a database with the same file path and file name but different replica IDs. When this occurs, the ICM will display a list of databases for the Web client to select the correct database.

- When the URL includes a replica ID, the ICM may have difficulty resolving the URL to a single database if multiple replicas of the database exist on the server. When the occurs, the ICM will redirect the client request to a server that contains at least one replica of the database and the Domino Web server will select a replica to serve to the user. You can specify the replica database to access by indicating the actual filepath to the replica in the URL.

- When the URL includes a NotesID item value, the ICM may not be able to locate the Notes document and process the URL. This is because the NoteID will be different for every database replica. Therefore, the NoteID should be avoided when generating URLs. The Universal ID is a better option because the Universal ID is the same among all the database replicas.

When using ICM, the availability and failover protection is not fool-proof. If the http client has been redirected to the Domino server and the Domino server subsequently fails, the http client will time out and a server not responding error will be sent to the Web client. The user is forced to go "back," reload or retype the URL, or refresh the page. At this point, the ICM will recognize that the Domino server is out of service and redirect the client to another available service. However, the http client will likely be challenged to authenticate (depending on the access settings for the server and Domino databases) unless the client had previously authenticated to the new server in the current session. If the browser and server support SSL3, the reauthentication will occur automatically.

Configuration of the ICM

Every cluster must have a dedicated ICM running on a Domino server. Because the ICM uses the local Domino Directory, it must be in the same domain as the Domino cluster.

The decision process when configuring the ICM is similar to the process of planning the original cluster. Some of the factors to include when planning the ICM are

- The number of servers to include in the cluster
- The processing power and drive space of the servers
- The anticipated traffic and load being carried by the servers
- The number of database replicas of each database to include and where they should be placed among the servers

- If a private LAN should be created for the cluster traffic
- Where the ICM should be located and running.

You have the following options when deciding where to place the ICM:

1. The ICM can run outside the cluster on a dedicated Domino server. This server can run minimal server tasks and contain only the databases required for the server to run. Because the server is dedicated only to minimal tasks and running the ICM, it maximized reliability and performance. If the ICM is running outside the server, you may want to use native operating system clustering capabilities.

2. You can further improve availability by setting up more than one ICM to handle HTTP requests outside of the cluster. If one ICM becomes unavailable, the alternate ICM(s) can handle the http request(s). This can be accomplished by running multiple ICMs on the same machine using Domino partitioned servers (explained in this chapter) or running the ICM on its own server running on its own machine. If running more than one ICM, they should be configured to use the same hostname in the Domain Name Server. Therefore, the failover occurs transparently to the user. This could increase performance if a single ICM would not be able to handle the load effectively. However, typically multiple ICMs will not increase performance.

3. You also can setup one ICM to handle http requests inside of the cluster. The ICM can run on any server within the cluster. Nevertheless, because the server will be required to handle tasks generated by the ICM and the Domino server will be doing more work than if the ICM was located on another Domino server, be sure to run the ICM on the most powerful or least burdened server in the cluster. When the ICM runs on a server in the cluster, it accesses the local Cluster Database Directory.

4. You also can improve availability by setting up more than one ICM to handle http requests inside of the cluster. The ICM can run on any of the servers within the cluster. Nevertheless, because these servers will be required to handle tasks generated by the ICM and the Domino server will be doing more work than if the ICM was located on another Domino server, be sure to run the ICM on the most powerful or least burdened servers in the cluster. When the ICM runs on a server in the cluster, it accesses the local Cluster Database Directory.

5. Finally, you can setup an ICM to handle http requests inside of the cluster and outside of the cluster. The primary server to handle http requests is the ICM cunning on the server outside of the cluster. When the server outside the cluster becomes unavailable, the second ICM located inside the cluster then handles the http requests.

When the cluster is configured for ICM and the ICM task is enabled, the Domino http server will direct all http clients to the ICM for all the databases stored in the Cluster Database Directory (`cldbdir.nsf`). This Domino database contains the information about the location of the databases in the cluster and the servers they are stored on.

When the ICM is running on a server outside of the cluster, it will select a server in the cluster to access the Cluster Database Directory. If that server becomes available, the connection will failover to another server within the cluster. The ICM will always use a local copy of the Domino Directory so the ICM must be in the same domain as the cluster.

The ICM is configured after you have already installed and configured the Domino clusters. The ICM is configured in the Server document located in the Domino Directory. Within the Server document, open the Server Tasks tab, then open the Internet Cluster Manager tab (see Figure 20.14).

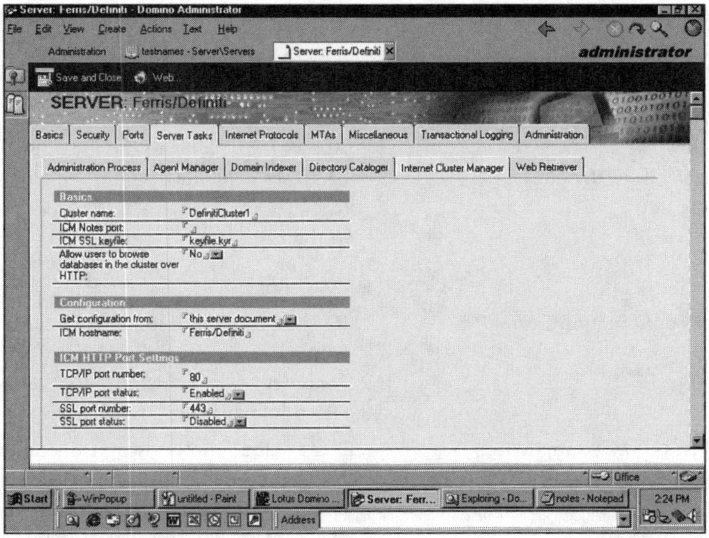

Figure 20.14 The Internet Cluster Manager.

Here are the steps to configure the ICM:

1. Open the Domino Administrator on an existing Domino server.
2. Click the Configuration tab.
3. Click the twistie to expand the Server category and click All Server Documents.
4. Open the server document you want to enable ICM (select the server document and click Edit Server, press Enter, or select File, Open from the pull-down menu or simply double-click on the server document).

5. Click the Server Tasks tab.

6. Click the Internet Cluster Manager tab.

7. Enter the fields for the ICM (see Figure 20.15), described here:

BASICS SECTION

Cluster Name	If the ICM is running on a server outside the cluster, enter the name of the Domino cluster the ICM will be managing. If the ICM is running on a server inside the cluster, this field is not required.
ICM Notes port	The Notes port the ICM will to communicate with the http clients. Entering a port value restricts the ICM communication to the specified port. You can leave this field blank (the default) which will allow the ICM to use any port to communicate with http clients.
ICM SSL keyfile	The name of the SSL key file containing the certificates to identify the ICM when communicating with https clients.
Allow users to browse databases in the cluster over http	Allows http clients to browse a list of the databases contained within the cluster (the uses can perform an ?OpenServer command in the URL).

CONFIGURATION SECTION

Get configuration from	If setting up multiple ICMs to use the same configuration, enter the name of the server document from which to retrieve the configuration information.
Obtain ICM configuration from	If the value "another server document" is selected from the "Get configuration from" field, this field specifies the name of the server that contains the server document to use for configuration information.

Disable Internet Database Browsing

It is generally a good idea not to allow database browsing for http clients, especially for Internet/Extranet configurations. Therefore, for added security you should disable this feature.

CONFIGURATION SECTION

ICM hostname	Enter the fully qualified host name the http clients will be accessing. This will most likely be the DNS name but could also be the IP address This field is required so that the http server can create URLs that reference the ICM. If the ICM task is running on the same Domino server as the http task, it is best to assign the ICM its own IP address in the "ICM host-name" field to avoid conflicts.

ICM HTTP PORT SETTINGS SECTION

TCP/IP port number	The port number for the ICM to use. If the ICM task is running on the same server as the HTTP task and the ICM does not have its own IP address, be sure to assign the ICM a different port number than any other port numbers on the server.
TCP/IP port status	Enable/Disable HTTP communication with the ICM
SSL port number	Enter the port number for SSL. If the ICM task is running on the same server as the HTTP task and the ICM does not have its own IP address, be sure to assign the SSL port number a differ-ent port number than any other port numbers on the server.
SSL port status	Enable/disable HTTPS communication with the ICM.

8. Save and close the Server document.

Continue modifying the ICM configuration document for all the servers in the cluster that are running the http tasks, regardless if the servers are running the ICM task itself. This is required because each Domino server uses the settings in the ICM document from its respective server document determine how to direct the http Web clients to the ICM. Once the ICM tasks starts (when the server is restarted), the ICM will use this information to find the cluster name, network address, host name, port settings, and so on.

As evident in the ICM HTTP Port Settings Section, ICM supports SSL. In fact, the ICM can use the same SSL certificates as the Domino Web server or a different set of SSL certificates. You can require SSL by modifying the Internet Cluster Manager of the Server document.

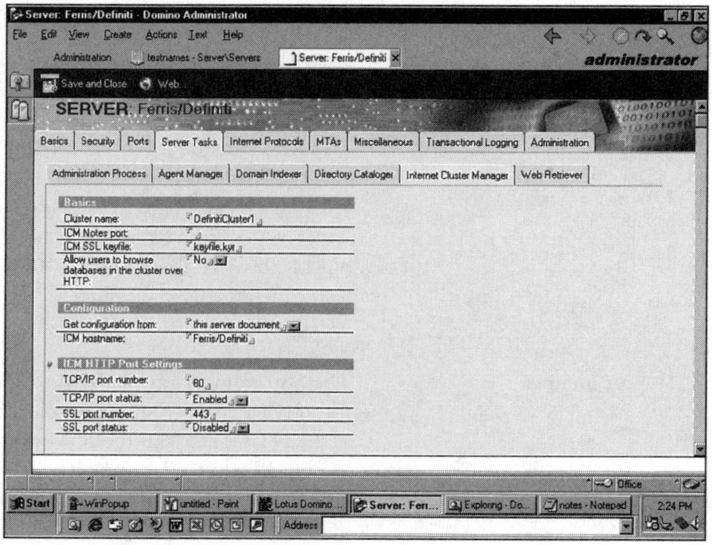

Figure 20.15 Setting fields for the ICM.

You can start the ICM tasks manually by typing "load ICM" at the server console. However, as with many other server tasks, you will need to add the task to the "ServerTasks" setting in the notes.ini file. An example of this is shown below:

```
ServerTasks=Router, replica, cldbdir, clrepl, http, icm
```

You can use the ICM in cluster configurations that have been in previous releases of Domino. In fact, the ICM will direct http requests to other Domino Web servers within the cluster, regardless of the Domino release. However, only R5 Domino servers can generate URLs that reference the ICM (described earlier in this section). After the client is redirected to a Domino server running a previous release, the ICM capabilities are lost. Therefore, some of the workload balancing and failover functions will be limited in a mixed cluster.

To avoid conflicts, give the ICM its own IP address on each Web server. Follow these steps to set this up:

1. Make an IP address available using the operating system.

2. Launch the Domino Administrator.

3. Select Files, Preferences, User Preferences from the pull-down menu.

4. Click the Ports icon.

5. Click New.

6. Enter a meaningful name for the ICM port (for example, ICMPort).

7. Select TCP as the driver (see Figure 20.16).

Figure 20.16   Setting the ICM Port.

8. The port location should default office network, therefore, you can leave this field alone

9. Click OK.

10. Click OK.

11. If this server contains the ICM, add the following line to the `notes.ini` file to set up the port:

    ```
    PortName=TPC, adapter # or network #, # of sessions, date buffer size
    ```

12. Add the following line to the `notes.ini` file. *PortName* is the name of the port configured in the Domino Administrator (in step 6):

    ```
    PortName_TcpipAddress=0, IpAddress
    ```

13. In the Domino Administrator, click the Configuration tab.

14. Click the twistie to expand the Server category and click All Server Documents.

15. Open the server document you want to enable ICM (select the server document and click Edit Server, press Enter, or select File, Open from the pull-down menu or simply double-click the server document).

16. Click the Server Tasks tab.

17. Click the Internet Cluster Manager tab.

18. Enter the name of the port you configured.

19. If you want to use port 80 for both the ICM and Web server:

    - Click the Internet Protocols tab.
    - Click the HTTP tab.
    - In the Host name(s) field, enter the IP address of the host name of the Domino Web server.
    - Select Enable for the Bind to host name field.

Managing/Monitoring the ICM

You can manage/monitor the ICM from the Domino server log file (historical data) or the statistics (current data).

To view the log file, you can do one of the following lists:

1. Open the Domino Administrator.
2. Select the server that contains the log file you want to examine.
3. Click the Server tab.
4. Click the Analysis tab.
5. Expand the Notes log.
6. Click the Miscellaneous Events (see Figure 20.17).

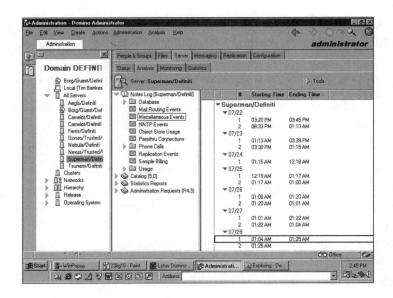

Figure 20.17   Viewing events from the Notes log.

7. Open the Log Entry document in the results pane.

Or

1. Open the Domino server log file (log.nsf).
2. Open the Miscellaneous Events view.
3. Open the Log Entry document to examine it.

To view the current statistics:

1. Open the Domino Administrator.
2. Select the server whose statistics want to examine.
3. Click ICM in the All Statistics list (see Figure 20.18).

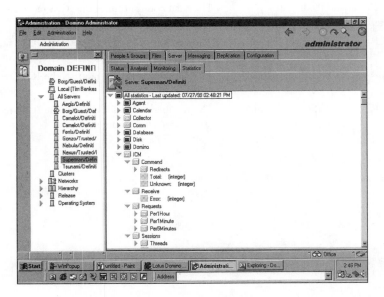

Figure 20.18   Viewing statistics from Domino Administrator.

Or

1. Type show **stat icm** from the server console.

Table 20.4 lists and describes the ICM statistics.

Table 20.4 **Internet Cluster Manager Statistics**

ICM.AvailablityIndex	The integer value from 0 to 100 indicating the server's availability (O indicates no resources are available, 100 indicates complete server availability)
ICM.Command.Total	The total count of URL commands the ICM received
ICM.Command.Unknown	The total count of URL commands the ICM did not recognize
ICM.Receive.Error	The total count of times the ICM could not process a client request as a result of a communication problem between the client and the ICM

continues

Table 20.4   **Continued**

ICM.Command.Redirects.Successful	The total count of times the ICM successfully redirected a client URL request to a cluster member
ICM.Command.Redirects. Unsuccessful	The total count of times the ICM unsuccessfully redirected a client URL request to a cluster member
ICM.Command.Redirects. ClusterBusy	The total count of times the ICM received a client request and all the servers were BUSY
ICM.Requests.Per1Hour.Total	The number of HTTP requests the ICM received in the previous hour
ICM.Requests.Per1Minute.Total	The number of HTTP requests the ICM received in the previous minute
ICM.Requests.Per5Minutes.Total	The number of HTTP requests the ICM received in the previous five minutes

Index

F

M

networks
connections, testing via tracert, 640
counters for monitoring
performance, 686
dialup connections, modems, 124–125
frame relay, benefits of, 30
installing Notes from, 188
integrating Domino with, 27–36
local area (LAN), failures, 36
named, 54–56, 87–88
names, routing mail to, 281–283
Notes named, mail routing, 273–274
performance
monitoring, NT Performance Monitor, 682
tuning, 741
Private, creating, 758
protocols supported by Domino and
Notes, 36–38
routing mail to, 281–286
security, 414
support, planning for Domino
rollouts, 25
timeouts, configuring to improve
Domino performance, 627
wide-area (WAN)
failures, 36
setting up, 30-31
nevent.exe. *See* **Event Manager service**
New Database dialog box, 179
new folders, moving mail into, 644
New mail sound setting, 531
new organizational units (OUs),
initializing renamed user to, 506
new services, 80
newsgroups, creating accounts, 246–247
Next option, 116
nhttp.exe. *See* **HTTP service**
nimap.exe. *See* **IMAP servers**
nldap.exe. *See* **Internet directory services**
nnntp.exe. *See* **Internet Newsgroup**
servers
NNTP Servers. *See* **Internet**
Newsgroup Servers
NNTP. *See* **Network News Transport**
Protocol

No access, 424
No access allowed field, 158
No option, 510
No proxy for these hosts and domains
field, 159
no retrievals field, 156
nodes, installing Domino on, 770–771
noise, electrical, 33
non-domain-related directories, 456
non-Domino servers, setting up access,
237–249
nonoptional standard Domino
services, 74
Not responding status icon, 708
Not running status icon, 708
Note ID documents
design, locating, 441
from logs, 563
Notes CD. *See* **Rich Text**
Notes Client, 19
Notes Compound Document. *See*
Rich Text
Notes cross-certification, 405–406
Notes Desktop client, 19
Notes Direct Dialup connection docu-
ments, 239, 230–234
Notes domains. *See also* **servers**
connecting to Internet, 301–309
mail routing, 272–273
Notes domains and aliases field, 308
Notes Dynamic Configuration, Mobile
Directory Catalog, 483
Notes field, 155
Notes fields to be removed from
headers setting, 341
Notes Group Registration Options
dialog box, 205
Notes Log (log.nsf), 560
monitoring replication, 388
troubleshooting mail routing, 342, 344
Notes Mail client, 19

P

Q-R

U

X-Z